A QUESTION OF INTENT

A QUESTION

OF INTENT

A Great American Battle

with a Deadly Industry

DAVID KESSLER

PUBLICAFFAIRS   *NewYork*

Book design by Mark McGarry, Texas Type & Book Works.
Set in Monotype Dante.

Library of Congress Cataloging-in-Publication Data
Kessler, David A., 1951–
A question of intent: a great American battle with a deadly industry / David Kessler.
p. cm.
ISBN 1-891620-80-0
1. Tobacco—Law and legislation—United States—History.
2. Nicotine—Law and legislation—United States—History.
3. United States—Food and Drug Administration—History.
4. Tobacco industry—United States History.
I. Title.
KF3894.t63 K47 2001
363.19′4—dc21
00–034152

FIRST EDITION
1 3 5 7 9 10 8 6 4 2

To Paulette
With whom all things are possible

For Elise and Ben

The guilty have a head start, and retribution
Is always slow of foot, but it catches up.

The Odes of Horace, BOOK III, ODE 2

CONTENTS

VERITAS

I called him "Veritas," and he was a mystery to me. Veritas spoke cautiously, using code words and elliptical phrases, a habit he had developed after many years in the upper levels of the tobacco industry.

"Mazes within mazes," he said. "People get lost in mazes."

I had no idea what he was talking about, but I nodded to keep him going.

"See the movie *The Name of the Rose*," he suggested. "The blind librarian. There's a parallel."

A parallel with what?

"It was life in the notebooks," he said. "Big, black notebooks. They were three-ring binders, and they looked innocent enough, but those books ... it was our Bible."

We sat facing each other in the lounge of a private club in downtown Washington. There was an air of shabby gentility to the place, the residue of better days. Veritas had made anonymity a condition of the meeting, and except for one waitress, we were alone in the room. I waited for him to explain, although such restraint did not come readily to me.

"There was a paradigm." Veritas pursed his lips, and made a noise like a buzzer. "They trained you ... *b-z-z* ... they programmed it into you ... *b-z-z* ... you had to study it like the Catechism ... *b-z-z*."

He intended the odd buzzing noise to mimic a conditioned reflex. I asked cautiously, "Those notebooks, did they actually exist?"

"Three-ring binders," he said. "They were real. Everything was scripted. The script was etched in stone."

His use of the word "script" brought the code words and phrases into focus, and I began to understand what he was getting at. Veritas was talking about the tobacco industry's strategy. Of course, there was a script, I thought to myself. Why hadn't I seen that earlier?

When we began our investigation of tobacco at the Food and Drug Administration, we had no idea of the power wielded by the tobacco companies, but we soon learned why the industry was for decades considered untouchable. Tobacco employed some of the most prestigious law firms in the country and commanded the allegiance of a significant section of the Congress. It also had access to the services of widely admired public figures, ranging from Prime Minister Margaret Thatcher to Senator Howard Baker. With its limitless resources and a corporate culture that was aggressively defensive, the industry perceived threats everywhere and responded to them ferociously.

Tobacco also reached out and bought the services of Charlie Edwards, a former commissioner of the FDA and one of my predecessors. He was a man I had respected—someone, ironically enough, who had been influential in my selection as commissioner. But after I began my investigation into the industry, he testified before a Senate committee and tried to discredit me. Later, I discovered he was on retainer from Philip Morris. There was nothing illegal about the transaction. It was his privilege to take the money; it was my privilege to think poorly of it.

I was at a disadvantage with Veritas. Over the years I had spoken with dozens of informants from the tobacco industry, but usually I had been with members of the team I assembled in the early 1990s. The tobacco team's assignment had been to ask whether nicotine was a drug and thus should be regulated by the FDA. Team members were trained professionals, men like Tom Doyle and Gary Light, with backgrounds at the Secret Service, the CIA, and the Army Criminal Investigative Division. I recruited others who had begun their careers on Capitol Hill and in journalism. Each had years of experience in the art of investigation. They had guided and protected me in the past, sometimes at considerable risk to themselves. But I was no longer FDA commissioner, and now I was on my own. I asked myself how Tom and Gary would have handled this situation.

"Let him talk," Gary would have said. "Schmooze with him, don't press him. Keep it light."

"He's all wound up, he's tight. He wants to talk, every informant wants to talk, that's why he's here."

"He's carrying around a load of guilt. You've got to let him work through that guilt. Just let him talk."

I never developed the interviewing skills that Gary and Tom possessed. But I tried to go slowly with Veritas each time we met.

"Tell me about the true believers," I said to Veritas, referring to the men who made tobacco their livelihood.

"You mean the southern gentlemen," he said. "The old-time guys, they were tobacco men, not businessmen. They were part of an agricultural society that saw tobacco as just another farm product. It was a highly profitable product, but it could have been soybeans or cotton as far as they were concerned. Profits were important to these people, but so was the tradition in which they had been raised."

Veritas continued, "They believed there was a controversy. The true believers were the moral part of the play."

I looked up from my notepad. I was struck by Veritas's long, drawn face. He seemed in complete control of himself, sitting utterly still as he spoke. He did not gesture or nod. "By the nineteen-eighties the farmers were out and the MBAs were in. The original proprietors were replaced by executives with little or no connection to the land. The lawyers created the paradigm."

Devised in the 1950s and '60s, the tobacco industry's strategy was embodied in a script written by the lawyers. Every tobacco company executive in the public eye was told to learn the script backwards and forwards, no deviation allowed. The basic premise was simple—smoking had not been proved to cause cancer. Not proven, not proven, not proven—this would be stated insistently and repeatedly. Inject a thin wedge of doubt, create controversy, never deviate from the prepared lines. It was a simple plan, and it worked.

"It made us look like horses' asses," said Veritas. But the industry never lost a case, and that was all that mattered to them.

Embedded in this defensive strategy to neutralize the cancer issue, however, was a secret that posed as great a danger to the industry: the addictive and pharmacological nature of nicotine. In the 1950s, this had not been considered a factor threatening to the tobacco interests. By the 1970s, the industry had come to recognize that research on nicotine's pharmacological effects could be useful, but it had to be done covertly. If it were ever discovered that the tobacco companies knew that nicotine was an addictive drug, the FDA might try to regulate cigarettes, and that was what they feared most. Because of this, the script that had been so carefully followed had to be broadened.

Industry dogma began to express two fundamentals: that smoking had not been proved to cause cancer and that there was no scientific proof that nicotine was an addictive substance.

"Did we get it right?" I asked Veritas, referring to our investigation, which had led the FDA to assert jurisdiction over the nicotine in tobacco.

Veritas looked nervously around the room. He obviously did not want anyone he knew to see the two of us together. "You hit the bull's eye three times," he said. "You were right to focus on nicotine as an addictive drug. You were right to elevate the discourse to the level of public health. You were right to focus on the addiction of children."

But being right did not mean we would win.

"You were really true believers," he added. I nodded, though we had not been true believers at the beginning.

"You became like them," he said. I started to object, but Veritas explained himself. "You became masters of shaping public opinion."

There was some truth there. We had focused on collecting evidence of what the companies knew. No one had ever done that before, and in the end, this evidence molded the public's view.

"All we did was ask a simple question," I pointed out, although I knew that was an understatement. None of us had ever done anything else with such intensity. "We asked whether or not nicotine was a drug. That was where the team was focused. Only over time did I realize that this question was aimed at the heart of the industry."

Veritas nodded. "Frankly, I'm surprised that you didn't come to see it sooner."

Of course, I thought, that's easy to say from your position. Your people created the maze. We had to find our way through it.

PART I

OPENING BATTLES

1

WHEN I was appointed commissioner of the Food and Drug Administration in October 1990, the newspapers said that I had been preparing for the job my whole life. There was some truth to that. I was trained both as a doctor and a lawyer, I had taught food and drug law, and I was running a teaching hospital in the Bronx. Reporters liked to add that I had also worked on Capitol Hill, though I had been only a part-time volunteer during my pediatric residency.

With encouragement from me, friends and colleagues began mentioning my name as a possible candidate to lead the FDA. My campaign for the job took a big step forward when I was summoned to see Louis Sullivan, President Bush's secretary of Health and Human Services, under whose authority the agency fell. Dr. Sullivan greeted me graciously, though he was always reserved and formal, and he escorted me into his spacious front office overlooking Independence Avenue. The dome of the Capitol dominated his view. The former president of Morehouse School of Medicine, Sullivan had come out of the same world of academic medicine as I had; there was every reason for me to feel at ease.

We walked together to his private dining room, where Sullivan asked, "What would you do with the agency?"

"Enforce the law," I said. It rang flat, even in my own ears. Sullivan did not react, but I felt a wave of panic, a catecholamine surge, wash over me. I had never experienced anything like it before. My back muscles went into spasm. I was afraid to pick up a fork, lest the secretary notice my shaking hands. I was the medical director of Albert Einstein Hospital in the Bronx, but here, in this setting, I was an unknown. Sullivan wanted to know what I would do if I had responsibility for an 8,000-person agency with a $600 million budget that regulated one quarter of every dollar Americans spent—from the food they eat to the drugs they take to the cosmetics they wear. For someone who had supposedly spent decades preparing for the job, I did not have a very articulate answer.

Early on, I knew that I wanted to work in Washington. I also knew that I would become a doctor; I had known that from childhood. Deciding to go to law school was harder for me, but I knew that legal skills would somehow prove useful.

In 1975, I took a leave from Harvard Medical School to attend the University of Chicago Law School. Paulette, whom I had married the previous summer, had already completed her first year of law school. She has a gift for argument, and on the exams in classes we took together, she always earned a higher score. We had met years earlier, on the porch of the three-story wooden Victorian house where she lived at Smith College.

At the time I was a student at Amherst College, immersed in a study of renal cancer in frogs and the viruses associated with it, and I needed an unending supply of amphibians with tumors. To find study animals, I traveled to large frog farms where I put on thigh-high wading boots and squeezed the bellies of thousands of animals, looking for masses. To others, it might have seemed routine, but nothing about science has ever been routine to me, not then and not now. In science it often seemed that the longer the road, the greater the reward, at least often enough to turn the dullest assignment into an adventure.

The evening Paulette and I stood talking, the trunk of my Oldsmobile was filled with croaking frogs, hundreds of specimens in plastic bins. She accepted my invitation to take a look, but I could not tell by the expression on her face whether she was impressed or repelled. It was the last time I saw her at a loss for words.

My fascination with frogs could be traced back to Oscar Schotté, one of the world's great developmental biologists and one of my most important early influences. I had been named an Independent Scholar during my junior year at Amherst, which exempted me from traditional classroom requirements and left me free to devise my own course of study. Although well past retirement age, Schotté, a professor emeritus, singled out one student each year to whom he served as mentor. Beginning in 1971 I spent two years in his laboratory, sometimes working through the night. My responsibility in those years was not to study a set curriculum in a predetermined sequence, but to learn the art of inquiry and investigation. I thrived in that unregimented environment.

Whatever else he taught me about science, Schotté also helped me understand that meticulous attention to detail and patience are as important to problem solving as a grand vision. In those years I also learned the importance of focusing fully on a task and sticking with it until it was done.

Schotté introduced me to his closest friend at Amherst, the great American historian Henry Steele Commager. Schotté and I agreed that Commager's class on the American Enlightenment was the one formal course I would take as an Independent Scholar.

Never afraid to take a stand, no matter how unpopular, Commager had opposed the Vietnam War as early as 1964, just as in the 1950s he had been one of the academic world's sharpest critics of Senator Joseph McCarthy. But he counseled patience in an impatient era. He cautioned us to examine carefully the long-term consequences of actions intended to remedy the immediate problems of the world, and he emphasized that important things in life are never achieved quickly, but rather through what he called "the long pull." He remains in my mind a model of citizenship, a man whose devotion to scholarship was combined with his commitment to public responsibility.

Schotté and Commager: one a scientist, the other a humanist. These were the models whose faces I saw before me as I began the journey that would take me from my private world to a very public life.

ALTHOUGH my first performance felt like a disaster, Louis Sullivan called me back for a second interview months later. We had barely begun talking when Michael Calhoun, the secretary's chief of staff, strode into the room. Slightly balding, trim and strong, Calhoun held himself erect and looked every inch a member of the Praetorian Guard. He was as direct as his boss was courteous. Without pausing to make small talk, he interrupted our conversation. "There is only one question. One issue. Are you going to be loyal to the secretary or are you going to be loyal to Hatch?"

The question surprised me. Calhoun was referring to my first experience in Washington almost a decade earlier, when I was a volunteer on the staff of Senator Orrin Hatch's Committee on Labor and Human Resources, the Senate's health committee. Since then I had not had much contact with Hatch. But shortly before my meeting with Sullivan and Calhoun, I had seen the

senator at a dinner to raise funds for medical education in South Africa. I half
expected one of his aides to whisper in his ear, "That's David Kessler, he used
to work for you." Instead, Hatch greeted me with a bear hug. "Remember
Uncle Orrin when you're commissioner of FDA," he said affectionately.

My early experience within the Beltway had been something of a proving
ground for me. To make it to Washington back then, I had to be persistent. In
college I wrote Republican Senator Jacob Javits of New York, offering to volunteer as a summer intern in his office, but I got nowhere. Later, with medical and legal degrees in hand, I tried again when Senator Ted Kennedy
chaired the health committee. Still no results. Finally, when the Senate passed
into Republican hands, I was welcomed. It was sheer luck—the committee
was in a period of transition that had left it short-staffed. At the time I cared
little about which political side I worked for.

I began in the spring of 1981, working at the Dirksen Senate Office Building where space was at such a premium that I was not given a desk. Squeezed
into a tiny ground-floor office with several colleagues, I made do instead with
a small telephone stand. One day the staff director rushed in, clutching a
stack of papers.

"Who knows something about the FDA?" he demanded. "We need someone to work on some legislation."

I spoke up. The interest in cancer that I had developed under Oscar Schotté's
tutelage had remained with me during law school. There I wrote for the University of Chicago law review, analyzing a controversial section of the law that
dictated how the FDA should regulate cancer-causing chemicals in food.

"Okay, this is yours," he said, tossing the papers at me. In that instant I
became the committee's resident FDA expert.

Now, as Calhoun interviewed me for the job of commissioner of the
FDA, I realized my early ties to Capitol Hill could count against me in a
different political circle. I tried to allay his fears. "Look, I know Hatch," I said.
"I don't have to earn my stripes with him. I can say things to him that someone coming in fresh could not." Calhoun seemed unconvinced.

THE FDA was an organization in trouble and most people in Washington
knew it. In truth, the agency had been under stress since its inception.
Although it was launched as a scientific agency, science had often clashed with
the realities of politics. Harvey Wiley, a visionary public servant, fought for

passage of the Federal Food and Drugs Act of 1906, one of the nation's first consumer protection laws. He was immediately opposed by a powerful lobby. Lawyers for the industries that would be subject to its authority—canning, drugs, and whiskey—came before Congress to plead for exemptions, claiming that the law was too harsh and would ruin their businesses. Wiley prevailed and became head of the Bureau of Chemistry, the FDA's predecessor.

In the decades that followed, the nation's food and drug laws were toughened considerably—in 1938, under the Federal Food, Drug, and Cosmetic Act, for the first time drugs had to be proved safe before they could be sold, and in 1962, manufacturers were required to establish that they were effective as well. Over the years, the range of products under the FDA's jurisdiction grew exponentially and the scientific challenges became more complex. But the resources with which to shape an appropriate response did not keep pace.

By 1990 virtually no one was happy with the FDA. Weakened by years of ideological intervention, especially during the Reagan era, from 1981 through 1988, the agency had become a political whipping boy. Much of its authority had been diluted by the Office of Management and Budget, which was used by the White House to pursue an aggressive and dangerous deregulatory agenda. The FDA was underfunded, understaffed, and demoralized. It lacked basic enforcement powers—it could not subpoena witnesses and documents, embargo unsafe or questionable food and drugs, assess civil penalties for most violations, or destroy unsafe imports. There was such confusion in the marketplace that even some of the industries the FDA policed wanted its authority restored. But real as doubts about the FDA's capacity to protect the American food and drug supply were, they were not what brought me back to Washington. It was fraud and scandal.

The scandal began with an informant, a private investigator, and an attorney. The attorney, Val Miller, who represented one of the nation's largest generic drug manufacturers, believed something was radically wrong at the agency. His client had been steadily winning approvals for many of its new products until 1986, when those approvals dropped off precipitously. The following year he found out why.

At the Holiday Inn in Rockville, Maryland, the Washington suburb that is also headquarters to the FDA, Miller had lunch with an FDA chemist who had left the agency a few months earlier. The nervous woman expressed concern about what was going on in her former office. Miller kept pushing gently for information, and the story began to unfold.

The chemist reported that some drug companies were delivering generous gifts—a fur coat, an expensive VCR—to her boss, Charles Chang. Not
coincidentally, Chang had taken away certain drug applications that the
chemist was reviewing and had reassigned them to someone else. Currently,
Chang was running three reviewers. Two were slow and methodical, while
the third was able to clear a swift 200 approvals a year. The drug makers who
paid off Chang had their applications read by the speedy reviewer.

Miller checked out the informant and decided she was credible. Nothing
gave him any reason to think she was either an attention seeker or a disgruntled employee. He decided to hire a private investigator, who later became
known to federal prosecutors as "Trash Cover" because of his careful
scrutiny of Chang's garbage. Twice a week during a six-week period in 1987,
Chang's trash produced a piece of a photograph. It was apparent that the
pieces were being carefully cut up and then discarded.

But Chang wasn't careful enough. Slowly, Trash Cover was able to put
together the pieces of the photograph. It was a picture of Chang with two
men, one the president of a generic drug company, the other a consultant to
the industry. They were standing in front of a Hong Kong tourist attraction.
This was the beginning of what came to be known as the generic drug scandal, which eventually led to the conviction of forty-two people and ten companies on charges of fraud or corruption. Charles Chang went to jail.

Although FDA Commissioner Frank Young was not implicated in the
generic drug scandal, he had been slow to respond to hints about it. I met
Young at about this time, when I invited him to give a lecture to the class I co-
taught on food and drug law at Columbia University's law school. From the
vantage point of the Morningside Heights campus that day, I realized that
something was wrong. Within minutes of his arrival, Young thumped on his
chest.

"I'm in body armor," he said.

According to Young, the FBI in New York had picked up a threat on his
life. An HIV-infected man had allegedly paid five hundred dollars to have
Young assassinated. Young asked my co-teacher, Hal Edgar, to identify an
escape route from the lecture hall, and he warned Hal that for his own safety,
he should not stand too close.

"Vortex," Young said repeatedly as he lectured our class. "FDA is in the
vortex." I had never heard anyone use that word so many times.

But it was not bullets that should have worried Young. After a series of missteps and misjudgments at the FDA, the Department of Health and Human Services, of which the FDA is a part, began to view the agency as more of a problem than an asset. Young's most notorious decision had been the embargo he placed on all fruit imported from Chile, largely on the basis of a single anonymous threat; the scare proved unfounded. The generic drug scandal was the crushing blow. Young was asked to resign in 1989, and a search for a new commissioner was launched.

At the same time, the Bush administration decided to create a blue-ribbon advisory committee to examine the FDA's problems and to recommend solutions. Charlie Edwards, who had headed the agency in the early 1970s, was put in charge. My academic articles on food and drug law and my time with Orrin Hatch helped bring me to Edwards's attention, and I was asked to become a member of his advisory committee.

By then, the reputation, as well as the abilities, of the world's premier food and drug safety agency had sunk to historic lows. In its final report, the Edwards Committee described "grave resource limitations" that imposed "sometimes staggering burdens on the Agency." The committee also expressed "doubts about the FDA's current capacity to conduct effective law enforcement," or to fulfill its many other statutory obligations.

What was unclear was how much any one leader could change things. An old story told by FDA field inspectors captured the sentiment within the agency. "The FDA is like one of those giant clowns carried in the New Orleans Mardi Gras parade," it went. "The body, moving under cover, is the agency itself. The head, called the commissioner, is pelted with rocks until the clown falls over. But the body picks up another head and keeps doing its business."

I received a call from the White House personnel office in late October 1990 to say that the President was going to nominate me as FDA commissioner. As I hung up I stared out the window of my Bronx hospital office, overlooking a barbed wire–enclosed subway yard, and for a moment I felt triumphant. That uncomplicated feeling did not last long. Within days I received a letter from a congressman asking in no uncertain terms that I turn a set of FDA documents over to his committee; on the bottom, he had written, "Welcome to Washington and good luck."

On learning of my nomination, Michael Calhoun told a high-level staffer in the legislative affairs office of the Department of Health and Human Services to "encapsulate" me. When the Senate Committee on Labor and

Human Resources, which was preparing for my confirmation hearings, asked me to respond to a list of questions, the Department tried to insist on writing the answers for me. Assuming it was my views that the senators wanted to hear, I refused.

"This is my confirmation," I said. "I'll answer the questions."

Everyone believed the congressional vote to approve my nomination would have to wait until after the holidays when the new legislative session began. But a sense of urgency took hold, as Congress and the White House decided that the FDA had gone long enough without a commissioner. There was a push past formalities, and in the end I was confirmed in a record eight days. Never again would I have it so easy in Congress.

I was thirty-nine years old, and I was supposed to clean up an agency in crisis. The giant clown in the Mardi Gras parade had picked up a new head.

2

SOON after my confirmation, I asked the acting commissioner to keep an eye on the agency's day-to-day business for a month while I prepared to take over. I wanted time to listen to my new colleagues and to think about my first steps. I hid away on the thirteenth floor of the Parklawn building, the FDA's Rockville headquarters. The gray behemoth is a regrettable example of institutional architecture, with mazes of offices branching off a confusing network of corridors. My makeshift space was barely big enough for two chairs and one rickety desk. I had come a long way since my days as a part-time Senate aide, but I still had not settled into an adequate office.

One of the first people to seek me out was Jeff Nesbit, the agency's associate commissioner for public affairs. Jeff was a paradox. Two of his heroes in Washington were Ralph Nader and the investigative columnist Jack Anderson, and by the time he was twenty-seven he had worked for them both. He was also a devoutly religious evangelical Christian who questioned authority at every turn. But Jeff was equally at home with the secular give-and-take of consumer advocacy. His road to Damascus had been on a bicycle. On a twenty-five-day coast-to-coast journey, he talked with hundreds of people and returned home inspired by the hope and optimism he encountered. His life's goal became pursuing social change through political action.

Much to the surprise of his colleagues, he turned to Senator Dan Quayle to do it. One of the first people to believe that Quayle was a viable vice presidential candidate, Jeff pursued a *sub-rosa* campaign in the summer of 1988 to get the Bush team to consider him for the ticket. Although he saw his goal realized, Jeff was never comfortable with the hard-nosed politicians who surrounded Bush. The discomfort was reciprocated, and after the Bush-Quayle ticket was elected, he was told to look for another job. In typical fashion, Jeff chose one of the toughest jobs in Washington: he came to work for the beleaguered FDA.

Now we sat together in a tiny cubicle. Jeff realized that I was thinking of replacing him with someone I already knew and trusted, and he wanted to fight for his job. He had done his homework before we met, reading everything that I had written and talking to reporters who covered me in Washington.

We started talking about his background. He told me that after writing an article about the Kentucky Derby that offended horse-racing interests, he had been fired from a job with a Kentucky newspaper. And when he discovered that he had made some errors in a piece he had written for Jack Anderson, Jeff argued adamantly that Anderson should print a correction. The columnist refused, and Jeff resigned a few weeks later. I began to think I liked this man.

Over time, I learned that we shared an indifference to ideological labels and a reluctance to view the political landscape in black-and-white terms. Public health mattered to us—we both wanted to work on issues that made a difference in people's lives—but party affiliation did not. I suppose that was a form of ideology in itself; certainly, it was a driving force for us both.

Jeff also understood something else, something that would take me longer to comprehend. The reality of Washington was that we would have to fight fiercely to make changes that mattered. I decided to keep him on.

I QUICKLY learned that the time required to develop sound public policy and to map strategy competed with the all-consuming nature of emergencies. And any notion that I might have had about leisurely charting an agenda for the agency quickly evaporated.

It was almost midnight on Saturday, March 2, 1991, and I was watching *Saturday Night Live*, when the telephone rang. I had been formally sworn in as commissioner only one week earlier. My family was still living in New York, and I was commuting home from Washington on weekends.

Jeff was on the line. He had just received a report from the FDA's district office in Seattle that Sudafed capsules laced with cyanide appeared to be circulating in the Pacific Northwest. A woman named Kathleen Daneker had died after taking one, and another woman had narrowly escaped death. I turned off the television.

The agency receives some three hundred reports of tampering every year, and though many are never confirmed, none can be ignored. In those situations, decisions that may involve life and death have to be made swiftly and without complete information. I had faced pressure as a pediatrician working in an emergency room and again when I was running the hospital in the Bronx. But this was different. In a tampering incident, the number of lives at risk is unclear. How many deadly capsules were out there? One hundred? One thousand? And where were they? Also different was my role in the unfolding drama. I was accustomed to dealing with emergencies on a hands-on basis. Now I was thousands of miles away.

Still, as Jeff started running through the facts, I felt calm. For the moment I was unfazed by the thought that I had never handled a tampering incident before. I interrupted Jeff to suggest a conference call so that I could speak directly to the frontline field people myself. Within minutes we had everyone who had so far been involved in the case, plus the top people at FDA headquarters, on the phone. (To be accurate, not quite everyone was there. When the conference operator awakened one veteran staffer and told him the commissioner was on the line, he assumed it was a crank call and hung up.)

"What do we know?" I asked.

Jim Davis, the chief investigator in the Seattle office, laid out the chronology. The story began a month earlier in Tumwater, a suburb of Olympia, at the southern end of Puget Sound, about fifty miles from Seattle. On the night of February 2, the town's fire department responded to a 911 call from Joseph Meling. His twenty-eight-year-old wife, Jennifer, was having seizures.

When the medics arrived they found her comatose. By the time she got to the hospital in Olympia, she was near death. Her stomach was pumped in the emergency room, but her blood sugar and lactic acid were so high and her blood pressure so low that the doctors thought she had gone into diabetic shock. They gave her insulin to lower the blood sugar, bicarbonates to counter the deadly level of acid in her blood, and a drug to boost her blood pressure.

By midnight she was still in a coma. The desperate doctors continued the treatment, using so much bicarbonate that they virtually exhausted the hospital's supply. But it worked. Over the next twenty-four hours, Jennifer Meling staged a dramatic neurological recovery.

Shortly before she had gone to bed, she had taken three different products: an iron tablet, an over-the-counter supplement, and a twelve-hour Sudafed capsule. A hospital blood test showed 6.14 milligrams of cyanide per liter in her blood—triple the amount that is normally lethal. She was lucky to be alive.

An FDA investigator had already gone to Tumwater to secure copies of Jennifer Meling's medical records and the statement she had made to a detective after her recovery. Meling had told the police that she had taken a Sudafed capsule from a box that her husband, Joseph, had purchased the week before. The interview also revealed a troubled marriage, including a 911 call to police three days before Christmas, 1990, and a huge increase in Jennifer Meling's life insurance policy.

The Meling case raised the eyebrows of the investigators—it had the scent of attempted homicide. A 1983 federal law had made tampering easier to prosecute; it was passed in part because no charges had been brought against a suspect in the Tylenol poisoning case, though that incident had resulted in the deaths of seven people. The statute defined tampering as the malicious adulteration of a consumer product that is already in commercial channels. If Meling had put cyanide into his wife's Sudafed, it was a matter for the Tumwater police. But if he had put cyanide-laced capsules back onto store shelves, it was a federal offense and a matter for the FDA and the FBI.

Davis said Burroughs Wellcome, the manufacturer of Sudafed, had reported the case to the FDA on February 15. Although I said nothing, I was dismayed that others at the agency had known about this for two weeks, and I was only learning about it now.

Jeff's call to me came only after cyanide had been implicated in the death of another Washington woman. Kathleen Daneker collapsed in her bathroom in Tacoma, twenty-five miles northeast of Tumwater, shortly after taking Sudafed for a sinus condition. For two days she lingered in a coma and on life support in St. Joseph's Hospital, and then she died. When laboratory results showed 6.49 milligrams of cyanide per liter of blood in her body, the medical examiner immediately alerted the FDA's Seattle office. Seattle investigators had not yet determined how, or even if, the two cyanide poisonings were related. I began pushing Jim Davis and the other participants on the conference call about possible connections between the two cases. Was there one culprit or two? Was there any relationship between Meling and Daneker? What was the risk that other cyanide-containing Sudafed capsules were on the market? Or in home medicine cabinets? No one had clear answers.

Davis told me about conversations his office had already had with Burroughs Wellcome. Each retail box contained one to four blister packs and was sealed on both ends with tape bearing the company's logo. Ten red-and-clear capsules sealed with a blue band were individually wrapped in a blister pack.

After the first incident, Burroughs Wellcome had analyzed the leftover Sudafed capsules from the batch Jennifer Meling had taken and pulled eighty-four boxes from the store where her medication had been purchased. Nothing unusual had been found.

Dick Swanson, who headed the agency's emergency operations section in Washington, D.C., was listening quietly on the line. "Dr. Doom," as he was known, had earned his nickname from years of handling product tampering and other health emergencies, from botulism in Bon Vivant, a canned soup, to the salmonella that had been used to poison salad bars in a small Oregon town, where cult members hoped to sicken enough voters to sway a local election. Swanson's other moniker, "Darth Vader," referred to his vaguely sinister persona, which was reflected in his preference for a dark office—usually a desk lamp was all that illuminated the room. Along with piles of books, Dick's office was strewn with product samples from previous investigations: a giant jawbreaker, malt liquor, cold medicine, a lollipop. On his desk in the center of the room was an antiquated phone that was just functional enough to accommodate conference calls. Swanson had served six commissioners. He generally worked directly with the FDA's field people, and I sensed that I had upset him by doing so myself, but I could do nothing about that now.

From his West Coast office, Jim Davis continued relaying the story. The first break in the case had come only that morning, he said. In the FDA's Seattle laboratory, Ruth Johnson had been assigned to examine the Sudafed blister pack from which Kathleen Daneker had taken a capsule. Ruth was a perfectionist who had been with the agency for more than twenty-five years. She pulled on white cotton gloves and looked at the four empty blisters under the microscope. There was no residual material. Using a scalpel to cut open the intact blisters, she removed the remaining capsules. Still nothing unusual. The blue plastic band sealing together the two halves of each capsule was intact. She slit open each capsule and transferred some of the contents into test tubes, dissolving them in water and adding a few drops of sulfuric acid. If cyanide were present, the acid would release a cyanide gas. It did not.

Giving up on the bench tests, Ruth checked out the packaging—and noticed a discrepancy. The number for the box was 8U2849 and for the blister pack, 8U2846. One number was different. It meant the capsules from one box had been put into another, a classic sign of tampering. Upon learning what Ruth had found, a colleague dashed down the hallway to look at a copy of the Tumwater police report on Jennifer Meling. The box of Sudafed capsules she had used bore the number 002847; the blister pack was 8U2846. Jennifer Mel-ing and Kathleen Daneker had used blister packs taken from the same box.

It was 12:30 A.M., March 3, on the East Coast, three hours earlier in the Pacific Northwest. Jeff Nesbit, who had been working with the public affairs people in the Seattle office, said we had fifteen minutes to decide whether to issue a statement for the 10 P.M. West Coast news broadcasts.

We needed to make a move. Our first decision was relatively easy—I sug-gested issuing a warning for the Seattle region in which we would release the product codes in question and urge the public to look carefully at any Sudafed they had at home. Everyone agreed, and Jeff signed off to call the local news stations.

The next decision was tougher. In a mobile society, a local tampering could quickly have national reach. Dick Swanson pointed out that someone could easily buy Sudafed in the Seattle area, pack it in a suitcase, and travel anywhere. And yet we had not found even one Sudafed capsule that showed any evidence of tampering. Should there be a product recall? If so, should it be national or regional? A measured response was vital. While erring on the side of caution often seemed prudent, public panic could jeopardize the agency's credibility, with potentially calamitous consequences for the future. We reviewed everything that had been learned and talked to everyone we could.

As we were agonizing over our next move, there was a sudden commo-tion over the speakerphone. An FDA investigator had just burst into the Seat-tle conference room-turned-command center. I glanced at the wall clock in my study. It was 2:40 A.M. in New York.

The announcement was clipped and brief: "There's been a third incident." In Lacey, Washington, a woman named Sabra McWhorter had been watch-ing the Channel 4 news in Seattle and heard our warning. She immediately called the television station and told them that two weeks earlier her hus-band, Stanley, had died after taking a Sudafed capsule.

A Vietnam veteran, McWhorter, forty-four, had been a healthy and suc-cessful commercial real estate broker. After two weeks of uncomfortable sinus problems, he bought a package of Sudafed. His wife stood nearby as he took a capsule. Almost immediately he said, "I'm going to quit taking these …I don't feel good. I'm getting lightheaded. I think I'm going to faint."

Those were his last words. He collapsed into his wife's arms, his eyes wide open, his right leg jerking. Paramedics rushed him to the hospital where he was put on life support; he died the next day.

Channel 4 called the FBI. The FBI called the county coroner. The coroner called the FDA.

The code on the McWhorter blister pack of Sudafed was 8U2846. Suddenly, I felt ill. I knew there was no need for further debate. I asked for the telephone number of Philip Tracy, the CEO of Burroughs Wellcome, woke him at four in the morning, and told him what had to be done. Within a few hours, we had issued a nationwide recall.

OVER the next few days, we found three packages of Sudafed capsules laced with cyanide. One was still on the drugstore shelves in Tacoma. The other two, purchased at different stores in the region, were already in home medicine cabinets. One tampered package had been opened but in a lifesaving twist of fate, the consumer had begun taking the capsules from the other end.

A week later, Swanson notified me of another cyanide-poisoning death linked to Sudafed. But chemical fingerprinting showed that the poison was from a different batch and we determined that it was a copycat crime of sorts— a suicide masquerading as a tampering. The dead man wanted his family to collect on his life insurance policy.

Almost eighteen months passed before the FBI completed its investigation and Joseph Meling was indicted on twenty criminal charges. He had traveled up and down Interstate 5 putting adulterated Sudafed on store shelves in an attempt to murder his wife and then mask the killing as an anonymous product tampering.

The Sudafed incident was my welcome to the agency. The morning after the national recall, a reporter asked me why we had not moved sooner. I began to understand just what I was facing.

3

When I told Secretary Sullivan before my appointment as commissioner that I wanted to enforce the law, my words sounded so obvious as to seem banal, even to me. But the FDA had not been known for its enforcement muscle, and that was something I was determined to change.

Within weeks of my arrival in Washington I made my first major public speech about the need to restore the FDA's credibility. As I stood at the podium of the annual meeting of the Food and Drug Law Institute, I looked across an area the size of a football field filled with food and drug lawyers and lobbyists. They all earned their livelihoods from their dealings with the FDA. I suspected that most of them were indifferent to my academic credentials and were uncertain that I had enough experience, political finesse, and judgment for the job.

I already knew something about this permanent Washington coterie of lawyers and lobbyists. Many were FDA alumni who had switched sides and were now representing the food and drug companies they used to regulate. Years earlier when I worked on the Hill, I had glimpsed the close relationships between regulated industries and congressional representatives. At that time the industries were demanding that the nation's food safety standards be relaxed, and their lobbyists readily gained access to key legislators, a lot more readily than when the FDA had been paying their salaries.

In my speech I emphasized that law enforcement—the frontline, field-based work so crucial to product safety—had been short-changed in recent years. In essence, we had a lot of scientists and lawyers on staff but not enough cops. "The FDA is the regulator, and you should know that I have no problem stating that fact," I said firmly, though I knew that deregulation was in vogue. "The FDA *must* stand for, it *must* embody, strong and judicious enforcement.... Let me remind all of you neither to underestimate the vigor of this agency nor the strength of its resolve."

The intensity of my delivery, more than the words themselves, led one prominent lobbyist to call this my "kick-ass speech." But not everyone was impressed. Malcolm Gladwell of the *Washington Post* said to Jeff Nesbit, who was a friend of his, "Wake me up when he does something."

WASHINGTON insiders tend to keep watch on newcomers, looking for hints that can help them understand what a person is really like. Pressed for time, I began jogging through the streets at all hours of the night. When word of my unconventional exercise habits reached the Department, a few people wondered whether I was a bit over the edge.

Hoping to do some of my learning outside the media microscope, and innocent enough to believe that was possible, I told Nesbit that I thought it would be best if the FDA could stay out of the press for my first six months as commissioner. I wanted to make some structural changes and streamline the bureaucracy, but I was not exactly shaking up the place. My focus was on finding the resources and staff to reinvigorate the battered agency and to improve both its efficiency and its morale.

Shortly after I became commissioner, I was summoned to John Dingell's office. The Michigan congressman, a legendary character with a verbal style like that of a prosecutor, was at once a harsh critic of the FDA and a staunch defender of its mission. After he had gotten wind of the generic drugs scandal, he had unleashed a lacerating investigation, holding more than a dozen hearings, blitzing officials with demands for documents and records, and creating a siege mentality at FDA headquarters. Dingell fired off so many astringent letters to the FDA that they became known as "Dingellgrams"—and any failure to satisfy him was likely to end in a personal roasting.

Congressman Dingell was leaning back in his chair when I arrived, yet he seemed to fill the room. He launched into a stern lecture about the deficiencies of the agency, an inventory of failings that he wanted me to address. Dingell had friendly sources throughout the FDA and was dangerously well-informed about its shortcomings. In the past he had known about problems at the agency long before the commissioner. If I was to avoid becoming the target of his wrath, I was going to have to find ways to change that.

I knew before I took the job that the FDA was the favored whipping boy of politicians and antiregulatory ideologues, of companies under its jurisdiction, and of often-dissatisfied consumer groups. It had been like that for decades, largely because the agency had influence over such a huge portion of the American economy and its decisions affected so many powerful interests. "A slow-moving target that bleeds profusely when hit," one former commissioner said of the FDA. No one could ever be fully prepared to run it.

Dingell was less concerned about the special interests outside the agency than about the bureaucracy within it. He viewed some of my predecessors as figureheads and knew that I could easily become captive to forces inside my own agency. Like others, Dingell understood that I had an opportunity to master the job and a chance of being destroyed by it. I realized little of this at the time, but I knew that I had one thing going in my favor. Usually, taking bold steps is the best way for the head of a federal agency to get into trouble. In my case, the FDA was under such aggressive attack for not responding appropriately to its problems that bold action would likely be tolerated, perhaps even welcomed.

One morning I visited the FDA's Center for Foods, and its enforcement arm, the Office of Compliance. Although a health claim on food was considered the equivalent of a drug claim, the FDA's efforts at enforcement had dwindled to almost nothing. After a decade of virtually no restraint from the agency, a free-for-all had developed as marketers looked for ways to gain advantage on competitive supermarket shelves. Outlandish health claims had become commonplace. One example was the unchecked use of the word "heart," as in "heart-lite," "heart choice," and "heart-healthy."

The FDA staff had set out a slew of branded food products for me to see. They were especially bothered by the unbridled use of the word "fresh" and they showed me two particularly flagrant claims, one involving tomato sauce for pasta, the other, orange juice.

Ragu sauce, produced by the multinational giant Unilever, bore the label "Fresh Italian." But like most mass producers, the company cut shipping costs by boiling fresh tomatoes until they were reduced to solids; this paste was then shipped to regional plants, where water was added to reconstitute the sauce.

The orange juice issue involved Procter & Gamble's Citrus Hill brand. The phrase "Fresh Choice" was three times the size of the brand name on the label and the description read: "Pure squeezed 100% orange juice." In smaller type were the words "from concentrate." On the paper cartons, the Citrus Hill blurb claimed, "We pick our oranges at the peak of ripeness. Then we hurry to squeeze them before they lose their freshness." Tropicana, a Seagram's brand, had complained that Citrus Hill was a blend of juices from Brazil and Florida that were reduced to concentrate through evaporation. Months later, water was added back, along with orange oil, orange pulp, and something described as "orange essence," in an attempt to restore flavor.

The law required that if a label was determined to be false or misleading, the FDA should seize the product and prohibit its sale. But to the frustration of our enforcement agents, the agency had not seized a food product on these grounds in years. The industry had come to believe that we never would.

The Ragu controversy went public in March 1991, when I was called to testify before the House Subcommittee on Health and the Environment, chaired by the California Democrat Henry Waxman. Knowing that Congressman Alex McMillan, a subcommittee member, had once run a retail food chain in his home state of North Carolina, the FDA's Center for Foods had passed copies of the "Fresh Italian" Ragu labels to his staff. McMillan picked up on it. When the floor opened for questions, he held up the labels and asked me about the use of the word "fresh."

I used his questions to telegraph my intentions. "I think the product is misbranded," I said. "We believe our experts will conclude that the evidence—and we are analyzing it—will support that determination. If that is in fact the case, and the use of the word 'fresh' remains on the label, the Food and Drug Administration will seize the product."

Unilever made a meaningless concession, adding a panel on the Ragu label saying "means fresh taste." Rather than wait until we could conduct new consumer surveys to determine whether the Ragu label remained misleading, we decided to move against Citrus Hill. The first step was to warn Procter & Gamble that we were ready to take action. The company's response was to argue, in essence, that everybody did it. No one, they insisted, sold juice that was squeezed directly from the fruit, then sealed into containers.

A young FDA lawyer named Denise Zavagno was put in charge of the Citrus Hill case. Denise understood that I wanted to clean up the anarchy in food labeling, and she recognized that the agency's credibility was at stake. In early negotiations, Procter & Gamble did not take us seriously, so we took the first step towards seizure, sending FDA representatives to a Minneapolis warehouse to collect product samples. The next day we received a call from company lawyers. Suddenly they were ready to negotiate. Over the next forty-eight hours, as conference call followed upon conference call, agreement seemed to be in sight.

Our warning letter to Procter & Gamble set April 24 as the deadline for compliance. By chance, I was scheduled to speak before a group of food industry lawyers that day in Palm Beach Gardens, Florida, and I hoped to be able to announce a settlement. At 9 P.M. on the twenty-third, the phone rang at the FDA. Procter & Gamble refused to sign the agreement.

Denise called Margaret Porter, the agency's chief counsel, to tell her that negotiations had failed. Margaret relayed the news to me in Florida.

"What do you want to do, David?" she asked.

Had I been more attuned to the consequences of seizing a mislabeled product after years of quiescence, I might have paused. Perhaps I should have asked myself whether I had come to Washington to confiscate cartons of orange juice. I ought at least to have considered whether I would be accused of taking on an "easy" target. But I had not been on the job long enough to think about such questions. It was not my intention to make a symbolic gesture. This was simply part of the FDA's job, or so I thought.

I answered Margaret's question with one of my own. "What did we tell them we would do?"

"We said we would seize the product."

"Well, go seize it."

I put down the phone and pulled out the text of my speech to the food industry lawyers. I needed to make some revisions.

THERE was a brief delay the following morning when the U.S. marshals, who had to accompany the local FDA staff to the site of the seizure, were sent instead to chase an escaped convict. They soon returned, having caught their man, and headed to the Super Valu warehouse, where they quickly encircled 24,000 half-gallon cartons of Citrus Hill with yellow tape. That, technically, was a seizure.

In Florida, about the same time, I began my speech. The food industry lawyers were dressed for golf.

I opened with comments about the agency's poor record in policing food and about the food industry's apparent belief that the only good FDA was a weak one. I reminded my audience that I had taught food law and written about it.

They did not seem impressed. I had not yet mastered the art of reading an audience, but I was reasonably sure this one was listening with only half an ear. I persevered, moving towards a discussion of enforcement. "Protecting consumers against fraud requires first of all a willingness to enforce the law, a characteristic that has not been sufficiently apparent in recent years," I said. This was still not enough to break their leisurely mood.

I added that I was convinced that the generic drugs scandal had happened because people thought they could get away with it. "If people perceive that their government is not protecting them against cheaters, they will not be confident that the same government is protecting them against unsafe or unwholesome food."

Not much reaction. I was coming to the end of my typed draft. '

"If the label claims that a product is low-calorie, we will see that it is low-calorie. If the container states that it contains juice, we will make certain that juice is what it contains."

I looked hard at them and said, "This is not the idle talk of a new commissioner. We have taken a firm position on the use of the term 'fresh' on the food label."

I paused before reading a new paragraph, written in longhand: "Today, the U.S. Attorney's office in Minneapolis is filing on the FDA's behalf a seizure action against Procter & Gamble's Citrus Hill Fresh Choice orange juice product, made from concentrate. The use of the term 'fresh' on their product is false and misleading and confusing for consumers. Today's action will send a clear message that the FDA will not tolerate such violations of the law. If you entertain any doubts about the steadfastness of the FDA where enforcement is concerned, please be disabused of this notion."

I finally had their attention. Suddenly, my words about the agency's enforcement powers, and our willingness to use them, took on new meaning. They decided their golf games could wait.

Within hours, the importance of media attention was made clear to me. Jeff Nesbit only learned about the seizure the night before it happened, but he immediately recognized it as an opportunity to publicize the agency's new activist role and to push me into the limelight.

Jeff had told me he planned to videotape my Florida speech, but I had given little thought to the implications. I certainly did not realize he was going to put a video news release of me announcing the seizure on satellite. That night the story was on national television, and the next morning it received major newspaper coverage. Some of the reports trivialized the seizure, calling it the United States versus 24,000 cartons of orange juice. But a few journalists realized that we had taken on a pillar of the food industry and were sending a strong signal that a new era in enforcement had dawned.

The agency's switchboard began to light up. Charities were asking for the 24,000 cartons of orange juice, which were quickly donated to a local food bank in Minneapolis.

Denise Zavagno received a call from her mother. "I read in the paper about you and the orange juice," she said. "You haven't got anything better to do with your time?"

My son Ben, who at the time had a passion for professional wrestling, created a poster of me in the wrestling ring facing down a carton of Citrus Hill.

Finally, the CEO of Procter & Gamble's beverage division called me directly and said the company had not thought we were serious. He admitted having made a mistake by walking away from the table. The company quickly relabeled its orange juice and the rest of the industry heard the message.

There was no need for further seizures. Unilever took "means fresh taste" off its Ragu tomato sauce, renamed it "Fino Italian," and agreed to amend the ingredient list to be clear that the sauce was made from tomato concentrate. Within a few months, twenty other firms had removed "fresh" from their processed-food labels.

Mark Green, New York City's commissioner of consumer affairs, praised the seizure. "The new FDA has done more about deceptive food claims in a week than it did in the past decade," he said. "After years of the Federal government regarding consumers as a four-letter word, it's wonderful to see the FDA metamorphosis from a lapdog into a watchdog."

The critics were not so delighted. The *Washington Times* ridiculed the action. "It's nice to know the FDA has found something to do besides stop AIDS patients and otherwise incurably ill people from trying drugs that the agency just isn't sure are effective."

My superiors at the Department of Health and Human Services were also less than enthusiastic, mostly because they had been caught off guard. Connie Horner, the deputy secretary, called me and spoke gently. She asked that next time I let the Department know in advance what was happening.

In truth, it had never occurred to me to go up the chain of command and inform the Department. I believed I was acting appropriately in my capacity as commissioner. But for Horner, the risks of appointing an unknown to the FDA had been demonstrated. When she interviewed me for the job months earlier, Horner said, "David, once you're Senate-confirmed, we lose all control." Now, I am sure she saw that she had been right.

Back at FDA headquarters, someone strung up a banner that read, "The watchdog is back and it has teeth." I was sending a wake-up call, an assertion of independence that the Washington establishment could not—and did not—ignore.

4

JEFF NESBIT kept watching me, wondering whether I had the will to do whatever it took to protect the public health. Slowly I began to earn his confidence, and after Citrus Hill he decided to broach an idea with which he had been wrestling for some time.

Jeff leaned his lanky frame against the doorjamb in my office, waiting for a meeting to end. Then, as the others were filing out, he came across the room. From the look on his face, I thought he had some ordinary business to discuss. Instead, he said, "David, I want you to take on tobacco."

Jeff's attitude was that if something could be done, and should be done, there was no excuse for not trying to do it. He was not one to wait until the moment was right; rather, he worked to create that moment. He did not ask me if I wanted to take on tobacco. He told me I should.

I had already discovered Jeff's knack for identifying broad and timely issues, but this one seemed off the mark. We were barely beginning to dig out from under the avalanche of external interference and internal corruption that had threatened to bury the agency. The orange juice seizure had been a guerrilla action—it was dramatic and effective, but lasting change could only come from a major commitment of resources. What we needed was to craft a long-term food-labeling policy, and that's what was on my mind.

Beyond that, I was still handling the basics. The agency needed expanded enforcement powers and more efficient management, and staff morale was only beginning to improve. I was also trying to build an Office of Criminal Investigations to fill the huge gap in the agency's capabilities that Sudafed had revealed. Relying on the FBI had taken too long; I wanted to be able to run our investigations quickly to meet the needs not only of law enforcement, but of public safety. I had just announced a plan to create a team of one hundred criminal investigators to do that.

Tobacco? I was not ready to grapple with it. I thought Jeff was crazy.

THE last time I had thought about tobacco regulation was in a Columbia Law School classroom. My co-teacher, Hal Edgar, loved teaching and loved the law. Nothing pleased him more than to demonstrate to students the untenable nature of their opinions. My approach was to focus on how decisions get made and how people can push a process to a conclusion. We were good foils for each other.

In May 1977, Action on Smoking and Health (ASH), a public interest group based at George Washington University, had submitted a petition to the FDA asking that the agency assert jurisdiction over cigarettes as a drug. Donald Kennedy, who was commissioner at the time, denied the petition, and ASH filed suit in U.S. District Court against the FDA.

Don Kennedy had his hands full in those days dealing with a proposed ban on saccharin, the artificial sweetener that had been shown to cause cancer in mice. At a congressional hearing, one senator asked Kennedy how he could propose to ban saccharin when he had done nothing to ban a much more dangerous product: cigarettes. Kennedy's response was short and pointed. "Senator, I'll be glad to go to work on the cigarette ban as soon as you give me the legislative authority to do so."

This assumption that the FDA did not have jurisdiction delighted the tobacco industry. Anyone familiar with the ways of Washington doubted that Congress, so beholden to the industry, would ever consider anti-tobacco legislation.

With that history in mind, I posed a question to my class of second- and third-year law students. "The question," I said, "is, why doesn't the FDA regulate cigarettes?" I wanted them to imagine themselves in the role of commissioner of the Food and Drug Administration and to consider whether they should regulate cigarettes as drugs.

To answer, the class had to understand the statutory definition of a drug. I directed them to the relevant section of the law, which defined drugs in part as "articles (other than food) intended to affect the structure or any function of the body." I emphasized the two components of the definition: a substance not only had to affect the structure or function of the body, but the

27

manufacturer had to intend that it do so. One of my students immediately understood the implications, and asked whether two manufacturers could make exactly the same product, one a drug, the other not. "The answer to that is yes," Hal Edgar said promptly. He expanded his point. "Suppose you're putting out sugar in a pill, and you are labeling this sugar 'Miller's Super Sugar will cure cancer.' Anyone doubt that Super Sugar is a drug?"

No one did. The health claim made it a drug. But the same sugar, marketed simply as "Bill Miller's Cane Sugar," was different. Nobody thought that was a drug.

That standard also applied to tobacco. In *ASH v. Harris*, the Court of Appeals upheld the FDA's decision not to regulate cigarettes as drugs because no evidence had been presented to demonstrate intent.

The discussion shifted to the political realities. "Is the reason cigarettes aren't regulated because of the tobacco lobby?" one student asked.

I thought not. "Don Kennedy and all these commissioners, they don't really care about the influence of the tobacco lobby. Congress may care…" I said.

Hal was indignant. "Don Kennedy doesn't care about the influence of the tobacco lobby? Does Don Kennedy have a budget?"

Everyone paused, but I continued to argue that the power of the industry had diminished over the past decade, and that in any case, Kennedy's job was to carry out the statute.

Returning to the *ASH* case, I asked, "Would you have brought this lawsuit?"

Hal said yes. Even predicting the likelihood of a defeat, he thought there was value in putting pressure on the FDA and forcing people to think about the issue. He added that *ASH* did not have to be the final word.

"I do not read this case as holding the commissioner can't change his mind if he wants to," Hal said. "Who knows what would happen if he did change his mind?"

IN subsequent years, the agency had deviated little from Kennedy's position. Premier, a supposedly smokeless cigarette under development by R. J. Reynolds in the late 1980s, during Frank Young's tenure as commissioner, offered one opportunity for the FDA to take action. Premier was unlike any cigarette ever seen before. It contained only a small amount of tobacco, and that seemed to have been added to diminish the chances that it would be regulated. The high-tech product had a carbon tip that, when lit, heated up tiny aluminum balls impregnated with nicotine that were called "flavor beads." Cut open, Premier looked like the shell casing of a bullet, and when it burned, it emitted an aerosol-type spray. Premier produced virtually no smoke and no tar at all. It delivered nicotine without burning tobacco. RJR wanted to market the product as an alternative to standard cigarette brands.

RJR knew it had to manage its government relations carefully in order to put Premier on the market "free of government interference or regulation," as a company memo said, and it developed an aggressive strategy for doing just that. Among the company's explicit objectives: "insure that FDA initially declines to assert jurisdiction... neutralize key members of the Administration and Members of Congress so that there is not an overwhelming sentiment to force FDA jurisdiction."

Whether Premier was a healthier product was not germane to the question of whether the FDA should regulate it. The question centered instead on intended use and its similarity to existing cigarettes. To FDA compliance officers—referred to as "puritans" by one RJR official—Premier looked like a novel nicotine-delivery system, but Commissioner Young seemed unable to make up his mind about taking action. Months went by, until finally he sent a letter to the chairman of R. J. Reynolds that was a model of ambiguity: "Whereas it is possible that we will decide the product does not come under our jurisdiction, it is also possible that we will decide that the product is subject to FDA regulation."

By the time Young sent his mixed message, Premier was beginning to run into problems of a different sort. Senior executives at RJR who lit up the "delivery device" were appalled by its foul taste, which they described with locker-room epithets. Despite its $68 million investment, RJR halted tests on Premier in February 1989. The product never went on the market, and the FDA never had to make a decision. But the image of those nicotine-coated balls stayed in the minds of some at the agency.

ALTHOUGH I did nothing to encourage him, Jeff Nesbit did not give up hope that I might eventually confront the question of tobacco regulation. Jeff was a master of the corridor confrontation, buttonholing people and making his pitch to a captive audience. He raised the issue whenever he could, with anyone who would listen. Most people he spoke with thought him naïve. The tobacco industry is too big and too powerful, he was told. Going after it is a fool's errand, political suicide. Nesbit heard the same message over and over: the industry and its friends would come after us.

One afternoon in the spring of 1991, Jeff got into a heated argument with Gerry Meyer, one of the agency's old-timers. It began when Jeff caught Gerry in the hallway and asked his oft-repeated question. "Why doesn't the FDA regulate cigarettes? It doesn't make any sense."

Jeff continued insistently. "This consumer product kills more Americans than you can possibly imagine, and you won't touch it. Why?"

"That's a crazy idea," snapped Gerry. "It's a crock."

Gerry and Jeff made a striking contrast. Jeff looked perpetually youthful, with the physique of a long-jumper, which he had been. His reputation as a careless dresser was second only to mine. Gerry was older, the professional who had seen everything and was implacable in his views. Despite his commitment to public health, he did not consider this an appropriate FDA issue. The agency risked losing the support of congressmen from tobacco-growing states, Gerry said, and might be putting its budget on the line. That could jeopardize its ability to do anything at all. Gerry knew that sort of thing had happened before. Once, after regulators pursued a beet processor who was grinding down larger, tougher beets to sell as the more tender small ones, the New York congressman in whose district the beet manufacturer operated slashed the agency appropriations, forcing extensive layoffs. Though the incident had occurred many years earlier, long-time staff had taken it to heart. Gerry was concerned that hostility from the Hill could again put us in serious jeopardy. "It's a no-brainer," he concluded.

Jeff was not convinced. I kept ducking his hints that I consider the case for tobacco regulation, and he kept ignoring my lukewarm response. Finally, to quiet him down, I agreed to schedule a briefing.

I wondered why Jeff kept pushing, but I did not ask. He did not tell me then that his father, a lifelong smoker who had often tried unsuccessfully to quit, was dying of cancer. His brother, ten years his junior, had also become an addicted smoker. Each day, before coming to the agency and again after work, Jeff visited his father at the hospital to say good-bye.

A "GOLDENROD," so-called because it was printed on a yellowish-orange paper, was generally circulated before a briefing of the kind that Jeff requested. A goldenrod set out the agenda and typically included some background to bring meeting participants up to speed on the issue of the day. According to the goldenrod, the formal purpose of the meeting was to discuss our position "on the regulation of cigarettes as drugs." Summaries of several citizen petitions, a tool used by individuals or groups outside government to persuade government agencies to act, were attached.

Two petitions, filed in 1988, asked the agency to regulate Premier as a drug. Another claimed that by advertising low-tar cigarettes as safer than brands with normal levels of tar, manufacturers were selling a product that warranted FDA regulation. There had been no response by the agency. Still another petition, filed within months of my arrival at the agency, asked that Next, a new Philip Morris product being marketed as a "denicotinized" cigarette, be classified as a drug.

More than a dozen FDA scientists, lawyers, and administrators were invited to the briefing. I considered it a good opportunity to learn something about the personalities and philosophies of people who were still relatively unknown to me.

At 3 P.M. on May 2, 1991, everyone filed into a conference room on the fourteenth floor. The building faced north, excluding direct sun; the only natural light came from windows on the narrow, far wall. Previous commissioners had sat at one end of the long table in a chair with a higher back than the others; the remaining chairs had been allocated in a descending order of rank. I abandoned the "throne," choosing instead to sit halfway down one side of the table in a low-back chair. I could see that the absence of hierarchy was unsettling for the junior people, who did not know where to sit.

Portraits of my fourteen predecessors hung on the wall. As I looked at the starched collar of Harvey Wiley, who had threatened the interests of industry for the sake of the public health, I remembered reading a comment of his that I found appealing. "I began my public career without any idea of being quarrelsome and belligerent," Wiley had declared. "But from my entry into public life I became a belligerent in, I think, the best sense of the term. I fought with all my power for what I considered to be right."

Then there was Walter Campbell, whose tenure from 1921 until 1944 was marked by a crackdown on quack medicines and lax food standards. There had been ten more commissioners between Campbell's departure and Frank Young's appointment in 1984, a succession accelerated by the agency's heightened visibility and political vulnerability. Many of the later faces gazing down on the conference room had dealt with the pressures of increasingly sophisticated industry lobbying and the intrusive political agendas of the White House and Capitol Hill. None had seriously challenged the hands-off policy on tobacco.

I ASKED Jeff to begin. He made a passionate case that smoking was such an overwhelming public health crisis that we could no longer ignore it. He used the grounds on which he felt the strongest, his sense of the current political climate, arguing that the White House was not likely to stand in our way if we explored the possibility of regulating tobacco. He believed that George Bush was likely to be more sympathetic than Ronald Reagan, who earlier in his career had appeared in advertisements for Chesterfields. Equally important, he thought that Secretary Louis Sullivan would back us. I thought Jeff was probably right about Sullivan; I was less sure about Bush.

Knowing that he was facing battle-weary veterans of wars on Capitol Hill, Jeff was careful to emphasize his belief that the power of the tobacco lobby was no longer secure. Though large segments of Congress had once been beholden to the tobacco industry, he thought that its hard-core influence had shrunk to five or six states. He also pointed out that even that influence had not been tested for many years because the legislative challenges to tobacco had been so few.

When Jeff concluded his presentation, I said nothing, although I knew that the dangers of smoking, however real, did not by themselves provide a basis for regulating cigarettes. I went around the table to ask for comments.

It was quickly evident that Gerry Meyer led the opposition forces. In a tangible sense, Gerry represented the agency's institutional memory. I was the seventh commissioner under whom he had worked. As he acquired seniority at the FDA, he had made it part of his job to protect the commissioner. Over the years, he had hired many of the senior staff and had worked hard to see that his perspective and opinions were given due weight when policy decisions were made.

On tobacco, Gerry's arguments had nothing to do with whether or not smoking was lethal. Unlike most of us in that conference room, he had seen that in clinical detail during a ten-year stint with the National Cancer Institute. In 1962, he helped to set up a medical school in Ghana. Because the West African program was short of staff, Gerry assisted with autopsies. He never forgot the sight of lungs black and gummy with tar of people who had been heavy smokers.

Yet he was convinced that the FDA was not equipped to deal with tobacco as a public health issue. Gerry's main thrust was a more decorous reprise of what he had said to Jeff in their hallway argument: investigating tobacco would burn up too many resources and invite reprisal from the Hill or the White House through budget cuts. He was also dubious about where Secretary Sullivan might stand. "Will he be there if you get into trouble?" he asked rhetorically. Gerry suggested that the whole issue be diverted to the Drug Enforcement Agency, which could consider regulating tobacco as a "controlled substance," like heroin or cocaine. I thought this a flier that nobody could take too seriously, but Gerry was in earnest.

Gerry's colleague, Dan Michels, was equally determined to leave tobacco alone, partly out of fear of reviving the kinds of pressures the generic drugs scandal had engendered. As the head of drug compliance, Dan had been embroiled with the Hill twelve hours a day, six days a week, for months on end, responding to exhaustive calls for documents, facing hostile interrogations, and seeing the honor of the entire agency tarnished by the outrageous actions of a few. They had been the toughest of his thirty years with the FDA. Standing over six feet, two inches and heavyset with a graying beard, Dan looked every bit a stern compliance officer. But the prospect of another bloodying on the Hill was too much for him to contemplate. He saw tobacco as "the big muddy," a swamp from which the FDA would not be able to extricate itself.

Dan Michels and Gerry Meyer sat together on one side of a divided agency. Catherine Lorraine, an attorney in the general counsel's office, sat on the other.

Catherine grew up in Richmond, Virginia, a city noted not only for its aromas of honeysuckle and magnolia but also for being a major center of the American tobacco industry. Her father was proud of his family's Virginia roots, and when Catherine was a child he made a point of taking her to places where his ancestors had lived or worked. To visit the railroad station where a great-grandfather had earned his living, they would drive past the tobacco warehouse district. Catherine always remembered the rich, sweet smell of curing leaves in the squat, brick buildings.

As a student in the 1960s, Catherine studied art history at Yale and worked as a paralegal at a New Haven law firm that defended black radical groups. Her venture out of the South to an Ivy League school in that politically charged era helped define her professional goals and her style. She held strong views but they were couched in a soft-spoken manner. When she graduated from law school at the University of Virginia, becoming the first woman in her family to pursue a professional career, she looked toward public service. Her first job was at the Department of Education, and in 1986 she signed on at the FDA.

Those were conservative times, and Catherine was frustrated when the FDA passed up opportunities to be more aggressive. By the time Jeff Nesbit called for his briefing, she was convinced that the tobacco lobby was as powerful as any single interest in the country, and she viewed it as ruthless. Catherine had been dismayed to learn that several of her predecessors in the FDA's general counsel's office had been seduced by its largesse, opting to work for the industry after tenures at the FDA. Ultimately, she was bothered most by the defection of Richard Merrill, who had been dean of the University of Virginia Law School and who helped to imbue her with an enthusiasm for the FDA.

Catherine wanted an opportunity to speak out, but Dan Michels and Gerry Meyer had made it seem foolhardy to take on tobacco. She glanced at me for some reaction, but I offered none. I was determined to remain neutral.

With only a few moments to compose her thoughts, Catherine sought some way to pack all of her feelings into a few words, without sounding too emotional. Her words lingered long in my memory. "This is the most important thing we can do," she said crisply. "If we take it up, I'm willing to spend the rest of my career working on it."

At this, Dan Michels rolled his eyes and muttered, "Oh geez, Catherine, come on!"

We moved on. After Catherine's quiet but passionate statement of support, it was the turn of her boss, Margaret Porter, the agency's chief counsel, to speak. Margaret had reviewed the petitions carefully and had seen an association that was only on the fringes of my awareness—the link between my commitment to stronger enforcement on public health issues and the challenge of tobacco. Without much elaboration, Margaret said that if I decided to tackle the issue she was ready to make the resources of her office available. I heard her words as elegant code for "taking this up is not such a dumb idea."

My gaze fell next on Kevin Budich, who had tried to push the agency forward on Premier. After ten years as a field inspector, where his job of monitoring product safety included visiting farms to ensure that pesticide levels fell within legal limits, making unannounced visits to drug-manufacturing plants, and assessing flaws in hospital equipment, Kevin had earned a reputation as a compliance hawk. He had also been involved in a number of nicotine-related issues over the years, but now he felt as if he were walking a tightrope. Knowing that his supervisors did not want any part of tobacco, he was noncommittal to the point of being evasive. I looked at him oddly for a moment, not quite understanding where he stood.

Nothing else that was said changed my sense of the divisions in the room. I revealed little of my own thinking as the briefing came to a close. "Look, there are a lot of other things that I need to take on first," I said. "But I'll get around to this."

With that message, I seemed to have satisfied the first law of neutrality, sending both sides away with a sense of victory. Leaving the room, Dan Michels said to himself, "We ain't going to do it."

Kevin Budich went back to his office and told his colleagues, "Something is going to happen here."

Others thought the fact that I had held the meeting at all was a sign of interest, and they may have been right, although I certainly was not focused on the subject. For one thing, I did not think the agency was ready. Although we were beginning to recover from the generic drug scandal, we had not yet earned a reputation for accomplishment, and many at the agency still felt highly vulnerable to attack. This wait-and-see attitude was reassuring to the tobacco industry, which had asked its contacts on the Hill how the agency was going to handle the citizen petitions. "Don't worry about a lot happening on this for the foreseeable future," one congressional staffer predicted.

A few months later, at a meeting of the National Cancer Advisory Board, I stammered uncomfortably when asked by a board member about the FDA's willingness to do something about tobacco. Then I said the decision was out of our hands. Our jurisdiction is vast, I said, but "there are a few things in life that probably aren't foods, drugs, medical devices, or cosmetics, things that fall between the cracks. A cigarette is one."

I said that day that once we classified cigarettes as drugs, we would be required to ban them altogether. "There is no alternative," I stated. Perhaps I was just looking for an easy out when I added that Congress sets the mandate for the agency and Congress would therefore have to give us new power to act. At that moment, despite my longstanding interest in cancer research and the time I had spent becoming an expert on the comparatively minor carcinogenic risks in food, I shrugged off the question.

Had I thought about it, I would have realized that my answer did not get to the heart of the laws that defined a drug—to the question of intent. But of course, no one had ever tried to determine the nature of the industry's intentions.

5

I WAS not being disingenuous when I told my staff that I had lots to do before I could grapple with tobacco. We were on the alert for product tamperings, and there were many. One sloppy extortion attempt revolved around a threat to inject AIDS-contaminated blood into meat; in another, baby food was the target. Then, an angry political group threatened to poison tea imported from Sri Lanka.

The challenges surrounding access to safe and effective drugs were always center stage for the agency. When New York City's health commissioner told me that a manufacturer had stopped producing a crucial drug to treat tuberculosis, leading to a dangerous shortage, we had to convince other companies to take over production. When we discovered that an ingredient in one diet drug swelled inside the body after use, leading to intestinal obstruction, we quickly decided to pull it from the market.

We also had to act when our inspectors found that some discount brands of canned tuna were subject to unusually high rates of decomposition and when state health departments complained that condoms manufactured in Thailand had high breakage rates. We had to decide what to do about reports that cholera-contaminated water was being brought to U.S. shores aboard South American ships and how to safeguard the blood supply when patients started dying from bacterial infections after transfusions.

And we were constantly accountable to Capitol Hill. A manufacturer complained that we were stonewalling approval of his product, a component of snake venom to treat AIDS, and his senator called me to demand an explanation. The staff of a congressman who prided himself on his aggressive defense of consumer rights developed the irritating habit of faxing complaints about agency activities to us late on Friday afternoons. Invariably, we would get a telephone call from the press asking for comment at almost the same moment that we first learned of the issue.

The need for answers often preceded the availability of data. Should we allow military troops to use therapies of uncertain safety and effectiveness in the hopes of protecting them against the risk of biological warfare? Were the minute quantities of lead detected in wine enough to create risk for human beings? How alarming was a single study suggesting a link between hair dye and non-Hodgkin's lymphoma? Had the safety of breast implants been demonstrated? Often, I had to base my decisions on sketchy science, with the media invariably nipping at the agency's heels. If we took no action in response to even a whisper of risk, we would be attacked. And if we did take action, we would often be asked why we had not done so earlier.

BUT I did not want my time to be spent exclusively on short-term emergencies. I soon realized that I had to move issues myself, or I would always be responding to events I could not control. I began keeping a mental list of my priorities, both large and small, so that I could push for action on them.

I had come to the FDA with one issue about which I cared deeply. As a physician who had worked in the Bronx during the 1980s, I understood what the AIDS epidemic was about, and I wanted to make it one of my top priorities. It was hard for those untouched by the brutal infectious disease to appreciate the level of desperation in affected communities. A few drugs were available to treat the opportunistic infections associated with AIDS, but there was nothing besides AZT to keep the virus itself in check.

Well-organized activists emerged to fight the bureaucracies they saw as impediments to effective treatment. They never followed a game plan. Instead, they just kept identifying obstacles to their goals and finding ways to storm past those obstacles. Two years before my arrival at the agency, demonstrators had targeted the FDA and surrounded the Parklawn building, carrying placards that read "R.I.P. Killed by the FDA" and "FDA red tape killed me." They hanged Frank Young in effigy.

The activists were demanding the right to try any new drug, regardless of how little was known about it. Ellen Cooper, a young and inspiring physician who headed the agency's antiviral division, insisted on first having scientifi-cally rigorous data to demonstrate that drugs worked. The law required that but it led to her being branded an inflexible guardian of FDA tradition. Although her dedication was never in doubt—she had worked almost around the clock to analyze the data on AZT, allowing the drug to be approved in record time—she became the lightning rod for a community's fury.

The worst moment came when she was publicly called a murderer. That flourish came from Larry Kramer, a New York City playwright and the founder of ACT-UP, the confrontational grassroots organization behind most of the visible protest activities of that era. The remark, though inappropriate and unfair, was vintage Kramer. It was in the tradition of "A Call to Riot," an April 1990 piece he wrote for *Outweek*. In that article he declared, "We are being royally fucked over, screwed to death. . . . [I]ntentionally allowed to die is no longer hyperbole, exaggeration, opinion—it is fact. The systems this government has in operation simply could not move any more slowly." The sentiments did not win him a lot of allies among my colleagues.

Such language had begun to diminish by the time I came to the agency. The ranks of the activists had been depleted by illness and death. I saw how exhausted the survivors had become—yet how determined they were to keep on fighting. I did not think it was right to leave them alone in their battles. I also thought there were sound public health reasons for addressing their con-cerns. For their part, the activists had become more sophisticated about how the drug development and approval process worked, and they were ready to work with the agency. The moment was ripe, it seemed to me, to look again at the rules that controlled access to treatment.

Ellen Cooper was too exhausted to stay and be part of the process. Within weeks of my arrival, she submitted her resignation, a victim of frustration and burnout. I asked her to reconsider, but she had made her decision. Dra-matizing the seesawing alliances that characterized the environment, Larry Kramer wrote an angry three-page letter about Cooper's resignation, sending copies to dozens of public health officials, activists, and journalists. This time, he offered a lament for Cooper. "We shall miss her terribly," he wrote. He also told a *New York Times* reporter, "She's been like Joan of Arc."

I began to widen the agency's contacts with the AIDS community. At first, I did a lot of listening. Over time, I came to respect Kramer, who was gentler and more thoughtful in private, and we became friends. I also developed a col-legial relationship with Martin Delaney from San Francisco. Delaney was in his fifties, older than many of the activists who dominated ACT-UP. He came to prominence as the founder of Project Inform, which taught people with AIDS how to smuggle unapproved drugs into the country from Mexican pharmacies. But he was also comfortable in a traditional business milieu, where he had worked for many years. While ACT-UP was at the barricades, bringing media attention and public sympathy to its cause, Delaney was concentrating on making the connections that gave him influence inside the system.

I let Delaney, Kramer, and other activists know that I was interested in strategies to put drugs into the hands of people with AIDS before the usual raft of studies had been completed. Even before my confirmation, I had begun thinking about a "conditional approval" process. The challenge was to identify an earlier-than-ideal point along the drug approval path when an urgently needed drug might reasonably be made available to patients. I did not want to wait until we knew beyond any doubt that the drug was ready for marketing. Instead, I wanted to make certain drugs available when there was some evidence that they could possibly slow, moderate, or relieve the advancement of disease in patients whose need was urgent. At the same time, I wanted a strategy that would allow the traditional battery of tests to continue so that the safety and efficacy of the compound could ultimately be documented.

Robert Temple, the FDA's most senior drug reviewer, had spent most of his professional life at the agency, and he knew more about the evaluation of drugs than anyone else there. He was dedicated to the FDA's mission, and though he did not embrace change lightly, he could be persuaded by powerful ideas. Shortly after I arrived, I asked him to develop a strategy to accelerate drug approvals, knowing that if he could design something with which he felt comfortable, I would be able to sell it to others and feel confident that our approval standards emerged intact.

I was convinced that we had to take risks. As a consumer protection agency, the FDA had historically focused almost single-mindedly on keeping unsafe or ineffective drugs off the market. Speeding access to urgently needed products was not nearly so deeply ingrained in our culture. The assumption was that good science was possible only through a painstaking analysis of a mountain of empirical data, regardless of how long the process took. Many drug reviewers had become accustomed to working at an academic tempo, largely devoid of deadline pressure. "Do you want it fast or do you want it right?" was a common refrain.

Temple proposed allowing significant new drugs to be approved on the basis of a two-stage evaluation. Usually the FDA required that a drug demonstrate clinical benefit, such as reducing the risk of heart attacks or extending life. But that takes time, and meanwhile, other evidence of a drug's effect—for example, the ability to lower cholesterol—often becomes apparent. Bob's idea was to approve a drug on the basis of an earlier "surrogate," while requiring that it continue to be closely monitored. If results did not live up to expectations, the drug could be pulled from the market.

Temple was filled with reservations about his own concept, haunted by failures from the past, particularly the cardiac arrhythmia suppression trial. In CAST, two drugs had worked as intended, suppressing the abnormal rhythms that increase the risk of sudden death in patients who had already had heart attacks. But the study showed, unexpectedly, that the people who had taken the drugs were two and a half times more likely to die than patients who had not. A symptom had been dealt with at the cost of exacerbating the disease. CAST was a stark warning to proceed cautiously with the use of surrogates.

I soon had an opportunity to test the conditional approval idea on a new AIDS antiviral drug called ddI. Our scientific experts told us that drugs that increased CD-4 cell counts, a critical barometer of immune strength, could reliably be expected to extend the lives of people with AIDS. That gave us a surrogate marker. We called the manufacturer, Bristol-Myers, which had already completed an early-stage clinical trial of ddI but had not yet analyzed the results, and asked for their data. Asking a pharmaceutical company to bring undigested data to the FDA so that our reviewers could conduct their own analyses was an almost unheard-of cultural change. Instead of saying, "Prove the merits of your drug," we were saying, "How can we get this drug through the system if it works?" It was also a significant risk. Our job as a gatekeeper was to be an objective evaluator of data, not an advocate of an unproven therapy.

The FDA's Antiviral Drugs Advisory Committee met in mid-July 1991 to consider ddI. Bristol-Myers's approval application was based on four studies that enrolled a total of only 170 subjects, not remotely balanced to represent a true picture of the AIDS population. The studies provided no comparative data on the baseline health of the different patient groups, the nature of the clinical care they received, or the impact of differences in study design. Furthermore, even if these early clinical trials had been better designed, they would have been expected only to establish some degree of drug safety, not to determine the drug's effectiveness. Had the company relied on the same level of data to ask us to approve a new painkiller or an anti-inflammatory medication, it would have been told to go back and finish its homework.

Although FDA reviewers added marginally to the case for declaring ddI safe and effective by describing their independent analyses of the Bristol-Myers data, the committee was alarmed. "These studies do not push the frontier of knowledge," said Alvin Novick of Yale University. "These totally undermine our confidence in how to do clinical trials."

It was a long, tense day. The meeting room was stuffy, the air conditioning inefficient, and everyone was frustrated. Advisory Committee members were pained by the inconclusive evidence. The activists felt that the human need for ddI was being sacrificed on the altar of exacting data. A representative from Bristol-Myers wondered out loud whether AIDS drug development was worth the trouble. When the meeting adjourned at 9 P.M., more than twelve hours after it began, everyone thought the ddI application was in trouble. At dinner late that night, committee members were somber. They wanted the drug to work, but desire was not enough. The evidence did not seem to be there.

But the agency had done something else unprecedented. On the second day of the meeting, FDA reviewers presented an interim analysis of a different study, one that Bristol-Myers had not even looked at. This study met all of the FDA's traditional design standards, with a single exception: it was a year away from completion. Nonetheless, the FDA review showed a consistent, if tiny, increase in CD-4 cell counts among patients using ddI.

As the advisory committee debated the evidence, I sensed that several members were undecided. I tried to convey the message that in this case, the greatest risk could be refusing to take a risk. In the end, an average bump of ten CD-4 cells among patients taking ddI was enough. The science, while far from conclusive, pointed in the right direction. By a vote of five to two, with one abstention and one member disqualified from voting because of his own ddI research, the committee recommended that the drug be approved. We finally had a model for accelerating the approval of drugs for serious and life-threatening diseases. Over the next nine months, more definitive trials were completed that confirmed the safety and effectiveness of ddI. And over the next few years, the same process was used for a dozen AIDS drugs, as well as for treatments for breast cancer, heart disease, stroke, diabetes, rheumatoid arthritis, and respiratory distress syndrome.

After that experience, my sense of what I needed to do as commissioner began to change. I saw that I could do more than merely bounce from crisis to crisis.

6

AFTER the seizure of Citrus Hill orange juice, I called a meeting with the senior people from the Center for Foods and asked, "What's next?" We decided to focus on the industrywide practice of proclaiming that vegetable oil had "no cholesterol." This, of course, was an absurd claim. As one newspaper editorial noted, vegetable oils have never contained cholesterol, which is found only in animal products, and the label wording was as relevant as saying "contains no nuclear waste." Yet to a health-conscious shopper, "no cholesterol" looked like good news. The labels met the legal definition of misleading, and we warned the manufacturers to change them. Within weeks they all agreed.

We now started taking enforcement action at a pace that Washington had not seen from the FDA in years. With our will to enforce the law no longer in doubt, the agency was treated seriously as a policeman in the marketplace, and our skirmishes became big news. Headlines and magazine cover stories trumpeted the new climate at the FDA. "Regulatory Chief Stirs Up Business," announced the *Wall Street Journal*. *Newsweek*'s cover read "Feeding Frenzy," and *Business Week* declared, "FDA Is Swinging a Sufficiently Large Two by Four." The *Washington Post* called me "Eliot Knessler," a play on the name of the Prohibition Era gangbuster. I could have done without the nickname, but if it was taken as a sign of the agency's renewed credibility, I was not going to object.

I knew that our aggressive stance was good for agency morale, but it took longer to discover that it was also something the public very much wanted. Consumers needed to know that the FDA would stand up for them, and that gave us a certain amount of independence. My relationships with the

Department of Health and Human Services were more delicate. The Bush administration believed in deregulation, and we were a regulatory agency. I had to remain accountable to my bosses, yet I was determined to enforce the law. I also had to consider questions to which there were no simple answers. How did the philosophy of deregulation apply to health and safety? Whose job was it to decide? And what did the President think? I had certain day-to-day responsibilities, but the chain of command between me and the President was lengthy. To date, President Bush and I had been together just once in the White House, for a photo opportunity when the accelerated drug review regulations were announced.

My early days in Washington were far from an unbroken string of victories. Tensions with the Department began to rise, and they were not always about policy. Michael Calhoun, Secretary Sullivan's chief of staff, was especially upset about all of the media coverage I was generating. When *The New York Times Magazine* ran a cover story on me, there was apoplexy on the executive floor of the Department. My political naïveté might have been showing, but I did not fully understand why my increasingly high profile was perceived as an act of disloyalty to Sullivan.

Having the media focused tightly on me and the agency had other perils as well. For one thing, I was a novice when the networks came calling, and I had not yet learned to think tactically about the role of the news media. Initially, the ability to formulate a crisp sound bite, or any sound bite at all, eluded me.

My worst moment came on *Good Morning, America* in May 1991. I was not sophisticated enough to prepare in advance, thinking neither about the questions I was likely to be asked nor about the message I wanted to deliver. Worse, I had no idea what to expect from an interview conducted via satellite. I was installed in a dark cubicle, facing a remotely controlled camera. The anchor, Charlie Gibson, was nowhere in sight, and I heard nothing until the lead-in to the segment. And then, suddenly, a voice began asking me questions through my earpiece. The interrogation felt Kafkaesque. Without any clues from body language, I did not know when to stop talking, so I rambled on, unable to complete a coherent sentence. I gestured with my hands as if they were disembodied objects. Gibson must have been astonished that the head of a federal agency could be so inarticulate. When it was over, I vowed I would never appear on television again.

Sharan Kuperman of the FDA's press office told me adamantly that I had to put myself in the hands of a media coach. I refused. She insisted, explaining that the agency had a contractual arrangement and that no additional costs would be incurred. I could not believe the government paid for this sort of thing. Eventually she wore me down, but I approached the whole exercise with a measure of hostility. When I was offered a sandwich on my first visit, I took out my wallet to pay for it. I did not want anyone doing me any favors. To me, there was something slick about being trained to talk to the press—which meant learning to deflect difficult questions and to stay on message—and I did not want to be slick. My perhaps innocent view was that if I had something substantive to say, I did not need to learn how to say it. I did not yet understand how the media could help advance an issue and create a safety net for me.

NOT only do the FDA's decisions have huge public health implications, but they also affect people with powerful interests and the resources to protect those interests. My first taste of what happens when a government official gets in the way of an industry with clout was when I had to testify before Henry Waxman's Subcommittee on Health and the Environment about the need for additional FDA enforcement powers.

The FDA desperately needed basic enforcement tools, including greater access to manufacturing, ingredient, and quality control records, more extensive powers to recall a product and issue subpoenas, and the ability to embargo suspect foods. The absence of those tools reflected an artifact of history: the agency had been empowered when regulatory agencies were few, and even in the flush of the reforming zeal of the New Deal, federal enforcement authority was less favored than action by the states. Congress was considering legislation intended to correct that and to give the FDA the clear-cut federal powers that newer agencies, such as the Environmental Protection Agency, took for granted. In the course of the debate, I learned a lesson about power, which took the form of what I came to call the incredible shrinking testimony.

Under an Executive Order issued by President Reagan, I was required to secure approval from the Office of Management and Budget for my opening statement in support of the enforcement bill. In recent years, OMB had developed a culture that fit comfortably within the Reagan and Bush administrations. To many of the OMB staff, there was no such thing as a good regulation. When OMB's cuts and revisions to my testimony were returned to me, I saw that they had utterly transformed my message.

Talking of our need to embargo products that were in violation of the law I had written, "FDA's current authorities in this area are very limited." The OMB version, written by an unknown hand, was "appropriately limited," completely changing the meaning.

On the agency's limited power to investigate, my draft read, "What may be surprising is that, except for prescription drugs and restricted medical devices... FDA inspectors lack the authority to examine records that may be crucial to an investigation...." The OMB censor removed the opening phrase so that it read, "For prescription drugs and restricted medical devices... FDA investigators *have* the authority to examine records...." Strictly true, of course, but not my point.

I had no way of knowing the extent to which the food, pharmaceutical, and medical device industries had mustered their forces to oppose the enforcement bill, but I knew that someone had more influence at the highest levels of government than I did. I also knew that I could never go in front of the Waxman committee and utter the testimony as OMB had rewritten it. OMB could prevent me from saying certain things, but I was not going to let it put words in my mouth.

JULY 1, 1991, was a sultry summer day in the Capitol. The chamber for the Waxman hearing was in the institutional hulk of the Rayburn House Office Building. Inside, men in tropical suits and women in summer dresses were already thinking about the upcoming holiday. I was in a dark, heavy suit, ready for roasting.

FDA testimony typically ran twenty or thirty pages, but with no alternative, I cut my remarks to less than one page. It took all of thirty seconds to deliver my opening statement, a transparently thin tissue of platitudes. I wanted to make sure the congressional committee knew that I had been muzzled. Congressman Mike Synar, an Oklahoma Democrat, commented, "In my thirteen years I cannot remember testimony so short on such an important subject."

But I had not given up. I had arranged to have four of the agency's most senior enforcement officers sit to my right at the table facing the congressmen. When I introduced these key people, I pointed out that together they represented more than one hundred years of experience in the field. They provided examples of the limits to our current authority, helping to make the case that I could not. They told stories of pesticide-contaminated food that the FDA did not have the right to embargo and product adulterations we could not effectively investigate.

We made no converts among the Republicans. To a person, they espoused an "enough is enough" philosophy. "The regulatory load on American consumers and businesses today has reached awesome dimensions," claimed William Dannemeyer of California, who had taken off his jacket and looked ready for a fight. Congressman Norman Lent of New York acknowledged me as a long-time constituent before alleging that we were asking for the kind of powers that Mikhail Gorbachev was at that moment dismantling in the Soviet Union.

There was little I could do to curb the rhetoric, but I should have realized that one of the provisions in the enforcement bill was a gift to its opponents. I asked that the right of our criminal investigators to carry firearms be formally established by law. In fact, agents engaged in certain dangerous activities, such as pursuing counterfeit drug dealers and smugglers, already did just that, but we wanted it codified. Ignoring the very real risks field investigators face in the underground world of criminal activity, the food industry urged its friends in Congress to ask why the FDA needed guns to inspect cereal. We gave our opponents a device to ridicule us, and the legislation died without ever reaching the floor. To this day, the FDA has not been given some of the most basic powers a regulatory agency should have.

Much later, I learned that Juanita Duggan, a former Reagan staffer who had moved on to represent the National Food Processors Association, had urged friends still in the White House to "kill the bill." They had obviously listened. Too late, I realized that I had been sandbagged by such lobbyists because I had overlooked a key tactical step. I should have lined up more support, especially in those corners where the power to defeat me rested. In the future, if I needed White House approval to make something happen, I had to get the White House on my side.

Within a few months, the sentiment in Washington had swung all the way from feeling that the FDA had to be goaded into action to fearing that somebody had better stop us. Had I not moved so aggressively on enforcement from my first days, the agency would have continued to be accused of laxity, and I might have received more support for the legislation I needed. But now ideologues and lobbyists feared giving the agency, and me, too much power.

7

SUMMONED by his former boss, Dan Quayle, Jeff Nesbit left the FDA in the summer of 1991 to help the vice president improve his image with the media. But Bill Hubbard, in the FDA's policy office, kept the tobacco debate alive inside the agency.

Bill knew more than most about tobacco. As a boy growing up in eastern North Carolina, he had spent a lot of time hanging around local farms. Sometimes he played with neighborhood kids in the tobacco fields, being careful to stay clear of the plants; he had been warned that he could get nicotine poisoning by rubbing up against them with bare skin.

Tobacco helped to put Bill Hubbard through college. In the 1930s, commodity prices had plummeted. In order to bring supply and demand into equilibrium, a New Deal crop support program was developed that gave a tobacco allotment to existing tobacco farmers. Without an allotment, a farmer was not allowed to grow tobacco commercially, but anyone who had an allotment had it in perpetuity—it was attached to the property and was passed along to any heirs. Bill's mother had inherited a ten-acre tobacco allotment from her father and had leased it out to a neighboring farmer in return for a share of the profits. In the 1960s, the allotment was bringing in several thousand dollars a year.

But gradually the value declined and the administrative hassles increased and Bill's mother eventually handed the allotment back to the U.S. Department of Agriculture. The family's stake in the product was gone by the time that tobacco moved onto Bill's list of responsibilities at the FDA.

Bill had spent most of his professional life with the agency. In 1972, at age twenty-three, he signed on at the lowest rung of the civil service and worked his way into senior-level management, becoming the second-ranking member of the FDA's policy office. With his self-effacing manner and ability to get things done, he was considered something of an institution. Bill's years on the job had given him personal connections in three vital places: inside the agency, at the Department of Health and Human Services, and on Capitol Hill.

NINE months had passed since the May 1991 meeting with Jeff Nesbit, and tobacco had barely broken the surface of my consciousness since then. Bill Hubbard did not seriously believe that the agency would unilaterally broaden its authority over tobacco products, but he was encouraged by my early actions and relieved to see the FDA awaken from its period of hibernation. He was also embarrassed at how long the agency had dragged its feet on the various tobacco-related citizen petitions clogging the FDA's docket and worried that the delays might make us vulnerable to criticism. He thought some sort of response was overdue.

Most of the petitions awaiting action were the handiwork of Scott Ballin, the chairman of the Coalition on Smoking or Health, which united the American Heart Association, of which Ballin was the vice president, the American Lung Association, and the American Cancer Society. Like Bill Hubbard, Ballin listened with interest to my vow to enforce the law and pointed out the analogies between tobacco and food labeling to anyone who would listen. If the FDA was serious about defining terms like "low fat" and "low salt," he kept saying, it should also be serious about setting standards for "low tar" and "low nicotine."

Ballin thought the appropriate federal laws to regulate tobacco might already be somewhere on the books, and for months he sat in his office studying them. "I was asking a very fundamental question," he told me much later. "If tobacco hadn't existed and if I manufactured cigarettes and tried to put them on the market, who would tell me I couldn't do it?" He scrutinized the laws governing toxic and hazardous substances, which were administered primarily by the Environmental Protection Agency, looked at the mandate of the Federal Trade Commission, and studied the legislation that applied to product safety and packaging. As it turned out, every major law included a variation of essentially the same sentence: "The term 'consumer product' [or "hazardous substance" or "chemical substance"] does not include tobacco or tobacco products."

Gradually, Ballin's focus narrowed to the FDA. He looked back at the agency's history and immersed himself in the Food, Drug, and Cosmetic Act of 1938 and its dozens of subsequent amendments, which gave the modern FDA its authority. He studied the circumstances in which the FDA had taken some type of action against tobacco products, which almost always involved explicit health claims. And he searched for the usual tobacco exemption. To his surprise, he did not find one. How could this be? Ballin wondered. Had the authority to regulate tobacco always been there but never applied?

Fellow tobacco control activists were unimpressed. No one thought there was much to gain by targeting the FDA. Michael Pertschuk, former head of the Federal Trade Commission and a strong advocate for tobacco control, dismissed the idea. "The FDA reacts to calls that it assume jurisdiction over tobacco products as if it had been tossed a red-hot coal," he said. Even Sidney Wolfe, director of the Ralph Nader–affiliated Public Citizen's Health Research Group and a long-time enemy of tobacco, thought the Coalition should not divert its attention from efforts to push Congress to impose new restrictions on tobacco. Wolfe faxed me a memo, stamped confidential, asking in strong language that I answer the petitions. "The only way the Coalition is going to stop beating its head against a wall on this issue is for the commissioner of FDA to *state unequivocally* that FDA either *will* or *will not* regulate conventional tobacco products," Wolfe wrote. "At this point, FDA implicitly points to Congress for the answer, while Congress points back." Wolfe privately urged me to deny the petitions.

Undaunted, Ballin kept bombarding us with citizen petitions, adding new ones to the docket on February 27, 1992. One petition asked the FDA to classify Merit Ultima, Philip Morris's low-tar cigarette, as a drug. Another argued that cigarettes being marketed as weight-loss products should be regulated as drugs. When the new petitions arrived at the agency's doorstep, Bill Hubbard sent a memo to his boss at the policy office, Mike Taylor. "As you know, we've historically said that cigarettes are intended only for pleasure, and we've only regulated those products that have made specific therapeutic claims," he wrote. With the agency's traditional perspective in mind, Bill added, "We presumably will deny these petitions, but I guess we ought to do so thoughtfully."

Hubbard wanted to bring together a few key people to discuss the issues the Coalition had raised. I was comfortable with that idea and suggested that we should eventually share our thinking with Jim Mason. I reported directly to Mason, the assistant secretary for health. Mason reported to the Department secretary.

Bill asked Ilisa Bernstein to take charge. Ilisa, who had a doctorate in pharmacology, had joined the agency in 1988 to review the new drug applications that had to be approved before manufacturers were allowed to market their products. At first she focused on reviewing cancer drugs but soon shifted to AIDS. In August 1991 Ilisa entered law school. Though she wanted to continue to work full time at the agency, she could not remain in the crisis-driven environment of the antiviral division. Bill Hubbard interviewed her and thought her energetic and ambitious. She accepted his offer to work in the policy office and reported to the fourteenth floor of Parklawn soon afterwards.

In mid-March 1992, Bill came into her small office with the tobacco assignment. After describing the pending Coalition on Smoking or Health petitions, Bill identified a few knowledgeable people in the agency and said, "Look into this. Find out the status of the petitions and what we're doing about them. Find out who is involved."

Ilisa was pleased. Her mother's smoking habit and her own battle with asthma in her twenties had confirmed her distaste for cigarettes. She always made it a point to give smokers a wide berth. Still, she doubted tobacco regulation had much of a future at the FDA and was only half joking when she gave Bill a big smile and said, "No wonder you're giving this to me, the new person in the office. I'm getting the projects that aren't going anywhere."

NEAR the end of April, my wife, Paulette, and I were scheduled to attend the Heart Ball, a black-tie dinner sponsored by the Washington affiliate of the American Heart Association. I had been selected as an honoree, largely for my work on truthful food labels.

Among the blizzard of nightly social events in the Capitol, we had been warned that the Heart Ball stood out for its formality. Congressman Mike Synar was a fellow honoree that night. Synar had recently introduced legislation putting the FDA in charge of tobacco regulation, although no one believed it had a chance of passing.

I knew Synar only as one of the faces looking down at me when I testified on the enforcement bill, and I remembered how irritated he had been by my bowdlerized testimony. Synar was said to be a fearless and principled congressman. He was also a good-looking bachelor wearing cowboy boots. Over veal medallions and mixed greens, Paulette chatted with Synar and found him charming. When she mentioned that our son, Ben, had a passion for collecting old baseball cards, Synar said that he had his childhood collection stored in his attic back home in Oklahoma. He seemed amazed to learn how valuable the old cards could be.

After dessert, most of the guests drifted away from the table, and the dance floor was soon full. I rose to mingle, but Synar collared me, and we returned to our seats. He turned his chair around and straddled it like a man on a horse, his cowboy boots visible from under his tuxedo. He wanted to talk, and I had the feeling that he no longer had baseball cards on his mind.

"You know, you need to do something on tobacco," he said. I waffled, avoiding any commitment, and no doubt confirmed the frustration with me that he had felt at the enforcement hearing. Our conversation was brief.

I looked around for Scott Ballin. I knew that he had a large say in who would be honored that night, and I wondered whether the whole thing had been a setup. Ballin later admitted that he had deliberately arranged for me to sit next to Mike Synar.

8

THE LAST TIME a United States president had been directly involved in an FDA decision was in 1908 when Theodore Roosevelt overruled the agency's ban on saccharin. Since then, a president's advisers had often exerted their influence, but it had been almost unheard of for the occupant of the Oval Office to dictate FDA policy. It was about to happen again.

When Congress passed the Nutrition Labeling and Education Act of 1990, it handed us an opportunity to recast our piecemeal attacks on misleading food labels into a cohesive strategy. Fundamental to the new law was its requirement that all foods list the amount of fat, saturated fat, protein, sodium, carbohydrates, and fiber they contain and place them in the context of a daily diet. Congress also wanted to establish definitions of health claims, such as "light" and "lite," as they apply to fat content. The simple idea underlying the legislation was that people would be able to choose healthier diets for themselves by reading accurate and meaningful information on food packages.

Like all ideas that have a natural utility, the "Nutrition Facts" information panel on food now seems unremarkable, so familiar as to be taken for granted. Most people never saw the political battle that made it happen.

The FDA's mandate was to develop regulations that would translate the labeling legislation into action. Not surprisingly, given the emasculation of the agency during the 1980s, the Democratic Congress had doubts about whether the agency was up to this task—or whether the Republican administration would allow the agency to proceed. Reflecting these concerns, an unusual "hammer" was placed in the legislation: the FDA's proposed regulations were to be complete by November 1991, and the final regulations were to be published a year later, on the eve of the 1992 presidential election. If the final rules were not issued by then, the proposed rules became effective instead.

I knew that diet accounted for the second largest cause of preventable death in the United States—tobacco, of course, was number one—and that improving how Americans ate was one of the most important public health actions we could take. My goal was not to dictate behavior, but to provide the information that would allow people to make educated choices.

Congress had mandated general requirements for the food label but had said nothing specific about presentation. The legislation had no design mandates and no requirements in terms of prominence and legibility. Somehow, we had to find a way to fit added information on thousands of different types of food packages, from pasta to peanuts, on hard packs, clear packs, candy wrappers, boxes of Cheerios, and cans of Coke.

We also had to develop standards for serving sizes. It had been a widespread industry practice to minimize sizes so that they bore little relation to the amount people actually ate—for example, the calorie content of "light" cheesecake was based on a "serving size" of half a slice. We were determined to close this loophole by requiring serving sizes to reflect the amount customarily consumed.

My point men, the officials who had to navigate myriad minefields to develop the regulations, were Mike Taylor, the head of the FDA's policy office, and his associate, Jerry Mande.

IF it had not been for red M&Ms, Jerry might never have come to the FDA. In the 1970s, as an undergraduate at the University of Connecticut studying nutrition and biochemistry, Jerry read that the agency had banned a red dye that gave M&Ms and many other red foods their distinctive color. That set him thinking about regulatory priorities, and wondering why the FDA focused more on cancer-causing trace additives, such as the dye, than on the macronutrients that dominated daily diets and had a far greater impact on health.

Jerry spoke with an accent that was a cross between Boston and Brooklyn, and his concern about health was reflected in his own exercise and fitness habits. An expert in health policy and the political process, he kept his television set permanently tuned to CNN. Now, Jerry took on the food label format as his personal mission, displaying a dogged focus that sometimes infuriated his colleagues. His office soon became a small museum of food labels. Jerry was convinced that existing information was being ignored by consumers for two reasons: it was confusing and it was hard to read. Since the food industry was going to spend billions of dollars reconfiguring its packaging to include the required new information about nutrient content, Jerry reasoned that we should make sure it could be read.

As required, we published one set of proposed regulations addressing the content of the food label on November 6, 1991. A second set of regulations, published in July 1992, outlined the best options for presenting information on the label. But we had not yet won support for our proposals from the Department of Agriculture (USDA), which regulated meat and meat products.

Although the Nutrition Labeling and Education Act applied only to the FDA, the USDA and the FDA had agreed that one label should be used on all packaged foods. For too long, the two agencies had been divided by absurd territorial disputes. Pizza toppings was one example: cheese and tomato came under FDA labeling rules, but if pepperoni was added, the USDA took charge. It was time for the federal government to speak with one voice.

One of the most controversial issues was where to fix the average daily total of calories. Our proposed label showed what percentage of the recommended daily intake of a nutrient was contained in one serving. That percentage was based on a total daily calorie count, making it the foundation of the label. In our initial proposals, we estimated a mean daily calorie intake of 2,350. The public health community complained that this number was too high, especially for women, and after reviewing the comments, I agreed and began to push for a 2,000-calorie count instead. But the food industry and the Department of Agriculture wanted the per-serving percentage of fat and other nutrients to be based on the 2,350-calorie count.

That was assuming they had to accept an average calorie count at all. What USDA preferred, to my surprise, was as little information as possible on the label—it was willing to allow the grams of a given nutrient to be displayed but did not want that figure placed in the context of a daily diet. The USDA designed an approach that would instead force every consumer to make a series of laborious calculations. Using flip charts, Mike Taylor and I showed Secretary Sullivan and his staff that USDA wanted to require every consumer to calculate individual calorie requirements and then to perform five separate mathematical steps just to determine what percent of a person's daily recommended intake of a given nutrient was in a single serving. The same process had to be repeated for total fat, saturated fat, carbohydrates, and protein. Different formulas were involved for cholesterol, sodium, and fiber. The disadvantages of the one-size-fits-all approach were far outweighed by the advantages of a clear label. I was looking for an easy-to-grasp consumer guide, not an exercise that required a calculator. The secretary saw immediately that USDA's idea was nonsense.

For USDA, the concern about labeling revolved around one word—fat. It was not uncommon for meat products to have nearly half the desirable level of daily fat calories in a single serving. Once the meat industry realized that our proposed label would make it far simpler for a shopper to gauge fat intake, it vigorously lobbied the USDA to follow a different course.

Compared to Ed Madigan, the secretary of agriculture, I was woefully outranked. I did not even report to a cabinet-level department head. Madigan, a veteran of the tough state house politics of Illinois, was known as a low-key, close-to-the-vest dealmaker. Madigan had been one of the principal forces behind the passage of the food labeling law during his tenure in Congress, but he was now being squeezed by the industry lobby and the 110,000-person bureaucracy he had inherited. One hint of the thinking within the USDA was reflected in a staffer's comment about the term "low fat." "The problem is that our products won't be able to make that claim," he said.

Our products. A confusion between the interests of the industries it regulated and the interests of the consumer it was supposed to protect seemed ingrained within USDA. It was not going to be easy for the two agencies to agree on the final rule.

EVERY August, our family spent a weekend in Margate, a small town on the New Jersey shore, south of Atlantic City, where Paulette grew up. En route one day in 1992, Elise and Ben clamored to go to a McDonald's. I agreed. As they ate their Chicken McNuggets and I sipped a Diet Coke and ate French fries, my eye fell on the tray liner. I was surprised to see that, against a background photograph of fresh vegetables, McDonald's had set out its own case for a healthy, balanced diet. In small type at the bottom, I spotted this statement: "Based on nutritional guidelines by the National Research Council. Fat recommendation based on a total daily intake of 2,000 calories."

There it was. In a temple of fast food, 2,000 calories was used as the standard. If 2,000 calories was acceptable to McDonald's, I thought, it should be acceptable to anybody. I walked through the restaurant and collected several more tray liners to take back to the office.

I was still trying to bring USDA on board. As a compromise, we suggested a footnote to the label that would make it clear that 2,000 calories was simply a reference point, but that individual needs might differ. Secretary Madigan was not mollified.

In the contentious environment that developed, Mike Taylor came to see me. He spoke in measured tones, but I knew he was disturbed. As the FDA's policy chief, Mike understood the forces deployed against us. He was convinced that the USDA's position was driven largely by the cattlemen and the meat industry. A revolving door between industry and government added to the potent political mix. Craig L. Fuller, who had been President Bush's chief of staff when Bush was vice president, was one of the more visible influences at the White House in the weeks before the 1992 election. More recently, Fuller had become a lobbyist with Philip Morris, whose food division included Kraft. Now, he was paid to defend American cheese, arguing that our criteria made it impossible for the company to develop a version that could be called "light."

From the White House, the pressure moved down to the Office of Management and Budget, which had the power to block our regulations. As required, we had submitted draft after draft of the final rule to OMB and often had it returned to us with industry-sought changes. More than once, OMB's wording had been taken almost verbatim from industry comments we had already carefully considered.

We were caught in a messy tangle of political ideology and special interests, Mike said, but none of it was out in the open and that opacity made it difficult to confront the problem head-on. He argued that we should go public with the debate over the label format and daily calorie counts, presenting it for what it was—a public health opportunity in jeopardy.

I decided to ask Marian Burros, a reporter and columnist at the *New York Times,* to meet me for lunch. Jeff Nesbit had taught me that to get a message across, it helped to work with reporters who became experts on their subjects, and Burros had followed the story from the beginning. I had been especially struck by how she had deconstructed surveys promoted by the food industry that purported to show that consumers favored the old food labels over the proposed new one. As we ate Mongolian barbecue in Washington's tiny Chinatown, I told her that I was not sure I could prevail on food labeling, given the strength of our opposition.

Although I did not say so explicitly, Burros understood that I was prepared to resign if the FDA was not allowed to publish its final regulations. On this issue, to compromise would have meant to allow corporate lobbyists to dictate public health policy. I wanted her to understand what was going on behind closed doors if USDA's position won out and I had to step down.

Burros helped inform the public about the agency's labeling proposals, and we also found support in the editorial pages of the *New York Times* and the *Washington Post*. In an October piece, Burros quoted an FDA official who accused the USDA of "just fronting for fat." I kept quiet about the source of that sound bite—the poker-faced Mike Taylor, who had given her the comment from his kitchen telephone. Ed Madigan was furious at being portrayed as a tool of the meat industry. The opportunity for a deal with USDA seemed to slip away.

Characteristically, Paulette soon became impatient with the delays. My wife has a no-nonsense style and a manner that never left others in doubt about how she felt. She began wearing a button that read, "Free the Hostage Rules."

FOOD labels, of course, were not all that was being discussed in Washington. It was the fall of 1992, and things did not look good for George Bush. Although preoccupied by the reelection campaign, the White House staff could not ignore the public scrap between the Departments of Agriculture and Health and Human Services. Two weeks before Americans went to the polls, the dispute was brought to the attention of James Baker, the President's chief of staff. A flurry of meetings followed, with OMB assigned to knock heads together to settle the matter.

I gave simple instructions to Mike Taylor, who represented the FDA at those meetings: talk as much as you like, but make no compromises. In a city where compromise is critical to getting things accomplished, I was standing firm on the 2,000-calorie count. The only problem: the USDA was not budging either.

9

TOBACCO remained a distraction for many at the agency, but the issue was gaining attention, if not actually much momentum, in the hands of Ilisa Bernstein. She had put together a small interdepartmental group to discuss ideas on regulation, pulling together talent from across the agency to brainstorm, study, argue, and recommend steps for action. But the divisions within the agency had not diminished. Gerry Meyer, in particular, continued to argue that "attempting to use the Food, Drug, and Cosmetic Act to ban the use and sale of tobacco is not a profitable use of anyone's time." Others disagreed. One agency official surprised Ilisa by declaring, "FDA has the power to regulate, but it never has."

File cabinets and computer hard drives began to fill with published tobacco research and notes from meetings with scientists. Novices were turning into experts on a variety of subjects: nicotine, addiction, tobacco control, the history of regulation, and the tobacco-related efforts of other agencies within the federal bureaucracy.

Jack Henningfield came in to speak with Ilisa's group. Henningfield headed the clinical pharmacology branch of the National Institute on Drug Abuse (NIDA) and had been a major contributor to several Surgeon General's reports, including the 1988 one that officially declared nicotine in cigarettes addictive. With more than two hundred publications to his credit, Jack was an expert on addiction in general and on nicotine dependence in particular.

He was also a veteran of the scarring battles that sometimes engulfed the tobacco issue. In the summer of 1982, Shook, Hardy & Bacon, a Kansas City, Missouri, law firm that had long been key counsel to the tobacco industry, received documents from a source at Harvard Medical School, including two

NIDA progress reports involving Henningfield's research. One used animals, the other human beings, but both showed that given the opportunity, the study subjects would administer nicotine to themselves—a defining characteristic of an addictive substance. Within a year, the Tobacco Institute, the industry's lobbying arm, was pressuring its congressional allies to prevent NIDA from studying the addictive properties of tobacco.

That kind of pressure soon came to a head. Carlton Turner, the Reagan administration's drug czar, visited NIDA's laboratories. Jack Henningfield showed him around proudly, talking at length about his work. Turner seemed interested, and Henningfield assumed that he had been impressed by the sophistication of the research.

Turner also spoke with Jerome Jaffe, who became NIDA's acting director. The next day, Jaffe summoned Jack into his office. Jack recalled Jaffe's description of his conversation with Turner vividly. The drug czar had pounded his fists on Jaffe's table and was reported to have suggested that if NIDA had so much money to waste studying the addictive properties of nicotine, then maybe NIDA did not really need its budget. Jaffe understood the implications, and he was glum. His predecessor had left his job weary, discouraged by a lack of enthusiasm among senior staff for working on tobacco, and Jaffe chose not to take a stand on the issue. "That's what bureaucracies know how to do," Jaffe told me.

"Jaffe put the burden on me," Henningfield recalled. "He said he was not going to shut down my studies but told me that if I persisted in doing them, I would threaten NIDA's budget and the budget of my colleagues next door, at Johns Hopkins University. His message was: this is bigger than just your laboratory."

Jack was stunned. "This is what happened in Russia," he thought, "not in America." The idea that someone in a high government position would make a demand that so obviously defied public health interests disturbed him deeply. But his options were limited. He told Jaffe he would complete testing of the subjects already in the pipeline and then bring those studies to a close. The abandoned research was never resumed, pockets of incomplete data were never published, and new efforts to explore tobacco addiction were delayed by several years.

Eager to share what he knew, Jack schooled Ilisa's group in many facets of nicotine and drug addiction. I was kept apprised of such activities and I occasionally stopped by meetings to listen or to offer a few words of support. But despite the group's efforts, tobacco was still a peripheral interest for me.

The industry wasn't paying much attention to the FDA, either. Although the tobacco control movement had achieved a number of victories in the previous two decades, pressures on the cigarette manufacturers had eased in recent years. There was still considerable concern about restrictions targeting the risk of secondhand smoke, which had made inroads on the public consciousness, but those restrictions were not coming from the FDA. At one Philip Morris meeting, participants were encouraged to brainstorm about strategic opportunities for changing the industry's image. With no holds barred, responses poured out by the dozens: "infiltrate the World Health Organization"; "create a bigger monster (AIDS)"; "make it hurt (political risk) to take us on"; "program for journalism and law schools"; "create science journal"; "organize 'spontaneous' protests on our issues"; "sue the bastards." Actions involving the FDA were nowhere on the list.

By the fall of 1992, Ilisa's tobacco group was ready to present me with a paper outlining options for responding to the Coalition's petitions. Everybody felt they understood the issues far better than they had when they began their studies. But there was also a sense of frustration, a recognition that they had not produced a convincing argument for reconsidering the longstanding position that cigarettes did not fall within the FDA's jurisdiction. When they reported to me, I had to agree. Nothing they said persuaded me to become more involved.

And so it might have remained. Smoking could easily have drifted in limbo, with some at the agency hoping for my eventual support and others sure that I would leave things as they were. What changed the course of events was the intervention of David Adams.

At the agency, David was viewed as strong-willed, creative, and maddeningly slow. A colleague called him a "freelance artist of the law." Others complained that he was not a team player. But while I valued cohesion, I also knew that iconoclasm could be useful to any large organization, and I respected David for the way his mind worked.

He had joined the FDA in 1978 after clerking for a federal judge. In the general counsel's office, David specialized in drug advertising and labeling and became an expert in the concept of "intended use." When a rumor circulated that Adams was planning to leave for private practice, Mike Taylor persuaded him to join the policy office instead, knowing that he would find colleagues there who appreciated his style.

David had been attending meetings of the tobacco working group since it was launched, but in typical fashion he had also been doing his own thinking. Now he had a legal theory, and he wanted me to hear it.

Normally anyone wanting to talk to me had to pass my vigilant executive assistant, Kay Hamric. Kay struggled heroically to keep me on schedule and relatively free from distractions, but I encouraged a certain level of informality, believing it helped to foster an exchange of ideas. By slipping through a door in the neighboring policy area, it was possible to walk directly into my private conference room, and then through a second door into my main office. A few days after I heard the report from Ilisa's group, David Adams cautiously opened the door from the conference room, poked his head around it, and asked politely, "May I have a minute with you, commissioner?"

He looked uncertain, knowing his idea diverged sharply from the agency's traditional perspective. David agreed with something I had said at an earlier meeting, that the petitioners' focus on low-tar products was narrow and misplaced. He was thinking about strategies for regulating all forms of tobacco.

"There is a way to regulate cigarettes, if you want to do it," he told me. He explained that Ilisa's group had learned that nicotine was a variable in tobacco, not an immutable constituent. "Cigarette manufacturers can take the nicotine out, but they leave it in. That goes to the question of intent."

The idea was powerful, as elegant as it was succinct, and I recognized it as a dramatic new way to approach an old problem. We had been thinking about how to regulate tobacco; Adams thought perhaps we should consider regulating *nicotine* as a drug. Knowing that he could never persuade the agency's old guard that his theory gave just cause to take on tobacco, he made his case directly to me.

Intellectually, the idea made sense. From that moment, and for the first time, I began to focus on tobacco.

I KNEW myself well enough to know that if I became engaged in the tobacco issue, it was going to require an enormous commitment of my time and energy. Once I got started, I would have to learn everything about tobacco that I could. But now I had a reason to finally start thinking seriously about it.

I decided to test the FDA's new idea on the Department. I scheduled a meeting for some of us with the assistant secretary for health, Jim Mason. The discussions with Mason took place in his rectangular conference room on the seventh floor of the Humphrey building in downtown Washington, which houses large parts of the Department of Health and Human Services. The lobby walls were decorated with a mural charting decades of public health accomplishments, beginning with the victory over smallpox. The legislation that created the FDA was one milestone; another was the date of the first AIDS drug approval.

As we walked into the meeting, I pulled Ilisa aside and asked her not to review her tobacco options paper in detail. I had other ideas.

I sat opposite Jim Mason and addressed him directly in my opening remarks, emphasizing that my goal was to discuss the issues, not to make any decisions. A conundrum discussed at that meeting, one that would challenge us again and again in the coming years, was that the FDA approved products on the basis of their safety and efficacy—and carcinogen-laden cigarettes could never be proved safe. Yet I said explicitly that the FDA would not head down the mine-laden road of prohibition. With some 50 million smokers in the United States, a total ban was out of the question. Mary Pendergast, my top troubleshooter for the agency, quickly backed me up, offering an analogy to saccharin. The FDA's efforts to remove the sugar substitute from the market in the 1970s had been blocked by an angry public and a wary Congress. Rather than a ban, I hinted that the FDA might have other, more creative, strategies in mind.

That was the cue David Adams needed to introduce his theory. A few hours earlier, I had told him I would give him an opening. Now, just as we had planned, he took the floor. "Perhaps the FDA should declare nicotine a drug," he suggested. "The fact that the manufacturers do not remove the ingredient hints at deliberate intent."

Michael Eriksen spoke up as soon as David had finished. Michael, head of the Office on Smoking and Health at the Centers for Disease Control (CDC) in Atlanta, had joined the meeting by video teleconference. In an earlier job, at M. D. Anderson Cancer Center in Houston, Michael had seen people in the grip of nicotine addiction. One of his patients had been fitted with a prosthetic device after her nose and part of her mouth were removed in a battle against nasopharyngeal cancer. A year later, she was back; the prosthesis had become discolored by the cigarettes she continued to smoke. Michael made two important points: one, that the FDA should be taking a more aggressive stance on tobacco, and two, that Adams was on the right track.

"Perhaps the petitioners have submitted the wrong petition," I said to Mason, hinting that nicotine might be a better focus. Then I stepped back a little and said that it would be difficult to establish nicotine as a drug. I did not want to oversell the point or promise more than I thought I could deliver. We had presented the issue, and Mason was interested. For now, that was enough.

His receptivity surprised a few people at the meeting. Like me, he was a political appointee of a hands-off Republican administration, and it would have been easy for him to hear us out without offering much encouragement. But Mason was genuinely concerned about public health, and as a Mormon, he had an abstemious perspective. He urged us to continue exploring the issue, to draw on the resources available at CDC's Office on Smoking and Health, and to report back in six weeks for further discussions.

At my request, Ann Witt joined the tobacco discussions. An attorney with the uncanny ability to predict the consequences of an action many steps down the road, Ann was not shy about arguing with me, a characteristic I appreciated. She was also a lucid writer with a knack for distilling key points from a mountain of material.

She joined the FDA in 1980 and had more than a decade of legal experience in foods and drugs by the time we began to think about tobacco. Some of those years had been difficult ones. When she took charge of the drug advertising division at my request, we were implementing regulations designed to prohibit pharmaceutical companies from promoting their products to doctors under the guise of education. At a meeting of the American Medical Association where she described the new policies, some of the participants—doctors—had actually thrown things at her.

Now, we were talking about tobacco. Ann asked what we expected to achieve—"before we are stopped."

I did not yet have an answer, but one thing was clear to me. Before we could even consider regulating nicotine as a drug, we had to build a case. If tobacco manufacturers intended their products to contain nicotine to satisfy an addiction, I was going to have to find the evidence to prove it.

Still, we were getting serious. "We seem to have passed the point of continuing to 'just say no' to the regulation of tobacco products," wrote one senior FDA manager to his colleagues.

By late November 1992, after a month of almost weekly meetings, the next step had crystallized in my mind. I suggested that we respond to the petitions by sending a letter to the Coalition on Smoking or Health that indicated a shift in our thinking. After I outlined the points it should cover, David Adams took the first crack at a draft. Catherine Lorraine, from the general counsel's office, and Ann Witt soon joined in to make revisions.

Things were going well, but there was one problem. George Bush had lost the election a few weeks earlier. Bill Clinton would be sworn in as the nation's forty-second president on January 20. Jim Mason would soon be out of a job. Most likely, so would I.

10

George Bush's defeat had also complicated the food labeling issue. A White House meeting between Secretary Louis Sullivan and Secretary Ed Madigan had failed to resolve the contentious issue of calorie counts, and Bush's staff had reluctantly agreed that it would have to go all the way to the Oval Office. Mike Taylor could not believe that the President would personally get involved in such arguments. He said as much to one White House official. "That's what he does for a living," responded the official. "He makes decisions."

I was not at all sanguine about the outcome. The forces deployed against us included the White House's Council on Competitiveness, a conduit for conservative, free-market industry views. And Madigan had won some sympathy by suggesting that we had inflated his original legislation beyond reason. In a letter to the *Washington Post* he wrote, "I would note that a 15-page bill has been turned into 4,000 pages of regulation, far beyond what was envisioned when it was passed."

I was more convinced than ever that I might be forced to resign. My fate as commissioner and the fate of nutrition labeling had become inextricably linked. If the decision went against us, I could not disobey an order from the President. For me as a political appointee, the only response to defeat was to leave.

The evening before the Oval Office meeting, Mike Taylor and I met with Lou Sullivan at his Alexandria, Virginia, condominium to discuss options. All three of us agreed that we could not compromise on the basic structure of the regulations. For the first time, I showed the secretary the McDonald's tray liner I had collected on the Jersey shore. He seized on it immediately and insisted on taking it to the White House. He also asked Mike to accompany him, in case details of the proposed label had to be argued.

I did not talk openly to Sullivan about quitting if the USDA stance was allowed to prevail, but he understood well enough now that this was a matter of principle for me, and he knew what my recourse would be.

THE morning of the White House meeting, Marlin Fitzwater, the President's press secretary, called the public affairs office at Health and Human Services to ask for clips of recent newspaper coverage on nutrition labeling. We read this as an encouraging sign. Attention was being paid to how the decision would play in the media.

Mike rode over to the White House in Sullivan's Lincoln Towncar. As they pulled into the driveway between the West Wing and the Old Executive Office Building, reporters called out questions, but Sullivan walked on. Leaving Mike to wait, he headed alone to the Oval Office.

The President sat in one of two wing chairs with his back to the fireplace. Vice President Quayle was at the President's side, a sign perhaps that the White House conservatives thought Secretary Madigan might need some help. Madigan and Fitzwater sat on a sofa, facing Sullivan, James Baker, and Baker's deputy.

It did not take long for the meeting to hit a wall. Sullivan said that if his Department were required to adopt the USDA approach to the label, it would first have to try to build a written record to support it, and then open up a public comment period, a process that could take at least six to eight months. This was not what the White House wanted to hear. Staff wanted the issue resolved before Bush left office.

Mike was summoned a few minutes later. Ever courteous, the President rose to shake hands and directed him to a chair next to James Baker. "I'm a little puzzled," the President said to Mike. "I'm being told that I can't just make a decision and have it promptly executed, that the Department can't just salute smartly and go execute whatever decision I make. Why is that?"

This question went to the heart of the legislation. Mike explained that the evidence in the record would not legally support the USDA format. Aware of the President's naval service, he used a maritime metaphor, explaining that even if we started to turn the wheel of the ship, it would take time to set a new course. Mike held his ground as the vice president challenged his premise. Then Baker intervened: "I think he has a point, Mr. President."

Mike was released, but he was asked to wait in the office of the President's secretary. As he sat in an antique chair, the President's dog, Ranger, walked over and offered Mike his head to pat. This was apparently a rare honor—and, he dared to hope, a good omen.

The meeting continued for an hour, with the President's staff becoming increasingly agitated because a call was expected from Boris Yeltsin. Brent Scowcroft, the national security adviser, arrived and started pacing nervously, concerned that a meeting on nutrition labeling was taking precedence over East-West politics.

Sullivan produced the McDonald's tray liner with a flourish, pointing out that the 2,000-calorie benchmark was deemed reasonable by a pillar of the fast-food industry. Madigan was taken completely by surprise. The President sat staring at the liner for a minute or two, studying the detail. Shortly afterwards, Mike was asked back, this time to explain what was meant by the phrase "total daily value." As he did so he noticed the tray liner prominent among the papers strewn on the sofa, but when the meeting came to a close, no decision had been made, and nobody felt able to predict the outcome.

The following evening, Paulette and I were in our room at the Waldorf-Astoria in New York, getting ready for a dinner sponsored by the American Federation for AIDS Research. We expected it to be a lively night, with entertainment provided by a well-known female impersonator. As we were dressing, my beeper went off. It was Secretary Sullivan's office telling me that the President's decision would be made known the following morning. I had no idea whether Bush was going to side with the USDA or with us.

I turned to Paulette and asked, "Is this resignable?"

"Absolutely," she said, without a moment's hesitation.

Paulette was a master of realpolitik, and there was no hard decision I made without her. In Washington it was considered proper form to keep one's spouse in the background, and only a few people understood our intellectual partnership. Although trained as a litigator, Paulette was generally more interested in the fate of the novel than the fate of the common law. Always a voracious reader—Trollope's political novels were great favorites, even before her exposure to the political life—she constantly turned to literature for a frame of reference. Nineteenth-century English fiction informed her sensibilities: everything would always work out in the end.

But it was not just her outlook that I valued. She was very shrewd, with a remarkable ability to consider issues from all perspectives. Although I did not keep her informed of every development in my work, I often turned to Paulette when a final decision had to be made. She was able to cut through artifice and had rare insights about motive and strategy. Even if she knew little of the background on an issue, she could grasp its essence immediately and usually gave me advice that was exactly on point.

Now she was insisting that if Madigan prevailed, there was no option but to resign.

I agreed. The issue went beyond the food label itself. I was not going to resign over the choice of 2,000 rather than 2,350 calories. I was going to resign because a decision against us would have meant that the meat industry had asserted undue influence over the White House. I felt that the FDA's credibility and independence were at stake. From the outset, I insisted that we were not going to allow political interests to outweigh public health. I could not go back to the staff that had worked so hard on this and say, "We'll have to do it USDA's way." Nor could I stand up at a press conference and tout the merits of a food label in which I did not believe.

I told no one, but I knew that if it happened, I would not be alone. Mike Taylor was not going to tolerate a sellout to USDA either. And Louis Sullivan had signaled that he, too, might resign.

I FLEW back to Washington early the following morning. Once again Mike Taylor accompanied Sullivan to the White House. Marlin Fitzwater and Bob Zoellick, the deputy chief of staff, were there.

"I asked Marlin to come," explained Zoellick, "because we want to go ahead and announce these decisions this afternoon."

He did not say what the decisions were. Instead, he ruffled through papers and pulled out one. "First, I want to talk about the format decision."

Sullivan and Mike still did not know which way it was going.

"This is the President's decision," said Zoellick, handing over the paper. "He wants option two-C." That option gave us a label with everything we wanted.

I never thought that the Office of Management and Budget would allow us to require one industry standard and had not actually expected the President to choose a specific design format. We were focused on a uniform calorie count, a realistic serving size, and a user-friendly way to calculate the percentage of each nutrient in a daily diet; the design options in our briefing book were intended only as examples of how that information could be presented. But the President had not only agreed to the 2,000-calorie count, he had chosen a specific layout for a nationwide, standardized nutrition label for all nonmeat and processed meat products.

Mike returned to the office and told me what had happened. "That's it," I said. "It is a presidential order. We are going to require that format."

"Nutrition Facts" would appear in bold type at the top, as the logo Jerry Mande wanted, with a fine black line around the panel. As a gesture to Madigan, the President agreed to a footnote explaining that the recommended allotment of 2,000 calories could vary depending on individual needs. He also made specific decisions about the definition of terms like "light," accepting most of our recommendations. We lost only one part of the argument. The President did not want restaurants included. Our rules would have required that health claims on menus meet the same standards as claims on packaged foods. It was a disappointment, but in view of the breadth of our victory, one I could easily accept.

THAT afternoon, we held a press conference to present the new format and to explain what we hoped to achieve by the revolution in nutrition labeling. Months earlier, in a widely reported comment, Lou Sullivan had likened the supermarket shelves to the Tower of Babel. Now, he said, "The Tower of Babel has come down." That sound bite led the news reports.

The labels began appearing in mid-1993, and within a year they were universal. The agency gained new credibility. Equally important, I learned more about what it took to tackle big issues. The challenge in Washington, I began to realize, was not getting a job, but figuring out what to do with it. The right combination of opportunities simply does not present itself all that often. For me, taking action began as a matter of survival. With the agency under close scrutiny from so many sources, I knew I had to act deliberately. But having recognized the need for initiative, I next had to decide what had the most significant impact on public health. With only so much time, energy, and resources—and with so many obstacles to making changes—it was foolish to expend capital on anything less. Still, it was some years before I realized that the food label was an opening skirmish, a battle I had to fight and win before I was ready to deal with tobacco.

11

IN THE two years since I had become commissioner, the animosity towards me had grown in some quarters. On more than one occasion, the *Wall Street Journal*'s editorial page had been brutally personal in its attacks. I did not know the President's views, although I heard that a journalist from *U.S. News & World Report* had asked John Sununu, then Bush's chief of staff, whether Bush was thinking about firing me.

"No," Sununu was reported as saying. "Kessler's got balls."

Michael Calhoun, by contrast, seemed to lose all reason when he heard my name. "Kessler, you're in free fall," Sullivan's chief of staff snapped at me before the President's defeat. "If Bush gets reelected, you're out."

Whatever his goal, Calhoun succeeded only in hardening my outlook. But others around Secretary Sullivan were also lining up against me. I learned later that some of them had been checked, to a degree, by the belief that I enjoyed the protection of powerful political backers, notably Senators Orrin Hatch and Ted Kennedy. In truth, I never had all that much political clout on the Hill, but it was useful to have my opponents believe that I did. With George Bush about to leave the White House, the deregulation advocates had taken off their gloves. No longer constrained, they were determined to make sure that I would not, under any circumstances, be allowed to continue as commissioner. According to Washington protocol, a change of administration is a time for political appointees to submit their resignations to the sitting president. Even before the election, President Bush's appointees had been asked for resignation letters, and I had complied. After his defeat, the White House personnel office again requested a letter. Assuming one was sufficient, I ignored the request. Several rather nasty telephone calls followed, accusing me of holding out. Finally, the personnel office sent over a courier, and I drafted a second resignation letter. At that point, I could have left the FDA with an easy mind. I had seen the food label through to completion, and the scientific review of potentially lifesaving drugs was moving much more swiftly. Paulette would have been happy to have us both out of Washington. But I learned that Donna Shalala, who had been named by Clinton to replace Lou Sullivan as Department secretary, pending Senate confirmation, wanted me to stay on. The same message had presumably been passed along to Bush's people, but the word was out that they were going to accept my resignation anyway. That meant I would have to be formally reappointed and reconfirmed by the Senate. There was no way that Paulette would agree to live through a process that promised to involve at least as much character assassination as substance. And in any case, it was a petty gesture that I felt sure was intended to punish me for my strong stance on enforcement and for my willingness to serve as commissioner under a Democratic president.

President Bush was above such tactics, and I doubted he had approved this one. I decided to ask the outgoing secretary to intervene. Sullivan took me seriously when I said that someone was playing games. Soon afterwards, I received a call from the head of the White House personnel office telling me that the President had decided not to accept my resignation after all.

Still, my reappointment was not a done deal. Al Gore was an ally who had let me know that he appreciated the agency's enforcement activities, but I was a stranger to Bill Clinton. In some Washington circles, a Republican political appointee was anathema to a Democratic administration, and I did not know the new President's view. In my own mind, I was not fully aligned with the views of either party. As a teenager I was a Barry Goldwater supporter, but over time my views had moderated significantly.

Behind-the-scenes discussions were still taking place at the Clinton White House when a story broke in the *Washington Post* that I had been asked to stay in the new administration. Bernadine Healy, head of the National Institutes of Health and one of the other holdovers from the Bush administration, had resigned on Friday, February 26, 1993, and both developments were carried in a single news article the next day. At seven that morning the telephone rang in my house. It was Donna Shalala, telling me to keep my head low while she handled the situation.

In truth, the final decision had not been made. The story, as I heard it, was that the new President picked up the Saturday *Post*, read about me on the front page, and asked, "Did I do this?" When the press called the White House to confirm my reappointment, questions were answered with fuzzy language about the new administration's intention to "work with me."

BY NOW I was committed to taking a visible position on tobacco. We polished the letter to the Coalition on Smoking or Health indicating that the FDA might consider regulating tobacco and kept it stored on Ann Witt's hard drive. But even after I was asked to continue in the new administration, I decided not to make tobacco a first-one-hundred-days issue. It did not seem like the right strategic move. Most of the key players at the Department were newly appointed. Although I had ties to many of them from our previous professional lives, we had not worked together in Washington, and they had no particular reason to trust me, a holdover from the Bush era. Besides, I was sure tobacco was not an issue a fledgling president would want to tackle immediately.

But I got off to a rocky start with my new Democratic colleagues anyway, raising their hackles when I tried to force through a regulation restricting the sale of body tissues from foreign sources. That strange episode began when I was given a copy of a letter offering for sale to American tissue banks an array of bone, tendons, and skin from deceased donors in the former Soviet Union at cut-rate prices. Incredibly, despite the risk of HIV, hepatitis, and other infectious diseases, there was nothing illegal about these transactions; tissue banks were run largely outside any existing regulations. Only body organs were strictly regulated.

When I approached Department senior staff, I encountered a resistance I had not expected. They argued that we did not have enough data—no cost-benefit assessment, no risk-benefit assessment, no hard evidence of the existence of bad practices in the tissue industry—to support regulation. Officials also viewed the issue as a distraction from health-care reform, which was consuming most of their energies. "Put this in your next budget," Department officials suggested. "Bring it up in November, and then we'll think about it." I was irritated by the response, but I also realized that I had perhaps been too casual in my approach. I had not worked hard enough to make my case.

Back at Parklawn I began to think about a strategy. Over the next few months, I set up an underground investigation that nearly led FDA investigators to buy body parts from Russian sources. My first step was to ask Jack Mitchell to take charge.

Jack helped run the FDA's Office of Special Investigations, which I had launched in July 1991 to combat the agency's unhappy knack for being the last to know when it had a problem. OSI was an ad hoc, seat-of-the-pants kind of office, ready to deal with the unexpected and the unusual. It served as a kind of early warning system, and Jack—with his background in investigative journalism, his experience as chief staff investigator for a Senate oversight committee, and his extraordinary range of contacts among legislators, policymakers, and the media—was the ideal man for the job. He was an independent operator with confidence and style and also possessed a curiosity that could not be blunted. Jack reported directly to me.

We decided to set up an undercover operation and negotiate directly with the tissue purveyors to see what was actually involved in making a purchase. One of Jack's colleagues said the process reminded him of watching his father bargain for furs on Orchard Street, the commercial heart of Manhattan's old Lower East Side. The Russian-born tissue broker wanted $5,000 per body, but he offered us a deal for one that had tested positive for hepatitis B. We offered $6,000 to purchase one "good" body and one that was infected, and after further sparring we upped the ante by another $1,000, and the deal was struck.

We never consummated the purchase, but armed with the evidence of trafficking in diseased bodies, I went back to the Department to push for new regulations. "Isn't this the same rule we rejected back in April?" asked one staffer with evident irritation. Everyone knew I was forcing the Department's hand. I felt an undertone of hostility, but I did not care. "We can go to the press with a story about contaminated body parts coming into the United States for transplantation, or we can go with a story about a regulation that makes this sort of thing illegal," I warned. "Which do you prefer?"

I had learned how to break through complacency, and the reluctance to support tissue regulation began to crumble. Soon, we were allowed to present our proposal to Secretary Donna Shalala. Shortly before our meeting, the University of Wisconsin had earned a place in the Rose Bowl, and Shalala, who had been its first woman chancellor, greeted me wearing the cheesehead that is the hallmark of the dedicated Badger fan. She invited me to try on her cheesehead, but I decided it was not the moment to look foolish.

Our meeting was a formality. The secretary had made up her mind to sign off on the new regulation.

MY STRATEGY for dealing with the underground tissue trade did not endear me to the Department, and I knew that I could not always rely on confrontational tactics. On tobacco, I was going to try to secure consensus.

Shortly after Shalala assumed leadership of the Department, I sent over a list of key policy issues facing the FDA. I played down the importance of tobacco—it was number seven on a list of about a dozen items. But it was there.

I began to lay the groundwork for action in a series of informal, confidential conversations with selected Department people during the first year of the Clinton presidency. These conversations were a way to begin moving tobacco onto the agenda and to provide what I thought of as "immunizing doses" against the glare of public scrutiny that would surely come when the issue heated up.

I knew several people in the new administration. Early in 1993, Paulette and I invited Harriet Rabb, the Department's new general counsel, to our house for dinner. Although I did not know her well, our paths had crossed occasionally, and we had a number of friends in common. Harriet had spent more than two decades at Columbia University's law school, first as a professor and then as vice dean.

She was new enough to Washington that she did not own a car, so I drove her home after dinner. As we headed down Massachusetts Avenue, I raised the tobacco issue, telling her, "If you put all the things the FDA does together and weigh them against the beneficial effect of stopping people from smoking, stopping tobacco use would have a bigger impact on health in this country."

That statement made an impression, just as I intended. "I thought it was a totally colossal assertion," Harriet told me later.

I also mentioned tobacco to Phil Lee, who had replaced Jim Mason as the assistant secretary for health. Phil was a friend and one of the giants in public health. Donna Shalala had brought him in to serve as an adviser during the transition between the Clinton and Bush administrations and then would not let him go. At the age of seventy, he was the grand old man of the Department. Phil had little use for the tobacco industry. I offered few details about how we might take it on, but I knew that when the time came, he would be with us.

Some time later, I had my chance to broach the topic with Bill Corr, who had been a key congressional aide before becoming a trusted member of the

Department's inner team. I asked for a private word with Bill when we were together at a two-day meeting, and we moved to a corner to talk. I quickly sketched out our early thinking on nicotine regulation, and as I spoke, I could see Bill grow excited.

Very tentatively, I also raised the tobacco issue with Ruth Katz. A confidante of Paulette's since childhood, Ruth had become one of our family's closest friends. Coincidentally, she was also counsel to Congressman Henry Waxman's Subcommittee on Health and the Environment. When I was first asked to come to Washington, Ruth made it clear to both Waxman and me that she would not allow politics to place a wedge between us. She and I scrupulously avoided discussing FDA issues overseen by her committee. But one wintry Friday, as we sat talking in a Hamburger Hamlet, I told her that I had a strategy for taking on tobacco. Ruth did not probe for information, but she warned me not to rush and suggested that I send out some tentative feelers to key people in Congress first.

PRESSURE from the advocacy community continued all year. At every possible public forum, Scott Ballin called for tobacco regulation and complained that politics was interfering with public health. After the *News & Record*, a Greensboro, North Carolina, daily newspaper, reported that tiny fibers from cigarette filters were lodged in the cancerous lungs of smokers, Ballin told reporters this would not happen if the industry were regulated by the FDA.

Ballin called it "courteous agitation," but I was getting annoyed. I needed him to back off a little. Mike Taylor and I decided to schedule a meeting with him. Over lunch, I hinted to Scott that the agency was prepared to tackle tobacco once we determined the right strategy and I pleaded for breathing room. The afternoon was cordial. When Ballin returned to his office, he excitedly called members of the Coalition on Smoking or Health's steering committee to report my interest. "We'll just have to wait and see," he said.

But he did not let up. In April, the *Wall Street Journal* published his letter entitled "When Shown Tobacco, FDA Dog Won't Hunt." Ballin wrote that the FDA's silence on tobacco was for "purely political reasons, namely the unmatched special interest status of the tobacco lobby."

In the late summer, the Coalition asked Phil Lee for a meeting to talk about the landscape of tobacco control, especially the possibility of raising the federal excise tax, intensifying international activities, and giving the FDA regulatory authority. I was asked to attend the meeting, along with representatives from the Centers for Disease Control. Phil had a knack for making people feel that their voices were being heard, and the discussions were amicable. But I was not ready to go public with my thinking, and I felt acutely uncomfortable that day. Even when Lee asked me directly to describe FDA activities on tobacco, I said as little as possible.

INSTEAD, without ever planning it, I continued to assemble the team that would eventually engage tobacco with a vigor not seen before at the FDA. Although no one was hired with tobacco in mind, I soon had a very talented group of people reporting directly to me.

Mitch Zeller came on board in 1993. A lawyer who hated law school, Mitch had never planned to work for the FDA. Two years earlier, as counsel for Congressman Ted Weiss's oversight committee, Mitch turned the FDA upside down in his pursuit of documents, subpoenaed me to appear before the Weiss committee, and threatened to hold me in contempt. At the time, he was trying to learn more about the drug evaluation and approval process. The White House had ordered us to withhold the documents. I was caught in the middle.

That was not the first time Mitch had pursued the FDA. Earlier, he had confronted the agency's Center for Veterinary Medicine, which monitored drugs used in food-producing animals, drugs that ended up being consumed by humans. Mitch's investigations into the lax regulation of drug use in milk cows and his willingness to be confrontational had generated tremendous hostility at the agency. And in a previous job at the Center for Science in the Public Interest (CSPI), an advocacy group focused on nutrition, he had angered FDA food experts when he pushed for a ban on sulfites, potentially dangerous food preservatives.

Though Mitch was jovial, teased his colleagues, and told bad jokes, he was intense and insightful behind his clean-shaven round cheeks and boyish face. Some at the agency were not keen on opening their doors to this outsider, but I wanted his tenacity.

12

ON JUNE 13, 1993, CNN reported that two syringes had been found in cans of Diet Pepsi. The story quickly gained national attention, and an avalanche of new complaints poured into the agency. Soon, it was apparent that many of the reported tamperings were hoaxes, but I could not ignore the possibility that at least some of them were genuine. I asked the FDA's fledgling Office of Criminal Investigations, which had started operations a year earlier, to step in.

OCI was a law enforcement office equipped with all of the tools the experts told us we needed. One of them was an internal polygraph unit. When Terry Vermillion, OCI's director, told me he wanted to bring in lie detectors, I looked at him as if he were asking for a witch doctor. I knew nothing about the scientific accuracy of polygraphs and questioned our need for such a unit at the FDA. But Terry explained that in the hands of a professionally trained law enforcement agent, a polygraph is a powerful investigative device. He saw it not so much as a test to be offered in evidence, but as a tool to get at the truth. In his experience, a trained investigator could use the device to elicit a confession. I soon learned that a polygrapher is not only an interrogator but also a keen observer of human behavior.

As the Diet Pepsi scare heated up, OCI's investigators flew from city to city to investigate tampering reports, and soon they were eliciting confessions from people who had fabricated claims and were making arrests. Once I was sure we were dealing with a series of false reports, I went on national television to underscore that such actions were criminal and to warn that we would prosecute every case. Almost immediately, the torrent of claims slowed to a trickle.

As the investigation drew to a close, Terry Vermillion came into my office, accompanied by a colleague. "I want you to meet a guy who has been key here," he said. "He's been flying back and forth around the country doing polygraph exams and getting one confession after another. He hasn't been home in weeks." I shook hands for the first time with Gary Light.

I soon turned to Gary with a very different sort of assignment. A potential tobacco informant had come to our attention in the fall of 1993, when Jerry Mande, in the policy office, received a telephone call from Matthew Myers, a long-time tobacco foe. Matt's call to Jerry had two purposes. First, he wanted Jerry to convince me to appear on ABC's weekly news magazine show, *Day One,* which was conducting an investigation into the manufacture of cigarettes. The producers had called Jerry a couple of weeks earlier asking for an interview with me, but I had refused. I was still laying the groundwork for releasing our letter to the Coalition on Smoking or Health and was not interested in speaking publicly about tobacco.

Matt's second item was far more interesting: he offered to link us to a whistleblower, a former R. J. Reynolds employee, who had been code-named "Deep Cough." Despite ongoing fears of legal retribution from the tobacco industry, Deep Cough was willing to describe RJR's manufacturing process to the FDA in detail. For the first time, we had an opportunity to get an insider's look at the industry.

As soon as Jerry told me about Deep Cough, I knew we had to handle the informant delicately. I could not use the FDA scientists and lawyers who had taken the first tentative steps into the world of tobacco. Instead, I needed professionals with law enforcement experience—bluff-proof investigators with the skills to test the credibility of a confidential informant.

GARY Light had joined the FDA's Office of Criminal Investigations just a few months before the Diet Pepsi story broke. A twenty-year veteran of the U.S. Army Criminal Investigation Command, he had been involved in undercover narcotics operations both in the United States and abroad, as well as in investigations of larceny, robbery, rape, and murder. He was one of the top instructors at the Department of Defense's Polygraph Institute, where all federal polygraph examiners are trained.

Gary accepted the assignment to interview Deep Cough, asking only for a partner he could trust. He named Tom Doyle. Tom began his career as a transit cop in New York City and then signed on with the Secret Service, earning his law degree along the way. After a brief period prosecuting juvenile cases, he worked at the CIA. He talked little about those years, but we knew he had been involved with overseas training.

It was the beginning of an extraordinary partnership. Tom, a Catholic school boy from the Bronx, was quiet and reserved. He was expert at encouraging people to be open and candid, an ability greatly aided by his resemblance to an altar boy, albeit a bearded one. Gary, a gregarious southern California native, stood six feet tall and wore a mustache. His special talent was reading people, listening for mistakes, and detecting misstatements or outright lies. They complemented each other well.

Both men dressed carefully and conservatively, either in sports jackets or blazers, wearing long-sleeved shirts and knotted ties, even in the hottest of humid southern days. They avoided dark suits, thinking that made them look too much like authority figures. In their investigations they used tricks of the trade that only a veteran would know. They addressed most of their subjects as "sir" or "ma'am," partly out of politeness, but partly as way of stroking fragile egos. On the other hand, if they felt a subject was too self-important, they skipped the honorifics. Another technique was to intrude into a subject's space, getting within three feet of the person in order to gain an edge of intimidation.

When I asked the investigators to question Deep Cough, I did not appreciate the culture clash that would result from their interactions with FDA headquarters personnel. After twenty years of dealing with criminals, Gary and Tom were cynical as only cops could be. They never took anybody at face value and were predisposed to make an assumption of guilt. The Parklawn staff was made of gentler stuff, and inevitably there were misconceptions on both sides. At first, Gary and Tom felt that some of the FDA people looked upon criminal investigators as lower forms of life, and they played on that. Once, Gary told some of the more gullible team members, with a straight face, that before questioning an informant, he generally locked that person in his car trunk and drove over a bumpy road.

But if some headquarters people saw Gary and Tom as cops pure and simple, the two agents saw others at the FDA as civilians who, while talented and well-meaning, knew nothing about dealing with informants. Gary and Tom were shocked when they heard that Catherine Lorraine and Jerry Mande had been making plans to interview Deep Cough at Jerry's home and promptly put a stop to that idea. Never let an informant know where you live, they warned; it was not only unprofessional, it was potentially dangerous.

THE investigators reached Deep Cough by phone on January 11, 1994. They had been warned that the informant was high-strung and very emotional. The purpose of the first call was to put the subject at ease and to lay the groundwork for future interviews.

Although the conversation was cordial, the anger and fear in Deep Cough's voice were obvious. The former RJR manager had been laid off and was afraid of being hounded because of the confidentiality clause that is a standard part of the company's employment agreement. Tobacco industry employees are routinely asked to sign such agreements, which the companies consider essential tools for safeguarding proprietary information. Deep Cough was also under strain because ABC was pressing for an on-camera interview. It took Gary a long time before the conversation moved from the *Day One* show to the topic of RJR. The informant clearly knew some of the details of the cigarette manufacturing process and mentioned that "vats of nicotine" were used in reconstituted tobacco. At that time, we knew nothing about the nature or use of reconstituted tobacco, let alone about the existence of vats of nicotine. Only later did we learn that as far back as the 1950s, the industry had developed a process that resembled papermaking for using stems, scraps, and other leftovers (or "trash," as one factory worker called it) from the tobacco plant. The manufacture of "recon" involves adding a solvent to the leftovers and creating a slurry that is then spread into a thin sheet. A certain amount of the nicotine contained in these scraps dissolves in the solvent and is concentrated and sprayed back onto the paper sheets. Reconstituted tobacco is now a constituent of virtually all American cigarettes. The industry describes it as a means to reduce waste and cut costs.

In a second telephone conversation a few days later, Deep Cough offered more details about RJR's marketing and product development processes. This time, the informant hinted that the company had conducted nicotine research on human beings under the auspices of a division called BIO/BIO.

I pushed Light and Doyle to interview Deep Cough in person. By now, I knew the question we needed to answer. Was nicotine a drug under the Food, Drug, and Cosmetic Act? Deep Cough was the first insider to whom we had access who might help us find out.

The meeting took place on January 20, 1994, at a seafood restaurant overlooking the ocean in Virginia Beach. In the wintertime, that corner of Virginia is a quiet, almost dreary place, and the three of them had the restaurant almost to themselves. Over a two-hour dinner, Gary and Tom gave the informant what they called the "schmooze," a chatty conversation designed to establish feelings of trust. Tobacco and nicotine were never mentioned. With dinner over, they adjourned to a hotel suite that Tom had booked earlier, and the actual interview began.

The atmosphere was relaxed as the two investigators told Deep Cough that the FDA was beginning to amass information about the cigarette manufacturing process, but that we needed someone to tell us what it all meant, what the research entailed, what was actually going on behind industry's closed doors. They appealed to the informant's sense of patriotism.

"One of these days the FDA may be regulating tobacco," emphasized Tom. "We don't know if that's going to happen, but if it does, we want it to be the right kind of regulation. That's where you can help your government." That was a theme to which Tom returned often. Even in a cynical age, it worked with Deep Cough.

Deep Cough's comments took the form of a rambling narrative that continued for several hours:

We were told never to use the word "nicotine." We called it either impact or satisfaction. One of the company lawyers told me never to use the word "nicotine," because that could open us up to regulation by the FDA.

One of the research projects based on market desires was the "Super Ultra-Low-Tar Cigarette." People in the tobacco business believe that the public associates cancer with tar, not with other ingredients such as nicotine. During this study we monitored the body fluids of volunteer employees who were smokers and who consumed a certain number of cigarettes each day. One of them walked around during the work day carrying a cooler that maintained his urine samples. He also provided saliva and blood samples. They told us that the Super Ultra-Low-Tar Cigarette was the wave of the future. They told us that smoking improves short-term memory, that smoking is equal to a cup of coffee, that cigarettes cannot specifically be shown to cause cancer.

The concern with Winston cigarettes was that the last puff did not have as much impact as the first. A new project was designed to put nicotine levels into the filter web of Winston products in order to provide puff-by-puff delivery for product consistency. The product was being test-marketed.

In one project where the product had little impact, there were directions to adjust the amount of nicotine or the pH, the alkalinity, to increase impact. The amount of nicotine within the cigarettes was increased.

Reconstituted tobacco is made by extracting nicotine from those parts of the plant that cannot be used. The extracted nicotine is then sprayed onto paper sheets, which are introduced into cigarettes at the desired level. Not only that, but R. J. Reynolds and the other tobacco companies buy nicotine extract from flavor houses.

Deep Cough went on, sometimes speaking in a low and controlled voice, sometimes building to a peak of excitement, occasionally giving in to emotion and shedding tears. At times the informant seemed to talk in code, using abbreviations such as STT, XB, and KDN Extract. By the time the interview was over, Tom and Gary had a mass of anecdotal information, much of which they did not understand. They tried not to let Deep Cough know that they were working mostly in the dark.

That night the investigators briefed me by phone. As they read their notes, I heard certain key words: "body fluids," "nicotine levels," "spray-dried tobacco extract," "buy nicotine extract from flavor houses," "adjusting the pH of the extract to affect nicotine delivery." If Deep Cough's statements were true, they were evidence of nicotine manipulation. And if the company was manipulating nicotine, that was evidence, under the drug definition, of the company's intent.

"Is the informant credible?" I asked.

Tom and Gary said it was too early to tell.

13

Day One kept pressing me to appear on its upcoming broadcast, but I stood firm. The producers were also pushing Deep Cough. Tom and Gary were fiercely opposed and urged the informant to remain out of view. ABC eventually called Gary directly. He had neither interest nor experience in dealing with the media, and his first reaction was concern. "I don't talk to ABC," he said. "Talk to the Office of the Commissioner. I don't get involved with this." His next thought was to extricate himself from the tobacco assignment as quickly as possible.

We were not the only people *Day One* producer Walt Bogdanich wanted to put on camera. I learned later that at the beginning of February 1994 he asked R. J. Reynolds to provide a source willing to talk about nicotine addiction. In exchange for RJR's cooperation, Bogdanich agreed to have the interviews videotaped and brought to a halt if the company felt he had been in any way deceitful. The interview was set for February 21.

Bogdanich also called Philip Morris. RJR had alerted that company to the upcoming broadcast, and so Philip Morris was expecting the call. "While *Day One* had been snooping around flavorings, etc., the story now is definitely about nicotine," read a Philip Morris e-mail before Bogdanich even requested an interview.

"I think you'll find me more open than other reporters," Bogdanich said to Philip Morris. "I really want to look at both sides here. . . . I'm not out to sandbag you." The company declined the interview, answering questions about its use of reconstituted tobacco and tobacco extract in a six-sentence fax, which included the following disclaimer: "Nothing done in the processing of tobacco or manufacture of cigarettes by Philip Morris increases the nicotine in the tobacco blend above what is found naturally in the tobacco."

A week before the RJR segment was scheduled for taping, members of the company's legal team began to prep the company scientists who were scheduled to appear on the show. Notes taken by RJR's director of public affairs show that the discussions centered on addiction:

> Company's position drives litigation—not addictive. At most a habituation/custom/practice. Critical issue to defend in litigation—people can quit. Voluntary—freely choose to take up and give up.
>
> Intoxication. Life destroyed. Smokers—don't have that—go to church, in clubs, etc. ... Don't keep taking more and more every day. ... If give up—they might have discomfort. ... Like a fanatic jogger with bad knees—goes through same discomfort when gives up. Less than half smokers have withdrawal. Compare to dieter. Not saying easy—like any other habit, may be difficult.
>
> If had son or daughter married—would rather spouse be a smoker, alcoholic, cocaine/heroin addict? Offends common sense. ... Cigarette smoking does not destroy families.

As the show date approached, RJR was busy. An internal memo written during this time was titled "High Nicotine G7 for Blendoff as G7-28." G7 was RJR's term for reconstituted tobacco. The memo read: "Attached is a list of G7 materials produced for R&D that are no longer needed. All these materials are made from the G7-1 blend recipe. The nicotine levels were raised by adding KLN extract to the G7 extract. ... All these materials have been relabeled...."

Raised nicotine levels? Relabeled? No longer needed? The memo seemed to suggest that a reconstituted tobacco with a high nicotine content in fact existed. Considering that *Day One* was expected to focus on the use of nicotine extracts, the timing of RJR's document was curious.

I SENSED that the time to release our response to the Coalition on Smoking or Health petitions was nearing, and I decided to use the pending *Day One* program as leverage. I handed the Department the latest draft of our three-page letter to the Coalition, told them about the upcoming broadcast, whose exact date had not yet been scheduled, and asked for the green light to send the letter. I knew that if *Day One* aired first, it would appear as though we were reacting to the show. We had worked too long and too hard for that.

On many issues there is a delicate dance between the Department and the FDA. In theory, I could simply have responded to the petitions on my own authority. Officially, no other sign-off on the letter was required. But I had grown to appreciate the value of being a team player, at least when I could get the rest of the team on my side. With an issue as big as tobacco, I wanted the Department to know what I was doing—and to sanction it.

It was fifteen months since Ann Witt, Catherine Lorraine, and David Adams had written the first draft of the letter, focusing on the question of whether nicotine was a drug. Despite numerous revisions, the substance of the letter had not changed in any major way, but we continued to debate the implications of every word and to fine-tune the language. The letter now opened with an explicit statement that it was not a formal response to the Coalition's petitions, but was an effort to "frame the issues for the broader public debate that will be necessary to resolve them." Then we suggested that the Coalition petitions were not sufficiently far-reaching. "The focus should be on the presence of nicotine in cigarettes in amounts associated with addiction," our letter read.

After laying out the framework that gives the agency jurisdiction over drugs and emphasizing the need to establish vendor intent, we touched on the FDA's historic reluctance to regulate cigarettes. "Although it has been well-known for many years that some people smoke for the drug effects of nicotine … cigarette vendors have in the past been given the benefit of the doubt as to whether they intend cigarettes to be used for this purpose, because some people smoke for reasons other than the drug effect."

Now, we said, we had reason to think that something else might be going on. "This evidence … suggests that cigarette vendors intend the obvious— that many people buy cigarettes to satisfy their nicotine addiction. Should the agency make this finding based on an appropriate record or be able to prove these facts in court, it would have a legal basis on which to regulate these products under the drug provisions of the Act."

We concluded with a nod to Congress. An earlier draft of the letter had read: "The proper forum for this discussion, and for resolution of these issues, is not the FDA, but the Congress." Now I thought that position was too weak. I wanted to walk the line between a unilateral assertion of authority by the FDA and deferring responsibility to Congress. My goal, to the extent that I had formulated one, was to goad legislators into action. The final text read: "We recognize that the regulation of cigarettes raises societal issues of great complexity and magnitude. It is vital in this context that Congress provide clear direction to the agency. We intend therefore to work with Congress to resolve, once and for all, the regulatory status of cigarettes under the Food, Drug, and Cosmetic Act."

I had no clear expectations about what would happen next nor even what I wanted to happen, although I thought it likely that Congress would have to respond. Perhaps, I thought, some legislators would encourage us to move ahead. More likely, they would define a limited role for us. Or, we might be told to step aside altogether and allow federal legislation to address the issue. I thought the most probable scenario was that somehow we would be stopped in our tracks.

THE clearance process within the Department was more informal and swifter than old agency hands like Bill Hubbard had expected. He visualized a sluggish series of internal meetings and a protracted struggle at every step, such as had happened with body tissues, before someone was willing to say, "Okay, take it to the next level." Hubbard wondered whether the sought-after approval would ultimately come at all.

Bill Corr circulated the letter quietly among a handful of top staff in the Department. His style, honed from years on Capitol Hill, was to touch base with the right people and to make sure they understood the letter and knew it would generate a lot of attention. Phil Lee, who had made a single change when I showed him an earlier draft, altering a "which" to a "that," had another chance to stamp the letter with his approval. Jerry Klepner, Shalala's assistant secretary for legislative affairs, worried about the final paragraph. He knew that if we were perceived as making an end run around the Hill, we would offend people who might otherwise have been our allies and who could find ways to stop us later.

I waited patiently until the last week of February 1994, and then I knew it was time to release the letter.

Tobacco had been in the news every day that week. McDonald's announced that smoking would be banned in all of the company-owned fast-food outlets. The Surgeon General held a press conference to release the twenty-third annual report on smoking and health, this one focusing on cigarette marketing to young people. And the *Day One* show had finally been scheduled to air; despite our admonitions, Deep Cough was going public.

Early on Thursday, February 24, I called Claudia Cooley, who headed the Department's executive secretariat, and told her how important it was for us to issue the letter before the broadcast. Later that day, I bumped into Bill Corr at the Humphrey building. He looked at me and said quietly, "You can go."

I echoed his words: "I can go?"

Bill nodded.

"I'll send it out tomorrow."

Until then, only a handful of people within the FDA knew we were working on the closely held letter. In recent weeks I had clued in the FDA's chief counsel, Margaret Porter, and Jim O'Hara, who ran the public affairs office. Mike Taylor, from the policy office, had been commenting on drafts all along, even though he had his doubts about the project. Weeks earlier he had looked straight at me and asked, "You're not actually going to regulate tobacco, are you?"

Someone had given a copy of the letter to Sharon Natanblut. I had recruited her from the public relations firm of Burson-Marsteller so that she could apply her "social marketing" skills to food labeling. As she read through the letter, Sharon was at once excited and deeply disappointed that she had not been involved. For a few minutes, she sat at her desk trying to work; then she marched down the hall and into my office, demanding a word with me.

"How could you do this and not have me be part of it?" she asked. "I just have to be working on tobacco."

I backed away from her, but she refused to let me off the hook. The official launch of the new food label was still several months away, and Sharon's involvement with the development of a public education strategy was crucial to its success. I told her so, but promised to let her work on tobacco as soon as that campaign was done. That was not good enough for her. Philip Morris had been one of her clients at Burson-Marsteller, and she regretted ever contributing to its public relations efforts. Sharon's exposure to the industry had convinced her that, in her words, it was "misleading and deceitful," that it sold a deadly product, and that it had extraordinary amounts of money at its disposal. That combination both angered and frightened her. She let me know that her involvement in tobacco was not negotiable.

A few key people needed to know that the letter was about to be released. I asked my assistant to organize a meeting as quickly as possible. The mood in my office was somber when we gathered that afternoon. The dozen or so senior people there ordinarily talked, bantered, and argued freely with one another. Now, they were subdued. We had been building to this for some time, and no one had been sure that we could pull it off. At any point, the Department or even the White House might have sent word not to go forward.

Everyone understood the weight of the moment. We were preparing to give wings to the letter, and no one could predict the direction in which it would travel.

Diane Thompson, head of the FDA's legislative affairs office and the agency's chief liaison with Congress, spoke up. A Capitol Hill veteran with acute political instincts, Diane knew nothing about the letter until that moment, but she immediately understood the magnitude of what I proposed to do. She also knew that though the letter had been a group effort, at the end of the day, my signature would be on it.

There was an intensity in her voice as she addressed me directly. "You know, David, no matter what the Department says to you before you issue the letter, you will be all alone if the reaction is unfavorable. I don't think you can count on anybody to back you up if things go wrong."

The room fell silent. Everyone recognized the truth in what she was saying. If I were skewered in the press or on Capitol Hill for overstepping the agency's jurisdiction or making a power grab, my support would quickly evaporate. Diane did not come out and say my career might be on the line, but the implication was clear.

A few seconds passed, and I broke the silence. "What's the worst that they can do to me?" I asked.

There was a touch of both arrogance and naïveté in my question. In truth, I had no idea what it meant to challenge the tobacco industry, nor did I fully understand what I hoped to achieve by doing so. But there was something else behind my response as well. After the battle over food labeling, when I had been prepared to resign for a principle, I had made a decision. As long as I could use my position to get things accomplished, I would stay on the job. But there were compromises I was not willing to make. There was no more debate.

EARLY that evening, with just a few people left in my office, I read and reread the letter, lingering over every sentence. Then, I decided to give Jack Henningfield a call.

Jack and I had never spoken directly, although he had been one of the first scientific experts Ilisa Bernstein had consulted during her information-gathering process. I reached him around dinnertime at his Baltimore home. Hearing family noises in the background, I apologized for the intrusion, told him that I could not reveal exactly what I was doing, and asked for his help. For more than an hour we discussed the passages in the letter that focused on addiction, and I asked about the supporting data. The letter had to be 100 percent accurate, totally unassailable. As a scientist, Jack understood the level of precision I needed.

We were finishing our conversation when Jack's older son pounded on the door, demanding that Jack come to dinner. The addiction expert walked into the kitchen and said to his wife, "I have no idea what we were working on. I don't know whether it will ever see the light of day. But if it does, this is a lot bigger than the Surgeon General's report on youth smoking that we just released." It was shortly after noon on Friday, February 25, 1994, when I called Scott Ballin and told him I would be faxing him a letter shortly. "I want you to understand fully where the agency is coming from," I said. I could tell that Ballin was euphoric.

There was no big celebration that afternoon. I brought Congressman Henry Waxman up to speed in a five-minute telephone briefing and met with Ed Rensi, the CEO of McDonald's. Rensi had been delighted that the McDonald's tray liner had helped persuade President Bush to adopt the 2,000-calorie standard for the new food label, and he wanted to talk about what the company might do as part of the official rollout. But he was skeptical about how useful the label would actually be, mostly because he thought the average serving size would not reflect American appetites. I knew otherwise. Not long before, Sharon Natanblut and I had sat on the floor of my living room counting out Goldfish snacks from a bag. A serving size had been estimated at fifty-five pieces. Even Sharon, a confirmed junk-food devotee, felt satisfied after she consumed that amount. Now, I went to her office and was not surprised to find her eating a bag of potato chips for lunch. She accompanied me back down the hall, showed Rensi the chips, and told him that the entire bag would be labeled as a single serving. Rensi was persuaded.

Later that day, Catherine Lorraine walked into my office and asked if I was going to have a signing ceremony. She looked disappointed when I held up a felt-tip pen and told her the letter had already been signed. I handed her the pen and told her to keep it.

A FEW minutes after the letter had gone out, Jim O'Hara headed back to his fifteenth-floor office to contact the news media. Jim brought to the agency almost twenty years of experience as an aggressive reporter on *The Tennessean*. His coverage of state politics had led the *Washington Post* reporter John Schwartz to dub him the "meanest man in Nashville," and when Jim left Tennessee to take a job at Burson-Marsteller, state legislators issued a joint resolution in his honor that read, in part, "Many of us will miss him like we would miss a migraine headache or a root canal." He hung a framed copy in his office when he came to Washington.

Jim and I met for the first time in early 1993 at the American City Diner in Chevy Chase, one of those places that capitalizes on 1950s nostalgia, complete with bubble gum–popping waitresses. He was dressed more like a downtown Washington lawyer than the typical federal bureaucrat; he was almost courtly in appearance. At six feet two inches, with reddish hair and a full beard and mustache, he stood out in any crowd.

We were scheduled to talk for an hour, but we hit it off immediately, and the meeting lasted twice as long. The trick to filling a high-level political position with one's preferred candidate is to convince a congressman or senator to submit the name directly to the White House. Then, when the White House sends over suggested candidates for the vacancy, the right person is already on the list. That is what I did, and soon after, Jim signed on at the FDA. O'Hara had a reputation among reporters for credibility. He still thought as they did and still answered the phone with a reporter's curt greeting: "O'Hara." From the beginning, we agreed that he would sit in on decision-making so that he could explain the agency's actions to the news media, and thus to the public, effectively.

Jim knew when to use enough hype to bring a story a little extra attention, and when to downplay it. At one point, we had to file an injunction against the American Red Cross, insisting on new measures to strengthen the safety of the blood supply. That sort of incident could create front-page news, but we were determined not to cause widespread fear. When he briefed reporters, Jim was so understated that the *New York Times* decided it was not even worth writing about; the other newspapers buried the story.

Now, we decided to alert a small circle of reporters to our letter, settling on Philip Hilts at the *New York Times* and John Schwartz at the *Washington Post*, who were both top science reporters, plus our contacts at the major television networks. The sun was streaming through the windows in Jim's corner office as he placed his calls, leaning back in his chair, his legs stretched over his desk. The telephone was cradled on his shoulder. I could picture Hilts at his perpetually messy desk in the Washington bureau of the *Times* at the other end of the phone. I had seen the newsroom and knew it was a fishbowl, with cubicle partitions only a few feet high; a private conversation was almost impossible.

O'Hara described the letter in his distinctive twang and measured tone of voice, avoiding overstatement, and then he sent a copy over by fax. Hilts was initially struck by the careful wording, but when he read the line about the FDA possibly having a legal basis to regulate cigarettes, he recognized it "as a complete break with the past."

Schwartz also understood its significance at once. "Holy shit," he gasped. Later he said, "I knew immediately that the world had changed."

Word of the letter began to get out around Washington and beyond, and reactions filtered back to me. Jack Henningfield said he was "stunned, awed, and amazed" when he learned of its release.

Margaret Porter began to wonder whether the agency would be sued.

On Capitol Hill, a staffer from the House Agricultural Committee asked for a copy and complained of a ruined weekend. Josh Kardon, chief of staff to Oregon Congressman Ron Wyden, wondered about our next steps and about our endgame. Rip Forbes, an aide to Congressman Waxman with a long-standing interest in tobacco control, said to himself, "This is going to make a great hearing."

Walt Bogdanich, producer of the *Day One* program set to air on Monday, dashed up a flight of stairs to talk to the editors who were putting together the nightly news. "This is going to be a huge story," he said breathlessly. When his editors did not immediately grasp the historic nature of the letter, he ran back downstairs to call both his mother and his wife, reading each of them every word.

The letter took the tobacco industry completely by surprise and officials quickly scrambled to find out how their intelligence networks had failed so completely. Steve Parrish, senior vice president for external affairs at Philip Morris, wondered whether we were bluffing to get the Coalition off our backs.

Judy Wilkenfeld, an attorney at the Federal Trade Commission, was sitting in her boss's office when word of the letter arrived. Judy had briefed Ilisa Bernstein's group about the tobacco-related activities of the FTC but had been very skeptical about our commitment. The letter caught her unaware. "We were stunned," she recalled. "Stunned and elated. We thought an atom bomb had gone off in Rockville."

SATURDAY morning I picked up the newspapers. The *Times* ran Hilts's coverage as a front-page story, and Schwartz's piece in the *Washington Post* was a few pages inside. Both articles accurately analyzed what we had done, positioning it as a fundamental shift in agency thinking, but not a unilateral declaration of action. Hilts quoted Brennan Dawson, a spokesperson for the Tobacco Institute, as saying, "We are surprised that this FDA letter is getting the attention it is. The bottom line of this letter is that FDA won't act without further action from Congress. Nothing has happened."

Schwartz had also gone to the industry for comment. Asked about the implication that cigarette companies might be artificially manipulating nicotine levels to maintain addiction, Walker Merryman, director of communications for the Tobacco Institute, said, "I don't know what they could possibly be talking about."

PART II

THE INVESTIGATION BEGINS

14

On Monday morning, February 28, any notion of sitting back and watching the reaction to our letter unfold vanished. One telephone call with Henry Waxman and Mike Synar and suddenly I was forced to come up with a new game plan. The congressmen were calling for hearings.

Surprisingly, the congressmen from tobacco-growing states were silent. Instead, it was the anti-smoking representatives who seized the opening we handed them. I should have anticipated their interest. Our turnaround on a major public health issue was too tempting for the anti-tobacco members on the Hill to resist. From a congressional perspective, our letter had the word "hearing" written all over it.

Waxman was a former smoker who had the fervor of a convert, and when the California Democrat was passionate about something, he threw himself into it completely. I had developed a good working relationship with Waxman, although it had taken some time to build. Neither one of us was particularly good at small talk, and we came to appreciate each other only after we became substantively engaged on issues that we both cared about. Waxman was a shrewd political player, but on some issues he was willing to walk away from a negotiation rather than compromise his principles. I admired the fierce loyalty he engendered in his staff.

Over the past several years, Waxman and Mike Synar had been the stalwart advocates of anti-smoking initiatives, persistently trying to push legislation through an unwilling Congress. For the most part they had hit a brick wall. Waxman knew that getting any sort of anti-smoking bill with teeth out of his subcommittee was an accomplishment and that getting one passed by both houses would be a miracle.

The only legislative breakthrough in recent years had been passage of the

Synar amendment to a bill that reorganized federal substance abuse and mental health services. The amendment required states to enforce laws against underage purchase of cigarettes as a condition for receiving mental health block grants. It had taken three years of very complex legislative maneuvering to get that on the President's desk in 1993. Yet neither Waxman nor Synar was deterred. Both understood the value of persistence, of keeping an issue in the public eye, even when defeat seemed inevitable.

The two congressmen made no secret of their enthusiasm for our letter, which could not have come at a better time for them. Tobacco control seemed to have stalled, and no one quite knew how to jumpstart it. For months, the failing Clinton health-care reform package, the ambitious initiative that would have restructured the nation's health system, had dominated the legislative agenda, pushing aside many other health issues. A possible shift in FDA policy concerning cigarettes offered a new focus. Waxman insisted gently, but firmly, that I come up to the Hill to set out the case to support the FDA's regulation of cigarettes.

"Case, what case?" I thought frantically. On the basis of an interview with just one informant, our review of a handful of documents, and the insights of experts in the field, we had preliminary indications that tobacco manufacturers were controlling for nicotine. But in my letter to the Coalition, I carefully wrote that if evidence existed that the companies intended nicotine's effects, the FDA would consider regulating tobacco. I never said that we were prepared to assert jurisdiction.

I headed back to Rockville, fully focused on the upcoming hearing. Congressional hearings play a crucial role in how the media frame an issue, and that in turn has enormous influence on the way the issue is seen by the American public. No date had been set, but I knew the hearing would happen within a few weeks. As I drove back to the office along the George Washington Parkway, I decided to pull together a team to learn everything possible about the industry's knowledge of nicotine and to determine whether the tobacco companies were manipulating and controlling nicotine levels. I called a meeting for that afternoon.

ROOM 1468, the commissioner's conference room, was the best the FDA had to offer, but it was a modest space, with pale-pink walls decorated with pastoral and floral prints. Rose-colored cushioned armchairs surrounded a large rectangular table and lined the walls. Those who could not fit at the table, or preferred to be less visible, sat along the side walls. There was a speaker-phone in the back of the room and a television set hung on a brace. The easel I had requested for this meeting stood near the door.

It had taken us almost three years—from the May 1991 meeting orchestrated by Jeff Nesbit to the release of the letter in February 1994—to move this far. Now we had three weeks, at most four, before the hearing. Room 1468 would soon house the tobacco team. I scanned the group that had been hastily called together. I had picked each of these people from an agency of 8,000, and I had crossed jurisdictional and bureaucratic boundaries to do it. Kay Hamric, my assistant, had told them only that the commissioner was holding a meeting on tobacco and that they were to attend. I was not yet sure what roles anyone would play. Some people there had been involved in tobacco since we first started exploring the issue, others knew little about it and were not sure why they had been invited. The majority had gotten their most recent information about the FDA and tobacco from newspaper and television reports over the weekend.

They were, for the most part, strangers to one another. I was the only one who knew them all. Even the most effective government workers are typically anonymous beyond their small circle of coworkers. Together for the first time, they regarded one another with some uncertainty and a little mistrust. But all were prepared to suspend their doubts about each other and about this new endeavor. Everyone sensed how serious I was.

Mitch Zeller, now a colleague rather than the adversary who had once subpoenaed me, was attending a tobacco meeting for the first time. Two days earlier, I had bumped into him at a Borders Books in Rockville.

"What are you doing for the next two weeks?" I asked.

"Anything you want me to do." Now Mitch waited expectantly at the conference room table, flipping the top of his pen between his fingers.

Ann Witt and Catherine Lorraine, the chief architects of our letter to the Coalition, sat next to each other. Both could have earned many times their government salaries working in a private law firm, but they preferred instead to be at this table. Jerry Mande, who had worked on the food labels, sat next to me.

Randy Wykoff, who headed the FDA's special office on AIDS and cancer, had lobbied for a spot on the team, and I had gladly offered him one. A pediatrician by training, Randy had also earned a public health degree and then headed a local health department in South Carolina before coming to the

FDA. He believed passionately that addressing the problem of nicotine addiction was one of the most effective ways to spend public health dollars.

Kevin Budich, who had worked on tobacco longer than anyone else at the agency, was there, as was Liz Berbakos, from the agency's executive secretariat. Liz was a master of keeping things on track. A "mother hen" sort, she had a knack for organizing massive amounts of material, and she used a curious combination of wheedling, scolding, and rewards to pull work from the people she supervised. Anticipating future needs, I also included Carol Knoth, a pharmacist who had become a research librarian, on the embryonic team. Carol, like some of the others in attendance, had never been invited into the commissioner's conference room before.

Tom Doyle and Gary Light from the Office of Criminal Investigations sat with their supervisor. I knew I needed the skills of the OCI for a longer, more intense period of time than I had originally thought. I hoped that Deep Cough would not be our last informant, and I wanted Gary and Tom loaned to me.

As I looked toward the back of the room, squinting into the afternoon sun, I could read the doubt on the faces of the criminal investigators. Years later, Gary and Tom admitted that they thought there was no way I would be able to tackle the industry. Both men were used to conducting operations with small groups, involving only those who had an absolute need to know about an investigation. Sitting in the crowded conference room, they saw a roomful of people who would be sharing information on a very sensitive issue, and I could sense that they were edgy.

Gary and Tom eyed Jack Mitchell, representing the Office of Special Investigations, with particular concern. Jack was colorful and iconoclastic. In his days as a journalist, he once ransomed a hostage in Colombia for $250,000 in cash. Jack thrived on sensitive assignments and felt most comfortable in the world of investigative reporters and congressional investigators, the two groups that made the law enforcement people in OCI most uneasy. Although he had orchestrated the investigation into the importation of human tissue, Jack was not a real cop, and Gary and Tom thought that was what the job required. Unrelated to tobacco, there had already been some skirmishes over territory between the two offices, and Gary and Tom felt protective. They were worried that OCI might be the fall guy if there were congressional fallout from our foray into tobacco.

Jack was equally apprehensive about the OCI investigators. Gary and Tom were strangers to him, and besides, they were cops. He doubted they had much political savvy. I knew Jack was hoping his colleagues at OCI would play the game according to his rules; if they didn't, he would be just as content to head out alone. Jack relied heavily on his instincts and hated to be told what to do. I could sense that he was salivating at the thought of investigating the tobacco industry.

MY ROLE was far different than it had been during Jeff Nesbit's tobacco meeting. Then, I had sat and listened. This time, I was on my feet. "We have a few weeks to prepare for a congressional hearing on tobacco," I said, emphasizing the need for evidence. "We have to find out everything we can about nicotine and its use in cigarettes. We need to be one hundred percent focused. We need to be one hundred percent right."

I ticked off some of the questions we had to answer: How are cigarettes made? How is nicotine related to addiction? Are manufacturers adding nicotine to cigarettes? How does the industry set nicotine levels? Where is the nicotine coming from?

"We need to crash," I said. Many people in the room thought they had a good idea of what I meant. We all knew how to work long days, into the night, and through the weekend on special projects. Still, lives were about to be changed. I gazed for a moment at Ilisa Bernstein, now six months pregnant with twins and attending law school at night.

As we reviewed what we had already learned, I was aware that everyone was listening closely. Jack Mitchell had yet to draw a doodle on his notepad, the ultimate indication that he was engaged. I was also struck by Jim O'Hara's attentiveness. As a former newspaperman, O'Hara had been dismayed when he discovered that in government there were not only meetings but also pre-meetings to prepare for the meetings. He tended to grow restless, and if he could not avoid a meeting altogether, he would drop in, listen briefly, and slip away as soon as he could. This time, he stayed.

I announced that we were going to divide the group into investigative, science, and legal teams. I was to be the coordinator, pushing people in new directions, absorbing what was being uncovered, and formulating new questions until I was satisfied that we had learned everything there was to learn. There was no obvious or easy way to begin looking for evidence of a company's intent, but I was determined to pursue every avenue, though I had no road map to show me which avenues even existed.

Tom, Gary, and Jack were assigned to the investigative team. Somehow these men, who traveled in such different circles, would have to work together. I charged them with finding out how cigarettes were made and how nicotine was used. I knew that finding informants who could give us a window into the industry would be a critical part of their assignment.

We put visits to cigarette manufacturing plants on the "to do" list, although we were not sure that the FDA had the authority to require the companies to allow us to inspect. Inspections of a fish processing plant or a drug manufacturer were part of the daily business at the agency, but it was unclear that we had the same rights when we were trying to determine whether a product should be regulated in the first place.

The investigative team also needed to fill in the very sketchy picture we had of the mysterious flavor houses mentioned by Deep Cough. What were they? Were they a source of added nicotine? No one around the table knew. Someone asked whether nicotine levels could be manipulated in the tobacco plants themselves and wondered who inspected the crop. There were more questions than answers at this stage.

"Who knows anything about patents?" I asked. Although there were several lawyers in the room, no one responded. Then Ilisa spoke up. "Well, I'm studying patent law right now." That was more than anyone else could say, and I put her in charge of the patent search. Carol Knoth, the librarian, approached Ilisa after the meeting adjourned and volunteered to help.

The legal team was to search pending and settled liability cases and to review the citizen petitions submitted by the Coalition for legal points. Its assignment was to think about credible regulatory options for the agency. Mitch Zeller was put in charge of contacting other federal agencies to find out what they knew about tobacco and what they did about it. We also needed to review every congressional hearing ever held on tobacco.

I asked the science team to learn everything possible about nicotine and addiction. How addictive is nicotine? What is the difference between a habit and an addiction? Who gets addicted and at what levels? Is nicotine in cigarettes for taste? "Bring in experts to help sort out the pharmacology and physiology of nicotine," I said. "We have to go to Waxman's hearing steeped in the best science available."

With the meeting drawing to a close, I looked around the room one last time. I sensed that the right men and women, most in their thirties and forties, had come together at the right time in their personal and professional lives. I felt now that our past work had somehow moved each of us inexorably toward this day and this task. It was as if we had all been preparing to take on the most powerful of industries without ever knowing it.

I reminded the team to watch the *Day One* broadcast, which was scheduled to air that evening. We had heard rumors that the producer was furious with us for releasing our letter days before his show aired, but that was not my real concern. I wondered what evidence the show would produce.

15

"THEY PUT NICOTINE in the form of tobacco extract into a product to keep the consumer happy," said Deep Cough. The voice had been altered and the face concealed for national television, but the words were crystal clear.

"They're fortifying the product with nicotine, is that correct?" asked John Martin, the on-air correspondent for *Day One*.

The answer was yes.

I had raced home to watch the broadcast, which was introduced with the comment, "Late last week when word of our investigation got out, the Food and Drug Administration announced that it is now considering whether to regulate cigarettes as drugs." So much for the two years we had spent in preparation.

"Now a lengthy *Day One* investigation has uncovered perhaps the tobacco industry's last, best secret—how it artificially adds nicotine to cigarettes to keep people smoking and boost profits," boasted Martin in a statement that would return to haunt ABC.

Calling cigarettes "a complex, scientifically engineered product," Martin claimed that the methods used by the cigarette companies to control nicotine levels precisely had never before been disclosed. Nicotine manipulation occurs, asserted the reporter, through the use of reconstituted tobacco.

"For years, growing and blending was an art," explained Martin. "But about thirty years ago, it began evolving into something quite different." He explained how stems and stalks of the tobacco plant, and even tobacco dust, were processed to create reconstituted tobacco as a way to save money. But there was a drawback from the industry's perspective. Reconstituted tobacco had "poor taste and less nicotine." To compensate, he said, the companies "apply a powerful tobacco extract containing nicotine and flavor to the reconstituted tobacco."

Powerful tobacco extract? Where was it coming from?

Footage of huge barrels flashed on the screen. The reporter explained that tobacco extract was manufactured by flavor houses and shipped to the companies. Picking up on Deep Cough's assertion that tobacco was fortified with nicotine, Martin pushed the informant about how much was added.

"That really depends on what level the process calls for," Deep Cough said. "In other words, I can say to you: I want it at one percent, I want it at five percent, I want it at ten percent, I want it at fifteen percent." The correspondent did not ask how that could be done, and the informant did not volunteer the information. To me, it was an enticing hint about manipulation of nicotine levels, but Deep Cough offered no evidence.

A number of highly regarded public health advocates appeared on the show. They, too, were convinced that manipulation was occurring.

"The industry manipulates nicotine, takes it out, puts it back in, uses it as if it were sugar being put in candy," said a tobacco control advocate, Cliff Douglas.

Congressman Mike Synar seemed to agree, saying that the industry did not want anyone looking at their product, "so that they can doctor it, they can alter it." But again, I heard no hard proof.

Jack Henningfield and former Surgeon General C. Everett Koop weighed in too, with Henningfield claiming that "the cigarette is essentially the crack cocaine form of nicotine delivery." Jack's point was that both nicotine and cocaine are most addictive when burned and inhaled into the lungs.

Industry denials were terse. "Why are you artificially spiking your cigarettes with nicotine?" Martin asked an industry spokesman.

"We are not in any way doing that," came the answer.

When the show ended, I turned off the television, feeling as much confused as educated. To me, the full story of reconstituted tobacco and nicotine extracts remained elusive.

The next day, Mitch Zeller and I sat together in the conference room, playing and then replaying the tape at critical points. I kept asking, "What facts do we have? Where's the new information?" I dissected every sentence.

Only one of the guests had ever seen the inside of a cigarette factory and been privy to production secrets. That was Deep Cough. I replayed the lines where Deep Cough hinted at nicotine manipulation and talked about the percentages of nicotine that result from "the process." The process? What process? The making of reconstituted tobacco? The processes that the company used during its research and development?

Despite my doubts about the informant's credibility, I returned to OCI's interview notes with Deep Cough. The statement that "the nicotine is extracted and replaced artificially in order to make the amount the same throughout the cigarette, in every puff" seemed to support *Day One*'s assertions of manipulation. On the show, the narrator said that a scientist had been asked to test the reconstituted tobacco portion of several brands of RJR cigarettes in order "to verify that nicotine was being added." Reconstituted tobacco ordinarily contained 25 percent or less of the nicotine in regular tobacco, stated *Day One*'s John Martin, but the samples tested by the scientist, Bogdan Prokopczyk, contained up to 70 percent. Prokopczyk could only guess why. "I was kind of surprised because I expected it to be less," he said. "The most likely explanation is that some nicotine has been added, either with flavoring agents or just by itself."

Mitch and I reached Prokopczyk by phone, and he agreed to fax us his analysis, but it quickly became clear that he was not an expert in the subject. He had never worked on tobacco before *Day One* approached him and had no hard evidence that nicotine had been added to the product. Under our insistent questioning, he began to doubt his own conclusions, and I thought he must be wrong. As it turned out, he was on to something, but none of us yet realized it.

At my request, Jack, Gary, and Tom visited a number of flavor houses. Some of them admitted to manufacturing nicotine-containing tobacco extracts used abroad by American companies. I later learned about a company that used a 9 percent nicotine solution to avoid a German law that required concentrations of 10 percent or higher to be labeled with a skull and crossbones. But we could not verify that the nicotine used in reconstituted tobacco domestically was coming from these flavor houses.

THE tobacco industry had long tried to stay alert to potentially threatening legislative activities. A Philip Morris memo, "Washington Outlook for 1994," identified the fight against the Clinton health-care reform plan, which would have been funded by a 75-cents-per-pack cigarette excise tax, as the biggest issue of concern. The industry also expected the Surgeon General's upcoming report on tobacco use among young people to create a firestorm. Anticipating a harsh indictment of tobacco marketing, Philip Morris set up self-described SWAT teams to minimize the report's impact on federal, state, and local legislation. The SWAT teams were responsible for ensuring a swift media response and for mobilizing third-party, seemingly autonomous organizations to carry the charge. A barrage of letters to newspaper editors was prepared in advance, some urging government to concentrate on "real issues of concern to the public," such as youth crime and weapons in the schools. Members of the advertising community were pressured to defend tobacco advertising practices on constitutional grounds. Alliances with retail outlets and wholesale suppliers, sports marketing firms, and stadium owners were also planned to discourage legislative action.

Amidst all of this activity, the threat of FDA regulation initially received little mention. Even after our letter went out, Philip Morris executives tried to shrug it off. Adopting an air of indifference that weekend, they fired off e-mails to one another. "Much ado about nothing," said one, describing the press response. "A rehash of everything already said … with a few antis thrown in."

But by Monday morning, an hour before the opening bell on Wall Street, they sounded decidedly less calm. One e-mail warned: "There may be some weakness in the stock this morning until things [are] sorted out."

The tobacco companies also became convinced that a coordinated attack on tobacco was under way. In a week that had included our letter, the *Day One* broadcast, the release of the Surgeon General's report, and McDonald's decision to go smoke-free, it may have been difficult for the industry not to feel under siege. But this mentality reflected a lack of understanding about the workings of government. I ran into Lloyd Cutler, who was then counsel to the President, at the White House. "Industry thinks this is all an orchestrated effort," he said. "They don't realize you are an independent agency. We don't even know what's going on." Of course, we were not an independent agency, but I understood the benefits to the perception that we were, and I did nothing to correct him.

At the Department, Judy Feder, a deputy assistant secretary, thought much the same thing. "Orchestrated?" she asked. She wasn't even sure whether Secretary Shalala had been alerted. "Did you tell Donna you were doing this?"

Donna did know about the letter. But I had never cleared it with the White House, and my hunch was that the Department had not either. In any case, whether or not industry officials truly believed our move was part of a broader conspiracy, they quickly rallied to respond. From then on, they did not risk being taken unaware by FDA activities.

ALMOST from the day our team began its work, I began loading my well-worn brown overnight bag with piles of industry patents, court cases, articles, and books whenever I headed home. Before long I outgrew that bag and just loaded cardboard boxes full of reading material into my car. Sometimes they had an extended layover in the trunk, but most nights I began reading as the rest of my family was falling asleep. From about 11 P.M. until 2 in the morning, I lay in bed, poring through everything I could get my hands on about the industry, tobacco, nicotine, and the modern cigarette.

I began with the basics, starting where cigarettes start—with the tobacco plant. I did not know until then that tar is not part of the agricultural product, but rather is produced by combustion when the cigarette burns. Nicotine, by contrast, is a natural component of tobacco leaves from the alkaloid family of molecules, which also includes heroin, cocaine, and caffeine. When it is extracted from a plant, nicotine is an oily, liquid poison. Absorbed through the skin, less than one tenth of a teaspoon of free nicotine can be fatal to humans. The warning Bill Hubbard had heard in childhood was more than just a folk tale.

In a 700-page tome titled *Tobacco and Tobacco Smoke* I learned that there are three types of tobacco used in the making of cigarettes, each with its own characteristics: Burley was air-cured and high in nicotine; Bright was flue-cured, sweeter, and smoother; and Oriental added flavor to the other two. Then I discovered that nicotine levels in tobacco plants vary not only from breed to breed, but also from one plant to the next. Even within a single plant, the leaf, stem, and ribs yield varying nicotine levels, depending on numerous factors. For example, the higher up a leaf is on the stalk, the greater its nicotine concentration. The amount of nicotine in a plant is also influenced by both genetics and environmental factors, including climate, locale, soil composition, and weather. A lot of rain, or a lack of it, is enough to alter nicotine content, as is the way a particular batch of tobacco is stored and processed. Despite all of that, every cigarette brand's nicotine level is strikingly uniform. Naturally, I wondered how this came to pass.

To find out, I needed a better understanding of what happens between the field and the final product. I began reading *The R.J. Reynolds Tobacco Company*, a comprehensive history written for public relations purposes, which explained the reconstituted tobacco process the company had developed in the 1930s and 1940s. "Few if any developments in the tobacco industry were more important than the fabrication of reconstituted leaf...," noted the book. I already knew that salvaging the tobacco stems and scraps had resulted in tremendous savings, but it was the potential opportunity for manipulation during the process that intrigued me.

Another book brought to my attention was *Nicotine Addiction: Principles and Management*, edited by C. Tracy Orleans and John Slade. Slade was a practicing internist with a longstanding interest in tobacco control. From his modest outpost at a New Jersey community hospital, where he witnessed the toll inflicted by smoking on a daily basis, Slade became passionate about tobacco, and the way in which the FDA might regulate it. Over the years, he scoured the libraries and read everything he could find about the history and public health aspects of tobacco. He asked friends in banking and advertising to funnel information about the industry to him and he subscribed to trade journals, including *Tobacco Reporter*, *Tobacco International*, *World Tobacco*, and *Tobacco Journal International*. When the journals offered annual supplements, which indexed industry suppliers and described the products used in cigarette manufacturing, Slade bought those, too. From the beginning of our investigation, he sent us a steady stream of information.

The first chapter of his new book examined nicotine delivery devices. One sentence described "the 'fortification' of reconstituted tobacco sheet with nicotine as a routine procedure at LTR Industries, a cigarette paper-making division of Kimberly-Clark." I circled the citations.

One of the best collections of tobacco literature was at North Carolina State University. Carol Knoth spoke with a fellow librarian there about the possibility of obtaining materials through interlibrary loans and encountered a bias that was unusual in a spokesperson for an information storehouse. "I think what you're doing is unconscionable," she said. "You're taking our jobs away from us."

I needed another approach, and so I asked a student intern to go down to

North Carolina State and scour the collection for articles we could use. She was young and I asked her to carry a backpack and wear jeans so that she would blend in. She eagerly agreed, eventually bringing back thousands of pages from journals, conferences, books, and reports. One gem was *Tobacco Encyclopedia,* which reproduced a copy of an LTR Industries advertisement. We blew up the ad and hung it in the conference room. Along the top half of the advertisement were rows of drawings of an Elizabethan-looking gentleman with a feather in his topper, high-ruffled collar, and a beard and mustache. The figure was identified as Jean Nicot, a French diplomat after whom nicotine was named. The color lightened from one drawing to the next, illustrating the words in capital letters in the center of the page: "MORE OR LESS NICOTINE."

Several times I read the small type in a box at the bottom: "Nicotine levels are becoming a growing concern for the designers of modern cigarettes, particularly those with lower 'tar' deliveries. The Kimberly-Clark tobacco reconstitution process used by LTR Industries permits adjustments of nicotine to your exact requirements. We can help you control your tobacco." There it was, in so many words.

EARLY one March morning, I made my way through a snowstorm to reach Union Station and the train to New York. I was scheduled to brief newspaper and magazine food editors about the new food label. Thinking I was leaving tobacco behind for the day, I settled in for the three-hour ride and opened the *New York Times.* The lead paragraph to Anna Quindlen's op-ed column, headlined "Where There's Smoke," read "Oh, what a smoothie that David Kessler is. The commissioner of the Food and Drug Administration recently set a fire beneath one of America's most pernicious public health issues. But he said Congress must decide how to put the fire out, knowing full well that many elected officials will want only to ignore the smoke and go about their business as usual."

I have been called many things in my life before, but smooth has never been among them.

"Take it as a compliment," Jim O'Hara suggested.

Back in Washington, the tobacco team was trying to second-guess my thinking. "What are we saying that we are going to do next?" asked Diane Thompson. Pushing hard for a clearer definition of our position, she warned that telling the Hill "we're working on it" was not going to be good enough.

Continuing to press, she asked, "At what point do we or do we not assert jurisdiction?"

Ann Witt jumped in. "Would FDA regulate? Is that a viable option?"

"What does Kessler want?" Thompson asked. "What is his intent?"

What they did not realize was that I did not know the answer to that question myself.

16

A WEEK had already passed since my conversation with Henry Waxman, and though a firm date for the hearing had not yet been set, I was sure it would be soon. I badly needed industry informants who could help me piece together the bits of information I had and make sense of it all. I began pushing the investigative team harder for leads, although I knew the industry's hold on its employees, both past and present, would make these people reluctant to talk.

Gary and Tom moved into a small office near mine, which they soon decorated with industry memorabilia. They were now working on the tobacco investigation full time. Bumper stickers reading "Pride in Tobacco" and "Do it Right, Grow Premium Bright," plastered their file cabinets, and a poster of Joe Camel aiming his cue at the heart of a cue ball was tacked to the wall. Meanwhile, Jack Mitchell, who worked one floor above Gary and Tom, began to tap his web of connections.

Our first break came in early March, when Jack handed me a quasi-legal document identifying Vedpal Singh Malik as the plaintiff. The defendants were eight Philip Morris employees who worked at the company's research center in Richmond. I read through the fifty-two-count complaint. Malik had been a senior scientist with Philip Morris, working on two projects that involved the techniques of genetic engineering. One had the goal of creating a nicotine-free tobacco plant, the other a plant that contained fewer carcinogens. Although Malik knew that his work was viewed with amusement, and even contempt, by many of his associates, he felt that he was making great scientific strides. Then, without warning, he was told that his projects were being shut down immediately and that he was out of a job.

Apparently driven by resentment, Malik spent the next few months developing his complaint against the company. The document, although sprinkled with legal jargon, was plainly a homemade job. It rambled too much to have been drafted by a lawyer, and I recognized a paranoid quality in it. Malik referred to a "privileged class" and charged that some Philip Morris employees had received their advanced degrees by "unconventional" practices. An Indian immigrant, he also claimed to have been the victim of racial discrimination and to have been punished for wanting "to remove the deadly chemicals from Philip Morris's flagship brand, Marlboro."

But some of the charges were interesting: that Philip Morris scientists had confirmed the carcinogenic effects of certain compounds in Marlboro cigarettes and in secondary smoke; that Malik had developed a process for removing those compounds from tobacco, but that management had suppressed the data; and that Philip Morris scientists had assisted in hiding from the public in-house research that showed the hazards of smoking. Malik also alleged that Philip Morris had dumped large quantities of nicotine into the James River in Richmond, and he talked about a secret laboratory called INBIFO, located in Germany.

I learned later that Malik had approached a *New York Times* reporter, Michael Janofsky, with his story. When Janofsky pursued it, asking Philip Morris to respond to Malik's charges, he was told pointedly that the scientist was unstable and threatening. The company also warned Janofsky about using "potentially libelous material." I eventually discovered that Philip Morris had outlined a plan for dealing with reporters who asked about Malik, and when Janofsky came calling, one executive sent a warning memo to colleagues: "Sounds to me like it could be an exposé on 'suppressed breakthrough research.'" Whether because of the uncertainties in Malik's claims or a reluctance to break new ground, the *Times* ultimately decided to let the story go.

Despite this baggage, I thought Malik might know something useful and asked Gary and Tom to contact him. Malik was still bound by a confidentiality agreement, but we soon discovered that he was an embittered and desperate man and that he was willing to talk.

They met at his workplace, the Medical College of Virginia. Because Malik had only a laboratory bench to call his own, he borrowed a tiny backroom office. When Gary and Tom arrived, he immediately turned out the lights and pulled down the window shade. The only light filtered eerily in through the rain-washed window and around the edges of the shade. The walls were plastered with stickers warning against hazardous materials. Malik was agitated. He told Tom and Gary that Philip Morris had already ruined him and that if word of this meeting got out they would take away what little he had left. He rambled on about a gun club at Philip Morris where employees practiced with rifles, about threatening telephone calls to his home, about his fears for the safety of his family.

Tom and Gary concluded that the informant's resentment toward Philip Morris cut deeply into his credibility. But mixed in with his personal problems were nuggets of information about the ways in which the company altered nicotine levels. The investigators were particularly interested when Malik said that the nicotine extracted from tobacco for Next, an experimental, nicotine-free cigarette, was added to Marlboro. I had read a reference to the nicotine removal process, called supercritical extraction, in one of the industry patents. It was analogous to the chemistry involved in extracting caffeine from coffee. Malik said supercritical extraction was used at Philip Morris's Bermuda Hundred plant outside Richmond, Virginia.

The OCI agents decided it would be worthwhile for me to speak with Malik directly, and we arranged a telephone interview. Gary and Tom stayed in Virginia with Malik while Jack Mitchell and Mitch Zeller joined me in my office. When Malik came on the speakerphone, I asked what was done with the extracted nicotine.

"They absorbed the nicotine onto the stems," Malik said. "Nicotine is soaked onto the stems."

I pushed him. "Are you absolutely certain they have taken the nicotine that was extracted in the Bermuda Hundred facility and added it to stems?"

"Yes," he answered, repeating what he had told Tom and Gary. The company had "added these stems to make Marlboro."

"How are you certain that occurred?"

"Because they told me."

Malik also quoted a senior manager as saying, "A cigarette without nicotine is like sex without orgasm."

Switching topics, I decided to follow up the references in his complaint to INBIFO, the German lab allegedly engaged in clandestine research for Philip Morris. "Are you aware of any studies done by the German laboratory?" I asked.

"The German lab is very top secret," Malik answered. But he had no further details to offer, and I moved on.

"Who else worked or used to work doing research?"

Malik identified several potential informants, including a chemist we code-named "Philip" and a behavioral scientist we called "Cigarette." Though I was skeptical about Malik, those two names made the time we spent cultivating him as an informant well worth our while.

PHILIP had been director of applied research at Philip Morris for five years, and he had detailed knowledge of both the research and the production processes. During his years with the industry, he saw himself as a lone company voice calling for the regulation of cigarettes. Philip believed that regulation would provide a forum in which industry could openly discuss issues of health and safety. It was a pragmatic approach to a business problem as much as a concern for the public welfare, but his concept gained him few friends. Philip left Philip Morris in 1984.

Gary reached Philip by telephone and assured him that he would be treated as an anonymous source if he agreed to speak. Philip, it turned out, had been half expecting, half dreading a call from the FDA. Although he had signed a confidentiality agreement with the company, his first conversation with Gary lasted more than two hours. Philip spoke frankly and provided Gary with something we badly needed—an understanding of how cigarettes are made. He confirmed that the technology existed to make tobacco that was free of nicotine and talked at length about reconstituted tobacco, nicotine salts, and pH factors, soon delving into areas that were beyond Gary's understanding. Philip also explained that the industry had its own sources of nicotine, including, as Malik had said, what it could collect from the nicotine-removal process.

At a pause in the conversation, Gary thought briefly of ending the interview and picking it up again at a later date. He figured he was well ahead of the game. What had begun as a preliminary contact had turned into a stream of information. Gary was accustomed to long interrogations, and he had been taking notes furiously, but he was dealing with a subject and a vocabulary unfamiliar to him. He knew that he needed time to absorb what had been said, and he thought it might be best to take a break. But Philip wanted to talk, and there was always the risk that he would later change his mind. Besides, Gary hated walking into my office, excited about an important find, only to have me ask the one question that he had not considered.

His professional instincts dictated that he stay with a subject who was willing and eager to cooperate.

By the end of their conversation, Philip pointed Gary in a new direction. In his notes, Gary put an asterisk by Philip's suggestion: look at Merit cigarettes.

WE WERE fortunate that Gary's initial conversation was so productive, because Philip subsequently became more guarded on the telephone and insisted on a different set of ground rules. Although he remained cooperative, his new approach was to point us in the right direction, while compelling us to think and to search for ourselves.

He gave three reasons for adopting this strategy. The first stemmed from his confidentiality agreement. He knew that the company took it seriously. Some years earlier, a reporter from his college alumni magazine had casually mentioned his name in a story, saying, in essence, that Philip had left Philip Morris, a producer of cancer-causing products, to pursue more worthwhile work. Although Philip had never met or spoken to the reporter, the story drew a sharp reaction from the company's lawyers, who assumed that he had somehow violated his agreement. They fired off a letter warning Philip against any similar incidents under pain of legal action.

The second reason that he pulled back was a lack of hard evidence. Without documents, laboratory reports, or data analyses to back his assertions, Philip thought he might be even more vulnerable to legal action. And third, he believed that we were in way over our heads. He did not think we had the background or experience in the field of tobacco to fully understand the science that was involved. And he knew we were going up against an adversary with virtually unlimited resources, the best lawyers, and scientific experts who had been working with tobacco for decades.

In the time that remained until the Waxman hearing, and for two years afterwards, we held a series of telephone conversations with Philip, which often began in mid-evening and sometimes lasted well past midnight. Typically, we would be dispersed throughout the neighborhoods of suburban Washington, connected by conference call. Philip had a standard opening. "First, I'd like to point out that all the information that I'm going to provide to you, you should be able to find in the open literature. I hope maybe I can help you find where it might be located." In these conversations, Philip seldom volunteered information, although he did try to answer specific questions. Since I was often unsure what to ask, I asked about everything.

I admired Philip's intellect and enjoyed our game of Twenty Questions. From the beginning, I identified with him, for science was his armor. He had known the deep satisfaction of scientific exploration from childhood, as had I, and had learned how to ask questions and how to look for answers. "I'd been a scientist since I was seven years old," Philip told me. "Philip Morris can't take away my science. Nobody can litigate you out of a way of thinking." Philip saw that as his defense if he were ever sued. He told me he imagined writing his own legal briefs and representing himself in court.

Philip's detailed technical knowledge helped me understand how sophisticated the tobacco industry's science really was. He talked about thermogravimetric analysis, used to measure where the nicotine was located in the smoke, and the gas chromatograph, also used to measure nicotine. He described a complex computer model that enabled the companies to input an array of factors about cigarettes—from the porosity of the paper and the design of the filter to the burn rate—in order to determine precisely how much nicotine a given brand of cigarettes would deliver.

I was intrigued by his description of the particles that contain nicotine, tar, and the many other chemicals that float in smoke. Too small, and a smoker does not retain those particles. Too large, and they become lodged in the back of the throat. "If you get the particles the right size, they get all the way down in your lungs," Philip explained. Elaborate chemistry was involved, one more indication to me that the tobacco companies devoted enormous resources to delivering nicotine in their products.

I kept coming back to the "flavor" extracts containing nicotine that had been featured on *Day One*. I wondered whether the extracts sprayed onto tobacco, particularly reconstituted tobacco, boosted the overall nicotine levels of the cigarette. One evening as we were talking, Philip began to work out a series of calculations in his head. Although he did not know the exact formulas in use—that was a secret closely held by very few in the company, he said—he hypothesized that even tiny amounts of added nicotine could be significant.

What I did not know then was that Philip Morris was almost simultaneously performing the same type of analysis. On the basis of its calculations, the company concluded that outside extracts contributed only a tiny amount of nicotine. Nonetheless, it decided to end their use. A week before the hearing, Philip Morris pulled all of its remaining extracts off the production line.

17

THE WAXMAN hearing was scheduled for March 25, barely two weeks away. I still did not know whether the tobacco industry was manipulating nicotine levels, and if it was, I certainly could not prove it.

But I had never really worried about the outcome of our investigation—until now. It hit me suddenly, one evening at dinner with my family. We were in a Bethesda restaurant, and Paulette, Elise, and Ben were talking and laughing. I was totally preoccupied, barely able to participate in the conversation. All I could think about was the rapidly approaching hearing, the blank pages of testimony I needed to fill, and the fact that I could barely move.

A twinge I felt weeks earlier had been the beginning of serious back pain. I had the red sofa from my office moved into Room 1468 so that I could lie on it while I was holding meetings. Sitting for any length of time had become too painful. Well-intentioned staff proposed various remedies. Mitch wanted me to try an injection that had helped him get through back problems. Liz offered me a back brace. But I was not a cooperative patient. I was going to tough it out.

Though I did not admit it to my colleagues, I knew that stress was a factor in my pain. Maybe I was wrong about what the tobacco companies knew about nicotine. Maybe they did not really intend its pharmacological effects. Maybe the nicotine levels in cigarettes were simply natural products of the tobacco plant.

I KEPT my panic to myself, giving no hint to the tobacco team, but I pushed everyone even harder to pursue new angles. They grew accustomed to my telephone calls, which could come at any hour of any day. "Are you finding anything?" I kept asking. "Where else should we look?" We could not afford to overlook a single lead, no matter how unlikely. I had some idea of what I was looking for, but I did not know where to find it.

Meanwhile, I had an agency to run. A particular priority for me was winning congressional and White House approval to build a consolidated campus for the FDA in suburban Maryland. The $900 million project would bring together some 8,000 employees now scattered across the Washington metropolitan area. I felt this was crucial to modernizing the agency and increasing its efficiency.

I also had to prepare for appropriations hearings on the FDA's Fiscal Year 1995 budget, which were coming up in the House in another week. Congressman Richard Durbin, an Illinois Democrat and a long-time foe of tobacco, chaired the appropriations committee. He was a strong ally of the agency, one of those members of Congress who believed wholeheartedly in good government and not at all in grandstanding. We arranged to meet shortly before his hearings. Durbin was interested in our tobacco activities and over lunch in the members' dining room, he asked me whether nicotine had flavor. I was embarrassed not to know the answer.

As soon as I returned to Parklawn, I looked up nicotine in my *Merck Index*, an authoritative encyclopedia of chemicals. Nicotine has an "acrid, burning taste," read the entry. I began thinking about the words the tobacco industry used to describe nicotine's function in cigarettes, words like "taste," "flavor," "satisfaction," and "impact." But what did all of that really mean? Were "satisfaction" and "impact" merely euphemisms for the drug effects that smokers get from nicotine? How does nicotine affect the flavor or taste of a cigarette? Why would something that produces "an acrid burning taste" be a flavoring?

Over the next few days, I kept walking into Ann Witt's office, interrupting whatever else she was trying to do, to wrestle with these questions. I was intrigued when I read an industry spokesperson's comment that nicotine provided "mouth feel," and I sought books to explore the subject. Soon I realized the absurdity of my search. This was not an issue of taste. Ice cream might have mouth feel; nicotine had an effect on the brain.

Documents I later discovered showed that RJR was also interested in this topic. Company scientists concluded that "at a minimum, nicotine appears to play important roles in both the sensory and pharmacological processes that contribute to smoking satisfaction." Another document, this one from

Brown & Williamson, indicated that the company knew that discussing nicotine's effects was dangerous. One official, trying to determine whether to receive research reports from British American Tobacco (BAT), its parent company, wrote, "[I]f the reports include discussions of pharmacological effects of nicotine, the information will not be interesting and would be helpful to the plaintiff." The company decided to begin receiving the reports, but to be prepared "to inform BAT to cease sending the data to B&W if the science is not interesting."

Despite the industry euphemisms, the subject went to the heart of our investigation. In order to declare nicotine a drug, we would have to show that it was intended to achieve physiologic effects, not merely to impart a desired flavor. And we still could not do that.

EVEN though the Surgeon General's 1988 report declared the nicotine in cigarettes addictive, the tobacco industry continued to dispute that claim, arguing, in defiance of a scientific consensus, that the lack of an intoxicating effect meant nicotine was not addictive. I recognized that understanding the nature of addiction was fundamental to our investigation. Over the years, the word had acquired multiple meanings, signifying one thing to a scientist studying brain chemistry and another to a layman simply judging behavior. The definition had also evolved over time. In the early 1960s, addiction was viewed as a personality disorder, and the assumption was that the addict was somehow to blame for a lack of willpower. The biological basis of addiction, and particularly how substances act on the brain, was not well understood until several decades later.

With just a few statistics, Randy Wykoff gave me a powerful way to think about the topic. "There are forty-nine million smokers in the United States," he said, opening one briefing. "Three fourths of them say they are addicted and two thirds of them say they want to quit. Seventeen million smokers try to quit every year but more than ninety percent of them fail." He then presented two other pieces of data that made the point better than any scientific definition. After surgery for lung cancer, nearly 50 percent of those who survive resume smoking. Even when a smoker's larynx is removed, 40 percent start smoking again.

Later in our investigation, I gave Randy one of his more unusual assignments, asking him to look into background levels of nicotine in vegetables, including potatoes, cauliflower, and eggplant. That request was generated by an industry statement, made in response to our letter to the Coalition, that nicotine is found in common foods. Although the industry surely knew that inhaled nicotine reaches the brain much faster than nicotine that is ingested, I wanted to have a ready reply. Randy's staff reviewed the literature on nicotine absorption through ingestion and after a careful analysis concluded that a person would have to eat about 355 pounds of cauliflower, 309 pounds of potatoes, 206 pounds of tomatoes, or 22 pounds of eggplant to equal the amount of nicotine in one cigarette.

To deepen our scientific understanding of addiction we again brought in Jack Henningfield. It was my first chance to meet him in person. I pushed Jack on the differences between caffeine and nicotine. The issue was being tossed around in the media and by those who opposed any movement by the FDA to regulate cigarettes. "Is FDA going to ban coffee next?" asked the critics.

Jack ticked off a number of differences. As he spoke, I went over to the flip chart, picked up a magic marker, and started writing. When the page was full, I ripped it off and taped it to a wall. Every inch of the wall was soon covered by my handwritten notes.

"One of the most distinguishing characteristics of caffeine, as compared to nicotine-containing products, is the enormous decaffeinated beverage industry," he explained. "That's just something you don't see with addictive drugs. You don't see tobacco cigarettes without nicotine surviving on the market. But there is a flourishing industry for decaffeinated coffee products, with a lot of people switching back and forth." He also emphasized another critical distinction. "People use nicotine products literally in the face of death."

Cigarette packs were scattered all over the conference room. Jack reached for a cigarette and asked for a knife. He began to conduct an autopsy on the cigarette, pointing out the different types of tobacco, the ventilation holes, the overwrap, and the fast-burning papers. He kept driving home the message that the modern cigarette is a highly sophisticated device. "Tobacco companies have become pharmaceutical houses," Jack stated flatly.

"How much nicotine does a cigarette need to deliver in order to addict a smoker?" I asked.

The question caught him unprepared. Although addiction experts know that users will seek out a threshold dose of addictive drugs, Jack had not previously thought about a precise level. He immediately realized that it was an important question, recognizing that there had to be some threshold for nicotine—below it, addiction might not occur; above it, it probably would.

Thinking out loud, he commented that smokers trying to quit typically "hit the wall" at twelve or thirteen cigarettes a day. On the other hand, a small number of smokers, known as chippers, can smoke about five cigarettes a day without becoming addicted. "That means that some place between ten and fifteen milligrams of nicotine per day [on average, about ten to fifteen cigarettes], it's extraordinarily likely that people are addicted," Jack said. He added that the vast majority of smokers fit within this group.

After our meeting, Jack began to explore nicotine addiction threshold levels with his colleague Neal Benowitz; they eventually coauthored a *New England Journal of Medicine* article on the subject. They suggested that by estimating the level of nicotine likely to produce addiction, regulations could be developed mandating a nicotine content below that level. Ann Witt seized on this idea and suggested that we consider notifying tobacco companies of the nicotine threshold; then, after a defined period of time, we could reasonably consider that any tobacco products with higher nicotine levels were intended to have addictive effects. I listened, but said nothing.

I FELT as if I were playing a connect-the-dots game, with no way to link the dots. Unable to see a pattern in the mass of information we had already accumulated, I kept pushing for more.

Ilisa Bernstein and I had by now obtained copies of more than one hundred patents. Though dry and technical, they offered me a window into the industry. With their descriptions of what the companies were allegedly trying to achieve, and what capabilities they had acquired over the past several decades, these patents dented the industry's armor of secrecy, if only slightly. Although their lawyers had surely limited the information in the patent applications to the minimum necessary to secure the patents, enough was present to be useful.

One patent, filed by Philip Morris in 1966, read in part: "Maintaining the nicotine content at a sufficiently high level to provide the desired physiological activity, taste and odor which this material imparts to the smoke, without raising the nicotine content to an undesirably high level, can thus be seen to be a significant problem in the tobacco art."

I wanted help in interpreting these patents and asked Bob Benson, a lawyer from the National Institutes of Health and a patent expert, and Charlotte Yaciw, a chemist in the FDA's addictive products division, to meet with me and a few members of the tobacco team. Bob explained the three criteria that make a claim patentable: it must be novel; it must not be obvious—that is, it cannot be the natural next step beyond what is already known; and it must have a practical application. He then picked up a patent and walked us through it, page by page. He warned that the abstract, which appears on the first page, is intended to summarize the patent but has no legal bearing and in fact is often wrong. At the end of the patent are the claims—what the applicant claims to legally own as intellectual property.

"If a company files a patent, does that mean they are using the technology?" I asked. We needed to know what we could conclude about company actions on the basis of their patents.

"Not necessarily," Bob responded. On the other hand, he pointed out that someone must have been thinking about potential use or there would have been no reason to file.

I had a pile of patents on the table and passed them out, like a dealer with a deck of cards. "Take a few minutes and read over each one of these patents," I told the group. "And then let's go around the table and summarize what we have."

One involved the transfer of nicotine from one tobacco to another. Patent #4,215,706 involved transferring nicotine from high-nicotine-content tobacco to "nicotine deficient" material, reconstituted tobacco, or tobacco filler. That caught my attention because I was still thinking about *Day One*'s suggestion that reconstituted leaf had unusually high levels of nicotine. But why would the industry want to shift nicotine from one tobacco to another? Did that somehow affect its impact on the smoker?

According to a number of patents, nicotine was added to filters, paper, or tobacco to increase the nicotine content in the smoke. One patent described the addition of nicotine levulinate, a salt. Others described the use of levulinic acid to reduce the harshness of nicotine, which allowed a smoker to tolerate it at an increased level. If nicotine was in cigarettes for taste, as the industry claimed, why would the manufacturer want to mask it? Equally puzzling was a group of patents to develop nicotine analogs, variants of nicotine's chemical structure. According to the patents, these compounds had use as insecticides. Why was the industry interested in developing insecticides?

The patents also included detailed discussions of lowering the pH of smoke, which apparently made the nicotine easier to inhale. Deep Cough had hinted, to the contrary, that the companies increased the pH to increase the impact of nicotine. Some patented techniques involved making smoke more acidic, others made it more basic. I was puzzled.

The industry seemed to be able to do virtually anything with nicotine. I began highlighting passages in the patents, sentences such as "It is another object of the invention to provide an agent for the treatment of tobacco smoke whereby nicotine is easily released thereunto in controlled amounts." And, "[P]rocessed tobaccos can be manufactured under conditions suitable to provide products having various nicotine levels." As much as possible, I intended to use the industry's own words in my testimony.

Obviously, the technology for manipulating nicotine was available. But had it been used? As we circled around that answer, I began to be haunted by a bigger question. Was tobacco really a drug? And was I prepared to deal with the consequences of declaring that it was? For a moment I wondered about the purpose of our entire investigation. Where did I think I was going with it? Given the history, longevity, and influence of tobacco in this country, labeling tobacco products as drugs would be an enormous leap. But I rejected the safe corollary—setting the whole thing aside—and my moment of doubt soon passed.

The hearing was drawing closer and I still had nothing firm to go on. I virtually moved into the conference room.

18

WHEN I was not holed up studying everything I could find on tobacco, I wandered the halls restlessly, stopping by the offices of various members of the tobacco team. Sharon Natanblut's office was just down the inner corridor from mine. As I had promised, I put Sharon on the tobacco team full time once the food label was successfully launched. Her office was decorated with all sorts of family memorabilia, including a handmade doll dressed in a satin gown, fur boa, and rhinestone broach that her father had given her years earlier. It was a cluttered space, and when I dropped by, I had to share the sofa with the doll.

Sharon was the only member of the tobacco team who had worked for the other side. We discussed what it was like inside the tobacco companies. Sharon emphasized that as people, industry officials were quite nice. "They'll talk to you about their family, they'll talk about the health concerns that they have for their kids, they're very human," she explained. "How do these people live with themselves? They compartmentalize what they do. They work for the tobacco companies, but they're not making any kid go out and smoke. If they define their work very narrowly, then there's no reason for them to feel bad."

Sharon told me about a briefing book used within the tobacco industry to help executives respond to difficult issues. Whenever the health point was raised, the proper response was to deflect the questioner. Thus, the important point was never health, it was economics or protecting the farmers or the smoker's right to choose. This tactic was not only strategically sensible, it was a way to avoid guilt, allowing those who sold tobacco not to face the knowledge that they were profiting from a product that caused widespread illness and death. But many within the industry also genuinely believed that cigarettes were not all that dangerous, just another risk in a world that was filled with them. I did not doubt that they were as dedicated to their mission as we were to ours.

Standing together against hostile forces created a sense of cohesiveness among company executives. They were offended by the accusations that they were doing something evil, and the sense of being misunderstood led them into a world of their own. Those living and working within it understood one another well. That was important because joining the tobacco industry closed off certain future job opportunities. When counsel for Philip Morris tried to attract new lawyers, the potential recruits were sometimes told, "You can tell people you worked for Kraft." At least one senior tobacco lawyer who had worked at the FDA understood the consequences of his career decision quite well. He told friends that after deciding to represent the tobacco industry, he never expected to be appointed to a position in government again.

Sharon knew that the industry's point man for the "freedom of choice" message—that people freely choose to smoke—had been Guy Smith IV, a senior executive at Philip Morris, who preached it at every opportunity. Smith was the company's cheerleader. He seized on the choice argument because he knew that it resonated both within and outside the company. Though articulate and intelligent, Smith expressed himself with such fervor that he became known by some in the company as "the bull in the china shop." In a December 1984 presentation to the company's board of directors, he showed a series of news clips reporting on the American Cancer Society's Great American Smokeout and called it social engineering that ran "counter to the very fabric of the American sense of individualism." Making a thinly veiled analogy to fascism, he continued, "This year we all witnessed cancer society–sanctioned projects that are quite frankly frightening in nature and clearly move into 'vigilantism'—startlingly reminiscent of a terrifying human trait seen earlier this century."

Smith believed that labeling anti-smoking advocates as enemies bent on destroying the industry was good for morale within the company, and he deliberately chose language that would enhance that perspective. "Zealots" was one of his favorite words for tobacco's critics, Sharon recalled. He would demonize the enemy, so as not to see it as a coalition of concerned citizens who cared about preventing 430,000 deaths from smoking every year. Instead, he characterized his opponents as fanatics willing to sacrifice the American way of life to further their goals. If Smith had remained at Philip Morris, I was sure he would have labeled me a zealot as well.

"It was all a game for him, and he loved the sparring," Sharon said. "He loved that he could actually succeed in putting down people who were accustomed to wearing the white hats." Despite his cocky manner, Guy Smith was a company man who enjoyed his job and the clout that came with working for an organization as rich and powerful as Philip Morris. He made that clear to Sharon one day when they were talking about a Burson-Marsteller public relations project. When the time came to discuss costs, Sharon offered, "You know, there's another way that we could do this. It would be more economical, more affordable."

It was a thought that most of her clients would have appreciated, but Smith turned to her with a bemused look. "Sharon, you just don't get it," he said. "We're Philip Morris. We've got more money than God."

RICH as it was, the industry was becoming nervous. Years after our investigation was complete, I learned that company executives had begun to debate the merits of an aggressive counterattack shortly after our letter to the Coalition had gone out. The response began with a memo labeled "VERY CONFIDENTIAL" that was sent on March 7 by the CEO of Philip Morris Companies, Mike Miles, to senior management. The subject: "Ferocious Defense."

Miles described the company's traditional strategy for responding to attacks on the industry as one of "passive defense," based on the theory that "it is better to let the anti's shadow box with themselves than for us to get into the ring with them in an active, aggressive way." Given the rising pitch of tobacco control efforts, including what he called "Kessler's recent trial balloon," Miles suggested it might be time to reconsider that strategy. "It seems to me that we need to seriously reconsider whether our current passive defense strategy is the right strategy, or whether we have 'less to lose' by being more ferocious."

Exploiting an instinctive American distrust of government, and especially a distaste for regulating personal behavior, Philip Morris began to develop its response: the FDA's real agenda was not to regulate cigarettes, but to ban them altogether. From the company's perspective, it was a smart move, one based on consistent findings that the word "prohibition" had overwhelmingly negative connotations.

Industry lawyers also began to insist publicly that intent could only be shown by specific marketing claims; if it was not on the label or in product advertising, there was no intent. We read the law differently—we believed that what a company knew, did, and said also revealed its intent. And according to meeting notes, Philip Morris lawyers privately understood this, telling their client that intent could be determined from many sources, including SEC filings and internal memos, "irrespective of what we say about it." At the bottom of that page of notes were four words written in capital letters: "THIS IS VERY DANGEROUS." Then: "The solution is political."

O UR search for hard evidence continued unabated, but even promising leads seemed to be going nowhere. Deep Cough had always been flighty, often refusing to take our calls or failing to return them, but the informant seemed even more elusive after the *Day One* broadcast. Gary would call from time to time, at odd hours, but the informant was obviously screening the calls. One evening, as he was driving home, Gary decided to try again. For no apparent reason, Deep Cough answered the telephone and was in a surprisingly chatty mood. As information about reconstituted tobacco began to emerge, Gary pulled onto the shoulder of the highway and tried to capture every word on paper. Rain was coming down in buckets and passing trucks sprayed cascades of water over his car.

Deep Cough began reading excerpts from documents. Hungry for the papers, Gary offered to make the four-hour drive at once to pick up copies. Deep Cough hesitated, then refused, apparently fearful of violating the confidentiality agreement so explicitly.

One document Deep Cough read over the phone that night seemed to confirm the informant's earlier assertions about BIO/BIO, the research division that allegedly collected urine, saliva, and blood samples from RJR employees. The image of workers walking around with coolers filled with urine had seemed bizarre, but now Deep Cough gave Gary the name of the lab that had analyzed the samples and identified a participating employee. To confirm the informant's credibility, Gary later made a cold call to that employee, identifying himself as "Dean Cooper," a technician from that lab. Dean Cooper was the undercover name that Gary Light had been using for twenty-five years. I was not comfortable with the idea of using pseudonyms, but in Gary's profession, that technique was not unusual. The fictional character had become almost an alter-ego for Gary. In a matter-of-fact voice, he asked whether the employee had provided a urine sample at his employer's request. Without hesitating, the man said he had done so.

The lead about the nicotine vats, on the other hand, fizzled. Deep Cough had originally told Gary about vats stored behind RJR's Research Center, but in a later conversation, the looming storage tanks had mysteriously shrunk down to stainless steel vials. That sort of inconsistency added to my doubts about Deep Cough's credibility, making me wonder whether any of the information would be useful. It was a long time before I realized that the fault may have been mine. At the time, I did not know how to ask the right questions.

THE wide net I cast in search of evidence eventually brought me to the Federal Court and Customs House, a massive stone presence in downtown St. Louis. There, tucked away on the top two floors of the ten-story building, was the FDA's drug analysis laboratory.

By mid-March I was talking with the St. Louis scientists almost daily. I also brought in our forensic chemistry lab in Cincinnati, which was built after the Tylenol tamperings in 1982, as well as our lab in Los Angeles to support our work. Had the technologies in the industry patents been put into practice? Could the labs scientifically establish that extra nicotine had been added to currently marketed cigarettes? What evidence existed that nicotine levels were being manipulated? I needed the skills of lab scientists and technicians to help me find out.

Most of the scientists had little experience with nicotine, although years earlier one lab had helped to investigate an attempted murder that involved nicotine-injected oranges. But they quickly developed techniques to measure nicotine levels in cigarette components. In one painstaking process, they removed the papers from cigarettes, cut off the filters, and placed the loose tobacco into small cylindrical stainless steel mesh baskets. These baskets were snapped onto long rods, inserted into a dissolution apparatus, and rotated in a beaker with extraction fluid for two hours until the nicotine was removed. The nicotine samples were then placed in tiny tubes and run through a high-performance liquid chromatography machine to be measured. This process was repeated hundreds of times, virtually around the clock. Other sampling techniques were used for papers and filters.

None of it was yielding useful results. The tests gave us data, but no answers. One day we put scientists from all three labs on a conference call. As we came to the end of a long conversation, I asked, in a pro forma way, "Anything else?" Someone mentioned finding crystal-like mica particles in a sample of tobacco. When I heard that, I recalled a patent in which metallic objects could be soaked with nicotine and put in a cigarette.

"Is there any nicotine on it?" I asked. The answer was yes.

Immediately, I insisted that the technicians probe further, and they spent weeks searching for particles of mica that might have been a source of added nicotine. Nothing useful showed up. Mica's consistency is such that it was quite possible to find nicotine on it, whether it had been intentionally added or had simply migrated there. Moreover, mica particles are common in dirt and could attach themselves to tobacco leaves during harvesting. I was beginning to feel that I was chasing my tail, but I did not know what else to do. The labs took the episode as a lesson: don't mention anything to Kessler unless you are reasonably sure there is something to it.

DURING one of my early conversations with our informant Philip, I summarized my basic understanding of how industry manufacturing processes had evolved. I needed to be sure I had the story right. I described the industry's concern, dating to the 1940s and 1950s, about using waste products—scraps, stems, and dust—economically. "Reconstituted tobacco was introduced at that stage," I suggested.

Philip agreed. Gary had been right when he said, "They use everything but the oink."

Paper processing and the extract process were developed after that? I asked. Again, assent.

I speculated that the next phase had involved a focus on nicotine levels to produce an impact, which occurred in the 1960s, but Philip interrupted my account. "You are missing one key factor," he said. "In the 1940s we had just regular old cigarettes. And then an important thing happened in the fifties when the filter cigarettes came in. And you can ask yourself, 'Why did filters gain such popularity?' Healthier cigarettes."

Filters were thought to reduce tar levels. Unfortunately for the industry, the techniques used to reduce tar also reduced nicotine, resulting in a less "satisfying" cigarette—to an addicted smoker, that is—and so the industry began to tinker with new approaches. Philip explained that one way to create a satisfying, low-tar cigarette was to use tobaccos that were richer in certain volatile compounds. Repeating a lead he had given to Gary, Philip suggested I look for the Merit cigarette ads that had appeared in the mid-1970s.

I spent one Saturday rummaging through used-book stores. It did not take long to find Merit ads in the back issues of *Time* and *Life* magazines. "Yes, You Can," shouted one, in boldface type. Then, in smaller print, the ad read: "You can switch down to lower tar and still get satisfying taste."

Another ad was even more interesting. "If a cigarette has less tar it has less taste too. In Richmond, a research team put a new technology to work. They cracked cigarette smoke down and isolated certain key flavor components. Natural components with the unique ability to deliver taste way out of proportion to tar. The discovery was called 'enriched flavor' tobacco and packed into Merit."

Enriched flavor was obviously a Madison Avenue term. What did it mean? And how was it done?

Philip told us about something called "super juice," reportedly potent, malodorous stuff. "People don't like to be in a room with ashtrays that have spent Merit cigarettes in them," Philip recalled. But super juice helped make Merit a commercial hit, he said, and a certain lore came to surround the product.

I asked what was in super juice. Philip said he had never been privy to that information, but he thought it had an acetic acid component. "The intent was to find those compounds that would give you the best—whatever word you want to use—acceptability, flavor, impact, et cetera—at the lowest tar level." Philip hypothesized that super juice was soothing, causing people to inhale smoke more deeply or more intensely. "There was a masking effect," he explained. "It's kind of like applying an astringent. It's like using Chloroseptic when you have a sore throat."

Super juice apparently produced the same sort of effect that some of the patented techniques had sought to achieve. I told the labs to make sure they included Merit cigarettes in their analyses.

PHILIP also urged me to look up the work of a Philip Morris scientist named Robert Jenkins. One afternoon, I arrived at the National Library of Medicine a half hour before closing time. The library had a closed-stack policy, and the circulation desk had just closed. No exceptions. I thought about identifying myself but resisted.

My eagerness must have been evident because the attendant relented and retrieved the article I wanted. Jenkins had put nicotine on the outside of the cigarette's tobacco rod, right under the paper, to study whether more of it was then transferred into the smoke. It was another suggestive study, but was not evidence of what actually went on in a manufacturing plant.

Meanwhile, the St. Louis lab continued to test and record nicotine levels. In the course of their work, the technicians noticed something surprising. Although the total weight of nicotine varied considerably from brand to brand, the percentage of nicotine from cigarette to cigarette in any one brand was remarkably consistent. This was amazing for an agricultural product. With its vast experience in prescription drug analysis, St. Louis pointed out that tobacco companies had achieved a level of uniformity using a heterogeneous crop that matched or exceeded what drug companies, using well-defined chemical entities, could achieve. Such consistency did not happen by accident.

The St. Louis work did not prove anything, but it did help dispel any notion that nicotine levels occur in cigarettes by chance. For the moment, it was the most useful thing the labs had given us. But it was not enough.

19

DESPITE the industry's reputation for keeping its employees tight-lipped, Gary and Tom kept getting leads on new informants. I wondered whether that was because the FDA's primary concern was for health. We were not looking to punish criminals but rather to protect the public, and that seemed to encourage openness. One morning, the OCI investigators briefed me about several promising leads and then began telling me matter-of-factly about a psychologist who had been employed by Philip Morris from 1980 to 1984. Hired soon after graduate school with a mandate to "clean up the product" and make a safer cigarette, he had established a behavioral pharmacology laboratory at Philip Morris's request. The scientist's mission was to study the effects of nicotine and other smoke components on the central nervous system and to pursue research on possible nicotine substitutes. Although rats were his study subject, he had been told that his work could lead to the creation of a nicotine analog that would inflict less damage on humans than nicotine itself. The ultimate goal was to produce a molecule that could either be engineered into or sprayed onto a tobacco plant.

Gary and Tom told me that the scientist and his colleagues believed they had succeeded in developing the nicotine analog. Philip Morris responded to their research by closing down their laboratory, destroying their work, and firing them. One of the company's lawyers recognized that conducting research on nicotine's effect on the central nervous system could lead to evidence that nicotine was addictive. And that was legally perilous.

I did not yet realize that Gary and Tom were referring to Cigarette, the behavioral scientist who had been mentioned by Ved Malik, but I knew immediately that this lead might prove critically important. "Go find him," I said insistently. "Whatever it takes. We need to talk to him."

Tom, of course, had been trying to do just that. On the phone, the informant had stalled, mentioning his confidentiality agreement with Philip Morris.

"Look, we just want to talk to you, we're not going to put you in any jeopardy," Tom said persistently. He told Cigarette that his real name would never appear in the files. For security reasons, he would be referred to only by his code name.

Cigarette made no commitment but much later he told me that he had long been expecting our call. As he hung up the phone, he took a deep breath and wondered what had taken us so long.

IT WAS just past noon and raining on March 15 as Gary and Tom headed to the Christiana Hilton in Newark, Delaware, to meet with Cigarette. The scientist had for the moment conquered his anxiety and was willing to talk, but only in a public place. Like many people who had once worked in the upper echelons of the tobacco industry, Cigarette had developed a full-blown case of industrial paranoia. He admitted to me that he had arrived an hour early for the meeting and had searched the lobby for cameras and other recording devices. He also scanned the lobby for anyone who was particularly well dressed. He had become an expert at spotting people who worked for the tobacco companies.

As they entered the hotel, Gary and Tom recognized Cigarette from the description he had provided. He was a dark-haired man dressed in jeans, a T-shirt, and a black leather jacket. They walked across the long stretch of lobby to the wing chair in which he sat. After a few minutes of introductory conversation, they began asking questions about his work at Philip Morris. Their voices were low and their tones were gentle, but the questions were pointed and insistent.

They quickly realized that Cigarette's mood swung wildly. One moment he seemed to be in the depths of anxiety, sure that he was the victim of a tobacco company plot and suspicious of both the motives and the identities of his interlocutors. The next, he was on the upswing, confident that their FDA credentials were real, and eager to tell them about his groundbreaking research.

Cigarette said that during his time at the company he had sought to discover what made nicotine "reinforcing." He steered clear of the word "addictive." In the first phase of his experiments, he tried to determine what laboratory rats would do to obtain nicotine, and how eagerly they would do it. The animals were given the choice of two levers to press; one administered a dose of nicotine, the other only a placebo of saline solution. Cigarette found that after a few preliminary tries, the rats ignored the placebo and invariably chose the nicotine dispenser. Over several days, the animals conditioned themselves to self-administer almost ninety doses of nicotine in a twenty-four-hour period. The experiments showed that the self-administration was controlled, at least in part, by nicotine levels in the blood or tissue.

Tom and Gary immediately understood the importance of Cigarette's story. Cigarette was telling them that his company had been running experiments on self-administration—a hallmark property of an addictive drug—while publicly denying any knowledge that nicotine was addictive.

After describing these experiments, Cigarette fell silent. His mind seemed to be wandering, and he was visibly nervous. He may have wondered if the conversation was being taped, or if he was actually talking to hired hands of Philip Morris, ready to make his life a living hell, as he said the company's lawyers had promised. Cigarette had a career and a family to sustain—a new family since his first marriage had fallen apart under the strain of his job loss —and he had never felt sure that he was finished with Philip Morris, or that Philip Morris was finished with him.

"What can you guys do to protect me?" asked Cigarette.

Tom assured him that his identity would not be divulged, but Cigarette was apparently not persuaded, because he asked next about a witness protection program. Tom told him that would not be necessary.

Cigarette pulled from his wallet a tiny photo of me, clipped from a magazine. "This is a friend of mine," he said. "You guys know him?" My face was much fuller and the reproduction was so poor that neither Tom nor Gary recognized me. This made Cigarette more nervous than ever.

Nonetheless, his panic seemed to pass, and he picked up the conversation again, describing his efforts to develop a safer cigarette. The goal had been to discover a molecule that would have the same biological effects as nicotine on the brain without the damaging impact on the heart. Cigarette said later that the "wish-list molecule" the company hoped to find would be as potent as nicotine in the brain—perhaps more so. He realized the difficulties involved, but together with an associate, Cigarette discovered in the early 1980s a nicotine-like compound, called 2'-methyl nicotine, that performed just as he wished. He was convinced that they had made an important discovery.

When Gary and Tom briefed me, I realized immediately that Cigarette's search for a nicotine analog fit perfectly within the tradition of pharmaceutical development. Manufacturers often develop slightly different forms of a basic molecule to produce new drugs. Cigarette's compound was among the patented molecules that the company claimed had value as insecticides. I had been trying for months to understand these. Now I knew it was the pharmacological properties that really piqued the industry's interest.

CIGARETTE and his associate also worked together on a research paper that changed the course of their careers at Philip Morris. Cigarette started to tell the story of that paper to Gary and Tom, but after a few sentences he stopped and then abruptly changed the subject, asking the investigators what part of the FDA they worked for.

Tom and Gary gave Cigarette a general idea of their work at the agency and their backgrounds in law enforcement, hoping to assure the informant that he was dealing with professionals who knew how to protect his interests, and then to move back to the subject of the paper he had written. They told him that they were with the Office of Criminal Investigations but were at the moment on loan to the commissioner's office. They also said that Tom had once been with the Secret Service, and that Gary used to work in the Army's criminal investigation unit.

If Tom and Gary had realized they were dealing with someone bending under a full load of irrational suspicions, they probably would have described their backgrounds differently. Cigarette later told me the way he heard it: that they were not really with the FDA at all but were on loan. That Tom was from the Secret Service, and Gary was with Army intelligence.

Cigarette's face darkened. He stood up, backed away from the table, and announced in a tight voice that the meeting was over. Tom and Gary tried to calm him but he was not listening. He edged around the table and walked rapidly across the lobby without looking back. In a moment, he was gone.

They waited a few minutes, then dialed Cigarette's car phone. He answered but refused to talk. Tom tried to tell him how to check their credentials, but the line went dead. Tom made a face, clicked off his phone, and slipped it back into his pocket. They had lost Cigarette at a crucial moment.

Cigarette had said he had written the paper with an associate. That was the man they had to find.

THE two agents tracked down Cigarette's former research associate the next day. He was employed at the Armed Forces Radiobiology Research Institute in Bethesda, Maryland, and he was willing to talk.

Tom and Gary met the man at his laboratory on March 17, St. Patrick's Day, just eight days before the Waxman hearing. He was code-named "Cigarette Jr." The name may not have been the best choice because it put him in a secondary role to Cigarette, and confidential informants often have a strong sense of status, but the name stuck and was never changed.

Cigarette Jr. was open and cooperative about his work at Philip Morris and did not bear the burden of suspicion that his colleague carried. He confirmed what Cigarette said, adding many details of his own. In retrospect, he said that he felt tremendously misled by Philip Morris, and that his years of effort had been wasted. He, too, said they had been given the mandate to produce a "safer" cigarette and he, too, had lost his job.

On reflection, Cigarette Jr. said he should have been more suspicious about the secrecy that surrounded their research. Such was the climate that even their laboratory animals were delivered surreptitiously. Their work, in fact, had been a secret within a secret. Several years earlier, according to Cigarette Jr., the entire tobacco industry had agreed to stop conducting whole-animal studies. Philip Morris had broken that agreement when it set up their lab, and so their research was not only kept secret from the outside world, but also from their allies within the industry.

Tom and Gary looked up from the notes they were taking and asked casually about the scientific paper Cigarette had mentioned.

Cigarette Jr. paused a moment, apparently surprised by the question, but then he explained that the two men had written a paper for the journal *Psychopharmacology*. Cigarette Jr. said it had never been published—and that Philip Morris made them withdraw it.

That's it, thought Gary. That's what we're looking for. Tom casually asked for more details.

Cigarette Jr. indicated that the paper was technical in nature, but at Tom and Gary's urging he began to describe the research. When he had finished, Tom asked whether he still had a copy of the paper.

Too many years had passed, and he did not, but he suggested that Cigarette might. That was no help. Tom said that Cigarette was not talking to them at the moment. Cigarette Jr. smiled understandingly, advising them not to pay any attention to his colleague's moods.

Changing direction, Tom asked Cigarette Jr. whether he would be willing to speak with others at the FDA. The informant agreed and a conference call took place the next day. The speakerphone was in the center of the table in my office. I decided it was best to remain silent and asked Mitch Zeller, whose legal background and oversight experience on the Hill made him an adept questioner, to take the lead. Never content to keep my ideas to myself, I scribbled questions and kept passing them to Mitch. With characteristic independence, Mitch asked only the questions that suited him.

Cigarette Jr. described his academic background and gave an overview of his work for Philip Morris, explaining the research that showed that rats would sacrifice food and water for nicotine. Both he and Cigarette thought the results warranted publication and they submitted a paper entitled "Nicotine as a Positive Reinforcer in Rats" to *Psychopharmacology* in January 1983.

Their timing could not have been worse. Shortly after the paper was sent off, Cigarette was summoned to a meeting with Philip Morris executives. A New Jersey woman, Rose Cipollone, dying from lung cancer, had filed a lawsuit against three cigarette companies, including Philip Morris, charging them with failing to warn her of the addictive nature of smoking and its potential consequences. Not surprisingly, the company did not want a description of nicotine-starved animals in its own labs to become public. "The data you're generating are inconsistent with our position in lawsuits," Cigarette was told by his boss. A top Philip Morris executive asked why Cigarette should be allowed to risk a billion-dollar enterprise for lever-pushing rats and instructed him to withdraw the paper from publication. Under the condition of his employment contract, the authors had no choice but to comply.

But they decided to make a silent protest. An abstract of the paper had already been published by the journal of the American Psychological Association—there was nothing that Philip Morris could do about that—and both authors had been invited to the APA's annual convention in Anaheim, California, to participate in discussions there. Philip Morris gave them permission to attend the meeting, but instructed them not to discuss the nicotine paper. Customarily, the authors of papers stand in front of posters describing their work, ready to talk science and to answer questions. Cigarette and Cigarette

Jr. put up a blank poster at the convention, and Cigarette stood in front of it for three hours, explaining to anyone who would listen that the poster represented data that he was not allowed to present.

The academic community at the convention was sympathetic to the scientists and outraged at the company. Nonetheless, on April 5, 1984, Philip Morris ordered the two scientists to kill all of their animals and suspend further experiments. Then, they were fired.

Eighteen months later they resubmitted the nicotine article to *Psychopharmacology,* hoping that enough time had passed to allow them to get away with it. Instead, Philip Morris exercised the confidentiality clause in their contracts, threatening legal action if they tried to publish. Again, they withdrew the paper. The company made it clear that it respected no statute of limitations on its willingness to sue and vowed to drag the researchers to court over and over again if necessary. They did not try to submit the paper again. In their view, Philip Morris had won.

With Cigarette Jr. still on the speakerphone, Mitch explained how eager we were to see the paper. The informant confirmed that he no longer had a copy. Mitch then asked who had edited the paper. After a long silence, Cigarette Jr. identified the editor as Herbert Barry, in the department of pharmacology at the University of Pittsburgh.

Mitch turned to me and gave a silent thumbs-up. His lips formed the word, *Bingo.*

20

On March 15, 1994, the same day that Cigarette fled his meeting with Tom and Gary, the *New York Times* printed a letter from William Campbell, president and CEO of Philip Morris USA. Referring to both our letter to the Coalition and a *Times* editorial that had raised questions about nicotine addiction, Campbell wrote:

> At several points, Dr. Kessler's letter and your editorial misrepresent the facts.
>
> Nicotine occurs naturally in tobacco. Nothing in the processing of tobacco or the manufacture of cigarettes increases the nicotine in our products above what is naturally found in the tobacco. Our manufacturing results in less nicotine in every cigarette we make than in raw, unprocessed tobacco. Moreover, consumer taste preferences have led to products with lower tar and nicotine levels. As a result, the overall nicotine content in cigarettes has declined more than 50 percent in the last 40 years.
>
> As for addiction, a Surgeon General's report states that more than 40 million Americans have quit smoking, and more than 90 percent of them did so with no professional help. These findings are not consistent with the behavior of individuals addicted to drugs like heroin or cocaine.
>
> Finally, I would like to clarify the process used in making reconstituted tobacco, which is designed to make efficient use of all parts of the tobacco plant. The first patent on tobacco reconstitution was issued almost 150 years ago. The level of nicotine in the finished, reconstituted tobacco is significantly lower than the nicotine level in unprocessed tobacco.
>
> Cigarettes are a legal product, and more than 50 million American adults choose to smoke. We are proud of the quality standards in making our product.

Campbell's letter, I thought, offered us an unprecedented opportunity. My assertions about nicotine had been flatly denied, and we had been told that we did not fully understand the cigarette manufacturing process. What better way for us to learn than to see it firsthand? It was worth a shot.

I quickly drafted a letter to Campbell, concluding, "We believe the best way for us to gain an accurate understanding of your processes would be, as a first step, for FDA representatives to meet with members of your research, scientific, technical, and production staffs and to review relevant information. We are prepared to do this immediately. Please let me know how we may make arrangements for such visits."

To our surprise, Campbell agreed to my request with alacrity. The head of a major tobacco corporation inviting the FDA inside? In the wake of *Day One*, it was clear that Philip Morris was eager to refute any charges that nicotine was artificially added to cigarettes. So eager, in fact, that they were giving us an opening we had not seriously considered possible before. The opportunity to visit Philip Morris in the final days before my testimony seemed like great luck. No one on the team had ever been inside a tobacco manufacturing plant.

On a conference call with the team on Sunday night, March 20, I reviewed the priorities for the visit and selected the group that would go. I chose Tom and Gary, along with Jack Mitchell, Mitch Zeller, and Kevin Budich. I also asked two chemists from the Baltimore office and two FDA field representatives from Virginia to join them, and we were able to get Bob Spiller for the trip. Bob was one of the top enforcement lawyers at the agency, so good at what he did that I always had to negotiate with his boss, Margaret Porter, for his time.

The following day, William Campbell conveyed his personal disappointment that I would not be joining the tour group, but pledged the company's full cooperation. As agreed, we then faxed Philip Morris a list of our areas of interest, emphasizing "tobacco ingredient processing" and the company's "understanding of the effects of nicotine and nicotine analogs on smokers, volunteers, and test animals." I hoped our team might begin its tour late Monday, and then have all of Tuesday and Wednesday for an extensive look at the facilities. But while they were en route to Richmond, some three hours away, we encountered our first hitch. Philip Morris called to say that contrary to earlier plans, it would not be ready to accommodate the FDA until nine the following morning.

As they arrived in town, team members headed to the Holiday Inn. It had been a long drive in heavy traffic and torrential rain, and everyone was a little frazzled. It did not help that the hotel adjoining the enormous Philip Morris compound smelled of smoke. Mitch and Jack were among the first to walk into the hotel lobby. Both immediately noticed a man and woman dressed in business clothes sitting together and in a slightly irrational moment assumed that they were the Philip Morris handlers. They turned out to be the representatives from the FDA's Virginia field office.

In a mood of high anticipation, mixed with anxiety, the group gathered in Bob Spiller's room that night to make final plans. Philip's remarks had made learning more about the manufacturing of Merit a priority. We also wanted to understand the supercritical extraction process and the Bermuda Hundred plant that Ved Malik had described. And we hoped to discover more about reconstituted tobacco and flavorings. Everyone planned to take copious notes and to ask as many questions as possible; there would probably never be a second visit. When Mitch called to check in with me, I reminded him to tell the group to be as polite as possible. Regardless of what happened, Philip Morris was our host.

Late that night, there was a second hitch. Philip Morris sent over a letter that read, "Your letter references certain issues that seem to be beyond the scope of the request of Dr. Kessler, specifically, pharmacological and behavioral data and the company's testing of its cigarettes on 'smokers, volunteers, and test animals.'... [I]t is not our intention to explore these issues with you at this time in the context of the present visit."

EARLY the next morning the team drove the short distance to the Philip Morris Operations Center, the administrative headquarters of the company's complex. The sweet smell of tobacco hung in the air, an odor very different from that of a burning cigarette. The cavernous lobby was dominated by an enormous display of plaques depicting the multitude of Philip Morris brands. Because packaging and brand names vary in different parts of the world, many of the names were new to the team, and the sheer number of brands was a revelation.

The group was escorted through a floor of office space, which looked like any other, except for one detail: most of the offices had ashtrays on the desks. The meeting room was large, modern, and comfortable, with a pastoral view. Harold Burnley, Philip Morris's director of product development, and David Merrill, director of environmental compliance and engineering, seemed eager to be of assistance. Arthur Levine and Donald Beers, former FDA attorneys now with the law firm of Arnold & Porter, were also in the room. Shortly before the meeting began, Arthur Levine had asked Bob Spiller, "So who are the two guys from the Office of Criminal Investigations?" Clearly, Philip Morris had done its homework. It was an unsettling beginning, but the tone of the morning was otherwise amicable, although Beers fell asleep within an hour.

Burnley, in his mid- to late forties, with salt-and-pepper hair, stood up and began to provide an overview of cigarette manufacturing. He used elaborate flow charts filled with numerical formulations: start with one hundred pounds of tobacco, separate out different pieces, blend so many parts Oriental leaf with so many parts Burley leaf, and so on. Details aside, the image was of a carefully controlled and complex process. Surprisingly, given the busy flow charts, Burnley's major point was the simplicity of Philip Morris's scheme. The goal was to use every part of the tobacco plant, he said. We do not want to waste anything. Not knowing if they would be given copies of the presentation, everyone on the team recorded the information in great detail—getting down literally every word, where possible.

Burnley moved on to reconstituted tobacco. Ears pricked up as he described it in detail—separating leaf, treating it, extracting, evaporating, and concentrating the liquid, drying leaf, adding back the liquid, drying again, cutting the sheets. Again the thrust of his message was that reconstituting tobacco was not about nicotine, but about the efficient use of the tobacco plant.

"Why do you add the water back?" asked Kevin Budich.

Tobacco is tobacco, whether in solid or liquid form, replied Burnley. He said the company was trying to be resourceful, trying to use every bit of the tobacco, even when it was concentrated in water.

As the morning wore on, Mitch and Bob began to ask more questions about nicotine manipulation. Mitch looked Burnley directly in the eye every time he asked a question. Did Philip Morris take steps to determine "correct" nicotine levels? he asked. Did Philip Morris ever add nicotine? Burnley said no, emphatically, and more than once; Philip Morris does not manipulate nicotine levels. Rather, there is an inviolate ratio of tar to nicotine—15:1, he said. As tar goes down, so does nicotine. Philip Morris's manufacturing process is designed for tar, he kept insisting. To the extent that nicotine content changes in a cigarette, it is because the tar level has been changed.

The group also asked about supercritical extraction, and Burnley called in a company specialist to answer some of the questions. We had seen this process described in early patents, but it was Ved Malik who had piqued our interest in the precise technique for removing certain chemicals. A few years earlier, Malik had said, when Philip Morris test-marketed Next, the company had spent hundreds of millions of dollars to build the Bermuda Hundred plant to extract nicotine from tobacco. But the nicotine-free cigarette had not been a commercial success, the project was eventually scrapped, and the plant stood unused.

What, we wanted to know, had Philip Morris done with all the nicotine it extracted before Next was declared a failure? Malik said it had been used in Marlboro cigarettes, but we did not ask specifically about that brand. The company flatly denied the use of nicotine extracts, claiming instead that the extra nicotine had been absorbed onto tobacco stems, packed in barrels, and discarded in landfills. It was a stopgap measure, a spokesman said. Had the Next brand succeeded, the company would have invested in costly scrubber technology to destroy the nicotine directly.

After the long and tiring morning, the team members welcomed a break from the smoky conference room. The Philip Morris representatives had been lighting up throughout the morning, David Merrill in a particularly effervescent fashion, as if each cigarette gave great pleasure. For the afternoon tours, the FDA visitors asked to be split into five groups of two apiece in order to see all the facilities, but Burnley said that Philip Morris wanted everyone to remain together.

This was a major problem. If the group did not split up, then it could only see a tiny fraction of the facilities. Maybe that was the company's goal, Mitch thought. A compromise was reached allowing the team to split into two groups of five each. Philip Morris was insistent about which facilities they would be allowed to view. The first group would visit Making, the plant that handled general cigarette manufacturing. Group two would tour Park 500 and Blended Leaf, the facilities where reconstituted tobacco was made.

ONE Philip Morris lawyer joined each of the groups. Don Beers and Harold Burnley accompanied those visiting Making, an immense warehouse-style facility that looked much like any highly automated industrial-agricultural manufacturing operation. Enormous cardboard boxes were stacked in a handling area, where the smell of tobacco was almost overpowering. Here, the leaves were measured, catalogued, and held at specific temperature and moisture levels. The boxes were stacked on pallets, emptied onto conveyor belts, then passed through gigantic sorters, blenders, cutters and the like, just as Burnley had described. That day's cycle, he said, was a normal production run. The plant was deafeningly noisy, and everyone stayed close together to avoid falling out of earshot.

The group asked frequent questions, raising their voices to be heard over the din. At every opportunity, nicotine was raised as an issue. Do you measure nicotine at this point? Do you do anything to nicotine levels here? Burnley occasionally summoned a worker to answer a question, but mostly he continued to make his central point. The industrial process was all about tar; nicotine, he said, was barely even a secondary consideration.

Meanwhile, the second group piled into a van, escorted by David Merrill and Arthur Levine. The drive to Park 500 took about thirty minutes. Along the way, Merrill pointed out the Bermuda Hundred facility, a gleaming white building, very modern in appearance, set back amid forest land, where the supercritical extraction process had been housed. "Want to buy it?" he joked. After all the money that had been spent, the plant was empty, its machinery maintained periodically, but otherwise left alone. Mitch Zeller asked again what had happened to the nicotine extracted in Bermuda Hundred. Merrill reiterated that it had been sent to landfills.

The equally modern Park 500 facility was one of the largest plants any member of the team had ever seen, the kind of operation it would take the FDA months to inspect, were it to conduct a formal inspection. As at Making, a surprisingly small number of employees were on hand to keep the facility running. As the team was led through the reconstituted tobacco process, three additional Philip Morris staffers joined the group. Mitch felt that he was being bird-dogged by one of the company's lawyers.

It was the team's first opportunity to look directly at reconstituted tobacco. In the main holding room, countless hexagonal cardboard boxes containing the scraps, stems, and dust of raw tobacco were stacked to the ceiling. The air smelled of the same slightly sweet aroma that permeated much of the Philip Morris compound. Each box was hoisted up by an enormous lift and then turned over and poured onto a conveyor belt for sifting.

The group passed through the main manufacturing floor, where conveyor belts, large and loud machines, vats of liquid, and thousands of pipes converged, with no end in sight. After sorting, the leaf was combined with liquid and pressed into a mush, much like papier-mâché. The liquid was then separated from the mush, centrifuged and heated in a series of vats, concentrated, evaporated, and eventually added back to the solid material.

As they walked, everyone took special care not to trip over pipes, which occasionally had labels—SEL (strong extract liquor, the liquid extracted in the early stage); CEL (concentrated extract liquor, that same liquid after evaporation); SBW (strong brown water); and RBW (rich brown water). Mitch also saw a pipe labeled "DAP" and asked what it was. "Diammonium phosphate," answered one of the guides. "Just another one of the flavors." Arriving at a series of large vats in a dark and humid part of the facility, they climbed a few steps to peer through small portholes at the sludgy material being heated inside. The place had the feel of a submarine, from the pipes overhead, underfoot, and alongside to the close quarters and the computerized equipment that monitored the process. So vast and complex was the operation that the company could have been adding nicotine at that very moment and no one would have known it.

The group passed through the plant's flavor center, where tobacco flavoring was added to the CEL through a multitude of small pipes. Each flavor was marked with a code; the company provided a corresponding list of flavors, which included such things as cocoa and licorice. (When I heard about this, I thought of Philip's instructions to study the products that are given off when chocolate is burned. I soon discovered that chocolate gives off theobromine, a chemical similar to theophylline, which is used in asthma treatment to help people inhale.)

At this point, Arthur Levine, who had been carefully following Mitch throughout the tour, seemed to get lost in the process. In what appeared to be his own excited curiosity, he simply wandered off. Would that our team could have done the same.

Despite all the electronics and the controlled appearance of the process, Philip Morris was eager to convey the impression that reconstituting tobacco was an art, not a science. On the way back to the Operations Center, David

Merrill asked lightheartedly, "Okay, so now you've seen our facilities. Are we spiking cigarettes with nicotine?"

Kevin Budich asked the size of Park 500. Seven hundred fifty thousand square feet, answered Merrill.

"Well, we didn't cover anywhere close to that area," Budich said.

By 6 P.M., both groups arrived back at the Operations Center and gathered again in the conference room. Philip Morris had arranged to have four representatives from Flavor Operations make a presentation about the use of flavor extracts. The team asked a lot of questions, but because of the level of secrecy within the company, the presenters did not even know the composition of the flavoring.

Finally, the exhausting day ended. The team was escorted out and headed back to the Holiday Inn. In small groups, everyone went to dinner to unwind. Later, they again gathered in Bob Spiller's room to discuss their tours and to formulate a game plan for the following day. All agreed they had learned only as much as Philip Morris wanted them to learn. When Mitch called me to check in, I urged him to push harder on the issue of nicotine control. How could they know their nicotine levels with such certainty if they were not testing, or adjusting, for nicotine during the manufacturing process?

At around ten that night, Bob asked Kevin to stop by. Bob had been studying data on tar and nicotine that the company itself had given us, trying to reconcile them with Burnley's claim that nicotine always followed tar in a fixed 15:1 ratio. Something did not seem right; on one of Philip Morris's low-tar brands, the ratio was closer to 10:1. Budich checked the math and agreed with Spiller's conclusion. There was no way that what Burnley had said could be true.

THE following morning, the group arrived at the Operations Center for a tour of Philip Morris's chemistry labs. They came first to the testing facility, where Philip Morris conducted tests for tar, nicotine, and carbon monoxide in their own cigarettes and those of their competitors. Smoke filled the air. For the first time, the group had a chance to see the Federal Trade Commission's bizarre-looking smoking machine. It was a four-foot cylinder with a hood over the top and tubes inside for holding cigarettes. Dozens of cigarettes were placed in the machine, the hood was closed, and a lighter ignited the cigarettes. The machine then simulated puffing on the cigarettes, and the smoke was "inhaled" into a filter pad, which trapped particulate matter so that it could be measured.

The group asked questions about the FTC tests and about this smoking machine. Did it really approximate the way people smoke? Though no two smokers are exactly alike, a Philip Morris employee replied, the test was industry standard, and the company was satisfied with it. I was skeptical when I heard about that, having already learned that cigarettes could be designed to trick the machine. Ventilation holes in the filter, which can easily be covered by a smoker's fingers, the speed at which the paper burns, and the length of the cigarette can all foster misleading numbers. One informant had told me that the tobacco companies themselves did not rely solely on FTC numbers, instead using their own data, which was based on simulations of how deeply smoke is inhaled, how long it is held, and how many puffs per cigarette are taken.

In response to the team's request, Burnley agreed to provide two pages of formulas for Merit. This was trade secret material, however, and Philip Morris requested confidentiality, to which everyone agreed. But Don Beers suddenly intervened, advising his client not to provide the information without some kind of written guarantee. Bob Spiller spoke up to say that FDA was experienced at maintaining confidentiality. Burnley seemed convinced by this, but in an odd, tense moment, he suddenly asked to see everyone's credentials. He walked around the table as everyone displayed their proof of FDA affiliation. Only then did he present the Merit formulas.

There was more discussion of manufacturing, focusing particularly on air flow and the exact composition of the cigarette rod. And, without prompting from the group, Burnley changed his position and acknowledged that the tar-to-nicotine ratio was not actually immutable. How did Philip Morris account for that? Burnley entered into a complicated explanation that no one fully understood, something to do with high and low boiling points within cigarettes, and the way in which nicotine can be momentarily trapped in condensation within the cigarette. His comments were not very convincing.

THE team members drove back in small groups to Parklawn. I was poring over a stack of files when Mitch Zeller came in to brief me, and as he waited, the most important lesson of the visit suddenly dawned on him. The Merit formulas that Philip Morris had given the group showed that different types of tobacco—each with a different level of nicotine—had been mixed together. Although the company kept saying it did not specify nicotine levels, Mitch realized that these blends allowed the company to control the bottom-line level of nicotine delivery.

"How did it go?" I asked Mitch.

We had only a moment to talk. "Fine, fine," Mitch said impatiently. "Look, David, they don't have to spike. They don't have to add nicotine."

"What do you mean?"

"I'm talking about blending. They can do it through blending."

21

WE DID NOT have much time and I still wanted a copy of Cigarette's never-published paper. I asked Mitch to call Herbert Barry at the University of Pittsburgh, whom Cigarette Jr. had identified as the paper's editor, though I knew it was unlikely that he had kept a copy of the paper for a decade unless he was highly organized or a pack rat.

Mitch placed the call to Pittsburgh and Barry called back several hours later. To Mitch's surprise, he remembered the submission of the article and the way it had been withdrawn at the insistence of Philip Morris, but he no longer had a copy of the manuscript.

This was bad news, but it could have been worse. Barry did have copies of his correspondence with Cigarette, whom Barry knew by his actual name, Victor DeNoble. He also remembered DeNoble's colleague, Paul Mele, our Cigarette Jr. Mitch asked Barry if he would be willing to send him copies of the correspondence, but Barry was reluctant; he wanted DeNoble's permission first.

That was not going to be easy. Mitch could not tell Barry that DeNoble was a confidential informant for the FDA, nor that, for the moment, DeNoble was not talking to the agency. But Mitch did the best he could. He said that he understood Barry's reluctance to release the correspondence, then added, "Please, I'm just asking you to think about it." Mitch urged, "Keep an open mind. Please call me back if you think you'd be in a position to share these papers with us."

Mitch reported his conversation with Barry to me. It seemed unlikely that we would make any progress on that front.

Liz Berbakos had better luck in her assigned task of securing the abstract published by the American Psychological Association. Someone at APA had been able to locate it and promised to fax a copy to her. It was the first step in the right direction.

The second step came at about seven that evening when Mitch returned to his office after an afternoon of meetings. On his desk were two sheets of paper, fresh from the fax machine. One was a cover letter from Herbert Barry. The other was a copy of a letter Barry had written to DeNoble, dated September 22, 1986. It read, in part, "I share the distress you expressed in your phone conversation of 18 September that the Philip Morris Company has issued an injunction against the publication of this paper."

Mitch read the letter carefully, read it again, then wheeled around and raced down the corridor. He burst into my office with a look of pure elation on his face.

I NEEDED to meet again with Jack Henningfield to learn more about the science underlying DeNoble's work on the self-administration of nicotine. Several of us gathered in the conference room, and I turned the conversation to nicotine as a reinforcer. "An addictive drug sets off a biological chain reaction in the brain producing a conditioning effect that the individual has little control over," Jack told us. I asked questions to clarify certain points, assuming Jack would not have any idea why I was interested. I had no reason to think he knew anything about DeNoble's work, but just to be thorough I asked, "Do you know if the industry has ever done any of its own research on self-administration?"

Jack began describing some of the studies DeNoble had conducted.

Despite what I was thinking, I tried not to appear overly interested in this. I closed the meeting as soon as I could and asked Jack if I could see him in my office. Once we were alone, I said, "Tell me what you know about DeNoble's work." He described it in greater detail. I knew that we were talking about the same material.

"Do you have any idea where I could get a copy of his paper?" I asked.

"Actually, I may still have a draft of his manuscript in my files."

Jack was one of the leading experts in the field, so it made sense that DeNoble might have shared the manuscript with him, but still, I could not believe my luck. He checked with his office, and within hours we had the paper. I knew we had a bombshell.

The next question was how to make it public at the hearing. To avoid taking the Department by surprise, I alerted Donna Shalala's legislative adviser and talked about the best way to release the information. I was concerned that if we played the story of Philip Morris suppressing research too boldly, it would overshadow the question of whether nicotine was a drug, and the broader messages of my testimony would be lost. I decided not to include it in my prepared statement, but to let it emerge in the subsequent question-and-answer period.

WITH only a few days before the hearing, and after weeks of immersion, countless dead ends, and vague hints from informants, some of the pieces of the puzzle were beginning to fit together. In the final hectic days, I sat alone at the large table in the conference room. I had with me all of the data generated by the St. Louis lab, which had been analyzing the nicotine content in twenty brands of cigarettes. The first ten entries were for the Merit family, and I studied column after column of numbers. Eventually, I saw that among the Merit products, the "ultra-low-tar" cigarette had the highest percentage of nicotine—approaching 2.0 percent. Regular Merit cigarettes, the so-called "full-flavor" cigarette, had 1.46 percent. I checked the figures again and again. What I saw was the opposite of what one would expect if industry claims for their cigarettes were true. The lowest-tar cigarettes should have the smallest percentage of nicotine. Instead, they had the most.

Was this laboratory error? If not, it was stunning. I contacted the St. Louis lab and asked them to recheck the Merit figures and to have another lab run the same tests. The figures that came back from the second lab were not identical to those of St. Louis but they corroborated the general pattern. The percentage of nicotine in Merit increased as the advertised tar level decreased.

SOON afterwards, I was in my office with six sheets of paper spread out in front of me. Weeks earlier I had learned that the tobacco companies provide the Federal Trade Commission with an array of data on every type of cigarette they make. On the basis of that information, the FTC had calculated industrywide sales-weighted values for tar and nicotine, for each year from 1982 through 1991. I had requested the data from the FTC, and now I sat staring at more columns of numbers, in type no larger than that found in a phonebook.

Alexander Spears, vice chairman and chief operating officer of Lorillard Tobacco Company, was going to be testifying at the upcoming hearing, and we had been given an advance copy of his testimony. One sentence stood out as I tried to make sense of the FTC figures. "We do not set levels of nicotine for particular brands of cigarettes," he planned to tell the committee. "Nicotine levels follow the tar levels. The easy proof that no nicotine manipulation has occurred may be found in the temporal tar and nicotine data from the 1950s to 1990s." It was the industry mantra once again. But the mass of FTC figures I was reviewing discredited the assertion that both tar and nicotine levels had dropped proportionately over the years. Instead, they showed that, overall, nicotine levels had gone up while tar levels had dropped. If tar and nicotine levels moved independently of each other, I thought it might be proof of manipulation.

I called Bob O'Neill, who had a reputation as the dean of FDA statisticians. He came to the agency in 1971 and played an important role in issues involving clinical trial design and analysis, sampling techniques, epidemiology, and the monitoring of drugs after they were marketed. When Bob arrived, I showed him the year-by-year FTC data. He quickly grasped the importance of the trends I was studying. "I need to think through this," he said. "Let me take a closer look." Sensing my urgency, he promised, "I'll get back to you tomorrow."

At 4 P.M. the next day, Bob appeared with a series of computer-generated graphs. When he plotted the nicotine data, the line had an upward positive slope, reflecting about a 10 to 15 percent increase in the average nicotine content of cigarettes between 1982 and 1991. Tar levels had fallen during the same time period. The graphs flatly contradicted the industry claims.

"How could the industry and FDA use the same data to reach such different conclusions?" I asked, thinking about Spears's prepared testimony. Bob pointed out that industry used a time span of many decades, which masked the changes we saw in the ten-year period that we had examined.

With the hearing fast approaching, the evidence was finally coming together. The patents had given us an insight into what the industry could do with nicotine but did not establish that its inventions were actually put into practice. Now the Merit and FTC figures gave us much more of a hint that nicotine levels were being manipulated and controlled. We could go to the hearing with data.

As I talked with the tobacco team about how best to present the statistical analyses and graphs we had generated, I received a letter from Congressman

Thomas J. Bliley Jr., a Republican representing Richmond, Virginia. Bliley was the ranking minority member of Waxman's subcommittee, and an official in Philip Morris's government affairs office had called him "our sentry" on that committee.

The two-page letter asked us to provide his office with a long list of information and documents prior to the hearing. Bliley wanted everything we had to support the statements in our February 25 letter, and then some. First on his list was "all evidence in the FDA's possession that suggests that cigarette manufacturers may intend that their products contain nicotine to satisfy an addiction on the part of some of their customers." Specifically, he wanted written summaries of all of our conversations and copies of all documents we had received in connection with this "allegation," along with the names, addresses, and titles of anyone who had provided us such information. The letter also asked for documentation supporting other statements made in our response to the Coalition and then, to be sure nothing was missed, asked for "All other information or 'evidence' brought to the FDA's attention or otherwise received by the FDA that you relied on."

The letter was dated March 18. It arrived at the FDA three days later. The closing line of the letter read, "Please provide this information to my office no later than March 21, 1994."

This was the first of numerous document requests that we would receive from members of Congress with strong ties to the tobacco industry. As head of a federal agency, I was obliged to take any congressional request seriously, but anyone who has been around Washington knows when a member of Congress is doing the bidding of a loyal supporter or constituent. Congressional staffers had seen Bliley ask questions or make statements at hearings and committee meetings as he read from binders they assumed to be the work of the tobacco industry.

It was apparent to me that Bliley's letter was a fishing expedition, intended to catch not only what we knew but how we knew it—he wanted our sources. I confirmed the influences on Bliley much later, when I obtained an internal Philip Morris document dating to this period that listed "letter to Kessler from Bliley" as one of its agenda items. The tobacco industry was using its friends in Congress.

Despite my suspicions, I could not ignore his request. I sent Bliley the list of published references we had drawn on for our letter to the Coalition.

22

THE OUTLINE of my congressional testimony had begun to take shape late one night when I was at home, too filled with ideas to relax. My mind was racing as I grabbed a pen and the nearest piece of paper with some blank space on it, which turned out to be the paperbound 1981 Surgeon General's report.

I began writing furiously in the blank space between the lines of type on the cover until I ran out of space at the bottom of the page. Then, I began to scrawl in the margins, winding around the edges of the cover until there was writing in every direction. When my ideas filled that page, I flipped the book over and began scrawling over the blank back cover. When I finished, I went back and tried to number this morass of ideas.

It was laughable, this book covered with barely readable scratches, but I thought I might have something. I had just outlined the centerpiece of my congressional testimony—the notion of free will.

For decades, the industry had trumpeted the cause of free choice for smokers, and the concept had struck a chord with the public by tapping into a libertarian instinct in American society. I had to reframe the debate. My job was to make the case that nicotine is addictive and that addiction robs people of choice.

I called Mitch at home that evening. "I need your help," I said.

Mitch arrived early the next day. I put the defaced Surgeon General's report on the coffee table in front of us. He glanced at it, looked at me, and laughed. I went over it with him, turning the page sideways and then upside down to follow my numbering, turning the book over to capture the thoughts on the back cover. His demeanor changed. I was relieved to have identified a key theme.

Of course, the tobacco companies understood the argument about free will long before I did and feared it could undermine them, shattering the defense that had thus far won them every product liability lawsuit the industry had faced. A 1980 Tobacco Institute document discussed this: "[T]he entire matter of addiction is the most potent weapon a prosecuting attorney can have in a lung cancer/cigarette case. We can't defend continued smoking as 'free choice' if the person was 'addicted.'"

We began drafting my written testimony over the next few days, working virtually around the clock. I called my speechwriter, Renie Schapiro, back from a long-planned vacation to produce an initial draft. For four almost sleepless days, she produced one revision after another as the team labored over every word. Mitch Zeller later compared the process to a forced march at night over swampy terrain. I wanted consensus as much as possible, and that meant arguing through sharp differences of opinion. That sort of contention could have threatened the entire effort, but it seemed to have the opposite effect, and the team emerged from the process closer than ever.

Eventually, we agreed on every word of the thirty-page testimony, and footnoted every statement. I wanted briefing books containing references for everything we said. We could not afford a single mistake.

PREDICTABLY enough, after the frenetic pace of the past few weeks, Thursday, March 24, 1994, the day before the hearing, was wild. It began with an announcement by Philip Morris of a $10 billion libel suit against ABC and against both the producer and the reporter on the *Day One* story. The suit charged that the network had made "false and defamatory" statements and sought $5 billion in compensatory damages and $5 billion in punitive damages.

According to the Philip Morris statement, "The essential allegations made by ABC on those broadcasts was that cigarettes are 'artificially spiked' with nicotine during the manufacturing process 'in order to keep people smoking.'"

"These allegations are not true and ABC knows they are not true," said Murray Bring, the company's take-no-prisoners general counsel. It would have been naïve of me to think that the timing of the lawsuit was not intended as a warning to me, but it had no effect. We were not changing course.

My written testimony was supposed to be handed to the congressional committee twenty-four hours before I was to testify. As required, I had submitted it to the Office of Management and Budget at the White House for clearance, but I did not hear back until eight o'clock the night before my appearance on the Hill. Incredibly, from an agency that had demanded major revisions in the past, OMB wanted only one change, and it was a sound suggestion. I was asked to eliminate a letter that I had included at the end of my draft testimony. The letter came from a woman whose father had died of emphysema. "His death was not the hard part," she wrote. "His life was the real horror story.... My most vivid memories were my dad's unforgettable words of despair. Not one day went by when he didn't say, 'I know these damn cigarettes are killing me, but I can't quit.'...I remember him being under the oxygen tent begging for a cigarette." The OMB official who reviewed the text had lost her own mother to a smoking-related illness, I later learned, and had cried when she read the story. But she thought the letter was too emotional for the hearing.

I alerted Waxman to the story of Victor DeNoble's suppressed research for Philip Morris, knowing it was likely to generate a stir at the hearing. I also decided it was best not to blindside Congressman Bliley. I reached him at home that night and briefly described what I planned to say. "It is going to come up tomorrow," I said. "I just don't want you to be surprised." I braced myself for his response, expecting a difficult conversation.

Bliley politely thanked me for calling, and the conversation was over. No questions, no reaction. I put down the phone, amazed. At the time, I concluded that he had not grasped the importance of what I said. The truth, as members of his own staff later told me, was that he always had to be thoroughly prepared before he would respond on a tobacco issue.

I began to practice my statement just before 10 P.M. Sharan Kuperman, from the FDA press office, timed me, and after a second read-through she said I could do it in less than thirty minutes only if I wanted to sound like a fast-talking pitch man. Waxman had given me only ten minutes, and I intended to argue for more time as soon as I saw him in the morning.

My staff wanted me to go through the testimony once more, but I insisted on going home. I wanted to get some sleep, and I was wary of being overprepared.

THE hearing was scheduled to begin at 9:45 the next morning. I deliberately arrived late for the scheduled rendezvous with the group at Federal Office

Building 8. I stay calmer when I am not around a lot of excited people, and that day, I had to be as calm as possible. I knew that my presentation would have a major impact on how the possibility of FDA regulation was viewed by the public.

At about 9:15, we took the elevator down to the building's underground garage. Our footsteps echoed across the concrete floor as we walked towards the van waiting to take us to the Rayburn House Office Building. I was in the center of a tight circle, surrounded by members of the tobacco team.

The van dropped us off at the horseshoe-shaped driveway in front of the main entrance of the Rayburn Building. A line of people hoping to watch the proceedings had formed outside the hearing room, one of the largest in the building. Although it can accommodate a few hundred spectators, all the seats were quickly filled. CNN was to cover my testimony live, and the camera crews were setting up. The industry had its observers there, as did the anti-tobacco groups.

I was focused on one person and one thing. I walked directly over to Congressman Waxman. After shaking hands and exchanging pleasantries, I got to the point. "I need more time. I need about thirty minutes for my opening statement," I said. I was informing, more than asking. My message was, "Trust me."

I could tell he was not pleased. Witnesses, especially government officials who are considered to be among the most boring speakers, typically get no more than five or ten minutes. Waxman would have to get Congressman Bliley's assent first, and it might even mean having to extend the time for industry witnesses as well. I don't recall waiting for an answer. I was determined to give my entire statement.

IN HIS introduction, Chairman Waxman said the morning's testimony would be about "drug addiction, which claims the lives of four hundred thirty thousand Americans a year. The drug is nicotine." He reviewed our letter and explained that I had been invited "to elaborate on the possible application of the Federal Food, Drug, and Cosmetic Act to tobacco products."

Then, he lashed into the tobacco company executives. The CEOs of the major companies had been invited to testify, but all had declined. They were instead represented by the Tobacco Institute's Charles Whitley, one in a long line of former congressmen hired to head the institute. Waxman entered into the record the letters from the CEOs declining his invitation and left no doubt about his feelings. Referring to Philip Morris's president, Mike Miles, Waxman said, "Mr. Miles had the time to hold a press conference and announce a lawsuit yesterday, but he wouldn't find the time to come before the Congress of the United States and talk about this very issue."

Waxman ended by commending Congressman Mike Synar for continuing to raise the issue of FDA regulation of tobacco over the years. Synar's passionate and tenacious efforts on tobacco control had long bedeviled the industry. I had already had a taste of that tenacity at our meeting at the American Heart Association dinner two years back.

Then Waxman turned to Bliley for his opening statement. It felt as if a cold front had suddenly passed through the room.

Reading from a prepared text, Bliley went after me directly. "I know that the tobacco industry is not very popular in some quarters, but that does not excuse federal officials from their duty to proceed cautiously and responsibly before leveling serious accusations. Commissioner Kessler has not done so in this instance. I view this hearing as an opportunity for Dr. Kessler to explain his precipitous and reckless conduct and to set the record straight."

It was a disquieting experience to be blasted ad hominem in public, but I steadied myself and let the attack roll over me, keeping my emotions in check. Shortly after he completed his statement, Bliley left the hearing, missing most, if not all, of my testimony.

THREE congressmen were on the first panel to testify: Richard Durbin of Illinois, James Clyburn of South Carolina, and Martin Lancaster of North Carolina. Of these, only Durbin was an ally, and, predictably, he urged greater regulation of tobacco. Clyburn argued that there was nothing new to prompt FDA's reexamination of this issue and accused me of "scaremongering" at the expense of his constituents. We later learned that prior to the hearing, the tobacco industry had generated a list of sympathetic people willing to testify on its behalf, Clyburn among them, and intended to "write one-two pagers" for them.

Lancaster, who sometimes served as a conduit between the Hill and the industry and who had written a "Dear Colleague" letter disputing claims that nicotine was added to cigarettes, commented that the FDA was having enough difficulty meeting its current responsibilities and should not take on the additional burden of tobacco. He did not mince words. "FDA's recent actions on this issue of nicotine in cigarettes suggests to me that the Agency, in its eagerness to come after the tobacco industry with both barrels blazing, has in fact run off with its pistols half-cocked and its barrels loaded with blanks."

Lancaster was soon rewarded for his loyalty. The following month, top Philip Morris executives were asked to make personal donations to his reelection campaign. "It is suggested that you give $200–250 and that you send a letter with the check indicating that you are an executive of PM," read the e-mail from within Philip Morris. Under federal election law such a request is legal, and in any case, Philip Morris did not need to ask for anything from Lancaster. The son of a tobacco farmer, representing a district that grew more tobacco than any other in the country, Lancaster looked out for his constituents and for his own political survival.

With Lancaster's invective still hanging in the air, Chairman Waxman invited me to speak. I took my place alone at the table, glanced over to make sure that my staff was ready with the charts, and began my prepared statement. "The cigarette industry has attempted to frame the debate on smoking as the right of each American to choose. The question we must ask is whether smokers really have that choice.

"Consider these facts. Two thirds of adults who smoke say they wish they could quit. Seventeen million try to quit each year but for every one who quits, at least nine try and fail. Three out of four adult smokers say they are addicted."

I continued with a few more statistics, and then I looked up at the chairman and set the tone for the rest of my testimony. "Mr. Chairman, the issue I will address today is simple: Whose choice is actually driving the demand for cigarettes in this country? Is it a choice by consumers to continue smoking? Or is it a choice by cigarette companies to maintain addictive levels of nicotine in their cigarettes?"

I described nicotine as "highly addictive," explaining briefly how it affects the brain and described the significance of animal self-administration studies. I pointed to a chart listing the major medical organizations that had declared nicotine addictive. Next, I began discussing the control of nicotine levels. While noting that all of the facts were not in, I said that "a picture is beginning to emerge.

"The public may think of cigarettes as no more than blended tobacco rolled in paper. But they are more than that. Some of today's cigarettes may in fact qualify as high-technology nicotine delivery systems that deliver nicotine in quantities sufficient to create and sustain addiction in the vast majority of individuals who smoke regularly." To support that statement, I went through the patents we had found, quoting verbatim from the industry.

"The research undertaken by the cigarette industry is more and more resembling drug development," I continued, offering several examples.

I went on to discuss actual nicotine levels in cigarettes, presenting our findings on Merit and the FTC data. A chart went up showing an inverse ratio between tar and nicotine levels. "We analyzed three varieties of one brand," I explained. "What surprised us was that the lowest one had in fact the highest concentration of nicotine in the cigarettes."

As I drew my testimony to a close, I emphasized the importance of the statutory word "intent" as we considered whether to regulate nicotine as a drug. I acknowledged the ramifications of FDA regulation. "Clearly, the possibility of FDA exerting jurisdiction over cigarettes raises many broader social issues for Congress to contemplate. It could lead to the possible removal of nicotine-containing cigarettes from the market, the limiting of the amount of nicotine in cigarettes to levels that are not addictive, or restricting access to them, unless the industry could show that nicotine-containing cigarettes are safe and effective."

I acknowledged that precipitous removal of nicotine could cause withdrawal among millions of Americans and could lead to a black market. And then I ended with "On these issues we seek guidance from Congress."

MY opening statement had gone well. Next came two rounds of questions from subcommittee members. As I motioned for key staff to join me at the table, Henry Waxman began to speak.

"Dr. Kessler, you have laid out a really astounding picture, not only of the tobacco companies manipulating the levels of nicotine, but by doing that, manipulating the American people who take up cigarette smoking." Then he began firing a series of questions at me. I knew that he was trying to put information on the record and wanted only the briefest of responses. Although I am not generally known for brevity, I obliged. Paulette later told me that she had never heard me be so succinct.

"Tobacco is an extremely serious health hazard," said Waxman. "It killed four hundred thirty thousand people last year. Is that correct?"

"That is correct," I said.

"Nicotine in tobacco is an addictive substance. It has all the hallmarks of addiction. Nicotine is why people who want to quit smoking can't quit. Is that correct?"

"That is correct."

Then he raised the issue of cocaine in Coca-Cola. "Until 1902, the Coca-Cola company added cocaine to Coke. Today such a company would not think of adding cocaine or any other addictive substance to soft drinks. Isn't it true that the Food and Drug Administration would not approve addictive levels of nicotine as an additive which could be added to food?"

I agreed, although I had never been sure that the Coca-Cola story was true. "We would not allow addictive substances to be in any product that we regulate without the most tight regulation."

Soon after this exchange, Bliley reentered the hearing room. Waxman raised a question at about the same time.

"Dr. Kessler, on the critical issue of the industry's intent, have you found any studies by the tobacco industry that would support the proposition that nicotine is retained in tobacco for addictive purposes?"

Before he had finished, I glanced over at Jack Henningfield as if to say, "Are you ready?"

I responded by reiterating that self-administration is a classic characteristic of an addictive substance and that self-administration studies had shown that nicotine is addictive. Continuing, I said, "We recently learned that a team of industry researchers had carried out such studies in the 1980s and reached similar conclusions." I explained that two papers had been accepted for publication in respected journals.

Having been forewarned, Waxman picked up on my comments immediately. "Are you saying, in other words, that the tobacco industry sponsored studies of animals that would indicate that nicotine was addictive to these animals?... What happened to these studies?"

I spoke carefully. "We have been told that both manuscripts were withdrawn by the researchers before publication. We have a copy of a letter from an editor of the journal to the researcher."

"In other words," Waxman said, summing up my comments, "the tobacco industry sponsored studies on their own where they found out that nicotine was addictive and before the public could know about it, they acted to suppress those studies?"

Waxman wanted me to identify the company, which I refused to do. I had been very careful in my testimony not to single out any one tobacco manufacturer. I did not want the hearing to end up targeting particular companies. I was targeting the entire industry.

Bliley spoke next, again reading a prepared text. As part of his statement, he presented charts demonstrating that tar and nicotine had declined together between the 1950s and the 1990s. It was a page straight out of the industry's play book. When he completed his presentation, he asked, "Would you explain to us why this data, which shows an essentially perfect correlation between tar and nicotine levels for the past forty years, does not categorically contradict your contention that nicotine is added to cigarettes to produce and sustain addiction?"

"I would be happy to, congressman," I replied. Using our charts, I again went through our findings. Bliley wanted to know why they differed from those he had just cited, but despite the sophistication of his questions, he was not prepared to engage me on the specifics of my analysis. He quickly concluded by asking that I submit the data to the committee.

Later, when Bliley had the floor again, he read a detailed explanation of the use of denatured alcohol containing minuscule quantities of nicotine. "Is your suggestion that manufacturers may be spiking their cigarettes based on the use of denatured alcohol?" he asked.

"I have never said that, congressman. I have never used the word 'spiking.' I have never even talked about denatured alcohol." We were talking past each other, which made more sense to me when I learned of Philip Morris's plans to provide "questions to Bliley for use in examining Kessler."

"Then how did you arrive at your statement to the smoking people on February the twenty-fifth that the manufacturers may be spiking their cigarettes?"

I almost crossed the line with my answer. "First of all, I didn't use the word 'spiking,' congressman, and I would be happy to go through my testimony again, but it was rather lengthy." I did not mean to be sarcastic, but I was not going to allow my presentation to be distorted.

That essentially ended my exchange with Bliley. I was confident that he simply was not well versed in the facts. Later, I learned that his committee staff just wanted the hearing to end as quickly as possible. Tobacco scared the committee staff, mostly because it was out of their hands. The industry usually dealt directly with Bliley's personal staff, the political operators, rather than the committee staff, who are generally more knowledgeable about policy. As a result, they always felt at risk of being surprised.

For the next few minutes, the Democrats plowed friendlier ground. "I don't think I would be exaggerating to suggest that we have just witnessed some of the most historic testimony in the history of Congress on any subject," Mike Synar said when I concluded my presentation. Then, it was over.

I headed for the double doors that took me into the corridor. As those doors opened, I found myself in a media crush. Microphones were thrust into my face, reporters with notebooks and pencils poised were shouting questions at me. Bob Arnot of CBS was so aggressive in his attempts to ask about Bliley's poor performance that an FDA press officer actually elbowed him out of the way.

A car was waiting as I left the building. Jerry Mande used his political-advance-man techniques to create a path for me through the reporters, and we climbed into the car. "It was a home run out of Yankee Stadium," Mitch shouted from the backseat, even before the car doors had closed.

Within a few minutes, the team reassembled in my downtown office. Although our investigation was far from complete, we had assembled a compelling body of evidence to suggest that the tobacco industry was engaged in pharmacological research and nicotine manipulation. All of the data pointed in the same direction. For years, the tobacco companies had trumpeted the notion of an adult choice to defend the marketing of its product. Now, for the first time, we had suggested that the industry deliberately intended to addict consumers. It was a new way to think about cigarettes and a powerful idea. By the time the Waxman hearings ended, both the friends and the foes of tobacco regulation knew something had changed. We had begun to put the case before Congress and the American people.

PART III

THE EVIDENCE MOUNTS

23

FROM the moment I sketched out the evidence suggesting that the industry manipulated the nicotine content of tobacco and said that we might have grounds for declaring nicotine a drug, the character of the debate began to change. But I knew we needed more definitive proof, and I had no idea where to find it. And even if I could find it, it might not be conclusive. We also needed to know why the industry was manipulating nicotine. Its spokesmen were claiming the only purpose was to enhance taste and flavor. We had to prove their real intent was to "affect the structure or any function of the body."

There was the briefest lull in our activities after the Waxman hearing. The tobacco team had been working intensely for more than a month—days, nights, and weekends—to prepare for the hearing, and everyone needed a break. Besides, I was still not committed to moving forward in any particular direction. At that point, I would have been happy to listen if someone had wanted to talk about a legislative initiative or industry concessions.

As I was returning from a Department meeting near Dulles Airport, my car phone rang. It was Ilisa, and she was chastising herself. She had been reviewing a stack of tobacco journal articles over the last few weeks but had not completed the job before my testimony. Now, she lamented, "If only I had seen this in time."

Buried in her pile was a 1981 report written by Alexander Spears, the same Lorillard executive who had told the Waxman committee that nicotine levels followed tar. Ilisa read me a sentence from his report, prepared for a conference of tobacco chemists: "Current research is directed toward increasing the nicotine levels while maintaining or marginally reducing the tar deliveries."

The research had obtained at least a measure of success, according to Spears, who noted that the lowest-tar cigarettes "show a significant difference in tobacco nicotine level... and a trend toward increasing nicotine over time." It was just as we had said, but this time it was in the industry's words. And it directly contradicted what Spears had said in his testimony.

Any passing thoughts of suspending our investigation evaporated with Ilisa's finding.

NONE of us realized at the time that industry officials had been surprised by my testimony. Their initial confidence that the FDA's efforts would go nowhere had been bolstered by the early predictions of stock analysts: "Kessler Testimony Is Mostly Noise, Threat of Regulation by FDA Is Limited," declared one respected Wall Street expert. But on the day of the hearing, not everyone was so placid. Steve Parrish, a high-level Philip Morris executive, had been among those watching my televised testimony at the Washington office of Burson-Marsteller, the company's public relations firm. Long after the event, Parrish described to me his growing sense of anxiety, recalling that day as the first time he became concerned about the FDA and tobacco. He said he had been struck by my intensity. "He's like a revival preacher," he told colleagues.

Philip Morris had not sat idle in the weeks after our letter to the Coalition. According to documents I saw later, the company had moved forward with its "ferocious defense" strategy, creating an Action Team to deal with the FDA investigation. Early-morning meetings were scheduled, and Craig Fuller was put in charge. I had tangled with Fuller in his capacity as a Philip Morris executive before, when he lobbied the Bush White House on behalf of Kraft to say that the food industry could never swallow the nutrition labeling we had proposed. We had won that battle. Now Fuller was defending the tobacco side of the company, and by mid-March his Action Team was meeting on a daily basis.

At a board meeting on March 30, 1994, a few days after my testimony, Philip Morris's general counsel, Murray Bring, called the FDA's initiative "by far the most threatening" of recent moves against the industry and labeled my recent activities "ominous." Referring to me, Bring stated, "If he were to declare that nicotine in cigarettes is addictive, and must be regulated, that action could affect the way in which jurors approach the issues of addiction and choice." Bring realized what I still did not—that our investigation was about more than FDA regulation.

An attorney from Philip Morris's outside counsel, Arnold & Porter, then summarized the company's intelligence on our investigation. He told the board that we had been interviewing industry employees and were using criminal investigators who had "received special training in investigative techniques and evidence development at the FBI Academy." Neither Tom nor Gary had FBI training, and both of them would have laughed at the assumption that they did. Still, the lawyers tried to be reassuring. "Philip Morris is mounting an intensive legislative effort to persuade members of Congress of the dangers inherent in the FDA initiative," said the lawyer from Arnold & Porter. Bring promised to provide more detailed information on strategies "to respond to these attacks and to seize the initiative wherever possible."

Following the presentations, board members had an opportunity to ask questions and make comments. "Do we have a profile on Dr. Kessler?" asked one. Historically, the industry had monitored the appointment of new Surgeons General and tried to influence the selection, but it had never paid much attention to the FDA commissioner. That was changing. A photograph of me was included in a slide show at a later board meeting.

The chance to talk more about industry strategies came in April at The Cloister in Sea Island, Georgia, a grande dame of seaside resorts in the South and long a meeting place for Philip Morris's board of directors. The draft text of a presentation by Steve Parrish included his description of a four-pronged Tobacco Strategic Attack Plan. The first approach was the "frontal assault," direct actions taken in Philip Morris's own name. The sweep of activities included opening other manufacturing plants to investigators from the FDA and the General Accounting Office, briefing government officials, running aggressive ad campaigns, and working at the state level to preempt local legislation.

Next came "surgical strikes," the company's individual lawsuits. "Each of these gives us tremendous media opportunities which we are continuing to exploit," commented Parrish. "For example, with one legal action—the filing of the ABC suit—the word "spiking" has dropped from the lexicon of the anti-tobacco crowd. Frankly, if that is all the suit ever does, it will have been worth it."

Third were "allied attacks, where friendly third parties are engaged on our side but without direct or obvious connection to the industry." The wisdom of this strategy was supported by poll results that showed almost any organization had more credibility than a tobacco company.

Finally came "air cover" via the newly formed National Smokers Alliance. Nominally a membership organization, NSA had been founded by Philip Morris, and the company continued to support it. "In every sense, this is our NRA!" proclaimed the presenter proudly.

But the industry was worried. On the same day its board was meeting, a legal group headed by the flamboyant lawyer Melvin Belli was filing a $5 billion class-action suit against the tobacco companies, accusing them of intentionally addicting their customers. I thought for a moment about that news and wondered whether a Florida columnist might actually have been prescient. A few weeks earlier, Waldo Proffitt, editor of the *Sarasota Herald-Tribune,* had called our letter to the Coalition "one of the most fateful documents of the twentieth century" and predicted that it would, in time, "wipe out the tobacco industry as it now exists." Proffitt speculated that our suggestion that nicotine levels had been intentionally manipulated would prompt a rash of lawsuits seeking billions of dollars in punitive damages. And he thought the plaintiffs would start winning those suits.

HENRY WAXMAN wanted the chief executive officers of the nation's tobacco companies to respond to my testimony. He knew that there was a risk that they would overwhelm the committee, a chance that they would "pull an Oliver North" and turn the tables on Congress, but he also saw opportunity in another hearing. For decades, the industry's public relations and advertising machines had shaped the public face of tobacco—which usually looked like Joe Camel or the Marlboro cowboy. Waxman's staff thought it was time to redraw that image.

Waxman chose to invite the CEOs, rather than subpoenaing them, although he was not sure they would appear voluntarily. In the past, they had always sent surrogates, usually from the Tobacco Institute. Now he had visions of a hearing room with empty chairs where the witnesses should have been.

But the industry seemed to recognize it was risky to ignore Waxman's invitation. In the end, Congressman Bliley made sure that the executives testified, warning that if they did not show up for the April 14 hearing, he would not provide them with cover. It was an unusual demand from such a loyalist, an indication that we were having an effect on the mood in Congress.

All seven CEOs agreed to appear. After two decades of legislative efforts on behalf of tobacco control, Waxman was about to get his first opportunity to question the heads of the companies directly. As I left my house the morning of the hearing, I predicted to Paulette that a photograph of the men being sworn in as a group would appear on the front page, above the fold, of every major newspaper the next day.

I was unable to watch the live hearing, since I was scheduled to participate in a government-industry AIDS meeting where data about the newest class of antiviral agents were to be presented. The drugs represented a major breakthrough in AIDS therapy, and new FDA programs to speed their approval were in place. I used a pay phone to call my office hourly seeking updates on developments as they unfolded on the Hill, and when I returned home that evening, I watched the hearing on videotape.

In his opening statement, Bliley made light of the tobacco control forces allied against him. Referring to news clips that described him as "the congressman from Philip Morris," he jokingly said, "Ladies and gentlemen, I would certainly like to know who is the antismoking groups' p.r. agent because this person has done more for the name I.D. of this small-town Virginia mayor over the past few weeks than all of my press secretaries combined."

Then, he focused on me. "I must say that I was saddened by what took place in this room a couple of weeks ago. I witnessed the commissioner of the FDA, who is both a trained scientist and a lawyer, take threads of truth and weave them into whole cloth of rumor and innuendo." It was a relief when Mike Synar took the microphone. He delivered his opening remarks with barely contained enthusiasm. "I am thrilled to be here, face to face, with the chief executive officers and chief researchers from the seven largest cigarette and oral tobacco companies in the United States."

During the first round of questions, Waxman asked the CEOs whether smoking caused cancer. The tobacco industry had long adhered insistently to the same line—the link has not been proved.

Jim Johnston of RJR was first to be asked that question. "It may," he conceded.

"Do you know whether it does?" Waxman persisted.

"I do not know."

Waxman moved on to Lorillard's Andrew Tisch. Like the others, Tisch had been prepped for a day and a half by industry attorneys before the hearing, as he told me later. He also said that he had walked in intending to be like "the Pillsbury dough boy," allowing the punches to roll off him, but that he had detested the entire experience. "In a deposition last year, you were asked whether cigarette smoking causes cancer," stated Waxman. "Your answer was, 'I don't believe so.' Do you stand by that answer today?"

"Yes, sir," Tisch replied.

"Do you understand how isolated you are in that belief from the entire scientific community?" Waxman asked.

"I do, sir," Tisch replied. Any thought that the CEOs were finally going to step away from the party line faded.

Turning next to Bill Campbell of Philip Morris, Waxman said, "Mr. Campbell, you were also deposed. And you said, 'To my knowledge, it has not been proven that cigarette smoking causes cancer'.... Will you ever be convinced?"

"Yes, I may be convinced," Campbell replied. But apparently not yet. "We don't know what causes cancer, in general, right now."

It was not the long-standing equivocation on whether smoking caused cancer that became the evening's big story. Rather, it was the answer to a question from Congressman Ron Wyden, a Democrat. "Let me ask you first, and I'd like you to just go down the row, whether each of you believes that nicotine is not addictive. Yes or no, do you believe nicotine is not addictive?"

In rapid-fire sequence, the CEOs all gave the same answer: "I believe that nicotine is not addictive."

Only Jim Johnston varied in any substantive way. "Cigarettes and nicotine clearly do not meet the classic definition of addiction. There is no intoxication."

None of them knew then that Paul Mele had already quoted to us the words of one Philip Morris executive: "We all know it's addictive. I'd shove it in my vein if I could."

MIKE SYNAR shifted the conversation to the closing of Victor DeNoble's laboratory. Expecting our testimony of three weeks earlier to shape the agenda of the hearing, Philip Morris's Washington office had warned Bill Campbell about what questions to expect.

Campbell denied the allegation that DeNoble's lab had been shut down because its findings were adverse to the industry, but a document written earlier by the company's outside counsel, Shook, Hardy & Bacon, suggested otherwise. "This kind of research is a major tool of our adversaries on the addiction issue," read the Shook, Hardy opinion. "The irony is that industry-sponsored research is honing that tool. In the final analysis, the performing and publishing of nicotine-related research clearly seems ill-advised from a litigation point of view."

With Synar taking the lead, the tone of the CEO hearing became argumentative. Synar asked Jim Johnston whether animal research was conducted in RJR labs. Then he asked Johnston to turn over any documents pertaining to that research.

"Those which do not involve proprietary product development—" Johnston began.

"Mr. Johnston, that is an unacceptable answer," Synar interrupted. "Proprietary information is available to Congress in confidential form. That is not a legitimate excuse for not providing it to the subcommittee."

Johnston retorted, "We will provide any reasonable data."

"No, that's not what I'm suggesting, Mr. Johnston."

I thought Synar needed to tone down his language, but I was not all that interested in the theatrics of the day. I was concentrating on what the CEOs would say about manipulating nicotine. An exchange between Congressman John Bryant and Bill Campbell finally addressed that issue. Drawing on the laboratory data I had presented in March, Bryant showed Campbell a graph of Merit cigarettes that illustrated our fundamental point—Ultima, the variety with the lowest level of tar, had the highest concentration of nicotine.

Campbell kept dodging the question about how the company achieved that result, but Bryant returned to it again and again. Finally, Campbell conceded that Philip Morris used blends with a higher concentration of nicotine in Ultima, compared to Merit filters, the regular brand. He quickly added that other tobaccos, with lower nicotine, were used to counteract the effects. But the admission of manipulation was now, finally, on the record.

In the days that followed the hearing, there was grumbling in the press that McCarthy-like tactics had been used to question the witnesses. In what some staffers suspected was an orchestrated event, callers to Waxman's office conveyed an almost identical message: Congressman Waxman is acting like McCarthy. Leave the CEOs alone.

The supporters of the executives under siege had found the only analogy, exaggerated though it was, that could arguably win them sympathy. To my mind, the aggressiveness of the attacks was unnecessary, but in the court of public opinion, where policy decisions often founder or thrive, the tone of the hearing was quickly forgotten. Etched into historical memory was the sight of seven CEOs swearing under oath to tell the truth.

Later, I would meet the senior tobacco executive I called Veritas, who had watched the event with interest. He knew that the industry's strategy of obfuscation and denial, decades in the making, was facing its toughest challenge. For the first time in recent memory, no trade association spokesperson was fronting for the nation's top tobacco executives on Capitol Hill; they were forced to speak for themselves. Though Veritas said that their testimony made them look like fools, he quickly added, "Life in the bunker can be filled with caviar." He suspected the event would test the CEOs' willingness to continue mouthing words that no one else believed. It seemed obvious that their script had stopped making sense, and early in the day, Veritas thought the executives might have been prepared to diverge from it. But apparently none of them knew what else to say. Within a few years, all seven were gone from their tobacco company positions.

The industry recognized that it was time to strengthen its armamentarium. Philip Morris sought out Mike Barrett, who had left his post as staff director of Congressman John Dingell's oversight committee, and asked if he would be available to provide advice to the industry on future congressional subpoenas. For that it was willing to pay generously. Over a five-year period Barrett was paid a total of $2.5 million, though by his own admission he did virtually nothing for the money. At one point the industry tried to reduce the fees to which it had already agreed, but Barrett refused. The problem, he told his client, was that accepting tobacco money had limited his future professional options. He felt that he had been tainted.

24

In early April, a team of FDA investigators headed to Winston-Salem, North Carolina, to meet with officials at R. J. Reynolds, the home of Joe Camel. Five weeks earlier, immediately after my letter to the Coalition, Jim Johnston had written me to deny that the company raised nicotine levels above what is found naturally in tobacco.

Shortly after receiving Johnston's letter, I wrote back asking about the possibility of visiting RJR. Richard Cooper, a food and drug lawyer I had known for more than twenty years, responded promptly. Cooper was a man of enormous intellect, a Rhodes scholar, a former Supreme Court law clerk, and a former chief counsel for the FDA. Now, he was representing R. J. Reynolds as a partner in one of Washington's most prestigious law firms, Williams & Connolly.

After some fairly amicable negotiations, eased by Mitch's assurance to Cooper that we had already been inside Philip Morris, the trip was arranged. The discovery during our first tobacco company visit that nicotine levels could be controlled by blending made me eager to see what else we could learn. I drafted more than twenty pages of questions, dealing with every aspect of cigarette production, from the leaf on the plant to the cigarette in the pack. I wanted the team to ask about the harvesting of raw tobacco, about how tobacco is graded, about the particulars of cigarette manufacturing, and about the company's marketing and advertising strategies.

The morning of the visit the team was ushered into a crowded conference room where RJR executives were gathered. Mitch took the lead in the questioning. Chuck Blixt, the company's personable in-house attorney, was in control for RJR, flanked by Cooper. Though blanketed in smoke, the day began in a relaxed atmosphere.

One of the first presentations was made by RJR's long-time master blend specialist, T. J. Porter, who confirmed what Philip Morris had told us, that stalk position correlates to a remarkable degree of accuracy with the nicotine content of a tobacco leaf. The highest content, he added, was in overripe leaves. Porter had a homespun manner, and when he said that he could simply roll up a raw tobacco leaf and smoke it to gauge its nicotine content, he seemed intent on promoting the notion that making cigarettes was less a science than a time-honored craft. But he spoke openly about the importance of nicotine, making one especially candid point: impact is basically a function of nicotine in tobacco. Impact is the feeling the smoker gets of being "hit in the chest," Porter explained.

A tour of RJR's vast manufacturing facilities came next. The group rode in company vans to the Brook Cove stemmery, where raw tobacco was received, processed, and graded before being shipped to the production plant. En route, one of the drivers, a woman with a strong North Carolina accent, gave a running commentary on RJR's benevolence: how it helped the local fire department, how it plowed roads free of snow in the winter, how the community relied upon the wages paid by the company.

At Philip Morris, the stemmery had been full of tobacco, bale upon bale of it, graded, tagged, and piled high. The RJR facility, by contrast, was deserted. Mitch had specifically requested the visit, but only after reaching the site did the Reynolds people mention that the stemmery had closed the previous Friday and would not reopen for several months. The plant, they said, was always closed during growing season. Inside the huge building, the size of several football fields, a few six-foot-square bales of tobacco stood in the middle of the floor, tagged with labels bearing bar codes that clearly stated the moisture, sugar, and nicotine content of each bale.

The next stop for the team was the lyrically named Tobaccoville, the Reynolds production facility, where tobacco became cigarettes. That visit began with a half-hour briefing by the plant's manager, a tall man in an open shirt who was unable to conceal his disdain for his government guests. Tobaccoville was vast, some 2 million square feet—forty-six acres—and at full capacity it could produce 8,000 cigarettes a minute, or 100 billion cigarettes a year. Employees used bicycles to move from one work station to another in a plant that typically consumed the amount of power required for 56,000 houses.

But not the day of the FDA team's visit. Coincidentally, that plant, too, was running well below capacity. Of more than a dozen production lines, only two were operational. It was, a Reynolds spokesman explained, a slow day. As they walked alongside one of the production lines, the team marveled at the cost to which Reynolds had apparently gone to scale back operations. And then someone suddenly noticed that over the ledge of a nearby window, a row of eyes was watching. Curious employees were apparently standing on boxes or tables in an adjoining staff room, peering silently over a high sill at the people from the FDA.

DEEP Cough had told us about BIO/BIO, the research division where human body fluids were tested. By measuring nicotine in the plasma, and cotinine, a nicotine metabolite, in the urine, the company could determine how much nicotine was in the smoker's bloodstream and the rates at which it was absorbed by and eliminated from the body. If Deep Cough was right, it was a strong indication that the company viewed its products as drugs. In a published monograph, RJR had compared cotinine levels in smokers using Premier, the novel smokeless cigarette it had abandoned in the late 1980s, to levels among those smoking regular cigarettes. I wanted to know if that sort of test had been conducted for any other products.

The FDA team began asking about human testing during the first day of the visit. Did RJR test body fluids? Chuck Blixt said the company did not conduct human studies, though he did acknowledge having measured nicotine in the urine of Premier smokers to ensure that the smoke delivery was not in some way unexpected and for research purposes. The team asked more questions on the same topic the following day. Was human testing done for low-tar cigarettes? For ultra-low-tar cigarettes? No. Human testing was done before Premier was test-marketed, insisted company spokesmen again.

Gary Light jumped in. "You're saying that you didn't do any cotinine research after Premier?" he asked. The answer was no.

The researchers in the room were perceptibly uneasy. Gary repeated his question in a slightly different form. Had they done research involving cotinine and urine or body fluids? Again, no.

Gary kept approaching the question from various angles, altering his phrasing to eliminate any chance of a legal nuance that would allow the company to answer in the negative while technically telling the truth.

Each time he repeated himself, the tension in the room rose. Finally, when he asked if there had been any research involving blood work, Rich Cooper snapped that the company had already answered that question. I don't care how you ask it or how many times you ask it, he said, the answer is still no. His anger was evident, and he left no doubt as to the company's claim.

Cooper was a lawyer known for good manners and a calm approach, but Gary's questions got under his skin. Later that day, he took Bob Spiller aside and asked him to remove Gary from the team, complaining that he was pushing too hard and trying to make the company look deceitful. Bob, of course, did no such thing.

Although it had no hard evidence, the team already suspected that R. J. Reynolds was engaged in human testing. Inside the plant, the team had seen several employees with small bandages on their inner arms, as though a blood sample had recently been taken. And Mitch made an inadvertent observation when he left the meeting to use the restroom. As he walked down a nearby corridor, he saw a Reynolds employee carrying a small cooler, the sort that would hold a six-pack of beer, open a door, and disappear into the room inside. Perhaps the man simply had his lunch in it—it was hard to imagine RJR would be collecting urine samples during our visit—but Mitch remembered Deep Cough's story about an employee using just such a cooler to deliver samples to the company. It was hard not to be suspicious but impossible then to be sure.

SOME time after the visit, the FDA team decided to test RJR's emphatic assertion that it had not conducted any studies involving bodily fluids since Premier. One of Gary's OCI colleagues telephoned Bellomy Research, also based in Winston-Salem, which Deep Cough had told us did contract work for the tobacco company. Posing as "Linda Benjamin," an employee of a fictional company, the investigator asked for an opportunity to discuss possible collaborations. The receptionist promptly connected her to Lacy Bellomy, the head of the company. The investigator then outlined a proposed research strategy, telling Bellomy that her firm wanted to draw blood samples from twenty-five people in each of four cities both before and after they used a smokeless tobacco product and then have the blood analyzed.

"I can work with you if it's smokeless," replied Bellomy. "I have a long-standing relationship with a tobacco company which prohibits me from working for any other tobacco cigarette company." Bellomy added that his was a marketing research company that did not actually do the technical work. "Our client has their own laboratories...with the nurses and the people to draw the blood and analyze it," he explained.

Then, a momentary note of caution crept into his voice. "Which smokeless company are you working with?" he asked. Linda Benjamin said she wasn't allowed to reveal that, which Bellomy understood.

Next, the investigator suggested that Bellomy talk with one of her colleagues, a man she called "Dean Cooper"—the undercover Gary Light. A week later, on the phone with Gary and Linda, Lacy Bellomy had become wary and suspicious. "I need to know a couple of things before we go any further," he said. His main concern was how we had gotten his name. Gary handled the question with his usual finesse, explaining that friends at RJR had made the recommendation. To reinforce the story, Gary dropped the names of a few Reynolds scientists, then added a dash of flattery.

Reassured, Bellomy began to talk more freely and seemed ready to do business. Gary told Bellomy that he would be traveling to Winston-Salem the following week. Fishing for more information, Gary said he planned to ask RJR about the use of its labs.

"That's what I was going to suggest to you," Bellomy interjected. "They probably are the leading people in the country or in the world in doing that stuff, you know."

Bellomy mentioned that he had last been involved in a project studying nicotine levels in blood about a year earlier and had worked on perhaps five separate studies with Reynolds since the late 1970s.

"This has been going on for a long time," he said.

"After Premier, also?" Gary asked.

"Before and after," Bellomy replied.

I HOPED that our third foray inside the walls of the tobacco industry, this time to Brown & Williamson's manufacturing facility in Macon, Georgia, would yield still more information. With each visit, we were building on what we had learned from the earlier ones, what our insider sources were telling us, and what we had observed. But Brown & Williamson was also better prepared. Company officials had spoken with RJR about a week earlier and received a synopsis of our visit. They knew what questions to expect and who would be asking them. A B&W notetaker had also jotted down a few comments about our cast of characters—Bob Spiller was called a "bully," Gary Light was labeled "aggressive" and "underhanded," and Mitch Zeller was a "zealot." Jack Mitchell "ran the show."

By any measure, Brown & Williamson is a more modest enterprise than either Philip Morris or R. J. Reynolds, despite being the American outpost of the huge British American Tobacco Company. Third largest among the tobacco companies, its cigarette brands include Kool, Capri, Barclay, Richland, Viceroy, and Lucky Strike, with these brands further subdivided into dozens of brand styles, such as Barclay 100s. Perhaps because it was a smaller company, Brown & Williamson was in some ways a less polished one. The personnel at Philip Morris and RJR had not seemed happy about playing host to a delegation from the FDA, but they nonetheless did so politely, Gary Light's altercation with Rich Cooper notwithstanding. The reception at Brown & Williamson was very different.

Mitch organized the details of the trip in a series of phone calls to Kendrick Wells, the company's in-house counsel. Mitch noticed that Wells seemed almost flat, devoid of personality, but he thought little of it at the time and was not anticipating any problems. They agreed on a two-day visit. Unlike Philip Morris and RJR, Brown & Williamson laid down no ground rules to limit the range of our questioning. No topic was declared off-limits. We had every reason to believe that this trip would prove to be our most fruitful yet.

THE FDA team was escorted into a conference room where the Brown & Williamson staff was waiting. Along with experts in leaf purchasing, cigarette manufacturing, and research and development, several attorneys were present. Gordon Smith and Gene Pfeifer (another ex-FDA lawyer) were both with the law firm of King & Spalding. Kendrick Wells headed the delegation.

Wells had thinning gray hair and pallid skin and he wore a gray suit. One of our informants had described him as the keeper of the company's secrets. A different metaphor came to Jack Mitchell, who immediately suspected that Wells knew where the bodies were buried. Kevin Budich thought him cantankerous and hostile. Mitch Zeller described him as a malevolent figure and nicknamed him "Doctor Death."

The atmosphere, if not friendly, was initially polite. But from the outset the company declined to answer certain questions, and as the meeting wore on, more and more of them were deferred or refused. With each unanswered question, adversarial feelings mounted.

By 11 A.M. the mood had worsened markedly. Kevin Budich, who had spent more than a decade doing in-the-field investigations for the FDA, asked about the use of extracts to boost the nicotine content of cigarettes. Kendrick Wells's response was swift and his tone sneering. Tobacco extract, he declared, contained such minute amounts of nicotine that it could not be measured in B&W's own laboratories, and it certainly had no effect whatsoever on the smoker. Tobacco extract was added, he said, solely to improve the taste of lower-grade tobacco. He said the company had previously disclosed full details of its tobacco extract usage to the Centers for Disease Control, and there was nothing to warrant further discussion.

Kevin knew this was a delicate subject, but he was unprepared for the vehemence of the reply. Wells's strident and contemptuous insistence that any investigation into the use of tobacco extract would prove to be a dead end made all the investigators wonder what he was hiding.

Wells may have genuinely thought we were wrong about tobacco extracts, or perhaps he was just less capable than the others of concealing his unhappiness at being forced to play host to the FDA. Bob Spiller guessed that Wells had occupied his position with Brown & Williamson long enough to remember when the companies could keep information off the record without being challenged and resented the shift. Whatever the reason for his anger, Wells began to pace the conference room and then he made an entirely unexpected announcement. We can't give you a second day, he said. We have a company to run here. The two-day visit had just been cut in half.

WHEN lunchtime came, Wells suggested a long break, during which the FDA team and the Brown & Williamson staff would dine separately. Infuriated by the abrupt cancellation of the second day, Mitch insisted on a shorter break; no one objected to sitting apart. Talking quietly, aware that they might be overheard, the investigators deliberated during lunch about the best use of their little remaining time and agreed on a list of questions to ask.

Then came a factory tour. Wells took long strides through the plant, staying ahead of his charges and mumbling to himself, clearly agitated. After their rapid run-through, the meeting reconvened in the conference room.

Mitch asked questions, many covering topics that had been raised and rebuffed earlier in the visit.

During the last round of questioning, Mitch passed a scribbled note to Bob. "We have been subjected to a much more sophisticated time-wasting here than at either PM or RJR," he wrote. At least Philip Morris and R.J. Reynolds had honored the agreed-upon terms of the visits. The team members simply did not understand what had happened to warrant the sudden change of plans. Had they stumbled on some valuable information but failed to recognize it? As they drove away from the Macon plant, everyone felt angry and perplexed. Later, reviewing the meeting, we speculated that at some point Brown & Williamson executives may have concluded that we knew more than they had thought. Perhaps they sensed we were not showing our full hand.

I did not have the same confidence in our own knowledge. One of our informants had suggested some questions, but he had been so sketchy and enigmatic that it was almost impossible to use his hints to advantage. Because we did not understand exactly what we were looking for, we did not know how to press the company for more information. And when the company gave us answers, we had no way to challenge them.

25

THE NETWORK of contacts that Jack Mitchell had carefully cultivated in his years as an investigative journalist and a Senate investigator was paying off. Résumés of industry insiders began to come his way.

Around the time of the first Waxman hearing, he had shown me the curriculum vitae of a Ph.D. biochemist who had once been vice president for research at Brown & Williamson. Jack had blacked out the name. He felt a tremendous sense of responsibility to potential informants, and protecting their confidentiality was always his first priority. I was impressed by the credentials of the scientist, but also cautious. We knew almost nothing about the man except what he had told Jack on the telephone—that he had been lured away from the pharmaceutical industry by Brown & Williamson at a salary of $300,000 a year with the assignment to reduce the toxins in cigarettes; that he began to feel isolated within the company; and that he was fired soon after arguing that coumarin, a tobacco additive, was toxic and should be removed from all B&W products. He looked like a promising contact but we could not be sure his story was true. Nor could we rule out the possibility that he was reporting back to B&W. I was focused on preparing for the hearing at that time and did not push Jack to pursue the lead.

But he stayed in touch with the scientist, who was soon code-named "Research." Over the next few weeks, Research slowly warmed to the idea of talking to the FDA—on two conditions. First, he wanted assurances that he would not be asked about his work with Brown & Williamson, which would have been a direct violation of his confidentiality agreement. He told Jack that industry defectors got "pummeled, discredited, and wound up losing everything they had, both financially and professionally."

His second condition was that he wanted to speak directly with me. He said that he did not want to "deal with anybody down in the bowels of the organization." He wanted to go to the "top of the pyramid." He thought I could benefit from his knowledge and would know what to do with it.

It was a highly unusual request. Although I had sat in on numerous phone interviews and had asked questions along with everyone else, I had never identified myself. Nor had I yet met face-to-face with a confidential informant or questioned one in my official capacity as commissioner. Jack did not close the door to Research's meeting with me in person but said that first he had to be certain of what the scientist knew and what he was willing to tell us. At that point, Research began to open up.

GARY and Tom were angry at the prospect of a private meeting, and they objected forcefully. Although they were cordial and always very professional in their interviews, they had no patience for coddling informants and wondered why Research considered himself special enough to warrant a private audience with the commissioner. A further objection to the meeting was more serious. Suppose, Gary and Tom told me, that Research went to the press and said, "Look, I told this to Dr. Kessler personally." Brown & Williamson might then be able to claim that I had encouraged him to abrogate his confidentiality agreement. The political and legal fallout could be serious.

There was also the possibility that Research was a disgruntled employee out for revenge. He had explained to Jack why he had been fired, but Jack had no way of knowing whether his version was accurate or self-serving. Gary and Tom, ever the cynics, doubted that he was as high-minded as his story suggested.

I knew the risks were real, and I listened closely as Jack, Tom, and Gary argued things out. I probably should have consulted our lawyers, but I did not want to get advice which I then might ignore. Finally, I made up my mind. I would talk to Research.

The visit on May 13, 1994, was a cloak-and-dagger exercise. No one except Jack knew who Research was or how senior he was in the industry. Only a few people at the FDA even knew that he was coming. My calendar for that day identified the appointment simply as, "Cigarettes/Mitchell."

Jack had sent Research a plane ticket by overnight mail. With him, as with all of our informants, we were careful not to pay for anything else; we did not want anyone to say we paid for information. Concerned that his movements might be traced, Research left his house two hours before flight time and took a circuitous route to the airport. Even though he was to be gone only for the day, he parked in a long-term parking lot. When I heard about his preparations, I thought they might be overkill, but I understood his anxiety. Research had already had a preliminary conversation with Henry Waxman's staff, which he dutifully reported to Brown & Williamson, in accordance with the terms of his confidentiality agreement. Soon afterwards, he claimed to have received an anonymous telephone call with the terse message, "Leave tobacco alone or watch your kids." A second threat was allegedly made shortly afterwards, followed by a series of hang-up calls to his unlisted telephone number.

Jack drove out to National Airport to meet Research. The men had exchanged descriptions of themselves, and they recognized each other easily. Research was a round-faced man of about fifty, of average height, stocky, with striking blue eyes and salt-and-pepper hair.

I was waiting for them in my office. Jack sat quietly as I talked to Research informally about his family and educational background. I also went into my own background, but that turned out to be unnecessary. Research had done his homework on me.

After a few minutes, I asked if I could bring in other staff to join us. Jack had warned Research that I would want to do that, and whatever his initial reluctance, he agreed. Mitch, Gary, Tom, and Kevin joined us around the table in my office.

During the first hour, Research talked generally about the cigarette development process and how a company designs a new product or revamps the formula of an old one. He was circumspect and nervous, his eyes darting constantly around the room, as he struggled with how much information to share. But his manner was at odds with his delivery, which was assured, fluent, precise.

Slowly, Research and I began to develop a rapport, partly because of my science background. During interviews with some other informants, Gary and Tom had been furious with me because I pushed too hard. I thought of it as being direct, but the pros called it hammering. With Research, I struck a better balance. After we had been talking for almost two hours, I asked if we could tape the discussion. I had wanted to turn the recorder on much earlier, but had not wanted to risk shutting him down. Research agreed.

For a while, the conversation ran through territory that had become somewhat familiar to us. In clipped and rapid speech, Research talked about impact, irritants, and leaf position, about reconstituted tobacco and the control of nicotine levels during manufacturing. He also mentioned that ammonia facilitates the release of nicotine. Just as I was reaching cerebral overload, Research mentioned plants that had been genetically manipulated for high-nicotine levels. I stopped short. "Did I hear what I think I heard?" I wondered.

Research continued. He explained that there were two ways of breeding for higher nicotine levels—hybridization and genetic engineering. Hybridization, the more traditional agricultural technique, involves crossing different plants and selecting out offspring with certain sought-after characteristics. But it has two problems—first, the process is slow and laborious, and second, hybrids tend to revert back to their original form over time. Genetic engineering, in which a gene for the desired trait is actually inserted into seed, is the newer approach. The methods could sometimes be used in combination, and Research said they had both been involved in producing a flue-cured tobacco with as much as an 8 percent nicotine level.

From my reading, I knew that the average nicotine level in flue-cured tobacco was between 2.5 and 3 percent. Genetic manipulation to achieve higher nicotine levels? I was stunned.

I HAD remained good friends with Jeff Nesbit, who was now working in the private sector but still keeping tabs on our evolving investigation. A few weeks earlier, Jeff had given me an important lead. He told me that a friend had been at a party with a prominent Washington tobacco lobbyist and had overheard him boasting that the FDA was looking in the wrong place. "It all begins in the fields," he said.

Now Research seemed to be confirming that. Without scaring him off, I wanted to learn as much as I could. First, I needed to put a name on the high-nicotine plant. Research made me work for information, often using jargon I did not understand, but I had already learned how to pose questions that he was willing to answer. "Let's do a make-believe formula of a cigarette," I said. "This stuff is both hybridized and genetically engineered. What do I call it?"

Y-1, or something like that, Research suggested.

Next, I needed to understand how the breeding was actually done. Research mentioned a genetic engineering firm in New Jersey but refused to identify it by name or to elaborate on its role in Y-1. I quickly moved back to safer ground, leading him into a discussion of agronomy. He told us about *Nicotiana rustica*, identifying it as a type of naturally high-nicotine tobacco that had been used in hybrid crosses. Research emphasized that *N. rustica* was agronomically weak and tended to be scrawny and limp, with a high susceptibility to disease and rot. On top of that, smoke from *N. rustica* was very harsh.

I asked what tobacco strains could be crossed with *N. rustica*. Look at the work of James Chaplin, he urged. I was already familiar with the name. Chaplin was a tobacco scientist formerly with the U.S. Department of Agriculture's Tobacco Research Laboratory in Oxford, North Carolina, and I had encountered his work while reading old tobacco journals. I knew that Chaplin had done extensive experiments with low-nicotine hybrids in the 1970s, but I had not read any studies with high-nicotine plants.

I began pushing Research about where genetically altered plants might actually have been grown. He mentioned several domestic farms, but hinted that the plant might have been grown in South America in larger quantities. That made sense. Under a government-sponsored price support tobacco program in this country, the nicotine content of tobacco had to fall within a certain range. The plants he was describing far exceeded the prescribed level.

Growing impatient, I asked more pointed questions. How would the seeds of this experimental tobacco be transported to the southern hemisphere? Where could I find records documenting their export? There probably were no records, Research said. As a result of a federal law designed to protect American tobacco farmers, it had been illegal through 1991 to ship seed out of the country without a permit, and those seeds could only be used for experimental purposes.

How could we find out where the plant had been cultivated? All Research would reveal was that Souza Cruz, a company located in a city of the same name and owned by British American Tobacco, was the largest producer of tobacco in Brazil. Research also said the seeds had been rendered sterile to protect them from competitors who might otherwise try to reproduce the plants.

Where would a high-nicotine tobacco, possibly grown in Souza Cruz, Brazil, enter this country? And how could we identify it from a customs invoice? Research did not know the port of entry.

I asked what cigarette brands might have used this high-nicotine tobacco. Research refused to name names.

Who would know more? A lot of people, said Research—the blenders, the developers, the leaf purchasers, the farmers who grew it experimentally.

Who would talk to us? Did he know anyone who had retired recently or had been fired? Research said that a lot of people were being laid off at B&W in the course of the company's move from Louisville to new quarters in Macon, Georgia. (Soon afterwards, he gave us one of our most valuable tools, a company telephone book.)

Five hours flew by before our conversation came to a close. Although I had only the beginnings of the Y-1 story, I knew I was hearing something important. As Research was readying to leave, he paused and advised me to watch the mail. He said that someone was sending us a large, white envelope containing some documents that we might find useful. Jack drove Research to the airport.

I ASKED the mailroom to keep a watchful eye. Eventually, someone spotted an orphaned package with my name handwritten on it. It had arrived much earlier and then sat unattended for days.

The envelope contained a selection of internal Brown & Williamson documents dealing with ammonia technology. Philip Morris and R. J. Reynolds were mentioned, making it clear that B&W was not alone in its work. A legal memo analyzed ammonia compounds, and sections from the *Handbook for Leaf Blenders*, code-named *Root Technology*, described a secret project utilizing ammonia to increase the potency of nicotine. That document was particularly explicit: ammonia, it said, "can liberate free nicotine from the blend which is associated with increases in impact and satisfaction." The subject of diammonium phosphate (DAP), an ammonia compound, had arisen before. Mitch had seen pipes labeled DAP at Philip Morris, and we had asked about it during our Brown & Williamson visit. B&W had deflected our questions, explaining that DAP was merely used to regulate the speed at which a cigarette burns. Now, we had documents suggesting otherwise. Apparently, the industry was looking for ways to intensify the effect of nicotine without increasing the amounts used.

Research never admitted actually sending us the package, but he certainly knew plenty about the subject. At a second meeting, he explained that ammonia acted as a scavenger to enhance the transfer and release of nicotine and speculated that it was the ingredient that gave Marlboro its appeal, helping to make it the most popular cigarette in the world. The chemists in our St. Louis lab later explained that ammonia made it possible to "free base" nicotine. This process changed the charge on the nicotine molecule, thus increasing the rate at which nicotine was absorbed into the bloodstream.

Jack Mitchell eventually got hold of the entire *Handbook for Leaf Blenders* and other documents that discussed ammonia, but he refused to reveal his source to me. He was visibly nervous when he handed me a brown accordion folder. Perhaps because I felt that I had just been entrusted with a rare and secret archive, or perhaps because I thought there might be some controversy about our access to these documents, I put gloves on and used a pencil eraser to flip through the pages. Within minutes, I realized the lunacy of my behavior, pulled off the gloves, and began to read.

RESEARCH urged me to look through patents to find documentation of Y-1. I pushed Carol Knoth, our librarian, feeding her every keyword I could think up. If the patent existed in the database, I was determined to find it. Carol found 286 patents in Brown & Williamson's name and 105 for British American Tobacco, but none of them was relevant. There were also thirty-six patents in the name of DNA Plant Technology, or DNAP, a New Jersey genetic engineering firm that Research had identified, but they, too, seemed irrelevant. I started pushing Research for names, and he told me that Roger Black, the chief blender at B&W, was in charge of the Y-1 project. His predecessor had been Phillip Fisher, who was now retired. On the DNAP side, he identified Janet Bravo as the Y-1 project manager and thought that she might be on leave from the company. As a bench scientist, Bravo had conducted a lot of the early experiments, helped to harvest the seed, and visited the farms where the experimental tobacco was grown. Research thought Bravo might be willing to talk. He doubted we could get to Fisher or Black. Research also said we should talk to "Chappy," the USDA scientist James Chaplin.

Research told us that B&W had enough seeds to grow Y-1 commercially and that field trials, or "scale-ups," had taken place on small, experimental farms in Wilson, North Carolina, and Cynthiana, Kentucky. I wanted the names of farmers on whose land the trials had taken place, but the only one Research could recall was Jones. I laughed at the idea of Farmer Jones and wondered how much of Research's story was actually true.

Then I asked how we could put our hands on an actual tobacco leaf with a genetically bred high-nicotine content. Research said we had to find it before it entered the manufacturing process; after that, it became an indistinguishable part of the blend.

"There's an inventory here in the United States of 6.2 million pounds," he claimed. That quantity, or anything close to it, suggested that Y-1 was far more than an experiment, that high-nicotine plants were being actively used in cigarette manufacture.

We were making incremental progress, but we were dogged by unanswered questions. We were still a long way from hard evidence that tobacco had been genetically bred for high-nicotine, grown offshore, using seeds that had been exported from the United States, then shipped back, blended into tobacco, and added to an American cigarette that was sold commercially. We did not know who had developed the high-nicotine seeds in the first place, nor who had carried them abroad illegally. I did not know what James Chaplin's role had been, and we had not yet determined the relationships among DNAP, Chaplin, and Brown & Williamson.

As I was winding down my second long interview with Research, I asked him if he knew of any B&W employees who might talk to us. He mentioned several likely prospects. Then, I began rifling through company documents, asking Research to identify people who were mentioned.

I had read halfway down the list when I asked, "Who's Jeff Wigand?" The name meant nothing to me at that moment.

Research looked around the room with a smile. Not appreciating the lengths to which our office had gone to preserve the confidentiality of its informants, he assumed I was joking. When no one smiled back, it dawned on him that I was serious. "I'm Jeff Wigand," he said.

26

PERHAPS even more important to our investigation than Wigand was a sarcastic and streetwise Brown & Williamson employee code-named "Macon." On May 24, Tom reached Macon through the company switchboard, but the scientist would not talk from the office. Their first real conversation unfolded slowly that evening. Macon had been with the company for many years, but still felt like something of an outsider.

Deliberately playing dumb, Tom asked his new contact how a low-tar cigarette could be made without losing its all-important "impact."

"You pump the nicotine," Macon said.

"How would you do that?" asked Tom. At that point, the informant became coy, answering Tom's question with another. "How do you think you do it?" came the response. Then Macon relented and said, "You would create a high-nicotine tobacco."

"Did they do it?"

Macon's cat-and-mouse game continued. "What do you think?"

"I think they would."

"You're right, they would." The chemist confirmed the existence of a program, ten years in the making, to engineer a high-nicotine tobacco plant. Macon said that B&W had successfully grown Y-1 in Brazil. Tom scheduled a conference call with the rest of the tobacco team.

CAROL Knoth patiently plugged away at the patent databases, trying some of the names that Wigand had given us, but she kept coming up empty. Finally, we asked, "Why does it have to be a U.S. patent?" The obvious answer was that the tobacco company involved would want to protect its interests in this country, but we had begun to wonder if a foreign patent might also exist. Carol broadened her search. Still nothing. Thinking the name Janet Bravo might somehow be wrong, she entered just the word "Bravo." That did it. Finally, after 450 unsuccessful searches, she found a patent in the name of Janis E. Bravo, Phillip R. Fisher, and Hubert A. Hardison. It was called "Genetically Stable Variety of Tobacco and Tobacco Plant."

We sent the listing directly to a patent service in Arlington, Virginia, asking for the abstract. That firm had to call in another service in the Netherlands, but before long we had the abstract in hand. Although the copy was barely legible and written in Portuguese, it made a clear reference to Y-1.

The next step was to obtain the full patent from Brazil. I asked our international affairs staff to track it down, but days passed with no sign of it. One explanation was that it was festival time in Brazil, and no one was working in the patent office. Another day, I heard that State Department protocol had to be considered. I was getting one excuse after another, running up against bureaucracy within my own agency. I finally lost my temper and summoned the international affairs staff to my office. "Either find me that patent, or get on a plane to Brazil and find it there," I said icily. Soon, I had the patent in my hand.

I did not have to speak Portuguese to know what we had: *A caracteristica importante que distingue a Y-1 ... de nicotina significativemente mais.* I quickly had the patent translated. Some of the language was arcane, but it confirmed what Wigand had suggested. According to the patent, Y-1 was

> ... a new variety of flue-cured tobacco that combines a high nicotine content and good agronomic and morphological characteristics. In addition, when this new variety is cured and processed by conventional processes and incorporated into a cigarette, it was found that the cigarette, when smoked, had an agreeable and acceptable taste and smell, unlike other tobaccos with high nicotine contents. The nicotine content of the leaf of this variety is usually higher than approximately 6 percent by weight on the basis of the dry weight of the leaf, which is significantly higher than any normal variety of tobacco grown commercially.

Armed with the patent, I knew we needed to speak with the patent holders. Mitch and Gary paid an unannounced visit to Janis Bravo at her New Jersey home. They arrived in the early evening in the midst of a pounding rainstorm, checked into a motel, and then drove out to her house, looking for all the world like a pair of overenthusiastic insurance agents making an evening call.

Bravo's husband met them at the door and, apparently taking pity on their sodden state, invited them in. To their surprise, Janis Bravo agreed to speak with them. They seated themselves in the living room, with Bravo some distance away in a rocking chair. Mitch and Gary decided not to take notes, rather than risk breaking the rapport they had quickly established. They listened with rapt attention as she breathed life into the patent.

Bravo described herself as the lead DNAP person for Y-1 throughout the life of the project. Her story differed from Wigand's in only one important way: DNAP had nothing to do with breeding a high-nicotine plant, she claimed. That work had already been done by the time the company entered the picture. She did not know who had actually done it, but DNAP had been hired by Brown & Williamson to make the Y-1 plant disease-resistant and male-sterile. In that form, the plant could generate seeds that would only produce pollen-free plants, giving competitors no reason to steal them, since they could not be reproduced.

Bravo said that DNAP had produced ten pounds of Y-1 male-sterile seed for B&W. It did not sound like a large amount until we understood that a tobacco seed is virtually the size of a speck of dust. Somewhere between five and seven pounds of the seeds had been shipped to Brazil for pilot production; the remainder had been sent to Louisville, where, under proper conditions, it could be stored indefinitely. Bravo said that she had visited some experimental farms in North Carolina and Kentucky where Y-1 was growing and had been to Brazil several times, as had James Chaplin and Phillip Fisher. She said she had dealt with them and also with Roger Black of B&W, characterizing all her contacts with the company as "low-level." Bravo described Y-1 as looking like a standard flue-cured tobacco plant but scrawnier, with smaller leaves. She claimed to have seen only small-scale experimental plots in Brazil and said she would be surprised if it were in mass production.

Although Mitch and Gary thought she was credible in her statement that B&W had already developed Y-1 before asking DNAP to make it pollen-free, they doubted her parallel claim that she did not know its nicotine content. And they were skeptical of her assertions that DNAP had neither performed any chemical analyses of Y-1 nor received that information from B&W.

Still, Bravo had been enormously helpful. We now had a patent holder who confirmed that a high-nicotine tobacco had actually been grown.

I DECIDED it was time to look for tangible evidence that Y-1 had entered this country. We knew we were not going to get documents from B&W. Nor was it likely that we would find a bale of tobacco leaves helpfully labeled "Y-1" in a warehouse somewhere. We needed to trace a paper trail through U.S. Customs and to hope that somewhere on it would be a reference to this high-nicotine tobacco.

I called the Office of Criminal Investigations and had them send over Tim Long, who had just been recruited from the Customs Service to help the agency track food and drug imports into the country. I told Tim what we knew about Y-1 and asked him to search for evidence that B&W had imported it into the country.

The Customs Service electronically collects a formal entry for every commodity import into the United States valued at over $1,000. Thousands of entries come in every day. Over the next few days, with help from his former boss at U.S. Customs, Tim devised a "data dump" to identify every tobacco importation in the last ten years. For fear of missing the crucial record, they wanted a complete list before sorting out Brown & Williamson–specific documents since the patent date of 1989. It took almost a week just to generate that data. And this was only a start. The name "Y-1" would likely appear only on the import invoice, if at all, and not on the computer record. That meant visiting every port anywhere in the country where B&W had received a shipment from overseas. Tim would have to visually inspect every single document.

Having launched Tim on his customs search, I turned my attention to Macon. When my conference call with the B&W employee began, I was still living mostly in a world of theory and possibility. By the time the call was complete, I knew how crucial Y-1 was to our investigation.

Macon had a cynical edge. As direct as Wigand was enigmatic, the informant called the Y-1 project "ill-conceived" and "dumb." Almost from its inception, Macon doubted that the costs and time involved in developing a genetically engineered strain of tobacco would ever pay off for the company. Nonetheless, the scientist had watched the clandestine development of Y-1 from the front row.

According to Macon, an early experiment using Y-1 in Barclay cigarettes had been disappointing; the product tasted terrible. But it certainly had impact. Y-1-enriched Barclay delivered "a buzz and a half," Macon said. "It would knock off your socks." To minimize the harshness while maintaining the sought-after "satisfaction," Macon told us that B&W had also tried to use Y-1 as expanded tobacco, which is cigarette filler pumped up with carbon dioxide. The first tests had been run in Viceroy 100s.

Our conversation drifted to the marketing side of B&W's business. Macon described charts that identified the age, sex, race, and income level of the sought-after consumer population for each brand. For example, the prototypical Kool smoker was a white male factory worker between the ages of forty-five and sixty, with an income below $25,000. The Barclay smoker was a white male white-collar worker, thirty-five to forty-five, with an income between $25,000 and $35,000. Salem was targeted at white females. Newport was aimed at blacks. The companies were a little more careful about age targets, Macon said, but they identified "starter brands" intended to appeal to "newcomers."

It was a fascinating digression, but I wanted to return to Y-1. "What is the status of Y-1 today?" I asked.

"Right now, it is in production," Macon stated confidently.

That was a bombshell. If we could show that Y-1 was actually being added to the cigarettes of American smokers, we would have direct evidence of nicotine manipulation.

Macon had done some homework to back up the assertion. On the basis of a review of the company's computer records, the informant stated that Y-1 was being used commercially in Raleigh King, Raleigh King Lights, Viceroy 100s, Viceroy King, Viceroy Lights King, Richland King, and Richland Lights King. It was an extraordinary claim—if we could prove it.

And there was more. Y-1 had been added to several of those brands only recently—in fact, just three days before the April 14 CEO hearing. "It looks like they are trying to use it up," Macon guessed. "With all the hearings going on, you really don't want to get tagged with a genetically engineered high nicotine flue-cured grade."

At first, I questioned the plausibility of this contention. If Y-1 were that controversial, I asked why the company would add it to more cigarette brands, rather than simply destroying the storehouse of tobacco. Macon's answer involved logistics and money. With millions of pounds of the stuff, getting rid of it was not a simple task. "You'd have to have a big bonfire or a big landfill," said Macon. Either way, B&W would be calling attention to its activities, as well as sacrificing profits.

Instead, the company defied production norms by using the same tobacco blend in numerous brands. The goal was to reduce the existing Y-1 inventory as quickly as possible. Macon also said the company had canceled its future agricultural contracts. Eventually, I saw Brown & Williamson documents confirming those facts. One memo, addressed to colleagues in Rio and Souza Cruz and dated April 19, 1994, just five days after the CEO hearing, read, "This is to confirm that B&W will not have a Y-1 requirement for the crop year 1994–95 and it is unlikely we will resume growing Y-1 in the future." Another described three blending options "to deplete B&W's Y-1 inventory." Following a technical description, the memo concluded, "Please read and destroy."

DURING our conference call, Macon offered a possible reason why we had been unable to find a U.S. patent. The informant thought that an application working its way through the approval process had been withdrawn only a month before.

"No more Y-1 contracts and they canceled the patent," stated Macon. We went back and looked at the Brazilian patent for clues. On my initial read, I had missed the significance of a number series on the first page but I now recognized it as a patent application number and asked our general counsel's office to request a copy from the U.S. Patent and Trademark Office.

Meanwhile, we decided to make contact with the other individuals listed on the Brazilian patent. On Saturday, May 28, two days after the Macon interview, Mitch reached Hubert Hardison at home.

The two men spoke for about fifteen minutes. Hardison sounded surprised to receive a call from the FDA, but not uneasy. Now retired, he had been a vice president for Export Leaf Technology, a company that had originally done tobacco research under contract with B&W and had subsequently been acquired by the company. Back in 1981, Hardison heard James Chaplin describe his *Nicotiana rustica* crosses at a tobacco industry conference. Hardison was intrigued and asked Chaplin to send him some sample seeds.

Mitch hung up with the strong sense that we needed to talk to James Chaplin. All of our Y-1 connections identified him as a key player. But first we scheduled another telephone interview with Jeff Wigand, which took place on June 1, the Wednesday after the long Memorial Day weekend. The big news from that conversation was the turmoil at B&W. "The company is going crazy," Wigand told us. Everyone had worked over the holiday. "The lawyers were in. The research guys were in. The marketing guys were in." He did not know what was going on but thought they might have gotten wind of the direction our investigation was taking.

During the team's visit to the company facilities weeks earlier, the team members had specifically asked whether B&W had conducted any genetic testing to raise or lower the nicotine content of tobacco plants. Initially, the response had been an unequivocal denial. After a pause, Kendrick Wells offered to clarify the answer. While Brown & Williamson did not itself do any such research, it may have supported some university studies into genetic breeding and engineering. His caution did not pass unnoticed, but nothing more was said. Now, the company must have realized how much we had learned.

27

As NEW INFORMANTS emerged and our investigation expanded, I began to realize that we were striking at the heart of a carefully constructed forty-year-old industrywide fiction designed to defend a product at all costs. The more I understood about nicotine, the more I wanted to understand the history of the narrative. At first I thought delving into the past was a diversion of only academic interest. But as I read everything I could find, I discovered parallels between the industry's approach to the pharmacological properties of nicotine and its early responses to the link between cigarettes and cancer.

THE dangers of cigarettes first came to widespread public attention in the early 1950s. At an historic meeting on December 8, 1953, a series of medical presentations linked smoking and cancer. Alton Ochsner, president of the American Cancer Society and the American College of Surgeons, predicted that unless steps were taken to remove the cancer-producing factor from cigarettes, the male population of the United States would be decimated. Scientists Ernst Wynder and Evarts Graham presented the results of mouse painting studies that demonstrated that mice whose bodies are painted with smoke condensates developed tumors.

This was revolutionary news. At the time, a link between smoking and cancer had not been acknowledged by the National Cancer Institute, the U.S. Public Health Service, or many distinguished members of the medical and scientific communities. At the nation's tobacco companies, there was talk of a conspiracy afoot to damage one of America's great agricultural products. Publicly, the industry quickly rebutted Ochsner's charges.

But its private face looked very different. At R. J. Reynolds, one top executive studied the evidence and wrote a detailed report that was circulated internally earlier that year, before Ochsner's presentation. "Studies of clinical data tend to confirm the relationship between heavy and prolonged tobacco smoking and incidence of cancer of lung," wrote Claude Teague. Teague believed that RJR's general counsel had the report "collected and destroyed."

A week after Ochsner's speech, six tobacco company presidents descended on the Plaza Hotel in New York to take stock of the threats they were facing. That meeting was followed by others with John Hill, founder of the public relations firm Hill & Knowlton. In those strategy sessions, the seeds were planted for what one tobacco company lawyer privately described as "the industry's ultimate public relations sham." It became the largest and longest-running public relations effort in the nation's history.

In the spring of 1994, hoping to learn more, I sent two FDA investigators across the continent to meet with a marketing professor named Richard Pollay at the University of British Columbia in Vancouver. Pollay was known as the "king of advertising," and his office was filled with memorabilia, including replicas of the Pillsbury dough boy, the Jolly Green Giant, and the Energizer Bunny. M&M and Coca-Cola Christmas tree lights draped his bookshelves. Pollay had studied John Hill's archives extensively, trying to understand how the tobacco industry had responded to the mounting scientific evidence linking cigarettes to lung cancer.

I next asked the FDA's historian to contact the Wisconsin Historical Society, where all of Hill's papers were housed. Soon we had copies of all of them. An early Hill & Knowlton memo put the challenge to the tobacco industry in psychological terms:

> There is only one problem—confidence and how to establish it; public assurance, and how to create it—in a perhaps long interim when scientific doubts must remain. And, most important, how to free millions of Americans from the guilty fear that is going to arise deep in their biological depths—regardless of any pooh-poohing logic—every time they light a cigarette.

Hill & Knowlton viewed its tobacco industry clients as remarkably unsophisticated about how the new scientific findings would change their world. Few in the industry knew much about lung cancer, and most still believed they would be able to respond to the charges with familiar techniques; small distortions of scientific facts and the strategic use of selected research and favorable quotes were techniques specifically mentioned.

But the firm recognized that its client was in danger and outlined four strategies for dealing with scientific critics: "(a) smearing and belittling them; (b) trying to overwhelm them with mass publication of the opposed viewpoints of other specialties; (c) debating them in the public arena; or (d) we can determine to raise the issue far above them, so they are hardly even mentioned; and then we can make our real case." In the end, each of these tactics was employed.

Hill & Knowlton had the tricky task of finding a way to identify the tobacco companies with a concern for the public good. The firm understood the challenge: "Honesty in science requires careful consideration and weighing of all points of view. The cigarette companies cannot hope to sponsor any public debate over cause and effect that would satisfy both smokers and scientists." Still, something had to be done.

The industry's first visible step was to run a full-page advertisement in 448 leading newspapers in 258 cities across the country. Titled "A Frank Statement to Cigarette Smokers," the ad read, "We accept an interest in people's health as a basic responsibility, paramount to every other consideration in our business. We always have and always will cooperate closely with those whose task it is to safeguard the public health." Accordingly, the ad announced an industrywide initiative to fund research into all phases of tobacco use and health. The proposal implied that the industry would pursue knowledge, wherever it might lead.

The Tobacco Industry Research Committee, later renamed the Council for Tobacco Research (CTR), was launched.

CLARENCE Cook Little, whom John Hill recruited as CTR's first scientific director, was an internationally renowned Harvard-educated cancer researcher and former university president. He had founded the Roscoe B. Jackson Laboratory on Mt. Desert Island in Maine, a pioneering facility for genetic research into cancer. Little had also played leadership roles at both the National Cancer Institute and the American Cancer Society.

The industry could not have invented a more effective spokesman. As intended, his stellar reputation helped attract other illustrious scientists to CTR's ten-member scientific advisory board. With his credibility and stature, all Little had to say was "It is not proven" and a shadow of a doubt could be cast over charges that smoking caused cancer. And that was all the industry hoped for—what came to be known as "the deadly delusion of an open controversy."

It scarcely mattered that most medical professionals accepted the new findings about cancer and cigarettes. For more than four decades, the industry continued to maintain that the link between smoking and ill health remained an open question. That claim was crucial to its unblemished record of victories in lawsuits filed by smokers and their heirs. "Everyone was molded according to the script," one industry official later told me. The industry knew that although, in the abstract, juries viewed the industry as a "venal and evil empire," they were also inclined to view smoking as a personal decision, making them reluctant to favor smokers in their verdicts. The defense capitalized on those reservations by developing arguments, often supported by paid scientists, built on the supposed uncertainties about the causes of cancer. Recognizing that they could not defeat the "cigarettes cause cancer" hypothesis, the attorneys could argue instead that "association cannot prove causation." As an analogy, one wrote, "[Y]ou can eliminate all standing water in the tropical and temperate zone to stop malaria...maybe you stopped or ameliorated the incidence of the disease, but you did not find the simple thing that caused it."

Building on that principle, industry lawyers spent millions of dollars trying to wear down their opponents in court. As the law firm of Jones, Day, Reavis & Pogue stated explicitly in a four-hundred-page analysis of corporate conduct, "The key defense strategy in smoking and health litigation is (and must be) to try the plaintiff." For example, one jury was told that Agent Orange or occupational exposure to chemicals might have caused a plaintiff's lung cancer. That the defense lawyers knew there was no detailed evidence of these exposures scarcely mattered. "A little alternative causation evidence goes a long way," according to an industry analysis of that case. "All of the jurors expressed doubts about the role of smoking." Not surprisingly, few cases ever reached a jury.

"Among friends," read a document drafted for the Tobacco Institute, many believe the industry has no "adequate defense." That did not stop it from presenting one. As damning charges continued to be leveled against cigarettes, CTR and its public relations allies responded with carefully worded statements that stressed contradictory evidence and emphasized knowledge gaps. Scientific experts were assigned specifically to find loopholes in arguments being advanced in litigation. Researchers were pressured not to publish critical findings, and when negative press reports appeared, CTR representatives met with the publication's editorial board to ask for equal time. These efforts worked, at least in the minds of some, and at least for a while. It was decades before the vast majority of the American public was fully persuaded that the risks of smoking were genuine.

I could not understand how C. C. Little, a man schooled in the scientific method, with a track record in cancer research, could stomach these strategies in his capacity as CTR's scientific director. At my request, the FDA's staff historian contacted her colleagues at the Jackson Laboratory and soon handed me a thick stack of Little's private papers. They offered few insights, but I learned that I was not alone in my bewilderment. An emotional letter from Charles Huggins, a Nobel laureate cancer researcher at the University of Chicago, struck me as particularly poignant. Huggins opened with an encomium, writing of his "boundless admiration" for Little. But then he pleaded, "Please leave [the] tobacco industry to stew in its own juice. [The] tobacco industry is criminal to promote smoking.... Only a knave or a fool can support [the] tobacco industry. It is dastardly. This is the Age of the Hollow Man. Let it not be known as the age when our finest thinkers sell out."

DESPITE the Council for Tobacco Research's attempt to follow the aggressive public relations strategy laid out by John Hill, new scientific evidence continued to accumulate. A crisis for the industry came in 1964, when the Surgeon General released the now-famous report that changed history by definitively linking smoking and cancer.

I bought an old copy at a used-book store in Bethesda. The findings were unequivocal. The average smoker had a nine- to tenfold increased risk of developing lung cancer, a heavy smoker at least a twentyfold increase in risk. Smoking far outweighed any other risk factor for lung cancer. Cigarette smoking, the report declared, was a health hazard of sufficient importance for the government of the United States to take appropriate remedial action.

Although the tobacco companies had no illusions about the dangers of the Surgeon General's report, Hill & Knowlton staff proposed a curious response—mailing a copy to every citizen in the country. The public relations experts counseled the industry to embrace the report, without necessarily agreeing with its conclusions. Their idea was to convey the message that adults should understand their risks and accept the responsibility of intelligent decision-making. Industry officials were outraged at the suggestion.

The head of public relations at Philip Morris had other ideas. "We must in the near future provide some answers which will give smokers a psychological crutch and a self-rationale to continue smoking." A further goal was "to point up weaknesses in the Report," and to identify contradictions and discrepancies.

Another company executive alerted his colleagues to a comment buried in the report: "There is no acceptable evidence that prolonged exposure to nicotine creates either dangerous functional change of an objective nature or degenerative disease." As it happened, that was not entirely true—there is an association between nicotine and the risk of cardiovascular disease. And in the fall of 2000, researchers suggested that nicotine could be directly converted to a potent lung carcinogen in the body. But none of that was known at the time, and the industry understood the importance of the Surgeon General's statement at once. For the moment, nicotine had been cleared of suspicion as a carcinogen.

AT each of our three visits to the tobacco companies, the lawyers had been very much in evidence. Now, as I plunged into the history of the industry, I realized how the power of those lawyers had expanded over the years.

Disappointed with CTR's output, David Hardy, of Shook, Hardy & Bacon, started searching for ostensibly independent scientists and physicians willing to accept the industry's position and to testify against the findings of the Surgeon General's report before Congress. In 1964 the Special Projects initiative got under way.

Born as an ad hoc response to the Surgeon General's report, Special Projects became a tool to defend the industry against the barrage of product liability suits that could put it out of business. Special Projects grants created a network of consultants, friendly witnesses whose interpretations of scientific studies always managed to be favorable to the industry. ("Rented white coats," said my high-level industry source, Veritas, during one of our discussions.) Enormous sums of money, millions of dollars in some cases, were paid to scientists and physicians willing to help the industry cast doubt on the health hazards of cigarettes. Experts who testified in congressional hearings and at other public forums on the industry's behalf were assigned a "keeper," a lawyer who carefully stage-managed public presentations. "The decision to have lawyers police the health controversy was probably a wise one," commented one Philip Morris official in a presentation to the company's board.

It took me time to piece together the nature of this amorphous entity. Special Projects had no official address, no incorporation papers, no board of directors, no by-laws, and no accountability. But industry documents showed that a Committee of Counsels, comprising the general counsels of the tobacco companies, were in charge, with a substantial amount of assistance from outside lawyers. Attorneys from Shook, Hardy and from the Washington, D.C., law firm Covington & Burling played prominent roles. Access to the offices of Special Projects was carefully controlled. Every decision, every research project, every public presentation went through the lawyers who worried about just one thing—liability.

"The Committee of Counsels protected the paradigm," Veritas said, referring to his view that industry officials were expected to respond with a single voice to the smoking and health controversy.

"Where did they cross the line?" I asked. After all, lawyers have a professional responsibility to protect their clients.

"When you commission the research and know the outcome, that's fraudulent," he said. "When you market that as the truth, that's evil." Veritas told me that the members of the Committee of Counsels were the high priests of the industry. He said the lawyers controlled what the company CEOs knew and heard.

Special Projects worked both within and apart from the Council for Tobacco Research, which continued to exist as a visible, incorporated grant-making body with a scientific advisory board. At times, the Special Projects lawyers used CTR's imprimatur and alleged independence to gain credibility, but just as often their activities were covert. Much of the Special Projects research had a predetermined outcome. "Clinical studies to be conducted... to show that duration and amount of smoking have no relation to the age of peak incidence of lung cancer," read one notation. The commingling went in the opposite direction as well, as the watchful Committee of Counsels increasingly assumed control over CTR's research grants and the publications that emerged from them. "CTR is NOT independent—because of what we have asked them not to do," a top official at Lorillard stated frankly.

Occasionally, the tactics surprised the uninitiated among the lawyers themselves. I read the comments of a recent law school graduate working at Wachtell, Lipton, another law firm representing the tobacco industry, feeling that I was reading a story of innocence lost. The young lawyer had been asked to review a Lorillard proposal to fund the work of a Georgetown pathologist in order to "keep him happy," even though there was no immediate value to his research. The proposal pointed out that the pathologist was a potential defense witness in a case against the tobacco industry.

The lawyer wondered about the propriety of using industry funds, administered through Shook, Hardy, for this purpose. He questioned whether the funds "were used to purchase favorable judicial or legislative testimony, thereby perpetuating a fraud on the public." Imagining himself for a moment in the role of a plaintiff—"assume the other side of the looking glass," was the phrase he used—he cautiously suggested that perhaps Lorillard was going too far and asked for guidance from his more senior colleagues.

I soon found other sources to substantiate the charge that the industry had put itself in the hands of its lawyers. Letters from David Hardy to the general counsel of Brown & Williamson addressed the risk of litigation. Hardy wrote that damaging statements made by tobacco company officials appeared "to demonstrate a belief on the part of company personnel that cigarette smoking has been established as a general health hazard or cause of some particular disease or diseases." That, he emphasized, would be "fatal to the defense."

I reread the letters. Was Hardy simply advising his client of the consequences of admitting that cigarettes caused cancer? Or was he telling his client what to say? When I showed them to Paulette, the lawyer in her pronounced them "shut-the-hell-up letters." I wondered who was in charge.

I READ every document pertaining to tobacco litigation that I could find in search of clues to industry strategies. One case I studied extensively was *Cipollone v. Liggett Group, Philip Morris, and Loews*, the product liability suit filed in 1983 by Rose Cipollone, a woman who had begun to smoke at age sixteen and whose case was pursued by family members after her death from lung cancer. The case was heard by Judge H. Lee Sarokin of the U.S. District Court in Newark, New Jersey. There, the tobacco industry won an early battle to protect some 1,500 internal documents from release. The defendants successfully argued that the papers, some apparently created by individual companies, others by the Council for Tobacco Research, were protected by attorney-client privilege; as a result, they were placed under court seal.

I saw another reference to that set of documents in a 1992 decision on one of the motions in *Susan Haines v. Liggett Group*, another product liability case. Sarokin was again the presiding judge. After hearing the plaintiffs argue vociferously that the documents should be released, Sarokin began to study them, grappling with a difficult legal question. Were they protected by the attorney-client privilege and therefore not subject to discovery and the inevitable publication that would follow? Or were the industry lawyers trying to cover up evidence of wrongdoing, in which case the privilege did not apply?

The judge was struck, as I was, by the extensive role the industry lawyers played in controlling scientific research at CTR, and in time he became convinced that the true motive was concealment. By deliberately putting certain elements of the tobacco business under the control of the lawyers, the industry was abusing the protection of the attorney-client privilege, he concluded. "The tobacco industry may be the king of concealment and disinformation," wrote Sarokin in his *Haines* opinion. I read and reread his decision, trying to understand more about the fraud that might have been committed.

Rather than releasing the full package of sealed documents, Sarokin decided to reserve the industry's right to confidentiality, pending appeal, and he allowed only five selected examples to become public. "We were afraid of discovery," an industry official said frankly in one of them. "We wanted to protect it under the lawyers. We did not want it out in the open." That was completely consistent with a story that a Philip Morris executive told me years later, about a company lawyer who tried to stamp "attorney-client privilege" on documents that emerged from research and development.

The industry itself acknowledged the public relations character of CTR in another document released by Sarokin. "It was set up as an industry shield .... CTR has helped our legal counsel by giving advice and technical information, which was needed in court trials. CTR has provided spokesmen for the industry at Congressional hearings.... On these projects, CTR has acted as a front."

As it turned out, there were no next steps towards a wider release of the secret papers. The industry went after Sarokin, complaining of bias, and the judge was removed from the *Haines* case in September 1992. The opportunity to break the seal on the elusive 1,500 documents was lost, at least for the moment.

I was not surprised that the tobacco industry used its money to purchase the cachet associated with prestigious institutions. Special Projects grants went to researchers at Harvard, UCLA, and elsewhere. But when I came across the name Sloan-Kettering Institute for Cancer Research, I was crestfallen. I had spent every summer during college working in one of its laboratories and had come to greatly admire Sloan-Kettering.

Beginning in the 1960s and lasting at least until 1970, Philip Morris had shamelessly contributed a total of $200,000 to the venerable New York City medical center, and following Philip Morris's lead, R. J. Reynolds, the American Tobacco Company, Liggett & Myers, Lorillard, and Rothman's, a Canadian brand, had also become generous contributors. I found a Philip Morris memo that mentioned Frank Horsfall, director of Sloan-Kettering, whom I had considered a legend in cancer research. Horsfall had "publicly expressed his doubt that smoking is implicated in carcinoma causation. Dr. Horsfall's opinion (coupled with his demonstrated liking for our Marlboro cigarettes) has been beneficial. As head of the nation's principal cancer research organization, he has tremendous influence."

Philip Morris was quite satisfied with its grants to Sloan-Kettering. One tangible result was to muzzle Ernst Wynder, who had conducted seminal mouse painting studies. According to one memo, Horsfall and other Sloan-Kettering officials began "subjecting Wynder to more rigorous screening procedures before letting him speak in the name of the Institute. This has had a proper and pleasing effect.... The deductible contribution to Sloan-Kettering is probably the most effective of all health research contributions."

Still another alliance involved the American Medical Association. In 1964 the AMA was vigorously lobbying against pending Medicare legislation while the tobacco industry was fighting efforts to place health warnings on cigarette packs. At the same time, the six major companies offered the AMA $10 million over a five-year period to fund research on smoking and health. On February 12, 1964, Francis Blasingame, the AMA's executive vice president, accepted the industry's offer. A little more than two weeks later, Blasingame sent a letter to the Federal Trade Commission, a strong advocate of warning labels. "With respect to cigarettes," he wrote, "cautionary labeling cannot be anticipated to serve the public interest with any particular degree of success."

This peculiar alliance fascinated tobacco executives themselves. "The AMA appears more concerned with safeguarding the financial interests of doctors through political lobbying than with the doctor's patients," observed

Sir Philip Rogers, head of the British Tobacco Association, on a visit to the United States.

If the industry was generous to its friends, it could be ruthless to its perceived enemies. Oscar Auerbach's "smoking dogs" studies, in which he induced cancer in the lungs of beagles, generated a particularly sharp response. With a budget of $500,000, the Tobacco Institute launched an advertising campaign intended to discredit the research and to embarrass the American Cancer Society, which had announced Auerbach's results. Some time later, industry officials also made plans to discuss possible cuts in Auerbach's funding with the Veterans Administration.

Not content to limit their activities to the domestic front, executives of seven tobacco companies met in secret at Shockerwick House, a large country house near Bath, England, in December 1976. They came together to address concerns that they "would be picked off one by one and that the domino theory would impact on all of us," and in the end agreed to create the International Council on Smoking Issues (ICOSI). The goal was to speak with one voice.

IT SEEMEd this industry did nothing by accident. From alliances with business and political leaders to "managing the social climate for tobacco use," the industry developed countless strategies over the years for influencing the national debate over tobacco and deriding its opponents. In media seen by young people it found ways to mock what it called the "new puritanism" and it commissioned a theater group to satirize "political correctness." And the industry tried to shift the argument from a focus on health, which was deemed unwinnable, to broader public policies. Thus, "[C]igarette taxes become an issue of a fair and effective tax policy. . . . [T]obacco marketing becomes an issue of freedom of commercial speech. . . . [T]obacco litigation becomes an issue of business liability reform to foster economic development. . . . [C]igarette-related fires become an issue of prudent fire safety programs."

Liaisons were formed with tourist groups to build support for the view that harsh smoking bans were unsuited to the supposedly more libertine European mentality. There was also a proposal to create "Parents for Priorities," a network of organizations that would push public officials to focus on such issues as crime and education rather than smoking. Though these were striking, there was one that I could hardly believe. The industry had developed a strategy for identifying Islamic religious leaders opposed to an interpretation of the Qur'an that would lead to a ban on tobacco use.

Another idea was a national survey "to determine if the public believes businesses should have the right to accommodate customers as they choose or if government should ban smoking." The intent was to involve a supposedly independent consumer group as sponsor of the surveys, but the industry was taking no chances. "Survey should be pre-tested to gauge response before approaching a sponsoring organization," advised one industry memo.

Notes from Committee of Counsels meetings suggest that proposals by Rosser Reeves, a titan in the field of public relations and advertising, generated particular interest. His proposal to the committee included commissioning books that challenged the links between smoking and health, to be published under the imprint of a mainstream publisher and to be mailed to hundreds of thousands of physicians and scientists. The idea was for industry to advertise the books in intellectual journals and the mass media. Reeves did not care if the books were read; he knew that the ads themselves would be more influential. He also proposed an "editor education" project—moonlighting editors from *Time, Newsweek,* and other magazines would be paid to write reports for the industry on the subsidized books. Reeves understood the benefits of enlisting "janissaries" who would come to "depend on it for their livelihood and whose zeal, consequently, often runs well ahead of their facts."

Reeves's ideas did not come cheap. He put together a $4.7 million proposal, and the Tobacco Institute budgeted millions of dollars to execute it. His objective was ambitious—to create a distorted picture of the world.

Occasionally, industry tactics bordered on the absurd. Guy Smith, the bull-in-the-china-shop whom Sharon Natanblut had encountered in her Burson-Marsteller days, was especially prone to far-fetched thinking. Before Philip Morris's board of directors, Smith enthusiastically championed a strategy he called "geo-attitudinal cluster-based targeting," which he claimed could reach millions of American adults. "Each of the 236 million Americans fits into one of the 40 mind-sets that can be appealed to and activated in support of a position," he said. "As we implement this system we will design measures to motivate people to act for us."

The industry sought allies wherever it could find them—in the ranks of think tanks, lobbyist groups, trade associations, antitax groups, foundations, and journalists in Washington and around the country. Some special interest groups were little more than fronts and relied heavily on tobacco money. More often, strategic links were forged with institutions that were philosophically in agreement with the industry and thus could give both cover and credibility to its positions. "This whole third-party concept in our defense structure is to give us clout, to give us power, to give us credibility, to give us leverage, to give us access where we don't ordinarily have access ourselves," explained a Philip Morris spokesperson. The message was "Be creative," and there was blunt talk about getting a "return on our investment" and the "Machiavellian" characteristics of the indirect approach.

Understanding whom "to neutralize" was part of the process, and explained why Philip Morris made donations to volunteer firefighters. The company claimed to have seen results: firefighters' willingness to say publicly that cigarettes do not cause fires. Philip Morris was also ready to assist when the National Women's Political Caucus asked for support to publish a directory listing all female public officials in the country. "Their priority was that they get credit for it," explained a speaker during one presentation. "That's fine with us. Our priority is that we get to distribute it and [get] open pathways of communications with the people who are listed within the directory."

On and on went the list of alliances, from the Heritage Foundation and the Hoover Institution on War, Revolution and Peace to the Manhattan Institute and the National Association of Manufacturers. Support for the National Journalism Center, which trained journalists in free-market political and economic principles, gave Philip Morris access to "journalists at print and visual media throughout the country . . . which has resulted in numerous pieces consistent with our point of view." Of comparable value were ties to the Washington Legal Foundation, a conservative think tank. "Have them publish an article, . . ." directed one company document. The Washington Legal Foundation also helped to "identify new legal scholars and marketing/public policy experts willing to write . . . 'White Papers,' 'Dear Colleagues' enclosures and testimony on specific tobacco advertising bills as well as on lower and high court decisions."

To reach minority communities, the industry provided support to the National Association of Hispanic Publishers, the National Newspaper Publishers Association, California Hispanic Publishers, West Coast Black Publishers, and the National Federation of Hispanic-Owned Newspapers. Aware of criticism that cigarette advertising was being specifically targeted at minorities, Philip Morris helped advance the argument that such claims were paternalistic and racist. To some extent they succeeded, as was seen at the 1993 meeting of the West Coast Black Publishers Association, where a resolution was passed endorsing the tobacco industry's right to sell its products in the black community. In a letter to Senator Ted Kennedy defending that resolution, the publishers association wrote, "It is offensive to the Black community or any other minority group to suggest that one group of individuals is less capable than another to exercise freedom of choice on whether or not to smoke. . . . There should not be any type of advertising ban against this industry."

International activities included lobbying developing nations and trying to undermine tobacco control efforts by the World Health Organization. "We must try to stop the development towards a Third World commitment against tobacco," wrote one industry official. "We must try to mitigate the impact of WHO by pushing them into a more objective and neutral position."

Perhaps even more chilling was the proposal at Philip Morris not merely to influence the media but to become it. The top-secret idea, part of a broader defensive posture code-named Operation Rainmaker, was to buy media outlets. "If we are to truly influence the public policy agenda and the information flow to the populace, we must be the media, we must be part of it," read notes prepared for a March 1990 meeting. "The only way to do this is to own a major media outlet. If we are not willing to take this step then we are not serious about really wanting to change the atmosphere."

The notes went on to propose an array of possible acquisitions: Knight-Ridder, the Copley News Service, United Press International, the publications controlled by Mort Zuckerman, or a major city daily linked to the international wire services. Philip Morris seriously considered proposals to acquire UPI.

IF MANY in the industry were focused more on image than on substance, the rare individual could be found who genuinely believed that smoking did not cause cancer. Frank Colby was one. Before his retirement from R. J. Reynolds, Colby had run a scientific literature retrieval system that gave him access to virtually everything that had been written about tobacco at any time, anywhere in the world. Industry lawyers used the vast library to find loopholes and contradictions in the statements of potential witnesses. Towards the end of his career, Colby moved onto the payroll of an outside law firm representing the tobacco companies.

Colby agreed to talk to me. He was a short, elderly, gray-haired man with a barrel chest, a bent back, and deep furrows across his forehead. Over lunch he laid out his position clearly, so that there would be no misunderstanding between us.

"We are farther apart now than ever," he said in a heavy German accent. "I totally disagree with your concept that smoking causes disease."

I was not there to argue, but to listen. I asked him to talk about his decades in the industry. As he spoke, I realized that I was dealing with an intelligent and sophisticated man, anything but a scientific hack. He called himself a contrarian, an independent spirit whose position was always in opposition to the accepted wisdom of the times. And it was this contrarian attitude that nurtured his views about the link between smoking and health.

But although he defended RJR's scientific research, Colby said that he had become embittered by the intrusion of the lawyers. In his mind, the Council for Tobacco Research had been a good idea, a place where genuine scientific freedom could exist. But that was not the case with the lawyer-driven Special Projects. To illustrate the point, he asked, "Do you know the story about the destruction of documents?" I did not.

He started talking about Henry Ramm, whose name I had already encountered in industry papers. Ramm had served as the general counsel of RJR for twenty-five years and had engineered much of the company's response to smoking and health issues. According to one document I read, Ramm's one great fear was that his company would do something that would enable the FDA to assert jurisdiction over cigarettes. Colby told me that back in the 1950s, Ramm had escorted him into the vault within the research and development library that contained all of the laboratory note-books. Ramm then ordered Colby to destroy certain documents.

"Which records?" I asked.

"Benzopyrene," said Colby, referring to a chemical carcinogen.

"Why was that?"

The reason was obvious, he said—concern about lawsuits from surviving families whose relatives had died from lung cancer. At first Colby refused Ramm's order to destroy the lab records. Then, remembering that everything had been microfilmed, he agreed.

"Ramm didn't know?"

"Of course not. He was an asshole. And a lawyer, which is synonymous."

His attitude towards lawyers prompted my next question. "Is it true that there was one script for all tobacco industry officials, that everyone really had to follow?"

"More or less, yes," answered Colby. "Certainly everybody had to be saying the same thing."

Despite his low opinion of the industry's lawyers, Colby was profoundly set in his convictions about smoking. He waved the banner of science, but his willingness to seize on bits and pieces of scientific data while ignoring the overwhelming weight of the evidence was profoundly unscientific. He told me, "It would be morally reprehensible to work for a tobacco company and believe cigarettes caused cancer."

28

OUR SEARCH for Y-1 continued. Macon had mentioned an experimental farm in Cynthiana, Kentucky, but we did not know who owned it or exactly where it was. I sent Jim Hunter, from Jack Mitchell's staff, down to Kentucky to see what he could learn.

He went first to a restaurant in the center of town that we heard was a gathering place for local tobacco farmers. Maps in hand, he approached a group of men seated together in the restaurant and asked whether they knew any farmers who were growing experimental tobacco. The group was friendly and open and mentioned a farm owned by "the Barnett boys." Jim spread his maps on the table and one of the farmers showed him exactly where to go, without asking who he was or what he wanted.

Following directions, Jim drove down a dirt road until he came to a farmhouse on a hill. The woman who answered his knock said she was Mrs. Barnett. After identifying himself as an FDA employee, Jim asked if the farm had ever grown experimental tobacco. "You're going to have to talk to my husband," she said quickly, inviting him in for tea.

Within a few minutes, a pickup truck drove across the field and two men got out. The younger was one of the Barnett brothers; the other was his brother-in-law, who had worked for Brown & Williamson for twenty years. When Jim identified himself, the brother-in-law went on the attack almost immediately. The FDA is ruining the tobacco farmer, he said. It has no right to investigate the industry. He was angry and abusive. Jim tried to calm him with words that had become standard in our investigation—the commissioner needs all the facts before making a decision. The man did not let up.

The farmer was more mild-mannered. "I wish you had time for me to show you what tobacco farming is really all about," he said. Jim leapt at the chance for a tour. As he climbed into the truck, the brother-in-law threw out a few more choice words and drove off.

For the next several hours, Barnett showed him his farm. Occasionally, Jim would ask a question about experimental plants, but Barnett recognized that Jim was fishing for information and he did not respond. Instead, he introduced him to his farmhands and gave him a simple lesson about the economics of farming—corn gave him $200 an acre, tobacco, $2,000. Jim asked if he could bring back a few plants. "I want Dr. Kessler to see this tobacco so he'll understand," he explained. Barnett had one of his hands pack up some plants for me.

I BECAME increasingly convinced that James Chaplin, the former USDA scientist, had played an important role in the development of Y-1. Gary called Chaplin and, without identifying our sources, reviewed what we had already learned. Chaplin agreed to talk with us by phone.

We also scheduled a call with DNA Plant Technology officials on the same day, June 10. Janis Bravo's candor had clearly upset her company, and she would not speak to us directly again, referring our calls to David Evans, a DNAP executive. It took several calls before the nervous Evans agreed to a telephone interview.

For both conversations, I needed someone at the table, other than me, who could speak the language of tobacco science. I preferred to avoid visible involvement with our ongoing investigation, although I sometimes took a risk and slipped in questions during a group interview, hoping my voice would not stand out. At other times, I wrote out questions for the team to ask, but I found the procedure frustrating because it was difficult to follow up properly.

I decided the best approach was to teach Mitch and Ann Witt the basics of plant genetics and genetic engineering so that they could ask targeted questions. My view was that anyone could learn anything, and these two were not just anyone; they were two of the smartest lawyers I knew.

A few days before the scheduled interviews, Ann and Mitch sat at the table in the small conference room in my office. I started writing diagrams and explanations on the board. They were very attentive at first, taking notes studiously, but it became clear in short order that they were absorbing almost nothing. Their faces were blank. I refused to give up. I spoke more slowly. I drew on the board. I repeated myself. The blankness in their faces began to give way to more active expressions of resistance. Ann started rolling her eyes; Mitch called me Professor Kessler. I persisted, explaining sexual reproduction in plants and the whole array of new genetic breeding techniques: somaclonal variation, anther culture, protoplast fusion. Finally, Ann declared that she had dropped out of tenth-grade biology. Mitch claimed never to have even taken it. It was a toss-up as to whether they were completely uninterested or, as Mitch later insisted, totally clueless. Either way, I finally gave up.

Still, someone had to take the lead. A member of the tobacco team had a technician bring over a voice synthesizer from the CIA, and I tried talking into it. The voice that came out had a stilted, inhuman, electronic quality; I sounded absolutely ridiculous, like someone who had sucked in too much helium. Although I was quickly convulsed with laughter, the thought of using the synthesizer made me uncomfortable. It was one thing to be on a speakerphone with six or seven other people and not to introduce myself; it was another to pretend to be someone else. I decided to sit in on the Chaplin and DNAP interviews anonymously. The team would have to forge ahead as best it could.

In preparation, I pressed Wigand for more information. He explained that Chaplin's original *Nicotiana rustica* crosses, done in the 1970s, had not panned out. As far as Wigand knew, Chaplin had never been able to grow agronomically viable high-nicotine cultivars. But Wigand believed that viable Y-1 seed had become available in 1988 and had subsequently been transported not only to Souza Cruz, Brazil, but to Zimbabwe as well. Mitch and I followed up that lead, calling the Tobacco Research Board at Kutsaga Research Station in Zimbabwe. Mitch asked an official there about any contracts to grow Y-1 or other high-nicotine tobacco plants. The man who spoke with him acknowledged having worked with Y-1 experimentally, but said he no longer did so and could not discuss it. Still, the call left us a little better off than we had been. We now knew for sure that Y-1 had been grown in Zimbabwe.

WITH the rest of us back in Washington, Gary Light and Jim Hunter drove down to Oxford, North Carolina, to sit with James Chaplin during his interview. We had wanted to talk with Chaplin while he was in his home—people tend to be less guarded there—but he had refused, instead arranging to use a room at the USDA's Tobacco Research Laboratory in Oxford, his former stomping ground. To facilitate the interview, Gary and Jim even brought along their own speakerphone.

At noon, Chaplin appeared. He was a distinguished-looking man of slight build, in his mid-seventies, with gray hair. Before the interview, Gary and Tom had code-named him "Limp," a reference to his straggly high-nicotine *N. rustica* crosses.

At the Parklawn building, Mitch, Ann, and a few others joined me for the Chaplin interview. Gary started with standard questions about his education and experience. Chaplin told us that he had been born and raised on a tobacco farm and that both his master's degree and his Ph.D. had focused on the science of tobacco. He said he had worked for the USDA for almost thirty years, retiring in 1985 as director of the Oxford lab. He had been a consultant ever since, providing services to Brown & Williamson until the early 1990s.

As long as the conversation focused on secondary topics, Chaplin's recollection was excellent. But as we telescoped in on the Y-1 story, especially the circumstances surrounding the transport of seed to South America and the scope of the commercial cultivation at Souza Cruz, Chaplin became markedly uneasy and began to claim ignorance.

After a short while I entered the conversation. I did not identify myself and Chaplin never asked who was talking. I opened with words of admiration and appreciation, an approach that was as much tactical as sincere. I told him it was an honor to speak with him and a great opportunity for us at the FDA to pick the brain of "one of the pioneers in plant breeding." Chaplin warmed to my praise. "Well," he said, "it's been a good career for me. A tobacco plant is one of the best plants that a geneticist could work with."

Chaplin began to explain the origins of his work. After the Surgeon General's 1964 report, Congress told the USDA to end its research into the best ways to grow tobacco. In line with that directive, Chaplin and his staff shifted their focus to lowering tar levels in cigarettes. As he cast about for a strategy, Chaplin came across a paper by an English tobacco scientist proposing to reduce tar without a loss of customer satisfaction by raising nicotine levels. Chaplin decided to pursue that idea by crossing *Nicotiana rustica* with standard tobacco plants. He explained that there were some forty varieties of the *N. rustica* plant, all with nicotine levels in the 6 to 8 percent range and all of which yielded only about 700 to 800 pounds an acre, a third of what normal tobacco plants would yield. He hoped that crossing *N. rustica* with a number of hardier, lower-nicotine tobacco plants would result in hybrids with the combination of attributes he sought. Instead, he produced plants that were invariably low-yielding, disease-prone, and scrawny.

As far as Chaplin knew, this research focus at USDA had been dropped when he retired. When he started working as a consultant for Brown & Williamson, Chaplin claimed the company already had a successful crossbred plant in hand and was almost ready to move into experimental planting. He said that he had been hired exclusively for his field experience.

"Who did the original crosses?" I asked.

Chaplin pointed to DNAP, claiming that it already had several lines of "high-alkaloid material" in its greenhouses. We knew that in the industry's parlance, "high-alkaloid" was virtually synonymous with "high-nicotine." Chaplin said he had no idea of the process that had been involved nor how long it had taken.

According to Chaplin, DNAP took hybrid seedlings from its greenhouses and planted them. When they were ready for harvesting, he was called in to help select the best lines. The Y-1 line had outperformed the others in several years of field trials, surviving chemical analyses of its alkaloid content and demonstrating genetic stability.

The task of selecting good lines was tricky, Chaplin said. B&W wanted a plant to meet four criteria: to be disease-resistant; to yield enough tobacco per acre to make it economically feasible; to be high-alkaloid; and to have "good smoking characteristics." Unfortunately for the company, these goals seemed to be incompatible. The high-nicotine hybrids tended to ripen early, making them susceptible to wilt and rot. They also smoked rough and tended to be low yielding. According to Chaplin, these problems had not been solved by the time he stopped consulting for the company in 1990. As far as Chaplin knew, the plant never achieved a yield higher than 1,500 to 1,800 pounds an acre, far better than the *N. rustica* parent but still some two thirds of the average tobacco plants.

Chaplin's open and conversational style shifted suddenly when we asked about offshore tobacco farms. Would *N. rustica* grow in South America? "I guess it would grow about like it does here," he answered vaguely. I kept pushing and he finally admitted seeing it grown on a few farms in Brazil. Then, he told us there had also been a Y-2. That was news.

The conversation turned to the subject of the seeds. Had he seen any seeds go down to Souza Cruz? Chaplin became very definite. "I never saw any," he said.

What about Fisher or Bravo? Had he seen either of them give seeds to anybody in Souza Cruz? He had not. "When we went down there, the plants were already grown," he said. "I don't know how the seed got down there."

I feigned ignorance and asked why this seemed to be a sensitive subject for him. He told me about the federal law against exporting tobacco seeds, except for experimental purposes.

"And this wasn't experimental, was it?" I asked.

He did not take the bait. "Every bit that I knew was still in experimental stages. It really was never in mass production, as far as I know." It seemed possible that Chaplin had never actually seen any commercial cultivation in Souza Cruz and so we asked about the U.S. farm where Y-1 had been grown. Did he know the farmer? Chaplin's memory improved incrementally. He could not pull up the name but he knew who we were talking about. "Big, fat fellow," he said, "I remember that. He died of a heart attack."

Was it Farmer Jones?

"That's who it was," he said. Lloyd Vernon Jones.

Gary pulled out his map, and Chaplin reluctantly located the Jones farm, about ten miles from Wilson, North Carolina, somewhere between Snow Hill and Stantonburg.

We ended the interview with Chaplin by trolling for names, but he told us only that the people he knew in Souza Cruz tended to be tight-lipped. Our interview ended at two in the afternoon. Ten minutes later, we were on the phone with DNAP.

I ASKED Sharon Natanblut to be part of that call, knowing she would be helpful on a tough interview. On DNAP's end, Clinton Neagley, an in-house lawyer, was joined by David Evans, the company's business manager. There was no mention of Janis Bravo, whom we had expected. Mitch protested her absence, but Neagley said firmly that she did not need to be involved. Apparently, in the eyes of the company, she had already done too much damage.

Neagley told us that he had been warned by B&W that DNAP was expected to uphold its "duties of confidentiality." As if hoping to appease us, the attorney added that B&W had carved out three exceptions to DNAP's confidentiality agreement, "three specific bits of information" he was permitted to disclose.

The first had to do with commercialization. Neagley had been instructed to say that "the project" had been "terminated some time ago," and that the work done on the patent had not been commercialized. When pushed to be more specific, Neagley said the project was terminated three years ago. He had not yet spoken the words "Y-1."

The second exception dealt with DNAP's involvement, which Neagley said had been "limited to making the variety described, Y-1, pollen-free" and doing some work on disease resistance. We sat up straighter; he had actually mentioned Y-1 by name. Consistent with Bravo, Neagley claimed that Brown & Williamson had handed them seeds that had already been bred for high nicotine.

The third nugget of information dealt with the techniques used in their work. Neagley claimed that genetic engineering had not been used to modify tobacco plants.

Virtually none of our subsequent questions elicited a straightforward answer. Because of her forceful edge, I wanted Sharon to take the lead, even though she was neither a lawyer nor an investigator. I passed her a note with the word "knife" on it; she got the message to push as hard as she could, but even so she made little progress. DNAP consistently denied any role in the development of Y-1, placing responsibility squarely with James Chaplin. "It is our understanding," said one official, "that the scientist in charge of that program at that time was one James Chaplin."

Fingers were being pointed in both directions.

The company was adamant that Y-1 had not actually been used in cigarettes, to the best of its knowledge—and indirectly admitted the company would have expected some financial benefit if it had been used. We asked the officials how much of the seed they had provided to B&W. They refused to answer. We were at a dead end.

Sharon Natanblut was annoyed, and she let DNAP know just how she felt. Afterwards, David Evans said the company would not do another call with us if "that woman" was on the phone. I told Sharon to take it as a compliment.

If we had not anticipated DNAP's behavior, we might have been disappointed, but asking the questions actually mattered to us almost as much as getting the answers. We were using the DNAP interview to send a message to Brown & Williamson. At this point, we wanted the company to know how much we had learned about the Y-1 story.

29

GARY and Jim were on the trail of Farmer Jones. Shortly after finishing the interview with Chaplin, they had driven sixty miles northwest from Oxford to Wilson. There was no highway linking the two North Carolina towns and so the trip had taken two hours, putting them into Wilson in the late afternoon. With Chaplin's directions in hand, they followed Route 42, looking for the landmarks he had mentioned—a burned-out gas station, a stand of plants, and a clump of four or five mailboxes. Just when they thought they were on a wild goose chase, each of the promised markers suddenly appeared. The last mailbox bore the name L. V. Jones.

The farmhouse sat at the top of the field that ran along the road. The farm itself looked to be about ten acres and did not seem to be much of a commercial operation. The house was modest, a brick ranch that appeared to have two or three bedrooms, perhaps twenty years old. They drove up the driveway and knocked on the door. No answer. They walked around the side to a screened-in porch. From where they stood they could hear someone inside. Eventually, a woman came out.

It was quickly apparent that she did not care much for the FDA. To Gary, the look on her face read "here-come-the-damn-Yankee-regulators." She said that her husband had died, and although he had done some work for Brown & Williamson, she did not know anything about the experimental plants. She doubted that she could be of help, but suggested they talk to "the nigger farmhand" who lived out back. Gary and Jim flinched at the word, which rolled off her tongue as easily as if she were speaking the man's name. It was a frustrating encounter. There they were, standing on the very spot where Y-1 had supposedly been grown, and they could not verify it. Gary wished

Tom were with them to break the ice. Tom had a "God Bless America" speech that could get anyone talking. He made it sound so reasonable. "We're trying to get the facts here, ma'am," he would say. "If we don't provide these facts, the commissioner is not going to be able to make the right decision."

Gary and Jim considered their options and decided to see what they could learn from a neighbor across the way. They drove into his driveway and a man appeared from behind the house a moment later, hand outstretched. He introduced himself as Johnny West and invited them onto his porch. Soon they had settled in for a chat.

As voluble as he was cordial, West told them everything he knew. He said that Jones had, in fact, grown experimental tobacco. He had just finished putting some tobacco in the shed when he had a heart attack and died in his fields. West remembered a lot of visitors—"Germans" and "foreigners," he called them—coming to the farm to look at the plants. He described someone who sounded like James Chaplin, but he could not recall the name.

According to West, Mrs. Jones knew more than she let on. The neighbor said she had kept written records for the farm. When Gary asked West what the experimental plants were called, he looked at them incredulously. "Tobacco," he said.

Then he suggested that if they really wanted to know what was grown out in the fields, they should "go talk to the nigger that works out there."

There it was again. "This is hard-core down here," Jim said to Gary as they left West's place. A Southerner by birth, he felt ashamed.

Behind the Jones farmhouse they saw a tiny tin shack. Tattered clothes hung on a clothesline strung between two poles. They knocked, and a black man, about sixty-five, skinny but strong, with only a few teeth remaining, came out. His name was Kirk Taylor.

At first Taylor seemed scared, but he soon started talking. He said that the farm had raised about two acres of Y-1 a year, much less of Y-2. He had tended the plants during that period for Jones and remembered them as shorter than usual and somewhat scrawny, but upright, erect. From the description, Gary and Jim knew they were on target. God bless Y-1's scrawny little heart, the investigators thought; you always know it when you find it. They took some photos of the farm, thanked Taylor, and drove off.

I felt a small sense of triumph when they reported to me. When I first heard the name Farmer Jones, I had laughed. The odds of actually finding the site where Y-1 had been grown in this country seemed remote. Now we were certain that the tobacco had left the lab and gone into the field, at least experimentally.

GARY and Jim had little time to congratulate themselves. While they were in tobacco country, they decided to see if they could find Phillip Fisher, the tobacco executive who was named on the Brazilian patent and who had supposedly been in charge of the Y-1 project for Brown & Williamson. That night they flew to Louisville and early the next morning set out for Fisher's house. His ordinary ranch house, set in the middle of fields, surprised them with its modesty. Fisher answered their knock dressed in jeans and a short-sleeved cotton shirt. He seemed shocked to find the FDA on his doorstep.

Again wishing Tom were along to get them inside, Gary plunged in with an easy question. "How long did you work at Brown & Williamson?"

Fisher was not at all hostile, but he was not going to be pushed. He declined to talk with them, citing his confidentiality agreement. Gary gave him the FDA's usual disclaimer. "We're aware that the confidentiality agreement exists, but we're part of the government and we don't believe it applies to us. All we want to do is talk about what you did for the company."

Without pausing, Gary asked another question. "When did you leave the company?" His strategy was to roll over any objection and keep moving.

Fisher did not buy it, insisting that he had to talk first to the Brown & Williamson attorneys. Besides that, he needed to go bale some hay. His hay had to be loaded on trucks by the end of the day, he said, and one of his helpers had not appeared.

Gary and Jim looked at each other. "Hey," Gary said, "we've got our suitcases in the trunk of the car; we can change. We'd be more than glad to help you."

The offer took Fisher aback because it was obviously sincere, but he laughed and said no. He wanted to talk first to Kendrick Wells, the general counsel, and asked them to call back in the evening. Gary's heart sank when he heard the name. He knew there was no way that Wells, Mitch's Dr. Death, was going to grant permission. Fisher had been very polite, almost friendly, but firm. They thanked him for his time and left.

Gary and Jim headed to town for lunch. Later in the afternoon they called Fisher and asked if they could come by that evening. This time Fisher sounded upset. He told them curtly that Wells insisted he have no further contact with them, except through a company lawyer. He said good-bye and hung up. Though disappointed, Gary and Jim did not think the effort had been wasted. B&W must be getting nervous, they thought.

DNAP's and Chaplin's mutual insistence that the other party was responsible for developing the original high-nicotine strain left us confused. DNAP did not mind acknowledging that it had tinkered with the seeds to make them sterile and disease-resistant. Chaplin had no concerns about describing field work intended to strengthen the plants, which were prone to toppling over. But neither wanted to be held responsible for using the breeding techniques that created a high-nicotine plant.

One afternoon in my office, I asked Gary to call Brown & Williamson's Souza Cruz affiliate in Brazil. Drawing again on his alter-ego, Dean Cooper, he reached Oscar Pontes, the man in charge, and asked whether high-nicotine hybrid plants were available, purportedly for a client in China. Pontes was cautious, explaining that Souza Cruz could grow the plants only if seeds were provided. I had never seen Dean Cooper in action before and listened, amused, as the conversation turned to soccer. The men talked about an upcoming World Cup match between Brazil and the Netherlands and about Diego Maradona, the Argentinian player who had been arrested for cocaine use. It was obviously an animated discussion, and Pontes seemed willing to stay on the phone for the rest of the evening, talking about anything except high-nicotine tobacco.

I thought I might do better trying to talk to Chaplin one more time. I was after a single fact. Who had done the original plant crosses to alter the nicotine content? When I got Chaplin on the phone, I started asking questions and I simply would not stop. I had learned that sheer persistence sometimes made a subject feel obligated to answer. That was the way it went with Chaplin.

I opened by telling him that DNAP claimed the original crosses in its possession had been done at his lab in Oxford.

"No, I don't recall that being done at Oxford, no."

"Did you specifically create Y-1?"

"I never created the Y-1."

I came at it again and again and Chaplin grew defensive. "I've never given DNAP anything," he insisted.

"I mean, it's fine, Dr. Chaplin," I said, now trying to sound reassuring. "We just need to know how they got there."

Finally, he broke down and told the truth. Chaplin admitted that he was the one who had actually succeeded in creating high-nicotine seeds. It had taken six years, and generation after generation of technical manipulation, involving such things as low-alkaloid tetraploids, fertile sesquidiploids, and multiple self-pollinations, but in the end the science had worked. James Chaplin had done the crosses that spawned the *Nicotiana rustica* hybrid that became Y-1.

Tim Long's customs search was now in its third week. After visits to Virginia, he had traveled to the ports of North Carolina, pulling records from Durham and Winston-Salem. Then he headed to the Jimmy Carter Records Center in Atlanta to search old files that had been archived. The Records Center was a huge warehouse filled with boxes that were piled in tiers and ran from floor to ceiling.

Each box held between fifty and one hundred customs entries and each entry ran anywhere from three to fifty pages; Tim had identified approximately 400 entries he wanted to see. In the dim light he climbed up and down a stepladder, pulling down boxes, thumbing through entries, searching for an invoice that hinted at Y-1. He scanned every page of every entry three times. It would be easy to miss a reference, especially since he had no idea exactly where it would appear. After two days of searching, Tim came up empty-handed. When Gary called for an update, Tim acknowledged he wasn't having any luck.

At Parklawn, the week started off with more promise. Macon had sent Tom some samples of Y-1. In our earlier conference call, the informant had offered to do just that, but we had not known whether to expect any follow-through. Now here it was, in the form of expanded tobacco. It resembled shredded tobacco, the kind we had seen in ordinary cigarettes. Packaged in Baggies with official-looking computer-generated labels, the samples strongly suggested a commercial product.

I was as pleased as the rest of the tobacco team to see the labeled samples, but when Ann Witt said we now had the "perfect piece of evidence," I had to disabuse her of that notion. We could not use the Y-1 without putting Macon at risk, and we were determined not to do that. Our search for evidence to document Y-1's use in American cigarettes was not yet over.

30

WHENEVER I could, I continued to search for information on what the industry knew about nicotine, and when. I still had the passion for library research that I had developed early in life, and it was important to me that I carve out the time to do at least some of my own. One Saturday, I decided to see what I could discover at the most public of places, the Library of Congress. I headed to the turn-of-the-century building on Independence Avenue, a few blocks from Capitol Hill. Sitting at one of the library's massive mahogany tables, which now hold computer terminals, I typed in a single search word—"nicotine"—and printed out a long list of books on the noisy dot-matrix printer nearby.

Then I moved into the octagonal Main Reading Room, a soaring space with a gilded dome. There was at least a ninety-minute wait for materials. While I stood in line to hand in my request slips, a woman recognized me and asked somewhat jokingly, "Do you do your own research?"

I smiled, without responding, and headed off to search other indexes until my book requests were ready. When they came, I began sifting through the piles. This was the unromantic side of discovery, but it was just the sort of work I had always enjoyed. Some of the volumes were edited collections; others, the results of symposia and conferences. Most dealt with how nicotine was metabolized in the body. I read the acknowledgments at the beginning of each volume, which usually thanked the Council for Tobacco Research for research funds. The published documents made it clear that hundreds of studies on nicotine had been funded by the tobacco industry.

Back at Parklawn I continued to pore through every source I could find. Eventually we created our own database, scanning all of our documents into a computer and then using a software program called Excalibur to conduct specific searches. One evening I typed "high nicotine" into the database. One hit, a 1956 report, *Measured Crop Performance, Tobacco,* suggested nicotine manipulation was not a recent phenomenon. In the 1950s, filter tips had been added to some brands of cigarettes to reduce tar. "With the increase in production of filter tip cigarettes, demand has increased for heavier bodied (tobacco) types that have full aroma and flavor and a relatively high nicotine count," read the report.

I also read the transcript of a 1957 congressional hearing in which the director of the tobacco division at the USDA acknowledged that industry "moved up the stalk," blending tobacco leaves found higher on the plant for use in filter cigarettes. In the back of the hearing record, I found a chart showing that regular-size filter cigarettes had a higher average nicotine content than the unfiltered equivalent. For the first time, I understood that filters, ostensibly used to address health concerns, removed not only tar but nicotine, and so the companies then sought ways to increase nicotine levels.

Essentially the same story was told in an obscure autobiography I found later, *Memoirs in a Country Churchyard,* written by a farmer named Floyd Nuttall. "There was a concern among our blenders and leaf men over the introduction of filter tip cigarettes," wrote Nuttall. "We knew we would have to cut down on some of the top grade brights and replace them with burley, which carried twenty-five to forty per cent more nicotine."

Nuttall doubted that filters would decrease the health hazards of smoking. Instead, he wrote, "the pro–filter tip people believed that through the use of stronger and faster burning tobacco, smokers would probably light up more often."

Continuing to comb the public record, I ordered all the back issues of *Mealey's Tobacco* and *Tobacco Industry Litigation Reporter.* The thousands of pages had to be one of the most extensive compilations of documents filed in tobacco litigation, but in the end, it was a record of the industry's safe landings. Until the *Cipollone* case, the tobacco companies had never lost a lawsuit, and that single defeat had been overturned on appeal. I found in these pages the ultimate irony—in the courtroom and at public forums, the industry claimed with one breath that the health risks associated with smoking had not been proved and with the next that if there was a risk, everyone knew about it. As Paulette reminded me repeatedly, this is what the lawyers had been paid to do.

Nonetheless, countless liability suits continued to be filed, including, on May 6, 1994, a class-action lawsuit on behalf of Dr. Howard Engle and other ailing smokers in Florida. No class-action case had ever even come to trial before, and I did not expect this one to go anywhere.

ONE evening, I reviewed notes that had been written more than a decade earlier, some by hand, others on a portable typewriter. Making sense of the hard-to-read papers that often lacked dates or titles took some doing, but I sensed it would be worthwhile. They came from the private collection of S. J. Green, director of research at British American Tobacco. Green had been more than just the company's chief scientist. Unlike Jeffrey Wigand, he also held a seat on the board of directors, giving him more insight into how the world of tobacco worked. In his later years, he decided to speak out about the industry that had given him his livelihood.

Green appeared in a BBC documentary after he turned renegade, and I was able to obtain some of his papers from a source there. Ann Witt secured others through connections that linked her to a lawyer working directly with Green's surviving family. Green wrote candidly about the industry's knowledge of the link between smoking and disease and the dominance of legal considerations. The strategy of denial, he wrote, "makes it very difficult for those in the industry to discuss safety evaluation, product safety, warnings and claims." That, he said, should change. "In my view, it would be best to be in a position to say in public what was believed in private."

But candor created its own problems. The thoughts Green committed to paper—that "nicotine is the most addictive drug," that addicted smokers "can no longer be said to make an adult choice," and that "a good part of the tobacco industry is concerned with the administration of nicotine to consumers"—could not be spoken above a whisper. Otherwise, industry fears that tobacco would be regulated as a drug in the United Kingdom might be realized, and that was dangerous. "The Americans were frightened that if this happened in Britain it would become a precedent for the world," Green said in an interview. There were "lots of lawyers, money spent on fighting this."

Instead, the industry chose the strategy it thought most likely to extend its life—"resist everything and then concede when necessary," said Green. Meanwhile, it viewed every year of continued existence as an opportunity for unexpected profits.

Green's words closely tracked what we were learning about the industry's thinking. In a particularly memorable note, he sketched a triangle symbolizing the reasons for smoking, with the three corners labeled "sensory rewards," "psychosocial rewards," and "pharmacological rewards." Clustered around "pharmacological rewards" were three more phrases—tranquilization smoking, stimulation smoking, and addictive smoking. The sketches looked to me like a powerful way to depict drug effects.

I knew that if I was going to use any of these unsigned documents to support our case for asserting jurisdiction over cigarettes, I had to be sure of their authenticity. If we tried to use them to support our arguments, someone would surely ask for proof that the industry scientist had written them.

Jack Mitchell discovered that Green had a surviving daughter, who we hoped would be able to authenticate them. It took weeks before he made his first contact with Megan Green, who traveled extensively, spending only a portion of the year in London. She was friendly and cooperative from the outset, but reluctant to become a public figure. After several telephone conversations, Jack mailed her copies of the documents we hoped to use. She was slow to respond, and, characteristically, I grew edgy. Jack counseled patience when I tried to convince him to fly to London to negotiate with her, and Megan Green did eventually authenticate the documents. "I have concluded that the handwriting and signatures that appear on the attached documents belong to my father," she declared in her affidavit.

The words of an industry insider supported our argument that nicotine was a drug. It was one more piece in our puzzle.

My FIRST encounter with William Dunn, known at Philip Morris as the "Nicotine Kid," yielded little. Dunn was a clinical psychologist who had done product testing for the company in the 1960s. Although we did not have a full picture of his work, I knew that he had hinted long ago that nicotine was a pharmaceutical product. "Think of the cigarette pack as a storage container for a day's supply of nicotine," Dunn wrote. "Think of the cigarette as a dispenser for a dose unit of nicotine."

One rare afternoon when Room 1468, the base of operations for the tobacco team, was empty, I slipped a videotaped deposition of Dunn from the *Cipollone* case into the VCR. His white hair combed in waves, Dunn faced the camera. Mark Edell, the attorney for the plaintiff, sat to his left. A Philip

Morris lawyer and a court stenographer were also present. Dunn was well prepared. In response to questions, he acknowledged spending four days readying himself for the deposition with the help of lawyers from Philip Morris and Shook, Hardy.

Edell showed Dunn a series of internal company documents and asked if he recognized them. The documents described experiments that involved the duration of a puff taken by a smoker, the changes in puff patterns, and the ways in which smokers modify their consumption of smoke to compensate for changes in the delivery of tar and nicotine. As he looked at one paper after another, Dunn replied that he recognized the general format, and his own signature, but not the actual contents. It was all too long ago, he claimed. The statement defied credibility. For years, these experiments had been fundamental to Dunn's daily work at Philip Morris. The questioning continued, interrupted frequently by objections from the lawyer representing Philip Morris.

Edell asked Dunn, "What is nicotine titration, sir?"

"That is a concept," Dunn replied.

"I know it's a concept, sir. Can you tell the jury and the court what kind of concept it is?"

"It was one of the hypotheses I had proposed that smokers adjust their smoke intake as a function of the amount of nicotine in the smoke."

I was familiar with the underlying theory—that a smoker will inhale more smoke if too little nicotine is present in the product. Dunn was careful to say that some research suggested the hypothesis might be valid, but other studies did not.

"Do you agree that nicotine is a powerful pharmacological agent?" asked Edell.

Again, Dunn hedged. "I would like to answer your question, Mr. Edell. My problem is, what's the definition of a powerful pharmacological agent? It's a very difficult question."

Edell was not getting very far. "During the time you were with Philip Morris, didn't your work include the question of whether or not cigarette smoke contained nicotine, and whether or not nicotine was a powerful pharmacological agent?" asked the lawyer.

"Which of those two questions would you wish me to answer?"

"Both."

"Our charter was to investigate why people smoked cigarettes," Dunn explained. "One of the hypotheses that we considered was that nicotine may be a reinforcing agent."

Edell then asked Dunn if he recalled an R&D program designed to reduce the carcinogens in cigarettes, possibly leading to a medically acceptable product.

"Could you restate the question more simply?" asked Dunn. "It was a complex question."

Edell did so.

"No, I was unaware."

"Participating in the selling and marketing of a product that might cause cancer in consumers at that time?"

"No, I was not."

"Were you ever interested in that?"

"Are you asking as a personal concern," said Dunn, "or as a scientist?"

"As a human being," said Edell.

There was an awkwardly long pause. Then Dunn said, "Restate the question for me, please."

"I withdraw the question," said Edell.

I switched off the VCR. *As a human being,* Edell had asked, *were you aware that you were participating in the marketing of a product that might cause cancer?* Not as a scientist, not as an employee of Philip Morris. Were you aware? Dunn had remained frozen in that long pause as he searched for the words he might use, any words at all, but there were none.

WILLIAM DUNN was by now in his early seventies and retired from Philip Morris. As we were debating how best to approach him, Tom Doyle simply picked up the telephone and dialed his number.

Tom starts from the premise that any person is reachable, and no subject is out of bounds. He hits you with breeziness—a good morning, how are you, do you mind if I come in—and before you can answer, Tom is through the door and sitting on the sofa. With total confidence he called Dunn, identified himself, and asked if he would be willing to talk to FDA investigators about his years as the top psychologist at Philip Morris. Dunn was caught off guard, but after only a moment's hesitation, he agreed to a meeting and gave Tom his home address in Richmond.

The get-together never took place. Tom, Gary, and Mitch arrived at

Dunn's doorstep, but he refused to talk, saying that he had to consult first with his former employer. Philip Morris eventually agreed to allow the interview, but only in the presence of lawyers. An appointment was rescheduled at law offices in Richmond, where Dunn was flanked by Arthur Levine, the ex-FDA lawyer whom we had met during the visit to Philip Morris, and by a Shook, Hardy attorney.

Mitch did not feel optimistic as he entered the conference room. He expected Dunn's lawyers to be argumentative and defensive, and he assumed Dunn would be a reluctant participant. To his surprise, those concerns were misplaced. Dunn's lawyers were virtually silent. During the two-hour meeting, they made sure that their client was comfortable and they took extensive notes, but they placed no restrictions on the subjects that were discussed and raised no objections to any of the questioning.

Dunn, far from reluctant, seemed to enjoy every moment of the meeting. He spoke with easy confidence of his work for Philip Morris in the 1960s, and of how he had expanded a core group of twenty housewives into more than 20,000 smokers who were studied to answer three basic questions: Why do they smoke? How do they smoke? What do they smoke?

Though Dunn spoke freely about people with whom he had worked at Philip Morris, Mitch began to see that while projecting an image of candor, he was deliberately vague in certain areas. He talked freely about work that existed on the public record, but his memory suddenly became faulty on other subjects. Over and over, Dunn claimed that he could not remember certain dates and places. And he never swayed from his insistence that his research had been done only for the advancement of science, not for commercial purposes.

During the interview, Dunn did not reverse his position that nicotine was the fundamental reason people smoked, although he insisted that this was a personal opinion, and one with which his former employers did not necessarily agree. We did not manage to learn exactly what he had been doing all those years at Philip Morris, but Dunn made it clear that he was proud of his contributions to an understanding of the psychology of smoking, as proud as the discoverer of a vaccine or a new surgical technique might be. He saw himself as a leader in social psychology, applying disciplines and techniques that the tobacco industry had never used before. He seemed to have no regrets. He was, as he boasted during his meeting with the tobacco team, the Nicotine Kid.

31

AT THIS point in our investigation into tobacco industry practices, we were deep in a maze.

I set up a conference call between the tobacco team and "Bio," a scientist with a background in immunology and oncology who had once worked for Philip Morris. Gary had already met with Bio several times. In an early meeting, Bio noticed that Gary had a holster under his sport coat. I preferred that our criminal investigators not carry weapons, and on subject interviews, Gary and Tom rarely did. But the Office of Criminal Investigations was a law enforcement office and its agents were professionals who had tangled with criminals. I could not deny them an opportunity to defend themselves if circumstances made that necessary.

As it happened, the notion that he was talking to an armed law enforcement officer put Bio at ease; it seemed to give Gary stature in his eyes and legitimized his inquiries. Bio agreed to talk with the tobacco team.

On our first call, he told us he had been hired by the scientist we knew as Philip. Our network of informants had doubled back on itself. We picked up the thread of human research. Although the visit to R. J. Reynolds and Gary's escapade with Lacy Bellomy suggested the tobacco companies were conducting pharmacological studies on human beings, we still did not have proof. Bio told us about the electroencephalography (EEG) group at Philip Morris, whose goal was to study how the human brain responds to cigarette smoke. Knowing that most psychopharmacologically active agents that affect the brain affect EEG results, researchers had positioned electrodes on the heads of their study subjects and then charted the differing patterns created by smoking different cigarettes. Drug research, I thought. Without a doubt.

Bio mentioned Frank Gullotta, a physiological psychologist who had been hired in 1977 to run the EEG program. Bio knew Gullotta quite well and said he had conducted some of the industry's most sophisticated human research. His tests of smoking showed that cigarettes with high levels of nicotine produced brain patterns suggesting alertness (low voltage, fast activity); by contrast, low-nicotine cigarettes had minimal effects. Gullotta kept refining his studies, employing ever more technologically complex and sensitive methods to pinpoint the electrophysiological changes associated with nicotine.

The real significance of Gullotta's work came when he shifted from basic science to practical applications. By testing the effects of specific doses of nicotine, he was able to identify levels that produced favorable physiological and behavioral responses. "Experiments conducted in our laboratory led us to the idea of how to produce an acceptable low-tar cigarette," boasted Gullotta in an internal industry memo. There was a touch of bravado in his next claim. "It was our work which led to the development of cigarettes with altered tar/nicotine ratios."

Bio assured us that Gullotta was not working in isolation. As we talked, Bio began describing what he called a "company within the company," the group that controlled Philip Morris's most sensitive research. In the early 1990s, members of this inner circle decided that Gullotta's EEG experiments should be moved out of the country to INBIFO, a company that had been established decades earlier by Philip Morris in Cologne, Germany. I assumed that moving the EEG research to Cologne was intended as a safeguard against litigation.

Our informant Ved Malik had also talked about the top-secret research at INBIFO, and an explicit industry document written by Thomas Osdene, the director of science and technology at Philip Morris, described procedures for handling sensitive company documents. Osdene instructed, "Ship all documents to Cologne ... keep in Cologne ... OK to phone and telex (these will be destroyed)....If important letters or documents have to be sent please send to home—I will act on them and destroy."

Bio had still more details to offer about INBIFO. Since its inception, he said, INBIFO had been deeply involved with studies of carcinogenesis and the pharmacology of nicotine. Bio emphasized that the overseas lab was considered an extension of Philip Morris's R&D facilities and said Philip Morris executives visited regularly. INBIFO was the first to develop an inhalation chamber that exposed rats and hamsters to smoke—and showed that the higher the tar levels, the lower the weight gain and survival rates. While the tobacco industry was publicly attacking the validity of the mouse painting studies conducted by early cancer researchers, INBIFO was secretly conducting its own such studies and acknowledging that mouse painting was the only "universally accepted bioassay" and resulted in "complete tumorgenesis."

I checked my watch and was surprised that it was midnight, three hours after we began the conversation and long past the time to end it. But now Bio seemed eager to keep going. He said that very few people at Philip Morris actually knew about the nature of the company's research. He said he was privy to the inside story only because he had personal connections.

OUR own attempt to learn from informants sometimes led us to dead ends and on occasion frustrated the investigators. "We're working with our hands tied," Gary once grumbled to Tom.

Tom knew what he meant. Although both men had an amazing capacity to earn the trust of strangers, they still had to rely on the goodwill of potential informants. Since the defeat of the enforcement bill early in my tenure at the FDA, I had never been able to get subpoena power for the agency, and we could not compel a subject to talk. We had no inducements to offer for cooperation, beyond an appeal to patriotism and civil obligation. Gary and Tom were also constrained by the need to proceed with great delicacy. They were aware that they carried the reputation of the agency on their shoulders and that they could not appear intimidating. It was a responsibility they took seriously. They were determined to be respectful at all times and never to give the tobacco interests a chance to accuse them of overstepping their bounds.

Still, new avenues kept opening, sometimes leading us to places we had not expected. Tom and Gary had been given the name of a product developer code-named "PC" who had been a participant in experiments involving cigarettes laced with toxic solvents. Tobacco companies routinely used developers to test new products, or variations of old ones, as a form of market research. A product developer for a bakery tastes various recipes for apple turnovers, cheese cake, or lemon cookies. A product developer for a tobacco company smokes different blends of cigarettes. But asking employees to smoke chemical solvents? That was different.

Although she was eight months pregnant and starting a new business venture, PC agreed to talk, and Tom and Gary flew to Colorado to meet with her. PC explained that in the spring of 1991, B&W began to receive a high volume of consumer complaints about an odd taste in their cigarettes. To test the theory that the taste came from solvents used in the packaging, B&W assembled smoking panels whose members had to smoke cigarettes injected with a variety of chemical compounds and to report any odd tastes. PC was drafted to participate.

During the studies she had kept her own list of more than thirty solvents used in the test cigarettes, and she willingly gave that list to Tom and Gary. It read like the inventory of a toxic dump site and included acetone, a flammable liquid; methanol, which is used as an antifreeze; and toluene, a product of coke-oven gas and coal tar. The individual solvents were injected into cigarettes, said PC, and each tainted item was then compared with an untainted control cigarette.

Tom asked if the panelists knew what they were smoking. Not at first, said PC, but after a few days, they were told about the solvents they were taking into their bodies. Eventually PC began suffering from persistent coughing, heart palpitations, bronchitis, and low-grade fevers, which she attributed to the study. When PC told Jeffrey Wigand, then the vice president of research, that she was quitting smoking for health reasons, he reminded her that smoking was a requirement of her job and suggested that she look elsewhere for employment. She left the company soon afterwards.

I ALSO had a conversation with "Critical," an engineer who had worked on Philip Morris's virtually abandoned Bermuda Hundred plant and the denicotinized Next brand it had been built to manufacture. The informant said the company had initially been very enthusiastic about Next. According to Critical, some smokers of low-tar, low-nicotine cigarettes attempt to compensate for the loss of nicotine by smoking more cigarettes. The company supposedly thought that even less nicotine might result in even more sales.

At first, Critical said, that is just what happened with Next. But not for long. Eventually, according to the informant, smokers reached a threshold where they felt forced to smoke a greater number of cigarettes than they could enjoy. As a cigar smoker, Critical understood the phenomenon. "If you give me one cigar I love it. I think it tastes great. But if you give me two cigars, that second cigar doesn't taste that good. And you almost have to hold a gun to my head to smoke a third cigar." Many smokers gave up the denicotinized cigarette, said Critical, and returned to their traditional brand. To the company's chagrin, Critical said, others stopped smoking. A Philip Morris colleague had told our informant that Next seemed to offer "the most effective way to stop smoking."

I never knew whether to believe Critical, but years after the FDA investigation ended, I searched industry documents seeking support for his claims. And I found something close in a research study comparing regular cigarettes to "alkaloid-reduced tobacco" (ART). Some participants reported "drawing harder on the ART cigarettes" and described them as irritating. The results also showed that some people "preferred the ART cigarettes because they were smoking less due to a decreased craving for cigarettes after smoking ART." The pursuit of denicotinized cigarettes was abandoned in the early 1990s.

ONE of the most disquieting conversations I had was with "Saint," a chemical engineer who once worked for Philip Morris. Philip had pointed us in Saint's direction, and Tom tracked her down at a southern university. Saint readily agreed to talk with the FDA, but made it clear that she did not want to testify or to come to Washington.

Saint was willing to talk openly about her research into the development of a safe cigarette. She had been recruited by Philip Morris because of her expertise in the field of thermodynamics and had been put in charge of supercritical extraction technology. We talked about both the science and the practical applications of her work. Along with denicotinizing tobacco, Philip Morris had been interested in employing the process to remove flavors and odorants from superior tobaccos that could then be used to upgrade inferior tobaccos.

As we talked, Saint made a comment about carcinogens that took me completely by surprise. I asked her to repeat it. She said that at one point she had been given a list of the carcinogens in tobacco and had been asked to conduct a pilot experiment, using the supercritical extraction process, to isolate and remove them. And then she said that she had been able to do exactly that.

It was a simple statement, but I had to struggle with the concept for a moment. A former chemical engineer at Philip Morris had just told me that she had been able to remove known carcinogens from tobacco by the same means used to decaffeinate coffee.

I became angrier as Saint continued to talk. She told me that management's attitude towards her work gradually began to change and that by 1984 she believed her days at Philip Morris were numbered. That year, she said, there was a sudden storm of activity at the company as projects were closed down, scientists were fired, and research animals were killed. I realized that Saint was describing what had happened to Victor DeNoble and Paul Mele. Her own project was not closed down, but she no longer felt comfortable working at the company and left a year later.

Though I thought the project Saint described was technically possible, I wondered whether I could believe her. I asked her to verify my understanding of the story one more time.

"You were given a list of carcinogens?" I asked.

"Yes," she said.

"And you were asked to see whether you could extract them from tobacco using extraction procedures?

"Yes."

"And you performed these experiments and you used supercritical extraction and you found you were able to remove many of those compounds on this list that they had supplied you?"

"Yes, that is correct."

"And you said to them, 'Okay, we can do this?' That's a fair statement?"

"Yes, that is fair."

After thanking Saint for her help, I ended the interview. In the past, we had heard about efforts by the tobacco companies to develop a safer cigarette, but in each case we had been told that those efforts had been unsuccessful. Saint's work had been a pilot project. Why wouldn't the company pursue it?

32

I ASKED for an opportunity to testify before Henry Waxman's congressional subcommittee. Tommy Sandefur, Brown & Williamson's CEO, was scheduled to appear before Congress in late June 1994, and I wanted to put our findings about Y-1 on the record first. I guessed that if B&W knew we were about to go public, the company would be more likely to be candid with us. Sure enough, about a week before the scheduled hearing, Mitch Zeller spoke to Gene Pfeifer, the former FDA lawyer now representing Brown & Williamson for the Atlanta firm of King & Spalding. The men agreed to a meeting.

Pfeifer was known to be honorable, but Mitch, though amenable, made it clear that we wanted to hear the full truth about Y-1. Mitch insisted that the right people be in the room to tell that story. The soft-spoken Pfeifer agreed to those terms, and a meeting was scheduled to take place in several days at the Parklawn building.

I had no illusions about motives. The company was nervous about what I would say on the Hill. Executives must have known we were preparing to present the full picture of the development and commercialization of Y-1. Along with legal liability, they surely feared the public relations impact of the story. Sandefur's last appearance before Congress, at the infamous CEO hearing, had been a debacle for the industry, and B&W did not want a repeat performance. The company wanted to be able to say it had come clean with us.

On the same day that Pfeifer called, we got more good news—a copy of the U.S. patent application for Y-1 arrived from the Patent and Trademark Office, along with several related legal documents. The mystery of why our librarian had come up empty-handed in her U.S. patent search was finally solved. Brown & Williamson had applied for a patent, but it had not been approved.

Brown & Williamson had filed an appeals brief on February 28, 1994, defending Y-1 as a significant, original invention. Our letter to the Coalition was released the same day. On March 16, B&W abandoned its application. The first Waxman hearing came a week later. And another week after that, the company withdrew its Brazilian patent. It was just as Macon had said.

I BEGAN to have visions of our customs expert, Tim Long, roaming, like the Flying Dutchman, from port to port, forbidden to rest or return home until Judgment Day.

In Charleston, he had found a number of Brown & Williamson entries indicating that tobacco shipments from Souza Cruz had passed through the port and had then been unloaded at Greenville. He headed there, where staff helped organize the records he needed and provided him space to work in privacy and comfort.

One midafternoon he came upon an entry dated September 21, 1992. Tim scanned the pages of the official documents: the entry summary page, the shipping letter, the certificate of origin, the transportation entry, the manifest of goods, the master in-bond, the duty record, the report of warehouse withdrawals, the packing lists, and the entry for immediate delivery. Nothing. Then, he looked at the attached invoice. One third of the way down the first page, he saw it: "Your order: Project Y1 13/08/92." There it was, in print. He could not believe it. He looked up in the air, made a prayerful sign, and let out a loud cheer.

The shipment had been what U.S. Customs called an "in-bond movement." The container had been shipped from Souza Cruz via the Cayman Islands into the United States at the Port of Charleston and then trucked to Greenville to be unloaded.

I knew that if anyone could have found the customs entry, it would be Tim, but until he called me with the news, I had not counted on it. It was such a long shot, even for an investigation that had already made many of them. I listened to his description of the document and then asked him to fax it to me immediately. At 4:16 P.M., on Wednesday, June 15, I held in my hand proof, usable proof, that Brown & Williamson had shipped almost half a million pounds of genetically manipulated high-nicotine tobacco into this country.

Two days later, nine members of the tobacco team gathered on the thirteenth floor to await B&W's arrival. I stayed in my office, trying to work. I was still keeping a low profile, but we devised a scheme for me to get interim bulletins. At a sign from Mitch, a surreptitious eye-roll toward the door, Liz Berbakos was to excuse herself from the meeting, ostensibly to use the restroom, and then come upstairs to give me a report.

The B&W group arrived at 2:15. Kendrick Wells, Drew McMurtrie, the company's director of product development, and Hubert Hardison, one of the original Y-1 patent holders, accompanied Gene Pfeifer.

The tension of the FDA's site visit the previous month lingered in everyone's mind. But the tone of this meeting, while somber, was far less antagonistic. Wells was not exactly friendly, but he was subdued. Mitch asked the B&W representatives to walk us through the full Y-1 story. Pfeifer turned first to Hardison, whom he called the "institutional memory" on that.

Hardison began his story with a folksy autobiography. "I was born in eastern North Carolina, back during the Depression on a tenant farm. Parents were farmers. I went to North Carolina State. Great distinction, the poorest man ever went to school." As he moved along to B&W's decision to lease the Jones farm to do "proprietary agronomic research," Hardison gave us some history. "The variety of tobacco production in America goes back; the first tobacco ever grown in America was done with smuggled seed, as you're aware of." Despite his colloquial style, he knew exactly what he was saying.

Hardison said he had started his experiments with Y-1 out of curiosity when he was working for Export Leaf Technology. James Chaplin supplied the high-nicotine seed without any expectations, either financial or proprietary. "Common practice of all the industry," he explained. "We could go to the research station, the land grant colleges, and all the research breeders to ask for cultivars. . . . That's the understanding. Friendly." Hardison started growing plants.

Ann Witt asked how Y-1 and Y-2 differed. "Well, you ever chew a dirty sock?" Hardison said. Apparently, that is what Y-2 smelled like. It was undesirable—in Hardison's words, a freak.

After Brown & Williamson acquired Export Leaf, B&W's Phillip Fisher heard about the project and asked for some seeds. Hardison and Chaplin were both brought in as consultants.

Hardison claimed Y-1 had been grown only on the Jones farm, at least while he was working at the company. "If you have a variety," he explained, "you don't turn it loose until you've got a patent." The FDA attorney Bob Spiller asked if B&W had applied for a patent. Wells, interjecting, acknowledged tersely that it had. The three patent holders—Bravo, Fisher, and Hardison—had released the patent to the parent company for a dollar. We asked next about DNAP's role in developing Y-1. Wells described work done to enhance the root system and strengthen the plant's ability to resist disease. But in sharp contrast to the detailed picture of the early breeding process, no one seemed able to speak knowledgeably about B&W's decision to pursue Y-1, or to launch crop production in Brazil. A note of frustration crept into the meeting, and everyone agreed to a short recess.

WHEN the interview resumed, Gene Pfeifer tried to be a conciliator. He said the meeting had been arranged at short notice and promised to make further details available at a later time.

Drew McMurtrie then began to talk about B&W's early interest in Y-1. With astonishing candor, he said the company was specifically interested in being able to use the tobacco to develop a product that maintained nicotine levels while lowering tar. Sharon asked why. "Nicotine is an important part of the smoking experience that the smoker expects to get," said McMurtrie. "As you lower and lower tar, that starts going away."

Mitch rolled his eyes and Liz excused herself from the meeting, practically running up the stairs to my office. It was an important point—not that the company had manipulated nicotine delivery, because we had little doubt about that by now, but that they had just admitted it in the offices of the FDA. Did they know what they were saying?

Mitch asked about the commercial use of Y-1. McMurtrie confirmed what our informants had said, that B&W hoped to develop a brand that could compete favorably with the market leader, Marlboro. Y-1 had first been tested in "light" and "ultra-light" products, but the results were disappointing. When Y-1 made up more than 30 percent of the tobacco, it gave a "totally off-balance smoke"; below that, it did not seem to contribute any unique taste characteristics. Knowing that certain tobaccos smoked better in some forms than in others, the company developed and tested Y-1 as expanded tobacco, just as Macon had told us. When they added conventional casings and flavorings, it made what they considered a great smoke. McMurtrie then listed the cigarette brands in which Y-1 had been used: Viceroy King, Richland King, Viceroy Lights King, Richland Lights King, and Raleigh Lights King.

At that moment, we knew definitively that Y-1 had been blended into cigarettes that were being sold to the American public. The list dovetailed closely with what Macon had told us weeks earlier.

"How much Y-1 was grown in Brazil?" asked Mitch.

They estimated an inventory of between 3.5 million and 4 million pounds. Actually, that figure was low. Wigand had given us a higher estimate, and I later saw a company memo listing the current U.S. inventory at 4 million pounds—with another 3.4 million stored in Brazil. But it was an astonishing admission, and Mitch signaled Liz, who excused herself again and dashed up to my office. "Boss," she practically shouted. Liz was the only person at the FDA who ever called me boss, and she did it routinely. "They've got millions of pounds of this stuff in warehouses."

The questioning moved into the area where B&W felt most vulnerable. How did Y-1 get to Brazil? No one seemed to know a thing.

"I had nothing to do with that end of it," said Hardison, who was the first to speak.

McMurtrie followed with a disclaimer of his own. "I don't know."

"I'm sorry," Pfeifer hedged. "I missed some of that."

Bob Spiller rephrased the question. "How do you get the process started?" he asked. "Do you send a guy with two seed packets and a hundred-dollar bill?"

Wells attempted to match the humor. "I don't know whether a hundred is enough." Everyone laughed, some nervously.

They had already volunteered other information that was much more important to us, presumably because they assumed we already knew it. But they had an exaggerated sense of the danger of admitting that they had moved seed from the United States to Brazil. Mitch rightly considered their fear an enormous miscalculation. Though federal law at that time did forbid tobacco seed exportation except in experimental quantities, a violation was a misdemeanor, and we had neither the authority nor the desire to prosecute them. Yet they were so focused on not telling us about the illegal shipment of seed that they were willing to reveal facts that moved us closer to declaring their products to be drugs. When I heard about this, I wondered for a moment what the other companies would have thought about Brown & Williamson's admissions that day.

Ultimately, according to Drew McMurtrie, the company concluded that Y-1 offered only a marginal benefit and discontinued production. We asked when that decision had been made and received a vague response. It was under consideration six months ago and had been finalized within the past few months. McMurtrie did not volunteer the obvious: this was just as FDA activities were heating up.

It was time to bring the meeting to a close. Reminding our visitors that during the previous month's plant tour we had been told specifically that the company had not conducted its own genetic tests, Mitch offered a final statement. "I take today's session, with all of the information that you shared with us, to be something of a correction of the record." None of us knew it then, but that remark helped spare Brown & Williamson from criminal charges that were later weighed, and rejected, by the Department of Justice.

WHEN the B&W group was gone, we gathered for a debriefing. Although unaware that Wigand and Macon were our informants, the company had confirmed everything that they had told us. I thought the admission that they had actually used Y-1 commercially in several cigarette brands, and still had millions of pounds on hand, was key, at least for the hearing four days away. Mitch thought that the comment about using Y-1 as "a blending tool" to lower tar while maintaining nicotine levels was the real revelation, and in the long run, he was right. We still did not know exactly how the seeds had gotten to Brazil, but that had never mattered much to us. I was ready to tell Congress the Y-1 story, beginning, middle, and end.

33

My testimony before Waxman was scheduled for Tuesday, June 21, 1994. I spent the weekend pulling the Y-1 story together and reviewing the documents on ammonia that had found their way into my hands, and I felt ready. I was convinced that the use of ammonia was as powerful an example of nicotine manipulation as Y-1, and I decided to include it as a prominent part of my testimony.

The Republicans were equally well prepared. Three months earlier, at the March 25 hearing, most of them had not been present. I had tangled with Tom Bliley and emerged unscathed. That was not going to be allowed to happen again. A tobacco lobbyist told me that the industry had sent an insistent message to its congressional allies: show up. This time, Bliley was flanked by Michael Bilirakis of Florida, Alex McMillan of North Carolina, Gary Franks of Connecticut, James Greenwood of Pennsylvania, and Dennis Hastert of Illinois, who later became Speaker of the House. The Democrats, on the other hand, were lightly represented. Only Mike Synar of Oklahoma, Ron Wyden of Oregon, and Mike Kreidler of Washington joined Waxman on this day. As I surveyed the subcommittee members, I felt momentarily apprehensive.

I walked over to the congressmen to say a courteous "hello." I approached Bliley, my hand extended, but he would have nothing to do with me.

Soon after, I took my place at the witness table and began laying out the Y-1 story, guiding the subcommittee through Chaplin's early experiments and B&W's field trials, through DNAP's work on male sterile seeds and the Souza Cruz contracts. I described the seed export law, the Brazilian patent, and the U.S. patent application, finally coming to the customs search for invoices, and our conversations with DNAP and Brown & Williamson. I had brought along cartons of cigarettes that had been manufactured with Y-1 tobacco and laid them before me on the table.

As I testified, Jack Mitchell began pacing in the back of the room. He was worried that I might be challenged to reveal specific sources, and he was poised to race out of the room, if necessary, to alert Jeff Wigand.

After Y-1, I moved on to ammonia technology, quoting from the copy of the *Handbook for Leaf Blenders* that had mysteriously arrived in our mailroom earlier. "'Ammonia, when added to a tobacco blend, reacts with the indigenous nicotine salts and liberates free nicotine.... [T]he ratio of extractable nicotine to bound nicotine in the smoke may be altered in favor of extractable nicotine.... [E]xtractable nicotine contributes to impact in cigarette smoke.'" I had no evidence that the tobacco companies had actually used ammonia for this purpose—and after the hearing they denied it vehemently—but there was no doubt that the process had been studied carefully.

Finally, I summed up. "Why spend a decade developing through genetic breeding high-nicotine tobacco and adding it to cigarettes if you are not interested in controlling and manipulating nicotine? Why focus on the enhanced delivery of free nicotine to the smoker by chemical manipulation if you are not interested in controlling and manipulating nicotine?"

Then, I shifted topics. I wanted to make the direct connection between nicotine manipulation and industry intent that was so crucial to our decision about regulating tobacco. Among other sources, I drew on documents sent to us by Macon that described consumer preference studies on desirable nicotine levels. Ultimately, the industry's own words were the most powerful tool I had.

At the time, I had no idea that Bliley's staff was working itself into a state of apoplexy over my testimony. As the details began to unfold, stunned Hill staffers summoned representatives of the industry trade associations into a side room. "What is going on here?" one agitated staffer demanded to know.

Back in the hearing room, I was girding myself for the question-and-answer period. I expected an attack. Jack's pacing grew more agitated.

WAXMAN opened the discussion, commenting that he had found my testimony "riveting." He commended the agency on its investigation.

Bliley was less impressed. He weighed in with a veiled defense not only of

Y-1, but also of Brown & Williamson's decision to develop it. "You appear to be suggesting that B&W did something detrimental to human health. Don't you know that the federal government through its Cancer Institute proposed just such changes in tobacco?" He went on to explain that G. B. Gori, a scientist at the National Cancer Institute, had posited in 1980 that increasing nicotine delivery, relative to tar, might be a useful way to create a less hazardous cigarette. Wasn't B&W doing precisely that? asked Bliley.

Inadvertently, the congressman was helping to make my case. "Mr. Bliley, I am not here to say what is right or what's wrong," I said. My point was that such activity was evidence of manipulation and control. "I believe that is relevant to the Food and Drug Administration's determination of whether nicotine is a drug."

Bliley, at least, had directed his comments and questions to the subject of my testimony. The rest of the Republicans completely ignored Y-1 and ammonia.

Congressman McMillan appeared to be following prepared remarks when he asked whether I had any evidence to prove that the tobacco companies added nicotine to their products, a claim that had been the foundation of the *Day One* broadcast. I tried to explain that there were ways of manipulating and controlling nicotine without "spiking" cigarettes, but he wasn't interested in my answers.

Then, alluding to my comments about the behavioral effects of nicotine, and in particular its tranquilizing properties, McMillan asked irrelevantly, "If that's the case, do you think that affected the ability of Winston Churchill and Dwight Eisenhower to conduct operations on D-Day? They were heavy smokers." I tried telling the congressman I had never said that smoking affected judgment. He ignored me.

In still another disconnected remark, McMillan commented, "It has been said to me by plaintiffs' attorneys that perhaps as many as ninety percent of those incarcerated in jail today . . . are there because of a crime related to drugs or alcohol. Would you include cigarettes in that category?" It was plain I would not get far trying to respond to these non sequiturs.

Congressman Bilirakis was next. He asked that I "please provide this committee for the record all the memoranda prepared by your investigators on their interviews and any memoranda or draft memoranda on the possible details and implications of potential FDA regulation of tobacco products."

I thought I knew where Bilirakis was going with his request. Three days

before I had written to the committee to warn them, "I am not in a position
to disclose the names of confidential sources or any information in my judgment that could lead to the identification of those sources." I called that limi-
tation "essential to protect the integrity of the agency's processes and its
ability to effectively investigate important public health issues" and consistent
with past agency practices.

Now, I told the congressman that I would be happy to work with the
chairman so that he could verify the accuracy of the quotes I had taken from
the documents. Bilirakis did not like my offer. He wanted everything.

"I am not willing to make available any document or any memo or any
information that could possibly jeopardize a confidential source," I said firmly.

Jack looked ready to run.

Bilirakis kept pushing. "This is the first time that I have heard anything
about confidential sources or anything of that nature. I am just flabbergasted."

Greenwood, McMillan, and Hastert rallied to Bilirakis's cause. "I am listening to this and it is kind of surreal," said Hastert. "You are going to give us
only that information that you are going to spoon-feed us."

I said that the agency would follow established procedures. Hastert cut
me off, and the exchange grew more testy.

"Tell me what those established procedures are," Hastert insisted. "Tell
us. What are the established procedures?"

I tried to answer, but Hastert cut me off again. "What are they? What are
the established procedures? You are telling us mumbo jumbo. Tell me what
the established procedures are."

"Congressman," I said, "we are engaged in an investigation..."

He cut me off again and again, growing redder with every interruption.
"No, no, no. Wait a minute. Don't go around. Either you tell me what those
established procedures are, or I think you are in contempt of Congress."

Waxman tried to intercede. "I think if you will give him a chance to
answer, you will find out what they are."

Hastert's harangue briefly subsided. I took the moment to retrieve the letter I had sent the committee earlier and read the relevant sections, but
Hastert wanted the last word. "When a person who works for the taxpayers,
such as you do, and who has some responsibility to Congress and its members, tells us that he can't give us this information to make decisions on, to
me that is contempt."

The Republicans continued to criticize me and the agency's practices until

Mike Synar stepped in. "I am disappointed by the tenor that this debate has taken, at least from the Republican side." Turning to me, he added, "The fact is that we have been here for three hours and not one fact you have presented has been refuted by either the tobacco industry or those people who would attack your credibility."

Synar's intervention moderated the tone of the debate, but the attacks continued, although at a lower decibel, until the end. In truth, it made little difference to me. By then, nothing could pull me off course. It had taken the evidence to bring me to this point, but I now believed so fully in what we were doing on tobacco that I did not care about the pummeling.

In the last minutes of the hearing, Bilirakis submitted six questions for the agency to answer, all relating to the possible regulation of tobacco products and all completely ignoring the day's testimony. "Isn't it true," went one question, "that under the current law, if the FDA asserts jurisdiction over cigarettes on the grounds that they contain nicotine as a drug, you would have no alternative but to eliminate all nicotine-containing cigarettes from the market because they would not be covered by any new approved drug application on file?"

The purpose of the inquiries seemed plain. Bilirakis was warning American smokers that if they did not watch out, the FDA would take away their cigarettes. We were given two weeks to respond.

One other incident occurred as the hearing came to an end. Gene Pfeifer, B&W's outside counsel, approached Jack, and after a few minutes of casual conversation, Pfeifer offered an apology. He told Jack that he regretted the way in which Y-1 had been handled and said he had not been given the whole story by his clients. It was rare for an attorney to acknowledge a lapse on the part of his clients, and I took it as a sign that Pfeifer, who was once an advocate for public health, was deeply troubled by his clients' behavior.

AFTER the hearing, we answered Bilirakis's questions as best we could, given their hypothetical nature. Eventually, I learned that he had not prepared them himself. RJR had drafted the questions and sent over a copy to Capitol Hill. Many of Bilirakis's questions matched, word for word, the RJR document.

Philip Morris had also contributed to the tone of the day. In a memo stamped "confidential," the company had developed a "Kessler Hearing Checklist." Among the suggestions:

"Require Kessler to give over documents (e.g., notes of interviews) relating to his investigation."

"Prepare a line of narrowly tailored hostile questions."

"Brief friendly Members and staff and prepare them to ask hostile questions."

The similarities between the proposed strategies and those that had been implemented were obvious.

The industry memos also confirmed something I had suspected. The information we had presented on Y-1 and ammonia had taken the Republican congressmen by surprise. Brown & Williamson knew it was coming, but the other tobacco companies apparently did not. As Mike Synar noted at the hearings, they could not refute the facts that I had presented, so they launched a diversionary attack on my credibility. And that assault was far from over.

34

SINCE our investigation had begun in earnest in late February 1994 I was repeatedly surprised at how much we were able to find. When we first began reading patents and analyzing tar and nicotine levels, I knew we were onto something, but I also knew that the evidence was circumstantial. I had no idea how much further we could go. After Y-1, I was confident that we had demonstrated nicotine manipulation. But to make a persuasive case for regulating nicotine, we needed direct evidence of the industry intent.

Months before the Y-1 hearing, Jack Mitchell had heard rumors that industry documents had been pilfered by a man named Merrell Williams. As a paralegal for a law firm that represented Brown & Williamson, Williams had been assigned to read and classify documents relevant to the company's efforts to defend itself against health-related liability lawsuits. Williams quickly realized the significance of what he had and began to spirit the confidential papers out of his Louisville, Kentucky, office to make copies. By the time his job ended, he had thousands of pages in his possession.

Williams, who had smoked Kool cigarettes, a Brown & Williamson brand, for thirty years, told no one about the documents until he faced emergency triple bypass surgery. After his recovery, he contacted a lawyer named Fox DeMoisey to discuss filing a personal injury lawsuit. DeMoisey, learning of the documents, believed that the papers might be protected by Brown & Williamson's attorney-client privilege. DeMoisey advised Williams to ship them back to his former employer—accompanied by a cover letter warning Brown & Williamson that it would be held accountable for Williams's health. Williams did just that, but he also kept a full set of the documents.

Brown & Williamson immediately launched a furious fight to prevent them from ever becoming public, securing a gag order so restrictive that Merrell Williams could not talk to his own attorneys about the documents.

Rumors of the papers' contents reached Jack Mitchell. He called DeMoisey, explaining that he was calling on my behalf. The attorney was willing to talk about his client, apparently assuming it would be to Williams's advantage to cooperate with a government investigation and perhaps to win a powerful ally. But he made it clear that Jack had no chance of getting a look at the documents.

Philip Hilts, the lead tobacco reporter for the *New York Times,* was more successful, managing to secure the documents from a congressional staffer to whom they had been leaked. When Hilts called B&W to ask for a comment, a spokesperson told him, "Those are stolen documents. They've been stolen from Brown & Williamson and you can't print them." That was all that Hilts needed in order to verify their authenticity.

On May 7, 1994, I picked up the *New York Times* and read the headline "Tobacco Company Was Silent on Hazards." Hilts quoted extensively from the documents, which showed that B&W had known about the health hazards of cigarettes and the addictive properties of nicotine since the early 1960s. One phrase jumped out at me: "We are, then, in the business of selling nicotine, an addictive drug...."

The line came from an internal memo written in 1963 by Addison Yeaman, then general counsel to Brown & Williamson. Yeaman recommended that the company "accept its responsibility" to disclose the hazards of smoking, despite the risks of litigation, so that it could openly pursue scientific studies aimed at identifying and eliminating the dangerous chemical components of cigarettes. In his memo, the industry executive also celebrated recent findings of nicotine's tranquilizing and appetite-suppressing effects, noting that it "delivers to the industry what may well be the first effective instrument of propaganda to counter that of the American Cancer Society."

Hilts also had documents showing that in the early 1960s, B&W had debated whether to disclose any information to the Surgeon General's office, which was then preparing its historic report. Ultimately, he wrote, "[T]he executives chose to remain silent, to keep their research results secret, to stop work on a safer cigarette and to pursue a legal and public relations strategy of admitting nothing."

As I read his article, I knew we had crossed an important threshold. I had never imagined that the tobacco companies would put in writing that nicotine was a drug, or that I would be able to get my hands on such documents.

After hesitating for a moment, I went into my study to call Hilts. The reporter covered the agency closely, and we had established a good working relationship. It was nonetheless the first time since coming to the FDA that I had initiated a call to a reporter to praise him, and I spoke cautiously. When Hilts answered the phone, I said, "I may be crossing the line here, but I'm calling to congratulate you."

Then I called Jerry Mande and asked him to get in touch with Rip Forbes, Henry Waxman's point person on tobacco. Forbes also had close professional contacts with the staff of Congressman Ron Wyden. Reading the Hilts story, I was reasonably sure that someone in those two congressional offices knew more about the Merrell Williams documents.

Forbes was willing to talk, filling Jerry in on details that had not been reported. He said Hilts had seen only a fraction of the Brown & Williamson documents and that the full set was available in his office. Questions about their legal status initially made Forbes leery about sharing them with us, but he agreed to provide Jerry with a few selections, including both the telling Addison Yeaman memo and *Intent to Deceive,* a draft of a book Merrell Williams had written about the industry. Forbes quickly made good on his promise and Jerry brought the material directly to my house.

That night, I lay in bed reading *Intent to Deceive.* Though poorly organized and written in a stream-of-consciousness voice, it nonetheless contained references to damning documents. One quote, from Sir Charles Ellis, head scientist for British American Tobacco, suggested much about corporate-sponsored research. "It is my conviction that nicotine is a very remarkable beneficent drug that both helps the body to resist external stress and also can as a result show a pronounced tranquilizing effect.... Nicotine is not only a very fine drug, but the techniques of administration by smoking has [sic] considerable psychological advantages and a built-in control against excessive absorption." *Intent to Deceive* was an extraordinary window into the tobacco industry.

WITHIN a few days we struck a deal with Waxman's office and agreed to sift through the documents to help them identify those of special importance. In exchange, we were allowed to take extensive notes, but not to make any copies of the material. Ann Witt and Mitch Zeller headed to the Gerald R. Ford House Annex. Years before, the Annex had been an apartment building for congressmen, with a room on the fifth floor reserved for poker games between the nation's elected representatives and its lobbyists. The offices were overcrowded, and the building was dingy and in such disrepair that staffers were told not to overload their bookshelves or to fill more than three drawers of their file cabinets, lest the floor collapse under the weight.

At the Annex, stacks of manila folders had been piled into boxes in random fashion, with no clear beginning or end. Ann and Mitch each took a box, picked up the first document, and started to read. Although the papers were largely summaries and indexes that served as a road map to other documents, they quickly grew excited. Their words of astonishment kept breaking the silence.

The papers were filled with references to research, primarily from the 1960s and 1970s, involving nicotine, nicotine manipulation, and the biological activity of tobacco. An internal memo suggested that the company planned to protect many of the documents from legal discovery by asserting claims of attorney-client privilege. Ann was struck by the blunt tone of the documents, a stark contrast to how the tobacco companies had been dealing with us. It was as if we had suddenly been shot into the inner workings of the industry. In short order, Mitch and Ann had taken some fifty pages of handwritten notes. Impatient for details, I raced between meetings to a nearby coffee shop and insisted they interrupt their work to join me and tell me what they had found.

Once they had a more complete feel for the documents, we gathered for a closed meeting in my office. Ann read me notes taken from the glossary of terms developed to guide Merrell Williams and his paralegal colleagues as they reviewed and coded the documents, presumably in preparation for litigation. "Confirmation of causation" was the label assigned to documents that confirmed the link between smoking and disease while the phrase "manipulation of research/data" was used for documents "suggesting that cigarette companies made recommendations to research organizations about how research should be performed...." I also noticed that "industry competition" was the code for documents that suggested the company might be trying to get a competitive edge by, for example, designing products that allow a smoker to "adjust his smoking habits (*e.g.,* compensate) to obtain greater delivery of nicotine."

Documents pertaining to the industry's advertising and marketing strategies were also coded, on the basis of their targeted audiences: "smokers 18 years of age or younger," "persons who have not yet started smoking," and "individuals attempting to quit...." Then there was a list of reports with names like Project Madhatter and Project Hippo, which gave us a glance at research conducted on the pharmacology of nicotine, the search for safer cigarettes, and compensatory smoking. Project 311–27 was described only as the "Nicotine Enrichment Study," while Project Ariel "deals with nicotine pharmacology and research for nicotine analogues or substitutes." Project Janus, a series of animal experiments that began in 1965, ran for more than a decade and documented the carcinogenic action of cigarette smoke on mouse skin.

One full-text document, "Report to the Executive Committee," dated July 1, 1965, was written by the head researcher at B&W. It read, in part, "[F]ind ways of obtaining maximum nicotine for minimum tar," and offered an array of specific suggestions, including "nicotine fortification of cigarette paper; addition of nicotine-containing powders to tobacco; and attention to blends."

For the first time, we had seen explicit industry documents demonstrating that the effects of nicotine were intended.

BROWN & Williamson thought the *Times* articles, and the coverage in other news media, might offer grounds for a libel action, but after considering the possibility, its attorneys advised that filing a suit would subject the company to discovery on all the nicotine-related information in its files. Another option, apparently taken seriously, was to file a defamation suit against Garry Trudeau, creator of a Doonesbury cartoon character who mocked the industry.

Meanwhile, we continued to build our case. The Merrell Williams documents were from only one company. But soon Jack Mitchell broke the lock on Philip Morris. What he found finally helped us to understand just what William Dunn, the Nicotine Kid, had been doing for all of those years.

When we started our investigation, I tended to ask a lot of questions before sending FDA investigators in pursuit of a lead. Not anymore. I had realized that the key to a successful investigation was to explore every avenue, even unlikely ones, because it was impossible to predict where a given clue might take us. I began taking the view that every piece of ground had to be covered. Jack thought a document archives in Houston might yield something of interest, and that was enough for me.

All we knew at the time was that the archives were under the control of a nonprofit organization called DOC, short for Doctors Ought to Care, which had been founded in 1977 by a physician named Alan Blum. We had heard that its archives contained a vast array of tobacco advertising, promotion, and other smoking-related materials, but I was not expecting much. Negotiations with the program director in charge of the archives were protracted, and more than once I was tempted to let the DOC documents go. Finally, with the arrangements made, Jack headed to Houston.

By the middle of the first day, Jack was sure that his search would produce nothing new or startling. Sensing his disappointment, one of the archivists suggested that he look at a collection of documents that had remained virtually untouched for years. The papers were something of a mystery; no one remembered how they had come into DOC's possession.

Jack began to sift through thousands of pages dating from the 1950s to 1981, many printed on Philip Morris letterhead. He soon realized he was reading internal research files, scientific charts, and laboratory reports. Many had been written by a group headed by William Dunn. There were two important messages in the papers. First, the behavioral and pharmacological effects of nicotine had been studied for decades, and second, industry research emphasized the manipulation of nicotine levels to produce a "satisfying" cigarette.

Research reports had titles like "Alpha Brain Waves and Smoking," "Smoking and Mental Concentration," "Puffing Behavior," and "Nicotine Control as Related to Cigarette Acceptability." In an outline of upcoming projects, Dunn described "tentative plans to inject subjects with IV nicotine to examine effects of nicotine spike, level, and 'the reinforcement characteristics of the substance.'" Another avenue of investigation was designed to ensure "that total nicotine in the system remains at or near the nicotine need threshold." In the study titled "Aggressive Monkeys," researchers observed, "[S]mall doses of nicotine have 'tranquilizing' effects." "Hyperkinetic Child as a Prospective Smoker" involved collecting data on elementary school children. Still another research proposal would give college students shock treatments to see whether they smoked more in times of stress.

One Dunn memo showed that the company's research sometimes was made deliberately invisible. He wrote that if a proposed study could demonstrate that nicotine had no withdrawal effects, then Philip Morris would want to "pursue this avenue with some vigor. If, however, the results with nicotine are similar to those gotten with morphine and caffeine, we will want to bury it. Accordingly, there are only two copies of this memo, the one attached and the original which I have."

Dunn also reviewed the fundamental mission of his smoker's psychology program. Given legal concerns about the pharmacological effects of smoke, "however beneficial that effect might be," he acknowledged that his studies could not be justified on the basis of their public relations value. But they could contribute to product development. "Smoking the cigarette is the lever press," he wrote, making an analogy to hungry rats. "The effect of that smoking act upon his person is the reward. That effect reinforces the smoking act. He comes to push the lever ten to sixty times per day. Our task is to understand the reinforcing mechanism, or process, whereby the habit is established and maintained."

In the end, Jack stayed in Houston for five days and photocopied 2,867 documents from the DOC archives. During the flight back, he never let them out of his sight. He hand-delivered the files to me the next day. I reviewed them immediately and realized that Dunn understood the implications of his work fully. "The psychopharmacology of nicotine ... is where the action is, for those doing fundamental research on smoking, and from where most likely will come significant scientific developments profoundly influencing the industry," he wrote.

But he also realized that this new research direction carried a risk. "It is where our attorneys least want us to be," he continued, brooding about the influence of the industry lawyers. The lawyers feared FDA regulation.

"Do we really want to tout cigarette smoke as a drug?" he asked a colleague. "It is, of course, but there are dangerous FDA implications to having such conceptualization go beyond these walls."

Dunn noted that the lawyers were likely to insist upon a "clandestine" approach to any research that treated nicotine as a drug, either implicitly or explicitly, lest it be "viewed as a tacit acknowledgement that nicotine is a drug," wrote Dunn. "Therefore although permitted to continue ... we must not be visible about it."

JACK was not the only one searching for documents. Soon after his return from Houston, Sharon Natanblut walked into my office. "You're not going to believe this," she said. A source had just described to her the contents of internal R. J. Reynolds memos under court seal in the case of *Haines v. Liggett Group.*

They dealt extensively with nicotine. Looking at her notes, Sharon read, "Nicotine should be delivered at about 1.0–1.3 mg/cigarette, the minimum for confirmed smokers. The rate of absorption of nicotine should be kept low by holding pH down, probably below 6."

I always suspected that if the tobacco companies thought about nicotine as a drug, they also thought about dose. And here was the target dose.

"The beginning smoker and inhaler has a low tolerance for smoke irritation; hence, the smoke should be as bland as possible," Sharon continued.

It was one thing to hear about the documents over the telephone and quite another to obtain hard copies, something that Sharon's source could not provide. Nor could we ask the court to break the seal on the documents, because that would jeopardize the informant. After consultation with an FDA attorney, it became clear that, for the moment, our only course of action was no action at all.

It was not long before we were able to tap another channel to the same papers. Mitch Zeller had cultivated a good relationship with a small group of high-profile lawyers who were pursuing class-action product liability suits against the tobacco industry. They were searching for industry documents, just as we were, and were eager to share what they found.

One of the lawyers, Ron Motley, a partner in a Charleston, South Carolina, law firm, had taken over the *Haines v. Liggett* case when the original attorneys abandoned it after spending $6.2 million of their own money and going ten years without a decision. Motley's team of investigative lawyers— he called them his junkyard dogs—flew around the country combing through documents. Ann Ritter, a trial lawyer and a partner in the firm, was among them. For ten days she had been sitting on the concrete floor of a cavernous Charleston warehouse, a place used exclusively to store files produced in tobacco lawsuits, plowing through boxes and boxes of files. Some were decades old and all were coated with a layer of dust and dirt. Among them were some of the long-missing 1,500 documents that had so disturbed Judge H. Lee Sarokin.

It was evening when the telephone rang in Mitch's house. When he answered, Ritter used the same words that Sharon had first used to me.

"Mitch," Ritter said, "you're not going to believe this."

The first of the documents, written by the RJR executive Claude Teague in the early seventies, began to arrive on Mitch's fax machine that night. As each page arrived, he grabbed it from the machine and read eagerly. When he was finished, he called me at home.

"This is what we've been waiting for," he said.

I ASKED the members of the team to meet at my house the next morning. When they were all in the living room, Mitch began reading:

"'Nicotine is known to be a habit-forming alkaloid, hence the confirmed user of tobacco products is primarily seeking the physiological "satisfaction" derived from nicotine—and perhaps other active compounds.

"'Thus, a tobacco product is, in essence, a vehicle for delivery of nicotine, designed to deliver the nicotine in a generally acceptable and attractive form. Our industry is then based upon design, manufacture and sale of attractive dosage forms of nicotine, and our Company's position in our Industry is determined by our ability to produce dosage forms of nicotine which have more overall value, tangible or intangible, to the consumer than those of our competitors.'"

Mitch looked up. "Listen to what he has to say about nicotine being used as a stimulant, a depressant, or a tranquilizer," he said. "'Many of these same effects may be achieved with other physiologically active materials such as caffeine, alcohol, tranquilizers, sedatives, euphorics, and the like. Therefore, in addition to competing with products of the tobacco industry, our products may, in a sense, compete with a variety of other products with certain types of drug action.'"

Everyone was watching Mitch with concentrated attention. He read without emphasis or drama.

"'Happily for the tobacco industry, nicotine is both habituating and unique in its variety of physiological actions, hence no other active material or combination of materials provides equivalent "satisfaction."

"'If nicotine is the sine qua non of tobacco products and tobacco products are recognized as being attractive dosage forms of nicotine, then it is logical to design our products—and where possible, our advertising—around nicotine delivery rather than "tar" delivery or flavor,'" he continued. "'We may survey the market and conclude that current cigarette products delivering about 1.3 mg of nicotine appear to "satisfy" the typical smoker. This, somewhat crudely, establishes a target dosage level for design of new products.'"

Mitch stopped reading for a moment. "This is what he has to say about the importance of nicotine to smoking. 'If...nicotine is the sine qua non of smoking, and if we meekly accept the allegations of our critics and move toward reduction or elimination of nicotine from our products, then we shall eventually liquidate our business.'"

One sentence was even more explicit than the rest: "'In a sense, the tobacco industry may be thought of as being a specialized, highly ritualized and stylized segment of the pharmaceutical industry. Tobacco products uniquely contain and deliver nicotine, a potent drug with a variety of physiological effects.'"

Mitch folded the papers. The Teague documents were the starkest and the most direct way imaginable to describe nicotine, and everyone recognized that. The room was silent.

WE DID NOT know everything. I was still unsure about reconstituted tobacco, and I doubted that the industry was telling the truth when it said we were wrong about ammonia's potency-enhancing effect on tobacco. And I was sure there was more to learn about nicotine manipulation. But those were unfinished details on a much larger canvas. The message contained in the documents was unmistakable. We finally had unequivocal evidence that the major tobacco companies knew that nicotine was a drug and had said so long before the FDA. Just as the industry lawyers had feared, the companies had given themselves away with their own words. The key question now was how to move forward on the evidence.

PART IV

TURNING DECEIT ASIDE

35

PHARMACIA, INC., a huge Swedish drug company, thought its nicotine nasal spray was ready for marketing. Like Nicorette gum and the transdermal nicotine patch, the spray was a nicotine-replacement product intended to help people quit smoking. The difference was that the nasal spray delivered nicotine to the bloodstream within minutes of use, making it potentially more effective—and more likely to be abused. Curtis Wright, who headed the FDA office that reviews products designed to treat addictive disorders, asked a board-certified toxicologist to review the approval application.

The physician was disturbed by what he saw in the data. Unlike the gum or the patch, the nasal spray could produce blood levels of nicotine that approached those in cigarettes, especially if the user administered several doses at once. A year after clinical trials began, some 40 percent of the participants who had quit smoking were still using the spray, and in some cases they were taking extreme measures to secure it. People had stolen dispensers or used the ones they had five or ten times as often as they had been told to use them. They sent their husbands and wives to the trial sites to request extra spray or begged for more themselves. Wright recognized this as addictive behavior and decided the FDA should ask its Drug Abuse Advisory Committee to assess the new drug for its abuse potential, which is a fairly common practice at the agency.

The committee, made up of a group of independent advisers that included clinicians and academic experts in addiction medicine, drug treatment, pharmacology, and related fields, was scheduled to meet on August 1 and 2, 1994. Realizing that the scientific forum offered an opportunity not only to evaluate the nasal spray but also to engage in a wider public dialogue about the addictive properties of nicotine, I decided to broaden the committee's agenda beyond the nasal spray. Specifically, I wanted answers to the questions I had asked Jack Henningfield months earlier. How much nicotine is needed to sustain dependence? And is there a safe level below which dependence is unlikely?

Anticipating media interest in the August meeting, Philip Morris went on the attack. One step was contacting newspaper editorial boards. "Any mitigating comments, let alone neutralizing one of these newspapers would be a powerful signal to Kessler and the administration," wrote Victor Han, vice president of corporate communications. "The window is approximately one week."

Two days before the event, we were flooded with industry comments from Philip Morris and R. J. Reynolds. The "paper dump" was a familiar industry tactic and meant that 2,000 pages of information had to be photocopied and distributed by overnight mail to the nine-member committee. Presumably to show how readily the concept of "addiction" could be trivialized, the companies had submitted articles with such titles as "Pinball Wizard: The Case of a Pinball Machine Addict," "Can Carrots Be Addictive?" and "Running Addiction: Measurement and Associated Psychological Characteristics." Another theme found throughout the documents was that many smokers managed to quit, and that personality played a role in their success.

WE booked the largest available meeting space, the Plaza Ballroom at the Holiday Inn in Silver Spring, and even that was overcrowded. In the highly charged room, everyone sensed what was at stake. The nasal spray offered an almost perfectly controlled experiment to confirm nicotine's addictive properties. The rituals involved in smoking, the images it supposedly evoked, and all of the sensory pleasures were irrelevant. The spray had no flavor, there was nothing to taste, and it had a harsh and burning sensation. One of our drug reviewers sprayed a dose into his own nostrils and said it was like snorting Drano. Some users developed nasal bleeding and nasal ulcers, and partially lost their sense of smell. Everything that allegedly led a smoker to use cigarettes had been taken away except the nicotine—yet many smokers found the spray almost as satisfying. By the day's end, the committee members agreed that people could become addicted to the nicotine nasal spray, and it was placed under tight regulation as a controlled substance.

Three expert witnesses for the tobacco industry were scheduled to speak the next day. Only one worked for a tobacco company. The others were receiving consulting fees.

Domenic Ciraulo, chief of psychiatry at a Veterans Affairs clinic in Boston, presented data showing that morphine, amphetamines, and gambling generated far greater euphoria than cigarettes. A former smoker who claimed it had been easy for him to stop, the psychiatrist asserted, "The mild nature of the withdrawal syndrome after smoking cessation also separates smoking from opioid, alcohol, or sedative hypnotic dependence and places it closer to coffee."

Taking pains to be courteous, I asked Ciraulo how difficult he thought it was to stop smoking. Shrugging slightly, he said that other substances posed greater challenges. I kept pressing. "If you look at the number of people who resume smoking after a diagnosis of lung cancer or even after a laryngectomy, how do you explain that?" I asked. "There, the danger is as real as it can be."

The Boston psychiatrist described the attitude of his patients as being, essentially, "Look, I've got cancer now, so why should I stop smoking?"

Michael Bozarth, an associate professor at the State University of New York at Buffalo, whose research focused on the biological mechanisms of motivation and reward in animals, made the final industry presentation. The scientist wore his long hair pulled back in a ponytail and talked in such a rapid-fire manner that it was sometimes difficult to follow his arguments. But his conclusion echoed that of his colleagues. "Research has failed to substantiate the claim that nicotine is addictive," he said.

I doubted these men were simply fronting for the tobacco companies. They were contrarian academics who had developed their own theories and the industry had seized on them. But they gave credibility to Veritas's assertion that "experts" could be found to testify about almost anything. In a private conversation I later had with him, Domenic Ciraulo acknowledged that he had been auditioned the day before the meeting by an array of industry representatives and attorneys.

Had we known more about the industry's research at the time, I might have asked other, more pointed, questions about the companies' knowledge of nicotine addiction. I doubt it would have made much difference. The "experts" had their own message to send, and no matter how deftly I questioned them, I was not going to change that.

With the presentations completed, the advisory committee began its public discussion. I knew how much was at stake. The FDA had never formally declared nicotine addictive. Any doubt now that it was would hand the industry an enormous victory. But with minimal dissension, the overwhelming majority voted with the committee member who stated without reservation that "cigarettes and other forms of tobacco are addicting, and nicotine is the drug in tobacco that causes addiction."

The committee was unable to pinpoint a threshold level at which addiction occurred. "My suspicion is that there probably is some sort of threshold dose for an individual below which dependent use is unlikely to develop," said one committee member. But she spoke for the majority when she added, "I don't think we have anywhere near the body of evidence necessary to begin to talk about what that dose may be."

It did not matter. The day after the meeting newspapers across the country headlined the committee's conclusion. "Panel: Nicotine Addictive," declared USA Today. Beneath the bold headline, the kicker read, "Regulation of tobacco possible, if FDA agrees." "Key FDA Panel Concludes That Nicotine Is Addictive," wrote the Los Angeles Times. The Baltimore Sun was even more explicit: "Panel Puts Nicotine Closer to FDA Control."

ARMED with the advisory committee's decision and the weight of all the other evidence we had collected, I asked a few members of the tobacco team to gather in the backyard of my Bethesda house one afternoon. It was one of Washington's legendary hot and sticky summer days, and we drank lemonade and tried to keep cool as we began to discuss next steps.

The longstanding assumption had always been that FDA regulation had to be an all-or-nothing proposition. Once the FDA classified nicotine as a drug, the tobacco companies would be required to file an application that showed cigarettes to be safe and effective; since they would be unable to do so, we would have to ban them. Now we had to decide whether a ban was, in fact, inevitable. Prohibition-style tactics were doomed to fail, but workable alternatives were elusive.

Then Ann Witt spoke up. "Why don't we regulate cigarettes and smokeless tobacco as restricted devices?" she asked. A copy of the Food, Drug, and Cosmetic Act sat open on her lap. The section of the statute governing medical devices—products as diverse as tongue depressors and CT scan machines—was enacted in 1976, almost forty years after the drug provisions. She argued that under the statute, the agency could restrict the sale, use, and distribution of cigarettes without banning them, if they were classified as medical devices.

There was a pause as the idea sank in. I realized almost immediately that Ann was onto something big, that this might be a near-perfect fit. Nicotine is the drug, the cigarettes and smokeless tobacco are drug delivery devices. Ann also pointed out that the device amendments permitted the FDA to regulate tobacco advertising; the drug provisions, by contrast, gave the FDA authority only over prescription drug advertising.

Ann's novel approach would allow us to assert jurisdiction over the product without banning it. It was the breakthrough we needed to move forward.

RECOGNIZING the value of thinking through our next steps without a lot of interruptions, I decided we needed to get away from the office for a few days. I wanted an opportunity to talk about the specific terms of the regulation we would draft to govern these restricted devices. Concerned about appearances, Jim O'Hara insisted that we keep our expenses to a minimum. Everything that the agency did on tobacco was subjected to microscopic scrutiny, and we had to make sure that no one could unfairly characterize the meeting as a junket. O'Hara lobbied hard for the 4-H Conference Center on Connecticut Avenue. "Maybe we should consider the bus station," one exasperated staffer suggested. Finally, we settled on Airlie House, a conference center in the Virginia countryside. My room had neither a television nor a telephone.

Twenty-two people gathered at Airlie House. "Any policy, any regulation, we come up with must be eminently reasonable," I said during the opening discussions. Those words—"eminently reasonable"—became my catchphrase, and although I was gently mocked for my repeated use of the term, I was serious. Whatever policy we developed had to meet the test of common sense.

In the early days of our investigation, I thought the real goal of FDA action was to push Congress to enact legislation. But with all that we had uncovered, I now told the group, "New legislation should remain an option, but it is not key." I also emphasized that the FDA should not attempt to resolve the tobacco dilemma alone; we needed to work with our sister public health agencies, especially the Centers for Disease Control and the Substance

Abuse & Mental Health Services Administration, which were already involved in tobacco control efforts.

Curtis Wright decided to add a personal note to our discussions. "My mother died of peripheral vascular disease that was due, in large part, to her total inability, even as a physician, to stop smoking," he said. "Myself, I probably made a solid three hundred quit attempts. I remember sitting in the lounge in the emergency room at Bethesda Naval Hospital where I was acting chief of emergency medicine and there would be a nurse and a corpsman, and me, and we would be getting ready to bag and tag somebody who had just had a fatal heart attack due to smoking, and we'd all be lighting up."

Then Curtis told a story about his seventeen-year-old son. "I raised Eric. I used to sit down and do his science projects with him and we did one on tobacco and health. One day he pulled out a Zippo lighter and wanted to show it to me. And I said, 'Son, there's only one reason to have a cigarette lighter. You're smoking, aren't you?'

"I'm sitting there looking at my kid, knowing that he's smoking, knowing that he's going to go through the same miserable experience trying to quit as I was. And there wasn't a damn thing I could do about it. I was utterly impotent when faced with all of the pro-smoking forces in society."

No one thought Curtis was being overly sentimental. Our move to regulate cigarettes was direct and personal for him.

The most intense discussion at Airlie House centered on the possibility of reducing the level of nicotine in cigarettes over time, with an eye towards eventually weaning smokers from the addictive agent. Ann Witt and Sharon Natanblut were convinced that the weaning strategy held promise. Each was a formidable advocate; together, they could be almost overpowering. "How would it be done?" I asked skeptically. "Would higher-yield brands be available for those who wanted them? Are there any studies demonstrating that this strategy works?" I was interested in the possibility of somehow modifying the product to make it safer, but I was not convinced that the science was available to tell us the best way to do this. We argued back and forth until I finally insisted we set the idea aside. Looking hard at Ann and Sharon, I said, "You're not going to implement national policy when you don't have any data, are you?" They reluctantly backed down.

By the time the long days of debate at Airlie House ended, we had outlined a set of advertising, marketing, and access restrictions that would form the core of the new rule. But the hard work lay ahead, in fleshing out the details. I wanted that job done in less than three months.

CATHERINE Lorraine, the lawyer who had helped write the letter to the Coalition, and Sharon Natanblut took charge of the team assigned to draft the proposed rule. I also brought over Judy Wilkenfeld from the Federal Trade Commission, who described herself bluntly as a "firecracker."

For many years, Judy had tried to keep the FTC involved in tobacco regulation, within the limits of the agency's mandate to police product marketing, sales, and advertising. She knew what it meant to face the wrath of the tobacco industry. After she was erroneously listed as an author of a journal article about the tobacco control movement, the U.S. Tobacco Company demanded that the FTC remove her from all tobacco matters, on the grounds that she was an advocate, not an impartial enforcer of the law. Judy became embroiled in a costly year-long battle to prove that she had acted appropriately. Although eventually absolved of any wrongdoing, she became disillusioned with an agency that chose to investigate her rather than come to her defense. Finally, when FTC commissioners refused to bring what she felt was an iron-clad case against RJR's use of the Joe Camel cartoon in advertising, Judy was ready to move. I invited her to join us at the FDA shortly after hearing a presentation she made to the tobacco team, and she jumped at the chance.

The rulemaking team started to work virtually around the clock. The air conditioning was turned off at the Parklawn building after hours, and without it the heat made working conditions almost unbearable. Eventually, I unearthed a monstrously large portable air cooler—it must have been at least six feet high—to keep the team from wilting.

While that group focused on the terms of the regulation, I turned my attention to the legal case we would have to build to support our decision to assert jurisdiction over tobacco. That decision hinged on the critical definition in the statute that we had discussed so many times—a regulated product must be "intended to affect the structure or any function of the body." To me, gaining that authority was far more important than the specific terms of the rule. I knew that whatever we proposed was likely to be relatively modest, at least initially. But if we could lay out a strong legal case, we could come back to the companion regulations and strengthen them over time, as necessary. Ann Witt and Mitch Zeller worked closely with me on the jurisdiction document.

Ann's assignment was to study the industry documents to see if they would prove intent. By now we had thousands of pages of tobacco documents in our hands; eventually, we scanned every one into our database. Week after week Ann sat alone, sifting through cartloads of paper and culling quotes to support FDA jurisdiction. I became her research assistant, taking home hundreds of pages every night, sometimes working until three in the morning to highlight passages I thought we should include. Back at the office I gave Ann the documents, with dozens of yellow flags poking out, and then bothered her constantly, asking whether she had remembered to include each one. By the end, we had so much documented evidence that we had to shrink the citations in the jurisdiction document down to six-point type.

IN THE summer of 1994, Mike Taylor, who had shepherded through the nutrition label, told me he was leaving to head the Food Safety and Inspection Service at the Department of Agriculture. Though I was sorry to lose him, I recognized it as an important opportunity to bring a public health focus to the USDA, the agency that had once stood in the way of the labeling initiative.

I recruited Bill Schultz to replace Mike in the policy office. Bill, a lawyer who had spent much of his early career at Ralph Nader's Public Citizen's Litigation Group, had often battled the FDA in court. When I worked for Orrin Hatch, Bill was fighting the senator's efforts to revise food safety laws, and when I came back to Washington as commissioner, he was counsel to Henry Waxman's subcommittee and a key congressional staffer on FDA issues. We had not always agreed, but I developed tremendous respect for his legal intellect. As was the case with Jerry Mande and Mitch Zeller, I saw Bill's contentious history with the FDA as a plus, not a minus.

Ann Witt and Bill had known each other for many years, and they, too, had often been at loggerheads. Bill had been opposing counsel on the first case Ann handled at the FDA. But the two lawyers had become friends, and now they became colleagues.

After a briefing from Ann, Bill immersed himself in a study of the word "intent." Traditionally, the FDA determined a company's intent from the label or the words used in advertising and elsewhere. Phrases such as "for temporary relief of pain" or "to prevent motion sickness" were assumed to show the purpose for which a drug was marketed. The tobacco industry was arguing publicly that the words on the label were the only basis for intent. But of course there was nothing on a package of cigarettes that implied an intent to create addiction.

Sitting alone in the open stacks of the Supreme Court library, Bill read dozens of cases that interpreted the word "intent" in the Food, Drug, and Cosmetic Act. When that library closed at five o'clock, he often went over to the Library of Congress.

In an ingenious move, Bill expanded his search beyond the Food, Drug, and Cosmetic Act, asking how intent had been interpreted under other statutes and by other federal agencies with regulatory authority. One day, as we puzzled over the issue in my office, I called Hal Edgar, with whom I had co-taught at Columbia Law School. Hal was the perfect person to help us understand intent as it is used in other legal contexts, and he graciously embarked on an in-depth and rather abstract discussion of culpability, purpose, knowledge, recklessness, and negligence. He crystallized the concept of subjective intent, a more nuanced legal principle than objective intent, with a classic example. An individual puts a valuable painting on an airplane and then plants a bomb on the plane. His intention is to collect insurance money for the painting, but when the pilot dies, he is charged with murder. Given the fact that the pilot's death is foreseeable, the law imputes an intent to kill.

As Bill began to shape a legal framework for asserting jurisdiction, I became his research assistant, too. Late into the night I ran computer searches on Lexis, the on-line legal database, using terms such as "willful blindness" and "ostrich defense" to learn what the law said about a manufacturer who ignored the uses to which its products were put. Another member of the tobacco team pointed us to a telling case in which a company had been marketing baby rattles as decorative ornaments for packages and clothing. The rattles were small enough for infants to put into their mouths and swallow, and the court ruled that the rattles fell under the jurisdiction of the Consumer Product Safety Commission statute because the manufacturer could reasonably have been expected to know how they would be used. The "foreseeable" aspect of this argument was readily extrapolated to tobacco— regardless of how tobacco was marketed, a cigarette manufacturer could anticipate that the product would be used for the druglike purpose of satisfying an addiction.

We developed a second legal theory focused on actual consumer use. Whatever the manufacturer's purpose, intent could be established by demonstrating that a product was used nearly exclusively for a druglike effect. Given the extent of smoker addiction, that was not hard to show.

Finally, we said that intent could be established by the manufacturer's explicit knowledge of the product's effect. Our ongoing investigation and the documents overloading our filing systems provided ample evidence on that score.

After months of effort, we felt confident that all three theories—foreseeability, actual consumer use, and explicit knowledge—provided a strong basis for declaring jurisdiction over tobacco. As sensible and straightforward as our legal analysis seemed to us, it was a pioneering interpretation of the Food, Drug, and Cosmetic Act.

36

CONFIDENT in our arguments for asserting jurisdiction, I began to look harder at industry marketing strategies. Understanding how the tobacco companies sold their merchandise, and to whom, was essential in order for us to decide how to regulate products used by 50 million Americans.

At the beginning of the twentieth century few women smoked, at least not publicly. George Washington Hill, the president of American Tobacco, became obsessed with cracking this huge potential market. He found his entrée in the "ideal of slimness." One of the pharmacological effects of nicotine was its weight-reducing properties, and Hill was willing to take advantage of that fact.

Hill hired the public relations guru Edward Bernays to launch an extensive campaign to sell Lucky Strikes by getting women to "reach for a Lucky instead of a sweet." The sugar industry was not pleased, but Bernays took the idea well beyond the promotion of a single brand of cigarettes. American women, already beginning to recognize the health benefits of weight loss, also responded to the concept of equating being beautiful with being thin. Bernays capitalized on that, encouraging commercial photographers and graphic artists to feature slender women and, as he said, "flooding fashion editors with photographs of thin Parisian models in haute couture dresses."

Bernays's efforts to influence the cultural milieu did not end there. Hill, concerned that the green packaging of Lucky Strikes did not match the predominant fashion colors of the times, ordered Bernays to "change the fashion." For six months, Bernays pursued every avenue to make green the preferred color for women's clothes and accessories. From the "Green Ball" staged as a high-society New York fund-raiser to the "Green Fashions Fall" luncheon at the Waldorf-Astoria for fashion editors and trade groups—where the menu featured green beans, pistachio mousse glacé, and crème de menthe—no detail was overlooked. By the fall of 1928, green was the color featured in department store windows and on the cover of *Vogue*.

The women's emancipation movement was well under way, and Bernays also worked to establish a link between cigarette smoking and the liberation of women. The psychoanalyst A. A. Brill, who had introduced Sigmund Freud's ideas to the English-speaking world, was brought in as a consultant to offer his views on why women might want to defy social norms by smoking. "Cigarettes, which are equated with men, become torches of freedom," Brill told Bernays. And so a torch parade was planned. On Easter Sunday, 1929, ten debutantes marched down New York's Fifth Avenue, cigarettes in hand, to protest the smoking taboo. That moment helped change public attitudes—and fostered a man-made epidemic.

Throughout the twentieth century the tobacco companies continued to use the theme of breaking taboos, recasting it as times changed. At one time, observed an industry writer, images of "elegance and glamour" were associated with smoking. But in a different era, a different marketing strategy was needed, and so images of a "more earthy 'sexiness' and 'machisma'" took hold. As one American Tobacco document explained, the goal was always to "consider a more contemporary and relevant lifestyle approach...to segment the female market on the basis of current values, age, lifestyles and preferred length and circumference [of] products." Particular attention was paid to poorly educated and minority women, who the industry knew were more likely to smoke.

After researching gender differences in the 1970s, some industry researchers concluded that women found it harder than men to quit smoking. "Women are more neurotic than men and more likely to need to smoke in stressful situations, presumably because they are less well able to deal with stress," theorized one official. The industry recognized the implications of this "neurosis" for product development. One was that "neurotic" women were thought more likely to respond to publicity about the health risks of smoking by switching to "lighter" cigarettes. The solution was to develop a "female-oriented" cigarette from which "considerably more nicotine could be obtained." Believing that it might be more difficult for women to stop smoking, industry executives cynically did what they could to make it harder still.

Another layer of risk may have been added when the "slim" cigarette, intended to appeal to women, was introduced. A British American Tobacco document found that not only does the amount of carcinogens inhaled increase as more tobacco is smoked, but there is an increased transfer of one of the most potent carcinogens from the tobacco to the smoke in cigarettes with smaller circumferences.

Industry marketing strategies played a role in the skyrocketing death rate from lung cancer among women, which now exceeds the number of deaths each year from breast cancer. Yet little outrage has been expressed, perhaps because the high fatality rate from lung cancer—compared to that from breast cancer—decreases the pool of potential anti-smoking activists. I suspect also that the industry's funding of many influential women's groups helped to maintain the silence. "We began intensive discussions with representatives of key women's organizations," one Tobacco Institute document noted matter-of-factly. "Most have assured us that, for the time being, smoking is not a priority issue for them."

TWELVE-HOUR rock concerts are not my preferred choice of entertainment, but my children, Elise and Ben, pleaded to go to one at RFK Stadium, and Paulette and I finally agreed to take them. I brought tobacco documents with me to read, but my earplugs did not entirely block out the loud music blaring from the center of the stadium, and eventually I gave up and surveyed the crowd. There were groups of kids wearing college T-shirts and young people with pierced eyebrows. There was a contingent of teenagers dressed entirely in black, and another wearing neat shorts, sandals, and tucked-in shirts. What they had in common, aside from their youth, was that many of them were smoking cigarettes. The day's events reinforced what a member of Lorillard's sales force had once written: "The base of our business is the high school student." Determining that nicotine was a drug suddenly seemed easy compared to finding a way to stop these young people from smoking.

One summer afternoon, as I was preparing to head again to the Jersey shore for my family's annual get-together, Sharon Natanblut handed me an index of nearly eight hundred industry documents that had been forwarded to her from the National Clearinghouse on Tobacco and Health in Canada. I identified the documents I wanted, and they began arriving at the beach by overnight delivery. Soon, I was immersing myself in the world of marketing to young people.

I became focused on two reports—"Project 16" and a follow-up entitled "Project Plus/Minus." Written by consultants for the Imperial Tobacco Company, the Canadian sister of Brown & Williamson, these were overt attempts on the part of the industry to understand why children start to smoke and why they want to quit. "However intriguing smoking was at eleven, twelve, or thirteen, by the age of sixteen or seventeen, many regretted their use of cigarettes for health reasons and because they felt unable to stop when they want to," read one document.

Project 16 quoted from focus groups with preteen and adolescent smokers, boys who once thought that smoking would make them men, and girls who believed that cigarettes would make them glamorous.

"I first smoked when I was 12. It was fun sneaking away and hiding."
"You were cool if you smoked. Girls looked up to you...."
"I thought I was a big boy. Tough. One of the crowd."
"It's either smoke or eat. I'd rather smoke...than eat and blow up."
"When I first started, it was in Junior High, and then you're just starting to find yourself...."

It was the regret of the children and adolescents that touched me most.

"I liked it. Now I hate it but it's still a habit."
"[W]e all said we'd do it for a few years and then quit, and we really meant it. Now, it's what? Five years later and I'm not so sure."
"I like to tell myself I don't have a habit, but really, I do."

The voices were composed in equal parts of teenage bluster and despair. I soon realized that the story rarely varied—experimentation, followed by addiction, and only later by the realization of addiction's grip. One boy who was interviewed likened his cigarette to a crutch that he held between his fingers. Another said when he saw a younger boy smoking, he wanted to punch him for his stupidity. A third wondered why cigarettes could be bought so easily, if they were so dangerous. Many envied friends who were not addicted.

"In high school, you never think that you're gambling with death....It's just a challenge to see if you can get away with it...."
"I never thought it'd become a habit....[A]fter you get smoking for a while you realize what it is. Then it's too late."

A single paragraph affected me more than anything else we had learned in our investigation. It noted how every young person was sure that he or she would not become addicted. "You never think you'll do any damage to yourself," said one of them. "You'll know how to control it."

But it was not so. As Project Plus/Minus stated, "[A]ddicted they do indeed become."

THAT preteens and young adolescents were experimenting with tobacco was not a surprise. What I had not fully understood until then was that those children were becoming addicted in their teenage years and finding it no easier than adults to quit smoking. Although I had briefly smoked a pipe, I had never been a cigarette smoker, and I did not have a visceral grasp of what it was to be in addiction's grip. A book called *Smoker: Self Portrait of a Nicotine Addict* gave me that sense. "One thing I don't decide, however, is whether to smoke," wrote the author, Ellen Walker. "For me, a forty-seven-year-old woman, that decision was made nearly thirty years ago by a first-year college student. And even she wasn't intending to make a lifelong decision; she was just going to try one cigarette. And then maybe just one more. Another, and then another, and at some point, she lost her power to choose."

I soon realized that children and adolescents were essential to the economic health of the tobacco industry. Claude Teague of R.J. Reynolds, who understood well the complex psychology of adolescents and how to manipulate it, knew that. "The fragile, developing self-image of the young person needs all of the support and enhancement it can get," he wrote. "Smoking may appear to enhance that self-image in a variety of ways.... This self-image enhancement effect has traditionally been a strong promotional theme for cigarette brands and should continue to be emphasized."

In the same report Teague also wrote, "At the outset it should be said that we are presently, and I believe unfairly, constrained from directly promoting cigarettes to the youth market, that is, to those in the approximately twenty-one-year-old and under group. Statistics show, however, that large, perhaps even increasing, numbers in that group are becoming smokers each year, despite bans on promotion of cigarettes to them. If this be so, there is certainly nothing immoral or unethical about our Company attempting to attract those smokers to our products."

Another RJR document noted that the fourteen-to-eighteen-year-old group was "an increasing segment of the smoking population." Teague was explicit about what RJR had at stake. "Realistically, if our Company is to survive and prosper, over the long term we must get our share of the youth market. In my opinion, this will require new brands tailored to the youth market; I believe it unrealistic to expect that existing brands identified with an over-thirty 'establishment' market can ever become the 'in' products with the youth group."

One obstacle to reaching young people was the unpleasantness that accompanies the initial smoking experience. Teague had some insights there. "For the pre-smoker and 'learner' the physical effects of smoking are largely unknown, unneeded, or actually quite unpleasant or awkward. The expected or derived psychological effects are largely responsible for influencing the pre-smoker to try smoking, and provide sufficient motivation during the 'learning' period to keep the 'learner' going, despite the physical unpleasantness and awkwardness of the period."

Once the learning period is over, the young person is hooked. "The physical effects become of overriding importance and desirability to the confirmed smoker, and the psychological effects, except the tension-relieving effect, largely wane in importance or disappear," Teague wrote. What is left is the need for nicotine.

I repeatedly came back to one telling paragraph: "[I]f we are to attract the nonsmoker or pre-smoker, there is nothing in this type of product that he would currently understand or desire. We have deliberately played down the role of nicotine, hence the nonsmoker has little or no knowledge of what satisfactions it may offer him, and no desire to try it. Instead, we somehow must convince him with wholly irrational reasons that he should try smoking...."

And convince them they did.

THERE were, of course, laws in every state that barred the selling of tobacco products to minors, but these were virtually ignored in most locations. To learn more about industry strategies to reach the youth market, I pushed Gary and Tom to track down new informants. "Doc," a scientist who had retired from RJR after a long and varied career that included a stint in research and development, knew a lot about the company's efforts to reach eighteen-to-twenty-four-year-olds through an ambitious Young Adult Smokers initiative, but he knew nothing about marketing to teenagers. He seemed genuinely astonished when I read him a memo from the RJR Sales Company in Sarasota, Florida, which instructed sales reps to identify stores "that are heavily frequented by young adult shoppers," specifically those in close proximity to colleges and high schools and to be sure to keep those stores properly stocked.

Doc did know that the company's official position was that targeting the under-eighteen set was taboo. When the *Wall Street Journal* ran an article about the Sarasota memo, RJR called it a rogue document written by a misguided employee. But Mitch Zeller located a similar memo from RJR Sales in Moore, Oklahoma. It, too, called for local sales representatives to identify accounts located near high schools and college campuses.

Doc led us to "Beach," who had conducted market research with college students on their spring break in Daytona Beach, Florida. When Tom Doyle first contacted Beach, he was not eager to talk. But in their inimitable style, Gary and Tom landed on his doorstep, and Beach, though wary, invited them in.

"What we are interested in is projects dealing with kids," Gary said. Beach's mood instantly changed.

"You're talking about the YAS, the Young Adult Smokers, aren't you?" he asked before the phrase had even been mentioned. With that, he opened up and began talking about his own kids. Beach told Tom and Gary that what his former employer was doing was wrong.

Beach helped us understand how RJR exploited the seventy-fifth year of selling Camel cigarettes to reposition that brand to appeal to young people. He described how the company pointedly referred to Camel's "birthday," rather than its "anniversary." The strategy was employed, he said, because "birthday" sounded young and fun while "anniversary" sounded like something that older people celebrate. He also talked about an expensive system to identify and study eighteen-to-twenty-year-old smokers and their smoking habits.

Another source was Gary Belcher, a former RJR manager who had been in charge of chain-store marketing. Tom and Gary drove to Belcher's house in Tampa early one afternoon. Belcher refused to let them in, but he suggested a meeting at a local restaurant at 7:30 that evening, and Tom and Gary agreed. They arrived early, took a booth, and ordered their usual iced tea. Five minutes later, two men walked in and sat nearby. They were tall and broad, with faces that were as set as masks. Gary stared hard at them. It was a cop thing called "gunning"—looking at someone slowly and carefully from the head down to the toes, and then waiting for a reaction. To his surprise, the men gunned him right back with the same hard stare. He turned to Tom, and muttered, "Did you see that?"

Tom nodded. "What do you think, cops?"

"Must be," said Gary. "Who else does that?"

"Ex-cops," Tom offered.

Within a few minutes, the informant arrived. It was obvious from the start that this was not going to be a pleasant interview. Belcher was surly, antagonistic, and deeply ambivalent about the interview. He believed Gary and Tom were trying to put good people out of work, but he also considered it his patriotic duty to talk to them. Belcher repeated that statement several times, like a mantra. When he began to talk, there was a sharp edge to his voice, but he confirmed everything they had heard about the Young Adult Smoker program and the marketing efforts targeted at convenience stores close to high schools and colleges. He talked for well over an hour, and then, abruptly, he stood up and left.

Tom and Gary gathered up their notes. Despite the subject's contentious attitude, the interview had been productive. Tom glanced over to the other booth. The two men were gone.

"What do you think?" Gary asked.

Tom shook his head slowly. "Doesn't mean anything."

They found their car, pulled out onto the boulevard, and started back to their motel. Three blocks down, they stopped for a light, and a car pulled up next to them. The same two men sat inside. They kept their eyes fixed straight ahead, and when the light changed they pulled away without looking over.

"Still could be nothing," said Gary.

"You really believe that?"

"Tell you the truth, I'm not sure."

They drove back to the motel and settled in, feeling uneasy. Gary filled several buckets with cubes from the ice machine, pushed a chair flat against the door, and piled the buckets onto the chair. Any intruder who managed to get the door open would have to push past the chair, setting off a cascade of ice that would serve as a simple but effective alarm system.

In the morning, all they had to show for their efforts were several buckets of ice water. When I heard that story, I did not believe that the tobacco companies would engage in physical harassment; on the other hand, a couple of renegade employees might. In any case, Gary and Tom caught the first plane out of town.

AT Parklawn, several of us often gathered around the speakerphone in my office to listen to former industry employees talk about the youth market's importance to the economics of the tobacco industry. "Bama" talked about the industry's recognition that "whoever gets the people starting wins the game." The goal was to keep them within a brand family. "They get them smoking Marlboro Red when they're, let's say, thirteen," explained Bama. "They smoke that until they're twenty-three [when they think] they may die one day." At that point, the company offers other Marlboro products, in keeping with the "line extension" marketing strategy.

"Bud," who had worked in marketing research at RJR until the late 1980s, also stressed the importance of early brand loyalty. He told us about RJR's FUBYAS concept, short for First Usual Brand Younger Adult Smoker. "When people turn eighteen, by and large, seventy to eighty percent of them have chosen a usual brand....One of the findings was, you've got to get these guys early. If you don't get them early, you're not going to get them."

Another RJR informant, code-named "Shaw," had worked as a division manager and sales representative for eighteen years. "We basically were looking at anything—any person—that was, say, fifteen/sixteen and could look over the counter and have enough money to buy a pack of cigarettes," he said.

"Did people speak specifically at any of the meetings about the ages fifteen, sixteen, or seventeen?" we asked.

"No, we didn't do that. I mean if we did, it was strictly among ourselves in our breakout meetings....We weren't fools. We knew the implications of what we were talking about if it ever went public."

Only after reading the industry documents and talking to a number of informants did I fully understand that there exists a window, an opening into the world of addiction, during the adolescent years. While that window is open, nearly 90 percent of the people who will become addicted to nicotine begin to use tobacco. Once that window is closed, at the end of the teenage years, far fewer will ever begin to smoke.

Nicotine addiction begins as a pediatric disease. As that fact sunk in, I knew we had to target our efforts at children.

37

MIKE SYNAR was, in every sense, a Washington anomaly: a liberal Democrat from a state of hunters and cattlemen. In Oklahoma, even Democrats tended to be conservative on government regulation, gun control, and the rights of ranchers, but Mike was an early advocate of tobacco regulations, a supporter of gun control, and a proponent of raising the fees charged to ranchers whose cattle grazed on federal lands. Despite differences with many of his constituents, his independence had long kept him in office.

Synar had been elected to the House in 1978 and had been easily reelected every two years until 1992. That year, tobacco interests poured money and manpower into Oklahoma in an attempt to defeat him in a four-way Democratic primary. It was a bitter campaign with a barrage of negative advertising. The opposition posted billboards along the Oklahoma highways juxtaposing his face with pictures of Hitler, Stalin, and Castro. The close results of the August primary forced a runoff between Synar and his strongest opponent. With the other two candidates out of the race, the tobacco industry worked hard to swing votes away from Synar.

Mike managed to win that runoff and the general election in 1992, but substantial damage had been done. Negative advertising often lingers in the minds of the electorate, and Mike carried that burden into the 1994 campaign. Once again he was forced into a primary runoff. Tobacco interests were less conspicuous that year, but the ranchers and the gun lobby worked hard to pick up the slack. They did their job well. Mike lost by a margin of two percentage points, and after sixteen years in Congress, he was out of a job.

Because of Synar's involvement with FDA oversight, I had stayed clear of any social contact, but when he lost the election, I wanted to express my regrets. One warm October evening, I drove into Washington to stop by the Sphinx Club on Fourteenth and K streets. Most politicians throw parties after winning an election. It was typical of Mike to throw one after losing. The party was in a huge, windowless basement ballroom, and as I walked down the stairs, I was struck by a wave of loud music and animated voices. The bar and the dance floor were filled with young people. My first impression was that I was the only one in the room over twenty-five and the only one wearing a suit.

Mike seemed to have invited half the Hill to his party, and some of his friends and family had flown in from Oklahoma. The walls of the ballroom had been decorated by his staff with oversized photographs of Mike at various stages in his career—a teenage Mike accepting a 4-H award; a mature Mike being sworn into Congress; Mike in Calcutta, in Bangladesh, in Alaska; and Mike in front of the Stillwell Café back home in Oklahoma.

The hard-core contingent that was still there when I arrived after midnight was the most enthusiastic of Washington partygoers, the congressional staffers, and the place felt a bit like a well-catered fraternity party. Mike was on the dance floor as I walked in, and while I was there he never left it. He danced with all of the female staffers, all of his current and former girlfriends, and anyone else who would get on the floor with him.

I worked my way through the crowd and across the dance floor to where Mike held center stage. He seemed to be dancing with three women at once, rotating from one to another. I waved to get his attention, and he smiled when he recognized me, but the band was pumping out music at a level that made conversation difficult. Raising my voice, I said whatever it is that one says to a politician who has just lost an election, and he thanked me with a grin composed half of frenzied elation and half of defiance. It was not the grin of a loser.

I waved my hand in a gesture of departure. Then I raised my voice again. "All right, now that you're out of office, let's have dinner sometime."

He nodded happily, waved good-bye, and spun around to reach for another partner.

IN THE months following his defeat, Paulette and I grew close to Mike. We shared a similar mix of cynicism and idealism, and we believed that the political system could be made to work better.

Mike loved to cook, and we had dinner with him regularly. Evenings with

Mike provided more than good food; they were also a theatrical experience, and everyone was expected to perform. The stage was his townhouse on Capitol Hill, the guests were his supporting cast, and he was always the star. Politics and statesmanship, conscience and cowardice, ethics and responsibility were his favorite themes. His heroes were always defiant. Joshua Chamberlain, the Union officer defying the Confederates from Little Round Top at the Battle of Gettysburg. Nelson Mandela defying the state from his island prison. He enjoyed playing the part of the gadfly, poking and prodding at people, provoking them into arguments that would leave them exhausted, but enriched, at the end of the evening.

Mike was searching for the next step in his life. He could have joined more than one Washington law firm, or used his years of experience in the House to become an influential lobbyist, but he turned away from that sort of thing. He was no longer a congressman, but he was still the maverick from Oklahoma, looking to do some good in his own way. He became the chairman of the National Bankruptcy Review Commission and a representative to the International Telecommunications Union. He also headed up the Campaign for America project, formed to advocate campaign-finance reform.

Mike threw himself into all of those projects, but he freely admitted that he missed the life on the Hill. He felt no resentment toward his former constituents who had turned him out, but he was still pained by the way in which the tobacco, gun, and ranching interests had combined to defeat him.

Some of that pain was eased one night when he told us that he was about to receive the John F. Kennedy Profile in Courage Award for 1995. The award, presented annually on JFK's birthday, is given to current or former government officials whose "abiding loyalty to their nation triumphed over all personal and political considerations ... who showed the real meaning of courage and a real faith in democracy."

After he had told us the news, Mike looked around the table and said that this was the proudest moment of his life. During his years in the House he had done what he had felt was right without expectation of honors or recognition. He was proud of his reputation as a maverick, even knowing that the fate of the maverick is often to battle alone against the odds and to face defeat without flinching. It was part of the life he had chosen for himself.

MIKE's defeat in the September primary proved to be a harbinger of things to come. On November 8, 1994, Election Day, the whole political equation was transformed.

I was on a conference call interviewing an informant as election results began trickling in from around the country. My attention was divided between the television news reports and the informant. Over the next several hours, it became apparent that the Republicans were going to gain control of the House for the first time in forty years. Henry Waxman would lose the chairmanship of the health subcommittee. In fact, the subcommittee would be eliminated altogether, and Tom Bliley would take control of its parent, the Commerce Committee, which had long been in the hands of the Michigan Democrat John Dingell. Newt Gingrich, the pugnacious Georgia congressman, would become Speaker of the House.

Three nights after the election, Gingrich was interviewed by Tom Brokaw on *Dateline NBC*. Calling him "the man who has spent years in Congress as the leading guerrilla fighter in the Republican war on Democratic turf," Brokaw said that Gingrich was known for being "casually reckless" in his attacks on his enemies.

The congressman immediately illustrated Brokaw's point by unloading on me. His criticism was scathing. He claimed that officials in the private sector, whom he did not name, had said I would "destroy" anyone who spoke out against me. Calling the remark "a very ominous charge," Brokaw pressed Gingrich for more information.

"Are you saying that Kessler has told these companies, 'I'll bankrupt you'?" he asked.

Gingrich replied, "I'm saying the companies have asserted that, yes."

"You are a powerful figure in Congress," Brokaw persisted. "Why didn't you simply pick up the telephone and call Dr. Kessler?"

Gingrich answered with scorn. "Call him and say what? 'Why don't you tell me that you are acting like a bully and a thug?'"

My car telephone rang as I turned into the cul-de-sac where I lived. It was the FDA's press office, telling me that NBC had just called. Tom Brokaw wanted my reaction to Gingrich's remarks. I suppose I should have expected that sort of attack, but I did not. I thought for a moment before I realized that the only appropriate response was none at all. "Tell them I'm not going to comment," I said. When I later saw the clip of the Brokaw interview, I watched Gingrich step from the tarmac onto a plane owned by a tobacco company.

In the weeks that followed the election, the press was filled with stories predicting the death of any attempt to regulate tobacco. The industry had donated more than $600,000 to the Republican National Committee during the election season, becoming its largest single contributor, and there was a widespread assumption that the payback was at hand. The lead of John Schwartz's election analysis for the *Washington Post* read: "Goodbye, Henry. Hello, Tom. Philip Morris, breathe easier." Bliley said that he saw no point in continuing to hold hearings on tobacco, because he did not think further legislation was necessary.

In that environment, FDA critics became bolder. In the name of what they termed "reform," conservative think tanks started developing proposals to farm out the agency's regulatory functions to the private sector or to dismantle them altogether. The Progress and Freedom Foundation, which had close ties to Gingrich and received substantial contributions from the pharmaceutical industry, called for a system of self-regulation, while the Competitive Enterprise Institute suggested that unapproved drugs and devices be allowed on the market with a label that merely identified them as such. The Washington Legal Foundation began running a series of advertisements in major national newspapers built around the out-of-date notion that the FDA was slow to approve new therapies: "If a murderer kills you, it's homicide. If a drunk driver kills you, it's manslaughter. If the FDA kills you, it's just being cautious." Some Republicans clearly saw the election as a mandate to discourage enforcement and advance their deregulatory agenda and they were wasting no time in waging ideological warfare against both me and the agency. The *Wall Street Journal* ran a column titled "First Step to FDA Cure: Dump Kessler."

Under the barrage of attacks, I decided to lower the FDA's profile slightly. A few days after the election, I canceled an interview with *Frontline*, which was producing an hour-long documentary about tobacco. Mitch Zeller appeared on the show instead, talking about the Y-1 investigation and what it illustrated about nicotine manipulation. It did not hurt to let people think that I might be backing off a little. But the assumption that the FDA had been cowed into silence was wrong. We were quietly moving ahead.

DESPITE the new political climate, or perhaps because of it, an unanticipated legislative opportunity arose. Soon after the Republican takeover, Bill Schultz told me that he wanted to talk with Tom Bliley's top aide, James Derderian, known as J.D., someone he knew from his years on the Hill. Bill was looking for a sense of what the new Commerce Committee chairman was thinking and how it might affect tobacco.

A couple of weeks later, Bill called my house one evening to tell me that he and J.D. had met privately. J.D. had a surprise for us. "Do you know what Nixon going to China means?" J.D. had asked Bill. The "congressman from Philip Morris" was thinking about drafting legislation to assert some sort of additional federal authority over tobacco. If Tom Bliley was seriously willing to deal, it could be an important opening.

To outward appearances, Bliley had been a consistent, sometimes shrill, spokesman for the tobacco industry's interests. But someone else was writing the harsh statements he read at hearings and some close observers felt his heart was not always in the job. Although he had never shown any previous willingness to negotiate on tobacco, Bliley did have a history of trying to work out compromises on controversial issues. Now, as J.D. explained to Bill, Bliley was thinking about his legacy. He occupied the chair held for so long by the formidable John Dingell, who will be remembered by history as a fierce advocate of consumer protection. Bliley knew that unless he did something dramatic, he would be remembered as the congressman who protected the tobacco companies. Assured that he could trust us to keep his efforts confidential, Bliley asked J.D. to arrange a private meeting with me.

Shortly after the new year, Bill Schultz and I walked down the long corridors of the Rayburn House Office Building, headed for a small side office near one of the hearing rooms. When we arrived, I literally hid from view behind a file cabinet in the hall while Bill entered. Bliley and J.D. then ushered the people out of the office and waved me in. I slipped through the door unseen.

The four of us sat in large blue chairs and Bliley immediately began to talk personally. For a moment, it was as if there had never been the least bit of animosity between us. After our very public run-ins on the Hill, the tone of the meeting started cordially and quickly became warm and open. Bliley said his wife was a longtime smoker who had tried unsuccessfully to quit and now her doctor was concerned about a rattle he was hearing in her chest. The congressman admitted that he was worried. I was surprised by his candor but recognized that his own experiences had helped to prompt the meeting. Bliley did not know whether he could even get the tobacco companies to agree among themselves. I let him know that we had the evidence to assert jurisdiction and that we intended to move forward. But I also indicated that if he thought he could bring the industry to the table, I was certainly willing to work with him.

After Bliley left the room, J.D., Bill, and I kept talking. I told J.D. that the FDA did not necessarily have to be the agency that oversaw any new regulations. What was important to me was getting regulations into effect. J.D. said that might give him the negotiating room he needed.

Ultimately, Bliley could not broker a deal. At least some in the industry were still more interested in a "ferocious defense" than in compromise. And nothing about his failed negotiations persuaded Bliley to become more supportive of the FDA's initiatives. In fact, after the industry walked away from the table, the distance between us only seemed to increase. Our moment of rapprochement quickly became a memory.

CHARLIE ROSE, chairman of the House Agriculture Committee and dean of the North Carolina congressional delegation, was also closely tied to tobacco. A moderate Democrat, Rose was in general more progressive than many southern members, but on tobacco, he was parochial. He viewed the federal government's tobacco support program, which ensured stable prices, as a key to the South's economy, as well as a way to keep the family farmer in business. Acre for acre, tobacco was far more profitable than any other legal crop, and for many of Rose's constituents, a few acres of tobacco meant the difference between eating and not eating, between whether some of their children went to college or not. Rose had no great love for the tobacco companies, whom he assumed to be mostly supporters of Republicans anyway, but he accepted and solicited their contributions. In a way, they were stuck with each other, and each made the best of the marriage of convenience. Philip Morris, in particular, paid close attention to Rose's fundraising needs.

The congressman took it upon himself to warn us about the risks he thought we were taking by pursuing tobacco regulation. One of his staffers relayed the message to me, through the FDA policy expert Bill Hubbard. Bill read me his scribbled notes of the conversation immediately afterwards.

"Do you guys really know what you're doing?" Rose's staff person had asked. "They can hurt you." I looked at Hubbard as he continued to read.

"What the tobacco companies want is, first, your scalp.... FDA has no right to take action on cigarettes.... Bliley will be coming after FDA big time.

He's preparing to send investigators all over the Agency looking for dirt.... He will also involve Appropriations staff.... Tobacco industry's goal is to dismantle FDA. The companies think you will bolt if dismantling begins. There would be thermonuclear warfare.... This is pure politics, not policy."

The bottom line was that the tobacco companies were betting that I would be gone from the agency within eighteen months, a victim of their relentless attempts to discredit me and weaken my agency. They assumed the tobacco initiative would die with my departure.

This was not the first communication from Congressman Rose. Even before the Republican takeover of Congress, Rose, like Bliley, had sent us a detailed request asking for all "memoranda, notes, reports, and correspondence" relating to our tobacco investigation. He also wanted the names of all FDA personnel who were involved and all of our contacts with anyone, either within or outside government.

Document requests are an appropriate part of oversight, but this request bothered me because I was sure that the tobacco companies were behind it. They wanted to harass us and to expose our informants. I had no intention of turning over anything the industry could not otherwise obtain through established channels.

Soon after I received Rose's letter, a colleague alerted me to a similar request Rose had made to Carol Browner, the administrator of the Environmental Protection Agency, when the EPA was trying to classify environmental tobacco smoke as a Class A carcinogen. I compared Rose's request to the EPA with court documents relating to the same issue that had been filed by the tobacco industry and quickly realized that the wording was far too similar to be coincidental. The letter to the FDA followed that same format. Years later, I learned that outside counsel to Philip Morris had drafted the Rose request to us.

Rose pursued his FDA document request until the Republican takeover cost him the chairmanship of the Agriculture Committee and then he pushed the new chairman, Congressman Thomas Ewing of Illinois, to renew it. Ewing sent out his own letter, and then Philip Morris, unsatisfied with my response, drafted another one for Ewing's signature. I continued to refuse to turn over documents that might put our informants at risk. Tensions escalated, and Rose and Ewing decided to launch a far-reaching investigation, asking the nonpartisan General Accounting Office to review the FDA's approach to its tobacco rulemaking procedures and to consider possible criminal charges that we had obstructed a congressional investigation.

The GAO quickly realized that the criminal referrals had no merit, but we clashed over our right to withhold confidential documents. The Department of Health and Human Services backed me up at a meeting with Congressman Ewing and the GAO investigators. "The agency must be able to depend on the public for a great deal of its information," said the Department's general counsel, Harriet Rabb. "Disclosure of the identity of individuals who worked with the agency could inhibit future cooperation." In truth, had it not been for the importance of protecting our informants, I would have loved to release the documents. Among them were Saint's story about the industry's ability to remove carcinogens, at least in pilot tests, and PC's description of being required to smoke tainted cigarettes.

As Harriet argued on our behalf, I glanced at the GAO representatives and wondered whether they had any idea that the tobacco industry was behind their inquiry. In the end, we agreed to allow the GAO to interview FDA employees who had been on the tobacco team, but we stood firm on not releasing the documents and they chose not to subpoena them.

As the meeting started to break up, Heidi Pender, counsel to Rose, looked at me and, apparently guessing my thoughts, said sharply, "I am not a shill for the tobacco industry."

38

SHORTLY after the Republicans' election sweep, we finished polishing a presentation to Secretary Donna Shalala. I had spoken about tobacco privately to her and she knew generally where I was headed, but my request for a formal meeting represented a step forward. I now felt confident enough in our strategy to start discussing details with the secretary.

I wanted her to understand how much thought we had already devoted to our proposals and to meet the people who had worked so long and so hard on tobacco. I wanted her to see firsthand the depth of Ann Witt's legal sophistication and Catherine Lorraine's grasp of regulatory nuances, to appreciate Sharon Natanblut's insights into public opinion and industry thinking, and to acknowledge Judy Wilkenfeld as one of the nation's foremost experts on tobacco advertising.

It was late afternoon and already dark outside on the November day we arrived at the Department. Shalala sat at the head of a long table, with Phil Lee, the assistant secretary for health, at her side. Other Department officials were scattered about the room. From where I was sitting, it was impossible to look simultaneously at Shalala and at her staff, so I addressed myself primarily to her.

I opened by redefining smoking as a pediatric disease. I was armed with the statistical evidence to make three key points: most smokers begin to smoke as youngsters; young people become as addicted as adults; and the prevalence of smoking among youth was on the rise, a marked contrast to trends of the recent past.

Our data were powerful and the implications were stark. We told the secretary that 3 million young people were smoking, that an estimated 516 million packs of cigarettes were illegally purchased by young people every year, and that 93 percent of the young smokers who try to quit report withdrawal symptoms. To underscore the message, I read a line from Imperial Tobacco's corporate marketing plan. "'If the last ten years have taught us anything, it is that the industry is dominated by the companies who respond most effectively to the needs of younger smokers.'"

I knew we had to capture the essence of the youth smoking problem with succinct and compelling numbers that would become part of the vernacular, and we had settled on two: three thousand children start smoking every day in this country, and one out of three of those will eventually die from their smoking. After Gary Giovino at the Centers for Disease Control checked out the methodology underlying the statistics to be sure we were right, I used those figures in the meeting with Shalala and over and over again in other forums.

Ann Witt spoke next, explaining why the FDA could legitimately claim jurisdiction over tobacco. She carefully laid out the evidence that the industry itself recognized nicotine as a drug.

Catherine Lorraine followed, putting the proposed regulation in a larger context. Our bottom-line objective, she said, was to prevent future generations of children from becoming addicted to cigarettes. "We are looking for ways to address both the supply side, through access restrictions that would make it more difficult for young people to obtain tobacco products, and the demand side, through advertising and promotion provisions designed to reduce the appeal of tobacco." Catherine emphasized our commitment to developing a regulation that was supported by the best available data and whose provisions met the three criteria I had insisted upon—that they be reasonable, that they be meaningful, and that they be comprehensive.

Next, Judy Wilkenfeld illustrated the explosive growth of advertising and promotion with a series of pie charts. In 1970, the industry's total marketing budget had been $361 million, which translated into $1.3 billion in 1992 dollars. Little more than two decades later, the figure had quadrupled, in real terms, to an annual $5.2 billion. The results were unmistakable. Before R. J. Reynolds introduced the Joe Camel cartoon character in 1988, Camel cigarettes commanded no more than 3 or 4 percent of the youth market; by 1991, that figure had climbed to 13 percent. The spending mix was also striking. After television and radio advertising were banned in the 1970s, event sponsorship accounted for a ballooning portion of the budget.

But Sharon Natanblut's primary emphasis that day was on public opinion. Broad support from the American people was crucial in the highly political environment of the Department and the White House, and Sharon reviewed a series of surveys that showed we had it. A Gallup Poll found that more than three quarters of the population favored restrictions on cigarette advertising that appealed to youth. Other studies showed that significant majorities also supported bans on free product samples and billboards and favored suspending the tobacco licenses of retailers who sold cigarettes to minors.

By the time Catherine, Judy, and Sharon were finished, the key components of our draft regulation had been summarized. Although a few of the terms were later modified, the changes proved surprisingly modest. In order to limit the appeal of advertising to children, we proposed ending the use of cartoon characters and colorful graphics in magazines. Ads in those publications would instead be restricted to a black-and-white, text-only format. Billboards, too, could only feature black-and-white text. We also sought a ban on such promotional techniques as giveaways linked to proof-of-purchase coupons and brand names on hats, T-shirts, and other non-tobacco products.

Sports and other events would be sponsored only under a corporate name, without mentioning specific cigarette brands, and access would be restricted by eliminating vending machines, free samples, mail-order sales, and the small-quantity cigarette packages known as "kiddie packs." The self-service displays often found near store cash registers would not be permitted, forcing every tobacco purchase to involve a personal interaction, and we proposed a system to hold the manufacturer responsible for ensuring that retailers did not sell to underage buyers. Finally, we proposed a "hammer" provision—if the goal of reducing underage smoking by approximately 50 percent had not been realized within five years, other restrictions could be put in place.

Shalala was impressed. From the lengthy set of provisions, she objected only to restrictions on sports sponsorship. She feared we would alienate the public if the tobacco industry pulled out of car racing, tennis, and other popular events. "We'll lose every sports fan in the United States," she predicted.

Taking their cues from the secretary, no one else in the room objected. Shalala gave no further orders, other than to say we would have to work with Department staff to get the rule into final shape. She did not establish a time frame for completing the assignment, but I thought we had just been given a green light. With a little fine-tuning, I assumed we would be ready to go.

I should have looked at Jerry Klepner, the Department's liaison with Congress. His face would have told a different story.

THE secretary's encouragement led to a series of evening meetings with senior Department staff early in 1995. People wrote cryptic notations in their appointment books and Department officials agreed that no one would be allowed to send a substitute. But I had no illusions that we could keep this entirely confidential.

Typically, we would start at about six and continue well into the night. We convened in the deputy secretary's conference room in the Humphrey building. The beige room was airless and overheated, and an unfortunate seating arrangement reflected the us-against-them tone of the early meetings—the FDA was on one side of the table; the Department, on the other. If someone arrived late and had to sit on the wrong side, there would be quiet chuckling in the room. All told, we were a group of about twenty.

Initially, the objective was to bring the Department up to speed on what we knew about tobacco. Kevin Thurm, Shalala's youthful chief of staff, became the facilitator. He played the role deftly, making sure that everyone's voice was heard without revealing his own thinking. "Educate us," he said. "Start at the beginning with kids, with advertising, with tobacco. Teach us everything."

We focused exclusively on the terms of the rule, how we would actually regulate nicotine once we asserted jurisdiction. As FDA commissioner, I deliberately assumed that I had the authority to make that assertion without involving anyone else, and to my surprise, no one ever challenged me. Of course, it would have been a significant political risk to take such unilateral action, though I did not mind having people wonder whether I might one day simply announce publicly our intention to regulate. But the Department's reluctance to interfere with our authority did not extend to the details of the rule itself. The secretary and the White House would have to sign off before it could become official, and that meant a rigorous vetting process.

In meeting after meeting, Sharon, Judy, and others walked methodically through the landscape of tobacco and youth smoking. It was an intensive education process, and the staff bombarded us with questions. To some extent, we welcomed them. We all wanted to implement the right regulation. But what lingered in the minds of many on the FDA team was the almost palpable skepticism in the room and a persistent effort to weaken our proposal. As soon as we passed one barrier, another invariably arose. It was hard not to feel defensive.

By this point my attitude about tobacco was "How do we win this policy battle?" Flush with our success in earlier public health initiatives, especially food labeling, I was not afraid of moving forward. The Department's attitude, on the other hand, seemed to be "How do we avoid losing?" They thought our timing could not have been worse. With both houses of Congress in Republican hands, the atmosphere was feverishly antiregulatory. No one was in the mood to take any action that could be tarred with the brush of "big government." Making matters worse, we were dealing with many of the same people who felt defeated by the collapse of health-care reform. In its complexity, its challenge to special interests, and its assertive use of government authority, tobacco regulation evoked health-care reform in ways that threatened to paralyze the Department. Only Shalala's enthusiasm barred some of her aides from dismissing us outright.

The Department representatives, for their part, were frustrated by what they perceived as our inflexibility. Some saw us as stubborn advocates, intent on persuading them to support positions we had already staked out, rather than being willing to weigh their concerns. When Judy Wilkenfeld jokingly referred to bars as "dens of iniquity," where tobacco could be sold and advertised without restriction, one Department staffer recalled thinking, "These are true believers."

The task of defending the proposal before Congress would ultimately fall to Jerry Klepner, who had almost two decades of experience on Capitol Hill. He was part of the secretary's inner circle, but he seemed to distance himself from this issue. After the health-care reform debacle, he did not think the administration had much political capital to spend on public health. From time to time he would look up at the ceiling and mutter, "You've got to be kidding. Do you think I'm going to sell this on the Hill?" He knew the nation's elected representatives had countless tools at their disposal to block any effort to regulate tobacco. At one especially demoralizing meeting, Jerry asked bluntly, "Are you people crazy?" At another, he said angrily that I was "mesmerized" by tobacco and accused me of steering a dangerous political course that left the agency vulnerable to attack from powerful congressional opponents.

As the meetings dragged on, I started pushing my chair away from the conference table, a partly conscious sign that I was withdrawing from the dialogue. My FDA colleagues wondered if I was abandoning them—Sharon later told me she felt like a decoy—but I felt it best not to voice my frustration. Our evenings invariably ended on a dispirited note, and as I walked the single block back to the parking lot with the team, grateful for the fresh, cool air, I sensed their bleak mood. Catherine, Judy, and Sharon were convinced we were headed nowhere. As we stood at our cars, I listened and tried to play the role of cheerleader, telling them that one way or another, we would be moving forward. I saw the painful process as a form of dues, the price we had to pay for the Department's cooperation, but nothing that was going to hold us back.

Bill Schultz tried to act as peacemaker. Hoping to ease the tensions that had developed, Bill invited Jerry Klepner to lunch one Saturday afternoon. For the most part, they steered clear of the details of the rule, talking instead about their families and swapping war stories from Capitol Hill. Jerry vented some of his frustrations with me and with the agency, complaining that we weren't giving his extensive legislative expertise due respect.

By putting the strongest advocates of action out front, I had shown the Department that there was real passion behind our policy. Now I had to prove that we were pragmatic as well. We had allowed ourselves to become vulnerable to criticism by making statements without having all the supporting facts behind them. Sensing weakness, Department representatives lunged, and that in turn made us more defensive. It was time for our arguments to become clearer, more focused, and more concise. I decided that everything we did must be totally data-driven.

Still, the pressure continued. It was especially difficult to persuade Jerry that the vending machine industry would survive a ban on selling cigarettes in their machines. He was concerned about the economic impact and the prospect that the tobacco industry would find ready allies in a coalition of small business owners. But Sharon reported that the youngest cigarette smokers were disproportionately dependent on vending machines—22 percent of thirteen-year-olds, compared to 2 percent of seventeen-year-olds, purchased their cigarettes from vending machines—and we were convinced that they had to go.

Some of the Department's strongest objections were reserved for the provision that would limit event sponsorship to the corporate name only, rather than allow the use of a brand name, such as the Virginia Slims tennis tournament. Department staff kept harping on the implications for motor car racing, wondering whether this would spell the end of the legendary NASCAR circuit. That was a familiar argument—when the tobacco industry was banned from television in 1971, some had argued that football would be in trouble—and we refused to budge. Some time later, Sharon collected all of the available data into a report that provided overwhelming evidence that sponsors of such events were reaching young children and adolescents in large numbers. Equally important, she found that race-car sponsorship was increasingly used by corporations other than the tobacco industry, disproving the argument that NASCAR would be devastated by the loss of tobacco company sponsorship.

But evidence was not enough. As she concluded a detailed presentation on NASCAR, Department official Kevin Burke, an expert on regional Democratic politics, spoke up. "What about rodeos?" he asked.

As it became clear that I could not depend on the Department to move the tobacco initiative forward, I realized I was going to have to develop an alternate strategy. Back at Parklawn, I started pushing Ann Witt and the jurisdiction team to complete its work. Once their document was finished, I would be ready to go public at any time with the announcement that cigarettes were subject to the FDA's authority. The exact terms of the regulation could come later.

The day before I was scheduled to testify at an appropriations hearing on the Hill, the document was finally ready. By then, we had moved to smaller morning meetings at the Department, sometimes starting at 7 A.M. I arranged to have an envelope hand-delivered to me there.

"I'm done," I said, when a secretary entered the meeting room and handed me the envelope. "This is the jurisdiction document. We have finished our jurisdictional determination."

Jerry Klepner pushed his chair away from the table, his breathing rapid and hard. He walked to the window, struggling to control his fury, and then walked back to the edge of the table. He looked directly at me and said, "I feel fucked."

"Jerry, if I wanted you to be fucked, I wouldn't be sitting here," I said. No one even glanced inside the envelope. It could have contained no more than blank pieces of paper.

A few days later, Secretary Shalala took us both to the Kennedy Center, where we sat in the presidential box and talked as friends. But the essence of our argument was set. And the signal I sent the day that Jerry Klepner exploded was clear. Whether the Department was with me or not, I was going to move the issue forward.

39

I DECIDED we should quietly establish our own channels to the White House. It was a risk to circumvent the Department, and I did not want to offend my overseers, but I needed support from other quarters.

President Clinton had reappointed me, but I was in no position simply to pick up the telephone and request a meeting with him. I had met the President for the first time not long before, at a White House Christmas party. Paulette and I had expected to be part of a large event, two among hundreds of guests waiting in line to have our picture taken with the President and the First Lady. Our first surprise was that only about one hundred people were there. I knew very few of them, although I recognized Pierre Salinger, who was on the board of the National Smokers Alliance, a Philip Morris creation. Then I saw Tommy Boggs, an influential Washington lawyer-lobbyist, coming our way. I had known him for years and knew he had clients across the political spectrum. I never knew which side of an issue he was representing at any given time. "I want to introduce you to someone," he told me as he shook my hand, turning to Philip Morris's top Washington lobbyist, Kathleen ("Buffy") Linehan. Linehan had a reputation as a "dragon lady" among some of her colleagues, and our greeting was as chilly as could be.

I had no idea why Paulette and I had been invited; it obviously was not an event for government bureaucrats at my level. I found the answer in the receiving line, when I met Mrs. Clinton. "I wanted you to come," she told me warmly. "I put you on the list. I really admire what you are doing. It's Orwellian to say that nicotine is not a drug."

The President mingled among the guests, greeting and talking with us individually or in small groups. Despite the festive season, there was a subdued feeling about the gathering. The President seemed resigned and weary. The Democrats had just lost control of both houses of Congress, and Clinton was using his conversations with guests that night to relive what had happened, and why.

At one point during the evening, Paulette and I found ourselves alone with him for a few minutes. The President was standing near a corner of the dining room where Abraham Lincoln's brooding portrait hovered over a huge gingerbread house. He clearly associated me with tobacco. "You know we lost the House because of two issues, gun control and tobacco," he said. I knew that several just-defeated southern Democrats had been telling him that trying to increase the excise tax on tobacco to fund health-care reform, combined with the ban on assault weapons, had cost enough votes to be decisive in key southern states. Congressman Martin Lancaster of North Carolina, who had lost his seat in the House despite support from the tobacco industry, told the President in a blunt letter written shortly after his defeat that the Democrats would never reclaim the "tobacco south" if the FDA were allowed to move forward on jurisdiction.

Paulette was immediately ready to argue. She would argue with anybody, even the President in his own house. "What was your choice?" she asked. "You had to take those stands."

I winced slightly, although I was secretly pleased. The President, bemoaning his loss, seemed to be saying that tobacco could not be tackled and Paulette was asking, "Well, why are you President, then, if it's not to take on things that matter?"

President Clinton was obviously surprised. "Of course those were the right stands to take. We just should have explained our positions better so that people would have understood them."

I knew I had only another moment of his time. "You know, there's a way we can do this, if we focus on kids," I said. Clinton was beginning to move away, but he turned back and gave a small nod.

I DECIDED to meet quietly with Abner Mikva, the White House counsel. Mikva had served five terms in the House, representing a swing district in Chicago and had also served as a federal judge, which made him one of a small group of Americans who had served in all three branches of government. Despite his unabashed liberal voting record in Congress, he managed to maintain warm relationships on both sides of the aisle, which helped him to win confirmation when President Jimmy Carter appointed him to a federal appeals court. Clinton's decision to install Mikva as White House counsel, after prevailing on him to give up his seat on the court, was hailed as a coup, just what the President needed. Mikva was well respected, and his ethics were beyond reproach. He was smart, sociable, still popular on the Hill, and still a regular at the House gym. In his late sixties, with a distinguished career behind him, he had nothing left to prove.

I had known Mikva since the early 1990s, when we both served on the University of Chicago Law School Visiting Committee, and I knew he would keep an open mind. Bill Schultz also knew him well, having argued a number of cases in his court, and I asked Bill to make the first contact.

On April 10, 1995, we entered the West Wing of the White House and were escorted upstairs. At Mikva's request, Chris Cerf, the associate counsel, joined the discussion. For the first time I laid out the core of our regulatory approach to tobacco in the White House, focusing on the potential public health advance and the opportunity we saw for the President. My goal was to convey the importance of taking action, but also to stress that ours was a reasonable strategy.

When we finished, Mikva acknowledged his relief. He feared we were going to push for a ban and admitted to being surprised by our measured response.

We also discussed *ASH v. Harris,* the 1970s court case upholding the FDA's decision not to regulate cigarettes. Coincidentally, Mikva had been one of the judges who ruled unanimously in favor of the FDA. As we talked, Mikva walked over to his bookshelf and pulled down the volume of *Federal Reporter* containing the decision. He told us that he had written the famous footnote: "Nothing in this opinion should suggest that the Administration is irrevocably bound by any long-standing interpretation. . . . An administrative agency is clearly free to revise its interpretations." According to the footnote, we needed only a reasonable basis for doing so.

I came away from that April meeting convinced that Mikva and Cerf were two strong allies. Enthused about the focus on children, Mikva urged us to begin making the case within the White House. "Go make noise," he said.

He also wanted me to send the jurisdiction document for review to Walter Dellinger, head of the Justice Department's Office of Legal Counsel. Mikva knew Dellinger had thought extensively about tobacco and would examine the document rigorously and give us an objective opinion on its validity. In retrospect, the entrée to Dellinger proved to be the most critical part of our meeting.

I believed that if we were talking to Abner Mikva, Secretary Shalala should be, too, and another meeting was arranged, this one over lunch in the secretary's dining room. During that conversation, I picked up hints that Mikva was already involved in negotiations with Charlie Rose, whom he had known for years, and with representatives of the tobacco industry. I did not have all the details then, but I later learned that Congressman Rose, like Bliley, thought he might be able to broker a deal. The tobacco companies saw negotiations as a possible way to forestall FDA regulation and agreed to participate in the talks, assuming two ground rules were respected. They did not want word of the meeting to get out, and they were unwilling to participate in any negotiations, either directly or indirectly, with the FDA. I was to be excluded completely from the process.

The possibility that the White House might strike a deal to gain political advantage, without adequately considering the public health impact of a settlement, was inescapable. It would surely be tempting for the President to position a compromise package as "pro kids" and appear to be standing up to the tobacco industry, while avoiding the major risks of pushing forward a comprehensive set of regulations.

Fortunately, Mikva and Cerf were determined to avoid a replay of a past mistake. The ban on the television advertising of cigarettes looked meaningful, but ultimately redounded to the industry's benefit at the expense of public health. Industry documents explicitly acknowledged this achievement. "The reduction in cigarette advertising seems to have made the industry stronger," wrote Brown & Williamson's chief counsel in 1976. "Profits have increased. ... Individual tobacco companies have benefited from government actions."

The tobacco industry representatives meeting in Rose's office soon realized that Mikva and Cerf would not yield to their will and discussions broke down. In the end, the congressman from North Carolina could get no further than the congressman from Virginia. The companies decided to gamble that the Clinton administration would not take the political risk of allowing the FDA to regulate tobacco.

News of the secret talks reinforced my determination to persuade the President of the merits of our approach. More than ever, I was becoming convinced that the outcome would be determined by where he stood. Mikva and Cerf had warned me that the fight to convince the President to back our proposals hinged partly on how vigorously we were opposed on Capitol Hill. Clinton was not going to take a risk on this issue if everybody else, including the congressional Democrats, was strongly opposed. I would have to wage what Chris Cerf called "the battle for the President's soul."

I DECIDED we needed the support of the people who had the President's trust. From the beginning, I knew that Al Gore could make the difference. He was critical to us for several reasons: his key role in reviewing executive branch regulations; his intense personal interest in the tobacco issue; his close relationship with the President; and, finally, the relationship I had developed with him. At an early meeting in a Senate office building, prior to my confirmation, we discovered that we had much in common, particularly a shared interest in science and technology. Subsequently, Gore let me know that he respected our aggressive pursuit of a public health agenda. He was an independent thinker with a mind for substantive issues, and over the past few years we had found ways to fuse policy and politics in several sensitive areas.

I asked Jerry Mande to approach the vice president. After working with him on Capitol Hill for almost a decade, Jerry knew how Gore thought. Knowing that Jerry was likely to have only a few minutes to lay out the case for FDA regulation, we carefully rehearsed his presentation.

The meeting was scheduled for four o'clock on May 5, but the vice president was running late and Jerry had to wait in the outer office. Barely big enough for one person, it was occupied by three staffers. He sat in a small chair between two desks and caught up with old colleagues as the minutes ticked by. The success of Jerry's presentation might well depend on whether Gore was rushed and impatient or relaxed and receptive, and the delay was working against Jerry.

Finally, he was ushered into the vice president's West Wing office. An oversized photographic print of the Earth as seen from outer space hung on the wall, a reminder of technological possibilities in an otherwise traditionally furnished space. As Jerry sat down across from Gore, he looked for some sign of the vice president's mood and sensed that he was giving Jerry his full attention. Jerry plunged in with a brief outline of the FDA investigation and handed over a copy of the jurisdiction document. He told the vice president that the agency wanted the White House to understand the issues that were involved and that we were asking for his help.

The vice president did not hesitate. He wanted to take the issue directly to the President, he said, on two conditions. We had to give him a few days, and he had to be the first person to speak to the President. The meeting lasted barely five minutes, but Jerry walked away with even more than we had hoped.

MIKE MOORE, the Mississippi attorney general, was scheduled to be in Washington and asked for the chance to stop by and see me. Moore brought Dick Scruggs with him. Scruggs, a private lawyer from Pascagoula, was working with Moore to spearhead Mississippi's lawsuit against the tobacco companies to recover the costs of smoking-related Medicaid expenditures. We had met for the first time after we sent the agency letter to the Coalition on Smoking or Health, and I knew that our activities had encouraged them in their suit. We stayed in touch as their litigation advanced, becoming allies in our related battles.

During our meeting, Scruggs alluded to a source in the inner councils of the White House and suggested he had an advocate there. Promising discretion, I persuaded Scruggs to identify him. It was Dick Morris, the controversial political consultant whose behind-the-scenes influence on Bill Clinton became a national news story shortly after our conversation. Morris had done some work for both Scruggs and for Senator Trent Lott, who was Scruggs's brother-in-law and later became Senate Majority Leader.

Dick Morris had been one of the architects of Clinton's Arkansas gubernatorial comeback in 1982. In the wake of the 1994 Democratic defeat in Congress, the Clintons turned to Morris once again. By the time I learned about his interest in tobacco, Morris was offering strategic advice directly to the President on a broad set of issues. These regular meetings were presentations, not debates, and they often lasted for hours, typically late into the night, in the Clintons' private residence on the second floor. Morris was intentionally kept in a kind of political quarantine, excluded from daily White House operations. In theory, he was also supposed to be kept off the press's radar screen.

At that time, Newt Gingrich's "Contract with America"—with its strategies for restructuring welfare, cutting taxes, increasing defense spending, and imposing term limits—was beginning to dominate the legislative agenda, forcing the President to weigh defensive strategies and to try to rebut charges that the election had rendered him "irrelevant." Morris believed the administration had to get back on course by taking the offensive with the right strategic initiatives. He argued that Clinton would not win the next election if he did nothing more than say "me too" to popular items on the Republican agenda and veto those he could not stomach. To gain ammunition, Morris orchestrated a comprehensive poll that tested every aspect of the GOP agenda. The poll included a series of questions on public attitudes toward the FDA and government regulation. What he found had major consequences for our efforts. When Americans expressed their enthusiasm for cutting government regulations, they were generally thinking about agencies such as the Internal Revenue Service. By contrast, the prospect of weakening the FDA filled them with concern, especially when they were asked specific questions about drug regulation and food safety.

As one of his midnight meetings drew to a close, Morris casually suggested that the President take on the tobacco industry. Morris, who did not share the President's view that tobacco had been instrumental in the election defeat, thought it was an issue that made good sense to champion. After consulting with Scruggs, Morris proposed that the White House somehow join the plaintiffs in the pending Medicaid-related state lawsuits. It was not a well-developed policy idea, and the President was noncommittal about any involvement with tobacco. Still, between Dick Morris and Al Gore, the seed of an idea had been planted.

FROM the day our tobacco initiative came to the attention of the White House, I was aware of internal divisions that could affect its outcome. Although the next national election was still eighteen months away, much of the opposition to FDA regulation within the White House came from those who feared the reelection risks to the President and to the Democrats in Congress. To them, the idea of confronting one of the most politically formidable and combative of all industries seemed a quixotic mission at best and dangerous folly at worst.

Deputy Chief of Staff Harold Ickes was known for his single-minded loyalty to the President, his capacity for hard work, his political acumen, and his bluntness. Personally he supported our effort, but he was counting electoral votes and he saw a down-to-the-wire race, with California and other states hanging in the balance. He thought adding tobacco to the mix could jeopardize the states that were still up for grabs. "Is this worth doing if it costs Kentucky and Tennessee?" Ickes kept asking. Succinctly put, his view was "great proposal, second term." And he was not alone.

The strongest and most consistent opposition inside the White House came from Pat Griffin, the assistant to the President for legislative affairs. Like Jerry Klepner in the Department, he had to face the Hill on a daily basis, and he was concerned about its response. He saw me as someone interested in pursuing my own agenda, regardless of the cost to Clinton.

I was aware of that perception. One day, Jerry Mande paged me as I traveled to the airport after giving a speech in western Massachusetts. Jerry had a source at the White House reporting to him on a meeting that occurred that day. The President's aides were worried that I would resign if a decision were made to bring my tobacco initiative to a halt or to compromise with the industry in order to reach a deal. The White House was trying to decide which would be worse—dealing with the fury my resignation would likely trigger, or with the political consequences of moving forward with regulation.

I was of mixed mind about the perception of me as an unknown but influential force, someone who could not be entirely predicted or controlled. It gave me valuable leverage in negotiations, which I was perfectly willing to use, but I wanted to win White House support and I could not do that if I were viewed as unduly independent. I made it clear that I was not interested in a power grab and that my main goal, as I had told Tom Bliley, was to get results. I was willing to forgo FDA jurisdiction to do that. I sent a message that I did care about the President's wider agenda. Up to a point, I wanted to be reasonable.

But only up to a point. Although I never said anything explicit, the fact that people thought I might resign over this was to my advantage.

DICK MORRIS and Mitch Zeller began sending feelers to each other, using Dick Scruggs as an intermediary. I asked Mitch to try to find out what Morris was thinking and what was being said at the White House. Morris, in turn, relayed questions about the FDA's work through Scruggs.

Eventually, Morris sent a message that he wanted to have direct contact with the agency. Mitch asked me how to respond. Talking directly to Morris, a political operator whose primary mission was to ensure the reelection of the President, seemed risky for a regulatory agency. But knowing that some White House staffers were pressuring the President not to support our regulations because of the political minefields involved, Mitch was willing to take the risk. Mitch and Morris exchanged telephone numbers through Scruggs, and a new line of communication was established. We were beginning to circle the White House.

40

PAULETTE was becoming increasingly frustrated that it was taking so much time for us to assert jurisdiction over tobacco products. Eager to have things settled, she began pushing me to release the document.

"Let it out," she told me. "If you wait, you may never have the chance. Once it's out, they can't do anything."

Paulette never tried to hide her outspokenness. It was typical of her that when the decision to nominate me as commissioner seemed stalled, she suggested that I tell the Bush administration to "pick me now or never." More recently, Jeffrey Goldberg of *The New York Times Magazine* had interviewed us at home about the FDA's tobacco campaign. In describing Paulette he wrote, "She is the hothead in this house, it seems." He then continued, "It is an odd thing about her husband, how coldly clinical he comes across on an issue weighted with such emotion." Paulette was not altogether pleased with the description of her, nor with the fact that the reporter had captured her aptly in a single sentence. "Compared to you," she remarked, "a potted plant is a hothead."

Still, I resisted her push to assert jurisdiction. I knew that the President's support, while technically not essential, would have a profound effect on the ultimate outcome.

I would have been less willing to wait had I known that powerful forces were beginning to converge with a unified objective: getting me out of my job. I already knew that I had become an anathema in certain circles. One tobacco industry official noted with satisfaction, "Perceptions of Dr. Kessler's overbearing presence are coming from increasingly varied sources." An article that appeared in the *American Spectator* in January 1995 called me a "Bush backstabber" and a "bureaucratic czar" with an "addiction to power." Philip Morris had met with the publisher months before that article appeared; within days of that meeting, an investigative reporter had been assigned to see what he could learn about me.

In another Philip Morris e-mail a company official wrote, "I obtained some cursory information regarding Kessler's status. Although limited in details, it is consistent with recent news reports comparing Kessler to 'Stalin' relative to his control and impact over the pharmaceutical industry. Apparently the DEA and some senior FDA people are gathering documentation to seal Kessler's fate in the near future (weeks or a few months). Apparently, Kessler's removal from his post is now considered very politically correct and consistent with Clinton using him as a scapegoat. The word is that Kessler will leave and very damaging information on Kessler will be made public in the process. Enjoy."

At the time, I knew nothing about these exchanges, but my sense of the hostile political climate made me sufficiently cautious to take contingency measures. I made copies of the jurisdiction document and prepared letters to each of the manufacturers explaining that nicotine had been classified as a drug and that cigarettes and smokeless tobacco were now considered drug delivery devices. Then, I asked Mitch Zeller to put a safe in his office, and I stuffed the cover letters and the jurisdiction document into large envelopes inside.

Mitch and I never spoke of what might happen to force him to take charge. But I knew that we were involved in a high-stakes fight now. And I knew that if the time came, Mitch would not allow those documents to languish in that safe.

ONE evening, my son, Ben, and I were on our way to Enriqueta's, a tiny Mexican restaurant in Georgetown. As I pulled into a parking space, we heard an advertisement on the radio. A woman with breast cancer was talking to a friend, complaining that the FDA had held up a therapy she urgently needed. The FDA needs to be reformed, the announcer concluded sternly. The implication was that the bureaucracy was too slow to approve drugs that could meet the needs of desperately ill people.

By the time I realized where the ad was going and reached out to silence the radio, the thirty-second spot was over. Had I been alone, I would have shrugged it off. I had learned to brace myself for the reaction that inevitably followed our every action. But now I heard the message through the ears of the nine-year-old sitting next to me—and the conversation sounded plausible, the announcer intelligent, and the critique damning.

For a moment Ben said nothing but I knew he was upset. "That isn't true, is it?" he asked.

In my son's eyes I was the FDA. I was silent, searching for the right words to answer him. It did not seem important just then to correct the distortions in the ad or to explain our policy for accelerating drug approvals. I did not want to engage him in a discussion about American ambivalence toward government. But I did want to help him consider context and to take away a larger message from what he had just heard.

"When you take on hard issues, people are going to come after you," I told him. "You have to be prepared for that." Ben did not look completely mollified, but I had little reason for concern. That fall he made his own small political statement when he dressed up for Halloween as Newt Gingrich.

The radio ad was the work of the Citizens for a Sound Economy (CSE), a self-styled "free-market" advocacy group based in Washington, D.C., whose funds came from an array of corporate sources in the chemical, oil, pharmaceutical, telecommunications, and tobacco industries. The ads were part of a careful strategy to create a public perception that the FDA did not protect consumers, it put them at risk: Death by Regulation. Once, while waiting in the green room to appear on a CNN television broadcast, I asked a representative of a libertarian think tank what he knew about CSE. He told me he considered it more of a public relations front than a genuine think tank. I found support for that claim later, when I read an e-mail from a Philip Morris executive who had learned that *Roll Call,* the Capitol Hill newspaper, was running a special supplement issue on the FDA. "Contact CSE about running an ad," Philip Morris advised.

CSE had a particular dislike for me. I was, said one CSE executive, the man "we all love to hate." Jeff Nesbit, whose interest in FDA regulation of tobacco had not flagged, worked briefly as the organization's communications director after the Bush-Quayle ticket was defeated. Shortly after his arrival, he accompanied Paul Beckner, CSE's combative president, to a meeting at Philip Morris headquarters in New York. CSE had already established several state-based groups to fight taxes and was ready to launch others. For an initial payment of $250,000, Beckner told Philip Morris, he could create a handful of new antitax groups in state capitols. Philip Morris understood the pitch—CSE would wear the mantle of a group opposed to taxes in general, but its first target would be the cigarette excise tax that was to have funded Clinton's health-care reform initiative. Jeff was astonished at the massive expenditure of time and money that Philip Morris was able to dedicate to its battles and disappointed by the cavalier gamesmanship he saw. He had not realized that Philip Morris was behind CSE's tax initiatives and left the organization soon afterwards.

When Jeff told me this story, he said there had been no explicit talk of a quid pro quo. But I knew that symbiotic relationships could be complex. A transcript from one Philip Morris workshop showed officials describing their efforts to educate newly elected female legislators. Claiming that this group was more likely to have entered politics after being involved with "women's issues" than with the private sector, Philip Morris discussed the need to explain to them "the quid pro quo system of how government and business can work together effectively."

WHILE hoping that President Clinton would not allow us to move forward, Philip Morris was carefully assessing its strategic options if he did. According to company documents, it could stop us in Congress or challenge us in the courts. It could launch an all-out attack on me and my congressional allies, with support from its surrogates, and get its message out on talk shows and in local newspapers. It could offer compromises and concessions, perhaps giving up billboards but not other forms of advertising, or it could deliver a counterattack with the kind of Harry-and-Louise advertising blitz that had sunk health-care reform. In its typical all-out fashion, the industry decided to pursue all of these avenues aggressively.

There was an irony to this. For many years, Philip Morris had privately assumed that Congress would force the industry to live with stricter controls on tobacco. In a 1988 memo, an executive noted that the company might agree to include informational inserts in its cigarette packages, abandon vending machine sales, and restrict the placement of billboards near schools. But after internal discussions, Philip Morris concluded, "[I]t would be a mistake to take any of these actions voluntarily at this time, because each of them may constitute an important bargaining chip in the legislative negotiations which are likely to occur within the next two years." No legislation was passed, and there were no changes in marketing practices.

The same sort of strategic thinking led to Project Rainbow, developed by Philip Morris to explore the possibility of a legislative compromise in which the industry would accept some level of restrictions on advertising and event promotion. Again, nothing happened. By 1993, recognizing a "pent-up demand" for legislation, Philip Morris's lobbyist Buffy Linehan asked the company's CEO to review a lengthy list of access, marketing, and labeling restrictions. Campbell carefully marked each option with comments such as "unacceptable," "modify," "reluctant give up," and "give away." After our letter to the Coalition was released, the industry sensed the time to act might be at hand. According to a strategy review, "Avoiding FDA regulation next year may well require selling a 'Rainbow compromise.'"

None of this meant that the companies were now eager to make concessions. As the prospect of FDA tobacco regulation picked up steam in the spring of 1995, they began calling in their chips with a vast network of third-party allies. "It is now or never as far as cutting this off at the pass," declared David Nicoli, head of government affairs at Philip Morris. "I am for the mass mob."

What he meant was a mass mobilization, and with his reputation as a workaholic, he was the sort of person who could help get that done. But it was expensive. Philip Morris estimated the cost of one proposed set of activities at $900,000—and its only concern was the adequacy of its mobilization budget should it have to mount a further offensive. A separate annual budget of some $1 million was used to pay a group of twenty-one public relations consultants monthly retainers to pitch journalists on local angles to national tobacco stories.

One part of the company's strategy at this time was to launch Action Against Access (AAA), a series of voluntary initiatives targeted at reducing tobacco sales to youth. By advocating modest restrictions on vending machines, bans on product samples through the mails, and other small steps, the company hoped to undercut momentum for more extensive regulation. A Philip Morris document preparing to announce AAA called it "an effort to preempt any press leaks and take the youth issue away from Kessler." AAA was also a means to provide cover to industry allies on the Hill. "They will not be as much on the defensive, and can attack FDA's move as a prime example of big government action aimed at adults."

Another angle was pursued through an international organization, called Libertad, created and funded by Philip Morris. Libertad was a coalition of businesspeople, academics, media representatives, and legal experts from around the world who were purportedly brought together by concerns about commercial free speech and in opposition to restrictions on cigarette advertising. At one Libertad dinner meeting, a journalist approached Craig Fuller, the corporate affairs executive at Philip Morris charged with addressing FDA issues, and broached the possibility of "writing a book about the evils of David Kessler."

The industry also put its friends in Congress to work. One of the priority items on my agenda continued to be the construction of a modern FDA headquarters that featured state-of-the-art laboratories and eliminated time-wasting inefficiencies. At the moment, the agency was spread across forty-eight buildings in twenty different locations around Washington. We urgently needed to relocate in order to improve the way we did our work. Recognizing that pulling the agency together would produce long-term savings, Congress began parceling out construction funds in fiscal year 1992, when the project enjoyed bipartisan support. For the 1996 fiscal year, we were hoping for a $65 million appropriation to purchase land in Clarksburg, Maryland.

But our chances vanished overnight when certain members of the House Appropriations Committee, and the outside organizations that goaded them on, launched a carefully orchestrated assault on the building project. In the process, its nature and scope were distorted beyond recognition. Congressman John Duncan, a Republican from Tennessee, claimed I was trying to create a "Taj Mahal" in Clarksburg. Later, the moniker "Kessler's castle" was tacked on.

Boyden Gray, the new chairman of Citizens for a Sound Economy, helped set the tone during his testimony. I genuinely liked Boyden. He had been President Bush's White House counsel when I was appointed FDA commissioner, and he had played an important role in choosing me for the job. Boyden had an academic perspective on policy issues, and though we had ideological differences about regulation, I thought him reasonable.

But his criticism of the agency revealed another side. Boyden began with a stale critique of the drug approval process, ignoring an array of published data that showed dramatic improvements in the time we were taking to evaluate new applications. Behind his rhetoric about "overregulation" and a "growing bureaucracy," he was attempting to show that the FDA could not be trusted to manage funds wisely.

Boyden's attacks were relentless. He even suggested that the very existence of the agency might be called into question. "The 104th Congress is currently in the process of identifying and eliminating federal agencies that have either outlived their usefulness, or whose mission can be best accomplished at the state level," he said. "Breaking ground on a government construction project of this magnitude is shortsighted—especially until the future of the FDA can be defined by the new Congress."

ONE of the most painful moments for me personally came when Charlie Edwards testified before the Senate Committee on Labor and Human Resources, chaired by Nancy Kassebaum. Edwards, a former FDA commissioner, had been a friend since the days just prior to my appointment. He had supported my nomination as commissioner, and he knew how far we had come in speeding up drug approvals and streamlining the agency.

The topic of the hearing was FDA reform. Because the event was not televised by C-SPAN, I arranged to dial in to *Hearings on the Line* for the live broadcast and I was listening on my cell phone en route to the Parklawn building. I was so focused on what Edwards was saying that I sat in the basement garage when I arrived, rather than miss a moment in the walk to my office.

As if recent attacks against us had been a spontaneous groundswell, not a carefully orchestrated strategy, Edwards commented, "Certainly the FDA has always had its critics, but I think it is rare, indeed, to have the criticism of the agency come from so many camps and to have so many different proposals for reform quoted at the same time.

"We have yet to ensure that those who are appointed as commissioner have the necessary qualifications for the job," said Edwards. "Far too often, the wrong person is in charge because it is easy but very wrong to assume that a medical degree or a prior post in academia is all that is needed to run this agency." He could not have been much more personal than that.

Then he criticized us for failing to live up to our "core mission." I had heard those words before and knew them as code to suggest that tobacco was a digression. "I also want to emphatically reiterate that the agency cannot continue its present bent to step beyond the bounds of its mission, especially when doing so diverts its attention from its core duties. Otherwise, the consequences will be devastating, not only for the agency and the industries it regulates, but also, and most importantly, for the millions of people in America who use FDA-regulated products."

I pressed "End" on the phone and took the elevator upstairs to my office. I felt as though I had just been punched in the stomach.

I had no way of knowing that Philip Morris had contacted Charlie Edwards more than a year earlier, just before I testified at the Waxman hearing in March 1994. I was also unaware that the company had proposed to establish a multi-million-dollar basic science research center at Scripps Research Institute in La Jolla, California, where Charlie had previously served as president.

Philip Morris's initial contact with Edwards had come in a call to his stateroom aboard an ocean liner heading for Singapore. A company attorney asked him to cut short his vacation so that they could talk, offering to send a corporate jet to Asia to fetch him home.

Edwards declined to end his vacation early, but told the Philip Morris lawyer that he would meet with the company upon his return. Originally, Philip Morris officials had hoped Charlie would call me and try to persuade me not to testify before Waxman. By the time he was back on American soil, it was too late for that, but Charlie continued to talk with high-level company officials, meeting with them first in California and then in New York. Two of his former FDA colleagues, Peter Barton Hutt, the agency's former general counsel, and Sherwin Gardner, who had been Edwards's deputy, accompanied him to the New York meeting.

Charlie argued that the industry needed to do something to improve its image. At the meeting, it quickly became evident that the Philip Morris executives were divided into two camps. Younger members of the group were ready to compromise to change the public perception of the industry, but the older hardliners seemed determined to maintain the status quo. Industry representatives then asked how best to keep the heat on the FDA. Edwards and Sherwin Gardner suggested areas in which they thought we were vulnerable and said the major trade associations would likely rally around the argument that tobacco regulation would divert FDA resources from other important responsibilities.

I knew nothing about these discussions as I sat listening to Edwards blast me in his testimony. Many of the statements matched, verbatim, those I later saw in a Philip Morris document that was part of the company's FDA media plan. Nor did I know that he was on retainer to that company. Edwards had been paid a total of $125,000 for his services as a consultant.

EVERY morning, it seemed, I would open the newspaper to see full-page ads from one of the tobacco companies, or its allies, attacking the FDA. R. J. Reynolds ran a whole series. One, showing citizens being thrown against police cars by law enforcement officers, was so overdramatic as to be laughable. My personal favorite was a photo of the Berlin Wall crumbling and a headline reading, "Where exactly is the land of the free?" Citizens for a Sound Economy had an anti-FDA ad campaign that never actually mentioned tobacco. Instead, one headline read: "Is the era of big government really over? Not at the FDA." Another, nastier, ad asked, "Does the FDA retaliate against its critics? If you said, yes, you're not alone." Though I was more amused than disturbed, I did not realize how much damage these ads were causing us.

In this charged political environment, I was not surprised to learn that Congressman John Duncan had proposed an amendment to appropriations legislation that would strike the funds for the next phase of our campus project. That move triggered another round of criticism. Ron Lewis of Kentucky was especially virulent, calling us incompetent and arrogant, "an agency run amok."

Ohio Republican John Boehner took a sarcastic approach. "As we go through this downsizing over the next couple of years, we will have ample room for the FDA, what is left of it, to be consolidated in some other empty buildings," he declared. I could not fathom Boehner's motives until much later, when it was reported that he was personally distributing campaign contribution checks from Brown & Williamson on the floor of the House, in direct violation of House rules.

By the time the Duncan amendment was put to a vote, I knew we were going to lose. The $65 million building request was killed by a vote of 278 to 146.

David Nicoli was watching the vote and circulated an e-mail to his colleagues the moment the project was dead. He noted with satisfaction that "tobacco was NOT mentioned during debate" and pointed out that "CSE orchestrated this and wrote most of the statements that were read against the FDA." The next step, he wrote, was to get the company's view of what the vote meant to the White House.

THE evening after our hopes for consolidating the FDA headquarters fell victim to the tobacco wars, I tuned into C-SPAN's live broadcast from the House floor. I was taken aback to watch Jim Bunning, a Republican from Kentucky, offer an amendment to the appropriations bill that included our funding for the upcoming fiscal year. "Mr. Chairman, this is a simple amendment. It strikes *all* funding for the Food and Drug Administration from the bill." We had no warning that the move was coming.

Nor had Congressman Joe Skeen, the Republican who chaired the Agricultural Appropriations Subcommittee. The usual protocol is for congressmen to alert floor managers of their own party to any amendments they plan to introduce. But Bunning had just charged down the aisle, livid, to make his announcement.

An attempt to cut our budget by 10 or even 20 percent would not have surprised me. In fact, I had long expected someone to propose a "no funds" rider that would have denied the FDA the right to use its appropriations to study the regulation of tobacco. But to zero out the agency on the spot? To end all federal funding to safeguard the drugs and foods used by the American public? It seemed ridiculous, but as I listened to the overblown language on the House floor, I was not absolutely certain that Congress would not take such a step.

Bunning made no attempt to hide his agenda. "The amendment is meant to send a shot across the bow of the FDA. It's a rogue agency that's out of control and Congress needs to slap it down." He launched into a familiar and unsubstantiated tirade about our work.

I vacillated between anger and amazement at the sudden burst of activity. The Speaker repeatedly tried to call the House to order.

When word of Bunning's move got around, Congressmen Richard Durbin and John Dingell came running in from their offices to join the fray. Dingell dared his colleagues to support the amendment. "Mr. Chairman, I am delighted to see the gentleman from Kentucky offer this amendment, and I congratulate him for it. . . . This is the kind of amendment that we Democrats love to see Republicans offer. It is the kind of amendment that will lead the voters of America and the consumers of America to vote the offeror out." With characteristic flourishes, Dingell offered a passionate defense of the agency, concluding, "America can look to its food, America can look to its cosmetics, American can look to its appliances, to its blood and every other commodity that affects health and that sustains life and know that it is safe because of the Food and Drug Administration."

Dingell's ringing endorsement was heartening, but not unexpected. The surprise of the day came from the California Republican Frank Riggs. "This is a shot across the bow of the FDA all right, but it comes from the cannons of the American tobacco industry," said Congressman Riggs. "The reason for this amendment is one reason and one reason only, and that is that the FDA in the face of overwhelming medical and scientific evidence is on the verge of classifying nicotine as an addictive substance." Until that moment, I had no idea Riggs was an ally.

Although the debate dragged on for some time longer, the worst was over. A few Republicans went to Bunning to argue against his move. "Don't make us stand up and vote," they pleaded. Bunning, who was known in the House for his temper, was still livid, yelling to be left alone. But he never called for a recorded vote, and in a voice vote, his was the only "aye" to resound loudly across the floor.

Apparently that was enough to satisfy him. "I just wanted to make my point," Bunning said, and then he withdrew the amendment.

41

I HAD KEPT publicly silent on tobacco since the November elections. Despite the hostility being directed towards the FDA, and towards me, I decided it was time to break that silence and I accepted an invitation to give a speech at Columbia Law School. As a courtesy, I first circulated a draft of my talk to a few key people in Secretary Shalala's office to make sure they were comfortable with my remarks.

But I refused to provide advance word about what I was going to say to anyone else, prompting a great deal of speculation within the tobacco industry. Only later did I learn that Philip Morris officials were convinced that I was going to announce a decision to regulate nicotine and sent representatives in force to hear me. The company was well prepared. Burson-Marsteller, its public relations firm, was set to fax an industry statement to five hundred media contacts the moment I made the announcement. Radio scripts were drafted, a conference room was set aside for the industry response, and a list of phone numbers was circulated for key staff and outside counsel. Steve Parrish of Philip Morris was to wait at Teterboro, a small New Jersey airport, for instructions on where to proceed. The company also prepared a press release announcing that it had filed a lawsuit seeking to overturn the agency's right to regulate nicotine.

None of it was necessary. In a crowded auditorium on the Morningside Heights campus, I outlined, for the first time in a public forum, the concept of nicotine addiction as a pediatric disease.

I told my audience that we needed to shift paradigms, to stop thinking of smoking as an adult problem, and to view it instead as a pediatric disease. "It is as if we entered the theater in the third act—after the plot has been set in motion, after the stage has been set. For while the epidemic of disease and death from smoking is played out in adulthood, it begins in childhood."

I went on to describe the all-too-familiar rite of passage. "It's the age-old story, kids sneaking away to experiment with tobacco, trying to smoke without coughing, without getting dizzy, and staring at themselves in a mirror just to see how smooth and sophisticated they can look.... It is a ritual born partly out of a childish curiosity, partly out of a youthful need to rebel, partly out of a need to feel accepted, and wholly without regard for danger."

As I discussed the addictive nature of nicotine, and its power over young people, I drew on the industry's words. "Of course it's addictive," a former CEO of one major tobacco company told the *Wall Street Journal*. "That's why you smoke." I described the industry's promotional strategies and their influence on young people. Two especially effective campaigns—the one that transformed the image of Camel cigarettes and the one that revived smokeless tobacco—demonstrated the power of marketing.

I was not ready to talk specifically about the FDA's thinking, nor did I reveal the discussions taking place back in Washington. But I did emphasize the need to prevent future generations of young people from becoming addicted to nicotine. Picking up on the industry's refrain that the decision to smoke is freely made, I concluded, "Of course we all want freedom for our children. But not the freedom to make irreversible decisions in childhood that result in devastating health consequences for the future. Addiction is freedom denied. We owe it to our children to help them enter adulthood free from addiction. Our children are entitled to a lifetime of choices, not a lifelong addiction."

The speech had its intended effect, letting everyone know the direction in which the FDA was headed, regardless of who controlled Congress.

UNCERTAIN about what I might do next, the industry took to monitoring my public appearances. When I gave a speech in Tampa, a court reporter with a stenographic machine sat in the audience taking down every word. I also continued to be a regular topic of e-mail exchanges at Philip Morris, including my favorite, "Clinton has an out-of-control whacko on his hands."

Philip Morris's twenty-third-floor conference room was designated the response hub to which personnel were to rush as soon as word came of the expected FDA announcement. The company ran detailed simulations, war games, to test its ability to reach key editorial page editors, dispatch op-ed columns around the country, and monitor and respond to media coverage. An hour-by-hour "battle plan" was developed for a number of possible scenarios. Other preparations included drafting one-minute speeches for sympathetic congressmen. In one, where I was called an "unelected bureaucrat," the text read, "Several of my colleagues on both sides of the aisle have described Commissioner Kessler's actions as outrageous, unbelievable, a power play. All those characterizations are true. It is also true that his actions yesterday were illegal. Yes, illegal. ... Commissioner Kessler has forgotten—or no longer cares—that he answers to the American people."

As industry activities intensified, I continued trying to win the Department's support. I suspected, though never learned for certain, that the vice president was responsible for prying loose some of the resistance. Whatever the reason, we finally began to make headway. As we toned down our advocacy, and the Department moved up the learning curve, tensions between the two camps eased. Ultimately, the hard questioning led us to discard a few ideas that we could not develop to our own satisfaction. We gave up the hammer provision, which would have tightened restrictions if underage smoking rates failed to drop. It was an easy place to compromise. Once we had jurisdiction, we could impose further regulations anyway, if necessary.

We were not, however, entirely happy with an agreement to lower access restrictions to age eighteen; I had proposed nineteen and would have even preferred the bigger impact on smoking rates that might come from imposing restrictions up to age twenty-one. But in the era of governmental devolution, there was too much resistance to a policy that would clash with state laws almost uniformly restricting tobacco sales to children under eighteen. The Department thought we were overreaching. Much as I would have preferred a higher age limit, I decided not to push.

Although we kept haggling over policy and details, we also began to talk about launch strategies when, and if, the day finally came that we were allowed to publish our regulations. Progress remained painstakingly slow. The Department kept suggesting alternate scenarios that had the President giving a speech on tobacco, and either calling on the industry to accept its responsibility for protecting young people or, at best, setting a deadline by which our rule would go into effect if the industry did not adopt a new code of behavior. I was not enthusiastic about these approaches, but I soon learned that they mirrored some of the options being considered in the White House at precisely the same time.

FOR MUCH of the spring of 1995, the White House staff resisted most of Dick Morris's suggestions. One observer said that Leon Panetta, the President's chief of staff, could barely stand to be in the same room with Morris, which hardly helped win support for his ideas. Once, when word got out that Morris was nearby, Panetta's assistant told me I had to get out of sight and whisked me away in the middle of a conversation. Panetta had no idea that we had already established our own line of communication to Morris.

One Sunday night in May, the President told a reluctant staff to give Morris a chance. According to Morris, the President said he was in a hole and had to "throw long." Morris's role was supposedly to help him do just that.

Morris held fast to the idea that one way for Clinton to regain the offensive was to take on the tobacco industry. Morris recalled that Clinton remained skeptical, convinced he would get one day of media attention, and lose five states in the election. Then he corrected himself, acknowledging that he would probably lose North Carolina and Virginia anyway, and that the issue might not have much impact in Georgia. But that left Tennessee and Kentucky, states the President felt he could not afford to lose.

Morris decided to test that assumption by commissioning a poll focused on the five states of concern. He presented the results at his weekly strategy session one June evening. Eight percent of voters in tobacco states made their living from tobacco or felt that their personal finances would be affected by regulations. Sixty-four percent of the voters backed government action to reduce teen smoking. An even larger percentage favored fines against store owners who sold to minors, a ban on vending machines to which children might gain access, and new warning labels aimed at young people. They also backed a ban on ads directed at children.

Morris liked ideas that were not controversial; 65 percent support was his cutoff. When polling told him that 75 percent of the population backed regulation if it applied only to young people, compared to 50 percent who would support regulation of adult smoking as well, Morris knew what to recommend. His objective was to convince the President and his staff that it would not be political suicide to go after smoking if the approach were targeted at kids—and to warn both the White House and the FDA not to become overly ambitious and launch a broader crusade against tobacco use by adults.

Jerry Mande managed to secure the results of the Morris poll from a source he had in the White House and gave them to me. Not long after, I took Ben to a minor league baseball game. As the first pitch passed over home plate, I began to study the data. The conclusions were unmistakable. Regardless of political affiliation, the American people did not want tobacco sold to children. Although I was not about to make decisions on the basis of a poll, the figures were reassuring.

The President was not so sure. He reportedly complained to Morris that having just completed the balanced budget, he had the whole world mad at him—and now he was being asked to come out against the tobacco companies. With every senator in the party content to see him dead, Clinton said, he could not afford more enemies.

Morris did not win converts among many of Clinton's top advisers. Panetta, in particular, found the poll results hard to believe. Harold Ickes continued to argue that tobacco should be saved for the second term. Both men saw compromise with the industry as a much safer approach.

But the vice president was convinced the time to confront the tobacco issue had arrived. He also said forcefully that it was the right thing to do, regardless of the political calculations. His was an influential voice. The President trusted Gore's judgment, and when the vice president took a strong position on an issue Clinton often deferred to him. As the White House debated its next move, the vice president kept up the pressure, both at his regular lunches with the President and in meetings with top advisers.

For all that, few people realized just how committed Gore was to tobacco control. One day, the vice president and I attended a State Department ceremony together. The Russians were struggling with food and drug safety challenges, and they had asked for our help. As we stood together to watch a treaty being signed, Gore leaned over and whispered in my ear, "Can't we do something about smoking in Russia?" I glanced at him, expecting to see the glint of a smile, but there was none. The vice president was serious.

The tobacco industry was aware of Gore's strong views and was eager to find ways to neutralize him. One Philip Morris official suggested trying to interest a columnist in writing a critical article about the vice president. The idea, he said, was to point out the contradiction in Gore's pursuit of his "reinventing government" initiative, intended to make federal agencies smaller and more efficient, "while simultaneously pushing hard for FDA to become the nation's smoking police and thereby greatly expanding the agency's powers and need for resources."

Despite President Clinton's reservations, our initiative fit into a framework that had recently begun to engage him. In a speech that he had written himself, Clinton called for "a relentless effort to change but not to eviscerate the government. We have tried weak government. ... It didn't work out very well." He claimed the Republicans had won Congress by running away from problems. From that vantage point, tobacco control had new appeal.

One evening in the Oval Office, Al Gore confronted Pat Griffin, who still advocated making a deal with industry. In full command of his facts, and with reference to the sister he had lost to lung cancer, Gore attacked that idea, speaking with such force and passion that he silenced the room. With a tone approaching moral indignation, he argued that the choice between compromising with the industry and allowing the FDA to regulate nicotine was not even a close call. Griffin later said that the vice president extinguished any breath of resistance that remained in him. The White House's willingness to assert leadership took a big step forward that night.

LEON PANETTA and Harold Ickes decided it was time to bring me to the White House. They wanted to meet the man Ickes sometimes called the "mad dog" and to determine whether they could work with me.

Panetta's usual management style was to delegate responsibility until an issue reached a decision or a crisis point and then to guide the process to a conclusion. But on tobacco, which he knew would have major implications for the administration on Capitol Hill and for the President in the election ahead, he became involved earlier and more directly. I knew he was never going to be a strong advocate for our position, nor did I expect him to be. I was simply hoping for a fair hearing on the issue. If he chose to oppose substantive action against tobacco, he could have scuttled our initiative altogether.

A meeting was set up in late June in Panetta's office. Donna Shalala was asked to attend, and she spoke first, describing our tobacco regulation as both a public health opportunity and a chance for the President and the administration to exercise leadership. She, too, had poll results—including a Robert Wood Johnson Foundation survey that showed broad support for an approach that emphasized children.

When I spoke, I reviewed the body of evidence that established nicotine as a drug and explained why tobacco was such a high priority for me. I spelled out the logic of focusing on children and mentioned other, more radical strategies that we could have proposed. I stressed that we had never considered a total ban. I also challenged the perceived political risks of taking action in tobacco-growing states and pointed out that there was also a political downside to doing nothing.

Ickes stood through the entire meeting, firing one tough question after another at us, and writing notes frenetically. Suspecting I might try to force the issue, or at least push it further into public view, even without White House support, Ickes wanted to keep as much control as possible.

WORD came back that our strategy of surrounding the President with advocates for our initiative was having an effect. But I could not influence the naysayers, and I knew that the President was listening to them, too. For one, Senator Chuck Robb, the Virginia Democrat, had asked the White House to announce that the FDA did not have jurisdiction over tobacco.

I continued to look for every opportunity to reach the inner circles of the White House, even asking Ann Witt to send a note to a childhood friend who wrote speeches for Mrs. Clinton. I wanted to contact anyone who had the President's ear. I was worried enough about the White House that I decided to enlist Mike Synar's help. Paulette and I were at his house for dinner one evening, enjoying a meal that featured his favorite twice-baked potatoes. I waited impatiently until the other guests had left.

"The White House wants to wait," I said. I had learned that one faction was strongly urging the President to make a speech challenging the industry to come up with an acceptable voluntary offer—or face regulation from the FDA. Proposals had surfaced for postponements of either thirty or sixty days. I saw these as delaying tactics, and as an invitation to the industry to put strong pressure on the White House not to make good on its threat to support FDA regulation.

Sprawling on the sofa, Mike shrugged. "That makes sense for them."

"But that's not the way to get something accomplished."

"I know, but you have to look at it from their point of view. That way it gives Clinton a chance to look like the 'New Democrat.'" Mike held up a hand and ticked off the advantages on his fingers.

"First, he gives industry a chance to act before the government acts. Second, it shows that he's open-minded, that he's willing to negotiate with the tobacco people. Third, if he does it this way there's always a chance of solving the problem without the government ever getting involved. Look, you know the President."

"That's just it, it would be bad for the President," I said. I shifted in my seat until I was sitting on the edge of my chair. "He delays the reg and he looks weak, it looks like he has no plan, it looks like he's caving in to special interests."

"Sure, but if industry walks away during the waiting period, then they're the ones who are acting in bad faith."

"That's a big 'if.' I'm trying to keep the message on kids. If we don't implement the rule now ... Mike, I can see the headlines. 'President Seeks Deal with Tobacco Companies.' Is that what you want to see on the front page of the *Times*?"

"Of course not." Mike was off the sofa and pacing the room. "But look what happens if the President goes for the rule from the start, and somewhere down the line his people negotiate a deal for something weaker. Then it looks like he's backing down, and he can't afford that."

"He can always say that he wants to work with Congress. Then he isn't backing down."

"The trouble with you," he told me, "is you want everything up front."

"That's the only way to get it."

"You're not being practical."

"When were you ever practical?"

"Plenty of times."

"Name one." I was on my feet now, matching Mike's pacing. "Clinton's best move is to announce a kids-oriented rule right now. That way he gets to wear the white hat, he gets to control the timing, and we get it done."

"Maybe you're right."

"I want you to help."

"Uh-huh." Mike looked at me thoughtfully. "You want another piece of pie?"

He started for the kitchen. I moved in front of him. "I don't want any coffee, and I don't want any more pie."

"Why are you dragging me into this?" Synar asked. "I'm out of office, I can't do anything."

"You may be out of office, but you never stopped being a congressman. You still have your networks, you still have your connections with the White House, don't you?"

After a moment, he nodded slowly.

"I want you to use them," I said. "I want you to speak to the political people at the White House. I want them to understand that this is the best move they can make. Not just for the country, not just for the kids. It's the best political move they can make."

42

BY THE MIDDLE of July 1995, the tide was turning on tobacco. While Panetta remained dubious, he was increasingly convinced there was little choice other than to allow us to move ahead. In his view the FDA's credibility and determination, coupled with the overwhelming weight of the scientific evidence, made it difficult for the White House to block regulations. Al Gore's voice on tobacco intensified the pressure, as did fears that I might resign on principle.

The odds had once been on taking no action. Now the issue was what kind of action to take. The White House began scrutinizing both our jurisdiction document and the details of the regulation. Walter Dellinger weighed in on our side. After reviewing our assertion of jurisdiction, at Abner Mikva's request, the senior Justice Department attorney reported that he accepted the validity of our four-hundred-page legal and scientific analysis and supporting documentation. Now I had backup from the Department of Justice.

On July 12, I was home with the flu when Jim O'Hara called to say that a team from the *Wall Street Journal* had found out that we were pushing the White House for a decision from the President. O'Hara revealed nothing to the reporters, but he called me with updates throughout the day as, bit by bit, they pieced together the story of our negotiations. By midafternoon, the *New York Times* also had the story.

As subsequent stories appeared in the press, the White House advisers became convinced that we were supplying leaks every time we detected hesitation on their part, but it was not true. Many of the stories read as if they seeped out of the porous White House itself. What was true was that they strengthened our hand, making it harder for the President to back away from our proposal. Although some of Clinton's advisers still hoped a less politically risky alternative could be found, everyone knew the issue was only going to become harder to resolve as the election drew near. The White House felt boxed in.

ONE summer evening, Paulette and I joined Mike Synar, Jerry Mande, and their dates for dinner at a restaurant across from the Uptown movie theatre in northwest Washington. As the others finished dessert, Mike and I went across the street to stand in line for tickets to *Apollo 13*.

It was the first time that we had been alone for a while, and Mike was not wearing his usual grin when he said there was something he wanted to tell me privately. We had never discussed any conversations he might have had with his friends in the White House, and now I wondered if he had bad news for us. In fact, the troubles were personal. He said that he had been having headaches for some time. He had been to several doctors, but no one had been able to explain the pain, and now he was worried. He was telling me this as his friend, but also as a doctor.

I listened and kept the impassive face that one learns to keep in medicine. I told myself that there could be a dozen different causes for those headaches, that I had been trained to avoid baseless suppositions, that I had learned over the years to remove emotion from the reasoning process. I was still telling that to myself on the following Friday as I boarded a plane for Boston with the films of Mike's MRIs in my briefcase. But I knew something was very wrong.

The headaches had increased in intensity in the days immediately after that evening, and Mike had begun to suffer from severe nausea. His doctors had ordered an MRI to be performed at Fairfax Hospital in Virginia, and I wanted the films to be read by a specialist at Brigham and Women's Hospital, not far from where I was to give a speech on biotechnology in Worcester, Massachusetts.

The neuroradiologist could not make a definitive reading of the MRIs, which showed a diffused pattern, not a single mass. Most likely, this meant Mike could have a brain tumor or an unusual fungal disease. A biopsy was the only way to find out. I conferred with Mike's friend Kathy French, a neurosurgeon. We had a choice between a "closed" biopsy, which would be done with a needle, or an "open" biopsy, a more invasive procedure. After consulting with her colleagues, Kathy thought the "open" was more appropriate, and arrangements for it were made at Fairfax.

As I drove home after visiting my daughter, Elise, at summer camp in Pennsylvania, Kathy called me on the car phone with the results. Mike had been diagnosed with a brain tumor, a central nervous system lymphoma. This was devastating news, but there was room for hope; CNS lymphomas are one of the more treatable types of brain tumors. But I knew that they could be readily confused with other primary brain tumors, and I decided we needed another reading of the biopsy.

I asked Paulette to take the slides up to Johns Hopkins in Baltimore and deliver them to Henry Brem, a friend from medical school who was director of the brain tumor service. Henry met her in the parking lot and escorted her to the office of Peter Burger, one of the world's foremost neuropathologists. Paulette gave the slides to Burger and then went with Henry to his office to wait for the results. After a delay that seemed interminable, Burger called. Henry listened, nodding, and hung up. In a quiet voice, he asked Paulette, "Do you know this patient well?"

"Yes," she said. "Very well."

"I'd better talk to David."

Henry called me and told me Burger's diagnosis. Mike did not have a CNS lymphoma; he had a glioblastoma, an even more aggressive form of brain tumor. The next day I had Mike admitted to the clinical center of the National Cancer Institute. The physician who would supervise his chemotherapy treatment, and who ultimately reduced her patient load to one, was Virginia Stark-Vancs, a young staff oncologist. In the months that followed, she devoted herself exclusively to Mike.

I deferred as best I could to Mike's primary doctors and limited myself to the job of coordinating his care—choosing the physicians, deciding which specialists to bring in, and insisting that all major medical decisions be discussed by the doctors as a group. Mike began chemotherapy, and during the next several weeks, he was in and out of the hospital on an irregular basis. He would come in for treatment, but he hated being there, and whenever he could he would run for home. At this point we were working to stabilize his condition by controlling the headaches and the nausea, both of which had worsened.

During one of Mike's stays at the clinical center, the President sent word that he wanted to come and visit. Mike asked me to be there; he felt that it would be a good opportunity to push the tobacco issue. I did not see it that way. I felt that the visit should be a private, not a political, moment. When the President arrived, I stayed in the parking lot behind the lines of yellow tape, beyond the Secret Service agents and away from the activity that surrounds a presidential visit. Only when the motorcade and the SWAT teams had left did I go up to Mike's hospital room. I knew that he was facing an uphill battle.

MY DISCUSSIONS with White House staff and the scuttlebutt I was hearing about the debate raging around the Oval Office made me hopeful that the President was coming around to our position. Leon Panetta told me that he wanted Donna Shalala and me to meet personally with the President.

In late July I returned to the White House, fully prepared to make our case. We were escorted upstairs to the President's second-floor study in his private residence. The President sat diagonally across the coffee table from the secretary and me. Vice President Gore, Leon Panetta, and Abner Mikva were also in the room.

I remember the President's first words at that meeting. He had been reading an article that summarized some of the Brown & Williamson documents revealing the company's knowledge about the effects of nicotine. "I want to kill them," he said forcefully. "I just read all those documents, and I want to kill them."

Then he asked me to set out our evidence and explain our strategy. I handed the jurisdiction document to the President. Paper clips marked pages with key quotes.

"Who said these things?" he asked as he read the Addison Yeaman quote. "'We are then in the business of selling nicotine, an addictive drug.'"

"Those are the words of industry officials."

"This is a powerful document you have here," he said.

I handed the vice president a clipping from the *New York Times* containing other quotes that I had circled. He read aloud Claude Teague's words, which described the tobacco industry as "a specialized, highly ritualized and stylized segment of the pharmaceutical industry."

I spoke directly. "Mr. President, it would not be credible for us not to move forward."

"All right, what are you proposing?" he asked, and the discussion shifted to the specifics of our proposed regulations. I described our goal: cutting children's use of tobacco products by half within seven years.

The President was interrupted with news of a Senate vote to lift the arms embargo on Bosnia. He was clearly exhausted, but he was listening. "In this environment you've got to get it exactly right," he said. "You can't overplay or underplay. You used to have room. Now you've got to get the policy exactly right the first time."

Then, Clinton turned to Mikva and asked about the constitutionality of the advertising restrictions contained within the rule. Mikva discussed the review at the Justice Department and said he thought the restrictions would pass constitutional muster.

The President concentrated on the arguments, and I sensed that he was with us. Some White House insiders thought we would not even have been asked to meet with him that day had he not already decided to give us his approval. Panetta thought the meeting itself had been the final persuading factor. "He was moved by the evidence," he said. "That meeting in the White House signaled that in the end the President was going to come down hard."

As I was leaving I turned to the President. "Thanks for visiting Mike Synar," I said. "It meant a lot to him."

"I love that guy," said the President.

THE PRESIDENT decided to give his blessing to the FDA proposals. The struggle for the President's soul was over. Or so we thought.

In fact, neither the President nor Panetta had entirely abandoned the possibility of a compromise with the industry. As a courtesy, the White House notified Senator Wendell Ford of Kentucky that the President planned to announce FDA regulations on tobacco and invited him in for a discussion. Southern and gentlemanly in manner, Ford was a Democratic leader in the Senate and a key Clinton ally. Ford's intelligence was good, and he already knew what was happening; he came armed with a counterproposal. Panetta listened closely and pushed Ford to wring more concessions from the tobacco companies, but he doubted Ford would be able to deliver all, or even most, of the fractious industry.

Meanwhile, Clinton was making a speech in North Carolina, a state dominated by R. J. Reynolds. While he was there, he also met with Governor Jim Hunt, a former colleague. Hunt, too, pressed hard the case that tobacco could hurt the Democrats, and he thought he had the President's ear. Hunt then called Ford and advised him to take another shot at winning support for a compromise, and Ford faxed a new proposal to the White House. Hours dragged by without a word. Ford was angry, but not surprised. He had long felt that no one cared much about tobacco farmers, and he also knew that we were pushing the White House forcefully to support us. Some time later he learned that Clinton had scheduled a public announcement of the FDA's proposed regulations for the next day, August 10, 1995.

I was escorted into the Oval Office to meet with the President briefly before his address. Clinton looked at me, putting his thumb and forefinger just a fraction of an inch apart, and said the White House had come that close to brokering a deal with the industry. I had known nothing about these other talks. It was then that I understood the saying within the White House that one never knows for certain that something is going to happen until the President steps up to the microphone to announce it.

Shortly afterwards, I took my seat in the East Room to one side of the President's podium. Donna Shalala sat in front of me, and a group of children were assembled nearby. Joseph Califano, who had served in Jimmy Carter's Cabinet and tried to launch a campaign against smoking in the Carter administration, sat by my side. That day, we made small talk. He waited until later to repeat a warning about the tobacco companies that he had once received from Tip O'Neill, the colorful Massachusetts congressman and long-time Speaker of the House. "You know, Joe," O'Neill had told him. "These guys can kill you." Califano said it took him a moment to realize that O'Neill meant what he said literally.

A mile from the White House, in the Stonehenge Room of the Department of Health and Human Services, the FDA tobacco team gathered together in a conference room to watch the announcement on television. Paulette was there, joined by many of the Department officials who had sat opposite FDA staff during those long, difficult meetings the previous winter.

And then the President walked down the red carpet and stepped up to the microphone to announce his support for the FDA's proposals to regulate tobacco, an initiative that most people outside the FDA would have thought unimaginable only months before.

43

MIKE SYNAR tried to follow our efforts from his sickbed. He had been fighting the odds in one way or another for most of his adult life, and though this battle outweighed all the others in personal terms, it still was a fight he intended to pursue with every resource available. He wanted to know all the details about his tumor, about his treatment, and about his future. For the most part, I told him.

At times when I saw Mike in his bed he seemed Gandhi-like in appearance—bald, shrunken, and swathed in white linen. But he tolerated the chemotherapy well, and over time we were able to ease his headaches and his nausea through a combination of medications. This helped give him the will to fight on.

Through it all, Mike was supported by family, in the broadest sense of that word. His mother had died a few years earlier, but his relationship to his father, Ed Synar, and his siblings was strong and enduring, and they came up from Oklahoma to be with him whenever they could. Then there was his congressional family, composed of staffers with whom he had worked over the years and with whom he had exceptionally close ties. The Synar softball team, captained by the boss, had always been known as one of the most competitive on the Hill. Although they no longer worked for him, at least one of his staffers was always at his side after he became ill. Even in the hospital they never left him alone, and when he was home, they cared for him continuously, working in shifts around the clock.

Mike retained a survivor's spirit. He set a visit to his hometown of Muskogee, Oklahoma, as a personal goal, and he made the trip, going back to the place he had often described to me, a large gray house with a swing on the porch and a fenced backyard where dogs could run. He spent time with his father. We considered it a triumph that we could get him well enough for that.

When Mike returned to Washington from Oklahoma, the call came that I had been dreading. His oncologist and I needed to meet in the hospital immediately. Mike had lost the feeling in his legs.

SHORTLY after the President's announcement, I did a live interview on the *MacNeil/Lehrer NewsHour*. As soon as the anchor finished my interview, she turned to Steve Parrish in New York for the Philip Morris perspective. "We may have a situation where cigarettes are banned from the market," Parrish declared. "That's Prohibition. I don't think anyone wants that."

The statement was absurd. We had just laid out the structure of our regulation in great detail, and the industry was claiming that what the FDA really wanted to do was to outlaw cigarettes. The industry's strategy was a carefully considered one, based on polls and focus groups that showed support for that message. "The prohibition theme is powerful," wrote Philip Morris's consultants. "It strikes a negative chord in the vast majority of the public and it puts the other side on the defensive...."

I should have taken the power of that message more seriously. I had seen it used years earlier, when we tried to address problems with dietary supplements, which were almost completely unregulated. The supplement manufacturers orchestrated a well-funded lobbying campaign designed to convince the public that we were intent on pulling all minerals and vitamins off store shelves. We had to contend with fliers shouting "kiss your vitamins good-bye" and advertisements showing soldiers storming a suburban home to confiscate vitamin C. Largely as a result, our public health efforts were defeated and products with fraudulent claims now fill supermarket shelves. We had not contemplated prohibition then, nor did we do so now, and I certainly believed both industries knew that. But I underestimated how much these scare tactics fed into the peculiarly American distrust of government.

In order to shift the tide of public opinion, industry public relations strategists also suggested identifying "hot button rhetoric" that could stir a visceral response. Two suggested "buzz phrases" were "war on the South" and "war on 50 million American smokers." The Republican pollster Linda DiVall surveyed fifteen hundred people to assess the impact of the President's announcement, and her findings offered support for potential industry attack themes, among them that I was overstepping the FDA's mandate and that the decision to smoke is an adult one that should be made by individuals, not by the government.

DiVall also identified several "winning arguments." Survey results showed that a majority of people did not see tobacco as a threat to teenagers comparable to violence, illegal drugs, and pregnancy and that smokers generally agreed that I was "regulating teenage smoking in order to severely restrict adult access" to cigarettes. Almost two thirds of respondents strongly agreed that "tobacco should not be regulated by the FDA like pacemakers, allergy medication, and insulin, but an aggressive campaign against teenage smoking should be waged."

Still, the industry was worried, and Steve Parrish admitted to Philip Morris's board of directors that the political climate had shifted dramatically over the past few months. "What happened?" he asked. "How did we get from late winter to late August where we had Kessler defending himself from congressional attack, and the White House clearly unwilling to stick its neck out, to a time where the President openly embraced Kessler and his radical proposals?"

Although Parrish left the question open, I knew the real answer lay in the weight of the evidence we had accumulated. But the industry was not giving up. "The FDA fight is yet to be won," concluded Parrish. "But win it we will."

THE PROPOSED rule was published in the *Federal Register* the day after President Clinton's announcement, triggering a period for public comment. By law, every comment on a proposed federal regulation—from concerned citizens, affected industries, and anyone else who wishes to express an opinion—must be read and given "full and serious consideration" by the agency proposing the rule. If we judged that a point was valid, we changed the rule. If not, we had to explain why we rejected it. Only after we had responded to every substantive comment, point by point, were we permitted to issue the final rule.

The industry saw the comment period as an opportunity to swamp us. By the first week of September, a trickle of comments had grown to a steady stream; by the third week of October, the stream had turned into a roaring torrent. Eventually, we received more than 710,000 comments, almost a sixteenfold increase over the previous record of 45,000. While some form letters were part of an effort initiated by anti-smoking organizations, the vast majority of these letters resulted from an industry-orchestrated campaign. A few of the correspondents carelessly sent in the instruction sheets they received from the tobacco companies. There was a 2,000-page comment jointly submitted from the industry as a whole, accompanied by 45,000 pages of supporting documents, and each company sent additional documents to address allegations directed specifically at them. Richard Merrill, the former FDA counsel, had signed industry submissions on behalf of both Lorillard and the Tobacco Institute.

We rented a warehouse a few blocks from the Parklawn building to process all of the responses and found space heaters to warm the frigid space. On a normal day the scene there was merely frenzied. On other days, as the bales and bundles arrived to be sorted, classified, and processed, it approached chaos. Dozens of people, many of them temps, worked in two shifts from eight in the morning to eleven at night. The first group registered the responses and entered the data into computer banks. The stacks of paper were then rushed to a second group, where each individual comment was read and categorized into one of hundreds of topics. More than five hundred samples of the various form letters sent to us were posted on the walls, allowing members of the crew to identify the nature of each comment quickly and to place it in its proper category. Finally, the responses were sped to a third team of professional FDA staff for careful analysis.

It was a scene of noise and confusion, but there was no other way to get the job done. The slightest letup would have sunk us in a sea of paper. At times, I almost camped out at the warehouse to monitor the responses and offer support. Liz Berbakos routinely supervised both shifts. She would sweet-talk the crew one moment and yell the next, lashing everyone through at a murderous pace, and then ordering in pizzas that she paid for out of her own pocket.

On the final day of the comment period, someone at the warehouse handed me a letter from the U.S. Senate. Thirty-two senators had declared their opposition to our regulatory proposals. It was, to say the least, a disconcerting moment. "Twenty senators have signed as of this morning," the Philip Morris executive David Nicoli had written earlier in an e-mail to colleagues. "Good news in that Senator Dole signed today. We will keep you posted."

I did not like that sort of surprise. I had not even known the letter was in the works, and I thought it did not bode well for our regulation. But when I got back to Parklawn, a colleague smiled and said, "You are looking at this all wrong. The best they could do was thirty-two. That means you have sixty-eight." I was not quite that confident.

BY THE time the comment period officially closed on January 2, 1996, our informant Jeff Wigand had gone public. Shortly before his television appearance, I received a telephone call from *60 Minutes* correspondent Mike Wallace. "You know who Jeff Wigand is?" Wallace asked, although he knew the answer.

"Mike," I responded. "You may know who I know, but I'm not going to talk to you about who I know."

I learned during that conversation that Wigand had sat for a four-hour interview with Wallace. I was dumbfounded. Here we had gone to extraordinary lengths to protect this informant, and then he deliberately opened himself to the press, apparently believing the interview would not air without his permission. I summoned Jack Mitchell and exploded. "I've been protecting this guy for a year and a half and he thinks he can sit down with Wallace and this isn't going public?"

By then, of course, there was nothing any of us could do about it. The industry went on the offensive, hiring detectives to try to discredit Wigand. Despite my anger, I wanted to ease some of the pressure on him. I called in Gary and Tom and said, "Open up another front." We pushed several other informants to go public, and when three former Philip Morris employees agreed to offer statements about how the company manipulated nicotine, I insisted on briefly reopening the comment period to get them on the record. My Department colleagues were appalled that I would create another opening for the industry lawyers, but it was a risk I thought we had to take.

As we began drafting the final rule, support for the industry was declining. Philip Morris consultants privately admitted the company's allies were "confused and pessimistic." Senators who had once been quiet supporters of the industry were now deemed likely to "go south" on a tobacco vote. One of Philip Morris's most trusted advisers wrote that Republicans had come to believe that "being involved with or having to vote on these issues will hurt anyone other than tobacco state representatives." A campaign being waged by activists against members of Congress who accepted tobacco money was also having an impact. Still, from the industry's perspective, all was not lost.

Company analysts concluded that "candidates act in their own self-interest, so few who have taken our money in the past will stop taking it."

THE loss of feeling in Mike Synar's legs had been caused by the growth of microscopic nodules of tumor along the roots of the spinal nerve, and despite aggressive radiation therapy, his legs became totally paralyzed over a period of three weeks. This proved to be more than a physical turning point for Mike. For the first time, he knew he was going to lose this battle. Soon, he resigned himself to that.

Nothing more could be done at the hospital, and arrangements were made to keep him comfortable at home. Entry ramps were installed in his house, and since his bedroom was on the second floor, a hospital bed was set up in the living room and nursing care was put in place. His congressional family took over the running of the house in round-the-clock shifts, some of them taking time off from their jobs to be with Mike. One evening, Paulette and I covered a shift for someone who could not make it, and we sat with Mike waiting for the night nurse to come on duty. Mike was irritable, and after a while he told us to go home. "Get out of here," he said. "The nurse will be here in ten minutes. I can take care of myself until then. You two go home. I'm not an invalid."

Rather than argue, we left, then sat outside in the car to wait for the nurse. She arrived on schedule, and we watched as she rang the doorbell. No one answered. I got out of the car and explained what had happened. "You'll have to use your key," I said.

"I don't have a key. Somebody always lets me in. Don't you have one?"

I shook my head. We were locked out, and Mike was inside and alone. Paulette pulled out the cell phone and started to call anyone who might have a key. She was still trying when the door slowly opened, and there was Mike. Weak as he was, he had somehow managed, just as he had said he would.

But his condition was deteriorating rapidly. My main concern was to see that his pain medications were adjusted on a continuing basis to keep him as comfortable as possible. Occasionally, he would insist on getting out of the house, and someone would maneuver him into a wheelchair and walk him around the block so that he could feel the cold air on his face.

His family came in from Oklahoma at Thanksgiving time and again at Christmas, and Mike rallied with each visit. The presence of his father was like medicine for him. Ed Synar was a rock of support, a gentle, plainspoken man with a dry sense of humor and strong family pride. He had seen his son go from a small town in Oklahoma to the highest councils in the country; he had seen him vilified in the last election; now he was watching him die. Through it all, he was unshakable.

Mike's condition worsened after Christmas. He talked frankly about what was coming, and more than once, I thought he was doing a better job coming to grips with his impending death than I was. As I sat by his bed, he said calmly to me, "I've accomplished what I set out to do in life. I'm at peace."

Mike Synar died on January 9, 1996. Sandy Harris, an ever-loyal member of his congressional family, had slept over the night before, and she called me at six in the morning. She said that she thought Mike was dead, and she asked me to come over and pronounce him, something that only a doctor can do. I was home alone with Ben. A blizzard had left huge piles of snow on the streets, making navigation difficult and treacherous without a four-wheel-drive vehicle. Under those conditions, I could not leave my son at home, and I did not want to take him with me. I called Kathy French, Mike's neurosurgeon, and asked if she could get to Mike's house and make the pronouncement. She said that she could, and did. That decision haunts me still.

MIKE was buried in Muskogee, Oklahoma, and on the morning of the funeral I flew from Washington to Tulsa. I had made no arrangements to get to Muskogee, but Dick Gephardt, the House Minority Leader, was on the same flight, and he offered to give me a lift. There were two funeral services, a private one for family and friends and a public service held in a huge church that accommodated the thousands who wanted to attend. There were four hundred cars in the funeral procession, and as it wound through the town, crowds gathered at every intersection. The police saluted as the flag-draped coffin passed by, and the townspeople stood with their hands over their hearts to honor the man they had so recently turned away at the polls.

The main eulogy was delivered by Frosty Troy, editor of the *Oklahoma Observer*. A month before he died, Mike had instructed Frosty not to "do any of that weepy stuff at my funeral," and Frosty obliged his old friend. He began by saying, "Now we know why Mike was always in such a hurry." Then he delivered a humorous and touching tribute that captured the essence of Mike Synar the maverick, the advocate, the delegate of the people.

He remembered when Mike first ran for office and said, "I supported him not because he was the best candidate. I just wanted to get rid of the incumbent." But he soon came to recognize the value of the man. "I was mesmerized," he told us, "by someone who really understood what public service was all about." Speaking of guns, he said, "If the life of one cop was saved, then Mike had done his job." Speaking of tobacco, he said, "If the life of one kid was saved, then Mike had done his job. He had a great mind, but he tied his heart to his head."

And then Frosty repeated what Mike had told him after he had lost his last election. "I always knew that this office belonged to the people, not me. Now they've made their decision, and I'm going on to do other things."

Going on to other things. There was a deep silence, and then it was time to bury Mike, close to where his mother lay, on a hill overlooking rolling Oklahoma farmland.

44

ONE less-than-admiring citizen wrote to inform me, "[Y]our hysterical attack on smoking is masking something more sinister in your psyche." Another expressed the hope that I would be emasculated. For better or worse, I had become the face of the FDA, and in my years there I made enemies in many places.

Tobacco generated mail that was sometimes misguided, often filled with anger, and occasionally desperate and heart-wrenching. A few writers likened me to Hitler, who had banned anyone under the age of eighteen from smoking in public. Crudely assembled letters and cards were sprinkled with swastikas, one of them overlaid on a photograph of me. Some wished me dead. As disturbed as I was by the hate they conveyed, I tried not to let the letters affect me. The FBI assured Paulette and me that people who mentioned their weapons seldom used them, although the Office of Criminal Investigations suggested that we trim back the shrubs in our front yard. For the most part, we did not allow the threats to impinge on our lives.

Although I became accustomed to the attacks, I was sometimes still surprised by their sources. In a medical journal article published in *Seminars in Respiratory and Critical Care Medicine,* I was accused of distorting data to "meet a political agenda." The article criticized our finding that on a sales-weighted basis, nicotine levels had risen since 1982 while tar levels had dropped. The article was written by Gary Huber, and I eventually learned that he was a physician whose research had long been funded by the industry's Special Projects. Huber had been independently preparing an article on nicotine, but when RJR sent him a package of information that included a critique of some of my congressional testimony, he took the company's perspective into account in his article. Years later, Huber admitted privately to me that our analysis of nicotine levels had been accurate.

In this environment, I anticipated some criticism when I had to testify at back-to-back House and Senate appropriations hearings in May 1996. But I did not anticipate the form it would take. Republican Congressman Michael Bilirakis said, without irony, that he was "troubled" by the agency's delays in promulgating regulations. I was a little flip when I said, "It's the first time I've heard a chairman in this Congress say we're not regulating enough." The next day, Senator Mitch McConnell covered exactly the same ground, offering two examples of delayed regulations. Essentially word for word, his criticisms were identical to those used by Bilirakis, and that was of course no coincidence—both men were following the industry's blueprint. I thought that if they wanted to criticize my stance on tobacco, they should have just come out and said so.

A draft letter written by Heidi Pender, the counsel to Congressman Rose, and intended for Rose's signature, was the hardest for me to stomach. It was addressed to Secretary Shalala, but a copy was sent to us by fax. Rose was announcing a press conference "detailing FDA's obstruction of a congressional investigation into the promulgation of the so-called tobacco regulation." That was in keeping with an earlier e-mail that had circulated at Philip Morris. "[W]e delivered a hearing outline...that urged the Subcommittee to hold a hearing or hearings focusing on Kessler's obstruction of Congress." Rose also promised to present evidence of certain *ex parte* contacts, including the fact that I had served Mike Synar as his "personal physician." I thought the letter set a new standard for low behavior.

There was more to come. I had long realized that my actions would be examined under a microscope, and I did everything possible to protect myself. I turned down upgraded hotel rooms and sent back gifts of flowers. I asked the FDA's financial office to audit my hotel and airline receipts to make sure that all of my travel expenses were in order. Still, I knew that people were looking for dirt, and intellectually I was braced for some sort of accusation. Every time Jim O'Hara walked into my office, I looked up expectantly, waiting for him to deliver the bad news.

Over several years, the National Legal and Policy Center, a virulently right-wing group funded by the Scaife Foundation, had filed more than 650 separate requests under the federal Freedom of Information Act. They asked for records of every sort, and ultimately $850 worth of travel receipts over a six-year period were challenged. I knew what had happened—taxi drivers handed me blank receipts and my support staff, who completed the voucher forms, estimated the taxi fare as best they could. But in the hostile climate in which we were operating, there was no such thing as an honest mistake. I wrote out a check for the disputed amount. Objectively, I knew I was overreacting, but to have my integrity challenged brought me as close to despair as I had ever been.

I WAS NOT the only one to feel the pressure. In the years since he broke the story of the Brown & Williamson documents in May 1994, Philip Hilts continued to cover the industry closely. Hilts was part of the old school of journalism, where experience counted for more than a formal college education. He had dropped out of Georgetown University in the mid-1960s and worked his way up through a series of local papers before moving to the Washington bureau of the *New York Times* in 1989. He had passion for the scientific details in a story, and, long before me, he had become fascinated by tobacco. Over time he maintained far more interest than most reporters. Until the mid-1990s, when revelations about the industry began to make headlines again, the hazards of smoking had become so well known, and the political response had been so predictably negligible, that the topic had been greeted for many years with boredom in newsrooms.

Hilts had generally managed to get his stories into print, but some editors at the paper seemed to grow tired of them. In time, a sense developed that the reporter had become overzealous and that the negative coverage of tobacco had lost its capacity to surprise. Several of his stories were killed. The most painful rejection came when editors turned down a lengthy, well-documented piece about marketing to children, which Hilts had labored over for weeks. Along with statistics about underage smoking and its correlation with the Joe Camel campaign, the draft quoted memos in which industry executives instructed their sales force on techniques for pitching cigarettes to young people. Hilts told the story of an R. J. Reynolds salesman who questioned his boss about that. Exactly who are the young people being targeted? asked the salesman.

The reply was as succinct as it was revealing. "They got lips? We want 'em."

An article about the manipulation of nicotine levels heightened the tension between Hilts and the tobacco industry. Drawing on remarks made by

Henry Waxman from the House floor, Hilts described a significant rise in nicotine levels relative to tar in Philip Morris's Benson & Hedges cigarettes. The altered levels matched those identified in recent company research as giving smokers an "optimal" amount of nicotine.

Philip Morris claimed to have no knowledge of why the ratios had changed and criticized Waxman harshly for "misleading the American people" by suggesting that nicotine manipulation was involved. The company also complained directly to Hilts, alleging that the fluctuations were associated with naturally occurring agricultural and climatic conditions. Hilts did not buy it. Then, Cathy Ellis, director of research at Philip Morris, called with an alternate explanation, suggesting that the Federal Trade Commission's data used to calculate the ratios were simply wrong. When Hilts pressed her on the changed ratios, Ellis finally said, "That, quite frankly, I don't understand myself." Hilts used the quote in a follow-up story.

Philip Morris was furious. This time, executives bypassed Hilts to complain directly to an editor at the *Times* and to ask for a correction. After a long and heated telephone conversation between Philip Morris and the newspaper, the *Times* told Hilts it believed no error had been made.

About a week later, however, Soma Golden Behr, assistant managing editor for national news, asked Hilts to come to New York. Hilts sensed it was not a social invitation. During a tense luncheon near the paper's offices in Times Square, Behr made it clear that Hilts was dismissed from the tobacco beat. The Hilts era of investigative reporting was over.

On the basis of the proximity of the Philip Morris complaint and the Soma Golden Behr meeting, it would have been easy to assume a cause-and-effect relationship between them. But the situation was doubtless more complicated. I knew that the *Times* had withstood corporate pressure when it published Hilts's original articles about Brown & Williamson; then, the paper chose to believe it was not bound by a court order blocking disclosure of the company documents. "Screw it," Max Frankel, the executive editor, had reportedly said. "If they are going to sue, they're going to sue."

Still, I wanted to understand what had happened, and years after Hilts was pulled from the beat, I discussed it with several people at the paper. It seemed that some senior editors had come to view Hilts as unrelenting in his coverage, pushing what they felt were increasingly unimportant stories. They concluded that his passion for the topic of tobacco came at the price of fairness. An added complication was Hilts's plan to write a book on the contentious subject while continuing to cover it for the *Times*; that was seen as a conflict of interest.

But the decision to reassign him caused concern among some at the paper. One colleague called him "a stellar reporter and a hero." Some regretted that the *Times* had, at least for the moment, run out of steam on the story. There was certainly more to uncover. Alix Freedman of the *Wall Street Journal,* who was as determined as Hilts to get out in front of the story rather than simply to follow it, subsequently won a Pulitzer Prize for her tobacco reporting.

IN MARCH 1996, I received a letter from Congressman Joe Barton, the chairman of the Subcommittee on Oversight and Investigations. "It is with great regret that I must inform you that I have reason to believe that one of your senior aides, Mitch Zeller, Deputy Associate Commissioner for Policy, has testified untruthfully in testimony given under oath before this Subcommittee on November 15, 1995 and December 5, 1995." Mitch was being accused of perjury. The congressman asked Attorney General Janet Reno to conduct a formal investigation on behalf of the Justice Department and to decide whether to file criminal charges.

The accusation dated back to hearings called to investigate so-called abuses of FDA authority. Mitch had told the subcommittee that during an agency investigation into the safety of a medical device, he had received certain documents under a court-ordered protective seal. The alleged perjury charge revolved around whether Mitch accurately stated which documents had been stamped "confidential."

When news of the perjury charge broke, Congressman Waxman linked it directly to the tobacco investigation, telling a *Washington Post* reporter that the hearings themselves had been part of a vendetta against the agency. "The Republicans are shamefully harassing FDA any way they can, and recklessly impugning the integrity of honorable government officials," said Waxman, observing that Zeller was the most visible agency official on tobacco, aside from me. I knew, too, that the FDA had no friends among Congressman Barton's staff. One staffer had worked in a senior position for the Washington Legal Foundation and previously tried to peddle the accusations about my travel expenses to the press.

Mitch and I both knew the charges had no merit, and we felt confident that he would be cleared. Still, he could do little except wait the months it took before the Justice Department announced it was dropping the case. It had been a classic *ad hominem* attack. "If you need to create a diversion because you don't want the agency involved, attack the agency," one tobacco company executive admitted to me later. "Throw everything at the wall and something will stick."

On an ABC news report that aired on June 27, 1996, Peter Jennings asked Joe Barton about the motives behind his attacks on Mitch and the agency. "Do you honestly believe that . . . the accusations of Mr. Zeller on perjury have nothing whatsoever to do with [his] position on regulating tobacco?"

Barton looked at Jennings for a long moment, then reached behind him and pulled out a Bible. "This is the Holy Bible," he said emphatically, placing his left hand on the book and raising his right. "I'm a United Methodist. I swear on everything that I hold dear to this country, and to my family and to my God, that my concern about FDA reform and my responsibilities and duties have absolutely nothing to do whatsoever with tobacco."

Jennings followed up with questions about contributions to Barton's campaign. "When the tobacco companies give you money, what do you think they want from you?"

"Well, not many do," he claimed.

Jennings had the information to contradict him. "Quite a number do," he said, reading from his notes. "RJR gives you money, Brown and Williamson, Philip Morris, U.S. Tobacco, the Tobacco Institute, Nabisco."

Barton was silent for an instant, then pursed his lips, shook his head slightly and said, "I've never had anybody directly relating a tobacco issue in this office."

Several years later, I read a Philip Morris report that included this highlight in an activity report dated October 20, 1995: "[S]ecured scheduling of two FDA oversight hearings at House O&I, in November, including one where Kessler will appear." The timing of the memo made it clear that he was referring to Barton's fall 1995 hearings. Perhaps the congressman did not meet with the tobacco industry in his office, but committee staff certainly had contact with it.

GARY LIGHT, too, faced recriminations. One August evening in 1996, he drove to West Laurel, Maryland, to watch his son play football. As he stood chatting with other parents, someone behind him asked, "Are you Gary Light?" Gary turned, his hand extended in greeting, and the man thrust legal papers into his outstretched hand. His neighbors backed away, embarrassed witnesses to the exchange.

Gary quickly read through the complaint, which accused him and an unidentified "John Doe" of three separate incidents of intimidation. They were alleged twice to have stopped a car in Richmond, Virginia, driven by a Philip Morris employee named Mark Deane, and subsequently to have made a threatening telephone call to Deane. "As a direct and proximate result of each defendants' [sic] malicious, intentional, and wanton actions ... Deane has been injured and damaged," read the complaint. It was a twelve-count charge, ranging from assault, false imprisonment, and infliction of emotional distress to violations of the state and federal constitutions. Deane asked for $2 million in compensatory damage and $4 million more in punitive damages.

Gary was not surprised to be sued. He and Tom had discussed that risk many times in the preceding two years. What he had not expected was to face legal action from someone he had never met, a man whose name meant nothing to him.

The idea that he had cut someone's car off was ludicrous. In the early days of the tobacco investigation, we had put a series of procedures in place to eliminate any appearance of coercion. Potential witnesses were to be told they could terminate their interviews at any time, decline to answer questions, and have an attorney be present. Gary and Tom were polished and level-headed, and they respected those guidelines as if they were religious canon. Until the tobacco investigation, no one had ever leveled a harassment charge against Gary.

Nothing about the case added up. At six feet tall and 217 pounds, Gary bore little resemblance to the six-foot-four-inch 250-to-260-pound man that Mark Deane described. The men who stopped him had identified themselves as FBI agents, and one had referred to the other as "Wheelhouse" or "Wheelheath," names that could not possibly be mistaken for Light or Doyle. Nor could the white Chevrolet Caprice the agents were said to be driving on the day of the first incident, or the burgundy Buick that was involved the second time, be readily confused with either of the FDA employees' cars.

Philip Morris hired a team of attorneys to represent Mark Deane. One of them brought the case to the FBI and volunteered Gary Light's name to investigators as a possible suspect. Yet a wealth of evidence established that

Gary had been elsewhere at the time of the alleged encounters. On the first date, he had taken off from work to launch his sailboat from the White Rocks Marina near Pasadena, Maryland, and had canceled checks and credit card receipts to prove it. The marina had a record of the afternoon launch, and in later depositions, his sailboat partner and the marina manager both confirmed the day's activities, under penalty of perjury. Gary also found receipts from a local service station, which had sent a tow truck with a gallon of gas after he sputtered to a halt on a nearby highway. In addition, his cellular telephone records showed two calls within the Washington, D.C. area, some one hundred miles from Richmond, at precisely the time Deane was allegedly harassed.

The documentation on the date of the second incident was equally persuasive. Gary and Tom had worked together at FDA headquarters throughout the day. Telephone records showed that several calls had been made from Gary's desk. Gary used a protected password to log onto his computer and exited a word processing program at the end of the day, which was reflected in the computer directory. The next day, both men were scheduled to fly to Los Angeles to interview an elusive informant. Mitch Zeller recalled a conversation with Gary late that afternoon about the upcoming trip, and cell phone records show that Gary made several local calls en route from the office to his home.

It seemed like an airtight alibi.

WHEN I learned about the lawsuit the day after Gary was served with papers, I was angry. The timing seemed no coincidence, and I held Philip Morris responsible. By casting doubt on the integrity of our investigation, the tobacco industry intended to raise questions about the legitimacy of our rule, which was scheduled to be published in final form in the *Federal Register* within days.

I did not mind asking my staff to work long days and nights, sometimes through weekends and holidays. I did not hesitate to ask people to be away from home for periods of time when travel was necessary to the investigation. Gary and Tom had both made enormous personal sacrifices, and their families had let them know that gifts they sent from every corner of the country did not always make up for their long absences. This was different. I felt that I had exposed Gary to danger, and now I was going to do everything

I could to extract him from it. Under other circumstances, I might sit down with an employee against whom an accusation had been made and ask, "Is this true?" I did not do that with Gary. We had worked closely together for two intense years, and I had absolute confidence in him. Instead, I called, apologized, and promised to do everything I could to help.

Next, I called the Justice Department. I stopped short of speaking directly to the attorney general, but not by much. In order for the government to provide legal representation for Gary, Justice first had to certify that the lawsuit stemmed from actions that fell within the scope of Light's employment. Ordinarily that process can take weeks. I received verbal approval within a day.

Soon after, in U.S. District Court in Richmond, Judge Robert R. Merhige asked for evidence that Mark Deane could identify Gary as the man who had stopped him. Deane was escorted into court from a nearby witness room. It was the first opportunity we had to take stock of the man, who looked at least twenty years older than his age of forty-one. Later we learned more about Deane's life, and I felt only pity; he was a pawn in a game he did not comprehend. With a tenth-grade education, he had been hired to sweep the floors at Philip Morris. Eventually, he moved into the position of a "cooker," which gave him narrow responsibilities for mixing chemicals on the floor of Philip Morris's Blended Leaf plant. He earned a little over twenty dollars an hour and sometimes worked as many as eighty hours a week. Deane had been treated for alcohol and drug problems and took medication for depression and high blood pressure. We also learned that he was a willing litigant who had filed three previous lawsuits, one for each of three car accidents.

As he walked tentatively down the aisle, shaking visibly, even Gary could not help feeling sorry for Deane. He was obviously terrified, avoiding eye contact with anyone in the room, indeed barely looking up at all. His voice matched his demeanor, and his testimony was almost inaudible.

"Are you the gentleman that made a complaint about somebody stopping you and questioning you?" asked the judge.

"Yes, sir."

"Do you see that man in the courtroom?"

Deane scanned the room slowly, his eyes resting briefly on Gary and then moving on. He stepped out of the witness box and looked around again, this time pausing longer at Gary. He hesitated and then glanced at the table where his lawyers sat. One nodded. Then, Deane nodded his head, too.

"That looks like him right there," he said, without conviction.

Judge Merhige pressed him. "It looks like him, but are you sure that this is the man?"

Deane asked Gary to stand and turn to the side. At that point, Gary made a critical error. "This way?" he asked in his distinctively raspy voice.

"Looks like him, but I am not sure," repeated Deane.

The identification had been so tentative that the judge decided to try a voice test. Not surprisingly, since Gary had spoken just a moment before, Deane identified his voice.

Merhige allowed the discovery process to begin. Months passed, and I came to believe that Deane's attorneys were trying to use the process to gather intelligence about both the nearly complete FDA investigation and the Justice Department's developing criminal probe into the industry. Justice was examining the question of whether the industry had lied to the FDA and to Congress about nicotine manipulation. Discovery also revealed to us how deeply Philip Morris was involved in the lawsuit. With the company paying all of the plaintiff's fees and costs, we knew litigation could last a long time.

BY THE TIME the depositions were completed in March, the weakness of the plaintiff's arguments had become apparent and the ongoing lawsuit seemed almost ludicrous. Deane's case came down to a single element: a flawed identification of Gary Light, one so tentative that the plaintiff had admitted his uncertainty under oath, and one that the court had called inadequate. Judge Merhige grew increasingly impatient with Deane's lawyers.

Finally, in April, the plaintiff asked to discuss the terms of a dismissal. The prospect of financial and professional penalties against the attorneys for pursuing a groundless charge must have finally convinced them that the game was over. On June 11, 1997, lawyers from both sides signed "a stipulation of voluntary dismissal," releasing Gary from all legal claims in return for his agreement not to countersue and to "waive all claims for costs, attorneys' fees and sanctions."

In two decades as a law enforcement officer, Gary had become accustomed to dealing with some of the worst of human behavior, but he had never come under so personal an attack. I thought the boundaries of ethical behavior had been crossed with that lawsuit.

Some time later, an Associated Press reporter asked me whether I thought the suit was intended to keep Gary and Tom from becoming involved with the Justice Department's criminal investigation. It certainly had that effect. I had already offered Justice their services, but shortly after the charges against Gary were filed, the department backed away from the relationship.

At one point, it occurred to me that Philip Morris may have orchestrated the whole thing, beginning with the initial harassment, but I thought it more likely that it had just seized on the opportunity when Deane came forward with his complaint. Years later a senior company official acknowledged this. "Sometimes you just want to believe something so badly," he said slightly sheepishly.

45

THE OBLONG Rose Garden at the White House, framed by osmanthus and boxwood, caught and held the summer heat. It was August 23, 1996, and the Washington weather was at its worst as we assembled to hear the President announce the publication of the final rule, giving the weight of law to the FDA's restrictions on tobacco. Tobacco industry analysts had estimated it would take the FDA three to seven years to review the hundreds of thousands of responses to our proposed regulations and complete our revisions. It took us twelve months.

A Herculean effort had been involved. Sharon Natanblut called it "the year of no sleep." People did not see much of their families that year. At one point, knowing we needed reinforcements, I recruited Phil Barnett, an attorney in Henry Waxman's office, to help us analyze the comments. I barely remember his leaving his tiny cubicle for months. Some team members clashed during this period, occasionally fiercely, though more from fatigue and stress than from any substantive differences. I deliberately ignored the tensions among them, figuring they would have to work through them, and somehow they did.

The temperature in the Rose Garden at midday was in the high nineties, and the banks of television lights that had been erected on scaffolds at the far end of the lawn intensified the discomfort as Vice President Al Gore made his opening remarks. "[B]eginning with the Secretary of Health and Human Services, Donna Shalala, and the commissioner of the Food and Drug Administration, David Kessler, and the entire team that has worked…"

There was applause at the mention of the team, and rightly so. I felt that the day belonged to the team's members, for it was their painstaking work that helped to change the public perception of tobacco. Had we simply declared back in 1994 that nicotine was a drug that should be regulated, we would have been stopped in our tracks. The team's investigation had brought us this far.

The vice president was saying, "[T]o those who market these products in ways that encourage our children to light up, today we say lights out.... That's not just my opinion.... That's the law of the land.... There's a reason why no other president in the history of the United States of America ever made this decision. This president stepped up to it."

My sense of satisfaction gave way to a more troubling thought. By "stepping up," the President had placed himself in a vulnerable political position, and I knew that his support for tobacco regulation might cost him the election, as some of his advisers feared. If that happened, it would be a very long time before any other president took on tobacco again.

President Clinton rose to speak. I listened to him develop the theme of triumph and accomplishment, but I found it difficult to treat this ceremony as a victory. This was a political occasion, based on the belief that a battle had been won, but in truth, many obstacles lay ahead. There was a distinct possibility that Congress would exercise its power to set aside the regulation within the next sixty days, and it was a certainty that the tobacco industry would challenge us in the courts. I had no idea how the appeals process would play out and little expectation that the Supreme Court of the United States would ever hear the case. Quite honestly, I thought the chances of that were slim. Somewhere along the way, I thought, something would surely happen to derail our efforts.

And then, too, I knew that the regulations we had developed were not the ultimate solution to the problem of youth smoking. I believed that they would make an important difference, that they would help to chip away at the social acceptability and ready access to tobacco products in American society. But I also knew that we were engaged in a protracted struggle against the industry's power to addict young people and that much more work lay ahead.

As the President spoke, I tried to set aside my misgivings. It had been a good month for the forces of tobacco control. Shortly before the White House announcement, I walked into the FDA's broadcast media office to hear CNN announce that the industry's long winning streak in the courts had finally snapped. A tobacco company had lost a liability suit. A Florida jury had just awarded Grady Carter, a sixty-six-year-old with lung cancer, $750,000 in damages from Brown & Williamson. To establish culpability the plaintiff's lawyers had relied heavily on industry documents that were now in the public record.

Still, I could summon no sense of triumph that day in the Rose Garden. I felt more like a military commander who had been recalled from the front lines to attend a victory celebration while the battle raged on.

THE TOBACCO companies could have filed their suit challenging the FDA's authority anywhere in the United States, but they chose the U.S. District Court in Greensboro, North Carolina. Greensboro lies in the heart of tobacco country, near Winston-Salem, where R. J. Reynolds built his first factory in 1875. The continued power of tobacco in North Carolina was reinforced for me personally when state legislators threatened to cut off funding to the University of North Carolina after I was invited there to participate in a seminar on tobacco control. And I heard that Senator Jesse Helms had donned a "Friends of Tobacco" cap at a political rally and stirred up the crowd by suggesting they get me to North Carolina and put me on one of their "fanny-kicking machines."

Although I was confident that our legal case was solid, I knew we were not on friendly terrain. William Osteen, the district court judge who would be presiding, was a true son of tobacco. His family owned a tobacco farm outside Greensboro, and he had been raised among the tenant farmers and sharecroppers who cultivated the crop. Before becoming a judge he had represented a group of North Carolina tobacco growers who had sued to uphold the federal tobacco support program. After he was appointed to the federal bench in 1991, he made several decisions in favor of tobacco interests, including a ruling that the industry could legally challenge the Environmental Protection Agency's finding that secondhand smoke was a carcinogen. At the same time, Osteen had a reputation for acting on his conscience, and more than once he had taken unpopular positions. In 1962, as minority leader in the North Carolina general assembly, he had defied local interests by proposing a tax on cigarettes to replace a food tax and had been highly criticized for his independent action. Judge Osteen was a complex man.

Snow was sprinkling on Greensboro when I checked into the Hilton Hotel on February 9, 1997, the night before the hearing. A squadron of tobacco executives, lawyers, and public relations experts had already arrived, as had reporters from all over the country. The hotel was packed, and I was told by the desk clerk that the only room still available was a smoking room.

The hearing began at 9:30 the next morning in a dimly lit and chilly courtroom. I took a seat in the front row. On my side of the aisle were the local U.S. attorney and three representatives of the Justice Department. Dozens of tobacco lawyers were seated across the aisle. Two lawyers would play key roles: Gerald Kell, representing the Justice Department on behalf of the FDA, and Richard Cooper, the former FDA counsel, representing the tobacco industry.

I saw Judge Osteen for the first time as he entered the courtroom. Tall, with silver hair and a square-cut face, he presented a distinguished appearance. Trial lawyers speak of a "cold" bench and a "warm" bench, distinguishing judges who hold themselves aloof from the courtroom from those who communicate more intimately. Within minutes it became clear that Osteen was going to provide counsel with a warm bench. It also became clear that he understood the historic nature of the argument. Despite the length and fullness of the record, he had read all the legal documents and their many footnotes.

Osteen addressed us all in a friendly but authoritative tone as he laid out the three questions that the court would have to decide. Had Congress ever intended the FDA to have jurisdiction over tobacco products? If the answer to that question was no, the case would be over, with the industry the victor.

If the answer was yes, the second question would come into play. Had the FDA appropriately classified tobacco products as drugs, as devices, or as a combination of drugs and delivery devices? Again, if the answer was no, the tobacco companies would win and the case would be over.

If the answer was yes, the court would reach the third question. Did the specific terms of the tobacco regulation promulgated by the FDA fit within the agency's mandate? If the answer was no, tobacco would have its victory. If the answer was yes, then the regulations would be upheld. On this question, the court could rule in favor of some, but not all, elements of the regulation.

Cooper opened the plaintiff's argument by stating that no matter what the FDA said to the contrary, the regulation was only the first step leading to an eventual ban on cigarettes. "Before us today is an extraordinary assertion of power by a federal agency," he said. "On the basis of a statute nearly sixty years old, never before applied to the tobacco products as customarily marketed, the Food and Drug Administration is asserting jurisdiction over virtually the entire tobacco industry; this, despite decades of categorical denials by FDA of just such jurisdiction; thereby, FDA is asserting the power to ban this industry. It is not going to exercise that power for now.... But it has expressly reserved that momentous power for the future."

Cooper went on to argue that for three decades, Congress had refused to grant the FDA authority over tobacco, that Congress, and only Congress, was the proper body to deal with tobacco, that Congress had never meant cigarettes to be regulated under the Medical Device Amendments to the Food, Drug, and Cosmetic Act, and that the FDA could not treat nicotine as a drug at the same time that it regulated cigarettes as a device.

It was a predictable response to a precedent-breaking action, but as a matter of law it was simply wrong. Congress had not identified specific products that the FDA could regulate; rather, it had established comprehensive definitions for drugs and devices. All products that met those definitions had to be regulated, unless an exemption was expressly created; there was no exemption in the Food, Drug, and Cosmetic Act for tobacco. Confronted with the evidence, the agency had no choice under its statute but to categorize nicotine as a drug.

Cooper also insisted that there had to be an affirmative therapeutic claim for a product to fall within the drug definition and meet the "intent" requirement of the definition. The government's attorney challenged Cooper's interpretation of intent. If that were the case, Kell said, then any manufacturer could put any drug on the market, not make any claims for it, and escape FDA jurisdiction. "That just can't be what the law is, and it is not what the law is," argued Kell. "Manufacturers can't put their head in the sand and ignore what tobacco products do, and say we don't intend that to happen."

Referring to explicit statements by the industry that we had uncovered, Kell added, "Cigarettes have been called addictive. They have been called a potential drug with a habit-forming alkaloid. They have been called a narcotic, tranquilizer, or sedative. They have been called pharmacologically active in the brain.... And the list goes on and on.... And the plaintiff's urging this Court to ignore all of this evidence would require the Court to turn a blind eye to maybe more evidence than I have ever seen in some seventeen years of litigating under the Food, Drug, and Cosmetic Act of the intent of the manufacturer of a product."

The hearing ended at three o'clock, and Judge Osteen told the packed courtroom that he hoped to deliver a decision within five to ten weeks. We came outside into the late-winter snowfall, and I spoke to the press. I praised the eloquent way in which the government lawyers had argued the case, adding, "The President stands firmly behind the regulations to try in a commonsense way to reduce the number of children who will become addicted."

On April 25, 1997, Judge Osteen issued a decision that was, for the most part, a resounding defeat for tobacco interests. The judge upheld the agency's 1996 claim that it had the authority to regulate tobacco, rejecting two of the industry's main points: that the FDA lacked congressional authorization, and that tobacco did not fit the agency's definition of a drug or medical device. He also upheld most of the sales and distribution provisions of our regulation. The industry won on only one point. Osteen ruled that the agency had exceeded its power when it ordered the tobacco companies to curtail advertising that influenced minors.

In the end, we won most of what we sought—getting the authority to regulate tobacco outweighed everything else. But the appeals process had not begun.

46

I LEFT the Food and Drug Administration before the lower court decided in our favor, resigning on February 28, 1997. Soon after, I became dean of the Yale University School of Medicine. The tobacco regulations upheld by Judge Osteen officially went into effect that same day. The FDA's right to assert jurisdiction was in the hands of the Justice Department now, and its lawyers would have to carry the case through the courts.

I had never wanted to establish a permanent home in Washington, and more than six years had passed since I became FDA commissioner. As I looked back over the years, I realized that a story told in retrospect tends to appear far more linear than it actually was. Although most people think about tackling complex issues in terms of charting a clear course to a predetermined goal, in my case, at least, nothing could have been further from reality. I had not come to the FDA intending to take on tobacco. My only goals back then had been to run the agency well and to enforce the law.

From the start, our efforts had been more of an improvisation than a master plan. We never had one destination in mind, and I never tried to predict the outcome of our work. Jeff Nesbit's persistence got me thinking about tobacco, and the team kept it moving. My own job was to create an environment that made it safe for others to take risks and then to give them cover so that they were not thwarted by bureaucracy or tradition. Inquiry and investigation were our vehicles—we led with a question, not an answer—and we groped along, sometimes reaching dead ends but eventually finding new tactical openings. Because the legal definition of a drug turned on intent, we had to look for evidence where no outsider had looked before—inside the industry. At the time, that industry seemed invincible.

Along the way, I learned that shaping public opinion could be as important as shaping policy itself and that I had to work hard to maintain focus on a set of issues that society has long found uncomfortable to address. I was tested in unfamiliar ways, and I had to learn not to act defeated, even when I felt defeated. When I first arrived, no one asked me whether I was willing to pay the price of commitment, and back then, I had not given the matter much thought. But towards the end—especially when my critics attacked me personally and directed their wrath not only at me but at many others within my orbit—I sometimes wondered whether I could recommend that young people consider a career in government.

Those dark thoughts never lingered long in my mind, and my departure was difficult, both for me and for some at the agency. For a number of intense years, we had been committed to a campaign focused on changing how the nation dealt with tobacco. And now, at least for the moment, our efforts were on hold. We could do little except wait for the court's ruling. I felt somehow that I was abandoning the people left behind, although I had been at the agency many times longer than the average presidential appointee. Newspapers noted that tobacco company stock prices rose on the day that I announced my departure; soon after, I walked out of the Parklawn building for the last time.

SOON after I left the FDA, the tobacco industry began to negotiate in earnest with the state attorneys general, led by Mike Moore and Dick Scruggs, who were suing to recoup the costs of tobacco-related diseases. Dozens of states were involved, and the prospect of being tied up for years in litigation with an uncertain outcome finally brought the tobacco companies to the table. I was invited to participate in the negotiations, but I declined. I thought secret talks, which would most likely require federal legislation and yet did not involve Congress, the White House, or many other affected constituencies, were not the right strategy. Matthew Myers, who had connected us to Deep Cough years earlier, was the sole public health voice at the negotiating table.

Eventually, the negotiators shook hands on a deal, subject to congressional approval, that appeared to represent a stunning victory for the forces of tobacco control. The settlement offered much of what we were fighting in court to secure, much of what we had determined would help reduce the rates of smoking in this country. The companies would pay hundreds of billions of dollars to the states, agree to an increase in the federal excise tax, and accept all of the provisions spelled out in the FDA rule. There was one catch— in exchange, they would be granted immunity from future lawsuits.

Congressman Waxman asked former Surgeon General C. Everett Koop and me to chair a committee of public health representatives to review the proposed settlement and report back to Congress. I read the terms carefully and became convinced that industry lawyers had managed to create an array of loopholes that would weaken the FDA's authority. Even more troubling were the immunity provisions. The more I considered the question, the more concerned I became that the settlement would confer legitimacy on tobacco and stability for the companies that sold it. Without the threat of lawsuits, they would be assured financial predictability, stable stock prices, and a less controversial environment in which to operate. Little wonder that under those terms, they had decided they could live with FDA regulation.

My attitude gradually began to harden. The clincher came when Matt passed along a comment by one of the industry negotiators, who said that what the companies really sought was "peace now, and peace forever." Knowing its history of turning government intervention to advantage, I felt we could not afford to accept a settlement that gave the industry what it most wanted.

I knew I was taking a tremendous risk in opposing a compromise. FDA's right to regulate might never be upheld by the higher courts. But I also saw that if the settlement moved forward, it would be recognized as a huge public health mistake in years to come. The legal environment appeared to be changing for the industry, and it was too early to close off the possibility of huge damage awards. As hard as I had worked for FDA regulation, and as badly as I wanted it, I knew that it was not worth the price the industry was demanding.

In the end, the attorneys general and the industry settled the state lawsuits privately for $246 billion, to be paid out over twenty years, and a more modest set of marketing restrictions that did not require federal legislation. There was no immunity clause.

JUDGE Osteen's decision in the district court in North Carolina was immediately appealed by both sides to the U.S. Court of Appeals for the Fourth Circuit. The appeals court does not usually hear cases during the summer months, but the government asked for expedited consideration, and oral arguments were scheduled for August 11, 1997, in the rustic Bath County courthouse in the hamlet of Warm Springs.

Warm Springs, a small patch of land in west central Virginia, is little more than an inn, an art gallery, and a post office in a hollow. Much of the land is mountainous and rich in wildlife, and much of it is perforated by hot thermal springs that deliver up to 5,000 gallons of mineral-rich water every minute. People come to Bath County for the waters, as they have for generations. A succession of presidents, from Thomas Jefferson to Franklin Roosevelt, have taken the waters there.

The people of Bath County are proud of what they have, and they are equally proud of what they lack. For one, they lack inhabitants. The population of the entire county is just under 5,000 people, and the local citizenry will call it a sad day when that figure is topped. For another, they lack a city, or even an incorporated town, and they have no intention of creating any. For a third, they have no traffic lights in the entire county.

There was, however, a county courthouse, guarded by the obligatory statue of a Confederate soldier, perched upon a hill. Built of red brick, in classic Greek Revival style, it features six massive Doric columns, gray slate steps, and a central rotunda and was completed in 1914 on the site of a previous courthouse. Despite additions over the years that have doubled its size and a balcony that sags so alarmingly it has not been used in years, the building retains a dignified air. Air conditioning has never been installed, and on warm days, when the courtroom windows are opened, the occasional bluebird or tanager has been known to fly in, perch on a rail, and observe the workings of the law. It would be easy to imagine this as the courthouse in *To Kill a Mockingbird*.

A group of us rendezvoused in Washington for the drive south to Warm Springs. Margaret Porter, Bill Schultz, and Mitch Zeller were there on behalf of the FDA. Harriet Rabb, the Department's general counsel, joined us, along with several Justice Department lawyers. Heading the contingent was Walter Dellinger, now the acting solicitor general, who had given us the green light on our legal claims two years earlier and who would be arguing the case for us now.

Attorney General Janet Reno met us, dressed for a Sunday morning hike. She made a point of seeing us off, a gesture we appreciated. As we divided ourselves into two groups for the trip to Warm Springs, Walter asked that I join him in the first van. He sat next to the driver with a book bag full of papers, including an outline of his oral argument. I sat behind, and as the van pulled away from the curb, I turned back to see the attorney general waving a small American flag, as if she were sending us off to battle. Walter spent most of the drive questioning me about the scientific aspects of the case, and he said he wanted to understand the larger public health issues involved. He wanted to go beyond the technical arguments about the FDA's jurisdictional authority and show that this was a reasonable and defensible initiative by an agency with substantial responsibility for public health.

Our conversation was interrupted only when it was time to stop for lunch. We left the interstate near Harrisonburg and turned onto a street lined with fast-food outlets. It was going to be fast food or no food, and the only question was which one to choose. The van full of lawyers began arguing the relative merits of Hardee's, Taco Bell, and Roy Rogers.

WE ARRIVED in Warm Springs in the middle of the afternoon. The van dropped us off at the King's Victorian Inn, a pleasant old Virginia house with a wrap-around porch and rattan rocking chairs. We were all thoroughly pre-occupied by the case. Though Dellinger had a reputation for preparing inten-sively for his cases, his wife, Anne, told me that she had never known him to be as consumed by a case as he was by this one. Conversation at the dinner table that evening centered on which judges would be chosen to hear the oral arguments. It dawned on me then that the scientific facts at our command, and our interpretations of the law, might carry less weight in the final out-come than the random selection of three judges. We would not know the selection until the following morning, but the Justice Department had devel-oped profiles of the fifteen judges on the Fourth Circuit panel and knew who was more or less likely to vote with us.

The next morning was the beginning of a perfect summer day in Warm Springs. Anne Dellinger told us that in a moment of quiet reflection, she had opened a Bible and read from the Book of Psalms. "The law of the Lord is perfect, converting the soul.... The statutes of the Lord are right, rejoicing the heart." We took it as reason to hope.

But our hope was premature. As I arrived at the courthouse, a Depart-ment of Justice lawyer rushed over and said, "It couldn't be worse." I looked at the sheet of paper he handed me with the names of the three judges on it.

Actually, it could have been worse, but not much. Judge Donald Stuart Russell, who was ninety-two, had been appointed in 1971 by President Nixon and was likely to decide against us. So, too, was Judge James Michael. Only Judge Kenneth Hall was a possible favorable vote. We were starting off with a two-to-one disadvantage.

In the courtroom, we rose as the judges filed in. Michael, who sat on the right, was tall and slender with dark hair, and dark, leathery skin. Russell was a dignified-looking man with an impressive head of white hair. Hall, also white-haired, seemed lively and engaging.

As soon as Walter began to speak, I knew that we were in for a long day and an uphill battle. Russell and Michael began at once to pepper the solicitor general with questions. They treated him with a distinct lack of courtesy, and their constant interruptions prevented him from developing his argument. He was never able to hit his stride.

In an effort to identify himself with the southern culture from which the bench had sprung, Walter mentioned that he had been raised in North Carolina and that he had always thought of tobacco as a natural product. He went on, however, to say that the "findings and conclusions of every major national and international health organization have found that these are highly manufactured products."

At this point, Judge Michael interrupted to ask, "Are any of those studies based on anything other than epidemiological studies?"

My heart sank. His comment was a gratuitous non sequitur, irrelevant to whether or not nicotine was a drug. "Epidemiological" had been used for decades by the tobacco industry as a code word for studies it claimed did not directly establish a link between cancer and smoking. My mind flashed to a 1972 Tobacco Institute document that offered a road map to the self-described strategy of "creating doubt about the health charge without actually denying it" and said explicitly that the purpose of the strategy was to manipulate judges, jurors, politicians, and public opinion. Michael's question made it plain that the industry's strategy had been effective.

Had I known about comments Judge Michael had made a few years earlier at an annual office Christmas party, I would have been even more certain of that. At that party, he was reported to have said insistently that there was "no evidence" of any link between smoking and lung cancer. His own staff was amazed.

As the morning progressed, it became clear that the appeals court's approach to the case differed substantially from that of Judge Osteen. In Osteen's courtroom, the case was tried primarily on the law, rather than on questions of science; this court took the opposite tack. But it was a peculiar science, one laced with myths, misunderstandings, and outdated concepts. In order to fully understand our case, the judges first had to be instructed in the more rigorous science that was the underpinning of our argument, for which they evidently had little patience.

Throughout the day, Russell and Michael interjected extraneous commentary into the discussion. At one point, Judge Russell complained that old photographs of President Franklin D. Roosevelt appeared in print with the cigarette airbrushed out of his hand. At another point, after Walter explained that the FDA had not moved against tobacco earlier because it had not had the evidence to do so, the discourse became silly. This exchange ensued between Judges Michael and Russell:

"The EPA didn't regulate the spotted owl for a long, long time; they could have," Michael said, adding that the agency had waited until it was scarce.

"What is the owl? What is the owl doing in this case?"

"That's an example."

"I was just wondering what the owl had to do with this case."

Walter, desperately trying to get the argument back on track, explained to Russell that Michael was reasoning by analogy.

The final blow came when Richard Cooper told the court that Congress never intended the FDA to have authority over tobacco products. At that point Judge Russell intervened. "Tobacco has political implications more than any other," he said. "And that's what makes it a different case. It has to sit on its own."

Frank Hunger, one of the senior Department of Justice lawyers sitting next to me, said softly, "I haven't heard that argument since 1954." Frank was referring to *Brown v. Board of Education*, in which the lower courts had argued that segregation was a political issue, not a legal one, and that political questions are not the province of the courts.

That was all that Cooper needed to hear. "That's the reason it should go to Congress," he said quickly. "Because . . . issues that have large political consequences, that cut across many interests in the country, issues about which people feel very strongly, are to be decided through the democratically elected Congress, not by an administrative agency."

He continued in the same vein. I listened carefully, but I knew it was over.

We had already lost Michael, and now it was clear that we had lost Russell as well.

As I walked out of the courthouse, a *Washington Post* reporter came up beside me, and said, "And that was supposed to be the higher court?" I could only shrug and keep on walking.

The ruling never came. Before any decision could be announced, Judge Russell died. The status of the appeal was in question for months. In the end, it was determined that Russell had not signed the decision before his death; the appeal had to be reargued. Judge Hall and Judge Michael were again seated on the panel, this time joined by Judge H. Emory Widener Jr.

The second appeal was heard in the federal courthouse in Charleston, West Virginia, a small city tucked into the confluence of the Kanawha and the Elk rivers. The court convened on June 9, 1998. This time, there was no heckling of counsel from the bench. Gone was the indecorous atmosphere that had marked the Warm Springs hearing; the Charleston court was at all times civil and restrained. But the Department of Justice's analysis predicted that Judge Widener was unlikely to be sympathetic, and that proved true. The Fourth Circuit voted 2–1 against us, and the case moved closer to the Supreme Court.

47

MY RELATIONSHIP with the law had always been odd. Although I graduated from law school, I had never practiced law. Mine had been a practical decision, a means of gaining certain tools, and no doubt my legal training helped me to do what I did. But my knowledge of the law did not mean that I knew a lot about lawyers. I still clung to an idealistic version of what a lawyer should be.

When I was in high school, a trial rocked my school district of Baldwin, Long Island. Maurice McNeil, a black biology teacher, had been wrongfully accused of molesting a young white student. In those days there were no more than a dozen black families in town, and McNeil was the only black teacher in the school. Rather than accept an offer to resign quietly with a good recommendation, McNeil fought to clear his name. Every day, I attended his school board hearing, which was held in the school auditorium, a place normally reserved for basketball games and Christmas pageants. A determined civil rights lawyer presented the defense, and I watched, riveted, as he proved that the accuser bore a grudge against McNeil because he had given her a low grade. Eventually, the teacher was cleared of all charges.

This was a testament to all the legal profession could be.

I WAS troubled by the statements submitted by the industry lawyers in response to the FDA's proposed tobacco regulations. Although their comments filled volumes, I condensed the thousands of pages to focus on two arguments: Nicotine is not addictive and the industry does not manipulate or control the nicotine levels in cigarettes. Based on what I knew, both arguments were false.

As I read those comments, I realized how little had changed. Perhaps I should not have been surprised. I had studied the industry's history and knew that the strategy to create false doubt about the health effects of smoking had been conceived and executed by lawyers decades ago. I knew that they had publicly denied that nicotine was addictive while privately admitting that it was and sponsoring research about the pharmacological properties of nicotine. I understood the power of the industry's Committee of Counsels and how it manipulated and suppressed research and documents, rather than risk revealing scientific knowledge to the public. And I remembered Paulette's comment to me when I began to study the industry's record of success in liability suits. "David, don't you know that this is what lawyers do?" she had said.

But those misrepresentations were in the past. Decades had gone by, enormous amounts of scientific information had accumulated. And still the rhetoric remained the same. A new crop of lawyers—many of whom had worked previously at the FDA—joined forces with some of the law firms that had been with the industry for decades and continued the charade. Had these lawyers simply done their job well, or had they committed fraud?

In legal ethics, the concept known as "dominant view" dates back almost two centuries, to Caroline of Brunswick's battle for the right to become Queen of England. "An advocate, in the discharge of his duty, knows but one person in all the world, and that person is his client," declared the barrister who defended her despite a widespread belief that she was guilty of adultery. "To save that client by all means and expedients, and at all hazards and costs to other persons, and in performing that duty he must not regard the alarm, the torments, the destruction, which he may bring upon others. Separating the duty of a patriot from an advocate, he must go on reckless of consequences though it should be his unhappy fate to involve his country in confusion."

Those representing the tobacco industry fully favored that sort of zeal. In their world, the lawyer is the agent of the client, and in that capacity, zeal is limited only by a requirement not to commit a crime. Truth is defined only as what is not known to be false. Ambiguity, sophistry, literalism—any of that goes, as long as the evasion is done with skill and the linguistic hook is credible.

NOT everyone sees a lawyer's duty in that way. I knew that John Langbein, a law school professor of mine at the University of Chicago and now a colleague at Yale, has a provocative minority view, one that is highly critical of the adversary system as it is ingrained in American law. I wanted to discuss the topic with him.

"The key problem with the adversary system is not that lawyers can make arguments on behalf of their clients," Langbein said, his head tilted forward and his piercing eyes fixed on me. "What is special is that we extend that from law to fact."

Instead of arguing on behalf of the individuals whose interests and lives are touched by the facts, Langbein claimed that lawyers actually challenge the facts themselves. "In the adversary system, the lawyers present two competing versions of what the facts are. We therefore have this extraordinary kind of relativism. It is a major flaw in our justice system—that we allow this privatization of the facts to occur. It's a combat system, not a truth system."

Shifting to the specifics of the tobacco industry, Langbein continued. "What I think was stunningly wrong was that the lawyers went from defending particular lawsuits to conditioning corporate strategy and corporation mission. It was utterly clear what the truth was—their clients were marketing a carcinogen and encouraging people to ignore the consequences."

But isn't that what lawyers are trained to do? I asked. To find arguments that are supported, however weakly, by some experts?

"That's the standard tricksterism of the American adversary procedure," Langbein insisted. "If you look at the back pages of the *American Bar Association Journal*, you'll find this list of experts available to testify. I can get a guy with a Harvard Ph.D. to testify that the Earth is flat. For enough money, I can find you somebody to testify to anything. That's the perverse nature of the system."

"It worked for decades," I reminded him. "The CEOs saw that it worked. They didn't lose a case. Why should they challenge it? Their survival was at stake."

Unconvinced, Langbein suggested the industry could have protected itself more effectively by acknowledging that the evidence of the health risks of smoking had changed, and then disclosing the new knowledge so that consumers could make an informed choice. "The industry wound up being poorly served because it continued to conceal, it continued to believe that hair splitting was going to work forever. It doesn't work forever." In the end, Langbein thought that the fatal flaw of the system had been to encourage concealment.

"The client is much more likely to be well served if you haven't set up a house of cards that will ultimately crumble," he said. "I always thought the cigarette defense would ultimately fail, that it was so transparently misrepresented that it had to fail. The question was not whether, but when."

"And the lawyers' commitment to zealous advocacy?"

"Zealous advocacy should be limited by a duty to the truth," insisted Langbein. "In every lawsuit, in every contact with authority, a lawyer should have a positive obligation not to be knowingly misleading."

"And the argument that there is no such thing as truth?"

"Well, that's postmodernism. And the truth is that none of us really believe it, including the people who say that. If you did believe it, you wouldn't eat a hot dog or a tuna sandwich or get in an airplane. The truth is that all of us rely all the time on objective truth."

"Are you saying that I can be a zealous advocate as long as I maintain a unique duty to the truth, as long as I am not misleading?"

"Yes, you are free to point out the discrepancies in the evidence, the things that genuinely point towards your client, but doing things that you know are misleading is wrong."

I asked about the argument that a lawyer's obligation to a client was paramount, regardless of what that lawyer personally knows or thinks.

"That's sophistry. You have a duty not to mislead, and your knowledge of the actual facts should be used for the truth."

"But the lawyer's job is to win," I said.

"That's what I meant about it being a combat system, not a truth system."

I KEPT thinking about how the lawyers had used the combat system to protect the tobacco industry. They believed that the companies' economic survival depended on it. Ernest Pepples, a lawyer at Brown & Williamson, wrote a memo that documented the bind. "If we admit that smoking is harmful to heavy smokers, do we not admit that BAT has killed a lot of people each year for a very long time?" he asked. "Moreover, if the evidence we have today is not significantly different from the evidence we had five years ago, might it not be argued that we have been 'willfully' killing our customers for this long period? Aside from the catastrophic civil damage and governmental regulation which would flow from such an admission, I foresee serious criminal liability problems."

What was Pepples to do? If his duty was solely to his client, one could argue that he had to obscure the facts, as long as he did not commit a crime. The adversary system gave him license to defend his client. And yet his quandary, and the conduct of numerous tobacco industry lawyers seeking ways to resolve that quandary, demonstrated the flaws within the adversary system.

When I was in law school, I was taught that the adversary system was fundamental to the legal system. Through a process of assertion and refutation—with each side putting forward its arguments and trying to destroy the case laid out by the opposition—the truth is supposed to emerge. But in my experience, this is not how the system actually works. The statements made by tobacco industry lawyers over the years, including their written comments to the FDA, did not lead us closer to the truth. To the contrary, a system that put duty to the client above all else cloaked the truth. Even now, after years of investigation, I doubted that I had learned the whole story about how the industry manipulated nicotine levels.

The adversary system is also supposed to guarantee that each party will have its rights successfully protected by an advocate. But important questions go unanswered if that is the case. Does the adversary system really permit a lawyer to knock down anything that comes in a client's way? And why should a client's rights matter more than the harm incurred by the rest of the world?

There is much to be said for Langbein's approach. But the dominant view serves the interests not only of the clients, but also of the lawyers. By telling themselves that they are following the rules of professional conduct, they are able to remain untroubled by conscience.

I am left with the realization that the dominant view—that an attorney's only loyalty is to his client—will remain the norm. But even so, the lawyers who wrote the industry script for decades crossed an ethical line, causing harm that ought not go without remedy. As I looked back over the history, I could not accept that they should be permitted to say anything, no matter how misleading, as long as their assertions were couched in half-truths. I could not accept that the legal profession could sanction the moral equivalent of lies.

A friend of mine who represented the tobacco industry tried to differentiate between those advocating on behalf of the industry in recent years, and tobacco lawyers of the past. "There's a difference between taking a set of facts or data and marshalling arguments about it in a legal context and being the person who purports to create the facts or data in the first place," he insisted. Referring to the latter category, he added, "They told the clients what to do, reviewed protocols, the scientists reported to them. The word 'deception' has been used to describe these guys. . . . They were engaged in an elaborate scheme to manipulate reality."

Although I thought that distinction deserved consideration, it did not exonerate the current group of tobacco lawyers. The old lawyers wrote the script; the new lawyers perpetuated it. Certainly the members of the Committee of Counsels were more than agents of their clients. Those lawyers helped create the positions of their clients. They interpreted the science for the industry scientists and then told the scientists what they could say. They also told the CEOs what to say. These lawyers were the producers and enforcers of the script. "They were supposed to be guardians of the truth, but they were protectors of the paradigm," said Veritas. "They had more power than the kings." They were co-conspirators.

48

THOUGH I was now at Yale, I could not completely let go of tobacco. One fall afternoon more than two years after my departure from the FDA, I sat parked in a rental car in front of a house on Peabody Lane, one of a row of detached single-family houses in a lower-middle-class Richmond, Virginia, suburb. The place looked abandoned. A yellow Renault sat on the ragged lawn, its trunk ajar. Dead bushes sagged against the steps, flattened cardboard boxes and sheets covered the windows, and bare wires jutted from the entry-way. Only an empty garbage can at the curb suggested that someone might be living there.

I was outside the home of Mark Deane, who had sued Gary Light for harassment back in 1996. I knew it was strange to have traveled hundreds of miles to try to find this man, but something about that incident gnawed at me. I thought that a conversation with Deane might shed light on what had been behind his lawsuit.

It took several hours before I was able to get a lead on Deane's where-abouts, but I finally learned that he had suffered a stroke and was staying with his family who lived about twenty minutes away. It was early evening, and the edge of the heat had begun to soften when I pulled up to a well-maintained house bordering Maymount Park, an urban oasis fronting the James River. I had spoken earlier to Deane's father, and I was expected.

A young woman dressed in white sat outside on the brick porch ledge, her back to the park, smoking a cigarette. Facing her was a stocky middle-aged man with a squarish face and a small beard and mustache. He was sitting in a flimsy folding chair, a cane by his feet. I had found Mark Deane.

I introduced myself by name and asked how he was feeling. Deane mumbled something about getting on well enough and then, seemingly bewildered, fell silent. His companion, as talkative as Deane was withdrawn, took over. Her name was Shirley, an old family friend. Deane dozed intermittently as she told me the story of the past few years of his life, a tale of addiction, mental illness, rehabilitation and relapse, a story of a life out of control.

As she spoke, Deane awakened and seemed to grow more alert. He raised his head and, speaking to no one in particular, said, "Philip Morris lied."

We swung our heads in his direction. He said it again, this time with anger in his voice. "Philip Morris lied."

"Philip Morris lied?" I repeated. "What did Philip Morris lie about?"

"It's a secret," said Deane, repeating the phrase over and over. "It's a secret. Don't tell."

I had to lean close to hear his words. Raw emotions were coming to the surface of his consciousness and his mood shifted swiftly. At times, he was close to tears. I asked my questions again, but he would not elaborate.

Turning back to Shirley, I asked what had prompted the lawsuit against Gary Light. She recalled Deane telling her that his car had been stopped by government agents identifying themselves as the FBI. The FBI, not the FDA. That jibed with what Deane had said in his original complaint.

But I pointed out that he brought a lawsuit against an agent of the FDA and asked, "Why did he bring the suit?"

Shirley answered quietly. "Philip Morris told him to bring the suit to get the government off its back."

"Say that again," I insisted.

Shirley repeated the words.

Then she told me about trips that Deane had taken, trips that had kept him away for days at a time. He had been coached on those trips, Shirley said, to say "what Philip Morris wanted him to say" during the depositions.

"Is that true, Mr. Deane?" I asked.

"Yeah," he answered without elaborating. He was obviously upset, and his arms and legs began to jerk. He groped for his cane and struggled to push himself out of his chair. "It's a secret," he gasped. "It's a secret. I can't tell."

Shirley calmed him, and he settled back into his chair. After a moment, I addressed him again. "Why did you file the suit against the government? Why did you file that suit?"

"Philip Morris," came the response.

"Philip Morris told you to do what?"

"Philip Morris told me . . . Philip Morris lied. Philip Morris lied to everybody."

AILING, with a history of mental illness and substance abuse, Mark Deane was the epitome of an unreliable witness. Throughout Gary Light's ordeal, we had pegged him as either a liar or a pawn. But for weeks after my conversation in Richmond, I kept wondering what was behind his accusations.

I thought about Deane's work as a "cook" for Philip Morris, where he had been responsible for adding chemicals to the slurry process involved in making reconstituted tobacco, the fabricated paper sheet that long ago had heightened our suspicions that the industry controlled the nicotine level in cigarettes. I also thought back to the *Day One* episode in which Deep Cough said that reconstituted tobacco was fortified with nicotine. A scientist who appeared on that show had been surprised at how much nicotine he found in recon and speculated that somehow it had been added to the product. But when I had gone looking for evidence to support these assertions, I had not been able to find it. To the contrary, the scientific documents I saw suggested they were wrong, that recon typically had a nicotine content of about 0.7 or 0.8 percent, which was far less than the tobacco leaves themselves.

Nor had I ever been sure that the companies actually enhanced, rather than manipulated, the amount of nicotine in their products. *Day One*'s accusation that Philip Morris "spiked" its cigarettes had led to the $10 billion lawsuit against ABC and so terrified the network that it had settled out of court with a face-saving apology. "There is no data," Philip Morris asserted flatly in one of the litigation documents, "which support the enhancement (spiking) of tobacco products in any aspect of our processing and/or manufacturing."

Perhaps, but I still was not convinced I knew all that there was to know, and now Deane's words gave me new reason to wonder. We had proved beyond doubt that the industry manipulated and controlled nicotine levels in a multitude of ways, but that was not quite the same as actually increasing the amount of nicotine in the smoke. Internal documents made it plain that the tobacco companies had tried in numerous experiments to put liquid nicotine in their products. Philip Morris had at one point test-marketed Marlboros with nicotine-soaked stems. Years earlier, I had doubted Ved Malik when he told us that such stems had actually been used in cigarettes. Apparently he was closer to the truth than I realized. RJR had also been unsuccessful in some of its efforts, eventually concluding that added nicotine presented taste problems and transferred less effectively to the smoke than naturally present nicotine. Thus, it had looked for other ways to achieve the same effect.

The distinction between control and enhancement might seem arcane to a casual observer, but to me it brought industry intent to a different level. The fight now was largely in my own head, with few policy implications, yet I was unable to stop searching for a fuller understanding of the industry's processes. Night after night, I went into the garage that served as my study and sat at the computer, searching through literally millions of pages of industry documents that had been released as part of an agreement between the state attorneys general and the tobacco companies. I read so many memos that I began to feel acquainted with some of the people who had written them. At one point, when I found a list of twenty-eight different types of recon manufactured at RJR, I suspected I was onto something. If recon was simply reprocessed waste, why had the company developed so many variants? Even more interesting to me was the fact that twenty-three of those types were listed as discontinued one month after I first testified to Congress in 1994.

One evening after midnight I saw a figure that did not make sense to me. The reconstituted tobacco in the plant where Deane had worked had a total nicotine content of 3.09 percent when it was picked out of a cigarette—more than four times the amount in the recon sheet prior to production, just as the scientist interviewed on *Day One* had thought. The documents suggested that I was not the only one surprised by a higher-than-expected nicotine level. Always engaged in competitive intelligence, the other tobacco companies had thought years earlier that Philip Morris was exploring opportunities to add nicotine to its recon.

Eventually, I found documents that helped explain what was happening. The process was far more sophisticated than simply pouring liquid nicotine into the tobacco blend. Instead, nicotine was transferred to recon from other higher-nicotine tobaccos by adding chemicals, such as ammonia and diammonium phosphate, that promoted complex acid-base reactions. "There is more than enough nicotine in our tobacco blends to yield any desired nicotine delivery if the transfer efficiency could be increased," wrote one Reynolds scientist. I realized that the challenge for the company had been that only a small percentage of the nicotine in tobacco normally ended up in the smoke.

I had strongly suspected for several years that ammonia could be used to increase the potency of nicotine by increasing the rate at which it is absorbed by a smoker. At one of Waxman's hearings back in 1994, I had described a patent, issued to Lorillard and titled the "Nicotine Transfer Process," that described how "nicotine-deficient" recon could be treated with ammonia so that it could receive nicotine from higher-alkaloid components. But the industry denied that ammonia had any nicotine effect, claiming instead that the chemical was added only to release pectin as an aid to tobacco processing. And Lorillard denied putting into use any of the patents that I had mentioned in my testimony. At the time I had no evidence to the contrary.

I decided to call Philip, the former Philip Morris physical chemist who had been such an important informant for us. It had been a long while since we talked, but he greeted me warmly and was glad to help. I faxed him the documents I had just read and asked him to confirm my interpretation of them. "Is this what it looks like?" I asked. "Am I reading this right?"

"Absolutely," Philip responded, confirming that the added chemicals forced nicotine out of the other tobaccos in the cigarette and allowed it to be captured on the recon. Other industry documents were explicit about the fact that ammonia increased nicotine delivery to the smoker.

Reflecting on the turmoil that *Day One* had generated with its use of the word "spiking," I hesitated briefly before asking my next question. "I know that people think of spiking as sitting there and pouring in liquid, but doesn't this accomplish much the same thing?"

"It's more efficient than spiking," Philip answered.

As he launched with his usual passion into the intricacies of nicotine chemistry, I had a powerful sense of how much the industry had kept hidden. Philip Morris had come close to destroying a group of reporters at ABC who, although they had not understood all the facts, were onto a critically important lead. And the company had gotten away with it.

I telephoned a colleague at the Department of Justice who had served on a task force that considered bringing charges against the tobacco companies on the grounds that they had lied or made deceptive statements to the FDA and to Congress. For five years, some twenty-five lawyers and FBI agents had conducted interviews, reviewed industry documents, and presented their findings to a grand jury, and some had become convinced there were grounds for indictments. But the case would have been difficult to prove, Justice was reluctant to pursue high-profile litigation that might result in defeat, and in the end, no criminal charges had been filed. Now, I described what I knew about how the nicotine level of recon had been enhanced. Although the grand jury deliberations were sealed, I had the impression that my colleague was not surprised by anything I said. "They beat us," she admitted. "They were too well lawyered. It kept them from being indicted."

"They got away with it," I said flatly.

"Did they?" my contact asked. "Sure, they won a series of major battles. But no one believes them anymore. There was a time when people did.

"Ultimately, they will lose because of what you did," she graciously assured me. "It is not over."

49

IT WAS a bitterly cold morning on December 1, 1999, as I walked into the United States Supreme Court. The oral arguments for *FDA v. Brown & Williamson et al.*, the case that would determine whether the FDA had the authority to assert jurisdiction over tobacco, was on the day's docket. Almost eight years had passed since Jeff Nesbit buttonholed me to talk about tobacco, almost six since we had taken the first public step by releasing our letter to the Coalition on Smoking or Health.

The loss in the court of appeals had been a blow. I hoped the Supreme Court would be more willing to listen to the statutory arguments. I was convinced that a strict interpretation of the law would result in a favorable decision for the FDA. I was equally certain that this was the most important public health case ever to come before the nation's highest court. Still, knowing that we were asking for a break with the past, I tried to ready myself for the court's skepticism.

There were no empty seats in the chamber, a dignified room with oak doors and marble floors and columns. Extra chairs had been provided for an overflow crowd of several hundred people. Members of the press who did not regularly cover the Supreme Court beat, along with those unable to get seats with a view, peered out from the openings in the ornate Art Deco brass doors along the side of the courtroom. Many members of the FDA team, some still at the agency, others scattered elsewhere in government and academia, had come back together to sit in the courtroom on this day. Paulette and I were squeezed into one corner next to Mitch Zeller and Sharon Natanblut. Senator Edward Kennedy and Secretary Donna Shalala were in the audience.

Unsmiling guards quieted the rows of spectators, warning us not to talk, although five minutes remained until the justices were to enter.

Mitch motioned to me as Richard Merrill, Tom Scarlett, and Richard Cooper walked up to the counsel's table, three former FDA chief counsels all now representing the tobacco companies. Cooper was arguing the industry's case. I was bothered less by the legal skills that these three were providing than by the support for the tobacco industry that their presence implied.

At the moment the hands of the clock struck twelve, the gavel sounded and we rose as the robed justices filed into the chamber and seated themselves on the raised bench, Chief Justice Rehnquist in the gold-trimmed robe he had designed himself after admiring a costume in a production of the Gilbert and Sullivan operetta *Iolanthe*. The Chief Justice sat in the middle of the bench, with the associate justices on either side of him in descending order of seniority. The marshal of the Court gave the traditional chant, ending with the phrase, "God save the United States and this Honorable Court." We took our seats, and the arguments began.

Arguing for the government, Solicitor General Seth Waxman opened his presentation by describing the pharmacological effects of nicotine and the ways the manufacturer manipulated them. "The FDA found that the manufacturers . . . engineer their products to deliver the precise doses of nicotine that consumers need to obtain its powerful effects," he explained.

He was interrupted, after a good start, by Justice Sandra Day O'Connor, who asked, "Is it the position of the government that the use of tobacco is safe and effective?"

Before Waxman could respond she added, "So, you know, it just doesn't fit." When I heard those words, spoken so reflexively, I wondered if it was all over. O'Connor was one of the pivotal swing votes, and I had hoped she would be on our side. From that moment forward, we were on the defensive.

"It strains credibility to say that these products can be safe, . . ." O'Connor continued. "I just don't understand how anybody could stand here and say fine, they're safe, so we'll permit them to be used." No one had made such a claim.

"Maybe we should have banned them after all," I whispered to Paulette.

Many of the comments and questions were unsympathetic to our position. O'Connor repeated the familiar tobacco industry charge that our theory would allow the FDA to regulate horror movies "because so many people go to them to get scared and get their adrenaline pumping." Next, the FDA would be regulating clothing, argued another justice. It took me a few minutes to understand the dynamics of the session—some members of the Court did not seem to understand that nicotine was a drug, or that cigarettes were drug delivery devices. I could not entirely blame them. When Jeff Nesbit first raised the issue of tobacco with me, I thought he was wildly off base. Even as a physician, I had not always viewed these products as drugs.

Chief Justice William Rehnquist demanded to know what had changed, pointing out that previous FDA commissioners had told Congress that the agency's governing statute did not cover tobacco. The solicitor general explained that overwhelming scientific evidence of nicotine's addictive properties had come to light, prompting Rehnquist to ask, "That certainly wasn't the first time that that scientific consensus evolved, was it?"

"Not five hundred yards from this courtroom," Waxman reminded Rehnquist, seven tobacco company CEOs had told Congress just a few years ago, under oath, that they did not think cigarettes were addictive.

"Nobody believed them," Rehnquist responded. Justice Antonin Scalia echoed his words, prompting muffled laughter throughout the courtroom.

Others on the bench picked up the theme that nothing was new, with Scalia asking why earlier findings about the dangers of cigarettes had not prompted the FDA to regulate. "Wasn't it clear from the early sixties? Indeed, wasn't it clear in 1938?"

I winced. Nineteen sixty-four was the year the Surgeon General's report was first released. Nineteen thirty-eight was when the FDA was first given the authority to determine whether products were safe before allowing them to be marketed. It was as if our investigation had never happened. They were unable to recognize how much had changed, how much more we understood, not only about the effects of nicotine, but about the extent of the industry's knowledge. We finally had evidence of intent. Why didn't they understand that?

"The evidence, that's what's different," I wanted to shout. "We never before had irrefutable evidence in the industry's own words." This new evidence had divided the agency's past from the present.

Then, it was Rich Cooper's turn to argue for the industry. Cooper began by discounting the importance of addiction as a factor in determining whether we had jurisdiction. "The nature of a product's effect ... does not determine FDA's jurisdiction," he said. "The relevant inquiry is simply whether a product has an effect on the structure or any function of the body."

Justice John Paul Stevens jumped in. "But only if there's an intent. Isn't that the key?"

Justice Stephen Breyer spoke up and tangled with Cooper on the question as to whether the FDA had authority to regulate products that did not make explicit claims. "The intent is derived from the claims in the marketplace," Cooper stated flatly.

We had argued strenuously in our jurisdictional document against this narrow way of viewing intent, and I was relieved that Breyer seemed to agree with us. Noting that everyone understood what cigarettes are, he asked why a claim was even needed. "Is the word 'safety' in this statute supposed to stop the FDA from looking at the real world?"

Later in the argument, Breyer was even more explicit. "Smokers are no longer able to kid themselves about this—that nicotine satisfies a craving caused by chemical addiction." That effect on the body, the justice suggested, fit the definition of a drug.

Paulette squeezed my hand.

Cooper took the perverse position of arguing for the danger of cigarettes. "We are bound on this record by FDA's findings, and FDA found these products unsafe....[I]f these were to be regulated as drugs, they would have to be found safe." The implication was that if we were granted jurisdiction, our next step would be to ban tobacco. The industry still perceived the fear of prohibition as its strongest argument. The irony was not lost on me. For forty-five years, it had denied there was a proven link between smoking and cancer. Now, before the highest court in the land, it argued that its products were so dangerous the FDA could not allow them to remain on the market, should it be given jurisdiction.

Cooper crossed swords next with Justice Ruth Bader Ginsburg when he argued for the limits of the agency's jurisdiction. Ginsburg asked whether heroin, if it were lawful, could be regulated by the FDA.

"If it doesn't purport to have a health benefit, it couldn't be regulated by the FDA," Cooper replied.

"Even if the product was harmful to health?" Ginsburg asked.

Cooper commented that thousands of harmful products did not fall within the agency's jurisdiction. Household cleaning fluids, he pointed out, are dangerous if swallowed. Ginsburg, who was seeking an example of a product in which the "core use is putting it into the body," rejected the analogy.

"I would submit that FDA's assertion of jurisdiction here is lawless," Cooper said as he began his concluding statement. "It is doing real harm to the Food, Drug, and Cosmetic Act, potentially expanding the agency's jurisdiction beyond limit, and severely weakening the consumer protection provisions of the Act in the interest of enhancing the Agency's discretion...."

I marveled at that stretch.

"Congress provided for the way these products are to be regulated, and if there are new facts, the precedent of 1964 should be followed when the Surgeon General made his report to Congress ... and Congress enacted a new statute. That's what should happen here."

I knew the industry's goal was to have the Court punt to Congress, where it assumed the issue would languish and die the lobbyist's death. But it was not a valid interpretation of the law. In 1964, there was only evidence of the health risks of tobacco. Now, we had clear evidence that nicotine was a drug.

After Cooper presented his argument, Waxman had two minutes for rebuttal, and then it was over. I was not encouraged. From a strict constructionist perspective, I thought the case was clear—given what we knew about nicotine's effect on the body and the manufacturer's intent, the FDA had the authority, indeed the obligation, to regulate it. But I feared the justices were looking beyond a legal framework, recognizing that a vote in favor of FDA regulation would be an assertion of government authority that they deemed unwarranted.

Still, I was struck that day by the extent to which perceptions of tobacco had shifted. Even the "everyone-knows-that" attitude that the justices took towards addiction was influenced by the evidence we had found. The FDA's investigation had changed popular thinking forever. Members of the court had come of age when attitudes towards smoking had been very different, and if they did not have the will to accept FDA jurisdiction, I knew that we had still made an important mark. No matter how many roadblocks remained to effective regulation, no matter how many charitable contributions the industry continued to make from its profits, no matter how much financial support the companies gave to those in public office, the world in which the tobacco companies did their business had been fundamentally transformed.

Still, it was hard to feel triumphant as I walked into the wintry air and down the long, storied steps of the Supreme Court to talk to a phalanx of reporters. I knew we had lost.

THE DECISION, handed down four months later, was 5–4. By the slimmest possible margin, the Supreme Court said the FDA did not have the authority to assert jurisdiction over tobacco. After hearing the oral arguments, I had thought we might win support from only two justices, but a narrower loss was not very consoling. The decision that could have saved hundreds of thousands of lives had been lost by a single vote. I thought I had steeled myself for defeat, but the news was painful.

Word came down shortly after 10 A.M., on March 21, 2000. Justice Sandra Day O'Connor's tone had been somber as she summarized the majority's opinion from the bench. She explicitly acknowledged smoking as "one of the most troubling public health problems facing our nation today," and said that we had "amply demonstrated that tobacco use, particularly among children and adolescents, poses perhaps the single most significant threat to public health in the United States." She seemed almost to be pleading with Congress to pass legislation that would grant the FDA regulatory authority. Nonetheless, she declared that "the FDA's assertion of jurisdiction is impermissible."

In the dissent he read that same morning, Justice Stephen Breyer showed that he understood exactly what we were trying to do. He called the majority's conclusion "counterintuitive" and declared that "tobacco products (including cigarettes) fall within the scope of this statutory definition. ... [n]icotine is a drug, the cigarette that delivers nicotine to the body is a device; and the FDCA [Food, Drug, and Cosmetic Act], read in light of its basic purpose, permits the FDA to assert the disease-preventing jurisdiction that the agency now claims."

The vote followed ideological lines. The split was not defined by a judgment on the industry's intent, or by the question of whether nicotine was a drug. I have to believe that attitudes towards government regulation determined the vote. I was convinced there was no evidence we could have presented to sway those five justices.

50

As FDA commissioner I had worked with the tools at my disposal, and for the moment there was nothing further the agency could do. I believed that the Congress would eventually vote to give the FDA jurisdiction over tobacco, and that this would help to reduce rates of youth smoking. But over time, I had come to understand the limitations of this approach. Regulation alone was not enough.

Although the Supreme Court had not been swayed by our evidence of the industry's intent, that evidence was hurting the industry in product liability suits. A string of defeats shattered its reputation for legal invulnerability. The evidence that showed that the tobacco companies deliberately sought to addict their customers, and that they hid what they long knew about the hazards of their product, was now being introduced routinely in civil suits. As a result, juries were shifting the burden of responsibility away from individuals, and towards the tobacco industry. The legal profession was making the industry pay for the strategies that had been designed by other lawyers. In Oregon, a jury awarded a plaintiff $32 million, most of it in punitive damages. Two verdicts of some $20 million apiece went against the industry in California. Like most awards, they faced long roads on appeal, but the trend was apparent. By the time the Supreme Court decision was handed down, hundreds of tobacco-related liability suits were pending.

At the same time, the tobacco companies' standing with the public continued to ebb, and tobacco company stock prices reached historic lows. Although the industry continued to generate huge profits, stockholders had reason to ask whether the companies were meeting their fiduciary responsibility to maximize investment returns.

In the face of these pressures, Philip Morris abruptly switched strategies and admitted in a public statement that smoking caused cancer and that nicotine was addictive. That reversal happened in the fall of 1999, before the Supreme Court heard the FDA's case. Barry Meier of the *New York Times*, who had energetically taken over Philip Hilts's tobacco beat after a two-year gap in coverage, called me to ask whether I considered the company's statement important.

The admission was loaded with caveats and I viewed it as a public relations gesture, as well as a strategy to influence the tidal wave of lawsuits. Still, Philip Morris was abandoning a position it had steadfastly maintained for fifty years. With only a moment to choose my response, I made a conscious decision to engage not only the issue, but the company itself. I told Meier the admission was indeed significant.

In the *Times* the following day I was quoted as saying, "It is a profound change. It really sets a new stage for regulation and legislation." I was deliberately sending a message to the company.

Steve Parrish seemed to respond to my overture during his appearance on ABC's *Nightline* that evening when he mentioned my name and talked about developing a dialogue.

A few days later Parrish called my office and asked what I thought of the company's announcement. Despite my public comments, I was not convinced that a genuine change in approach had taken place. But when he asked, I agreed to a meeting.

Parrish had for many years been one of the FDA's most outspoken critics. I recalled viewing a Philip Morris videotape that had been shown to company employees in 1994 to boost their flagging morale. On that tape, Parrish recapped my appearances before Henry Waxman's subcommittee and then said, "Many of Dr. Kessler's comments contained untruths, distortions, and factual errors." He all but called me a liar. For my part, although I had always made it a point not to demonize the tobacco industry or its leaders, I had certainly used tough language about them in my public statements. Now, we were getting together on neutral ground to talk.

I was early for our scheduled meeting, in a coffee shop in southern Connecticut, and had a moment to wonder where this conversation would lead. Even after we issued a detailed regulation that carefully avoided a ban on cigarettes, Parrish repeatedly accused the FDA of advocating prohibition. The company's polling told him that raising the specter of prohibition would help win public support. He had called the notion of FDA regulation a "radical idea" and vowed to his board that the battle against us would be won. He was part of an industry of master strategists with an unparalleled record of turning virtually every regulation to its advantage. I was wary of his motives.

Parrish arrived on time. A year older than I, he had been brought up in the Midwest and lived in a Connecticut suburb. Parrish was at once self-confident and approachable. I quickly understood why he was well liked in his company. We broke the ice talking about our families and about the child we would each be sending to college in the fall.

I was still thinking about the role of the industry lawyers, and I had come to the meeting hoping to learn more about that. To his credit, Parrish did not bristle or withdraw when I pushed him, although he insisted that Philip Morris believed what it was saying. "There are people who feel very strongly that we never said anything inaccurate," he said. But he admitted that the company had grown isolated, and complained that a "bunker mentality" had taken hold. "When you are talking only to yourselves, you begin to believe your own bullshit," he said candidly. "We assumed that everybody who disagreed with us was a prohibitionist, and was out to get us, out to destroy us."

Beginning with the FDA's first public expression of interest in tobacco, I became a prime adversary. "Our initial reaction in 1994 to what FDA was doing was the same reaction we'd always had," Parrish said. "It was defensive."

"You were going to kill us?"

"Yes. The way we saw it, this was something that this wacko at the FDA was for, and so it must be bad for us. Therefore, we have to defeat this, we have to be prepared to litigate this, we have to be prepared to lobby against this, we have to be prepared to run advertising against this, we have to be prepared to defend, defend, defend."

I asked Parrish what he thought we had gotten right.

"I think one thing you got right was that there needed to be more regulation of the industry," he answered. "We were different from other industries... in terms of the level of regulation and the lack of comprehensive regulation of an industry of our sort. If you have a product that harms people, kills people, and if many of those people are addicted to it, although the product is legal, what do you do about it?"

Although Parrish added no special emphasis, the words "harms," "kills," and "addicted" echoed in my ears. He was asking the same question that we had asked, and his conclusion was remarkably similar to ours. "I think what you do is to regulate it in a lot of different ways."

I sensed that Parrish was speaking very deliberately, that perhaps he had planned to say this to me from the outset. Another comment of his surprised me. "After a while it was no longer a question of winning lawsuits," he said. "It became a question of obtaining permission from society to continue to exist."

I looked at him closely; he seemed perfectly serious. Permission to exist? This was coming from an executive of an industry that had built a reputation over the decades for corporate arrogance and legal impregnability. I did not push the point. Instead, we talked about the possibility of legislation that would give the FDA the authority to regulate tobacco.

"No deals," I said, thinking back to the settlement offer with the state attorneys general that I had opposed. "No immunity." Parrish promised to get back to me.

ONE ASPECT of tobacco continued to bother me more than almost anything else—the enormous resources that remained in the hands of the industry. FDA regulations had been designed to reduce the appeal of tobacco products and to make it harder for children to buy them. Within the limits of our jurisdiction, that made sense. But historically, the companies have had so much power that they have managed to circumvent every measure designed to reduce sales of their products. Their drive to increase revenue had invariably trumped all other considerations. Unless we focused not only on the product, but on the purveyors of the product, I realized that the situation was unlikely to change.

I also began to think about the importance of removing the vestiges of social acceptability from tobacco in order to prevent future generations of children from becoming addicted to nicotine. I knew that changing priorities and attitudes, and ultimately creating new norms, is a far more complex task than achieving legislative victories, but in the end that is probably what it takes to reduce rates of smoking. Legislation and court decisions are simply milestones along the way. As a society, we have allowed the tobacco companies to shape public perceptions of cigarettes for far too long. Even now, with all that the FDA uncovered about nicotine manipulation and industry deception, it is too easy to be swayed by the argument that tobacco is a legal product and should be treated like any other. But a product that kills people—when used as intended—is different. No one should be allowed to make a profit from that.

As I considered the implications of this, I thought more about my conversation with Steve Parrish. Shortly afterwards, when I was invited to participate on a panel exploring the future of tobacco policy, I recognized the opportunity to learn something more about his intentions. The panel was part of a three-day conference on substance abuse organized by the National Center on Addiction and Substance Abuse (CASA), the brainchild of Joseph Califano. I served on CASA's board, and when Califano asked me to participate, I agreed—and urged him to invite Parrish as well. Parrish agreed to come.

A few days before the March 2000 event, Parrish called me at home. This time he wanted me to know that he was going to announce at the conference that Philip Morris believed cigarettes should be a regulated product. The company was going public.

I was noncommittal, but my mind was racing. Was there anything credible here, or was this just more public relations?

"You're advancing the issue," I said, but as I hung up from the call, I thought that whatever the motive, the company's goal was to gain legitimacy. All of our studies told us that regulation could cut rates of youth smoking, yet I was nervous to learn that the tobacco companies themselves now wanted regulation. The industry's phrase "Peace now, peace forever," came back to me. By defining a framework in which they could sell cigarettes and other tobacco products, presumably with rigorous prohibitions against sales to children, they knew that regulation had the potential to make their products less controversial. We had helped make the tobacco companies pariahs, and I wanted to be sure that nothing I did would help put the stamp of government approval on tobacco now. Yet I knew we should not lose an opportunity for no-strings-attached regulation.

STEVE PARRISH and I flew to the California conference together, talking during much of the five-hour flight. I told him bluntly that I saw the industry's enormous resources as the biggest barrier to reducing rates of smoking. Only then did I learn that Parrish believed his company to be acutely vulnerable. He told me that the punitive damages expected imminently in a Florida class-action case might bankrupt Philip Morris USA. And then he said he would give away the tobacco company if he could.

I had called Veritas after my earlier conversations with Parrish and now his comments came back to me. "You've hit the numbers guys exactly where they live," Veritas said. "They can project risk. You're making the game not worth the costs to them." He knew before I did that tobacco had become more of a liability than an asset.

He also knew the industry was taking a chance. "There is a crack in the Holy Grail," he said. "They're rolling the dice, they could lose it all here."

"You've been closer to victory than you realized," Veritas continued. "You're coming down the Ho Chi Minh Trail with more and more troops and they're backing up towards the helicopter." Not quite, I thought.

In any case, I was not ready to push Parrish further on those points in a public forum. Instead, I decided to see if I could get him to say that nicotine was a drug—on the record and before hundreds of the nation's leading public health experts and the national media. I suspected that he was going to be looking for wiggle room, and I wanted to make it as hard as possible for him to back away from the course he had set.

"Is this a genuine epiphany?" asked the panel moderator, Sander Vanocur, a former correspondent for ABC News.

"It is an honestly held, good-faith belief on my part that there needs to be more than just some regulation," Parrish answered. "There needs to be serious regulation of the tobacco industry at the federal level."

Vanocur then turned to me. I praised Parrish for appearing at the event, then I turned to him to ask the question that lay at the heart of the FDA investigation. "Is nicotine a drug?"

To my surprise, he did not hesitate to acknowledge that it was, although he added a caveat. "I do not believe that merely because nicotine is a drug that it should be regulated as a pharmaceutical or as a medical device under the Food, Drug, and Cosmetic Act. . . . I want to sit down and talk to you . . . about what is the right regulatory regime for tobacco, not as a pharmaceutical or as a medical device but as a tobacco product, which is addictive—I've conceded that—and which causes harm to some people."

"But no problem saying that it is an addictive drug?" I asked. Parrish agreed again that it was.

"The rule that FDA promulgated had two essential pieces: restrictions on access and reducing the advertising and promotion directed at young people. Anything wrong with anything in that rule?"

"I don't think there is anything wrong with those approaches," said Parrish, adding that the specifics would depend on further discussions with members of Congress and the public health community.

"There can't be any deals," I warned. I said firmly that I would not support a quid pro quo that exchanged regulation for immunity from liability.

"That is not what I intend to do. . . . I want to talk about the regulatory regime, not litigation."

I kept peppering Parrish with questions, and for the most part he gave me the answers I was looking for. During the audience question-and-answer period, he went even further. "Has your company taken a position on raising the age of smoking to twenty-one?" asked one listener.

"It is something we wouldn't rule out," Parrish stated.

That was a big step and I said so. FDA data had told us that raising the legal age would lead to a significant decrease in the number of people who smoked.

I must have heard the phrase "the devil is in the details" a dozen times that day, and I knew it was too soon to predict the significance of Parrish's overture. For decades, the industry had used the strategy of denial to erect a barrier against liability, but that approach finally stopped working. Now, Parrish was employing the strategy of concession, perhaps to achieve exactly the same goal. I was sure he wanted to improve his credibility. It was equally apparent that the tobacco companies, or at least Philip Morris, recognized the need to change their tactics. The industry that once boasted of having more money than God was in trouble.

ON July 14, 2000, the Florida jury weighing the first class-action suit ever to reach trial leveled a punitive damage award of $144.8 billion against the industry. The industry lawyers had done what they could to prevent the defeat, pleading that the tobacco companies had changed their ways. That was the new public relations strategy. Philip Morris's Internet site began providing detailed information about the health risks of smoking, the importance of keeping tobacco out of the hands of young people, and the findings of the Surgeon General. It even cited statistics collected by the FDA tobacco team and provided an electronic link to the full text of our tobacco regulations. Of course, it was the industry itself that had ensured that the regulations were not in effect.

But I did not know whether the Florida verdict would stand. And meanwhile the companies continued to sell a product that has killed 12 million Americans since the 1964 Surgeon General's report was issued. Three thousand American children were still beginning to smoke every day. And despite its conciliatory language, the industry had not stopped fighting regulation. In the wake of the Supreme Court decision, congressional legislators introduced a bill that would have given the FDA authority over tobacco. The industry lobbyists opposed it, claiming it was not the sort of regulation they had in mind.

There were other troubling developments. Tobacco stock prices continued to fluctuate and I knew investor sentiment could be unpredictable. The state attorneys general said publicly that they did not want the tobacco companies to be pushed towards bankruptcy. It was, of course, all about money. I realized that their top priority now was to protect the flow of settlement funds into their coffers—$246 billion over twenty years was a tempting windfall. State legislators were no better; they, too, were worried about putting the settlement at risk.

My understanding of the industry's power finally forced me to see that, in the long term, the solution to the smoking problem rests with the bottom line, prohibiting the tobacco companies from continuing to profit from the sale of a deadly, addictive drug. These profits are inevitably used to promote that same addictive product and to generate more sales. If public health is to be the centerpiece of tobacco control—if our goal is to halt this manmade epidemic—the tobacco industry, as currently configured, needs to be dismantled.

Considering the number of addicted smokers, nicotine has to remain available. But the entire infrastructure that promotes it, and that has such political clout, should not continue to exist. Instead, tobacco companies should be spun off from their corporate parents. Congress should charter a tightly regulated corporation, one from which no one profits, to take over manufacturing and sales. Many models, each one with unique characteristics, have been created over the years to promote varying public policy objectives—to provide transportation, to stimulate the flow of credit to home buyers, farmers, and students, and to deliver energy. In this case, the entity would supply tobacco products to those who want them, but with no economic incentives for sales. Promotion in any form should be banned. No more Marlboro Man, no successors to Joe Camel, no more colorful packaging. Ultimately, cigarettes should be sold in brown paper wrappers, with only a brand name and a warning label. Distribution should be tightly controlled to prevent access by children and adolescents. Sales revenues should be used only to underwrite manufacturing and distribution costs, with the remainder going into a fund created to pay liability claims and fund medical research and programs to counter youth smoking. It would be the end of the industry as we know it.

These are strong measures, but that is what is needed to deal with a product as dangerous and as addictive as tobacco. Dismantling is the only appropriate way to handle an industry that has engaged in the greatest of conspiracies and, in the process, knowingly put the nation's health at risk.

The question is how best to accomplish this. Litigation has emerged as the strongest weapon to chip away at the power of the industry, but liability claims against the tobacco companies also provide the greatest incentive for them to stay in business—they need to sell their products to earn the revenue to pay off accumulating debts. Because they will continue to incur new liabilities as more awards are handed down, there is no end to the cycle in sight. The only way out is for the companies to shed their tobacco business.

Without legislation, liability attaches to everything owned by the parent companies of the tobacco companies. If, however, the tobacco companies were to transfer their tobacco assets to a new entity, their non-tobacco businesses could be protected. Some sort of a government buyout will doubtless also be necessary. This is not the sort of immunity I have opposed fiercely in the past, not an immunity that would allow the companies to continue business as usual. I have something entirely different in mind. I want to give them an incentive to walk away from the tobacco business.

It was not my goal to dismantle the industry when the FDA first undertook its investigation, but it has become apparent that nothing else will work. Small steps are not enough to curtail the power of the tobacco companies, or the damage they do. The industry's response to this proposal is predictable. No matter how explicitly I reiterate that nicotine will remain legal and available, the industry will parade out its tired defense, and claim that the forces of prohibition are massing. It is not true—it was never true—but it is an effective technique because it frightens the American public. It will require committed leadership inside government to resist this characterization and to move, step by step, to change the role of tobacco in this country forever. Dismantling the industry will not happen quickly or easily, but it is the direction in which we should be advancing.

Whatever the challenges, the industry cannot be left to peacefully reap billions of dollars in profits, totally unrepentant, and without thought to the pain caused in the process. For that remains its intent.

Principal Characters

David Adams, director, Policy Development and Coordination Staff, FDA

Scott Ballin, chairman, Coalition on Smoking or Health

Liz Berbakos, special assistant to the commissioner, FDA

Ilisa Bernstein, senior science policy adviser, FDA

Thomas Bliley, member, U.S. House of Representatives (R–Virginia)

Kevin Budich, compliance officer, FDA

James Chaplin, tobacco scientist, Tobacco Research Laboratory, U.S. Department of Agriculture

Richard Cooper, lawyer, Williams & Connolly, representing R. J. Reynolds

Mark Deane, cooker, Philip Morris

Victor DeNoble ("Cigarette"), researcher, Philip Morris

John Dingell, member, U.S. House of Representatives (D–Michigan)

Tom Doyle, special agent, Office of Criminal Investigations, FDA

William Farone ("Philip"), director, Applied Research, Philip Morris

Jack Henningfield, chief, Clinical Pharmacology Research Branch, National Institute of Drug Abuse

Phil Hilts, Washington correspondent, *New York Times*

Bill Hubbard, associate commissioner for policy coordination, FDA

Paulette Kessler, adviser and helpmeet

Jerry Klepner, assistant secretary for legislation, U.S. Department of Health and Human Services

Carol Knoth, medical librarian, FDA

Arthur Levine, lawyer, Arnold & Porter, representing Philip Morris

Gary Light, special agent, Office of Criminal Investigations, FDA

Catherine Lorraine, director, Policy Development and Coordination Staff, FDA

"Macon," informant

Ved Malik, senior scientist, Philip Morris

Jerry Mande, executive assistant and special adviser to the commissioner, FDA

Paul Mele ("Cigarette Jr."), research scientist, Philip Morris

Richard Merrill, lawyer, Covington & Burling, representing the Tobacco Institute and Lorillard

Gerry Meyer, deputy director, Center for Drug Evaluation and Research, FDA

Jack Mitchell, commissioner's special assistant for investigation, FDA

Sharon Natanblut, associate commissioner for strategic initiatives, FDA

Jeff Nesbit, associate commissioner for public affairs, FDA

Jim O'Hara, associate commissioner for public affairs, FDA

Steve Parrish, senior vice president, Philip Morris

Gene Pfeifer, lawyer, King & Spalding, representing Brown & Williamson

Margaret Porter, chief counsel, FDA

Charlie Rose, member, U.S. House of Representatives (D–North Carolina)

Bill Schultz, deputy commissioner for policy, FDA

John Schwartz, staff writer, *Washington Post*

Donna Shalala, secretary, U.S. Department of Health and Human Services

Bob Spiller, associate chief counsel for enforcement, FDA

Louis Sullivan, secretary, U.S. Department of Health and Human Services

Mike Synar, member, U.S. House of Representatives (D–Oklahoma)

Mike Taylor, deputy commissioner for policy, FDA

Diane Thompson, associate commissioner for legislative affairs, FDA

"Veritas," senior tobacco industry executive

Kendrick Wells III, general counsel, Brown & Williamson

Jeffrey Wigand ("Research"), vice president for research, Brown & Williamson

Judy Wilkenfeld, special adviser to the commissioner, FDA

Ann Witt, special assistant to the deputy commissioner for operations, FDA

Henry Waxman, member, U.S. House of Representatives (D–California)

Mitch Zeller, associate commissioner, FDA

Notes

Although this is a first-person narrative, based primarily on my tenure as FDA commissioner from October 1990 through February 1997, I believed that it was important to draw not only on my own memory but also on the recollections and interpretations of others at the FDA, the Department of Health and Human Services, Congress, the White House, and elsewhere, and to seek perspectives from tobacco industry representatives as well. After leaving the FDA, I spent three years interviewing more than two hundred people, some of them many times, for that purpose. I also searched millions of pages of industry documents that have been made publicly available as a result of a series of lawsuits, which provide both an historical outlook and a view of industry activities during the period covered in this book.

Interviews conducted during the FDA's tobacco investigation are labeled "FDA interviews." Interviews conducted as part of my research for this book are labeled "author interviews." Interviewees are cited by last name only, and an alphabetical list of all interviewees cited in the book is provided on page 453. The professional affiliations listed for the interviewees reflect those most relevant to the narrative. Only tobacco industry informants who eventually spoke out publicly are identified by name.

Individual tobacco companies, tobacco trade associations, and other organizations assign numbers to their documents according to the Bates numbering system. The location of quoted material is indicated at the end of the run of Bates numbers, for example, "ID 2022854068–69, at 68." Some industry papers are unsigned, undated, unpaginated, or untitled; the citations for those documents reflect the available information.

Epigraph
The Odes of Horace, transl. David Ferry (New York: Farrar, Straus & Giroux, 1997), p. 161.

Veritas
xii   **Margaret Thatcher:** "Mrs. Thatcher would be available to consult with us for an initial three-year period.... [T]he fee we would pay for those services would consist of a $250,000 annual payment to her and a $250,000 annual contribution to the Margaret Thatcher Foundation ... we are of like mind" (Michael A. Miles, Philip Morris [hereinafter cited as PM] memo, 20 July 1992, PM ID 2022854068–69, at 68); "Lady Thatcher has extensive expertise and knowledge about geopolitical issues in many of the countries in which we currently do busi-

ness, or hope to do business. She is a consultant with us" (PM draft briefing book, annual meeting, 1993, PM ID 2022842565–694, at 678).

xii   **Howard Baker:** "Senator Baker's attachment to this Company gives us an effective high-level advocate of our policies.... [I]f the Company needs to be publicly identified in a positive way with an issue, he can do it best" (James Dyer, PM memo to David Greenberg and Buffy Linehan, "Senator Howard Baker," 29 June 1989, PM ID 2041252693–94, at 94). A call from Baker to John Sununu, President Bush's White House chief of staff, is discussed in James Dyer, PM memo to David Greenberg, "Louis Sullivan," 8 March 1990, PM ID 2022839660–61.

xiii   **Retainer:** "[P]ayments should be sent to Dr. Charles C. Edwards..." (Charles R. Wall, PM memo to Steve Parrish, "Retainer Fee for Dr. Charles Edwards," 20 May 1994, PM ID 2047710586).

xii   **Done covertly:** W. L. Dunn, PM memo to R. B. Seligman, "The Nicotine Receptor Program," 21 March 1980, PM ID 2022249518.

xi–xiv   **Veritas:** I conducted a series of interviews with "Veritas," a tobacco industry executive, in 1998, 1999, and 2000.

Chapter One

3   **Mentioning my name:** A common path to senior jobs within the executive branch is through prior congressional staff work, which provides connections to the people whose advice may be sought in filling the jobs. Often, loyalty and personal relationships matter more than political ideology. There may also be a formal search committee, as there was for the FDA commissionership; it sent 2,500 letters seeking nominations from medical groups, trade associations, and academic institutions, as well as from current and former government officials. Most members of the search committee also had their own potential candidates. The key to getting an appointment is to be on as many lists as possible.

4   **Oscar Schotté:** In an academic evaluation of me, Schotté wrote that "while he always is exceptional in the rapid learning of the theoretical premises ... and he might become a brilliant originator of experiments, there is certain clumsiness in performance—he will not be a brilliant technician...." He also called me "a master of uncovering information in whatever domain." See also Richard A. Liversage, "Oscar E. Schotté," *American Zoologist* 18(4):825–27 (Fall 1978).

5   **Henry Steele Commager:** Commager's influence emanated partly from his writing and teaching about the American character, which he characterized as "incurably optimistic," "never knowing defeat," "inventive," "practical," and personified by a belief that nothing was beyond reach. See Henry Steele Commager, *The American Mind: An Interpretation of American Thought and Character Since the 1880's* (New Haven, Conn.: Yale University Press, 1950).

6   **Interest in cancer:** When I was under consideration to become commissioner, the White House counsel, Boyden Gray, enlisted the help of Chris DeMuth, head of the conservative American Enterprise Institute, who had previously worked in the Reagan White House, asking for a "readout on me." DeMuth was reassured by my article questioning the wisdom of the anticancer clause (known as the Delaney Clause) in the Federal Food, Drug, and Cosmetic Act, which prohibited use of any additive that had been found to cause cancer in laboratory animals. See Comment, "Implementing the Anticancer Clauses of the Food,

Drug, and Cosmetic Act," *University of Chicago Law Review* 44(4):817–50 (Summer 1977).

6   **Harvey Wiley:** For historical background, see Oscar E. Anderson Jr., *The Health of a Nation: Harvey W. Wiley and the Fight for Pure Food* (Chicago: University of Chicago Press, 1958); James Harvey Young, *Pure Food: Securing the Federal Food and Drugs Act of 1906* (Princeton, N.J.: Princeton University Press, 1989).

7   **Authority restored:** "The efforts by Ronald Reagan's White House to reduce the FDA's interference in private industry have had an unexpected effect: the industry itself has joined with consumer advocacy groups and Congress in calling for the agency to be strengthened" (Philip J. Hilts, "Ailing Agency—The F.D.A. and Safety; A Guardian of U.S. Health Is Buckling Under Stress," *New York Times,* 4 December 1989, p. A1).

9   **Edwards Committee:** *Final Report of the Advisory Committee on the Food and Drug Administration* (Washington, D.C.: Department of Health and Human Services [hereinafter cited as DHHS], May 1991).

9   **FDA commissioner:** The official qualifications for the job included a medical or other advanced scientific or health-related degree, plus substantial management, policy, and decision-making experience. One trade association offered a different job description: "HELP WANTED: Beleaguered federal agency long on challenges but short on cash seeks qualified, tireless chief to streamline agency bureaucracy, respond to national health crises, assure safety of nation's food supply, enforce surveillance programs for controversial human and animal drugs, and monitor marketing of all new products. Ideal candidate will be able to meet and exceed above challenges, as well as supervise a professional staff of 8,000. Interested parties should submit detailed resumes to: President, United States of America" (*AHI Quarterly* 12[1][January–March 1991]).

10   **Approve my nomination:** Senator Albert Gore sponsored legislation in 1989 that required the FDA commissioner to be confirmed by the Senate. Holding hearings before my confirmation would have meant a delay until January, and Senators Orrin Hatch and Edward Kennedy both wanted greater haste. Gore agreed to a vote on my nomination on condition that hearings be held after I officially became commissioner. On October 27, 1990, in the closing hours of the congressional session, I was unanimously confirmed.

Chapter Two

14   **Tumwater:** Jennifer Meling, Statement, Tumwater (Wash.) Police Dept., Case #91–0680–02, 6 February 1991.

14   **Medical examiner:** John Howard, a Pierce County medical examiner, knew a great deal about the Stella Nickell case, a tampering involving Excedrin. That familiarity aroused his suspicions when he was confronted by Kathleen Daneker's sudden and unexplained death. Although the state toxicology lab that identified the lethal cyanide dose in Daneker's blood did not realize that a threat to public safety was involved, Howard did. His call to James Davis at the FDA undoubtedly saved lives.

17   **Joseph Meling was indicted:** The prosecution relied heavily on many hours of taped conversations between Meling and his parents, taken from an FBI wiretap and a planted microphone. FBI agents heard Meling admit that he had been to a

store where "they do something with chemistry." A clerk at Emerald City Chemical in Kent recalled selling a pound of sodium cyanide to one "Richard Johnson," a man wearing a blue denim jacket with white fleece lining. A guest at a family Thanksgiving dinner recalled seeing Joseph Meling with such a jacket. Meling was ultimately convicted of a scheme to murder his wife and collect $700,000 in insurance proceeds. See *United States v. Meling,* 47 F.3d 1546 (9th Cir. 1995).

Chapter Three

19   **Lacerating investigation:** David Nelson, Congressman John Dingell's chief of staff, was a leading investigator in the generic drugs scandal and perhaps the most zealous. FDA staffers told me bitterly that their encounters with Nelson left the innocent scarred. Carl Peck, who had joined the FDA to head the Center for Drugs when the scandal was breaking, found the garbage in his suburban garage rearranged one summer morning. Much later, an innocuous memo that Peck believed could only have come from his garbage turned up among the papers of Dingell's investigators.

19   **Dingellgrams:** In my first two years on the job Dingell wrote me 175 times. See Malcolm Gladwell, "Anatomy of a Dingellgram," *Washington Post,* 10 September 1992, A27.

21   **Called to testify:** House Committee on Energy and Commerce, Subcommittee on Health and the Environment, hearing, *Food and Drug Administration Oversight,* 102nd Cong., 1st sess., 13 March 1991, serial no. 102–25.

22   **Speech to the food industry:** David Kessler, Food and Drug Law Institute speech of 24 April 1991, reprinted as "Restoring the FDA's Preeminence in the Regulation of Food," *Food Drug Cosmetic Law Journal* 46: 395–402, May 1991.

24   **New era in enforcement:** Malcolm Gladwell, "FDA Adopts Fresh Approach to Labeling," *Washington Post,* 6 May 1991, A10; Miles Orvell, "The Metaphysics of Orange Juice," *New York Times,* 1 July 1991; "The Juice Police," *Washington Times,* 29 April 1991, p. G2.

     Mark Green: Warren E. Leary, "Ragu Agrees to Take 'Fresh' Off Sauce Labels," *New York Times,* 2 May 1991. A syndicated columnist wrote that the move sent a message that "the regulators are back in the business of regulating"—but added that "tobacco remains the glaring renegade" (Ellen Goodman, "The Missing Entrée in Regulatory Menu," *Boston Globe,* 30 May 1991, p. 19). Years later, cigarette manufacturers warned tobacco farmers: "Will FDA agents—whose powers are broad and include criminal law enforcement—be trampling through tobacco fields and seizing crops? Will tobacco farmers be subject to heavy fines? Don't laugh. Early on in the Kessler era, FDA agents confiscated made-from-concentrate orange juice from a warehouse because the carton labeling included the word 'fresh'"(Lorillard report, 1995, Lorillard ID 91715449–51, at 49).

Chapter Four

27   **Announced a plan:** Philip J. Hilts, "New Chief Vows New Vitality at F.D.A.," *New York Times,* 27 February 1991, p. B7.

27   **ASH filed suit:** Citizen petition, filed by Action on Smoking and Health, on 26 May 1977; rejected by FDA, 5 December 1977; upheld by the U.S. Court of Appeals, District of Columbia Circuit, 19 December 1980, 655 F.2d 236.

27   Statutory definition: 21 U.S.C. §321 (g)(1)(C) (1994).

28–29   Premier
       Small amount: R. J. Reynolds (hereinafter cited as RJR) report, "Project Alpha
Review," 25 July 1985, RJR ID 504946252–57. Government relations: RJR draft document, "Federal Government Relations Plan," 21 August 1987, RJR ID
505988438–52. One of RJR's objectives was to "ensure FDA does not regulate"
(RJR document, "Alpha Federal Action Plan," RJR ID 50636203133, at 31). Explicit
objectives: RJR report, "SPA [Premier] Government Relations," RJR ID
506008904. Puritans: R. A. Kampe, RJR memo to F. R. Johnson et al., "SPA
GR/PR/SA Plan," 1 September 1987, RJR ID 505988556–58, at 56. Peter Barton
Hutt, a food and drug lawyer and a former FDA general counsel, came to Parklawn on RJR's behalf to make a presentation on Premier. After touting the product's virtues, he admitted, "Without nicotine, you don't have a cigarette" (DHHS
memo, meeting between Peter B. Hutt and Daniel L. Michels, Sammie R. Young,
Rudolf Apodaca, and Kevin M. Budich, 23 October 1987).

31   Belligerent: Harvey W. Wiley, *Harvey W. Wiley: An Autobiography* (Indianapolis:
Bobbs-Merrill, 1930), p. 236.

35   Stammered uncomfortably: National Institutes of Health, National Cancer Advisory Board, transcript of 81st meeting, 27 January 1992, pp. 112–16.

Chapter Five

37   Product tamperings
       Meat: James F. McCarty, "Man Says He Injected HIV Into Meat," *Cleveland
Plain Dealer,* 31 March 1993, p. 5B. Baby food: FDA report, "Suspected Tampering
—Baby Food," 18 October 1991.

37   Had to act
       Diet drug: FDA Talk Paper, "FDA Orders Nature's Way Guar Gum Diet Pills
Off Market," 18 March 1992. Tuna: FDA Talk Paper, "FDA Announces Mislabeled
Canned Tuna Seizures," 25 March 1992. Condoms: Ruth Merkatz, FDA back-
ground document, "Viral Penetration Testing in Condoms," 29 October 1993.
Cholera-contaminated water: FDA Talk Paper, "Ship Ballast, Holding Tank
Waters to Be Checked for Cholera," 20 November 1991. Blood supply: Gerald V.
Quinnan, FDA memo to FDA commissioner, "Yersinia Contamination of Red
Blood Cells," 16 December 1990. Snake venom: Hugh Cannon, FDA memo to
David Kessler, "Heads-Up for Hatch Meeting—New Issue," 22 May 1991.

38   Need for answers
       Biological warfare: Mary K. Pendergast, FDA memo to Philip Lee, "The Use
of Pyridostigmine During the Persian Gulf War," 9 June 1994. Lead detected:
David A. Kessler, FDA memo, "Lead in Wine," 30 August 1991. Hair dye: S. H.
Bahm, "Use of Hair Coloring and the Risk of Lymphoma, Multiple Myeloma,
and Chronic Lymphocytic Leukemia," *American Journal of Public Health*
82(7):990–97 (July 1992).

38   Breast implants: I questioned the safety of breast implants after reviewing internal documents suggesting that Dow Chemical had rushed its product to the market despite concerns that the device's outer shell might rupture. One employee
wrote: "We ended up saying the envelopes were 'good enough' while looking at
gross thin spots and flaws in the form of significant bubbles. The allowable flaws

are written into our current specifications" (Tom Talcott, Dow memo, "Comment on Mammary Prosthesis Quality...," 15 January 1976). A retrospective analysis of thirty-five studies documented that implants had a 30 percent rupture rate at 5 years, a 50 percent rupture rate at 10 years, and a 70 percent rupture rate at 17 years. See J. S. Marotta et al., "Silicone Gel Breast Implant Failure and Frequency of Additional Surgeries: Analysis of 35 Studies Reporting Examination of More Than 8,000 Explants," *Journal of Biomedical Materials Research* 48(3):354–64 (1999). There is no evidence of significantly increased risk of connective tissue disorder associated with breast implants. See B. G. Silverman et al., "Reported Complications of Silicone Gel Breast Implants: An Epidemiologic Review," *Annals of Internal Medicine* 124(8):744–56 (15 April 1996).

39   **Larry Kramer:** Larry Kramer, "A Call to Riot," *Outweek,* 20 April 1990.

     Joan of Arc: Gina Kolata, "Citing Stress, FDA Aide Wants Out," *New York Times,* 22 December 1990, p. 12. See also John Leo, "The AIDS Activist with Blurry Vision," *U.S. News & World Report,* 9 July 1990, p. 16.

41   **CAST:** CAST investigators, "Preliminary Report: Effect of Encainide and Flecainide on Mortality in a Randomized Trial of Arrhythmia Suppression After Myocardial Infarction," *New England Journal of Medicine* 321:406–12 (1989).

41   **DdI**

     Surrogate marker: FDA Antiviral Drugs Advisory Committee, transcript of meeting, 13 February 1991. **Approval application:** FDA Antiviral Drugs Advisory Committee, transcript of meeting, 18 July 1991.

42   **The greatest risk:** Ann Witt, a senior FDA lawyer, was among those who once feared that anything done in the interests of speed might weaken agency standards. Looking back, she said of the resistance to accelerating the approval of drugs for serious and life-threatening illnesses, "We were totally wrong. It was an absolutely essential safety valve. Had we not found ways to make experimental drugs available, I think there would have been much more pressure to lower the approval standard."

42   **Accelerating the approval:** FDA, "New Drug, Antibiotic, and Biological Drug Product Regulations; Accelerated Approval; Proposed Rule," *Federal Register* 57:13234–42 (15 April 1992).

43   **What I needed to do:** John W. Kingdon offers a useful analysis of how an issue gets placed on the political agenda in *Agendas, Alternatives, and Public Policies,* 2nd ed. (New York: HarperCollins College Publishers, 1995). Kingdon suggests that issues gain "agenda status" when three streams come together: the problem is recognized as a result of some sort of "focusing event" or symbol, policy proposals are generated and refined, and there is receptivity from the public or influential political forces. In my view, people play a greater role in driving issues and policy changes than Kingdon or others generally recognize. What jobs people seek, their decisions about what issues to tackle in those jobs and how to frame the issues for the public, the pursuit of political support, and the ability to prevent their efforts from being derailed all determine what problems are confronted and how they are addressed.

Chapter Six

46   **Media coach:** When the agency inaugurated media training in the midst of the generic drug scandal, the prevailing attitude was "Just nail me to the cross," according to my media coach, Judy Leon. She said that FDA staff assumed, "The public safety advocacy groups, they're lying in wait. The committees on the Hill are lying in wait. The potential victims are lying in wait." No one was perceived as an advocate for the agency. The media training handbook Leon prepared for me read, "If you are afraid or apprehensive about doing a media interview, it's no wonder. Reporters in general, T.V. reporters in particular, hold all the cards, and the deck is stacked against you."

46   **Considering legislation:** "Food, Drug, Cosmetic, and Device Enforcement Amendments of 1991," H.R. 2597, 7 June 1991.

46   **Shrinking testimony:** Malcolm Gladwell, "FDA Chief Displays the Art of Avoidance," *Washington Post*, 18 July 1991.

46   **OMB:** The Office of Management and Budget (hereinafter cited as OMB), launched as the Bureau of the Budget during President Lyndon Johnson's administration, was created to review budget proposals objectively and to insulate the President from the competing budgetary claims of its cabinet officers. Its authority was subsequently expanded, becoming under President Ronald Reagan a means of transferring regulatory power to the White House. Under Reagan's Executive Order 12291, all major government regulations had to be screened by the OMB, theoretically for a cost/benefit analysis. In practice, the order gave enormous influence to the advocates of deregulation, sometimes allowing relatively low-level desk officers to thwart regulations proposed by a cabinet secretary.

47   **Waxman hearing:** House Committee on Energy and Commerce, Subcommittee on Health and the Environment, hearing, 102nd Cong., 1st sess., 17 July 1991, Serial No. 102–47.

Chapter Seven

51   **Red-hot coal:** Michael Pertschuk, "Opportunity Knocks; Will We Open the Door?" keynote address, "Tobacco Use: An American Crisis," Washington, D.C., 9–12 January 1993, reprinted in *Final Conference Report and Recommendations from America's Health Community* (Chicago: American Medical Association.

51   **Memo, stamped confidential:** Sidney Wolfe, Public Citizen's Health Research Group memo, "FDA Needs to Make a Clear Statement Regarding Its Willingness to Regulate Tobacco Products for Health and Safety."

Chapter Eight

54   **Nutrition Labeling and Education Act:** PL 101–535, passed 8 November 1990, 101st Cong., 21 USC § 301 (1994). The absence of a legal framework to guide the FDA's approach to health claims on food became a public health concern in the 1980s, when the marketing opportunities in such claims were recognized. The FDA proposed uniform scientific guidelines for health claims; OMB altered the proposal beyond recognition, in essence allowing food manufacturers to make any claims they wished. Agile marketers subsequently went in search of medical endorsements of every kind.

55   **Preventable death:** The most prominent contributors to mortality in the United States in 1990 were tobacco (an estimated 400,000 deaths), diet and activity patterns (300,000), alcohol (100,000), microbial agents (90,000), toxic agents (60,000), firearms (35,000), sexual behavior (30,000), motor vehicles (25,000—which excludes deaths attributed to alcohol and drug use), and illicit use of drugs (20,000). See J. M. McGinnis and W. H. Foege, "Actual Causes of Death in the United States," *Journal of the American Medical Association* 270(18):2207–12 (1993).

56   **Laborious calculations:** If the Department of Agriculture's approach were adopted, the consumer would have to do the following calculation to determine a product's fat content: (1) Determine how many calories the individual should consume in a day (within the range of 1,600 and 2,800). (2) Recognize the maximum percentage of calories from fat recommended (30 percent of calories from fat). (3) Multiply individual calorie needs by recommended percentage of calories from fat (*e.g.*, if calorie needs are 2,000 calories, 2,000 × .3 = 600 calories from fat). (4) Determine the maximum daily number of grams of fat (a gram of fat is about 9 calories; 600 calories divided by 9 calories = 65 grams of fat per day). (5) Determine the number of grams of fat in this product, from the label (*e.g.*, 9 grams). (6) Calculate how much this food contributes to the individual's daily fat goal (9 divided by 65 = .14, or 14 percent).

57   **Outranked:** Bruce Ingersoll, "Kessler's Vigor as FDA Food Regulator Leaves Farm Agency's Madigan with a Lot on His Plate," *Wall Street Journal,* 15 July 1991, p. A12; Daniel P. Puzo, "The Battle of the Bureaucrats," *Los Angeles Times,* 30 May 1991, p. H28.

58   **Craig L. Fuller:** Mark Landler, "Philip Morris' Top Lobbyist Could Use a New Rolodex," *Business Week,* 15 February 1993, p. 62.

59   **Inform the public:** Marian Burros, "Eating Well: The New Battle over Food Labels," *New York Times,* 1 July 1992, p. C4; "Labels New and Improved," *Washington Post* editorial, 10 October 1992, p. A26; "Honest Food Labels? Fat Chance," *New York Times* editorial, 18 November 1992, p. A26.

        Fronting for fat: "The Food and Drug Administration and the United States Department of Agriculture are in one of their nastier cat fights. . . . And off the record, they are happy to tell you why the other fellow is being stupid, stubborn, even venal. . . . [M]uch of the disagreement revolves around fat and how it should be listed on the label" (Marian Burros, "Eating Well: A Turf War in Washington Over Food Labels," *New York Times,* 14 October 1992).

Chapter Nine

60   **Harvard Medical School:** Nancy Mello, professor of psychology at Harvard Medical School, and one of her colleagues were consultants to the tobacco industry and were paid $15,000 per year for reviewing scientific material. See PM chart, "Special Account #4: Research Projects," 1982, PM ID 1005048380–81; Nancy K. Mello (Harvard Medical School), letters to Patrick M. Sirridge and Bernard V. O'Neill (Shook, Hardy & Bacon), 29 July 1982, PM ID 2062775975–76, and 30 September 1982, PM ID 2062775977–78; Greenspan & Yelon (CPAs), audit report, "Special Account #4," 23 April 1984, PM ID 2015048544–46.

61   **Industry's lobbying arm:** Fred Panzer, Tobacco Institute (hereinafter cited as TI) memo to David Henderson, "Rider on Addiction Study," 17 May 1983, TI ID TIMN 357897.

61 **Carlton Turner:** Author interviews with Henningfield, 7 November 1997; Jaffe, 9 September 2000; Pollin, 9 September 2000; Turner, 14 September 2000.

 Need its budget: Henningfield and Jaffe recall that Turner made a similar comment publicly at a scientific conference. Turner denied ever having challenged the agency's budget, although he admits to being outspoken in his view that "tobacco was more of a habit than an addiction, certainly not as addictive as heroin or cocaine."

62 **Strategic opportunities:** PM conference notes, "Project Down Under," 24–26 June 1983, PM ID 2021502102–33.

65 **Just say no:** Daniel Michels, FDA memo to Carl Peck et al., "Tobacco," 19 November 1992.

Chapter Ten

67 **4,000 pages:** Edward Madigan, "More Thought for Food," letter to the editor, *Washington Post,* 19 November 1992.

71 **New format:** The Nutrition Facts label was designed by Burkey Belser, a graphic designer in Washington, and won the President's Design Award, which called it "a superlative example of design at the service of the government and of government at the service of the consumer."

Chapter Eleven

72 **Brutally personal:** "The FDA's Brain," *Wall Street Journal,* 8 April 1992, p. A20.

72 **John Sununu:** "Some drug and food companies complain to the White House about the FDA chief's tough enforcement tactics on issues such as prescription drug promotion and food labels.... But Kessler is seen by the White House as more of a political asset than liability" (*Wall Street Journal,* "Washington Wire," 20 December 1991, p. A1).

74 **Array of bone:** The letter, dated December 11 1992, announced the launch of the Baltic Tissue Bank "in cooperation with the Kriolaboratory of St. Petersburg Institute of Traumatology and Orthopedy, one of the biggest in Russia." It concluded: "Sizes and your requirements in respect of preparation, conservation and control of tissue materials may be discussed during negotiations. We should mention that barter is also acceptable. And we are quite interested in finding a partner to establish joint venture company.... Sincerely yours, Dr. Pavel E. Blumenberg."

75 **Tissue broker:** "A few things can be arranged," said Gary Karsh, a California dentist with a heavy Russian accent, one of the tissue brokers, in a telephone conversation. Of the hepatitis B in the bodies, he said, "Yeah, yeah, that's what is coming out sometimes—hepatitis B or maybe C or this kind of stuff sometimes." But he tried to be reassuring: he had not seen a single AIDS case for almost eighteen months.

77 **Courteous agitation:** Coalition on Smoking or Health, "A 30-Year Report Card for the Federal Government on Tobacco Control Policies," 11 January 1994. The grades: Congress, D-; USDA, F; DHHS, D; U.S. Department of Justice, F; Department of Veterans Affairs, B; Environmental Protection Agency, B+; Federal Trade Commission, F; FDA, F; Occupational Safety and Health Administration, D-; U.S. Trade Representative, F; the White House, F.

77   **Silence on tobacco:** Scott D. Ballin, "When Shown Tobacco, FDA Dog Won't Hunt," *Wall Street Journal,* Letters to the Editor, 7 April 1993, p. A15.

Chapter Twelve

79   **Two syringes:** The Diet Pepsi tampering scare began when Earl Triplett, eighty-two, and his wife, Mary, seventy-nine, shared a can of Pepsi. When Earl looked inside the can for the symbol that would win him a trip to Alaska, courtesy of the local Pepsi bottler, he found a syringe instead. After a second complaint, the story began to be reported around the country, and with each report, new allegations surfaced in the area of the report. The FDA's Office of Criminal Investigations (OCI) spent months unraveling more than 400 complaints. A man in West Virginia had stuffed his cans with bits of trash collected from the back of his pickup truck. A lawyer in New York had tried to extort $400,000 from Pepsi after she forced a live mouse into a can. One legitimate screw was found. The case that precipitated the hoax was never resolved. The final cost to the agency was 14,000 investigative work hours and $104,000 in investigative travel expenses. And Pepsi? One distributor later told my wife's father, "If it hadn't been for your son-in-law, I'd be selling potato chips now."

79   **Office of Criminal Investigations:** Until OCI's launch, in December 1992, the FDA had the resources to investigate regulatory violations effectively, but not criminal matters. OCI staff were drawn from the Customs Service, the Internal Revenue Service, the Postal Service, the FBI, the CIA, the Bureau of Alcohol, Tobacco, and Firearms, and other federal law enforcement agencies. All agents were college graduates, some with law or other advanced degrees, and all had been trained at the Federal Law Enforcement Training Center. From the beginning we had a veteran professional organization. The average agent had 12.5 years of federal investigative experience; the average manager, 22 years.

80   **Come to our attention:** Two years earlier, the confidential informant Deep Cough had approached Cliff Douglas, who had long been active in tobacco control, and volunteered to talk about the inner workings of the company. Cliff became "Deep Cough's" confidant, and he later shared certain information with a colleague, Matt Myers. Matt called Jerry Mande at the FDA; their relationship dated back to Mande's tenure on the staff of then-congressman Al Gore.

82   **Vats of nicotine:** "The CI [confidential informant] knows the details of the cigarette production process and is aware of the vats of nicotine that make up the reconstituted tobacco. The CI cannot detail the chemical process involved but knows where the extraction and reconstitution occurs." FDA interview with "Deep Cough," 11 January 1994.

82   **Second telephone conversation:** FDA interview with "Deep Cough," 16 January 1994.

83   **Rambling narrative:** FDA interview with "Deep Cough," 20 January 1994.

Chapter Thirteen

85   **Walt Bogdanich:** Bogdanich was a Pulitzer Prize–winning investigative journalist who had already produced one tobacco program for *Day One,* which aired in November 1993. "Secret Sickness" presented a stark picture of how harvesters, some of them children, routinely contracted nicotine poisoning through skin

contact with damp tobacco leaves. He sent his cameras into a hospital emergency room where stricken workers were retching uncontrollably. Asked to comment, the head of the tobacco growers cooperative implied that actors had been hired to play the role of the workers.

85   **Upcoming broadcast**

   Asked R. J. Reynolds: Walt Bogdanich (ABC), letter to Peggy Carter (RJR), 14 February 1994, RJR ID 508748864. **Snooping around flavorings:** Victor Han, PM e-mail to Tara Carraro et al., 4 February 1994, PM ID 2024015016B–17A. **Sandbag you:** PM e-mail to Karen Daragan et al., February 1994, PM ID 2024015016B–17A. **Six-sentence fax:** Victor Han, PM memo, "ABC Day One," 25 February 1994, PM ID 2022847057–58.

86   **Began to prep:** Peggy Carter, RJR notes, 14 February 1994, RJR ID 508749040–49.

86   **Raised nicotine levels:** Gray Flinchum, RJR memo to Ron Sells, "High Nicotine G7 for Blendoff as G7–28," 23 February 1994, RJR ID 512853870–72. In response to my inquiry about this memo, which implied that G7 tobacco was to be blended into other tobacco products, RJR sent me a later document, which read: "[U]pon further examination of this material, along with analytical data, it has been decided that this material should not be used in any of our products" (R. E. Sells, RJR memo to Carol Stafford, "Dispositions of Test G7," 28 February 1994).

86   **Latest draft:** Shortly before I gave the Department a copy of our letter to the Coalition, I drafted two formal "decision memos" to Secretary Shalala. The first asked for guidance on the issue of nicotine in cigarettes under the Food, Drug, and Cosmetic Act. The second sought official approval to respond to the Coalition's petitions. Ultimately, I chose not to send either memo, opting instead for a more informal sign-off.

92   **American Red Cross:** Inspections of several American Red Cross sites revealed that more than 2,400 unsuitable blood products had been released. Problems included an inadequate donor deferral system; poor records on the disposal of 138 blood components from donors who subsequently tested positive for HIV antibodies; 50 reports of posttransfusion HIV infection that were not completely investigated, some for as long as four years; failure to promptly trace previous blood products from 12 donors who later tested HIV-positive; and two cases of posttransfusion hepatitis that had not been investigated. See Ellen F. Morrison, FDA memo, "FDA Briefing of American Red Cross," 13 April 1993; Anna J. Baldwin, FDA memo, "The American Red Cross," 6 January 1993; FDA presentation, "Compliance History American Red Cross, 1998–Present."

94   **Steve Parrish:** Author interview, January 1998, pp. 12–13.

94   **Coverage:** Philip J. Hilts, "U.S. Agency Suggests Regulating Cigarettes as an Addictive Drug," *New York Times,* 26 February 1994, p. A1; John Schwartz, "In Policy Shift, FDA Is Ready to Consider Regulating Tobacco," *Washington Post,* 26 February 1994, p. A4.

Chapter Fourteen

97   **Push legislation:** In 1986, when Congressman Mike Synar introduced legislation to ban the advertising or promotion of tobacco products, the industry took note: "[T]his will require a full court press. The strategy will have three prongs—the American Civil Liberties Union, the advertising community, and the unions. They

will all strongly attack the Synar proposal as one of the most unconstitutionally preposterous proposals to be introduced in Congress in years" (P. C. Bergson, RJR memo to M. B. Bass, "Synar Ad Ban Legislation," 10 June 1986, RJR ID 504983466–67). On 27 February 1992, Synar introduced legislation to give the FDA authority over tobacco, an effort that was revived by Synar and Congressman Richard Durbin the following year. None of the bills advanced in committee.

99 **Bureaucratic boundaries:** Bureaucracies tend to stress rules—who can be hired, what staff will do, how lines of supervision will be drawn—but the FDA tobacco team operated outside of traditional bureaucratic norms. For a discussion of bureaucracies, see James Q. Wilson, *Bureaucracy: What Government Agencies Do and Why They Do It* (New York: Basic Books, 1989), and Richard J. Stillman II, *Public Administration: Concepts and Cases* (Boston: Houghton Mifflin, 2000).

Chapter Fifteen

106 **Nicotine is extracted:** FDA interview with "Deep Cough," 18 February 1992.

106 **Flavor houses:** Flavor houses were as secretive as the cigarette manufacturers who purchased their products. They knew that if they divulged information about their additive formulas, they could face legal action from their customers. Not surprisingly, although we called or visited two dozen flavor houses, we learned little from our inquiries. Typical was the claim by Givauden, a flavor house in Clifton, N.J., that their tobacco extracts represented only a small part of their business and that they had no knowledge of how this extract was used by their customers, which included RJR, PM, and Brown & Williamson (hereinafter cited as B&W).

106 **Skull and crossbones:** Gray Flinchum, RJR memo to Gary Burger, "German High Nicotine Extract," 22 November 1993, RJR ID 510783956.

106 **Potentially threatening:** Kathleen M. Linehan, PM memo, "Washington Outlook for 1994," 29 December 1993, PM ID 2025774681–98.

107 **SWAT teams:** James Boland, PM memo to Josh Slavitt, "Surgeon General Plan," 17 January 1994, PM ID 2048213804–805; PM report, "Surgeon General's Report on Youth and Smoking & Healthy People 2000 Report," PM ID 2044779440–45; PM document, "SGR Response Plan, Communications Overview," 18 February 1994, PM ID 2023960047–49.

107 **Much ado:** Barry Holt, PM e-mail to Ellen Merlo, 28 February 1994, PM ID 2045995373.

Weakness in the stock: Nicholas Rolli, PM e-mail to Craig Fuller et al., "Times Article: FDA Regulation," 28 February 1994, PM ID 2045995375. **Coordinated attack:** "The timing of these events . . . could have only been done with the blessing and encouragement of the Administration" (Barry Holt, PM e-mail to Craig Fuller, 27 February 1994, PM ID 2045995373D–74). See also RJR report, "Overview," 11 April 1994, RJR ID 512716537–40.

107 **Independent agency:** The term "independent agency" generally means that the principal officers are protected against removal at the will of the President. But the FDA is not an independent agency, and under the terms of my appointment, I served "during the pleasure of the president of the United States for the time being."

108   **Fatal to humans:** Industry scientists estimated a lethal dose of nicotine, absorbed through the skin, for a 170-pound man to be 0.359 ml (J. D. Heck and H. S. Tong, Lorillard research report, "The Acute Toxicity of Nicotine Applied Dermally to Rats and Mice," 21 February 1977, Lorillard ID 982458–63). The Alza Corporation, which produced the nicotine patch, described its standard procedures for handling nicotine: "[J]umpsuit, booties, hoods and gloves will be donned once inside the process room and before beginning operations.... [I]f a nicotine spill should occur, notify the Emergency Response Team at once" (Alan Svec [Alza], letter to Andrew Lazerow [FDA], 17 March 1994).

108   **700-page tome:** Ernest L. Wynder and Dietrich Hoffmann, *Tobacco and Tobacco Smoke: Studies in Experimental Carcinogenesis* (New York: Academic Press, 1967).

109   **Public relations purposes:** Nannie M. Tilley, *The R. J. Reynolds Tobacco Company* (Chapel Hill, N.C.: University of North Carolina Press, 1985).

109   **Fortification:** C. Tracy Orleans and John Slade, eds., *Nicotine Addiction: Principles and Management* (New York: Oxford University Press, 1993). See also Donald A. Silberstein, "Flavouring Reconstituted Tobacco," *Tobacco Journal International* 1:26 (1985).

110   **More or less nicotine:** Ernst Voges, ed., *Tobacco Encyclopedia* (Federal Republic of Germany: *Tobacco Journal International*, 1984), p. 152.

110   **What a smoothie:** Anna Quindlen, "Where There's Smoke," *New York Times*, 2 March 1994, p. A15.

Chapter Sixteen

112   **Vedpal Singh Malik:** Malik's complaint reached us through Anne Morrow Donley, a founder of the all-volunteer Virginia-based organization Group to Alleviate Smoking in Public (GASP). At a Philip Morris stockholders' meeting, which Donley attended as the owner of a single share of stock, Malik approached her and said that he had important information to share. Months later, Malik gave her a copy of his complaint. Donley passed it along to Richard Daynard, chairman of the Tobacco Products Liability Project at the Northeastern University School of Law, who sent it to us on February 27, 1994. The complaint: fewer carcinogens, count 13; out of a job, count 33; privileged class, count 39; racial discrimination, count 21; unconventional practices, count 38; remove the deadly chemicals, count 16; secondary smoke, count 20; suppressed the data, count 21; hazards of smoking, count 38; James River, count 31; INBIFO, count 38.

113   **Michael Janofsky:** "Looks like a hot potato to me!" (Barry Holt, PM memo to Vic Han et al., "Janofsky Confirmation," 9 March 1994, PM ID 2046012469).

       Potentially libelous: Barry Holt, PM memo to Craig Fuller, "Janofsky Interview Today," 16 March 1994, PM ID 2023029476. **Dealing with reporters:** Victor Han, PM memo to Ellen Merlo and Steve Parrish, "Malik," 23 August 1993, PM ID 2047720538–43.

113–114 **Willing to talk:** FDA interviews with Malik, 14 and 21 March 1994. Author interview with Light and Doyle, 18 December 1997.

       Gun club: Author interview with Light and Doyle, 18 December 1997, p. 9. **Marlboro:** FDA interview with Malik, 21 March 1994, p. 8. **Nicotine is soaked:** Ibid., p. 4. **Orgasm:** FDA interview with Malik, 14 March 1994, p. 2. **German lab:** FDA interview with Malik, 21 March 1994, p. 12.

115–116   **Philip spoke frankly:** FDA interviews with Farone ("Philip"), 12 and 18 March, 29 April, and 16 May 1994; 4 May 1995; 21 February 1996. Author interviews with Farone, 14 February and 7 March 1998.

   Free of nicotine: FDA interview with Farone, 12 March 1994, p. 3. **Reconstituted tobacco:** Ibid., p. 3. **Nicotine salts:** Ibid., p. 6. **pH factors:** Ibid., p. 6. **Look at Merit:** Ibid., p. 5. **Three reasons:** Author interview with Farone, 7 March 1998.

117   **Outside extracts:** PM notes, "Calculations Based on Information from Flavor Operation Section," 22 March 1994, PM ID 2031128520–23.

   Pulled its remaining extracts: PM chart, "Compounded Flavors Containing Tobacco Extracts," 1994, PM ID 2031128493. According to one FDA informant, all Philip Morris operations involving its L&M brand had to be shut down in March–April 1994. "We were given a period of time to get everything that was associated with those blends out of the factory." Asked why, he said, "Because FDA was coming to inspect" (FDA interview with informant, 12 February 1996).

Chapter Seventeen

119   **Whether nicotine had flavor:** I found a book on flavoring tobacco that listed some 1,000 flavorants; interestingly, nicotine was not among them. See J. C. Leffingwell and H. J. Young, *Tobacco Flavoring for Smoking Products* (Winston-Salem, N.C.: R. J. Reynolds Tobacco, 1972). I also found a patent (no. 4,620,554) that used the word "hazardous" to describe the taste of nicotine.

   Mouth feel: Brennan Dawson (TI), in an appearance on *Face the Nation,* CBS, 27 March 1994.

119   **Sensory and pharmacological:** J. H. Robinson and J. C. Walker, RJR memo to W. Juchatz, "Sensory Aspects of Nicotine," 21 March 1994, RJR ID 51253501–12, at 11. By contrast, pharmaceutical effects were mentioned in an industry speech: "The nicotine in the blood acts upon the central nervous system and produces in the average smoker a sensation one could describe as both stimulating and relaxing. It is important to note that an individual who smokes regularly thoroughly enjoys this sensation" (M. Senkus, RJR speech, "Smoker Satisfaction," 4 August 1976, RJR ID 501142643–54, at 45).

120   **Not be interesting:** J. K. Wells III, B&W memo to E. Pepples, "BAT [British American Tobacco] Science," 17 February 1986, B&W ID 682419469–70, at 70.

120   **Nicotine in cigarettes:** *The Health Consequences of Smoking: Nicotine Addiction: A Report of the Surgeon General* (Washington, D.C.: Government Printing Office, 1988), p. 248.

   Lack of an intoxicating effect: J. H. Robinson and W. S. Pritchard, "The Role of Nicotine in Tobacco Use," *Psychopharmacology* 108:397–407 (1992). **Personality disorder:** American Psychiatric Association, *Diagnostic and Statistical Manual, Mental Disorders* (Washington, D.C.: American Psychiatric Association, 1952), p. 39; *Preventing Tobacco Use Among Young People: A Report of the Surgeon General* (Washington, D.C.: Government Printing Office, 1964), p. 351. **Three fourths** and **two thirds:** R. M. Thomas and M. D. Larsen, *Smoking Prevalence, Beliefs, and Activities by Gender and Other Demographic Indicators* (Princeton, N.J.: The Gallup Organization, 1993). **Try to quit:** "Smoking Cessation During Previous Year, Adults—U. S., 1990 and 1991," *Morbidity and Mortality Weekly Report* 42(26):504–7 (9 July 1993).

Lung cancer: G. Davison and M. Duffy, "Smoking Habits of Long-Term Survivors of Surgery for Lung Cancer," *Thorax* 37:331–33(1982). Smoker's larynx: Sarah Himbury and Robert West, "Smoking Habits After Laryngectomy," *British Medical Journal* 291:514–515 (24 August 1985). See also Thomas A. Burling et al., "Smoking Following Myocardial Infarction: A Critical Review of the Literature," *Health Psychology* 1(3):83–86 (1984).

121 **Found in common foods:** "Nicotine naturally occurs in a variety of common vegetables including tomatoes, potatoes, eggplant and green peppers" (House Committee on Energy and Commerce, Subcommittee on Health and the Environment, testimony of RJR, hearing, *Regulation of Tobacco Products (Part 1),* 103rd Cong., 2d sess., 25 March 1994, Serial No. 103–49.

121 **Ban coffee next:** The coffee analogy was raised many times in the course of our investigation. "The enclosed petition requests that FDA consider regulating caffeine beverages as drugs, and/or devices. It argues that the criteria set out by FDA in its pending proposal to regulate tobacco products may apply to such beverages" (Sam Katzman, Competitive Enterprise Institute petition, 25 October 1995, PM ID 2046557698); "[T]hank you for Philip Morris' $50,000 contribution..." (Fred L. Smith Jr. [Competitive Enterprise Institute], letter to Thomas Borelli [PM], 11 May 1994, PM ID 2046558291–94). The head of the Grocery Manufacturers of America called this petition "frivolous, bordering on absurd," adding, "The FDA will see it for what it is—a publicity stunt usually employed by extremists, not conservative think tanks" (*Food Chemical News,* 30 October 1995).

122 **Nicotine addiction threshold:** Neal Benowitz and Jack Henningfield, "Establishing a Nicotine Threshold for Addiction: The Implications for Tobacco Regulation," *New England Journal of Medicine* 331(2):123–25 (14 July 1994).

122–124 **Patents**

Maintaining the nicotine: PM patent 3,280,823 (25 October 1966). **Transferring nicotine:** Loew's Theatres patent 4,215,706 (5 August 1980). **Filters, paper, or tobacco:** Bavley and Resnik patent 3,109,436 (5 November 1963); Loew's Theatres patent 4,215,706 (5 August 1980); RJR patent 4,830,028 (16 May 1989); RJR patent 4,836,224 (6 June 1989); RJR patent 5,031,646 (16 July 1991); Imperial Tobacco patent 3,861,400 (21 January 1975); RJR patent 4,715,389 (29 December 1987); RJR patent 4,595,024 (17 June 1986); PM patent 3,280,823 (25 October 1966); PM patent 3,584,630 (15 June 1971); RJR patent 5,105,834 (21 April 1992); Advanced Tobacco Products patent 4,676,259 (30 June 1987); Gallaher Limited patent 4,236,532 (2 December 1980). **Levulinic acid:** RJR patent 4,830,028 (16 May 1989). **Nicotine analogs:** PM patent 5,138,062 (11 August 1992); PM patent 5,015,741 (14 May 1991); PM patent 4,590,278 (20 May 1986); PM patent 4,155,909 (22 May 1979); PM patent 4,321,387 (23 March 1982); PM patent 4,220,781 (2 September 1980); PM patent 4,442,292 (10 April 1984); PM patent 4,452,984 (5 June 1984); PM patent 4,332,945 (1 June 1982). **pH:** RJR patents 5,031,646 (16 July 1991) and 5,065,775 (19 November 1991). See also K. D. Brunneman and D. Hoffman, "The pH of Tobacco Smoke," *Food and Cosmetics Toxicology* 12:115–24 (1974); Gio B. Gori, Neal Benowitz, and Cornelius J. Lynch, "Mouth Versus Deep Airways Absorption of Nicotine in Cigarette Smokers," *Pharmacology, Biochemistry and Behavior* 25:1181–84 (1986). **Nicotine is easily released:** PM patent 3,584,630 (15 June 1971). **Various nicotine levels:** RJR patent 5,031,646 (16 July 1991).

Chapter Eighteen

125   **Inside the tobacco companies:** Author interview with Natanblut, 29 January
2000.

Briefing book: Ibid., pp. 2–3.

126–127   **Guy Smith:** Author interviews with Natanblut, 29 January 2000, and Smith, 22
September 2000.

Bull in the china shop: PM notes, "Notes for a Discussion with Guy Smith,"
PM ID 2023277482–84, at 82. **Social engineering:** Guy L. Smith, PM presentation
to the PM board of directors, December 1984, PM ID 2025434718–32, at 18.
Zealots: Guy L. Smith, PM presentation to the PM board of directors, 6 December 1988, PM ID 2025867229–34, at 29. **Game:** Author interview with Natanblut,
29 January 2000, pp. 3–4. **More money than God:** Ibid., p. 25.

127   **Ferocious defense:** Mike Miles, PM memo to Bill Murray et al., "Ferocious
Defense," 7 March 1994, PM ID 2022843127–28. For decades, industry representatives had differed on their public posture. "Reynolds has blown hot and cold as to
whether we should have an aggressive policy in the smoking and health field or a
passive and quiet one. . . . Philip Morris has been most consistent in advocating
aggressive public action" (Report, "Public Relations in the Field of Smoking and
Health," January 1963, B&W ID 0012694174–87, at 80).

127   **Develop its response:** "Test the prohibition message as an 'attack' message" (PM
report, "Tobacco Strategy Review," 22 March 1994, PM ID 2048917800–30, at 11);
"Prohibition does indeed provoke considerable negatives" (Dave Richardson,
Wirthlin Group memo to Craig Fuller, "Issues and Image Results," 18 April 1994,
PM ID 2031599618; "[T]he majority of the public has a decidedly negative view of
the federal government's performance . . ." (Roper Starch Worldwide, RJR con-
sultant study, "The Federal Government: Its Performance, Involvement in Private
Lives, Regulation of Smoking," June 1994, RJR ID 511423011–34, at 14).

128   **Many sources:** "In determining whether a product is intended for use as a drug,
FDA will consider representations made by the manufacturer in any forum"
(Peter Barton Hutt and Richard A. Merrill, *Food and Drug Law: Cases and Materials*,
2nd ed. [Westbury, N.Y.: Foundation Press, 1991], p. 386).

Solution is political: PM notes, "FDA-Kessler Session," 10 March 1994, PM ID
2022841536–39, at 36.

128   **Samples from RJR employees:** FDA interviews with "Deep Cough," 20 January
and 3 March 1994. Author interviews with Light and Doyle, 19 and 26 November
1997.

130   **No answers:** We kept hitting dead ends in our efforts to find out whether the
industry added nicotine to tobacco. Eventually, we called in Dan Harter, a
botanist from the Missouri Botanical Gardens, who used tweezers and a microscope to painstakingly separate the reconstituted sheet tobacco from cigarettes.
Our chemists then sought analytic techniques to distinguish synthetic nicotine
from natural nicotine, but their efforts did not bring us any closer to answers.

130   **Mica particles:** Author interview with Fricke, 11 March 1998.

130   **Chasing my tail:** One of the labs told me that dark spots were visible on some
cigarette paper wrappers. Thinking of a patent I had seen, I wondered whether
the spots might contain nicotine and asked the labs to analyze the wrappers. I
also ordered a dissecting microscope and examined the paper myself. As it turned

out, the spots had nothing to do with nicotine, but there were chemical traces of nicotine on the papers. The lab rolled cigarettes and wrapped them in plastic to see whether the nicotine might be migrating from the tobacco rod, rather than being deliberately applied to the paper. Soon enough, they discovered that high levels of phosphate in some of the papers trapped the migrating nicotine. I thought then that I was following another false lead; only later did I wonder whether the manufacturer might actually use phosphorous-rich paper to set a nicotine trap.

130 **Manufacturing processes:** FDA interview with Farone, 18 March 1994, p. 28.

131 **Super juice:** FDA interviews with Farone, 18 March 1994; 4 May 1995; 16 February 1996. Author interview with Farone, 14 February 1998. See also R. M. Ikeda, PM memo to F. L. Daylor, "Super Juice Constituents," 7 November 1975, PM ID 1003720260.

131 **Philip Morris scientist:** R. W. Jenkins Jr. and R. A. Comes, "Exogenous vs. Endogenous Transfer of Nicotine During Smoking," *International Journal of Applied Radiation and Isotopes* 27(5–6):323–24 (May–June 1976).

132 **Suggestive study:** Eventually I found evidence of extensive industry research on the migration of nicotine to cigarette paper and filters, including results that demonstrated that impregnating cigarette paper with acids can cause nicotine to migrate to the periphery, elevating the delivery of nicotine in mainstream smoke. See Lorillard Research Center, "A Progress Report on Acid-Induced Nicotine Migration," 15 July 1980, Lorillard ID 00304969–80; Lorillard Research Center, "Migration of Nicotine," 1977, Lorillard IDs 01410204 (project request), 01344569 (patent application), and 81072813 (status report); Lorillard Research Center, R&D project request and subsequent status reports, "Nicotine Manipulation, Migration & Reaction Mechanisms," 1980–82, Lorillard IDs 80640901; 80640944–58; 81072695; 81072698; 81072701; 81072713; 81072715; 81072718; 81072721; 81072723; 81072725; 81072730; 81072733; 81073060; 81073066; 81073068; 00370132–33; 00041736; 00041738; 80000243; 81072691–93; 81073042; 81073045; 81073047; 81073052; 81073055; 01322548–61.

132 **Remarkably consistent:** FDA memo, "Analysis of Packages of Cigarettes," 4 April 1994.

Chapter Nineteen

133 **Clean up:** FDA interview with DeNoble ("Cigarette"), 11 March 1994. Author interview with DeNoble, 3 February 1998.

133 **Legally perilous:** P. M. Sirridge, PM draft memo to F. S. Newman, "PM Counsel to PM Counsel Regarding DeNoble Manuscripts," 27 July 1983, PM ID 2021424402–12.

134–136 **Meet with Cigarette:** FDA interview with DeNoble, 15 March 1994. Author interviews with DeNoble, 11 January and 3 February 1998.

Hallmark property: Alan Leshner (National Institute on Drug Abuse), letter to Congressman Henry A. Waxman, 13 April 1994. **Goal:** House Committee on Energy and Commerce, Subcommittee on Health and the Environment, testimony of Victor DeNoble, hearing, *Regulation of Tobacco Products (Part 2),* 103rd Cong., 2d sess., 28 April 1994, Serial No. 103–153. **Wish-list molecule:** Author interview with DeNoble, 3 February 1998. **2'-methyl nicotine:** PM table, "Nicotine

Program Review, Revised," 18 October 1982, PM ID 2029039689–702; V. DeNoble and L. Carron, PM memo to W. L. Dunn, "Research Progress Concerning Discrimination and Prostration Studies," 18 August 1980, PM ID 1000128797–804; M. Sawyer, PM report, "Philip Morris Behavioral Research Program," PM ID 2025768107–66.

137 **Cigarette Jr.:** FDA interviews with Mele ("Cigarette Jr."), 15, 17, and 18 March 1994. Author interviews with Light and Doyle, 7 September 1999, and Mele, 9 September 1999.

    Misled: FDA interview with Mele, 15 March 1994, pp. 9, 20. **More suspicious:** Author interview with Mele, 9 September 1999, pp. 15–16. **Surreptitiously:** FDA interview with Mele, 15 March 1994. **Secret within a secret:** Author interview with Light and Doyle, 7 September 1999, p. 11. **Whole-animal studies:** FDA interview with Mele, 17 March 1994, p. 2.

138 **Summoned to a meeting:** FDA interviews with DeNoble, 15 March 1994, and Mele, 18 March 1994. Author interviews with DeNoble, 3 February 1998, and Mele, 17 January 1998.

    Position in lawsuits: Author interview with DeNoble, 3 February 1998, p. 19. **Billion-dollar enterprise:** House Committee on Energy and Commerce, Subcommittee on Health and the Environment, testimony of Victor DeNoble, hearing, *Regulation of Tobacco Products (Part 2),* 103rd Cong., 2d sess., 28 April 1994, Serial No. 103–53, p. 51.

138–139 **Silent protest:** FDA interviews with Mele, 17 and 18 March 1994. Author interviews with DeNoble, 3 February 1998 and 5 August 2000; and Mele, 9 September 1999.

    Kill all of their animals: Author interviews with DeNoble, 3 February 1998, pp. 18–19, and Mele, 9 September 1999, p. 31. **Threatening legal action:** FDA interviews with Mele, 17 and 18 March 1994. Author interview with Mele, 9 September 1999, p. 37. **Statute of limitations:** Author interview with DeNoble, 25 August 2000.

Chapter Twenty

140 **New York Times:** William I. Campbell, "Decrease in Levels," *New York Times,* Letters to the Editor, 15 March 1994 p. A22; "Addiction by Design?," *New York Times,* editorial, 6 March 1994, p. A14.

141 **Inviting the FDA inside:** David A. Kessler, letter to William I. Campbell (PM), 17 March 1994; William I. Campbell, letter to David A. Kessler, 18 March 1994.

141 **Philip Morris called:** Ronald Chesemore, FDA memo of telephone conversation with Steven Parrish (PM), "Facilities Inspection/Visit," 21 March 1994.

142 **Second hitch:** Steven Parrish (PM), letter to Ronald G. Chesemore (FDA), 21 March 1994.

142–146 **Philip Morris Operations Center:** Author interviews with Budich, 28 January 1998 and 4 February 1998; Spiller, 28 April 1998; Zeller, 1 February and 8 December 1998 and 6 January 1999; Budich, FDA notes, 22 March 1994; Robert Spiller, FDA notes, 22 March 1994; Mitchell Zeller, FDA notes, 22 March 1994.

    Tobacco is tobacco: Author interview with Budich, 28 January 1998, p. 35. **Inviolate ratio:** Author interview with Zeller, 1 February 1998, pp. 43–44; Mitch Zeller, FDA notes. **Flatly denied:** Author interviews with Spiller, 28 April 1998, p.

43, and Zeller, 1 February 1998, p. 54. **Lighting up:** Author interviews with Budich, 28 January 1998, pp. 24–25, and Zeller, 1 February 1998, p. 28. **All about tar:** Kevin Budich, FDA notes. **Want to buy it?:** Author interviews with Budich, 28 January 1998, p. 51; Zeller, 1 February 1998, p. 51. **Sent to landfills:** Author interview with Zeller, 1 February 1998, p. 54. **Being bird-dogged:** Author interview with Zeller, October 2000. **Had labels:** Author interview with Budich, 28 January 1998, p. 61. **No one:** Author interviews with Spiller, 28 April 1998, p. 38, and Zeller, 6 January 1999, p. 21; and 1 February 1998, p. 58.

146–147   **Plant's flavor center:** Author interviews with Budich, 28 January and 4 February 1998, and Zeller, 1 February and 8 December 1998.

       Chocolate: Author interviews with Farone, 14 February, 7 March, and 18 March 1998; William A. Farone, draft document, "Thoughts on Philip Morris Response on Manipulation and Control: The Use of Casings and Flavorings," 27 March 1996, p. 3. An expatriate American called me anonymously to say that the Brazilian flavor house in which he had worked for thirty-seven years supplied chocolate extracts for PM's Marlboro and that he believed chocolate and nicotine had synergistic effects. **Arthur Levine:** Author interviews with Zeller, 1 February 1998, p. 79–80, and 8 December 1998, p. 22. **Not a science:** Author interview with Zeller, 1 February 1998, p. 70, and 8 December 1998, p. 18. **Spiking cigarettes:** Author interview with Budich, 4 February 1998, p. 11. **Level of secrecy:** Author interview with Budich, 28 January 1998, p. 69.

147   **Smoking machine:** One of our informants believed that the rule of thumb was that actual tar and nicotine intake was 50 percent higher than what the FTC machine reported. FDA interview with "Doc," informant, 11 August 1994, pp. 69–71.

148   **Ventilation holes:** L. T. Kozlowski et al., "The Misuse of 'Less-Hazardous' Cigarettes and Its Detection: Hole-Blocking of Ventilated Filters," *American Journal of Public Health* 70:1202–3 (11 November 1980).

148   **Everyone's credentials:** Author interview with Budich, 4 February 1998, pp. 49–50; FDA notes of Budich and Spiller.

Chapter Twenty-one

152   **Merit figures:** Henry Drew, FDA memos to Ilisa Bernstein, "Summary of Phase I Cigarette Study," 17 March 1994, and "Summary of Nicotine Analysis in Cigarettes," 23 March 1994. Thomas Layloff, FDA memo of telephone conversation with James Saunders (USDA), "Collaborative Testing of Cigarette Samples, March 23, 1994.."

152   **Federal Trade Commission:** Although the FTC maintained an extensive collection of data and had been dealing with tobacco since the 1940s, it had no mandate to look into nicotine control. Unlike the FDA, the FTC is not a public health agency; rather, it is a law enforcement agency that polices marketing, sales, and advertising and looks for distortions in the marketplace. It had never asked the questions that the FDA was asking.

153   **Levels of nicotine:** House Committee on Energy and Commerce, Subcommittee on Health and the Environment, testimony of Alexander Spears (Lorillard), hearing, *Regulation of Tobacco Products (Part 1),* 103rd Cong., 2d sess., 25 March 1994, Serial no. 103–49

153   **Proof of manipulation:** FTC chart, "Tar, Nicotine and Tar/Nicotine Ratios by Year" (sales-weighted 1982–91); FDA graphs, "Sales-Weighted Nicotine and Tar Levels in Smoke as % of 1982 Levels: High Tar Category, Low Tar Category and Ultra-Low Tar Category."

154   **Thomas J. Bliley**

     Sentry: Gregory R. Scott, PM memo to Gene A. Knorr, "Rebuilding Our Relationship with Tobacco-State Congressmen," 25 August 1986, PM ID 2025854686–89, at 88. **FDA's possession:** Congressman Thomas Bliley, letter to David A. Kessler, 18 March 1994. **Read from binders:** Author interviews with Forbes, 17 April 1998 and September 2000. **Kessler from Bliley:** Action Team, PM notes, 16 March 1994, PM ID 2022838682–83, at 82; PM report, "Report for Government Affairs," March 1994, PM ID 2046044450–51.

Chapter Twenty-two

156   **Most potent weapon:** Paul Knopick, TI memo to William Kloepfer, 9 September 1980.

156   **Single mistake:** I knew any mistake would be used by the industry as an excuse to attack me. Michael Pertschuk, former head of the FTC, said one of the tobacco industry's key tactics was looking "for small injustices." A professor of his called that strategy "juggling the oranges so successfully that the judge never saw the elephant walk by" (author interview with Pertschuk, 16 February 1997).

156   **Essential allegations:** "Philip Morris Teleconference Announcement of Lawsuit Against ABC's 'Day One,'" 24 March 1994, PM ID 2024014040–59.

156   **Warning to me:** Philip Morris lawyers acknowledged that the "spiking" issue was not directly related to our activities, but added, "[T]he false claim by ABC is infecting the FDA issue. The claim is now embraced as true by various hostile Congressmen and the antis, and is being relied upon by them as a basis for arguing that the FDA should assert jurisdiction" (Murray H. Bring, PM memo to Michael A. Miles, "Rationale for Lawsuit Against ABC," 18 March 1994, PM ID 2023002738).

157   **Horror story:** Pat McGlothlin (Hollywood, Fla.), letter.

158   **Testimony:** House Committee on Energy and Commerce, Subcommittee on Health and the Environment, hearing, *Regulation of Tobacco Products (Part 1),* 103rd Cong., 2d sess., 25 March 1994 Serial No. 103–49.

159   **One-two pagers:** Kathleen Linehan, PM memo to Robert Reese and Gregory Scott, "Waxman FDA hearing," 17 March 1994, PM ID 2023029473

159–160   **Martin Lancaster**

     Conduit: Gregory Scott, PM memo to Kathleen M. Linehan, "Congressional Staff Briefing on FDA Regulation of Tobacco Products," 18 March 1994, PM ID 2023193512. **Dear Colleague:** Congressman H. Martin Lancaster, letter. PM circulated copies of the Lancaster letter internally, noting this was the final version sent before the Easter recess. See Gregory Scott, PM memo to Kathleen M. Linehan, "FDA re: Lancaster 'Dear Colleague,'" 30 March 1994, PM ID 2023173709–11. **Personal donations:** Ellen Merlo, PM memo to Fred Laux et al., "Lancaster Contribution," 19 April 1994, PM ID 2041166362.

163   **Questions to Bliley:** Action Team, PM notes, 23 March 1994, PM ID 2023322819.

Chapter Twenty-three

167   **Buried in her pile:** A. W. Spears and S. T. Jones, "Chemical and Physical Criteria for Tobacco Leaf of Modern Day Cigarettes," *Advances in Tobacco Sciences,* 35th Tobacco Chemists' Conference, Winston-Salem, N.C., 1981. See also congressional report, "Majority Staff Analysis of Chemical and Physical Criteria for Tobacco Leaf of Modern Day Cigarettes," House Committee on Energy and Commerce, Subcommittee on Health and the Environment, April 1994.

168   **Mostly noise:** Ira Loss, Andrew Schwartz, and Kelly Baldrate, Natwest Securities Corp. analysis, "Kessler Testimony Is Mostly Noise: Threat of Regulation by FDA Is Limited," 24 March 1994, PM ID 2023462123–24.

168   **Sense of anxiety:** The evening of my testimony, Steve Parrish met his wife at a fundraiser in their hometown in Connecticut. She looked at him and thought to herself, "My God, they're killing my husband" (author interview with Parrish, January 1998; p. 15).

          Revival preacher: Ibid., p. 17.

168   **Action team:** Mike Miles, PM memo, "Ferocious Defense," 7 March 1994, PM ID 2022843127–28.

168–169   **Board meeting:** Murray Bring, PM presentation to PM board of directors, 30 March 1994, PM ID 2022813447–73; Arnold & Porter attorney presentation to PM board of directors, 30 March 1994, PM ID 2022813560–74.

          Profile on Dr. Kessler: PM note, "Questions and Comments from Directors Following Messrs. Bring and Levine's Presentations," 30 March 1994, PM ID 2023312333–34, at 33.

169   **Surgeons General:** Philip Morris established an internal group to review President Bush's potential candidates for Surgeon General and to identify and vet some of their own. Given the importance of the post, the group agreed "to consider ways to impede the viability of candidates openly hostile to our industry." Also, "[I]t was agreed that politically it would be wise to involve some of our friends on the Hill and in the Republican Party" (David Greenberg, PM memo, "Update of Surgeon General Project," 19 July 1989, PM ID 2041252696).

169   **Photograph of me:** Worldwide Regulatory Affairs, PM presentation to PM board of directors, Sea Island, Ga. (slide 36), 29 April 1995, PM ID 2041645354–62, at 58.

169   **Sea Island:** Steven Parrish, PM draft presentation to the PM board of directors, Sea Island, Ga., 11 April 1994, PM ID 2048310347.

          Four-pronged: Ibid., p. 4. **NRA:** Ibid., p. 11.

170   **Melvin Belli:** "In what we would characterize as a nuisance suit... Melvin Belli et al. have initiated an international class action suit against all America's major tobacco companies" (R. Morrow [Smith-Barney, Shearson], note, "Who's Suing Who—Nicotine Controversy Stirs Old Warrior," 30 March 1994, PM ID 2031578327).

170   **Most fateful documents:** Waldo Proffitt, "Death Knell for Tobacco Industry," *Sarasota Herald-Tribune,* 9 March 1994.

170   **April 14 hearing:** House Committee on Energy and Commerce, Subcommittee on Health and the Environment, hearing, *Regulation of Tobacco Products (Part 1),* 103rd Cong., 2d sess., 14 April 1994, Serial No. 103–49.

172   **Dough boy:** Author conversation with Andrew Tisch.

172   **Shove it in my vein:** Author interview with Mele, 9 September 1999, p. 4.

172   **Questions to expect:** Kathleen Linehan, PM memo to Bill Campbell and Steve Parrish, "Testimony—Critical Issues," 11 April 1994, PM ID 2023194419–22.

172   **Our adversaries:** P. M. Sirridge, PM draft memo to F. S. Newman, "PM Counsel to PM Counsel Regarding DeNoble Manuscripts," 27 July 1983, PM ID 2021424402–12.

173   **Days that followed:** William Campbell, in a speech to PM management after the CEO hearing, said, "I want to tell you about the experience on a very personal level right here and now, so that we can all then put it behind us and move ahead. Regarding the spirit in which the hearing was conducted, if I'm the horse's mouth in this, then let me tell you, I was looking across the table at more than one horse's ass" (PM speech, William I. Campbell, PM USA management meeting, Norfolk, Va., 27 April 1994, PM ID 2024008057–105, at 97). Also after the hearing, Andrew Tisch of Lorillard wore a watch with a picture of Waxman within the cross hairs of what was presumably a gun's sight.

173   **Orchestrated event:** Author interview with Schiliro. Whether or not it orchestrated the calls, PM played on the McCarthy theme, drafting opinion pieces that called the Waxman hearing a "finger-pointing inquisition reminiscent of the commie-seeking circuses better known as the McCarthy witch hunts" (PM draft op-ed, "Smokers' Alliance," August 1994, PM ID 2046563595–98, at 95); Ernest Pepples, B&W memo to Michael Prideaux, 4 August 1994, B&W ID 502575847.

173   **Court of public opinion:** Not everyone thought the CEOs had performed poorly. "They not only never laid a glove on you, they didn't even know where you were a lot of the time . . . a series of tours de force" (Ernest Pepples [B&W], letter to William Campbell [PM], 22 April 1994, PM ID 2040411406). Letters of congratulations came from the public as well: "I saw you before that pinko congressional committee on C-SPAN and I think you did a great job..." (Irv Rastin [Athens, Ohio], letter to William Campbell [PM], 15 April 1994, PM ID 2045740621).

174   **Mike Barrett:** Author interview with Barrett, 2000.

Chapter Twenty-four

175   **Jim Johnston:** Jim Johnston (RJR), letter to David A. Kessler, 28 February 1994. Perhaps unthinkingly, Johnston acknowledged RJR's control over nicotine. "In addition to traditional tobacco blending techniques, various other techniques are available to cigarette manufacturers," he wrote, naming several of them. "The processing of certain tobaccos enables us to manufacture cigarettes consistent with the published 'tar' and nicotine levels despite the nicotine variations from leaf to leaf and crop to crop." An internal company fact sheet that circulated at RJR a few weeks earlier stated in so many words that the amount of nicotine applied to reconstituted tobacco could be varied. See T. A. Perfetti, RJR fact sheet, "Tobacco Reconstituted Sheet Material (G7)," 1 March 1994, RJR ID 511755345.

175–178   **Visiting RJR:** Author interviews with Budich, 23 April 1998; Light, 31 March 1998; Mitchell, 23 March 1998; and Zeller, 30 March 1998. FDA notes of Eileen Bargo, Kevin Budich, Barbara Frazier, Jack Mitchell, Diane O'Brien, Robert Spiller, and Mitchell Zeller, 11–12 April 1994.

Who confirmed: Author interview with Budich, 23 April 1998, pp. 11, 14, 16, 17, and 19; FDA notes of Kevin Budich, Diane O'Brien, and Eileen Bargo. **Impact is basically:** Author interviews with Budich, 23 April 1998, p. 18, and Zeller, 30 March 1998, pp. 22, 24, and 26; FDA notes of Kevin Budich, Jack Mitchell, Robert Spiller, Mitch Zeller. **Specifically requested:** Author interview with Light, 31 March 1998, pp. 15–16; FDA notes of Kevin Budich and Robert Spiller. **Bar codes:** Author interviews with Budich, 23 April 1998, p. 36; Light, 31 March 1998, pp. 14, 20, 21; Zeller, 30 March 1998, p. 16. **Slow day:** Author interview with Light, 31 March 1998, p. 12. **Scale back operations:** Ibid., p. 13; FDA notes of Jack Mitchell. **Row of eyes:** Author interview with Light, 31 March 1998, p. 12. **Human testing:** FDA notes of Mitch Zeller and Malcolm Frazier. **Before Premier:** FDA notes of Kevin Budich. **After Premier:** Author interview with Light, 31 March 1998, p. 30. **Perceptibly uneasy:** Ibid., pp. 30 and 38. **Various angles:** Ibid., pp. 30–31. **Remove Gary:** Ibid., p. 54. **Team had seen:** Author interview with Zeller, 30 March 1998, p. 10. **Saw a Reynolds employee:** Author interview with Light, 31 March 1998, p. 35. **Cooler:** Years later I asked RJR about the coolers that the tobacco team had seen. I was told they were used by employees who were smoking certain experimental products that primarily heat, rather than burn, tobacco and collecting "their urine to be analyzed for mutagenicity." RJR wrote, "These employees had coolers with them at all times to facilitate collection and storage of all urine produced during the specified collection periods. The results of RJR's studies were later publicly reported by RJR scientists" (Richard M. Cooper [Williams & Connolly], letter to David Kessler, 19 October 2000).

178 **After the visit:** Richard Cooper complained that we were distorting RJR statements. In a heated exchange of letters months after the FDA visit, the attorney wrote, "I am advised by R. J. Reynolds that studies of nicotine and cotinine in human body fluids are not conducted by R. J. Reynolds for the purpose of establishing nicotine content or yields of cigarettes under development" (Richard Cooper [Williams & Connolly], letter to Eric Blumberg [FDA], 18 November 1994). See also, "Planning meetings with the Brand R&D representatives continued in an effort to relate . . . plasma nicotine measures to product development and consumer testing" (RJR report, "Time [Min] Relative to Lighting Plasma Nicotine 'Boost' [ng/ml]," 1987, RJR ID 505857222–23; J. H. Robinson, RJR memo to Human Research Review Committee, "1986 Plasma Nicotine Study to Support Brands R&D," 23 May 1986, RJR ID 506216330–32).

178–179 **Bellomy research:** FDA transcripts of telephone conversations with Lacy Bellomy, 5 and 11 October 1994.

Long-standing relationship: Ibid., 5 October, p. 5. **Become wary:** Ibid., 11 October, p. 4. **Going to suggest:** Ibid., 11 October, p. 12. **Perhaps five:** Ibid., 11 October, p. 15. **Before and after:** Ibid., 11 October, p. 19.

179 **Spoken with RJR:** B&W notes, B&W ID 682637362–841, at 579.

180–182 **Brown & Williamson:** Author interviews with Budich, 14 July 1998; Mitchell, 7 July 1998; Witt, 8 July 1998; and Zeller, 7 July 1998.

Delegation: B&W list, "Brown & Williamson representatives." **Thinning:** Author interview with Witt, 8 July 1998, p. 25. **Company's secrets:** Author interview with Mitchell, 8 July 1998, p. 21. **Bodies were buried:** Author interview with Mitchell, 7 July 1998, p. 21. **Cantankerous and hostile:** Author interview with

Budich, 14 July 1998, p. 13. **Doctor Death:** Author interview with Zeller, 7 July 1998, p. 38. **Deferred or refused:** Ibid., pp. 18–19. **Tobacco extract:** Author interviews with Budich, 14 July 1998, pp. 14–21, and Zeller, 7 July 1998, pp. 37–40. **Company to run:** Author interview with Zeller, 7 July 1998, p. 51. **Mumbling to himself:** Author interview with Witt, 8 July 1998, p. 50. **Sophisticated time wasting:** Author interview with Zeller, 7 July 1998, p. 49.

Chapter Twenty-five

183   **Research:** FDA interview with Wigand (Research), 13 May 1994. Author interviews with Mitchell, 7 July 1998, and Wigand, 9 February 1998.

      Pummeled: Author interview with Wigand, 9 February 1998, pp. 7–8.

188   **Ammonia technology:** B&W document, *Root Technology: A Handbook for Leaf Blenders and Product Developers,* February 1991, PM ID 2060538953–86.

189   **Freebase nicotine:** The addition of ammonia converts nicotine particles to a more volatile free-base form that is more rapidly absorbed in the respiratory tract (James F. Pankow et al., "Conversion of Nicotine in Tobacco Smoke to Its Volatile and Available Free-Base Form through the Action of Gaseous Ammonia," *Environmental Science Technology* 31:2428–33 [1997]). An RJR report read, "In essence, a cigarette is a system for delivery of nicotine to the smoker in attractive, useful form. At 'normal' smoke pH, at or below 6.0, essentially all of the smoke nicotine is chemically combined with acidic substances, hence is non-volatile and relatively slowly absorbed by the smoker. As the smoke pH increases above about 6.0, an increasing proportion of the total smoke nicotine occurs in 'free' form, which is volatile, rapidly absorbed by the smoker, and believed to be instantly perceived as nicotine 'kick.'... [M]arket performance of various brands correlates positively with the total amount of 'free' nicotine.... [A]ll brands surveyed having over about 35 micrograms of 'free' nicotine/cigarette increased in market share in the period studied... (RJR report, "Implications and Activities Arising from Correlation of Smoke pH with Nicotine Impact, Other Smoke Qualities and Cigarette Sales," 2 October 1973, RJR ID 509314122–54).

190   **Second long interview:** FDA interview with Wigand, 17 May 1994.

Chapter Twenty-six

191   **Macon:** FDA interviews with "Macon," 24 and 26 May 1994. Author interview with Doyle and Light, 21 July 1998.

      Cat-and-mouse game: Author interview with Doyle.

192   **Patent from Brazil:** B&W patent PI9203690A, "Variedade de fumo geneticamente estavel e planta de fumo."

192   **Janis Bravo:** FDA interview with Bravo, 25 May 1994. Author interview with Zeller, 2 March 1998.

195   **In production:** FDA interview with "Macon," 26 May 1994, p. 12.

      Use it up: Ibid., pp. 13–16.

196   **Y-1 requirement:** R. R. Black, B&W memo, "Y-1 Production," 19 April 1994, B&W ID 510300232.

      Read and destroy: R. R. Black, B&W memo, "Options for Blending-Off Y-1," B&W ID 361001029.

196 **Hardison:** Author interview with Witt and Zeller, 16 June 1998.

197 **Going crazy:** FDA interview with Wigand, 1 June 1994, p. 92.

Chapter Twenty-seven

198 **Conspiracy:** RJR document, "Industry Background," January 1978, RJR ID 500281959–2002.

198–199 **Rebutted:** RJR's president scoffed at the new findings. "One of the best ways of getting publicity is for a doctor to make some startling claim relative to people's health regardless of whether such statement is based on fact or theory" ("Cigarette Scare: What'll the Trade Do?" *Business Week*, 5 December 1953). The president of American Tobacco (hereinafter cited as AT) took issue with the "loose talk on the subject." He pointed out that "no one has yet proved that lung cancer in any human being is directly traceable to tobacco or to its products in any form" (Paul M. Hahn, AT press release, 26 November 1953, PM ID 2025017717–19). "There are just three men in the medical fraternity who are advancing the lung-cancer-cigarette smoking theory, and they are apparently enjoying the publicity they are receiving" (E. A. Darr [RJR], letter to A. B. Gross, 10 December 1953, RJR ID 502407669).

199 **Confirm the relationship:** C. E. Teague, RJR report, "Survey of Cancer Research with Emphasis on Possible Carcinogens from Tobacco," 2 February 1953, RJR ID 501932947–68, at 63.

 Collected and destroyed: RJR memo, "RJR Research and Development Activities—Fact Team Memorandum," vol. 3, 31 December 1985, RJR ID 515873805–929, at 897. **Public relations sham:** "Our position continues to mislead the public—with a wink" (PM report, "Some Additional Thoughts," March 1990, PM ID 2021157133–43, at 35).

199 **Richard Pollay:** In the mid–1980s, Pollay was asked by Marc Edell, the plaintiff's lawyer in the *Cipollone* product liability case, to survey tobacco advertising. He drew first on his own book, *Information Sources in Advertising History* (Westport, Conn.: Greenwood Press, 1979), the leading reference to primary sources. Pollay was interested in how institutions gained power through advertising and how social values are changed in the process. See Richard Pollay, "Propaganda, Puffing and the Public Interest," *Public Relations Review: A Journal of Research and Comment* 16(3):39–54 (Fall 1990).

199 **Wisconsin Historical Society:** After learning that Pollay had visited the Hill archive several times, lawyers for the tobacco industry went too, and concluded, "While the documents contain no 'smoking gun,' a plaintiff's attorney might use them effectively to supplement and support existing charges against the industry" (Allen R. Purvis, B&W memo, "Summary of Important Documents in John W. Hill Collection," 7 May 1990, B&W ID 68910328–37).

199 **Challenge to the tobacco industry:** Hill & Knowlton memo to members of the Planning Committee, ID 00060860–68. Also in that memo: "They've competed for years—not in price, not in any real difference of quality—but just in ability to conjure up more hypnotic claims and brighter assurances for what their own brand might do for a smoker, compared to another brand. And now, suddenly, they feel all out of bounds, because the old claims became unimportant

overnight...." That the burden of proof has shifted is "almost too terrible for most of the industry's men to realize."

200 **Council for Tobacco Research:** Shook, Hardy & Bacon, *Brown and Williamson— Council for Tobacco Research Issues Notebook,* October 1991, B&W ID 682631909–2261.

200 **Clarence Cook Little:** At the press conference where his appointment as scientific director was announced, Little denied that the link between cigarettes and lung cancer had been proved. "Maybe people who are heavy smokers are a certain type, physically, glandularly, nervously.... Is it the fact that they smoke that means that some day they may have cancer, or is it the other way around?" A reporter suggested that if research were to establish a direct relationship between cancer and tobacco, the tobacco industry would be in effect "digging its own grave." Little denied that. "I think that they want to find that out, if it is there. They don't want to fool themselves. They don't want to kill people" (Tobacco Industry Research Committee, transcript of press conference, University Club, New York, 15 June 1954).

201 **An open question:** In the mid-1960s, the TI's public relations agency, Tiderock Corp., decided to develop a program that "re-establishes the cigarette controversy" (Tiderock Corp., "The Cigarette Controversy, An Action Program," 20 November 1967, cited in Jones, Day, Reavis & Pogue, draft report, "Corporate Activity Project," p. 53, B&W ID 681879254–715). "Our basic position in the cigarette controversy is subject to the charge, and may be subject to a finding, that we are making false or misleading statements to promote the sale of cigarettes" (William Kloepfer, Tiderock memo, 15 April 1968, cited in Jones, Day, Reavis & Pogue, draft report, "Corporate Activity Project," B&W ID 681879254–715, at 319).

201 **Deadly delusion:** Jones, Day, Reavis & Pogue, draft report, "Corporate Activity Project," B&W ID 681879254–715, at 273.

Molded: Author interview with former PM employee, 2000. **Venal and evil** and **Association cannot:** Janet Brown (Chadbourne, Parke, Whiteside & Wolff), memo, "Theories for Defending Smoking & Health Litigation," 20 August 1985, B&W ID 680712251–260, at 254–55 and 258. **Try the plaintiff:** Jones, Day, Reavis & Pogue, draft report, "Corporate Activity Project," B&W ID 681879254–715, at 273. **Alternative causation:** Richard G. Stuhan, *"Kueper v. R. J. Reynolds Tobacco Co. et al.,* Analysis of Post-Verdict Juror Interviews," 16 June 1993, B&W ID 536480002–285, at 49. See also Jones, Day, Reavis & Pogue memo, "Smoking and Health Litigation Tactical Proposals," 10 August 1985, B&W ID 68071226–337.

201 **Among friends:** TI document, cited in Jones, Day, Reavis & Pogue, draft report, "Corporate Activity Project," B&W ID 681879254–715, at 318.

202 **Researchers were pressured:** One researcher, Herbert Silvette, hired to write a monograph on tobacco research, discovered that what the Council for Tobacco Research (CTR) actually wanted was "an account of any published scientific information concerning the beneficial effects of smoking; that I should disregard whatever else had been published... and, above all, that I should display my 'judgment and discrimination' by carefully hiding them under a bushel-basket." CTR grantees Cecile and Rudolf Leuchtenberger were urged to delay publishing their research. "An immediate publication of existing results would probably be

regarded by most people as merely confirming the dangers or evils of smoking...
. I hope you will agree with me that some delay in publication is indicated here
on *purely scientific* grounds [emphasis in original]." Freddy Homburger was told in
more definitive language "not to publish without our approval." He scheduled a
press conference, intending to report the industry's efforts to suppress scientific
information, but the event was canceled without his knowledge by an industry
representative. See B&W report, "Independence of Research," B&W ID
682011473–96, at 79, 82–83, and 90.

202   **Particularly poignant:** Charles Huggins (University of Chicago), letter to C. C.
Little (CTR), 17 January 1968.

202   **1964:** "The consensus is that the industry is in a grave crisis," wrote one public
relations official, commenting on the anticipated 1964 Surgeon General's report
(J. V. Blalock, PM memo, "Tobacco Institute, Tobacco Industry Research Committee, and Hill & Knowlton," 18 June 1963, TI ID TIMN 1801.01). Philip Morris
called the report a "verdict against cigarette smoking" and urged the company to
conduct its own medical research to show that its products are not harmful (PM
Research Center PM report, "Smoking and Health: Significance of the Report of
the Surgeon General's Committee to Philip Morris Incorporated," 18 February
1964, PM ID 1000335612–25).

202–203   **Curious response:** PM counsel to PM counsel, PM report, "Affirmative Action
Program," 1 August 1988, PM ID 20224969102–24, at 108.

    Outraged: A former Hill & Knowlton employee claimed to me that the TI
wanted to run an advertising campaign urging young people to wait until they
were grown to decide whether or not to smoke. Supposedly, some at the public
relations firm felt that such a campaign was, in a backhanded way, tantamount to
an invitation to smoke, and the firm's affiliation with the TI ended in 1968.

203   **Psychological crutch:** George Weissman, PM memo to Joseph Cullman III, "Surgeon General's Report," 29 January 1964, PM ID 1005038559–61, at 59.

203   **Cardiovascular disease:** N. L. Benowitz and G. A. Gourlay, "Cardiovascular Toxicity of Nicotine: Implications for Nicotine Replacement Therapy," *Journal of
American College of Cardiology* 29(7):1422–31 (June 1997).

203   **Cleared as a carcinogen:** H. Wakeham, PM memo to members of the Research
and Development Committee, "Nicotine," January 1964, PM ID 1001502928–29.

    Directly converted: Stephen S. Hecht et al., "2'-Hydroxylation of Nicotine by
Cytochrome P450 2A6 and Human Liver Microsomes: Formation of a Lung Carcinogen Precursor," *Proceedings of National Academy of Sciences,* 24 October 2000,
early edition.

203   **Disappointed with CTR's output:** PM Legal Department, draft letter to H. H.
Ramm (RJR), 31 January 1963, PM ID 1005102050–61.

    Ostensibly independent: "The 6 General Counsel should at all costs continue
to be the guiding force" (meeting notes, "Discussion of Tobacco Institute," AT ID
ATX 927549—1049–55, at 52).

203   **Friendly witnesses:** "Lawyers cannot testify; we need people who can" (Committee of General Counsel, meeting notes, 10 September 1981, PM ID
2048925570–77). Occasionally, witnesses became less friendly if they felt they had
not been treated fairly by CTR. Of one witness an attorney wrote, "Dr. Sprunt...
wants something more than the hope they will approve his grant application

before he takes further public position on our behalf. . . . Dr. Sprunt's present attitude is that he is prepared to testify in Washington (including assuring an adequate statement by accepting our help in preparing the final form...) but feels that before he does so, we should adopt a more positive attitude towards his situation" (Edwin Jacob [Cabell, Medinger, Forsyth & Decker], letter to H. H. Ramm [RJR], 25 January 1965, RJR ID 500887112–13).

203 **Millions of dollars:** List of special projects funded by the Tobacco Industry Research Committee and the Council for Tobacco Research, PM ID 2048925665–704 and 2048925706–70.

204 **Keeper:** Author interview with Huber, 1 June 1998, pp. 51–52.

204 **Stage-managed:** Edward J. Cooke Jr. (Davis Polk Wardell Sunderland & Kiendl), memo to Janet Brown et al., 15 August 1967, PM ID 1005109800–801; ibid., 31 August 1967, PM ID 1005109806–807; ibid., 11 September 1967, PM ID 1005109792; ibid., 14 September 1967, PM ID 100510863. See also David R. Hardy (Shook, Hardy, Ottman, Mitchell & Bacon), memo to Janet Brown et al., 1 September 1967, PM ID 1005109766; Edwin J. Jacob, memo to D. R. Hardy et al., "Memorandum of Conference with Dr. Arthur Furst," February 1967, PM ID 100513741l–13; David R. Hardy (Shook, Hardy, Ottman, Mitchell & Bacon), letter to Alexander Holtzman, 27 October 1966, PM ID 1005154393; B&W document, "A Confidential Counsels' Memorandum of Surgeon General's Advisory Committee Report for Use in Preparing Witnesses," B&W ID 0012692604; PM counsel, PM documents, "Summary of Witnesses' Statements," August 1968, PM ID 2016002073–81 and PM ID 2016002192–96 and 1969, PM ID 2016002096–103.

204 **Police the health:** PM draft presentation to the PM board of directors, "Smoking and Health Controversy," 23 August 1982, PM ID 2015022483–85, at 85.

204 **Committee of Counsels:** Committee of Counsels, meeting notes, 10 September 1981 (B&W ID 0012687548, PM ID 2048925570–77, PM ID 2048925563–67).

Prominent roles: Covington & Burling memo, Herbert Dym to Juchatz et al., "Waxman Hearings," 22 April 1988, B&W ID 682007791–93. **Lawyers controlled:** Author interviews with "Veritas," 21 March 1998, and 27 January 1999. See also J. Kendrick Wells III (B&W), letter to Robert B. Northrip (Shook, Hardy, & Bacon) and Gordon A. Smith (King & Spalding), 23 November 1993, B&W ID 293002121.

204 **Grantmaking body:** "[I]f CTR is to be useful, ways must be found to bolster its reputation so it can be useful to 'launder' industry money" (PM notes, New York meeting, 15 November 1978); "There should be no written record of what transpired issued for distribution" (R. B. Seligman, draft memo to CTR file, "Meeting in New York, 15 November 1978," 17 November 1978, PM ID 1003718428–32).

204 **Predetermined outcome:** "Let's face it. We are interested in evidence which we believe denies the allegation that cigarette smoking causes disease" (H. Wakeham, PM memo to J. F. Cullman III, "'Best' Program for CTR," 8 December 1970, PM ID 2022200161–63, at 61).

Clinical studies: Special Projects, SP–118, 6 October 1966. **Not independent:** James Bowling, PM notes, quoting Alexander Spears at meeting of Industry Research Study Committee, 19 April 1979, cited in William L. Allinder (Shook, Hardy & Bacon), letter to K. F. Bixenstein (Jones, Day, Reavis & Pogue et al.), 22 October 1992, PM ID 2048925020–25, at 21; "CTR Special Projects should continue under CTR to give investigators an aura of independence" (AT meeting notes, 7

May 1979, AT ID MNATPRIV00034812–13, at 12). See also report "Independence of Research," B&W ID 682011473–96. Jeffrey Wigand also told me that industry lawyers told their "scientists how to interpret the science."

205 **Innocence lost:** David M. Murphy, Wachtell Lipton memo to Herbert M. Wachtell et al., "Lorillard/CTR study," 28 April 1992, Lorillard ID 87715635; David M. Murphy, Lorillard note, 30 April 1992, Lorillard ID 87715633.

205 **David Hardy:** David R. Hardy (Shook, Hardy, Ottman, Mitchell & Bacon), letter to DeBaun Bryant (B&W), 21 July 1970, B&W ID 681805313–19, at 13; David Hardy, letter to DeBaun Bryant, 20 August 1970, p. 7.

205 **Cipollone:** An industry summary of the case read: "Plaintiffs' Themes: Cigarettes kill. ... Rose Cipollone was never adequately informed that cigarettes cause lung cancer. ... Even if she had been informed, she was not responsible for her lung cancer because she was addicted and did not have a free choice to stop smoking. Defendants knew far more than they ever told the public about the hazards of smoking. Defendants advertised in such a way to minimize the known hazards of smoking. ... Defendants conspired among themselves and with third parties to deceive smokers about the hazards of smoking.

"Defendants' themes: Rose Cipollone was fully aware of the alleged risks of smoking ... Rose Cipollone knew that cigarette smoking was habit-forming before she began smoking. Rose Cipollone chose to continue smoking after an adequate warning was provided. ... Advertising does not cause anyone to begin or continue smoking. ... Tobacco companies conducted reasonable research into the alleged risks as soon as reputable scientists began to postulate a link between cigarette smoking and serious diseases. They disclosed the results to the government and the public" (Steven Parrish, Shook, Hardy & Bacon memo, "The Cipollone Case," 31 August 1988, PM ID 2022885364–86, at 74–75).

206 **King of concealment:** Sarokin's decision included the "afraid of discovery" and "industry shield" quotes here, plus others from the five documents the judge selected to be made public (*Haines v. Liggett Group, Inc.,* 140 F.R.D. 681 [ED.N.J. 1992]). Shook, Hardy & Bacon complained about the judge's "erroneous characterizations" of the five documents ("Background Paper on 'Crime/Fraud' Opinion in *Haines v. Liggett Group, Inc.,*" PM ID 2048925520–39).

Attorney-client privilege: Author conversation with Steven Parrish, 29 February 2000. **Went after Sarokin:** *Haines v. Liggett Group,* 975 F.2d 81 (3d Cir. 1992).

207 **Prestigious institutions**

Harvard: The importance of the Harvard grant "continues to be viewed by some as relating wholly to the name of Harvard" (Janet C. Brown, memo to Arnold Henson, "Industry Research Review Study Group," 4 November 1978, p. 17, B&W ID 0012684784). **UCLA:** "The industry also funded a project at UCLA Medical School, but only after the Medical School reassured the industry that nothing damaging to the industry would be discovered" (Jones, Day, Reavis & Pogue, draft report, "Corporate Activity Project," B&W ID 681879254–715, at 452). **Sloan-Kettering:** C. H. Kibbee and J. C. Bowling, PM memo to Joseph F. Cullman III, "Sloan-Kettering Institute for Cancer Research," 18 February 1970, PM ID 2024774530; J. C. Bowling, PM memo to C. H. Kibbee, "Sloan-Kettering Contributions," 23 November 1964, PM ID 1005038364.

207–208 **AMA:** "Ultimately, the companies contributed $15.005 million from 1964 to 1972"

(Shook, Hardy & Bacon, "Brown and Williamson—American Medical Association Issues Notebook," January 1990, B&W 682623623–788, at 628); F. J. L. Blasingame (AMA), letters to Joseph F. Cullman III (PM), 12 February 1964, PM ID 1002905198–99; to Morgan J. Cramer (Lorillard), 12 February 1964, PM ID 2015055651–52; and to the FTC, 28 February 1964, PM ID 1005037378–80.

Sir Philip Rogers: "Report on Policy Aspects of the Smoking and Health Situation in the U.S.A.," October 1964, PM ID 1003119099–135, at 102.

208   Smoking dogs: William W. Shinn, memo to Charles L. Bacon, "Auerbach Dogs," 15 April 1971, TI ID TIMN 221636; Jones, Day, Reavis & Pogue, draft report, "Corporate Activity Project," B&W ID 681879254–715, at 671–78 and 691.

208   Shockerwick House: Report, "Position Paper," PM ID 2501024522–25; Hugh Cullman, PM memo, 3 December 1976, PM ID 2025025286. When Philip Morris (Europe) seemed likely to diverge from the spirit of the group, a strong letter of concern was sent from O. H. Stewart Lockhart (BAT) to R. W. ("Bill") Murray (PM), 28 June 1977, PM ID 2501024528.

208   Business and political leaders: An "Influence Wheel" diagram that was part of a Philip Morris presentation showed spokes leading to the many factors affecting "legislative decisions" and to the Philip Morris programs designed to influence them. Some of the factors were the following: "Ideology: When an excise tax proposal emerges ... we know who the key legislators are and their positions"; "Pet Causes: We also make sure that we know the legislator's—and his or her spouse's—favorite philanthropies and try to support them"; "Direct Contact: A legislator is never too busy to talk about things like political contributions, fundraising for a coming election campaign and programs to benefit his district"; "Media: We have to get our point of view into print as often as possible. We try to have a third party, like an authority on taxes, write articles on our behalf" (Tina Walls [PM], 30 March 1993 speech, "Grasstops Government Relations," PM ID 2024023252–65; charts, "PM Decision Wheel," June 1993, PM ID 2044341613–18; chart, "PM Programs to Affect Legislative Decisions," PM ID 2047079565–66).

208–209   Social climate and tourist groups: PM presentation, "Managing the Social Climate for Tobacco Use," 1993, PM ID 2501342761–85.

New Puritanism and political correctness and survey: Burson-Marsteller report, "Smoking Bans/Accommodation Communications Program," 4 March 1994, PM ID 2023915422–28. Shift the argument: "Philip Morris U.S.A. Plan to Counter the Anti-Tobacco Lobby," PM ID 2023916383–442, at 402. Parents for Priorities: PM report, "New Project," April 1993, PM ID 2046662829–37, at 29. Qur'an: Draft PM report, "Corporate Affairs Plan," 25 November 1987, PM ID 2501254715–23, at 18.

209   Rosser Reeves: Rosser Reeves, Tiderock Corp. memo to Anne Hetfield et al., "The Study of a Propaganda Phenomenon," 18 July 1967, B&W ID 690014108–11; AT notes, meeting with Reeves, 27 July 1967, B&W ID 0012687516.

Proposal: "The Cigarette Controversy: An Action Program," Tiderock Corp., 20 November 1967, TI ID TIMN 70816–21. Millions of dollars: Tiderock Corp., TI budget, TI ID TIMN 0071439–41; "Reestablish cigarette controversy ... make it massive" (PM notes, 18 December 1967, PM ID 1003059283–85, at 83).

209   Geo-attitudinal: Guy L. Smith IV, remarks to PM board of directors, December 1984, PM ID 2021280135–49, at 42–44.

210 **Third-party concept** and **volunteer firefighters** and **National Women's Political Caucus:** Transcript of PM workshop, "Dealing with the Issues Indirectly: Constituencies," held in Rye Brook, N.Y., 13 September 1984, PM ID 2025421934–2000.

210 **List of alliances:** Twenty-five third-party allies were identified in a PM strategy report, "Tobacco Strategy," March 1994, PM ID 2045741542–48: Acton Institute for the Study of Religion and Liberty; Alexis de Tocqueville Institution; Americans for Tax Reform; Cato Institute; Center for the Study of American Business; Citizens for a Sound Economy; Citizens for Tax Justice/Institute on Taxation and Economic Policy; Claremont Institute for the Study of Statesmanship and Political Philosophy; Consumer Alert; Grocery Manufacturers of America; Heartland Institute; Heritage Foundation; Hoover Institution on War, Revolution and Peace; Institute for Research on the Economics of Taxation; Mackinac Center for Public Policy; Manhattan Institute; National Association of Manufacturers; National Center for Policy Analysis; National Empowerment Television; National Journalism Center; National Policy Forum; Pacific Research Institute for Public Policy; Tax Foundation; Texas Republic; and the Washington Legal Foundation.

210 **Washington Legal Foundation**

Have them publish: Craig L. Fuller, PM memo to Michael A. Miles, "February Monthly Report," 17 March 1994, PM ID 2023439346–51, at 47. **Legal scholars:** PM report, "Business Issues Tools," PM ID 2047720688–92, at 89.

210–211 **Minority communities:** PM budget, "Outreach/Constituency Development," PM ID 2048226950–60; Karen Daragan, PM e-mail, "FDA and Hispanic Publishers," PM ID 2047029044A–D.

Paternalistic and racist: PM report, "Business Issues Tools," PM ID 2047720688. **Black community:** Bernie Foster (West Coast Black Publishers Association), letter to Senator Edward M. Kennedy, 16 April 1993, PM ID 2026171599–600, at 599.

211 **International activities:** WHO report, Committee of Experts on Tobacco Industry Documents, "Tobacco Company Strategies to Undermine Tobacco Control Activities at the World Health Organization" (Geneva: WHO, July 2000), p. 88.

211 **Operation Rainmaker:** PM notes, "Top Secret: Operation Rainmaker," 20 March 1990, PM ID 2048302227–30, at 28; "Do something about the declining media climate" (PM notes, "Operation Rainbow," PM ID 2048302054–56).

Acquire UPI: Author conversation with Parrish, 29 February 2000. Author interview with Smith, 22 September 2000.

211–212 **Frank Colby:** Author interviews with Colby, 6 August and 7 October 1998 and 14 June 1999. When I asked RJR about Colby's allegation that Ramm had destroyed documents, the company referred me to the document retention policies it set forth in response to discovery requests in tobacco litigation.

Loopholes: Alan Rodgman, RJR memo, "The Collection of Tobacco Smoke—Health Literature for Legal Counsel," 2 June 1966, RJR ID 560536768–69, at 68. **One great fear:** RJR memo, "RJR Research and Development Activities, Fact Team Memorandum," vol. 3, 31 December 1985, pp. 27–28, RJR ID 515873805–929, at 867–68.

Chapter Twenty-eight

214 **Cynthiana, Kentucky:** Author interview with Hunter, 2 April 1998.

216 **Agronomically viable:** FDA interview with Wigand, 9 June 1994. Author interview with Witt and Zeller, 16 June 1998.

216 **James Chaplin:** FDA interview with Chaplin, 10 June 1994.

219 **DNAP:** FDA interview with Neagley and Evans, 10 June 1994.

Chapter Twenty-nine

221 **Farmer Jones:** Author interviews with Hunter, 2 April 1998; Light, 3 April 1998; and Light and Doyle, 21 July 1998.

223 **Phillip Fisher:** Author interviews with Light, 3 April 1998, and Light and Doyle, 21 July 1998.

224 **Original plant crosses:** FDA interview with Chaplin.

225 **Tim Long:** Author interview with Long, 17 May 1998.

225 **Baggies:** Author interview with Light, 3 April 1998.

   Piece of evidence: Author interview with Witt and Zeller, 16 June 1998, p. 37.

Chapter Thirty

227 **Filter tips**

   High nicotine: Guy L. Jones and W. K. Collins, "Measured Crop Performance, Tobacco," Dept. of Field Crops, North Carolina State College, Raleigh, N.C., December 1956. **Moved up the stalk:** House Committee on Government Operations, Subcommittee, hearings, 85th Cong., 1st sess., 18–19 and 23–26 July 1957, pp. 188–89. **Obscure autobiography:** Floyd H. Nuttall, *Memoirs in a Country Churchyard, A Tobaccoman's Plea: Clean Up Tobacco Row!* (Lawrenceville, Va.: Brunswick, November 1996). During the "tar derby" of the late 1950s, the companies "made extraordinary claims" for their new filter brands. "In most cases, however, the smoker of a filter cigarette was getting as much or more nicotine and tar as he would have gotten from a regular cigarette" (Ernest Pepples, B&W report, "Industry Response to Cigarette/Health Controversy," 4 February 1976, B&W ID 680099136–45, at 37).

227 **Industry claimed:** I read about the "everyone-knows-it" defense in a brief filed by industry lawyers in an Indiana court case. "There can be no serious suggestion that ordinary consumers... have not long been well aware that it may be very difficult to stop smoking." The lawyer wrote, "The alleged habituating or 'addicting' properties of cigarettes" was "common knowledge" (Appellee's Brief in Reply to Appellant's Opposition to Petition for Transfer, *Rogers v. R. J. Reynolds Tobacco Co. et al.*, 557 N.E.2d 1045 [Ind. Ct. App. 1990], [No. 49A02–8904-CV–164]).

228 **S. J. Green:** The Green documents, many personal ruminations and informal notes to colleagues, included "Smoking, Associated Diseases and Causality," "The Association of Smoking and Disease," and "B.A.T. Group Research; Research Problems and Policy," 9 April 1968.

   Lots of lawyers: Christopher Hird, reporter's notes of Green interview, February 1981.

229 **Think of the cigarette:** William L. Dunn, PM report, "Motives and Incentives in Cigarette Smoking," November 1981, PM ID 2056121547–64, at 51.

Videotaped deposition: Deposition of William Dunn by Mark Edell in *Cipollone* case, 20 November 1987.

232   Two-hour meeting: Author interviews with Doyle and Light, 1 April 1998, and Zeller, 11 April 1998. See also PM meeting notes, "Memorandum on FDA Interview of Dr. Dunn," 10 May 1994, PM ID 2023918978–93.

Chapter Thirty-one

233   Bio: FDA interviews with "Bio," informant, 8 June 1994 and 21 December 1995.
      Electroencephalography: FDA interview with "Bio," 8 June 1994, p. 5.
234   Frank Gullotta: FDA interviews with "Bio," 8 June 1994 and 21 December 1995.
      Brain patterns: F. P. Gullotta, C. S. Hayes, and B. R. Martin, PM memo to H. L. Spielberg, "Electrophysiological and Subjective Effects of Cigarettes Delivering Varying Amounts of Nicotine," 21 August 1990, PM ID 2025986595–601. See also PM report, "Protocol Summary for Testing of Cigarettes with Various Levels of Nicotine Delivery," 12 April 1994, PM ID 2050975543–44. Technologically complex: PM report, "Summary of Research Conducted at Philip Morris by Frank Gullotta," 1994, PM ID 2028812433–40; PM chart, "Human Smoking Behavior," PM ID 2500126796–862. Acceptable low-tar: F. P. Gullotta, C. S. Hayes, and B. R. Martin, PM memo to C. K. Ellis, "Raison d'etre," 8 November 1990, PM ID 2028813366–68, at 66. In this memo Gullotta wrote, "We have shown that there are optimal cigarette nicotine deliveries for producing the most favorable physiological and behavioral responses.... Our laboratory has demonstrated that all forms of nicotine are not behaviorally or physiologically equal. This observation is important for evaluating research cigarettes where the addition of nicotine is necessary."
234   INBIFO: FDA interview with "Bio," 8 June 1994, p. 64. The name INBIFO is a contraction of the name Institut für Biologische Forschung (Institute for Biological Research).
      EEG research: H. Wakeham, PM memo to C. H. Goldsmith, "Acquisition of INBIFO," 7 April 1970, PM ID 2022244451. INBIFO offered "a locale where we might do some of the things which we are reluctant to do in this country." One advantage was that "[e]xperiments can be terminated at will or required without delay" (PM report, "INBIFO," 11 October 1979, PM ID 1002974049–80, at 52). The company had thought about a similar strategy a decade earlier, when it considered shifting the animal laboratory run by Victor DeNoble and Paul Mele abroad, where the work could be more easily concealed. The scientists were consulted about the layout of a new laboratory in Germany, but the move was abandoned. Top-secret research: PM report, "INBIFO," 11 October 1979, PM ID 1002974049–80. Ship all documents: PM note, PM ID 1000130803.
235   Dead ends: Tom Doyle and Gary Light tracked down William Osdene, PM's retired director of research. The man was a master of evasion, willing to talk only about a volcano model, part of his son's science project at school, perched on his living-room table. When the investigators asked Osdene whether he had been born in England, he told them that there were no volcanoes in Great Britain. When they asked about his work as a cancer researcher in Dallas, he told them that there were no volcanoes in Texas either. When they asked him a ques-

tion about carcinogens, he started talking about the eruption of Vesuvius in A.D. 79. The meeting was as frustrating as it was unprofitable. See author interview with Light and Doyle, 1 April 1998.

235 **"PC":** FDA interviews with "PC," informant, 31 May 1994; 8 June 1995. Author interviews with Doyle and Light, 14 April 1998, and "PC," 14 May 1998; "PC" affidavit, 5 August 1994.

    Toxic solvents: "PC" maintained lists of the solvents she was evaluating. See "PC" notes, 29 August and 13 September 1991; FDA draft summary, "The Smoking of Ink Solvent Compounds by Brown & Williamson Sensory Panels."

236 **Odd taste:** B&W meeting reports, "Stale / Odd Taste in Kool / 236," 23 April 1986, and "Kool Stale Taste" / 236," 13 June 1986; B&W reports, "Microbiological Investigations Related to the Stale Kool Problem," 29 September 1986, and "Primer on Determining the Origins of Off–Taste Problems," 27 October 1987; B&W note, "What We Have Collectively Learned About Kool's 'Stale Taste' / 236," 19 June 1986.

236 **Cigarettes injected:** D. V. Cantrell, B&W memo to T. F. Riehl, "Packaging Solvents / 236," 24 October 1986; R. A. Gonterman, B&W memos to T. F. Riehl et al., "Domestic Product Development Status Report–August / 393," 10 September 1991, and "Domestic Product Development Status Report–September / 393," 2 October 1991; R. H. Honeycutt, B&W memo to B. A. Reasor, "Consumer Inquiry Odd Taste Investigation–Tax Stamp Inks / 130," 8 November 1991; B&W meeting reports, "Consumer Inquiries Steering Committee / 130," 11 November 1991, and "Residual Solvent Task Force Meeting / 130," 2 January 1992; B&W notes, "Ambient Aging Study of Best Candidate / 327," 11 November 1991, and "Determination of Packaging Solvents on Cigarettes / 162," 28 January 1992.

236 **Jeffrey Wigand:** Statement to FDA by "PC," 5 August 1994; FDA interview with Wigand, 1 June 1994.

236 **Critical:** FDA interview with "Critical," informant, 21 April 1994. Author interview with "Critical," 12 September 2000; PM report, "Extended Smoking Test of Doral Lights v. ART AB," October 1987, PM ID 2057044481–83; Kathleen Bates, PM memo to Melissa Jeltema, "Extended Smoking Test of Doral Lights v. the ART AB Sample," 24 July 1987, PM ID 2057724010–15.

237–238 **Saint:** FDA interviews with "Saint," informant, 25 and 26 April, and 7 July 1994. Author interview with "Saint," 12 September 2000.

    Supercritical extraction: FDA interview with "Saint," 26 April 1994. **Flavors and odorants:** Ibid., p. 26. **List of carcinogens:** Ibid., p. 98.

Chapter Thirty-two

239 **Patent application:** "New Variety of Tobacco Plant" (U.S. patent no. 761,312); patent was applied for on 17 September 1991; the claims were rejected on 10 July 1992; an appeal was filed on 28 February 1994; it was abandoned on 16 March 1994.

240 **Tim Long:** Author interview with Long, 17 May 1998.

240 **Proof, usable proof:** Souza Cruz Overseas shipment to B&W, 21 September 1992, shipping entry no. 014–1200134–7.

241 **B&W's arrival:** FDA transcript of B&W meeting, 17 June 1994.

Chapter Thirty-three

245   **Show up:** Author interview with Schlagenhauf, 23 March 1998.

245   **Laying out the Y-1 story:** House Committee on Energy and Commerce, Subcommittee on Health and the Environment, hearing, *Regulation of Tobacco Products (Part 3)*, 103rd Cong., 2d sess., 21 June 1994, Serial No. 103-71.

246   **Consumer preference studies:** BAT report, "Consumer Perception of Product Quality," B&W ID 581109368–84.

246   **Going on:** Author interview with Schlagenhauf, 23 March 1998.

248   **Not in a position:** David A. Kessler, letter to Congressman Henry Waxman, 20 June 1994.

249   **Pfeifer offered:** Author interview with Mitchell, 10 May 1998.

249   **RJR had drafted:** B. C. W. Leonard, RJR draft questions, "Must Ask Questions," 20 June 1994, RJR ID 515903356–96.

249   **Hearing checklist:** M. Firestone, PM memo to M. Bring et al., "Kessler Hearing Checklist," June 1994, PM ID 2023195342–43.

Chapter Thirty-four

251   **Fox DeMoisey:** Jack Mitchell, FDA notes, 11 March 1994.

252   **Secure the documents:** The chain of events that put the documents in the hands of the *New York Times* began with an anonymous fax to Donald Barrett, an attorney who was part of the Mississippi legal team that was filing the first state lawsuit to recoup the state's Medicaid costs for tobacco-related illness. Barrett tracked down the sender, Merrell Williams, and persuaded him to fly to Jackson, Mississippi.

     After weeks of subsequent telephone conversations, Williams finally agreed to turn over his papers to Barrett and his colleague, Richard Scruggs. Barrett then contacted the ABC News journalist Keith Summa. Summa and the ABC producer Walt Bogdanich pursued the story, but the network refused to touch it without a source who was willing to be named. Barrett then showed samples of the documents to the attorneys involved in *Castano v. American Tobacco Co.*, the first-ever federal class action lawsuit against the tobacco companies, which was filed in New Orleans.

     Soon, a box arrived at the office of Joshua Kardon, chief of staff to Congressman Ron Wyden, who shared its contents with a Waxman aide, Ripley Forbes. Shortly afterwards Kardon said to Philip Hilts, "I have something for you."

252   **Stolen documents:** Author interview with Hilts, 2 February 1998, p. 62.

252   **Addison Yeaman:** A. Yeaman, B&W memo, "Implications of Battelle Hippo I and II and the Griffith Filter," 17 July 1963.

253   **Intent to Deceive:** Merrell Williams, *Intent to Deceive*, working draft, January 1993.

253   **Beneficent drug:** Charles Ellis, "The Smoking and Health Problem," *Smoking and Health—Policy on Research* (Southampton, England: BAT Research Conference, 1962), pp. 15–16.

254   **Handwritten notes:** Mitchell Zeller and Ann Witt, FDA notes, "Master Summary of B&W Document Review," May 1994.

255   **Project Janus:** At my request, Bern Schwetz, the FDA's associate commissioner for science, reviewed the Project Janus studies and told me just how much the industry knew. "The carcinogenic potential of cigarette smoke condensates was

confirmed in the early studies of this series of experiments" (Bern Schwetz, FDA memo to FDA commissioner, 3 January 1995).

255 **Maximum nicotine:** R. B. Griffith, "Report to the Executive Committee," with attached note, 1 July 1965.

255 **Libel action:** J. Kendrick Wells III (B&W), letter to Jonathan W. Lubell (Morrison, Cohen, Singer & Weinstein), 25 May 1994, B&W ID 689105375–81; Arlene R. Smoler, memo to Michael J. McGraw and J. Kendrick Wells III, "Allegation of 'Lying' as a Basis for Commencing a Defamation Action," 11 June 1994, B&W ID 689105408–17.

255 **Broke the lock:** Jack Mitchell, FDA memo, Texas archival files, 1 May 1995.

256 **Research reports:** FDA document summary, "Mitchell Index of DOC Files."
     Alpha brain waves: W. L. Dunn, "Summary of Projects in Smoker Psychology Program," 9 May 1974, PM ID 1003288125–26. **Mental concentration:** W. L. Dunn et al., "Smoker Psychology Program," 6 June 1974, PM ID 1001521338–40. **Puffing behavior:** F. J. Ryan, "Summary of Projects in Smoker Psychology Program," 9 May 1974, PM ID 1003288125–26. **Nicotine control:** "Project 0302/Nicotine Control as Related to Cigarette Acceptability," 20 December 1962, PM ID 1001900308–10. **Inject subjects:** W. L. Dunn, PM memo to T. S. Osdene, "Plans and Objectives—1981," 26 November 1980, PM ID 1003293130–37. **Total nicotine:** W. L. Dunn, PM memo to T. S. Osdene, "Plans and Objectives—1979," 6 December 1978, PM ID 1003293151–59. **Aggressive monkeys:** W. L. Dunn and F. J. Ryan, "Project 1600 Consumer Psychology, July 16 – August 15, 1970," 1 September 1970, PM ID 1003288241–42. **Hyperkinetic child:** W. L. Dunn, PM memo to T. S. Osdene, "Quarterly Report, July 1 – Sept. 30, 1975," 26 September 1975, PM ID 1003287972–75. **Shock treatments:** F. J. Ryan, PM memo to W. L. Dunn, "Proposed Research Project: Smoking and Anxiety," 23 December 1969.

256–257 **Deliberately invisible**
     Bury it: W. L. Dunn, PM memo to T. S. Osdene, "Proposed Study by Levy," 3 November 1977, PM ID 2046754690. **Smoker's psychology:** W. L. Dunn, PM report, "Smoker Psychology Program Review," 19 October 1977, PM ID 2060564018–26. **Where the action is** and **clandestine:** W. L. Dunn, PM memo to R. B. Seligman, "The Nicotine Receptor Program," 21 March 1980, PM ID 1000127789–90. **Dangerous FDA implications:** W. L. Dunn, PM memo to H. Wakeham, "Jet's Money Offer," 19 February 1969, PM ID 1003289921–22.

258 **Target dose:** Claude E. Teague Jr., RJR memo, "Research Planning Memorandum on Some Thoughts About New Brands of Cigarettes for the Youth Market," 2 February 1973, RJR ID 502987357–68. One of the key principles of pharmacology is that a drug's effectiveness is tied to its dose. Too small a dose and the drug is ineffective; too large and it is potentially toxic. A number of documents underscored the industry's interest in finding the optimal level of nicotine. "Goal—Determine the minimum level of nicotine that will allow continued smoking" (Richard E. Smith, Lorillard memo to J. R. Ave et al., 13 February 1980, Lorillard ID 01394380–81, at 80); "Determine minimum nicotine to keep normal smoker "hooked," R.A. Tamol, P.M. employee notes, 1 February 1965."Maintenance of the smoking habit demands that smokers receive an 'adequate' dose of nicotine" (BAT document, BAT ID 105082406); "Define the optimum nicotine level in cigarette smoke required to maximize smoker satisfaction. Determine the existence

of a minimum or threshold value of nicotine required for satisfaction" (D. H. Piehl, RJR memo to Alan Rodgman, "Nicotine and Smoker Satisfaction," 4 January 1978, RJR ID 504701645–50, at 45); "The physiological response to nicotine can readily be elicited by cigarettes delivering in the range of 1 mg of nicotine" (William Dunn, "Motives and Incentives in Cigarette Smoking," 1972, p.4); "The minimum amount of nicotine necessary to produce pharmacological effects is referred to as the threshold level to satisfy 'nicotine need'" (William Dunn, PM memo to T. S. Osdene, "Plans and Objectives, 1979," 6 December 1978); "Objective: To select an intravenous dose of nicotine that will (1) produce peak plasma concentration between 20 and 40 ng/ml..." (J. Don DeBethizy, RJR research study description, "Intravenous Dose Selection," 17 February 1987, RJR ID 505856230).

258   **Claude Teague:** Claude E. Teague Jr., RJR report, "Research Planning Memorandum on the Nature of the Tobacco Business and the Crucial Role of Nicotine Therein," 14 April 1972, RJR ID 500898378–86. A decade before us, industry attorneys reviewed internal documents, including some by Teague, and deemed them "problematic" (Jones, Day, Reavis & Pogue, "Corporate Activity Project," draft, B&W ID 681879254–715, at 616).

260   **Nicotine manipulation:** One industry document summarized the methods for increasing nicotine "kick": "increasing the amount of (strong) burley in the blend ...reduction of casing sugar on the burley and/or blend...use of alkaline additives, usually ammonia...addition of nicotine to the blend...removal of acids from the blend...special filter systems to remove acids from or add alkaline materials to the smoke and...use of high air dilution filter systems" (Claude E. Teague Jr., RJR memo to W. D. Hobbs, "Implications and Activities Arising from Correlation of Smoke pH with Nicotine Impact on the Smoke Qualities and Cigarette Sales," 10 October 1972, RJR ID 509314122–54, at 27). See also the document that states that one of the industry's objectives was to: "[i]mprove our ability to make better use of current nicotine levels in smoke...[d]evise means of 'making smaller amounts of nicotine work harder ...'" (BAT document, BAT ID 105082406). Manipulation did not always involve increasing nicotine levels. Some types of tobacco contained more nicotine than the industry could use. R. J. Reynolds's 605 processing plant, for example, steamed and ammoniated burley, a hard, high-nicotine form of tobacco, to achieve nicotine levels "meeting the consumer needs." In the heyday of the process, 25 percent of all tobacco used in the manufacture of the company's cigarettes was treated at the facility. See RJR document, "Long Range Plan—605 Processing," RJR ID 511904495–503, at 495).

For more on nicotine manipulation, see RJR document, "New Technologies—Tobacco Blending: Nicotine Control," RJR ID 504216637–38; R. N. Wiley, PM memo to R. E. Blackmore, "High Nicotine to T.P.M. Ratio..." 19 March 1962, PM ID 1001885914–15; C. L. Neumann and T. A. Perfetti, RJR memo to J. P. Dickerson, "Optimum T/N and Product Recommendations for Nicotine Control," 18 March 1982, RJR ID 512974263–71; Frank C. Colby, RJR memo to R. A. Blevins Jr., "Cigarette Concept to Assure RJR a Larger Segment of the Youth Market," 4 December 1973, RJR ID 501166152–53; J. P. Dickerson, RJR memo to D. H. Piehl, "Nicotine Control, Ammoniation Strategy," 29 December 1981, RJR ID 512973998; RJR presentation, "Nicotine Control Program," 13 March 1990, RJR ID 512335552–72; Alan

Rodgman, RJR memo to A. H. Laurene and R. H. Cundiff, "Nicotine and Smoking Satisfaction," 5 January 1978, RJR ID 504701644.

Chapter Thirty-five

263–264   **Scientific forum:** FDA Drug Abuse Advisory Committee, transcripts of FDA meetings, 1 and 2 August 1994, in Silver Spring, Md., "Abuse Liability Assessment of Nicotine Nasal Spray" and "Issues Concerning Nicotine-Containing Cigarettes and Other Tobacco Products."

   On the attack: "FDA Talking Points," August 1994, PM ID 2047774763; Victor Han, PM draft memo, "FDA meeting," 26 July 1994, PM ID 2045691544–46.

264   **Paper dump:** "Submission of Philip Morris USA and the American Tobacco Company to the Drug Abuse Advisory Committee [DAAC] in Connection with Its Meeting on 2 August 1994," 29 July 1994, vol. 1.

   Pinball wizard: Ibid., p. 38. **Can carrots:** Ibid., p. 20. **Running addiction:** Ibid., p. 21.

265   **Expert witnesses:** Yumiko Ono and Suein L. Hwang, "Tobacco Dream Team: Experts Who Insist Nicotine Isn't Addictive," *Wall Street Journal*, 23 March 1995, p. B1.

265   **Private conversation:** Author interview with Ciraulo.

266   **After the meeting:** To counter the media barrage, PM planned to tell newspaper editorial boards, "Kessler is grand standing, playing to media, following personal/political agenda, diverting attention from other issues such as AIDS, breast implant fiasco, medical device backlog" (Victor Han, PM memo to Steven Parrish et al., "WP Editorial Board Meeting," 10 August 1994, PM ID 2047720659–60). The industry also forwarded copies of statements from supposedly independent researchers to congressional staff. See David Nicoli (PM), letters to congressional staffers in the offices of Congressmen Thomas Bliley, Alex McMillan, and Wendell Ford, 5 August 1994 (PM ID 2047992940–43, 2047992947–50, 2047992952–53, 2047992994–95). See also PM report, "Deliberations of the DAAC," 2 August 1994, PM ID 2040401664–77.

266   **Restricted devices:** 21 U.S.C. §520 (e) (1994), the restricted-device provision of the Federal Food, Drug, and Cosmetic Act.

267   **Airlie House:** Kevin Budich, FDA meeting notes, 21 July 1994.

269   **Embroiled:** Author interview with Wilkenfeld, 27 November 1997.

   Iron-clad case: Two years after deciding against undertaking a suit, the FTC charged on 28 May 1997 that the Joe Camel advertising campaign did, in fact, violate federal law. The FTC dismissed its own case on 27 January 1999, deciding that the relief it sought for "unfair and unlawful marketing" had been accomplished by the settlement between the state attorneys general and the industry.

Chapter Thirty-six

273   **George Washington Hill:** Edward L. Bernays, *Biography of an Idea: Memoirs of Public Relations Counsel* (New York: Simon & Schuster, 1965); Larry Tye, *The Father of Spin: Edward L. Bernays and the Birth of Public Relations* (New York: Crown, 1998).

274   **Elegance and glamour** and **earthy:** Hugh Bain Research, "The Psychology of Significant Moments and Peak Experiences in Cigarette Smoking: The Motivations

and Semiological Significance of Smoking," report prepared for B&W, November 1993, B&W ID 500287512–96, at 31.

274   **Segment of the female market:** C. I. Humphrey and C. W. Willoughby, AT memo to R. E. Smith, "New Female Brand," 29 October 1993, AT ID 970357877–79, at 78.

274   **Poorly educated:** RJR report, "Less-Educated, Today's Trend, Tomorrow's Market???," RJR ID 502753458–66.

274   **More neurotic:** R. E. Thornton, BAT "restricted" research report, "The Smoking Behaviour of Women," 12 November 1976, B&W ID 776193337–65.

274–275   **Slim cigarette:** "All cigarettes targeted to women have similar product characteristics. The six major female brands all have reduced circumference (Slim or Super Slim) and extra length (100's and 120's)" (C. I. Humphrey and C. W. Willoughby, AT memo to R. E. Smith, "New Female Brand," 29 October 1993, AT ID 970357877–79, at 77).

     Increased transfer: W. D. E. Irwin, BAT report, "The Effects of Cigarette Circumference Change on Nitrosamine Deliveries," report no. RD 2120, 19 July 1988, B&W ID 620000151–71.

275   **Marketing strategies:** Nancy Kaufman and Mimi Nichter, "The Influence of Media, Fashion and Promotion: Effects of Tobacco Use by Women and Girls," presentation at the World Health Organization International Conference on Tobacco and Health, 14–18 November 1999, Kobe, Japan; Virginia L. Ernster, "Mixed Messages for Women: A Social History of Cigarette Smoking and Advertising," *New York State Journal of Medicine* 85:332–40 (July 1985); Virginia L. Ernster, "How Tobacco Companies Target Women," presentation at the Interagency Committee on Smoking and Health, October 1990, condensed and reprinted in *World Smoking and Health* (American Cancer Society) 16(2):8–11 (1991); Norbert Hirschhorn, "British American Tobacco Documents in the Minnesota Depository: Focus on Women," briefing paper no. 14, July 1999.

275   **Influential women's groups:** Myron Levin, "The Tobacco Industry's Strange Bedfellows," *Business and Society Review* 65: 11–17 (Spring 1988); Marjorie Williams, "Tobacco's Hold on Women's Groups; Anti-Smokers Charge Leaders Have Sold Out to Industry Money," *Washington Post*, 14 November 1991, p. A1; Marjorie Williams, "The Funding Habit Women's Groups Can't Resist," *Washington Post*, 14 November 1991, p. A16.

     Intensive discussions: Susan Stuntz, TI memo to Peter Sparber, August 12, 1986, first cited by Myron Levin, "Women, Blacks Courted; Big Tobacco Buying New Friendships," *Los Angeles Times*, May 22, 1988. p. 1. At a Philip Morris workshop, Jeannine Dowling, a company official, laid out PM's involvement with political, professional, and activist women's organizations in detail. The political groups, she said, were "the most obvious targets for us in terms of giving us an immediate return." For example, the company sponsored fellowships organized by the Congressional Caucus for Women's Issues, which sometimes led the fellows to jobs with members of Congress. "You can't ask for better access," commented Dowling. Among the targeted professional organizations, Philip Morris sponsored a leadership training program for Hispanic women through the Cora Foundation and an awards program for the National Association of Negro Business and Professional Women. Dowling noted that the "payoff" came when the president of NANBPW went to Washington to testify on Philip Morris's behalf. Finally, the company supported activist groups, including the Women's Equity Action League. That, too, "paid off very nicely. . . . When we have a problem as we did on the excise tax, we can call them." See transcript of PM workshop, "Dealing with the Issues Indirectly: Constituencies," 13 September 1984, Rye Brook, N.Y., PM ID 2025421934–2000.

275   **Base of our business:** T. L. Atchey, Lorillard memo to Curtis Judge, "Product Information," 30 August 1978, Lorillard ID 03537131–32.

275   **Eight hundred industry documents:** "Index to Authors and Corporate Sources," National Clearinghouse on Tobacco and Health, Ottawa, Canada. See also "Selected Excerpts from Imperial Tobacco Limited Internal Documents," National Clearinghouse on Tobacco and Health, Canada, January 1992.

        Project 16: Kwechansky Marketing Research Inc., report for Imperial Tobacco Ltd., 18 October 1977. **Plus/Minus:** Kwechansky Marketing Research Inc., report for Imperial Tobacco Ltd., 7 May 1982, RJR ID 502987357–68.

277   **Addiction's grip:** Ellen Walker, *Smoker: Self-Portrait of a Nicotine Addict* (St. Augustine, Fla.: Hazelden, 1989).

277–278   **Claude Teague**

        Developing self-image and **survive and prosper:** Claude E. Teague Jr., RJR report, "Research Planning Memorandum on Some Thoughts About New Brands of Cigarettes for the Youth Market," 2 February 1973, RJR ID 502987357–68, at 58 and 64. **Fourteen-to-eighteen-year-old:** RJR Research Department report, "Planning Assumptions and Forecast for the Period 1976–1986 for R. J. Reynolds Tobacco Co," 15 March 1976, RJR ID 501630269–88, at 83. **Attract the nonsmoker:** Claude E. Teague Jr., RJR report, "Research Planning Memorandum on the Nature of the Tobacco Business and the Crucial Role of Nicotine Therein," 14 April 1972, RJR ID 500898378–86, at 82.

278–279   **Young Adult Smokers initiative:** FDA interview with "Doc," informant, 11 August 1994, pp. 96, 100–4.

        Identify stores: J. P. McMahon, RJR memo to sales representatives, "Young Adult Market," 10 January 1990. **Article:** "Tobacco Critics See a Subtle Sell to Kids," *Wall Street Journal,* 3 May 1990, p. B1. **Oklahoma:** R. G. Warlick, RJR memo to sales representatives, "Young Adult Market SIS Account Grouping," 5 April 1990.

279–281   **Beach:** FDA interview with informant, 8 September 1994.

        Belcher: FDA interview with informant, 15 December 1994. **Bama:** FDA interview with informant. **Bud:** FDA interview with informant. **FUBYAS:** FDA interview with "Bud," pp. 6–8. **Shaw:** FDA interview with informant, 30 November 1994.

281   **90 percent:** *Preventing Tobacco Use Among Young People: A Report of the Surgeon General* (Washington, D.C.: Government Printing Office, 1994), p. 65.

Chapter Thirty-seven

282   **Tobacco interests:** "I am writing to ask your support for Drew Edmondson" (letters from William Campbell [PM] to Andrew Tisch [Lorillard] and others, 10 June 1992, PM ID 2060370887, 2022849721, 2057174641); contribution solicitation,

"Edmondson for Congress ... Paid for by PHIL-PAC, the Philip Morris Political Action Committee ...," PM ID 2060370888).

Juxtaposing: Author interviews with Weiss, 10 December 1998, and Varma, 29 January 1999. **Out of a job:** Synar "became the first Democrat to fall in the '94 GOP tidal wave, losing his primary bid to a 71-year-old retired teacher with no political experience. The National Rifle Association proudly took partial credit for the defeat" (Lois Romano, *Washington Post,* 15 January 1996, p. C1).

285 **Bully and a thug:** *Dateline NBC,* transcript of broadcast, 15 November 1994.

286 **$600,000:** Michael Isikoff et al., "Of Tobacco, Torts and Tusks," *Newsweek,* 28 November 1994, p. 30.

286 **Payback was at hand:** John Schwartz, "Change Is in the Air for Tobacco Industry," *Washington Post,* 11 November 1994, p. A1.

Progress and Freedom Foundation: Peter H. Stone, "Ganging up on the FDA," *National Journal,* 18 February 1995. **Competitive Enterprise Institute:** Philip J. Hilts, "FDA Becomes Target of Empowered Groups," *New York Times,* 12 February 1995, p. 24. **Washington Legal Foundation:** PM considered WLF "a significant ally on many of the issues of interest to us" and proposed to "seriously consider increasing our contribution" (Charles R. Wall, PM memo to Mark Bodden, "Washington Legal Foundation," 21 July 1993). WLF was grateful: "Thanks for your support. You can be assured that WLF will continue to alert the free enterprise community to emerging legal trends of immense consequence." (Daniel J. Popeo [WLF] to Roy Marden [PM], 6 May 1994, PM ID 2024687311).

286 **Dump Kessler:** James Bovard, "First Step to an FDA Cure: Dump Kessler," *Wall Street Journal,* 8 December 1994, p. A18.

287 **Bliley:** William Schultz, FDA notes of discussions with Congressman Tom Bliley and Bliley's staff, 1, 9, 14, and 28 February 1995 and 10 March 1995.

288 **Fundraising needs:** Kathleen M. Linehan, PM memo to William Campbell, "Charlie Rose Request to Host Leadership America PAC Fundraiser in New York on May 23," 12 April 1994, PM ID 2025767629.

288 **Your scalp:** William Hubbard, FDA notes, 26 April 1995.

289 **Detailed request:** Congressman Charlie Rose, letter to David A. Kessler, 24 June 1994. A follow-up letter was sent to me on 27 October 1994, and to Secretary Shalala on 14 December 1994.

289 **Environmental Protection Agency:** Congressman Charlie Rose, letter to Carol Browner (EPA), 23 June 1994; I compared this to the legal document Plaintiff's First Request for Production of Documents, *Flue-Cured Tobacco Cooperative Stabilization Corp. et al. v. EPA,* No. 6:93CV370 (M.D.N.C., filed 20 July 1994).

Outside counsel: "This is what is being sent to Rep. Rose for his review and, hopefully, transmittal to the FDA" (Arnold & Porter, fax cover sheet with draft letter attached, 7 June 1994, RJR ID 515786099–107, at 99).

289 **Thomas Ewing:** Congressman Thomas Ewing, letter to David A. Kessler, 30 May 1995.

Unsatisfied: "We delivered a draft letter to Kessler from Ewing renewing his demand for documents from FDA that Rose requested last year and that Ewing renewed in May, which of course Kessler has ignored" (David Nicoli, PM e-mail, "AG Committee FDA Hearings," 12 September 1995, PM ID 2047027206C). A follow-up letter from Ewing to me was sent 30 October 1995.

289 **General Accounting Office:** Congressmen Thomas Ewing and Charlie Rose, letter to Charles A. Browsher (General Accounting Office), 28 November 1995.

   FDA's approach: General Accounting Office, *Food and Drug Administration: Regulation of Tobacco Products* (Washington, D.C.: General Accounting Office, September 1997).

290 **Shill:** Congressman Charlie Rose and his counsel, Heidi Pender, focused on the tobacco farmers of their district. "They've been growing the products, and they don't understand why they've suddenly became the devil," Pender told me (author interview with Pender). Philip Morris understood Rose's complex view of the industry: "Charlie Rose is Mr. Tobacco" and "has committed himself to us in the future," but "... tobacco-state congressmen are creatures of *their* constituents, *not* the cigarette manufacturers.... The producers' view [of] the manufacturers will determine the willingness of their representatives to act on our behalf" (Gregory R. Scott, PM memo to Gene A. Knorr, "Rebuilding Our Relationship with Tobacco-State Congressmen," 25 August 1986, PM ID 2025854686–89).

Chapter Thirty-eight

292 **3 million young people:** *Preventing Tobacco Use Among Young People: A Report of the Surgeon General* (Washington, D.C.: Government Printing Office, 1994), p. 5.

292 **516 million packs:** J. R. DiFranza and J. B. Tye, "Who Profits from Tobacco Sales to Children?" *Journal of the American Medical Association* 263(20):2784–87 (1990); K. M. Cummings, T. Pechacek, and D. Shopland, "The Illegal Sale of Cigarettes to U.S. Minors: Estimates by State," *American Journal of Public Health* 84(2):300–302 (1994).

292 **Withdrawal symptoms:** "Reasons for Tobacco Use and Symptoms of Nicotine Withdrawal Among Adolescents and Young Adult Tobacco Users—United States, 1993," *Morbidity and Mortality Weekly Report* 43(41):745–50 (1994).

292 **Corporate marketing:** Imperial Tobacco Ltd., marketing plan, "Overall Marketing Objectives," 1988, p. 6.

292 **Three thousand children:** John P. Pierce et al., "Trends in Cigarette Smoking in the United States," *Journal of the American Medical Association* 261(1):61–65 (6 January 1989).

292 **Total marketing:** FTC report, "Report to Congress for 1993, Pursuant to the Federal Cigarette Labeling and Advertising Act," 1995, Tables 3 and 3D.

292 **Joe Camel:** Youth smoking data on Camel cigarettes is described in Barbara S. Lynch and Richard J. Bonnie, eds., *Growing Up Tobacco Free: Preventing Nicotine Addiction in Children and Youths* (Washington, D.C.: National Academy Press, 1994), pp. 70–71. R. J. Reynolds, seeking to "youthen the brand," first introduced the "Joe Camel" cartoon in France. See James S. Carpenter, RJR memo to RJR Tobacco Brand Management, "'Funny' French Camel Design," 5 March 1985, RJR ID 506768857. "I think the French advertisement for Camel Filters is a smash. It would work equally well, if not better, for Camel Regular. It's about as young as you can get, and aims right at the young adult smoker Camel needs to attract" (Dana Blackmar, RJR memo, "French Camel Filter Ad," 7 February 1974, RJR ID 502303940).

293 **Gallup poll:** Gallup Organization, survey conducted for the Coalition on Smoking or Health, "The Public's Attitudes Toward the Regulation and Advertising of Cigarettes," April 1993.

294 **Evening meetings:** Author interviews with Burke, 18 May 1998; Cooley, 3 April 1998; Eriksen, 29 December 1997; Feder, 12 March 1998; Giovino, 27 February 1998; Klepner, 1 February 1998; Lorraine, 6 March 1998; Natanblut, 8 February 1998; O'Hara, 12 March 1998; Rabb, 31 January 1998; Schultz, 3 February and 3 March 1998; Thurm, 13 January 1998; White, 10 April 1998; Wilkenfeld, 8 February 1998; and Zeller, 28 February 1998.

296 **Data-driven:** It helped to be able to present a Robert Wood Johnson (hereinafter cited as RWJ) Foundation survey that revealed strong public support for limitations on youth access to tobacco, including proof-of-age requirements for cigarette purchases, restrictions on advertising designed to appeal to children, and a ban on cigarette vending machines. See Richard Strouse and John Hall, "Youth Access Survey: Results of a National Household Survey to Assess Public Attitudes About Policy Alternatives for Limiting Minors' Access to Tobacco Products" (Princeton, N.J.: RWJ Foundation, December 1994).

296 **Vending machines:** Response Research, Inc., "Study of Teenage Cigarette Smoking and Purchase Behavior" (Chicago, Ill.: National Automatic Merchandising Association, June–July 1989), p. 23.

296 **Event sponsorship:** RJR's comment about the FDA's proposed tobacco rule, submitted 2 January 1996, stated, "No matter what FDA might claim, there is no credible evidence that events sponsored by Reynolds are attended, or even seen, by significant numbers of children and adolescents." In fact, 64 million children and adolescents viewed auto racing on television in 1993. See Joyce Julius and Associates, Nielsen National Audience Demographics, "Sponsors Report."

Chapter Thirty-nine

300 **Lancaster:** Congressman H. Martin Lancaster, letter to President William Jefferson Clinton, 18 November 1994.

301 **Mikva and Cerf:** Author interviews with Cerf, December 1997; Mikva, 8 February 1998; and Schultz, 20 January 1998.

    Famous footnote: *Action on Smoking and Health v. Harris*, 655 F.2d 236, 242, n.10 (D.C. Cir. 1980).

302 **Charlie Rose:** Author interviews with Cerf, December 1997; Mikva, 8 February 1998; and Pitts, 5 March 1998. Chris Cerf, White House memo to Leon Panetta, "Overview of Prior Discussion re: Tobacco," 12 June 1995.

302 **Profits have increased:** Ernest Pepples, B&W report, "Industry Response to Cigarette/Health Controversy," 4 February 1976, B&W ID 536102368–77, at 75 and 77.

303 **Al Gore:** Author interview with Mande, 14 January 1998.

304–305 **Dick Morris:** Author interview with Morris, 9 February 1998.

    State lawsuits: Morris's briefing book for the President, 23 March 1995.

305 **Internal divisions:** Author interviews with Griffin, 17 February 1998; Ickes, 9 April 1998; and O'Connor, 17 February 1998.

Chapter Forty

308–309 **Overbearing presence:** Steven Parrish, draft remarks to PM board of directors, "Worldwide Regulatory Affairs: Issues Review, Prospects and Plans," Sea Island, Ga., 29 April 1995, PM ID 2044046538–650.

    Bush backstabber: James Bovard, "Double-Crossing to Safety," *American Spec-*

tator, January 1995, p. 24. **Met with the publisher:** Craig Fuller, PM memo to Bill Murray and Geoff Bible, "Weekly Information Items," 19 August 1994, PM ID 20440410461–62. **Kessler to "Stalin":** Cathy Ellis, PM e-mail to Marc Firestone, "Kessler," 12 December 1994, PM ID 2057069586.

310 **Citizens for a Sound Economy:** Marlene Cimons, "FDA Faces New Pressure to Speed Approval Process for the Record," *Los Angeles Times,* 14 April 1996, p. A1.

    Array of corporate sources: Ken Silverstein, *Washington on $10 Million a Day: How Lobbyists Plunder the Nation* (Monroe, Me.: Common Courage Press, 1998), pp. 121–41; Peter H. Stone, "Grass-Roots Goliath," *National Journal,* 13 July 1996, p. 1529. **Contact CSE:** David Nicoli, PM e-mail to Ellen Merlo et al., *"Roll Call/*FDA-October 9," 26 September 1995, PM ID 2047027442B. **Love to hate:** Silverstein, *Washington on $10 Million a Day,* p. 130. See also interview with Silverstein, 14 May 1998. **Meeting at Philip Morris:** Author interview with Nesbit, 29 June 1998.

311 **Women's issues:** Transcript of PM workshop, "Dealing with the Issues Indirectly: Constituencies," Rye Brook, N.Y., 13 September 1984, PM ID 2025421934–2000.

311 **Strategic options:** David Doak, Strategic Communication Group memo to Linda DiVall and Bob Carpenter, "Message Testing," 26 August 1995, PM ID 2047183610–11; David Bushong, PM memo to David Davies, "FDA Contingency," 14 July 1995, PM ID 2501211618–19; PM notes, "Re: Steven Parrish presentation," December 1994, PM ID 2047720208–15; David Nicoli, PM e-mail to Marc Firestone et al., "Smokers Advocate," 19 July 1995, PM ID 2046620254A; PM budget, "1995 Government/National Media Plan," 8 August 1995, PM ID 2047852617–20; Derek Crawford, PM e-mail to Karen Daragan, "FDA and 3rd Party Spokespeople," 4 August 1995, PM ID 2048328279; Chris Donahue, PM memo to Ellis Woodward, "FDA Mobilization Options," 9 February 1995, PM ID 2047024035–38; David Nicoli, PM report, "FDA Regulation of Tobacco," PM ID 2062526590–91.

311–312 **Stricter controls**

    Bargaining chip: Murray H. Bring, PM memo to Hamish Maxwell, "Smoking and Health," 20 December 1988, PM ID 2015023961–63, at 62. **Strategic thinking:** Murray H. Bring, PM memo to Hamish Maxwell and R. W. Murray, "Project Rainbow," 24 January 1991, PM ID 2048143656–59. **Pent-up demand:** Kathleen M. Linehan, PM memo to R. W. Murray, "Waxman Bill," 6 December 1993, PM ID 2022890917–18, at 17. **Lengthy list:** Kathleen M. Linehan, PM memo to Bill Campbell, "Analysis of Legislative Options Facing the Tobacco Industry in the 103rd Congress," 15 December 1993, PM ID 2022890818–42. **Rainbow compromise:** PM report, "Tobacco Strategy Review," 22 March 1994, PM ID 2048917800–30, at 814. See also PM report, "Rainbow II," PM ID 2022882101–105.

312–313 **Mass mobilization**

    Mass mob: David Nicoli, PM e-mail to Vic Han and Ellen Merlo, "FDA Action Alert Costs," 19 July 1995, PM ID 2046620269. **Expensive:** "Do you have all the money for FDA mob ($2.5 million) in your budget...?" James Spector, PM e-mail to Ellen Merlo, 28 September 1995, PM ID 2047027494B. **$900,000:** Ellen Merlo, PM e-mail to David Nicoli, "FDA Action Alert Costs," 19 July 1995, PM ID 2046620269A. **Separate annual budget:** PM draft budget, "Media Affairs, 1996 Plan and Budget," PM ID 2048226946–48. **Action Against Access:** "Talking Points for Ford, Bliley, et al.," PM ID 2047992385–87; **Libertad:** Minutes of PM staff meetings, 26 August 1986, PM ID 2023270039–40, and 24 October 1986, PM ID

2023270000–001; Tom Hamburger and Greg Gordon, "Tobacco Firm Linked to Travel By Judges," *Star Tribune*, 19 July 1998, p. A1. **Evils of David Kessler:** Craig Fuller, PM memo to Bill Murray and Geoff Bible, "Weekly Corporate Affairs Highlights," 15 July 1994, PM ID 2040410591–97, at 92.

313   **Building project**

     Taj Mahal: Gretchen Lacharite, "FDA Consolidation Plan Hit as a 'Taj Mahal,'" *Washington Times*, 1 February 1995, p. C6. **Kessler's castle:** U.S. Congress, House of Representatives, Congressman Gilchrest's amendment to Congressman Duncan's amendment to the Treasury, Postal Service, and General Government Appropriations Act, 1996, 19 July 1995. The FDA's need for modern, consolidated facilities had been clearly established. One newspaper described the archives building, which was housed in an old chicken coop, and the aquaculture research lab, whose back wall had been eaten away by termites. See Malcolm Gladwell, "Officials Warn: FDA Infrastructure Could Be Hazardous to Its Work," *Washington Post*, 5 June 1991, p. A17. The General Accounting Office (1989) and the General Services Administration (1990) also documented "serious" structural problems.

313   **Boyden Gray**

     Stale critique: Kenneth L. Kaitlin and Elaine M. Healy, "The New Drug Approvals of 1996, 1997, and 1998: Drug Development Trends in the User Fee Era," *Drug Information Journal* 34:1–14 (2000). **Rhetoric:** House Appropriations Committee, Subcommittee on Agriculture, testimony of C. Boyden Gray (chairman, Citizens for a Sound Economy), hearing, 31 January 1995. **Existence of the agency:** House Appropriations Committee, Treasury, Postal Service, and General Government Subcommittee, testimony of C. Boyden Gray, hearing, 21 March 1995.

314–315   **Charlie Edwards:** Senate Committee on Labor and Human Resources, testimony of Charles C. Edwards, hearing, *The FDA and the Future of American Biomedical and Food Industries*, 104th Cong., 1st sess., 5 and 6 April 1995.

     Philip Morris had contacted: Author interview with Edwards, 14 June 1998; PM notes, PM counsel, "Mtg. re: FDA," 5 April 1994. **Persuade me:** PM Action Team notes, 16 March 1994, PM ID 2022838682–83. **Statements matched, verbatim:** The two PM documents containing language matching that used by Edwards were PM ID 2044771450–54 and "Fixing Fundamentals Instead of Treating Symptoms Key to FDA Reform," PM ID 2044771447–49. When I asked Charlie Edwards about his testimony, he said that he "ran it through" Chuck Wall at Philip Morris and others for their input. He also said that the company "was very anxious that I get it [the testimony] published" (author interview with Edwards, 20 October 2000). **Retainer:** "Will you please arrange for payments to Dr. Edwards … [P]ayments should be sent to Dr. Charles Edwards [address given]" (Charles R. Wall, PM memo to Steven C. Parrish, "Retainer Fee for Dr. Charles Edwards," 20 May 1994, PM ID 2047710586). When I told Jane Williams, a member of Senator Nancy Kassebaum's staff, of Edwards's retainer, she said, "I was so naïve."

316   **Our campus:** U.S. Congress, House of Representatives, Congressman Duncan amendment and subsequent debate, Treasury, Postal Service and General Government Appropriations Act, 1996, *Congressional Record*, 19 July 1995.

Contribution checks: "Boehner's Blunder: Handing Out PAC Money Makes a Poor Floor Show, Leader Learns," *Cincinnati Enquirer,* 23 May 1996, p. A18. **Noted with satisfaction:** David Nicoli, PM e-mail to Murray Bring et al., "Round Two on FDA Campus," 19 July 1995, PM ID 2046620272B–73.

317 Strikes all funding: U.S. Congress, House of Representatives, Congressman Bunning amendment and subsequent debate, Agriculture, Rural Development, Food and Drug Administration, and Related Agencies Appropriations Act, 1996, 20 July 1995.

Chapter Forty-one

319 Well-prepared: Ellis Woodward, PM memo to Victor Han et al., "Preparations for Kessler's Speech," 8 March 1995, PM ID 2047035270–72; PM draft radio scripts, 28 February 1995, PM ID 2047035251–62; PM draft press releases, PM ID 2045671901–3.

319–320 Morningside Heights: David A. Kessler, Samuel Rubin Lecture, Columbia Law School, New York, N.Y., 8 March 1995.

It's addictive: E. Shapiro, "Big Spender Finds New Place to Spend," *Wall Street Journal,* 6 October 1994. **Smokeless tobacco:** In 1970, the population group most likely to use smokeless tobacco was over age 50; young men were among the least likely. By 1985, young men were twice as likely as men 50 or older to chew tobacco. See Barbara S. Lynch and Richard J. Bonnie, eds., *Growing Up Tobacco Free: Preventing Nicotine Addiction in Children and Youths,* Washington, D.C.: National Academy Press, 1994, p. 58. "We hope to start a fad," one U.S. Tobacco official said at a marketing meeting (Alix Freedman, "How a Tobacco Giant Doctors Snuff Brands to Boost Their 'Kick,'" *Wall Street Journal,* 26 October 1994, p. A14).

320 Out-of-control whacko: Steven Parrish, PM e-mail to Gregory Scott and Ellis Woodward, "Re: Kessler Speech," 19 October 1995, PM ID 2047028864A.

321 War games: PM draft report, "FDA Crisis Communications Plan," 25 May 1995, PM ID 2045671818–39; Burson-Marsteller simulations, "FDA Scenarios," 29 June 1995, PM ID 2048333400–82; 2047005151–55; 2047005124–44.

Unelected bureaucrat: Chris Donahue, PM memo to Ellis Woodward, "FDA Mobilization Options," 9 February 1995, PM ID 2045672047–50.

321 Bigger impact: The data generated from the National Household Survey on Drug Abuse suggests the onset and course of nicotine addiction. Among adults in their thirties who had ever smoked daily, 82 percent had tried a cigarette before the age of eighteen; 91 percent, before twenty; and 98 percent, before twenty-five. Fifty-three percent began smoking daily before age eighteen; 77 percent, before twenty; and 95 percent, before twenty-five. See *Preventing Tobacco Use Among Young People: A Report of the Surgeon General* (Washington, D.C.: Government Printing Office, 1994), pp. 65–67.

322–323 Morris's suggestions: Author interview with Morris, 9 February 1998.

Throw long: Ibid., pp. 7, 31–32. **One day:** Ibid., p. 2. **Commissioning a poll:** Dick Morris's briefing book for the President, 21 June 1995. **Whole world mad:** Author interview with Morris, 9 February 1998, pp. 39–40.

323 Reinventing government: David Nicoli, PM e-mail, "Article Ideas," 8 August 1995, PM ID 2047027690A.

324 **Eviscerate the government:** President William Jefferson Clinton, "Responsible Citizenship and the American Community," remarks made at Georgetown University, Washington, D.C., 6 July 1995.

324 **Pat Griffin:** Author interview with Griffin, 17 February 1998.

324 **To the White House:** Author interviews with Ickes, 9 April 1998; O'Connor, 17 February 1998; and Leon Panetta, 29 July 1998.

325 **Wants to wait:** A White House memo outlined options for dealing with youth smoking and the pros and cons of each. Although "Do nothing" was on the list, it was deemed "probably not a realistic option." Alternatives included allowing us to publish the tobacco rule, submitting legislation to Congress, or entering into negotiations with the industry. "All strategy options carry the risk of appearing either weak or unduly intrusive ... because of the public climate surrounding this issue, time presses" (Leon Panetta and Harold Ickes, White House memo to the President and vice president, "Reducing Youth Tobacco Use," 14 July 1995).

Chapter Forty-two

332 **Wendell Ford:** Author interviews with Ford, 24 September 2000; Hickman, 16 December 1998; and O'Connor, 17 February 1998.

333 **FDA's proposals:** U.S. Food and Drug Administration, *Regulation of Cigarettes and Smokeless Tobacco Under the Federal Food, Drug, and Cosmetic Act*, volume 1, *Proposed Rule, Jurisdictional Analysis & Appendices, and Related Notices* (Washington, D.C.: Government Printing Office, 1995).

Chapter Forty-three

335 **Prohibition theme:** James Lindheim, Burson-Marsteller memo to Craig Fuller et al., 13 June 1994, PM ID 2051825286A–87, at 86A. Numerous other industry documents show the enthusiasm for this strategy. "Commissioner Kessler is trying to use the youth smoking issue as a Trojan horse to gain jurisdiction over the tobacco industry. His real agenda is prohibition" (PM outline, "FDA Message Points," 12 September 1995, PM ID 2501211638–67, at 43); "Raise the fear of prohibition ... strong base in public opinion ... not a clear and present danger, easily undercut by anti's, easy to lampoon" (PM presentation, "Operation Breakthrough," PM ID 2045657118–40, at 20); "Prohibition will give organized crime a boost as the prohibition against alcohol did in the 1920's" (PM media plan, "Audience and Message," PM ID 2044771400–403, at 402); "Regardless of how FDA regulation is packaged, the net effect will be to prohibit the manufacture and sale of tobacco products" (RJR-prepared sound bite, "Prohibition/Dr. Kessler's Consent to Congress," RJR ID 511404211).

335 **Dietary supplements:** Public concern about the regulation of dietary supplements generated more communications to Congress in 1993 than either health-care reform or the North American Free Trade Act (NAFTA). Although we found evidence of hundreds of products making unsubstantiated claims, passions were inflamed; in one public setting, an angry man shook his fist in Mitch Zeller's face and screamed that the FDA was out to deprive him of his rights as an American. In the fall of 1994, Congress passed the Dietary Supplement Health and Education Act; theoretically there must now be a basis for health claims, but the legal burden of proof falls on the FDA's shoulders.

335   **Hot button rhetoric:** David Nicoli, PM e-mail to Ellis Woodward, 8 August 1995, PM ID 2047027690B.

        Republican pollster: Linda DiVall, PM memo to Marc Firestone, "Key Observations—National Survey #2," 17 August 1995, PM ID 2047010640–43.

336   **What happened?:** Steven C. Parrish, PM presentation to the PM board of directors, "FDA Issues Update," 30 August 1995, PM ID 2047690071–90, at 76 and 90.

336   **Public comment:** The comment period for a federal regulation, which is opened by federal agencies hundreds of times a year, exists to provide concerned citizens with a means of communicating their opinions to their government. Under the Administrative Procedures Act, every substantive comment must be recorded, read, analyzed, and categorized by the FDA.

        Changed the rule: Public comment resulted in several changes to the proposed tobacco rule. Originally we had banned mail-order sales of cigarettes, but we altered that to allow a two-year trial period. Likewise, instead of banning all cigarette vending machines, as we initially proposed, the final rule allowed vending machines where access by minors could be restricted.

337   **Richard Merrill:** In addition to having the signature of Merrill of Covington & Burling, the tobacco industry's comments were signed by Andrew Krulwich for B&W, James Kearney for Liggett Group, Peter Grossi for PM, and Charles Blixt for RJR.

337   **Twenty senators:** David Nicoli, PM e-mail to Marc Firestone et al., "Senate Letter to FDA Docket," 19 December 1995, PM ID 2047014501A.

338   **Reopening:** Three new public comments were added. See Ian L. Uydess, "Declaration of Ian L. Uydess, Ph.D.," 29 February 1996; William A. Farone, "The Manipulation and Control of Nicotine and Tar in the Design and Manufacture of Cigarettes: A Scientific Perspective," 8 March 1996; Jerome K. Rivers, "Declaration of Jerome K. Rivers." 61 *Federal Register*, 11419–20 (7 March 1996).

338   **Confused and pessimistic:** Black, Manafort, Stone & Kelly memo to David Nicoli, "Political Assessment of the Industry," 28 March 1996, PM ID 2047300321–22, at 21.

        Having to vote: John F. Scruggs, PM memo to David Nicoli, "Requested Situation Assessment," 28 March 1996, PM ID 2047300295–97.

340   **Funeral:** At a memorial service in Washington for Mike Synar, President Clinton repeated the words of William Faulkner which Mike had used when he accepted his Profile in Courage Award. "Never be afraid to raise your voice for honesty and truth and compassion against injustice, and lying and greed. If people all over the world would do this, it would change the Earth." And then the President said, "Our good friend, he changed the Earth."

Chapter Forty-four

342   **Enemies:** Though some hate mail was signed and some was anonymous, names are omitted here.

        Hysterical attack: Postcard, postmarked Chicago, 23 June 1994. **Emasculated:** Postcard, postmarked San Diego, April 1994. **Likened me to Hitler:** Letter, "Reich Fuhrer Heir [*sic*] Kessler," postmarked Brookfield, Ill., 24 June 1994; letter to "Dictator Heir [*sic*] D. Kessler," postmarked Brookfield, Ill., 3 August 1994. **Wished me dead:** Letter, postmarked Los Angeles, 28 February 1994, and postcard, postmarked Dallas, 8 August 1994. Not every threat had to do with tobacco. A dying man who thought I was keeping a drug from him wrote, "If I am going to senselessly and needlessly die, I will drag at least 20 of you goddamn killjoy un-American dictator bureau fucks to hell with me.... [Y]ou will not know until the bombs obliterate your building and as many of you FDA fuckers as efficiently possible." He crossed out his return address, but it was readable enough for investigators to see.

342–343 **Medical journal:** Gary L. Huber et al., "The Role of Nicotine in Smoking Behavior," *Seminars in Respiratory and Critical Care Medicine* 16(2):134–54 (March 1995).

Admitted privately: Author interview with Huber, 1 June 1998, pp. 22–23.

343 **Delays in promulgating**

Bilirakis: House Committee on Commerce, Subcommittee on Health and Environment, hearing, 104th Cong., 2d sess., 1 May 1996, Serial No. 104–99. **McConnell:** Senate Committee on Appropriations, Subcommittee on Agriculture, Rural Development and Related Agencies, 104th Cong., 2nd sess., 2 May 1996. **No coincidence:** "FDA's inadequate resources have led to significant delays in its rulemaking process," claimed a PM report (PM ID 2046864857–61, at 57).

343 **Heidi Pender:** Heidi Pender (counsel to Congressman Charlie Rose), draft letter to Donna Shalala (DHHS), 25 October 1996.

Urged the Subcommittee: David Nicoli, PM e-mail to Marc Firestone et al., "AG Committee FDA Hearings," 12 September 1995, PM ID 2047027206C–7.

343 **Looking for dirt:** Tim Friend, "Kessler Travel Investigation Called a Smear," *USA Today*, 21 February 1996, p. 1D.

National Legal and Policy Center: Author interview with Kenneth Boehm. The Washington Legal Foundation and Congressman Joe Barton, whose counsel had worked at the WLF, were also investigating my travel expenses.

344 **Grow tired:** Author interviews with Hilts, 2 and 22 February and 3 May 1998.

344 **They got lips:** Philip J. Hilts, *Smoke Screen: The Truth Behind the Tobacco Industry Cover-up* (Reading, Mass.: Addison-Wesley, 1996), p. 98.

345 **Benson & Hedges:** Philip J. Hilts, "Lawmaker Applies Pressure for Regulation of Nicotine," *New York Times*, 1 August 1995, p. A12.

Don't understand myself: Philip J. Hilts, "Philip Morris Denies Charge by Lawmaker," *New York Times*, 2 August 1995, p. A9.

345 **Dismissed:** Author interviews with Hilts, 2 and 22 February and 3 May 1998, and Parrish, January 1998. Senior PM executives believed that "we got him [Hilts] in trouble with his editor," although subsequent conversations I had with *New York Times* editors persuaded me otherwise.

345 **Going to sue:** Author interview with Liptak, July 1998, p. 4.

346 **Perjury:** Author interviews with Zeller, 23 March and 24 June 1998; *Preliminary Staff Report on Investigation of Sworn Testimony of Mitch Zeller, FDA Deputy Associate Commissioner,* House Committee on Commerce, Subcommittee on Oversight and Investigations, 104th Cong., 2d Sess., March 1996.

Great regret: Congressman Joe Barton (chairman, Subcommittee on Oversight and Investigations), letter to David A. Kessler, 26 March 1996. **Protective seal:** The core of the accusations against Mitch dated back to a telephone call from a lawyer, John Coale, who claimed to possess documents that hinted at wrongdoing by certain FDA officials. Mitch felt obligated to review the charges, and Coale passed along two sets of documents about pedicle screws, a device used in surgery to stabilize the spine. Some of the documents were under a court's protective order, and the subcommittee eventually challenged Mitch's comments about which of them were under court protection. He was also accused of stating falsely that he had no previous dealings with John Coale. The subcommittee's primary evidence of the existence of a personal relationship: the cover letter on Coale's first shipment read, "Dear Mitch."

346   **Abuses of FDA authority:** House Committee on Commerce, Subcommittee on Oversight and Investigations, hearings, *Allegations of FDA Abuses of Authority*, 104th Cong., 1st sess., 25 July, 15 November, and 5 December 1995, Serial No. 104–51.

346–347   **Vendetta:** John Schwartz, "FDA Official's Testimony Questioned; Accusation Is Part of GOP's Harassment of Agency, Critics Say," *Washington Post*, 2 April 1996, p. A11.

      Dropping the case: "No Perjury Evidence Against FDA Official in Pedicle Testimony," *Mealey's Litigation Reports*, 23 August 1996. **Ad hominem:** Author interview with Schlagenhauf, 23 March 1998. **Jennings asked:** *ABC News Report* with Peter Jennings, 27 June 1996. **Secured scheduling:** David Nicoli, PM memo, "Weekly Direct Report," 20 October 1995, PM ID 2047993169–72, at 69.

348   **Complaint:** Summons in a Civil Case, *Deane v. Light & Doe*, C.A. 3:96CV693 (E.D. Va., filed 21 August 1996).

348   **Nothing about the case:** Timothy P. Garren (U.S. Department of Justice [hereinafter cited as DOJ]), letter to Ronald L. Garnett, Esq., 19 September 1996; author interviews with Doyle, 26 February 1998; Light, 8 February 1998; Light and Doyle, 1 March 1998; Taylor, 8 and 18 March 1998; and Zeller, 4 March 1998. See also Gary Light, notes, receipts, travel vouchers, and phone logs; *Deane v. Light & Doe*, C.A. 3:96CV693 (E.D. Va.), depositions of James Dahl (FDA), 8 January 1997; Thomas Doyle, 2 January 1997; George Gross (private investigator), 7 March 1997; John E. Holleran (PM), 13 March 1997; Charles Kelly (private investigator), 7 March 1997; Gary Light, 19 December 1996 and 10 March 1997; Tracy McCloud (Bell Atlantic), 13 March 1997; Richard Priddy (boat co-owner), 13 March 1997; Jerome Rivers (PM), 13 March 1997; Mitchell Zeller, 28 January 1997.

348   **Philip Morris hired:** *Deane v. Light & Doe*, C.A. 3:96CV693 (E.D. Va.), depositions of John E. Holleran, 13 March 1997, pp. 39–41, and Mark Deane, 4 March 1997, pp. 295–96.

      Volunteered: Erwin A. Jack (FBI), notes, 20 May 1996; Ronald L. Garnett (Cooper, Liebowitz, Royster & Wright), letter to Erwin Jack (FBI), 17 May 1996.

350   **Robert R. Merhige:** Transcript of *Deane v. Light & Doe*, C.A. 3:96CV693 (E.D. Va., 25 October 1996).

351   **Company paying all:** *Deane v. Light & Doe*, C.A. 3:96CV693 (E.D. Va.), deposition of John E. Holleran, 13 March 1997, p. 41.

351   **Terms of a dismissal:** Stipulation of Voluntary Dismissal, *Deane v. Light & Doe*, C.A. 3:96CV693 (E.D. Va.), 11 June 1997. Light had the benefit of two of the government's best lawyers, Timothy P. Garren and John Taylor from FDA.

352   **Believe something:** Author conversation with Parrish, 29 February 2000.

Chapter Forty-five

353   **Final rule**: FDA, *Regulation of Cigarettes and Smokeless Tobacco Under the Federal Food, Drug, and Cosmetic Act*, volume 2: *Final Rule with Jurisdictional Determination* (Washington, DC: Government Printing Office, 1996). A record of the FDA's evidence that nicotine in tobacco is a drug is contained here, and in the proposed rule. See *Regulation of Cigarettes and Smokeless Tobacco Under the Federal Food, Drug, and Cosmetic Act*, volume 1, *Proposed Rule, Jurisdictional Analysis & Appendices, and Related Notices*, (Washington, DC: Government Printing Office, 1995.)

354   **Grady Carter**: Ron Word, "Jury Awards Cancer-Stricken Ex-smoker $750,000," Associated Press, 9 August 1999.

355   **Fanny-kicking**: Helen Dewar, "Gantt Hopes Centrist Message Will Attract 'Jessecrats' in Rematch," *Washington Post*, 1 November 1996, p. A21.

355   **Son of tobacco**: Joel B. Obermayer, "Tobacco Lawsuit Not Easy for Judge," *The News & Observer*, 9 February 1997, p. 14A.

356   **Hearing**: Transcript of Argument, *Coyne Beahm, Inc., Brown and Williamson, Liggett Group, Inc., Lorillard, Philip Morris, and R.J. Reynolds v. FDA and Kessler*, 966 F. Supp 1374 (M.D.N.C. 1997) (No. 2:95CV591), 10 February 1997.

358   **Decision**: *Coyne Beahm, Inc., Brown and Williamson, Liggett Group, Inc., Lorillard, Philip Morris, and R. J. Reynolds v. FDA and Kessler*, 966 F. Supp 1374 (M.D.N.C. 1997).

Chapter Forty-six

360–361   **Negotiate in earnest**: Peter Hardin, "Possibility of Deal Seen in Smoking Fight: Some See Industry Moving Toward Legislative Settlement," *Richmond Times-Dispatch*, 2 February 1997, p. A12.

    Proposed settlement: John M. Broder, "The Tobacco Agreement: The Overview; Cigarette Makers in a $368 Billion Accord to Curb Lawsuits and Curtail Marketing," *New York Times*, 21 June 1997, p. 1. **Report back to Congress**: C. Everett Koop and David A. Kessler, *Final Report of the Advisory Committee on Tobacco Policy and Public Health*, July 1997; John M. Broder, "Health Panel Set to Attack Tobacco Deal," *New York Times*, 28 June 1997, p. 6.

361   **Peace forever**: The notion of "peace" had been an industry goal for some time: "Defeat/minimize limits on domestic cigarette regulation and in the process secure five-year peace that minimizes impact on our business" (PM draft report, "Government Affairs Objectives," 9 January 1992, PM ID 2023200297–305, at 300); "What must the industry do with respect to full disclosure, adult use, and advertising/promotion...in order to achieve some lasting peace?" (PM report, PM counsel to PM counsel, "Affirmative Action Program," PM ID 2024969102–21, at 103); "Explore...the possibility of achieving a legislative compromise...anticipate a five-year period of 'legislative peace'" (Murray H. Bring, PM memo to H. Maxwell and R. W. Murray, "Project Rainbow," 24 January 1991, PM ID 2048143656–59, at 56); "Terms of negotiation...FDA regulation off the table... period of peace: 3 Congresses" (PM outline, "Project Rainbow II Elements," 21 March 1994, PM ID 2022838666–67, at 66).

361   **Settled the state lawsuits**: *Master Settlement Agreement*, 23 November 1998. See also Carrick Mollenkamp, Adam Levy, Joseph Menn, Jeffrey Rothfeder, *The People vs. Big Tobacco: How the States Took on The Cigarette Giants*, Princeton: Bloomberg Press, 1998.

361 **Court of Appeals:** Transcript of Argument, *Brown & Williamson et al. v. FDA and Kessler*, 153 F. 3d 155 (4th Cir. 1997), (No. 97–1604).

364 **Creating doubt:** Fred Panzer, TI memo to Horace R. Kornegay, "The Roper Proposal," 1 May 1972, TI ID TIMN 0077551–54, at 51.

364 **Comments Judge Michael:** Reported by employee of Charlottesville, Virginia, federal courthouse. I asked Judge Michael to respond, but he declined comment.

366 **2–1 against us:** *Brown & Williamson et al. v. FDA and Kessler*, 153 F. 3d 155 (4th Cir. 1998).

Chapter Forty-seven

367 **Trial rocked:** Roy R. Silver, "Baldwin Is Astir Over Charges Against Teacher," *New York Times*, 5 September 1967. p. 35.

367 **Two arguments**

    Nicotine is not addictive: For example, "The effects of nicotine are not comparable to those of addictive substances," and "there are no data to support FDA's position that the levels of nicotine in commercial cigarettes cause 'addiction' or have a substantial pharmacological effect" (TI, comments on FDA's proposed tobacco rule, vol. 3, comment #58385, Docket Nos. 95N–0253 and 95N–0253J). **Manipulate or control:** For example, "leaf blending is not used to artificially affect nicotine yields in cigarette smoke" (TI, comments on FDA's proposed tobacco rule, vol. 4, comment #58385, Docket Nos. 95N–0253 and 95N–0253J).

368 **Suppressed research:** For example, "We do not foresee any difficulty in the event a decision is reached to remove certain reports from Research files. Once it becomes clear that such action is necessary for the successful defense of our present and future suits, we will promptly remove all such reports from our files. As a rule, we invalidate about 15 reports each year for various reasons.... [W]e can cite misinterpretation of data as reason for invalidation.... As an alternative to invalidation, we can have the authors rewrite those sections of the reports which appear objectionable" (M. Senkus, RJR memo to Max Crohn, "Invalidation of Some Reports in the Research Dept.," 18 December 1969, RJR ID 500284499).

368 **Legal ethics:** See Deborah L. Rhode and David Luban, *Legal Ethics* (Westbury, N.Y.: Foundation Press, 1992); Deborah L. Rhode, *Professional Responsibility: Ethics by the Pervasive Method*, 2nd ed. (New York: Aspen, 1998); Richard Zitrin and Carol M. Langford, *The Moral Compass of the American Lawyer: Truth, Justice, Power, and Greed* (New York: Ballantine, 1999); Lincoln Caplan, *Skadden: Power, Money, and the Rise of a Legal Empire* (New York: Farrar Straus & Giroux, 1993); Charles W. Wolfram, *Modern Legal Ethics* (St. Paul, Minn.: West, 1986); Thomas L. Shaffer and Robert F. Cochran Jr., *Lawyers, Clients, and Moral Responsibility* (St. Paul, Minn.: West, 1994); Timothy W. Floyd, "Realism, Responsibility, and the Good Lawyer: Niebuhrian Perspectives on Legal Ethics," *Notre Dame Law Review* 67:587 (1992); Richard H. Underwood, "The Professional and the Liar," *Kentucky Law Journal* 87:919 (1998).

368 **Dominant view:** William H. Simon, *The Practice of Justice: A Theory of Lawyers' Ethics* (Cambridge, Mass.: Harvard University Press, 1998).

    Caroline of Brunswick: J. Nightingale, ed., *Trial of Queen Caroline*, vol. 2 (London: J. Robins, Albion Press, 1820–21), p. 8. **Not known to be false:** W.

William Hodes, "The Professional Duty to Horseshed Witnesses—Zealously, Within the Bounds of the Law," *Texas Tech Law Review* 30:1343 (1999).

368   **Lawyer's duty:** Author interview with Langbein, 26 October 1999.

370   **Ernest Pepples:** Ernest Pepples, B&W draft memo, "New Strategy on Smoking and Health," 1980, B&W ID 680051009–14.

371   **Adversary system:** David Luban, *The Good Lawyer: Lawyers' Roles and Lawyers' Ethics* (Totowa, N.J.: Rowman & Allanheld, 1984); Marvin E. Frankel, "The Search for Truth: An Umpireal View," *University of Pennsylvania Law Review* 123:1031 (1975).

371   **Harm incurred:** Deborah L. Rhode, "Conflicts of Commitment," *Stanford Law Review* 52:269–350 (2000).

371   **A friend:** Author interview with an industry lawyer.

Chapter Forty-eight

373–374   **Mark Deane:** Author interviews with Deane and McMillon, 27 August 1999; Deane, September, October, and November 1999.

       Philip Morris lied: Author interview with Deane and McMillon, 27 August 1999, p. 2. **It's a secret:** Ibid., p. 2. **Philip Morris told him:** Ibid., p. 7.

375   **Liquid nicotine:** T. A. Perfetti, RJR memo to J. S. Thomasson and M. F. Dube, "Preparation of High Nicotine Processed Sheet (G7 HN) Materials for XB," 10 September 1990, RJR ID 511282821-22; T. M. Larson and J. P. Morgan, Lorillard research report, "Application of Free Nicotine to Cigarette Tobacco and the Delivery of that Nicotine in the Cigarette Smoke," 6 May 1976, Lorillard ID 94672382–92; H. J. Minnemeyer, Lorillard memo to A. W. Spears, "Present Status of the Nicotine Enrichment Project," 13 April 1977, Lorillard ID 00044787–99; J. P. Morgan, Lorillard memo to S.T. Jones, "Nicotine Addition and Transfer in Tobacco Blends and Reconstituted Leaf Samples," 26 May 1994, Lorillard ID 88358066–67; J. P. Morgan and T. M. Larson, Lorillard research report, "Enrichment of Reconstituted Leaf Nicotine Content by Direct Addition of Nicotine Alkaloid to the RL Slurry," 12 April 1977, Lorillard ID 00398474–84; R. M. Irby, RJR memo to J. B. McCarthy, "Nicotine Content of Reconstituted Tobacco," 5 June 1974, RJR ID 514804771–74.

375   **Nicotine-soaked stems:** Chip Jones, " '90 Nicotine Project Gets FBI Scrutiny; Treated Stems Experiment Here Was Canceled," *Richmond Times-Dispatch*, 23 March 1997, p. A1. See also RJR memo, "New Philip Morris Patent," RJR ID 512331600; and T. B. Greene, RJR memo to G. R. Dimarco and W. M. Hildebolt, "Intercepted Philip Morris Products—Nicotine/Flavor Enhancement Technology," RJR ID 506911427–31.

376   **Added nicotine:** Donald H. Piehl, RJR presentation, ' "Tar'/Nicotine Control and Smoking Satisfaction," 9 May 1978, RJR ID 502742965–81.

376   **Types of recon:** RJR list, "Processed/Reconstituted Tobacco, Revised," 17 December 1993, RJR ID 513000117.

       Discontinued: RJR list, "Processed/Reconstituted Tobacco, Revised," 29 April 1994, RJR ID 511908676. RJR responded to my questions about the many types of reconstituted tobacco: "The only item on either list that was a high-nicotine item was G7-18, which is shown on the December 17 list as experimental and on the

April 29 list as discontinued. The G7-18 related to experimental projects. The discontinuation of G7-18 was not related to the 'Day One' program" (letter, Richard Cooper [Williams & Connolly] to David Kessler, 19 October 2000).

376 **Did not make sense:** R. G. Uhl, PM memo to H. Alonso, "DAP [diammonium phosphate] Content in Competitor Sheet Materials," 16 October 1987, PM ID 2056135299–306.

    Not the only one: "The alkaloid content of the reconstituted portion of the Marlboro blend appeared unreasonably high" (C. C. Bright, PM memo to J. E. Wickham, "Alkaloid Content of Reconstituted Materials Separated from the Cigarette Blend," 29 October 1985, PM ID 2022997570–72).

376 **Competitive intelligence:** Alan Rodgman, RJR memo to Roy E. Morse, "Clarification of My 07/22/80 Memo on Nicotine Additive," 8 September 1980, RJR ID 501522720–26; PM table, "Summary of Chemical Analyses," PM ID 2056135306; Harvey J. Young, RJR memo to Delwin P. Johnson, "Analysis of Marlboro Type I and Type II Reconstituted Tobaccos," 26 June 1973, RJR ID 504421353–58.

376 **Transferred to recon:** R. G. Uhl, PM memo to H. Alonso, "DAP Content in Competitor Sheet Materials," 16 October 1987, PM ID 2056135299–306; C. C. Bright, PM memo to J. E. Wickham, "Alkaloid Content of Reconstituted Materials Separated from the Cigarette Blend" (updated), 25 November 1985, PM ID 2056135446–50; B&W draft report, "Ammonia Technology," 3 November 1989, B&W ID 681001134–39; Thomas A. Perfetti and Lawrence E. Hayes, RJR report, "Improved Ammoniated Reconstituted Sheet," 30 January 1978, RJR ID 508880315.

376 **More than enough:** D. H. Piehl, RJR presentation, "'Tar'/Nicotine Control and Smoking Satisfaction," 9 May 1978, RJR ID 5027442965–81.

377 **Ammonia could be used:** J. M. Johnson, Lorillard research report, "Summary of the Effects of Ammonium Carbonate, Ammonium Bicarbonate, Urea and Diammonium Phosphate on Smoke pH, Smoke Data and Leaf Chemistry," 18 September 1996, Lorillard ID 89291533–45. Documents appeared to suggest that two weeks after my first congressional testimony Philip Morris privately confirmed that its "RCB" reconstituted tobacco had more than twice the amount of nicotine further on in the production process than it did originally (PM tables, "Nicotine Results," PM ID 2501303730–32). One document stated as "reasons for use" of ammonia that ammonia "increases the efficiency of transfer of nicotine from tobacco to sheet" (C. I. Ayres, BAT report, "Use of Ammonia/Ammonium Compounds/Urea," BAT ID 303636914–22).

377 **Putting into use:** House Committee on Energy and Commerce, Subcommittee on Health and the Environment, testimony of Andrew H. Tisch (Lorillard), hearing, *Regulation of Tobacco Products (Part 1)*, 103rd Cong., 2d sess., 14 April 1994, Serial No. 103–49.

377 **Call Philip:** Author interview with "Philip."

378 **Criminal charges:** The DOJ's decision not to bring criminal charges against the tobacco industry disappointed some of its investigators, who believed the industry had lied in its statements on addiction and nicotine manipulation. The case would undoubtedly have been hard to win. B&W had made false statements to the FDA when it said it had not genetically bred high-nicotine plants, but it later corrected the record, after being pressed by the tobacco team. Though PM claimed Victor DeNoble had not been fired because of his research, the claim

was not sufficiently material to warrant prosecution. A single word, "independently," protected industry witnesses, one of whom told Congress, "Philip Morris does not manipulate nor independently control the level of nicotine in our products." As for the statements that nicotine is not addictive, executives testifying before congressional committees claimed to be expressing personal beliefs, making perjury charges difficult to pursue. The most ambitious avenue of investigation, into whether an industry conspiracy dated back decades, ran aground in the absence of living witnesses and the challenge of proving that certain activities were company policy, rather than the actions of individuals. The lawyers who scripted the public statements did their job well, aided by an industry whose ranks were virtually sealed. One FBI special agent told me that although he had conducted investigations into organized crime, he had never seen an instance where so few people were willing to talk.

Though there was no criminal indictment, the Justice Department made a separate decision to file a civil suit against all the major tobacco manufacturers, seeking several billion dollars for federal health costs incurred and profits gained because of the industry's fraudulent conduct.

Chapter Forty-nine

379 **Supreme Court:** Transcript of Argument, *FDA et al. v. Brown & Williamson Tobacco Corporation et al.*, 120 S. Ct. 1291 (1999) (No. 98–1152), 1 December 1999.

384 **By a single vote:** *FDA et al. v. Brown & Williamson Tobacco Corporation et al.*, 120 S. Ct. 1291 (2000).

Chapter Fifty

385 **Product liability suits:** Joe Ward, "Tobacco in Court: Have Lawsuits Inflicted Damage or Is the Industry Holding Its Own?" *The Courier-Journal*, 25 July 1999, p. 1E.

Oregon: *Estate of Williams v. Philip Morris, Inc.*, No. 9705 03957 (Ore. Cir. Multnomah Co., 13 May 1999). **California:** "Judge Orders Henley to Accept $25M in Punitives or Face New Trial," *Tobacco Industry Litigation Reporter*, 9 April 1999, p. 4; Dennis J. Opatrny, "Tobacco Giants Hit With $20M in Punitives," *The Recorder*, 28 March 2000, p. 1.

386 **Profound change:** Barry Meier, "Philip Morris Admits Evidence Shows Smoking Causes Cancer," *New York Times*, 13 October 1999, p. A1.

Developing a dialogue: *Nightline*, ABC News, 13 October 1999. **Videotape:** "Rebutting Kessler," Reuters Corporate TV, PM ID 2040119701–702. **Conversation would lead:** Author interview with Parrish, 4 November 1999.

389 **Might bankrupt:** Author conversation with Parrish, 29 February 2000.

Give away the tobacco company: Philip Morris had considered getting out of the tobacco business a decade before my conversation with Parrish. CEO Bill Murray saw a deteriorating environment and wrote, "If we think that my worst-case scenario is likely, and that we cannot do much to improve the environment, we should get rid of our tobacco business. . . . If at the end of two years it looks like it is not working, we should implement Option A and get rid of the tobacco business" (R. W. Murray, PM notes, "The Background," September 1990, PM ID 2023027920–49, at 30 and 46).

390 **Epiphany:** National Center on Addiction and Substance Abuse (CASA), "Substance Abuse in the 21st Century: Positioning the Nation for Progress," transcript of panel discussion held at Simi Valley, Calif., 2 March 2000; "Verbatim: Big Tobacco's Changing Tune," *Washington Post*, p. B4, 5 March 2000.

391 **First class-action:** "Florida Tobacco Trial: Jury Awards Plaintiffs $145 Billion," CNN Breaking News, 14 July 2000.

392 **Introduced a bill:** Ira Teinowitz, "Congress Might Revive Tobacco Ad Rules; Bill's Author Claims Key Congressmen Support Extending FDA's Authority," *Advertising Age*, 24 April 2000, p. 36. **Lobbyists opposed:** Author conversation with Parrish, 17 August 2000.

392 **Pushed towards bankruptcy:** Bruce Bartlett, "Government Addicted to Tobacco Tax Revenues," *Detroit News*, 27 July 2000, p. 14; Barry Meier, "Florida Measure May Ease Lawsuit's Threat to Cigarette Makers," *New York Times*, 31 March 2000, p. 23; "States Prepare for Big Tobacco Bankruptcy as Miami Case Nears Verdict," *The Bulletin's Frontrunner*, 20 March 2000.

List of Author Interviews

David G. Adams, director, Policy Development and Coordination Staff, FDA

Michael J. Astrue, general counsel, U.S. Department of Health and Human Services

Lawrence Bachorik, deputy associate commissioner for public affairs, FDA

Douglas G. Baird, Harry A. Bigelow Distinguished Service Professor of Law, University of Chicago Law School

Scott D. Ballin, chairman, Coalition on Smoking or Health, and vice president and legislative counsel, American Heart Association

John F. Banzhaf III, executive director, Action on Smoking and Health

Philip S. Barnett, counsel, Subcommittee on Health and the Environment, Committee on Energy and Commerce, U.S. House of Representatives; director of policy research, FDA

Don Barrett, partner, Barrett Law Office

Michael F. Barrett, staff director, Subcommittee on Oversight and Investigations, Committee on Energy and Commerce, U.S. House of Representatives

Herbert Barry III, professor, University of Pittsburgh

Kim K. Bayliss, legislative director, Congressman Mike Synar (D–Oklahoma)

Soma Golden Behr, assistant managing editor, *New York Times*

Elizabeth G. Berbakos, special assistant to the commissioner, FDA

Lowell Bergman, producer/reporter, *60 Minutes*/CBS News

Ilisa B. G. Bernstein, senior science policy adviser, FDA

Kenneth F. Boehm, chair, National Legal and Policy Center

Walt Bogdanich, investigative producer, *Day One*/ABC

Kevin M. Budich, compliance officer, FDA

Miriam R. Burbach, supervisory investigator, FDA

Kevin J. Burke, special assistant, Office of the Assistant Secretary for Legislation, U.S. Department of Health and Human Services

Marian Burros, reporter and columnist, *New York Times*

John R. Cady, president and CEO, National Food Processors Association

LaJuana Caldwell, chief of editorial staff, FDA

Michael J. Calhoun, chief of staff, U.S. Department of Health and Human Services

Joseph A. Califano Jr., secretary, U.S. Department of Health, Education, and Welfare (1977–1980)

Angelo P. Capparella, associate professor, Department of Biological Sciences, Illinois State University

Christopher D. Cerf, associate counsel to President Bill Clinton

Domenic A. Ciraulo, M.D., professor and chairman, Department of Psychiatry, Boston University School of Medicine

Howard Cohen, health counsel, Committee on Energy and Commerce, U.S. House of Representatives

Frank Colby, director of research information, R. J. Reynolds; manager of scientific information, R. J. Reynolds; associate director of scientific issues, R. J. Reynolds

Glen Collins, business reporter, *New York Times*

Claudia Cooley, executive secretary to the U.S. Department of Health and Human Services

Ellen C. Cooper, M.D., director, Division of Anti-Viral Drug Products, FDA

William V. Corr, counselor to the secretary, U.S. Department of Health and Human Services

"Critical," informant

Lloyd N. Cutler, special counsel to President Bill Clinton

James A. Dahl, assistant director, Investigative Operations, FDA

Robert Damus, general counsel, Office of Management and Budget

James A. Davis, director, Investigations Branch, Seattle District, FDA

Cornelia Dean, deputy Washington Bureau editor, *New York Times*

Mark Deane, cooker, Philip Morris

Joseph A. Dear, assistant secretary of labor, Occupational Safety and Health Administration

Martin E. Delaney, founding director, Project Inform

Anne M. Dellinger, professor of public law and government, University of North Carolina Institute of Government

Walter E. Dellinger, acting solicitor general, U.S. Department of Justice

Victor J. DeNoble, research scientist, Philip Morris

Philip S. Derfler, associate chief counsel for foods, FDA

Anne Morrow Donley, executive director, Group to Alleviate Smoking in Public (GASP)

Clifford E. Douglas, director, Tobacco Policy Advocacy Institute

Thomas P. Doyle, special agent, Office of Criminal Investigations, FDA

Henry D. Drew, chief, Drug Monitoring Branch, FDA

Juanita D. Duggan, executive vice president for government relations and communication, National Food Processors Association

Edwin V. Dutra Jr., director of regulations policy and management staff, FDA

Harold Edgar, Julius Silver Professor of Law, Science and Technology, Columbia Law School

Charles C. Edwards, M.D., commissioner, FDA (1969–1973)

Bradford D. Elder, regulations editorial staff, Office of Policy, FDA

Michael P. Eriksen, director, Office on Smoking and Health, U.S. Department of Health and Human Services

William A. Farone, director, Applied Research, Philip Morris

Judith Feder, principal deputy assistant secretary for planning and evaluation, U.S. Department of Health and Human Services

David W. Feigal Jr., M.D., director, Division of Anti-Viral Drug Products, FDA

E. Ripley Forbes Sr., staff associate, Subcommittee on Health and the Environment, Committee on Energy and Commerce, U.S. House of Representatives

Wendell H. Ford, member, U.S. Senate (D–Kentucky)

Michael A. Forscey, partner, Wunder, Knight, Forscey & DeVierno

Allan M. Fox, managing partner, Fox Kiser

Malcolm Frazier, special assistant to the regional director, Office of Regulatory Affairs, FDA

Alix M. Freedman, investigative reporter, *Wall Street Journal*

Frederick L. Fricke Jr., director, Forensic Chemistry Center, FDA

Martin H. Gerry, assistant secretary for planning and evaluation, U.S. Department of Health and Human Services

Gary A. Giovino, chief, Epidemiology Branch, Centers for Disease Control and Prevention

Malcolm T. Gladwell, staff writer, *Washington Post*

C. Boyden Gray, counsel to President George Bush

James C. Greenwood, member, U.S. House of Representatives (R-Pennsylvania)

Patrick J. Griffin, assistant to President Bill Clinton, director of legislative affairs

Anne Brooks Gwaltney, special assistant to President George Bush and associate director of presidential personnel

C. McClain Haddow, C. M. Haddow & Associates

Sandra Kay Hamric, executive assistant to the commissioner, FDA

Daniel K. Harder, associate curator, Missouri Botanical Gardens

Sandra Z. Harris, staff director, Subcommittee on Environment, Energy and Natural Resources, Committee on Government Operations, U.S. House of Representatives

Geoffrey C. Hazard Jr., Trustee Professor of Law, University of Pennsylvania

Bernadine Healy, M.D. director, National Institutes of Health

Jack E. Henningfield, chief, Clinical Pharmacology Research Branch, National Institute of Drug Abuse

R. Harrison Hickman, president, Hickman-Brown Research

Philip J. Hilts, Washington correspondent, *New York Times*

Kathleen S. Holcombe, acting associate commissioner, FDA; professional staff, Committee on Energy and Commerce, U.S. House of Representatives

Jeffrey R. Holmstead, associate counsel to President George Bush

John D. Howard, M.D., chief medical examiner, Pierce County, Wash.

William K. Hubbard, associate commissioner for policy coordination, FDA

Gary Huber, M.D., director of Harvard Smoking and Health Research Project

James R. Hunter, associate director for science, Office of Special Investigations, FDA

Harold Ickes, deputy chief of staff to President Bill Clinton

Jerome H. Jaffe, acting director, National Institute of Drug Abuse

Joel Jankowsky, senior partner, Akin, Gump, Strauss, Hauer & Field

Michael Janofsky, national correspondent, *New York Times*

Sharan (Kuperman) Jayne, director of broadcast media, FDA

Ruth Johnson, analytical chemist, FDA

Joshua R. Kardon, chief of staff, Congressman Ron Wyden (D–Oregon)

Nancy J. Kaufman, vice president, Robert Wood Johnson Foundation

Ronald C. Kaufman, deputy assistant to President George Bush for political affairs

Steven Keith, M.D., professional staff member, Senator Edward Kennedy (D–Massachusetts)

Steven B. Kelmar, assistant secretary for legislation, U.S. Department of Health and Human Services

Donald Kennedy, commissioner, FDA (1977–1979)

Carol M. Kerner, supervisory chemist, Division of Drug Analysis, FDA

Jerry D. Klepner, assistant secretary for legislation, U.S. Department of Health and Human Services

Carol Knoth, medical librarian, FDA

Larry Kramer, writer and founder, ACT-UP

L. Robert Lake, director of compliance, Center for Food Safety and Applied Nutrition, FDA

Thomas P. Layloff, director, Division of Drug Analysis, FDA

H. Martin Lancaster, member, U.S. House of Representatives (D–North Carolina)

John H. Langbein, Chancellor Kent Professor of Law and Legal History, Yale University School of Law

Andrew D. Lazerow, public affairs specialist for the broadcast media staff, Office of Public Affairs, FDA

Joseph A. Levitt, deputy director for regulation and policy, Center for Devices and Radiological Health, FDA

Philip Lee, M.D., assistant secretary for health, U.S. Department of Health and Human Services

Judy Leon, senior vice president and director for media training, Powell Tate

Patricia Levy-Zuckerman, policy intern, FDA

Gary D. Light, special agent, Office of Criminal Investigations, FDA

Adam B. Liptak, senior counsel, *New York Times*

Timothy Long, investigative specialist, FDA

Catherine C. Lorraine, director, Policy Development and Coordination Staff, FDA

Roger L. Lowell, district director, Seattle District, FDA

Jacqueline M. Lowey, special assistant to the deputy secretary, U.S. Department of Transportation

James B. Macrae Jr., acting administrator, Office of Information and Regulatory Affairs, Office of Management and Budget

Vedpal Singh Malik, senior scientist, Philip Morris

Jerold R. Mande, executive assistant and special adviser to the commissioner, FDA

Robert J. Mangas, chief of staff, Senator Wendell H. Ford (D–Kentucky)

Joseph F. Marx, senior communications officer, Robert Wood Johnson Foundation

Sharon Lindan Mayl, senior policy adviser, FDA

Shirley McMillon, friend of Mark Deane

Paul C. Mele, research scientist, Philip Morris

Victor A. Meo, investigator, Seattle District, FDA

Gerald F. Meyer, deputy director, Center for Drug Evaluation and Research, FDA

Daniel L. Michels, director, Office of Enforcement, Office of Regulatory Affairs, FDA

Abner J. Mikva, counsel to President Bill Clinton

M. Val Miller, attorney

John Howard (Jack) Mitchell, commissioner's special assistant for investigation, FDA

Dick Morris, political consultant for President Bill Clinton

Matthew L. Myers, consultant, Coalition on Smoking or Health

Sharon L. Natanblut, associate commissioner for strategic initiatives, FDA

David W. Nelson, special assistant, Committee on Energy and Commerce, U.S. House of Representatives

Jeffrey Nesbit, associate commissioner for public affairs, FDA

Amanda Bryce Norton, chief mediator and ombudsman, FDA

Jennifer M. O'Connor, special assistant to President Bill Clinton

William E. O'Connor Jr., chief of staff, U.S. Department of Agriculture

James A. O'Hara III, associate commissioner for public affairs, FDA

Robert T. O'Neill, director, Office of Epidemiology and Biostatistics, FDA

Janice F. Oliver, deputy director of systems and support, Office of Compliance, Center for Foods, FDA

Leon E. Panetta, White House chief of staff for President Bill Clinton

Steven C. Parrish, senior vice president, External Affairs, and general counsel for Philip Morris, USA; senior vice president, Worldwide Regulatory Affairs, Philip Morris; senior vice president, Corporate Affairs, Philip Morris

"PC," informant

Kim R. Pearson, publisher, *FDA Insider Report*

Carl C. Peck, M.D., director, Center for Drug Evaluation and Research, FDA

Heidi Pender, special counsel to Congressman Charlie Rose (D–North Carolina)

Mary K. Pendergast, deputy commissioner/senior adviser to the commissioner, FDA

Michael Pertschuk, chairman, Federal Trade Commission; codirector, Advocacy Institute

Thomas F. Piekarski, compliance officer, FDA

Wayne L. Pines, associate commissioner for public affairs, FDA (1978–1982)

Keith Pitts, staff director, Subcommittee on Risk Management, Research and Specialty Crops, Agriculture Committee, U.S. House of Representatives

S. Jay Plager, associate director, Office of Management and Budget

William Pollin, director, National Institute of Drug Abuse

Ruth C. Pontius, technical writer and editor, Office of the *Federal Register*, National Archives and Records Administration

Margaret Jane Porter, chief counsel, FDA

Bogdan Prokopczyk, head, Bioorganic Chemistry, American Health Foundation

Jack Quinn, counsel to President Bill Clinton

Harriet. S. Rabb, general counsel, U.S. Department of Health and Human Services

Robert B. Reich, secretary, U.S. Department of Labor

William K. Reilly, administrator, Environmental Protection Agency

Kim A. Rice, operations supervisor, Office of Criminal Investigations, FDA

Ann Kimmell Ritter, partner, Blatt & Fales

Alan Rodgman, director of research, R. J. Reynolds

Stephen Roth, branch chief, Visual Information Service Branch, FDA

"Saint," informant

Timothy K. Sanders, clerk, Subcommittee on Agriculture, Rural Development, FDA, and Related Agencies, Committee on Appropriations, U.S. House of Representatives

H. Lee Sarokin, U.S. district court judge

Philip M. Schiliro, chief of staff, Congressman Henry A. Waxman (D-California)

Jeffrey Schlagenhauf, president, Smokeless Tobacco Council

Tom R. Schori, senior scientist, Philip Morris

William B. Schultz, deputy commissioner for policy, FDA

John R. Schwartz, staff writer, *Washington Post*

Richard F. Scruggs, partner, Scruggs, Millette, Bozeman, & Dent, PA

Thomas A. Scully, deputy assistant for domestic policy to President George Bush

Ken Silverstein, author and investigative reporter, *Harper's Magazine*

John D. Slade, M.D., associate professor, Department of Clinical Medicine, Robert Wood Johnson Medical School

Guy L. Smith IV, vice president, Corporate Affairs, Philip Morris

Douglas Sosnik, counselor to President Bill Clinton

Robert M. Spiller Jr., associate chief counsel for enforcement, FDA

Virginia Stark-Vance, M.D., clinical investigator, Investigational Drug Branch, National Institutes of Health

Bernice Steinhardt, director, Health Services, Quality and Public Health, General Accounting Office

Jur Strobos, director, Policy Research Staff, FDA

Wendy Strong, deputy assistant secretary for legislation, U.S. Department of Health and Human Services

Reid P. F. Stuntz, staff director and chief counsel, Subcommittee on Oversight and Investigations, Committee on Energy and Commerce, U.S. House of Representatives

Barbara E. Suhre, supervisory editor, Office of the *Federal Register*, National Archives and Records Administration

Louis W. Sullivan, M.D., secretary, U.S. Department of Health and Human Services (1989–1993)

Richard C. Swanson, director, Emergency and Investigational Operations, FDA

John Mack Taylor, associate chief counsel for enforcement, FDA

Michael R. Taylor, deputy commissioner for policy, FDA

Nancy E. Taylor, health staff director, Labor and Human Resources Committee, U.S. Senate

Diane E. Thompson, associate commissioner for legislative affairs, FDA

Larry Thompson, Office of Public Affairs, FDA

Kevin Thurm, chief of staff, U.S. Department of Health and Human Services

Carlton Turner, deputy assistant to President Ronald Reagan and director of drug abuse policy

Vivek C. Varma, chief of staff, Congressman Mike Synar (D–Oklahoma)

"Veritas," senior tobacco industry executive

Terry L. Vermillion, director, Office of Criminal Investigations, FDA

Nicholas Wade, science news reporter, *New York Times*

Jimmye S. Warren, senior trial attorney, U.S. Department of Justice

Henry A. Waxman, member, U.S. House of Representatives (D–California)

Craig E. Weatherup, president and CEO, PepsiCo, Inc.

Amy Weiss, press secretary, Congressman Mike Synar (D–Oklahoma)

Jan C. West, consultant abstractor, Council for Tobacco Research

Jacquelyn Y. White, deputy executive secretary to the department, U.S. Department of Health and Human Services

Michael White, director of legal affairs, Office of the Federal Register, National Archives and Records Administration

Jeffrey Wigand, vice president for research, Brown & Williamson

Judith D. Wilkenfeld, special adviser to the commissioner, FDA

Jane B. Williams, health policy adviser, Committee on Labor and Human Resources, U.S. Senate

Ann H. Wion, deputy chief counsel for program review, FDA

John Wiskerchen, lab director, Seattle District, FDA

Ann M. Witt, special assistant to the deputy commissioner for operations, FDA

Roger M. Witten, partner, Wilmer, Cutler & Pickering

Curtis Wright, M.D., deputy director, Anesthetic, Critical Care and Addiction Drug Products, FDA

Randolph F. Wykoff, M.D., associate commissioner, AIDS and Special Health Issues, FDA

Frank Young, M.D., commissioner, FDA (1984–1989)

Denise M. Zavagno, associate chief counsel for enforcement, FDA

Mitchell Zeller, associate commissioner, FDA

Robert Zoellick, White House deputy chief of staff for President George Bush

READINGS

Political scientists traditionally believe that it is almost impossible for individuals in large bureaucracies to make a difference. Bureaucratic routines, the influence of interest groups, and the divided nature of government are seen as placing insurmountable obstacles in the way of people trying to tackle large public issues. In my view, this pessimistic conclusion needlessly discourages people from entering public service. The following books and articles help answer the question of how individuals, both within and outside government, can bring about effective change.

Responsibilities of Public Officials

Moore, Mark H. *Creating Public Value: Strategic Management in Government.* Cambridge, Mass.: Harvard University Press, 1995.

Moore, Mark H., and Malcolm K. Sparrow. *Ethics in Government: The Moral Challenge of Public Leadership.* Englewood Cliffs, N.J.: Prentice Hall, 1990.

Reich, Robert B. *Public Management in a Democratic Society.* Englewood Cliffs, N.J.: Prentice Hall, 1990.

Initiating Policy Change

Baumgartner, Frank R., and Bryan D. Jones. *Agendas and Instability in American Politics.* Chicago, Ill: University of Chicago Press, 1993.

Cobb, Roger W., and Charles D. Elder. *Participation in American Politics: The Dynamics of Agenda Building.* Baltimore, Md.: Johns Hopkins University Press, 1972.

Doig, Jameson W., and Erwin C. Hargrove. *Leadership and Innovation: A Biographical Perspective on Entrepreneurs in Government.* Baltimore, Md.: Johns Hopkins University Press, 1987.

Kingdon, John W. *Agendas, Alternatives, and Public Policies.* New York: HarperCollins College Publishers, 1995.

Polsby, Nelson W. *Political Innovation in America.* New Haven, Conn.: Yale University Press, 1984.

Framing Public Debate

Derthick, Martha, Bruce K. Maclaury, and Paul J. Quirk. *The Politics of Deregulation.* Washington, D.C.: Brookings Institution, 1985.

Edelman, Murray Jacob. *The Symbolic Uses of Politics*. Urbana, Ill.: University of Illinois Press, 1964.

Majone, Giandomenico. *Evidence, Argument and Persuasion in the Policy Process*. New Haven, Conn.: Yale University Press, 1989.

Neustadt, Richard E. *Presidential Power—The Politics of Leadership*. New York: John Wiley, 1961.

Reich, Robert B., ed. *The Power of Public Ideas*. Cambridge, Mass.: Ballinger, 1988.

Stone, Deborah. "Causal Stories and the Formation of Policy Agendas." *Political Science Quarterly* 102(2):281–300 (1989).

Yankelovich, Daniel, and John Immerwahr. "The Rules of Public Engagement." In *Beyond the Beltway*, edited by Daniel Yankelovich and I. M. Destler. New York: W. W. Norton, 1994.

Political Strategy Within Government

Allison, Graham T. "Model III: Governmental Politics." In *Essence of Decision—Explaining the Cuban Missile Crisis*. New York: HarperCollins, 1971.

Haass, Richard N. *The Power to Persuade*. New York: Houghton Mifflin, 1994.

Harris, Richard A., and Sidney M. Milkis. *The Politics of Regulatory Change*. New York: Oxford University Press, 1996.

Heymann, Philip B. *The Politics of Public Management*. New Haven, Conn.: Yale University Press, 1987.

Levin, Martin A. and Mary Bryne Sanger. *Making Government Work*. San Francisco, Calif.: Jossey-Bass, 1994.

Kobrak, Peter. *The Political Environment of Public Management*. New York: HarperCollins, 1993.

Porter, Roger B. *Presidential Decision Making*. New York: Press Syndicate of the University of Cambridge, 1980.

Rubin, Barry R. *A Citizen's Guide to Politics in America*. New York: M. E. Sharpe, 1997.

Van Horn, Carl E., Donald C. Baumer, and William T. Gormley, Jr. *Politics and Public Policy*. Washington, D.C.: Congressional Quarterly, 1989.

Role of the Press

Clore, Harry M., ed. *The Mass Media and Modern Democracy*. Chicago, Ill.: Rand McNally College Publishing, 1974.

Gans, Herbert J. *Deciding What's News*. New York: Vintage Books/Random House, 1980.

Linsky, Martin, Jonathan Moore, Wendy O'Donnell, and David Whitman. *How the Press Affects Federal Policymaking*. New York: W. W. Norton, 1986.

Role of Congress

Aberbach, Joel D. *Keeping a Watchful Eye*. Washington, D.C.: Brookings Institution, 1990.

Arnold, R. Douglas. *Congress and the Bureaucracy*. New Haven, Conn.: Yale University Press, 1979.

Ogul, Morris S. *Congress Oversees the Bureaucracy: Studies in Legislative Supervision*. Pittsburgh, Penn.: University of Pittsburgh Press, 1976.

Role of Interest Groups

Browne, William P. *Groups, Interests, and U.S. Public Policy*. Washington, D.C.: Georgetown University Press, 1998.

Quirk, Paul J. *Industry Influence in Federal Regulatory Agencies.* Princeton, N.J.: Princeton University Press, 1981.

Understanding Bureaucracy

Downs, Anthony. *Inside Bureaucracy.* Boston, Mass.: Little, Brown, 1967.

Heclo, Hugh. *A Government of Strangers.* Washington, D.C.: Brookings Institution, 1977.

Kaufman, Herbert. *The Administrative Behavior of Federal Bureau Chiefs.* Washington, D.C.: Brookings Institution, 1981.

Lynn, Laurence E. Jr. *Managing the Public's Business.* New York: Basic Books, 1981.

Meier, Kenneth J. *Politics and the Bureaucracy: Policy Making in the Fourth Branch of Government.* 3rd ed. Belmont, Calif.: Wadsworth, 1993.

Robinson, Glen O. *American Bureaucracy: Public Choice and Public Law.* Ann Arbor, Mich.: University of Michigan Press, 1991.

Stillman, Richard, II. *The American Bureaucracy.* Chicago, Ill.: Nelson-Hall, 1996.

Wilson, James Q. *Bureaucracy.* New York: Basic Books, 1989.

Wilson, James Q. "Organizational Maintenance and Incentives." In *Political Organizations.* New York: Basic Books, 1973.

ACKNOWLEDGMENTS

As I hope this book makes evident, during the 1990s at the Food and Drug Administration an extraordinary group of men and women came together to work. They brought a passionate commitment to the agency. They were willing to make sacrifices, professional and personal, every day. To all who served with me at the FDA I am forever grateful. To the tobacco team, in particular, my unending thanks.

As soon as I left the agency, I began work on this book. Its creation has proved a long and wrenching experience for me. I could not have done it without the talents and insight of Karyn Feiden. Over the last three years, Karyn labored painstakingly with me. Her standards were the highest, her energy never flagged—her commitment to this book never wavered. I am in her debt.

Some say great editors no longer exist, but I certainly found one. A year into the project, Jonathan Harr introduced me to Dick Todd. Dick stands above all others in his ability to structure a story. His vision helped shape this book.

Had it not been for the considerable skills of Darcy Bacon, Herbert Burkholz, Clive Irving, Susan Rieger, and Renie Schapiro, I would be toiling still. They worked on specific sections of the manuscript with me, as did Nathan Lump, Stephen Whitlock, and Jill Cutler. Clive cared deeply about this project and saw the issues in a larger context. Herb with his flair and Renie with her policy perspective have given their all since FDA days and I appreciate it.

Numerous students, in the age-old tradition of hardworking students everywhere, helped me search through document warehouses, computer databases, and footnote sources. My thanks to Aaryn Cohen, Lisa Frankamp, Julie Furber, Reena Gupta, Elizabeth Johnson, Byron Kennedy, Jennifer Kenney, Swapnil Maniar, Monique Muggli, Kate Pearson, Eric Rosenthal, Laura Shaffer, and Judith Watt.

Deb Friedman, Maggie Hume, Caroline Polk, and Denise Wolk were my fact checkers—stout of heart, and thorough. Chris Jerome was a valiant proofreader.

Transcription services were meticulously handled by Dan Hawkins, Linda McNicol, and the ever-faithful Olga Papach.

Assistance with huge computer databases was critical. My thanks go to John Chepren, Robert Guarnieri, John Guidone, Kate Latimer, Phillip Simon, and Rosie Whitcraft.

I appreciate the gifts of time and energy expended by Lincoln Caplan, Malcolm Gladwell, Jeffrey Goldberg, and Jonathan Harr in their reading and commenting on the manuscript in its various incarnations. As is customary to say, and in this case as is accurate, any remaining flaws are my own.

The staff in the Dean's Office at the Yale University School of Medicine worked tirelessly. Kelly Edwards, Gerri Emerling, Eloise Glick, Elinor Lutch, and Helen Mann were indefatigable. Elinor Lutch I thank in particular for her ability to manage anything.

Publicly available tobacco databases and websites were of special value, especially those provided by Gene Borio, Anne Landman, and Michael Tacelosky.

Douglas Baird, Virginia L. Ernster, Geoffrey Hazard, Ronald A. Heifetz, John Langbein, Robert Jay Lifton, David Luban, and Richard Pollay were very generous with their time helping me to analyze painstakingly complex issues.

Anna Greenberg, Steven Kelman, Gary Orren, Linda Reivitz, and Richard J. Stillman II helped steer me toward useful public policy readings.

The book would never have been written without my colleagues who helped me run the Food and Drug Administration. They include Jane Henney, Mike Friedman, Mike Taylor, Bill Schultz, Sharon Holsten, Carol Scheman, Mary Jo Veverka, Robert Byrd, Kay Hamric, and the peerless Mary Pendergast.

At Yale, Irwin Birnbaum, Ruth Katz, Carolyn Slayman, Joseph Warshaw, and the department chairs and faculty gave me time to write and to think. Yale's president, Rick Levin, and the provost's office were unstinting in their support and encouragement.

I am grateful for the support of the Robert Wood Johnson Foundation, the Henry J. Kaiser Family Foundation, and the California Wellness Foundation. My special thanks go to Drew Altman, Steve Schroeder, Nancy Kaufman, Gary Nelson, and especially Joe Marx for their belief in the importance of telling this story.

Peter Osnos, publisher of PublicAffairs, cares deeply about books. I am very glad Chris Drew introduced me to him.

At PublicAffairs, Geoff Shandler, Paul Golob, and Robert Kimzey were valuable shepherds. Evan Gaffney added his creativity; Kevin Goering, his legal expertise. Bob Marsh, as indexer, and Kate Scott, as copyeditor, contributed the final touches.

I thank Bob Barnett for his always outstanding lawyering. David Black and Harry Evans were enthusiastic early on about this book's prospects.

Terry Dagradi, Jerry Domian, and Byron Kennedy hiked the tobacco fields with me, and with Mark Saba produced the photographs for the jacket.

None of this could have been accomplished without Frank Pearl, whose vision and commitment to the field of publishing is unmatched anywhere.

Throughout my life, I have depended on the loyalty and love of Roslyn Kessler, Irving Kessler, Paul Steinberg, Dee Steinberg, the late Elise Steinberg, Barbara Koltun, and Suzanne Gibbons-Neff.

I would also like to acknowledge the memories of David Ifshin, Martha Stone, and Mike Synar, whose brave struggles for life took place during much of the time chronicled in this book and whose battles served as an inspiration.

Writing this book was as difficult as anything I have ever done. As always, Paulette, Elise, and Ben made it all worth doing.

FDA TOBACCO TEAM

David Adams
Lawrence Bachorik
Lisa Barclay
Eileen Bargo
Philip Barnett
Elizabeth Berbakos
Ilisa Bernstein
Margaret Bierwirth
Eric Blumberg
Lawrence Braslow
Kevin Budich
Jennie Butler
Thomas Cairns
LaJuana Caldwell
Lawrence Cannady
Philip Chao
Kin Chiu
Laura Ciolino
Bernice Collins
Christine Congleton
Philip Derfler
Thomas Doyle
Henry Drew
Edwin Dutra Jr.
Michael Eriksen
Brenda Lee Evelyn
William Fairweather
Linda Felten
David Fox
Frederick Fricke Jr.

Gary Giovino
Steven Gitterman
Richard Geyer
S. Kay Hamric
Belinda Hayes
Alan Heaton
Jack Henningfield
David Horowitz
William Hubbard
James Hunter
Sharan (Kuperman) Jayne
Suzanne White Junod
Patricia Kaeding
Erica Keys
Anne Kirchner
Michael Klein
Carol Knoth
Douglas Kramer
Thomas Layloff
Andrew Lazerow
Gary Light
Timothy Long
Catherine Lorraine
Jerold Mande
Sharon Mayl
Susan Meadows
Michelle Migdal
Jack Mitchell
Michele Mital
Diane O'Brien

James O'Hara
Robert O'Neill
Sharon Natanblut
Karen Nelson
Margaret Porter
Diane Prince
Stephen Roth
Beverly Rothstein
Renie Schapiro
Joshua Scharfstein
Karen Schifter
Sharon Schneider
William Schultz
Kennon Smith
Brian Somers
Robert Spiller
Dan Spyker
John Taylor
Diane Thompson
Larry Thompson
Terry Toigo
Terry Vermillion
Roger Withers
Rosie Whitcraft
Judy Wilkenfeld
Ann Witt
Curtis Wright
Randolph Wykoff
Mitchell Zeller

INDEX

PublicAffairs is a new nonfiction publishing house and a tribute to the standards, values, and flair of three persons who have served as mentors to countless reporters, writers, editors, and book people of all kinds, including me.

I.F. STONE, proprietor of *I. F. Stone's Weekly*, combined a commitment to the First Amendment with entrepreneurial zeal and reporting skill and became one of the great independent journalists in American history. At the age of eighty, Izzy published *The Trial of Socrates*, which was a national bestseller. He wrote the book after he taught himself ancient Greek.

BENJAMIN C. BRADLEE was for nearly thirty years the charismatic editorial leader of *The Washington Post*. It was Ben who gave the *Post* the range and courage to pursue such historic issues as Watergate. He supported his reporters with a tenacity that made them fearless and it is no accident that so many became authors of influential, bestselling books.

ROBERT L. BERNSTEIN, the chief executive of Random House for more than a quarter century, guided one of the nation's premier publishing houses. Bob was personally responsible for many books of political dissent and argument that challenged tyranny around the globe. He is also the founder and longtime chair of Human Rights Watch, one of the most respected human rights organizations in the world.

———

For fifty years, the banner of Public Affairs Press was carried by its owner Morris B. Schnapper, who published Gandhi, Nasser, Toynbee, Truman and about 1,500 other authors. In 1983, Schnapper was described by *The Washington Post* as "a redoubtable gadfly." His legacy will endure in the books to come.

Peter Osnos, *Publisher*